DARK PSYCHOLOGY

AND

MANIPULATION

HOW TO ANALYZE & INFLUENCE PEOPLE

NLP SECRETS, HYPNOSIS, BODY LANGUAGE, PERSUASION

MIND CONTROL TECHNIQUES

EMOTIONAL INTELLIGENCE AND UNLIMITED MEMORY

13 BOOKS IN 1

ROBERT DANIEL BRADBERRY - TRAVIS JAMES CARNEGIE - KEVIN GREENE HORSLEY - DALE CLEAR GREAVES - JEAN DAN GOLEMAN

PERSUASION 15

Introduction 16

Chapter 1: What is Persuasion? 17

Chapter 2: Fundamentals of Persuasion 19

Chapter 3: Techniques of Persuasion 22

Chapter 4: Weapons of Persuasion 25

Chapter 5: Main Persuasion Skills 28

Chapter 6: Other Persuasion Skills 31

Chapter 7: Why and How people persuade? 35

Chapter 8: Theories of Persuasion 39

Chapter 9: Forms of Persuasion 42

Chapter 10: Ethical Vs Dark Persuasion 43

Chapter 11: Persuasion Vs Manipulation 45

Chapter 12: Emotional Persuasion Tactics 47

Chapter 13: Self-persuasion 50

Chapter 14: Why Read and Analyze Before Persuading 53

Chapter 15: Tips on How to Talk to Anyone 56

Conclusion 59

HOW TO ANALYZE PEOPLE..............60

Introduction 61

Chapter 1: The basics of dark psychology.........................62

Chapter 2: The Dark Triad 68

Chapter 3: Dark Psychology Tactics................................70

Chapter 4: Deception Tactics 75

Chapter 5: Skills and Tools 77

Chapter 6: How to Analyze People 80

Chapter 7: The Benefits of Dark Psychology......................83

Conclusion...85

DARK PSYCHOLOGY AND MANIPULATION86

Introduction 87

Chapter 1: What is manipulation. 88

Chapter 2: Ways to Manipulate and Persuade People. 98

Chapter 3: Behavioral musts to be adopted to become a perfect manipulator. 103

Chapter 4: Mistakes that make you vulnerable to manipulations. 108

Chapter 5: Types of Emotional Manipulation 110

Chapter 6: Psychological Tactics of Manipulation 114

Chapter 7: Difference Between Being "Nice" and Being "Manipulated 116

Chapter 8: environmental tactics and ideas. 119

Chapter 9: Dealing with an abusive or manipulative partner 121

Chapter 10: Laws of Manipulation 122

Conclusion 127

MIND CONTROL TECHNIQUES 128

Introduction 129

Chapter 1: An Overview to Dark Psychology versus Normal Psychology 131

Chapter 2: How to Use Dark Psychology to Manipulate Others 135

Chapter 3: Analyzing People through Body Language................................137

Chapter 4: Emotional Intelligence...139

Chapter 5: Importance of Emotional Intelligence 144

Chapter 6: Mind Control 149

Chapter 7: Mind Control Techniques...153

Chapter 8: The Secrets of Neuro Linguistic Programming.............................156

Chapter 9: Manipulation and Persuasion 161

Chapter 10: Characteristics of Manipulators.....................................167

Chapter 11: Hypnosis 174

Chapter 12: Brain washing 176

Chapter 13: Preventing Manipulation 178

Conclusion...181

HYPNOSIS.................182

Introduction 183

Chapter 1: Dark Manipulation 184

Chapter 2: Main Types of Manipulation (Examples of Manipulation and How to Apply Them).. 191

Chapter 3: What are the psychological manipulation techniques? 193

Chapter 4: How to Understand If Others Are Manipulating You 200

Chapter 5: The Importance of Manipulation 205

Chapter 6: Techniques to Defend Yourself from Manipulation 206

Conclusion... 215

BODY LANGUAGE... 216

Introduction 217

Chapter 1: Understanding the Psychology of Body Language 218

Chapter 2: Our Bodies and The Way They Speaks 221

Chapter 3: BODY LANGUAGE 224

Chapter 4: The Meaning of Body Posture...226

Chapter 5: How to Control and Body Language.....................................230

Chapter 6: Understanding People Through Body Language 233

Chapter 7: Body Language Myths...240

Chapter 8: Guide to Effective Body Language.......................................241

Chapter 9: Body Language & Work..245

Chapter 10: Using Body Language in Flirting and Dating...........................251

Chapter 11: Body language Others..255

Conclusion..258

GASLIGHTING 259

Introduction 260

Chapter 1. Gaslighting 261

Chapter 2. Understanding the Ins and Outs of Gaslighting 263

Chapter 3. How to spot a Gaslighter 268

Chapter 4: Cognitive Dissonance | How Manipulation Affects You 269

Chapter 5. How Gaslighting Narcissists operate to make their Victim Think that they are Crazy 273

Chapter 6. The Effects of Gaslighting 277

Chapter 7. Signs you are Being Manipulated with Gaslighting 279

Chapter 8. Things Narcissists Say During Gaslighting. 282

Chapter 9. Empowering Ways to Disarm a Narcissist and Take Control 284

Chapter 10. Ways to Stop a Deceiver in Their Tracks 289

Chapter 11. A Match Made in Hell: Narcissists and Empaths 294

Chapter 12. How to stop being manipulated by a deceiver 298

Chapter 13. Narcissistic Personality Disorder 301

Chapter 14- Toxic Relationships Recovery 306

Conclusion 311

UNLIMITED MEMORY 312

Introduction 313

Chapter 1: What is Memory?.................................315

Chapter 2: Memory and the Brain 318

Chapter 3: Types of Memory 320

Chapter 4: The Nature of Memory.......................324

Chapter 5: What factors affect memory?.............325

Chapter 6: Train Your Brain.................................328

Chapter 7: Upgrade Your Brain Power.................330

Conclusion..333

EMOTIONAL INTELLIGENCE 335

Introduction 336

Chapter 1: What is Emotional Intelligence? 339

Chapter 2: What are Emotions For? 341

Chapter 3: How to Understand Your Level of Emotional Intelligence 344

Chapter 4: Understanding Empathy 346

Chapter 5: How to Develop Empathy in Your Everyday Life 348

Chapter 6: Self-Awareness 351

Chapter 7: How Environment, Home and Work Influence Your Emotions 355

MENTAL TOUGHNESS

.... 357

Introduction 358

Chapter 1: What Is Mental Toughness? 359

Chapter 2: Characteristics of Mentally Tough People 362

Chapter 3: Assessing Your Mental Strength 365

Chapter 4: How to Develop Habits and Set the Right Goals 366

Chapter 5: How to Change Your Mental State and Increase Mental Toughness for Personal Success 370

Chapter 6: The Psychology of Willpower, Motivation, and Discipline 373

Chapter 7: Disciplined Like A NAVY SEAL 376

Chapter 8: How to Develop State of Mental Strength.....................380

Chapter 9: Improving Your Emotional Intelligence Using Mental Toughness .383

Chapter 10: Risk Management Toughness 386

Conclusion..392

MENTAL MODELS 393

Chapter 1: What are Mental Models? 395

Chapter 2: The Origin of Mental Models 397

Chapter 3: Principle of reason 400

Chapter 4: Writing and Inquisitive? The Best Mental Models to Help You 404

Chapter 5: The Role of Mental Models 406

Chapter 6: Cognitive Bias 410

Chapter 7: Fundamentals of Problem Solving 414

Chapter 8: Mental Models for Clear Thinking 417

Chapter 9: Mental Models For Critical Thinking 420

Chapter 10: Mental Models For Personal Happiness 424

Chapter 11: Using Mental Models for Decision Making 427

Conclusion 429

EMOTIONAL AGILITY 2.0 431

Chapter 1: Emotional Intelligence at Home.........................432

Chapter 2: Emotional Intelligence at Work...................................436

Chapter 3: Benefits of EI 439

Chapter 4: Practical Ways to Use Emotional Intelligence.................441

Chapter 5: Signs of High Emotional Intelligence in People...............443

Chapter 6: Practical Exercises to Develop Emotional Intelligence 448

Chapter 7: Busting the Myths About Emotional Intelligence 450

Chapter 8: Obstacles to the Improvement of EQ 453

Chapter 9: How to Improve Yourself 455

Chapter 10: Guidelines on Managing and Expressing Your Emotions 458

Conclusion 460

HELPFUL STUDY SKILLS FOR MEMORY IMPROVEMENT 461

Introduction 462

Chapter 1: How to Improve Your Memory?..................... 466

Chapter 2: Helpful Study Skills for Memory Improvement............................ 469

Chapter 3: Steps for Memory Formation........................... 472

Chapter 4: The Memorization Process................................ 476

Chapter 5: Health Lifestyle to Improve Memory 478

Chapter 6: Harnessing Your Concentration 482

Chapter 7: Accelerate Your Learning................................ 484

Chapter 8: Bring Information to Life 489

Chapter 9: What is Photographic Memory? 494

Conclusion.. 497

PERSUASION

Introduction

We are going to be talking about persuasion a lot in this book, so maybe we should take a minute to define what we are actually talking about. For our purposes, we're going to be talking specifically about intentional persuasion techniques. Intentional persuasion takes many forms. It could be words, pictures or environment. The words we hear, the things we see, the experiences we have all influence or persuade us to act in a particular way, either immediately or in the future. When someone deliberately molds their words, composes images, or creates an experience to elicit a particular response, that is intentional persuasion.

Intentional persuasion comes at us in many ways. Yes, we are all aware of advertising, and that deliberate attempt to persuade us to do something the sponsor wants us to do. But what about the not-so-obvious? Friends tell you things they think you should do. Blogs post articles on information they want you to have, presented in a way they want you to have it. The upscale decor and excellent treatment at your favorite restaurant keep you coming back every week.

Think about all the decisions you make each day. How aware are you of *how* you came to that decision? Did an actor get you to try a new insurance company? Did you ask your friend about what veterinarian she uses for her pets? Did your landscaper tell you that he recommended trimming your hedges? Did you get a coupon for a free sandwich from your local fast-food chain? Has your partner been talking a lot about the great travel blog he or she has been reading? Who did you vote for? These and millions of other decisions we make all the time are the products of some subtle (and some not so subtle) forms of persuasion.

You can use the powers of persuasion techniques yourself. Intentional persuasion can be used in all types of areas of our lives to achieve outcomes that we want, and that is what we will discuss here. Our primary focus will be to show how to use persuasion to effect change and to show how to counteract persuasion used on you for someone else's gain. Also, we will discuss times when unintentional persuasion may be keeping you from achieving your goals, and how you can exchange those accidental techniques for intentional methods that can get you back on track.

Chapter 1: What is Persuasion?

When people think about Persuasion, many different responses will emerge.

Some might think of the commercials they see around, advising we buy a specific product over another. In contrast, others think of Persuasion regarding politics and how candidates might influence voters' opinions to get their vote. Both are examples of effectiveness because the message tries to change the way the subject thinks.

Can find Persuasion in everyday life, and it is a beneficial force and a significant impact on the subject and the community. Depending on how Persuasion works, advertising, the mass media, legal decisions, and politics will be influenced, and in turn, will encourage the argument. There are noticeable differences between Persuasion and other types of mind control.

Brainwashing and hypnosis will need to be isolated to change their minds and identity. The control to achieve even a single final goal will also work on a single individual. On the other hand, Persuasion can be done on a single subject and on a larger scale so that you can persuade an entire group or even society by changing what they believe in. This can make it a lot more effective and perhaps unsafe because it can change the minds of lots of people at one time rather than the intention of just a single subject.

Many people believe they are not affected by the effects of Persuasion. They think they can find every type of sale made in their way, after which they can understand what is happening and through their reasoning find a conclusion.

In some situations, this will be real; no one succumbs to everything they hear. They use logic, specifically if it goes totally against their beliefs, no matter how intense the argument might be. Most people will avoid specific messages about buying expensive cars, televisions, or in the latest and trending article on the market. Sometimes, however, the act of Persuasion will be less evident, and therefore it will be difficult for the subject to form his point of view on what he is listening to. Influence is seen more by people in a negative light; they will think of a scammer or a salesman who will convince them to change their mind by continuing to annoy them until the change occurs. This procedure is thought of as negative, but we can use it positively and not in a harmful way.

There are forms of Persuasion that can improve a person's life, such as public service campaigns that help people quit smoking or encourage the person to recycle. It all comes down to how Persuasion is used.

Aspects of Persuasion

Like other forms of mind control, there some aspects to look at when it concerns Persuasion.

These elements help specify what Persuasion is. According to Perloff, Persuasion is defined as A process in which communications try their ideas and habits or mindsets regarding a concern, passing a message that may appear to be of free choice. This is one of the essential differences in distinguishing Persuasion from other forms of mind control; usually, the subject is free to make his own choices, even if the persuasion strategies try to mislead his

mind with specific instructions. The issue has two options now: choosing to buy an item or listening to the evidence behind the Persuasion and thus changing her mind.

Component of Persuasion

A couple of parts presents in the Persuasion assist in specifying it further. These elements consist of:

Persuasion is Symbolic.

This means that it uses images, words, and noises to point across. Persuasion will include the representative intentionally trying to affect the subject or group. Self-persuasion is a significant part of this process. The issue usually is not pushed, and instead, they are offered the flexibility to pick their decision. There are many ways that clear messages can be transferred, including face to face, web, television, and radio.

Communication can also take place nonverbally or verbally.

Let us consider these points critically.

To persuade someone, you must explain why they should change their thoughts. This can do through words, sounds, or images.

Photos, for example, are a way to show enough evidence to entice someone to do one way or another. There are also non-verbal suggestions, but they will not be as effective as using words and images.

The second secret is that Persuasion is going to be used in an intentional order to affect the way others are believing or acting. This is obvious; if you are not deliberately trying to influence others, you are not using Persuasion to get them to change. The persuader is going to try various ways to get the subject to think the same way that they do. This might be as simple as having a dispute with them or presenting proof that supports their perspective.

On the other hand, it could get far more involved and consist of more misleading forms to change the subject's mind.

The unique feature of Persuasion is that it allows free choice. The subject is permitted to make their option along the way. For the most part, no matter how difficult somebody tries to convince them of something, they do not have to go for it. The subject may listen to a thousand commercials about the absolute best cars and trucks to purchase. However, if they do not like that brand or do not need a new car, they will not buy it. If the subject is against abortion, it will not change their opinion no matter the number of people who come out to say how great abortion is. The subject most likely will not change their mind. This allows many flexibilities of options than what is discovered in other kinds of mind control, which might describe why lots of people do not see this as a kind of mind control when asked.

Persuasion is a kind of mind control that can happen in various ways. While brainwashing, adjustment and hypnosis must occur on a face-to-face basis, and in many cases in total seclusion, Persuasion can occur in other ways. You can find examples of Persuasion everywhere, when you talk to people you know, on radio and TV or on the internet. When using verbal strategies, you need to deliver clear messages through spoken and non-verbal means because it is much more effective. Persuasion has existed for several years since the days of ancient Greece. This does not mean that the procedures are the same as they used to be. There have been many changes over the years. Modern Persuasion Five ways modern Persuasion differs from how it used to be.

Chapter 2: Fundamentals of Persuasion

Persuasion works to change the subject's thoughts like all other forms of mind control; when you become convinced that everyone is trying to persuade you, it becomes easier to ignore the coming's persuasion. For example, when a conversation is going on, there is some form of influence. People will try to use all ways of power to their advantage. When people think about persuasion, they usually come up with various responses. One could think of advertisements that lead to purchasing a specific product rather than another. Others might think about persuasion about politics and how candidates might influence the opinion of voters and thus win the vote. Both can be called objects of persuasion because you are trying to change your thinking. Effectiveness can be found in everyday life and is a powerful force because it dramatically influences society. While can only persuasion on one topic to change their mind, it is also possible to use it on a larger scale to persuade an entire group or even society to change their thinking. This is perhaps dangerous because it can change many people's minds all at once rather than the mind of a single subject. Sometimes the act of persuasion will be less noticeable, and it may be more difficult for the person to create their own opinions on what they are told. When it comes to the act of persuasion, most people will see it in a negative light. They will think of a salesperson or scammer trying to get them to change all their beliefs and push and annoy them until the change occurs. While this is undoubtedly a way to think about persuasion, we can often use this process positively rather than just in a negative way. For example, public service campaigns can help people quit smoking or recycle; they can improve people's lives. Elements of persuasion

Elements of persuasion

The power to influence others, the ability to change minds and win hearts - all of this is yours, once you master the elements of persuasion. What are these elements? They are confidence, body language, Communication, storytelling and confirmation. We're going to look into that now.

Body Language

Mastering body language is a necessity for becoming more persuasive. It is one of the most important elements of persuasion - you will never see a big statesman or another influential person with poor body language. Studies show that body language has a much bigger impact on how others perceive us, and evaluate our message, than anything else. So make sure that you use it to your advantage.

Communication Skills

One of the best elements of persuasion you can have as an individual is having good communication skills. Consider the fact that a lot of people, if not the majority, will also try to refute your statements. There will definitely be individuals who initially cannot accept or understand your view, which explains why you need to learn how to respond appropriately.

Listen to what they need and want, and then respond. You also have to find the right words and arrange them properly to best suit the situation. There are communication strategies you can use, like rephrasing, asking questions, focusing, and many more. These will greatly improve the message channel so that ideas and views remain constructive and positive.

Storytelling

Storytelling is another important element of persuasion - because it is entertaining. And we human beings are addicted to entertainment. We crave it, because otherwise we feel bored. There are many ways we can satisfy our craving to be entertained, and people differ in their ways - but nobody is immune to stories.

Confirmation

And finally, we all have a deep-seated desire to have our dreams, hopes and wishes confirmed. And if you can provide the confirmation that what they secretly hope for is indeed not only possible, but attainable for them, then they will want to hear more of it, and they will be ready to accept a lot of other things as long as they can continue to get that confirmation.

Adjusting To Others

If you want to persuade others, you need to speak their language and adapt to a situation that they are most comfortable with. Let others feel that they are in control of themselves, their thoughts, and actions. You need to interact according to how they like it. Flexibility and open-mindedness are important, but be sure to stick to your main goal of influence. The two other elements of persuasion mentioned above can effectively follow once you've set the right mood and environment.

You now have gotten a brief introduction to the four elements of persuasion. The next step is to think about ways how you could use at least one of these even today. You could practice telling someone a story. You could practice your body language in front of the mirror, and try out different ways to bring a message across more persuasively. You could think about the desires and hopes of other people, and how you could confirm them.

Factors

Before you attempt to persuade anyone, some groundwork goes into the process that must be done beforehand. You will not just walk up to a stranger in the street and try to convince that person that they should buy a house or even a piece of paper from you. You have not assessed that person to determine if they need what you are selling or if that person has the means to buy the item. That scenario is farfetched, but the same principle applies to any situation where persuasion is being used.

It will help if you put thought into how and why you will approach the person or group of people you would like to persuade. The first factor that needs to be assessed is how easily this person or group of people can be influenced. You need to know how much work needs to be placed into making the individual(s) see things in the way you do.

The first factor that determines how easy it will be to influence other people is whether you are part of their group. Groups can mean several things. Groups can tell family, workplace, gym, or even a social media group. Being part of the group you would like to persuade does the job that much easier because you are seen as one of them. That relatability makes you more trusted. You also have insider knowledge of what makes the group tick. You know their views on particular matters and are less likely to step on toes when implementing the art of persuasion.

Certain qualities make certain people more comfortable to persuade compared to other people. A person's mental health is one of those qualities. Persons who suffer from depression and other mental health issues are more easily swayed to see things from someone else.

This is mainly because this person is likely to be lacking in aggression and has low self-esteem, both qualities that also make a person more easily persuaded. This is a point that can tip the scale in any direction, though, as a person with a mental health issue might agree with you to avoid the conflict if they do not but are not convinced or persuaded to your point of view.

As it relates to a lack of aggression, people who are typically not prone to showing aggressive tendencies are more agreeable and less likely to challenge the point you bring across to them. People with low self-esteem do not hold themselves or their abilities in high regard.

Therefore, they value the opinion of other people more than their own. As a result, they are typically easier to persuade. Slouching posture and the confidence in a person's tone as they speak are indicators of self-esteem levels.

If a person is upright and open in their body posture and speaks with high confidence, this person likely has high self-esteem, while the opposite is exact for low self-esteem.

People who are socially inept and more comfortable to convince than social butterflies. This is because people who are impaired when it comes to social interactions place the burden of the conversation on other people and are less likely to give their opinion freely; this ups the likelihood that they can be persuaded without challenging the person who is persuading them.

Once you have determined why a particular individual or group needs to be approached for persuasion and have learned how you will address the factors that affect how easy it will be to persuade then, you need to figure out how you will cross that bridge to start the process of persuasion naturally. Coming across as awkward or unsure will immediately put your target's guard up, hence making it less likely that you will sway them to your point of view.

If you are not part of the group that you would like to persuade, you need to get the right introduction into that group. Walking or calling will likely not work as we as human beings are naturally suspicious of people we do not know.

This person does not identify you or what you stand for and, therefore, will not trust what you have to say. This is why salespeople who could call have so much trouble getting a foot in to make the sale. The potential customer does not know or trust the salesperson.

Getting someone that the target already knows and trusts is better for forming that bridge. People tend to think that the connections of the people they already know and trust are likely to be trustworthy because people tend to build relationships with people who hold similar views and beliefs.

Sometimes, it is impossible to get an introduction through a mutual connection.
Therefore, as a persuader, you need to be still able to finesse your way into building that connection with the intended target from scratch. Even though cold calling is a sales strategy that many salespeople hate participating in, many salespeople find great success with the technique because they have mastered making the potential customer or client comfortable in their company and, further, trusting of the message that they are delivering. This mastery comes from having great listening and communication skills.

The first thing that active listening does is to allow the persuader to observe the language of the target. When I speak of language, I am not talking about English, Spanish, French, or any of the dozens of other languages said around the world (although I would certainly help if you speak the same language). Language, in this instance, refers to the jargon that the target understands or recognizes as applicable. A computer salesperson will have to learn a particular language that includes memory capacity, hard drive space, and monitor resolution. He cannot hope to sell anything to a computer fanatic if he does not understand these terms and others related to computers.

A master persuader knows how to ask questions that allow him or her to gather information about the one to be persuaded and then listens effectively to gain pieces of information that can make it easier to persuade the target. For example, a door-to-door salesperson can walk up to your door to make a sale. However, if he wants to have an effective campaign, he will not just start selling to you. Even if you want or need the product or service that he is selling, you will be wary of this stranger who has come up to your door and is not very trusting of what he has to say.

Instead, a savvy salesperson will work to get you comfortable, perhaps asking about your day or even picking up on your body's cues about how you are feeling. If you are feeling harassed, he might sympathize with you. If you are in a festive mood, he might enhance that feeling by being equally expressive, hence building a sense of camaraderie between the two of you.

Next, he will ask questions and make the meeting about you and fulfill your needs. Many salespeople's mistake is talking about themselves rather than allowing the customer to discuss their needs and wants. Always make it about the person you are trying to persuade.
Asking questions and listening to the target makes him or her think that you care about their needs and wants. You are respecting their beliefs and, thus, have their best interest at heart. This creates conditions where this person is more likely to actively listen to what you have to say and, therefore, be persuaded.

Even when the conditions are prime for stating your point, remain subtle. There is a notion in marketing that people are less likely to buy when they know they are being sold. The same applies to the art of persuasion. Suppose a person knows that you are actively trying to change their perspective. In that case, if that is plainly stated, the person will likely put up mental guards to prevent them from being persuaded even if the material being imparted is helpful to them. A person is more likely to be influenced if their guards are down. Therefore, you need to be low key about how you impart your persuasion. That is not to say that there are not instances where being blatant with influence does not work, but most often, the indirect route yields faster and better results. Subtle methods of persuasion include storytelling, drawing comparisons, and recognizing the integrity of the target.

It is also vital that you learn to agree with your target even when you do not agree with their view. You will never see eye to eye with anyone all of the time, and that applies to the target of your persuasion as well. While you must agree with your goal as often as possible to indicate that you value their opinion, it is also okay to disagree at times. It would be best if you disagreed since you are trying to convince the target to take on a different point of view. The key is to do so diplomatically and respectfully. Keep your posture and body language open and engaging. An agreeable attitude must be maintained even when you are disagreeing.

Chapter 3: Techniques of Persuasion

Other names can often call persuasion techniques; for example, they can be persuasion strategies. There is no way to encourage someone to act or think in a particular way. As the representative talks to the subject, she may provide evidence to change the subject's mind, using some force or pulling at the problem, performing some services for the issue, or using other types of techniques.

Use of Force

Depending on the situation, the representative might use some force to convince the subject to think like them. This can happen if the ideas don't match correctly, if regular talking doesn't work, or if the agent gets frustrated with the conversation turn. Force is used as a frightening tactic because it allows the subject to find time to reason about what is going on when a regular conversation takes place, compared to the force used when the rep has been less successful using the other means of persuasion that are given. Starting with power can therefore be a perfect thing. It can also strength used if the agent starts to lose control or presents inconsistent evidence to the agent and the agent ends up getting angry. Using force in persuasion procedures is often not a good idea because subjects may feel in danger seeing the use of power when they see that the representative will not offer another option to their request. The natural appeal of persuasion is leaving the subject a choice. However, if fraud is used, the freedom of choice vanishes, and the issue will likely begin to feel threatened. If they feel threatened, they are less likely to listen to what the agent says; this may not complete the process. Therefore, the use of force is not recommended and should be avoided in the persuasion process, unlike other forms of mind control.

Defense of Influence

Another technique that can be used to encourage the subject to lean a specific way is to use the weapons of control.

Weapons of control that can make the agent effective in their purpose are commitment, reciprocity and consistency, material evidence, scarcity, preference, and authority. These six weapons of influence are crucial to the representative, considering that they are part of a change in their subjects.

Reciprocity

The first weapon of control is the principle of reciprocity. This concept postulates that when a single person, the agent, gives the other person, the subject, something of value, the issue will try to pay back in kind. This generally applies when the agent performs some service, the matter will feel they have an obligation to render a comparable service to the agent for a long time. While the two functions might not equal, they have the same kind of worth so that the responsibility of each is equated out.

When reciprocity ends, it produces a sense of responsibility in the subject, which the representative will use as a powerful tool when he wants to use persuasion. The rule of reciprocity is beneficial because it helps the representative bring the subject into the right mindset by submitting him with a sense of commitment. Therefore, the representative can convince the issue to act in a particular way because the subject will feel that sense of responsibility on him. Another advantage to the agent in using interchange is that it is not just a moral position that will put the obligation on the subject; it is also a position supported by social codes. The agent does not need to worry whether the issue will return the favor if they do not feel like doing so; the agent has some tools to get this action.

As a community, people don't like irresponsible people in returning a favor or payment when they receive a free service. If the representative does not believe that the subject is about to pay him back, she will inform the social group. They can tell other friends or colleagues how they preferred the topic, but the subject didn't return it when they should.

Now the agent has imposed social requirements in this regard, making it appear that he will push the subject to do something. For the most part, the issue will be more than happy to reciprocate without requiring any outside force. To not seem greedy and self-centered, the subject will try in every way to repay the agent when the favor has been given. The representative may provide the individual with an option to repay the debt; the subject will appreciate this easy option and most likely will go as the rep desires.

Consistency and Commitment

The next weapon of control is commitment and consistency. The agents need to use both of these if they wish to convince anyone to change their perspective. They are much easier to understand and can assist the subject in making their choices much better when things are consistent. The subject refrains from doing well for the agent to change the facts they are using or change other information needed to help the subject work out the details. Avoiding consistency will make the representative appear as a false person who cannot trust, thus leading to the failure of persuasion. Character is one of the most challenging aspects of the persuasion procedure.

This is because:

Consistency is highly valued in society: most times, individuals like to have things remain a certain way. While there is many variety in day-to-day life, individuals feel safe knowing that everything will stay pretty constant. It allows them to remember what happened, know what to expect, and be prepared if changes occur. If there were no consistency, things would be complicated to plan, and there would be more and more confusion around. If you want to encourage a subject on a particular item, you should ensure that your facts correspond and make sense.

Consistency results in benefiting the everyday life of most individuals. Have you ever tried to prepare a day when something unexpected shows up?

It can make things complicated, and it may wind up feeling like a disaster. Many individuals like consistency because it gives them a way to understand what to do and what will happen. The character serves as a shortcut to everyday problems. Life is hard enough, so it makes no sense to include other futile things. Having eternal experience makes things so much easier.

Thanks to consistency, the subject can make the right choices and work out the details. They need to be sure their message is consistent if the representative wants to persuade the subject successfully. There is no room for wrong proof that can appear sooner and mess up the entire procedure. Keep the facts concise and sincere, and it is far better for convincing the subject.

There is something that connects consistency, and it is the act of commitment. Therefore, it is essential to have a responsibility to understand if the subject is convinced. In marketing, for example, this can mean that the issue will buy the product; in politics, instead of the subject will vote for this candidate so that it can vary according to the nature of the persuasion.

According to the principle of consistency, if an individual makes up his mind to do something, either in writing or verbally, they are likely to honor the decision they made.

It has been found that all of this is more real in terms of written commitments since there is strong evidence that they have accepted the dedication, and therefore, the topic will be emotionally more concrete. A lot of people will say to do something or that they will fix something to reverse and refrain from doing it. Some people will do what they said to do maybe because they didn't promise to do it. However, it is still tough to get results in this way. Also, there is no chance to back it up, given that an oral agreement will end up being what he said, and no one would win.

On the other hand, if the representative can produce a dedication from the subject, he receives proof that the essential things have been done. The important thing for the representative is to get the issue to accept the dedication, as the subject will have more propensity for the brand new topic and therefore will act to adapt to that job.

From that moment on, the issue will begin to participate in self-persuasion for the cause. Also, they will provide themselves with many reasons to support the commitment, thus avoiding any problems with the agent. If the representative can work on that point, the representative will have a lot less work to handle.

Social Proof: Persuasion is a type of social interaction. Therefore, it will follow the social rules where it is happening; its people will influence the subject.

They will be ready to do what others are doing instead of doing their own thing. The subject will base his or her beliefs and act according to what others are doing around him, how these same individuals act, and what they believe.

If the subject grows up in a city, he is likely to behave like the inhabitants who come from that city; on the other hand, those who grow up in a very spiritual neighborhood will likely spend most of their time doing good works and praying. It has become almost a fascinating charm to imitate what others do, even if people will say they want to be different and be an individual. Doing what others are doing can be an example.

If the host says, "Operators are waiting, please call now," the subject may feel like operators are sitting there because no one is calling them for anything. Therefore, the issue does not name because he thinks that if another person is not calling, they should not yell. If the host changes a few words and says, "If the operators are busy, call again," there could be a very different result.

The subject now assumes operators are busy with calls from many other topics, so the product must be the best. The issue will likely call at once and not postpone.

Chapter 4: Weapons of Persuasion

What are you trying to do when you try to persuade someone? In its very nature, persuasion is the ability that allows you to influence your goal in allowing a new belief in your system. You do this by making sure the confidence you instill in your target fits the way he thinks.

You also do this by challenging the authorities he listens to and assuming that you are the authority of the new belief you want him to acquire.

At this point, you will begin to realize that a persuasion is a potent tool. Influence allows you to move in and drop your target's defenses by placing them in a situation where their beliefs changed.

Beliefs are compelling in creating comfortable people, which dictates what they had done repeatedly. They are not 100% correct, and according to experience, they are malleable. Because they can change depending on one's world experience, you, the controller, will be able to challenge them and make your expectations view their environment as something else. It sounds easy, but it is not, of course.

The obstacle you face as you step into persuasion is your goal's definition of comfort. People would always want to believe what makes sense to them, such as their religion, their choice of products, and their entire lifestyle. We do not care about anything else.

Now, you should dispute the notion and offer damning evidence that some (or all) of your convictions may be incorrect. How are you doing this? It would help if you found a way to get them to listen and make sure you are on the same page, and get them to accept that you make sense. It would help if you stepped in for the kill when that happens.

One of the most effective ways to convince the target is by admitting a weakness, downside, detriment, or disadvantage before the other person does. For hundreds of years, this principle has been known, understood, and applied. The reason you admit a flaw in your case, or you state that you seem to be more truthful to the other party and your target by doing so.

For today's society, where everyone is cynical, this will be useful—being skeptical means that people in today's society will usually not believe a case or claim if the only advantages, benefits, and other arguments are admitted in their favor.

As such, they typically expect people to be on the lookout for a capture.

In other words, you will be automatically regarded as an honest and trustworthy person by accepting a harmful, fault, or drawback of your argument, idea, or case at the outset.

This strategy is one of most people who sell their proposals or services using the best tactics; this works well because the dealer would always give a personal brand testimony by making his recent experience so much better than his past life. The comparison makes the objective more conscious of what he wants–he never wants to experience the trouble you have been through, and anything you have tried and used personally will save him the situation.

Why is this tactic going to work? Because this makes them know that you can make mistakes that make them feel you do not have your defenses all the time, and you can relax in front of them. Moreover, your target will feel more comfortable with your presence because you do not seem too enthusiastic about persuading him or her to buy your claim, proposal, or case.

Instead, you are providing them with an opening they can test. So, which makes the entire statement a fascinating proposition, it becomes fascinating about which they would like to find out more. As such, the moment you are trustworthy in the eyes of your target is the moment to strike ideally!

You can better convince your target if you have done something that will be in his or her favor.

Offer your assistance. Any form of help is appreciated. The target will be more comfortable with you in this way. The target will also have a particular relation to you–implying that he sees you just like him or her. Once your goal becomes comfortable with you, your mental defenses will be lowered; this is the perfect time to convince him or her in your plan, statement, or case at the end of the day when he or she lowers his or her mental defenses.

Here's what a lot of self-help gurus would do–they are giving themselves a little background, and that'd always be about when they weren't successful. Once they find an easy way to change their lives, they turn up and tell you. They had told you their methods worked because they were trying the hard way to do things. However, they are willing to show you how to do something that would make your life tremendously better just the way you want it –the easy way. The technique appeals to many people because these accomplished people are willing to share what they have been through and are eager to share the secret without the recipient having to go through the bad experiences to gain the information.

It would also be advisable to point out that you are like your target and offer your claim because you think you are very similar. By making people believe that people with the same rank can easily exchange experiences, you can always persuade people. Now, they had found they could relate to an expert like you!

Knocking off the socks of your target means you are giving it a pleasant surprise. How are you going to do this? Blow off your goal with a fantastic fact, a remarkable statement, or just something that only a few people would learn. Make a claim, case, or suggestion that you can make. Or, you can teach them that has never been done before; this can also be something that can change the way the idea or statement is perceived; this will open their minds in such a way that they will accept new ideas and thoughts. It positions them in a state of relaxation and acceptance, in other words. The psychology behind this is that people enjoy being pleasantly surprised in general. If your target has been pleasantly surprised, making him or her say yes to your proposal, claim or case will be relatively easy. Why do you know? Because if you help such a person discover some fantastic new reality, deciding to pursue another person (you) will always be relatively more straightforward. It will be relatively easy to decide to give in to your statement or suggestion because you intend to feel more comfortable and receptive.

There is a reason why people believe in success stories. In essence, everybody always wants to find the easiest way to do things, and they are willing to buy anything that a person used to get out of a terrible situation that is also likely to happen to them. When you sell a parachute, the belt that people usually use is made of strings used to hold a parachute together; keep in mind that they likely wouldn't find themselves falling out of a plane and using a parachute to save their lives. However, if you tell people that a parachute can hold more than 500 kilos of weight so that they can use it tow their cars, and that it is the favorite bracelet for hunters and adventurers because it can serve as a tourniquet, a fishing line, or something to tie up their tents, they had to buy one from you for three times the price.

That is because these are the information that would make you think the service is much more important than it appears. Another useful tip linked to this technique of persuasion is the last introduction of the plan you want to be accepted or the item you want to purchase; this indicates that you have spent a considerable amount of time asking for approval of a plan or buying an item from your target. Because of your actions, the target would usually have to accept a single item or service after being removed from the start of the discussion. As such, you are placing your most crucial proposal or product at the end of the presentation or conversation would be strategically advantageous.

Be precise. You should be clear and specific in specifying details to your target audience if you want to add an element of credibility and credibility to your statements. The explanation for this is that if your words contain clear and detailed information, it means you know how they affect other things. When you understand how specific issues can be influenced by your plan, argument, or event, your claims are more difficult to attack. Moreover, most people unconsciously feel better when precise and accurate information is given.

Why are figures and percentages of all sorts of convincing people? It is because they get a sense of security from specific numbers. Of course, people do not think that something would work 100 percent of the time. They had wanted something that is almost foolproof because the "almost perfect" object they might get is even better than all the other products they've tried. That is why consumers often prefer to buy items that use numerical adjectives like most, almost all, and 9 out of 10. But if you insist that your product is perfect, notice the number of questions you get. That is because people do not think about perfection. They would instead get something that can be flawed, but they are still guaranteed to work if they fulfill the conditions. That makes the brand more attractive and trustworthy for people.

Suppose you are a consultant for operations management, for example. How can you apply the principle to your target dealings? Okay, you can say your target that his or her revenue will increase by 46 percent in 6 months by using your consultancy services. That is unique now! But if you tell someone you can promise a hundred percent increase in his revenue; then your goal will be more likely to go away.

That is because you do not get your target as a buyer unless you can show him some big-time customer who can back up your story.

Benefits Offer: What is a good offer? An offer should look like it is, not just for your help, for the use of your target. It would help if you made an offer that would build the same appeal for that reason.

Bear in mind that most people are more self-interested, not you. They are more likely to be aware of themselves, and they definitely wouldn't be following your interests. If you are going to make them act on what you are thinking of, make sure you make it look like they are getting more benefits than you would.

Chapter 5: Main Persuasion Skills

You understand that the ability to convince people to do something from your mindset is not a natural God-given gift, as many people perceive it to be. You can practice it and eventually be among the people who can speak their mind and make others follow their ideas. The following are the major skills of persuasion that you should equip yourself with whenever you want to sway people towards your thinking or make them accept your advances. Remember practice makes perfect and so you should have these skills ready so that you do not struggle when communicating to people. It should not appear as if it is a script you have mastered to use whenever you are persuading people, because if you are too uniform and monotonous you will not last long in this profession of persuasion.

Boldness

Being courageous of what you are doing offers you a sense of authority, and when it comes to persuasion, you will have an upper hand in handling the situation. You are the boss of your ego and hence have the right to control your actions, which should be in line with positive expectations of human conduct. A person who wants to have the ability to persuade others should be dignified to put himself at a respectable pedestal. Respect is earned and you should earn yours by recognizing the rights of your prospect, otherwise you your boldness will appear negative as if you are trying to be a controller and not a guide.

Boldness enriches the confidence in you where you get the energy to push on even if you encounter resistance. Never show weakness on your face when you are under pressure from a difficult prospect because you will meet many such characters in the process of conversation. The way you portray yourself tells people how they should treat you. Politeness is part of being assertive because you get the chance to be reasonable in your persuasion. Avoid a situation where the prospect will struggle to understand your motive. Be open with whatever you are saying to guide your listener to understanding your aim. Naturally, one cannot succeed in persuading others without having an assertive character. It has to be entrenched in you so that you can convince others to do something because a weak person will never conquer the minds of people who are ready to correct you in a bid to keep your advances at bay.

A victorious persuasion is not hard if you can understand your rights first and take your stand in the conversation. The next thing should be to arrange the persuasion tools you need to deploy such as making the audience feel that you control the situation. Some things you do in the initial stages of the persuasion determine the grip and control you will have, for instance, invoking the right mental setup of the person you are speaking to, which depends on the level of assertiveness you apply.

Understand what Fuels You

Yu ought to understand what motivates you to want to persuade others to do certain things. You have to know what is in store for you, or what you will achieve when you persuade a person successfully. The concept works just like in the case of an employee who works hard for the monthly payment. The caregiver who focuses on patients' progress to ensure that they recover and eventually feels great after they are well. Another example is a manager who ensures all is well for the smooth running of a company to maintain his position and prosper. Similarly, you should strive for something that would come after the persuasion, so that you can have the will to push on.

The people you enter into a dialogue with have an ultimate reason for engaging you in the dialogue, and when you understand what they need you will have an upper hand over them. Do not try to block their objective of dialoging with you, and instead hold a dialogue that makes them see that they have a lot to gain when they comply with what you are telling them. Hide your needs in what the person wants from the talk and in that case, you will have your way and win the debate very easily.

Because you definitely want the person to agree with you, you will have to weigh the benefits you offer to find out if they can serve his needs, because only then he can agree to your persuasion, and you will have won clean and square.

In our normal human lives, we have ten main requirements or needs that need to be satisfied in the things we do on a daily basis. You should hence try to understand those needs of the person you want to persuade, and identify the ones that are pressing him the most at that particular time. When you note it, you can then carry on with phrasing your request so that he will have no other option but to agree to your request and satisfy the need.

Use Rapport

Rapport has a magical link to persuasion. This technique is a balanced way of using words to pass a message so that everyone will want to listen to you. Unlike the past styles of persuasion that we have read about, this one is a bit physical and does not involve tricking the minds of your listeners. You have to learn how to arrange your words to influence others. However, you can combine the technique with the pasts to manipulate their thinking to your advantage.

Rapport assists you to create a harmonious attachment when you handle yourself at the same level as your listener. As a result, the prospect will be more comfortable and trustful. A comfortable environment emanates bringing the two of you together through attraction, and at such a time, persuasion becomes very simple.

To get a clear picture of how this works, try to remember any of the conversation you ever held with another person before, and why it always reflects on your mind. The things that made that special moment be etched on your mind are the power of rapport. The attachment of such a conversation is always powerful to an extent that you can tell the next words that are to come from the mouth of your partner. It becomes a balanced communication where both of you are patient and very attentive when one is speaking.

Rapport grows where there is a liking between the two of you, but that does not means physical attraction. The balanced exchange of words and information brings about the attraction. When both of you are drowning deep into the conversation, it appears like a dream.

The best thing about this tool is that it can be faked when you want to persuade someone. It will generate a situation just like the one in a genuine situation when done professionally. You need to make your listener feel the attachment to surrender and engage you in the conversation that will lead to your requests. The first step is to make the person like you or feel like you have the same ideologies. In that case, you need to gather information about that person or simply ask him some questions before the dialogue, and you will have an idea of what the person is like.

You will also need to make the person feel some similarity between the two of you, because it is human nature to feel safe around people who we share similarities.

It makes the mind relaxed so that you can persuade him with simplicity. As long as you can make the person like you, you will have won the persuasion halfway.

You can generate rapport in various ways to make the person be attracted to your style, but you do not have to pick any style of generating it because you can combine all of them to create a stronger approach to persuasion. You may have experience a situation where a friend of yours tends to change is tone and accent just to be at the same wavelength of the person he is speaking to. This mostly comes naturally when you want to bring yourself at the same wavelength and ease the tension that your varying accents and tones may generate. When you want to simplify the situation, you can then try to copy the person you are speaking to, so that you can both be at a neutral conversing level. The fun about this tool is that you can be like many people in different situations when you want to persuade them.

Be Persuasive Verbally

The verbal technique is a great to persuasion. It is the technique that salespersons use to thrive in their trade, and you can perfect the same too if you want to b a great persuader. The technique requires a precise arrangement of phrases and words guided towards a definite objective. The point where the rapport left the job of persuasion is when verbal persuasion takes over. It is used to make your motives clear on the minds of your listeners and hence make them do or believe something.

You need to be keen on how you arrange your words, phrases and paragraphs in a balanced sequence that will keep the listener glued to you not to lose a word so that he can understand your conversation. Spice your talk with examples that you can take from the surroundings, keeping in mind that the success of your effort will at times depend on the situation and surroundings. You ought to deploy the technique with care to achieve maximum success.

One of the best ways to achieve positive results in persuasion is to presuppose that what you want to do has already been done, or the person has already agreed to your requests and the result is positive. In that case, you are supposed to phrase your talk in a past tense form, in a manner that denotes that your listener has already agreed to your proposal. To keep yourself going you will need to tell your mind that your listener is enjoying your talk, a technique that will make you try harder to please your listener and make him yield to your request.

Chapter 6: Other Persuasion Skills

Persuasion is the combination and permutation of several critical skills that standalone and inspires trust from the listener. You must learn to use them all if you want to become unbeatable at persuasion. As you will observe, each one builds on the other, and hence, each one is important in its own right.

Communication Skills

This is one of the most critical skills if you want to succeed. Without communication skills, nothing can be achieved. Every person whom you will find at the top will have mastered the art of communication. If you cannot communicate your concept with perfect clarity, there is no chance of selling it – and hence, there would be no positive action.

Communication is often much too hyped of a concept. If you had to define it quickly, it is best said that "communication is putting across an idea in the simplest possible terms." Clarity is the core of communication skills. Other "ingredients" of good communication skills are:

Conviction

It would help if you believed what you are saying, and it should be clear that you do.

The greatest motivators (read that as persuaders) are those who come across as believing what they are saying 100%. The strength of your argument should come from your heart; it should be clear that you are 100% behind what you are saying.

Accuracy

Would you believe someone whose facts keep getting mixed up? It would help if you did your homework when you say something to persuade them to do something. Become the devil's advocate and look at the argument from both sides – for and against. Anticipate questions – even if you are giving a speech – and answer them to put your listener at ease.

Put yourself in the other person's shoes and counter the doubts that may arise from your proposition. The more accurate your facts are, the better are your chances to persuade the other person to your point of view.

Eloquence

Fluency of articulation is another essential skill when communicating an idea across. What you want to say should flow out effortlessly. People should like to listen to you because what you say makes sense and hangs well together. Therefore using the right words, correct phrases, and right expressions is very important.

To ensure that you have mastery over the language, you need to work hard at your vocabulary and use it. People should like to listen to what you have to say when you start talking because you can hold the argument together in a most eloquent manner.

Humor

There is nothing more attractive than having the power of making people laugh when you speak. In most cases, the most potent and beautiful humor is addressed to self, but occasionally taking a jibe at the listener can also be endearing. When you laugh at yourself, you look vulnerable and part-of-the-crowd and immediately accepted.

It is essential to keep in mind that you should NEVER use humor unless you can do this well. Practice saying it aloud in front of your friends and the mirror or videotaping what you plan to say until you perfect it. If you are among those rare people to whom humor comes effortlessly and intuitively, you will do good to use it as often as possible. For those who need to learn it, use it only when you are 100% sure that you have mastered it.

Listening Skills

Communication is incomplete without listening skills. No matter how well you put your ideas across, if you do not listen to the response and learn how to act upon it, you will never establish a robust connection with your audience. You must listen to your audience's cues and swerve your discussion to cover those points.

You must listen more and talk less in most cases because when people speak, they are most vulnerable. They tell about themselves, what they believe, what drives them, what they would like to do, what they find offensive, what they are happy about – and so on.

Listening will give you a hold on your audience, and you will know how to direct your discussion to get your audience to do what you want.

Listening also does one more thing – it connects you to your audience and builds a rapport. Whose company would you prefer? A person who listens to what you say patiently and attentively or one who never stops talking? People love to talk about themselves; all you have to do is ask open-ended questions and listen attentively.

Leadership Skills

You need to come across as a leader to be taken seriously. Leaders are charismatic speakers, avid motivators, and solution finders, among others. Charisma is often thought to be a trait that you are born with. Not true; it is just mastering the art of connecting with people.

Charismatic people instill trust and attract followers – and this happens when you feel confident about yourself and what you are doing. Confidence is something that puts you in the lead wherever you go. They say that you'd recognize a king or a queen in a crowd no matter how they are dressed because of how they carry themselves. They move like they are in total control of the world, which is exceptionally inspiring.

Timid people, people with low self-esteem, would not be able to persuade anyone because of their lack of self-assurance. It is impossible to want to listen or be convinced by one who is not sure of himself.

Problem Solving Skills

There are only two kinds of people in this world you will never forget, the problem solver and the problem maker. Who do you want to be? You would rather be the problem solver. People tend to respect those who can look beyond a crisis and find solutions. People like to be around such people because it makes them feel safe.

How do you develop problem-solving skills? It is not easy, of course. However, contrary to common belief, it is not too difficult either.

Next time you are facing any type of crisis on a personal or professional level, try these steps:

- Remove yourself from the immediate crisis and calm your mind. You may use meditation, deep breathing exercises, or simply take a long walk.

- Resist the temptation to find someone to pin the blame, even if that someone could be you. Do not bother with the why at this time.

- Look at what-next step. What needs to be done immediately to minimize the harm and prevent further damage? What is the first step that needs to be done?

- Take action. Take action now. Put one step in front of the other if you cannot see too much of what needs to be done. If you start taking action, you will find that one thing leads to another, and suddenly you would stumble upon the solution. People, however, will remember and appreciate you for the strength that you showed when you took that first step of action.

Learning-On-Your-Feet Skills

You will often land amid people who speak a totally different language (belong to another school of thought). They could be from a different world, different culture, and different outlook and hence, try your best; you could not connect with them on the premises you have ready for persuasion. In such cases, you need to learn on your feet.

You need to use your observation and communication skills to understand what they want and what they don't and guide your dialogue accordingly. Learning-on-your-feet is a skill that will come in handy anywhere you go, but it is beneficial when you are trying to persuade anyone and find that they do not share your bandwidth.

Observations Skills

Observation skill is the very foundation of leadership and communication. You need to master the art of reading a person within the first one minute of meeting him. With a larger audience, you need to do your homework well, plus feel their pulse when you talk so you can improvise accordingly.

The way a person dresses is groomed, talks, stands/ sits, holds his head, etc., tells you something about the person. Sharpen these skills by practicing, practicing, and practicing. A person with great observation powers will suffer from no set back because they would be relying upon their astute observation powers to learn about their audience. Observation skills are like having a dossier on the person you are talking to; hence, you know what to say and when so you could get him to do what you want.

Motivation Skills

The ability to motivate people is essential. Motivation is, however, a little different from persuasion. When you encourage someone, you need to connect the person to the five needs, i.e., esteem needs, social needs, safety needs, and psychological needs. Persuasion, on the other hand, focuses on a 6th need, i.e., YOUR needs.

Persuasion requires that you include and find a connection between your needs and your audience's needs. Motivation skills are essential because these teach you how to identify your audience's personal needs and how to link them with your purpose.

Selling Skills

Selling skills are among the essential foundation skills for persuasion. Selling includes almost all the gifts we spoke about earlier:

Education or Awareness

Selling requires that your audience be educated on the proposal's merits vis-à-vis their own needs and setting.

Collaboration

It also requires a primary platform for collaboration between you and your audience where both benefit. Persuasion means you get the person to do something you want him to do, but also beneficial to him.

Listening

You cannot sell without learning to listen. Listening will tell you what is essential to your audience and gives you a foot-in-the-door towards your goal.

Understanding

Understanding has two meanings here, i.e., understanding what your audience wants and building on it; and understanding how to use a particular situation to your advantage to persuade your target to do as you want them.

Helping

Selling means helping your audience to do something better, more accessible, faster – you bring in a change that is beneficial to their life in some manner.

Finding Solutions

Selling almost always offers a solution to a problem or difficulty. The better your ability to highlight the situation and your solution, the quicker you have the target accept your answer; the quicker you can persuade them to do what you want.

Connecting

An integral part of selling is building trust, a rapport where the other person believes that you have his best interest at heart. Without connecting with the person at core levels, you cannot achieve much.

Achieving Goals

Selling is showing the target the larger picture. Say you are selling medicine; you will connect it to the goal every person has to stay healthy and pain-free. Your methods need to build and highlight the roadmap to achieving these goals to be persuasive.

Chapter 7: Why and How people persuade?

Why people are persuasive

What makes a person convincing? Why are they persuasive, and you aren't? This is the answer we're going to pursue in this e-book, but I'm telling you now, there is no single, short answer to that question.

What makes this persuasive influence so tricky to pin down and elusive is its almost mosaic quality. It's the result, the perfect merger of several vital aspects that you wouldn't usually attribute to such an influence.

These aspects of their being don't only affect them but also affect us. That's the fascination around it. It's all psychological; it's an overwhelming and sometimes unintentional psychological influence on the people around them.

Confidence is the absolute most crucial aspect when it comes to persuasion. There's no doubt it's been scientifically proven that it's easier to persuade people when you're confident. That's because it's just assumed you're an authority on the topic, and they'll listen to you because they have no knowledge or experience, but you seem to have both.

It's also crucial to understand that humans are doubtful creatures. We're not very confident, and we don't believe in our abilities or even experience, so when someone comes along and appears to be sure and to know more, we follow them like a herd of dim sheep.

Persuasion is just as much about the impression you leave upon people as it is about your actual skill. Like many other times in life, appearances are more "real" than virtual reality because it's all other people will ever know about you. It doesn't matter if deep inside, you're insecure or you don't think you know what you're doing.

On the outside, you're this dazzling, confident creature that can persuade anyone into anything because you've mastered all the essential contributing factors: confidence, eye contact, body language, manner of speaking, tone, facial expressions, as well as your general demeanor.

Benefits of Persuasion

Persuasion is a potent and valuable skill that not everyone has, but everyone should have. It comes in handy throughout your life in virtually any aspect of your existence, from sweet-talking your way into free movie tickets to convincing your boss you deserve a raise.

Your relationship with your spouse

Far from being unfair or manipulative, having the ability to convince your significant other can improve your relationship because you have fewer fights about your disagreements and lack of compromise. Now you can use all that extra time and energy to implement your superior decisions.

Your relationship with your kids

Having the persuasion skills and absolute power and authority to convince your kids to do what you tell them to is as close to magic as you can get. If you don't believe me, try it!

Your relationship with your friends

We all have that one friend who always makes terrible life choices, and no one can get through to them and steer them towards the right path except you, that is. If you have influence and persuasion skills, don't keep them yourself. Use them for good, not evil.

Get paid what you deserve.

Negotiating falls under persuasion, so absolutely everyone should have this skill. No matter if you're haggling at the market or discussing a higher salary, you need to have the ability to convince your 'opponent' that you deserve this, and you should have it.

It's primarily applicable in the workplace, where – let's be honest – no boss will ever willingly part with their money and hand it over to you. So, it's your job to convince them to do it. You've earned it, you deserve it, and it's rightfully yours. You have to ask for it, but you have to know-how, and persuasive skills help with that.

Earn the trust and respect of your boss.

You can accomplish that by becoming their go-to person. Offer your bright ideas, come up with solutions to problems the company is facing, persuade them to implement your suggestions, and that they're the contribution the company needs right now. In time, you will reap the rewards when your boss comes to consult with you first.

Be a good leader to your colleagues.

Your persuasive abilities will prove invaluable to a position like this if you want people to respect you, your work, and your ideas. It should be evident for everyone that your way is the right way, and there will be minimal dissent if you have the necessary influence over them.

Get out of paying tickets.

How to Persuade People

The ability to influence someone during a conversation and make a decision is necessary to become one of the most influential people in the world today. This ability is helpful in business negotiations and everyday life.

In general, the impact on people is not so noticeable. The basic idea is that people their people'stheir simple subconscious desires often guide people's behavior. And to achieve your goals, you need to understand the simple desires of people and then make your interlocutor passionately wish for something.

It should be noted that to influence people; you should NOT try to impose or force them to make a hasty decision. It may seem incredible, but the person who wants to reach mutually beneficial cooperation becomes a huge advantage compared to those trying to impose something on others.

If you are willing to put yourself in the shoes of another person who wants to get something and understand their thoughts, you do not have to worry about your relationship with the person.

The secret lies in the ability to help the self-affirmation of the interlocutor. It is necessary to make sure that your companion looks decent in their own eyes. First things first, six fundamental principles will affect any of your interlocutors.

To achieve their goals, people often use psychology, which helps to manipulate a person.

Even in ancient times, it can be seen that priests ruled the people, instilling in them that religion is harsh and everyone will be punished if they cannot follow the established rules and practices. Psychological influence powerfully acts on the subconscious, causing the victim to be influenced to be led by a skilled manipulator.

If you want to succeed and learn how to manage people, these words of the great American entrepreneur should be your philosophy. You will grow your personality only when you are in close cooperation with the community.

From childhood, we develop the basic patterns of behavior and outlook produced by humankind's long historical, biological, and mental development.

To influence and control another person, it is required that you know their personality and behavioral traits. Most importantly, learn how to use this knowledge to master the specific methods and techniques of influence and control the behavior of the other, based on his outlook, character, personality type, and other critical psychological features.

If you want to learn how to manage people, secret techniques in this article will let you know the theoretical aspect of the question and allow the use of this knowledge in real life.

This method of direct influence on the psyche, whose essence consists of the introduction of the narrowed state of consciousness, makes it easy to control someone else's suggestion and management.

The ability to manage people, primarily, is to combine the knowledge of human psychology and their characteristics. They help change their behavior so that this change will cause the desired reaction in others.

Try to be more observant while communicating; it will help you better understand the individual psychological characteristics of the interlocutor. Based on this knowledge, try using the following methods and techniques to help you manage people correctly and efficiently.

To learn how to manipulate people, you must know how it feels to be on both sides. After all, you need to understand the feelings and emotions experienced by each side.

Just focus on the moral side of the issue. If you are ashamed to receive from people that are important to you, do not accept selfish purposes - better close and do not hurt their highly moral consciousness of the information received.

Legally, a ticket is a mandatory consequence of breaking the law in some way, by speeding, failing to wear your seatbelt, talking on your cell while driving, etc. Practically, however, a ticket can be a negotiation, as long as you have the necessary skills.

Get into coveted clubs or restaurants.

If you're persuasive enough, you can influence any menial gatekeeper and convince them to just let you through without needing to jump through fiery hoops or grease the well-meaning palms of anyone. Talk about some sweet perks!

Get important information.

If you can talk well enough, you can convince anyone to tell you anything. Gossip from your friend preferred customer sales dates from sales attendants, where they keep the extra free peanuts from the flight attendant you get the idea. Sweet talk yourself into perks and valuable info.

Deception

Deception means the act— massive or small, toxic, or kind— of motivating followers to accept data that is not true. Lying is a popular type of deception — the statement of something identified to be false with the intention of deceiving.

Though most people are usually honest, there are times when even those who adhere to honesty participate in deception. Research suggests the typical citizen lies multiple times each day. Some of such lies are major ("I've never betrayed you!") but more frequently than not; they are tiny white lies ("That suit looks perfectly fine") employed to escape awkward circumstances or to protect the sentiments of someone.

Trust is the foundation stone of all types of social life, from the love story and parental involvement to government. This is often compromised by deceit. Since truth is necessary for a human company, which focuses on a shared vision of reality, most individuals assume that everyone else is sincere in their connectivity and dealings. Many traditions have strict societal prohibitions against deception.

Several forms of deception may occur. According to the Interpersonal Deception Theory, there are five specific forms of deceit discovered. Some of these have been demonstrated in other aspects of mind control, showing that some overlap can occur. The five significant types of deception usually involve:

Lies

This is where the operator makes up information or offers data opposite to reality. This information will be presented to the target as fast, and the target will see it as the reality. It may be risky because the subject is not likely to know that they are being given fake facts; if the target realized the facts were inaccurate, they would certainly not speak to the operator, and there would be no deceit.

Equivocations

This is where the agent renders inconsistent, vague, or conditional comments. This is executed to lead the target into confusion and not know what's happening. It could also help the operator save face when the target returns sooner and accuse them of misinformation.

Concealments

This is one of the most prevalent forms of deceit used. Conceals are when the operator omits valuable data or relevant to the setting or purposely engages in any conduct that would hide the information pertinent to the target for that specific context. The operator may not have lied explicitly to the issue, but they would have assumed that the required crucial knowledge will never reach the target.

Exaggeration

This is where the agent overestimates an aspect that twists the facts a little to transform the narrative the way they want. While the operator may not be telling lies directly to the target, they are trying to do the complete opposite of exaggeration in that the operator will understate or lessen elements of reality.

Persuasion is a deliberate effort to change or alter a person's opinions, beliefs, or attitudes toward an issue, situation, object, or person. It is usually achieved by transmitting a message that could be verbal or symbolic.

While it could use persuasion in a manipulative sense, it is, in an actual purpose, different from manipulation. It is because, when persuading a person, he/she is usually aware of your efforts at changing their point of view and willingly or reluctantly allows you to try. In this instance, the person listens and concentrates on what you are saying and then tries to rationalize your ideas with reality before then putting whatever conclusions they come to comparison with what they believed.

Your role in the entire dynamic is to state your reasons for the change you are prescribing, give illustrations and evidence supporting your views and try to convince the target of your advances that your line of action or advice is their best bet. The main goal of this is getting them to switch to a state of reasoning. In this, persuasion resembles manipulation because your goal is still to push the target towards an outcome that they might ordinarily not have considered correct.

The success attained in persuasion usually depends on the target's preconceptions and their strength, perception of the person sharing the new message or idea, their perception of the message or view, and finally, their perception of the conclusion on offer. Upon outlining these reasons, it should be clear to you that the subject of your effort would probably possess ideas that are at least dissimilar. If not contradictory to yours and as such, the entire process would either hinge on your persuasion being very convincing or the target's ability to meet a compromise between the conflicting ideas that would majorly mirror the changes you want.

Below are six major theories that explain how the human mind absorbs and reacts to information. Knowledge of these would significantly increase the odds of persuasion if you could pinpoint it in your target.

The Attribution Theory

It concludes that people would either attribute actions and characters to people and objects, respectively, relative to the context they are being considered in or according to their emotional disposition.

When they attribute using context as a guide, they are likely to come to decisions that consider the environment of origin and situational factors. Such is seen when a person refrains from calling a product inferior or calling a person insensitive, instead of arguing that the product has been made from the best possible items available to the manufacturer. The person is merely reacting as he has learned from his childhood environment.

However, when considering their emotional disposition, they tend to believe that whatever is convenient for them is the only right decision or approach for every other person. Consider this situation:

You meet a person at an event or gather and try to start a conversation with them, but instead of giving you a polite audience, the person appears preoccupied with their thoughts or acts aloof. Angered or annoyed, you walk away, and when asked for an opinion on the person, you characterize them as proud, arrogant, or self-important.

In this case, the characterization you have concluded is based solely on your emotional disposition and does not consider the situation or possible problems the other person might have. The idea is not to determine whether you're mistaken or correct but instead to analyze how you are likely to process information about people and things. You might be right about the person.

Another situation is when you have been accused of doing something wrong, and you claim that your accusers have failed to see things from your perspective and are only interested in their point of view.

It is a perfect example of considering things as regards context. In this case, probably because the things said are negative, you'd notice the emphasis placed on contextual understanding of actions. There is also a minor hint of the dispositional thinking coinciding.

The Conditioning Theory

In this case, the person is likely to do things. It is if they are conditioned to look like their own decisions instead of coercion. It is mostly utilized in the advertising industry where commercials, advertisements, and billboards convey information that would provoke positive feelings in the population of interest.

They then connect such sentiments to their products, making you feel that the work would bring such a feeling into your life since you are more likely to purchase their product, thinking that your decision was an independent one.

It is usually possible because we generally perceive things based on our emotions and are more likely to buy things because they make us feel good.

The Cognitive Dissonance Theory

Based on this theory, it is assumed that people tend to aim for consistency in their thoughts, attitudes, and decisions. It is the cause why most individuals create principles that they strive to follow. Most people also seem intent on reconciling the contradictions as much as possible until they feel comfortable. I would give two examples of this.

Example 1

You have an extreme and deep-rooted need for canned food, either due to the laziness of having to cook meals or the frustrations at having to wait in queues for food. Then you are told that such canned meals could lead to cancer, and you don't want to have cancer. But you also don't want to stop eating canned food. So, instead of stopping with the habit, you comfort yourself that millions of people like you have the same pattern and never have cancer.

The cancer theory might be untrue, but your eagerness to dispute the fact or at least make the consequences seem less severe is your way of changing your mind or making the points you have just learned seem less important or valid. It is one of the ways of dealing with cognitive dissonance theory.

Example 2

Imagine a criminal with a conscience. It is probably hard to envision, but they do exist. Their criminal tendencies are clashing with their tender hearts and causing a bit of discomfort in such a situation. Such a person is very likely dealing with his/ her problems by giving in to the rationale that a criminal and wealthy life far outweighs the benefits of having a clean conscience or right heart. Again, I am refraining from judging whether such a rationale is sound but am more focused on the fact that the person seems to give in to a motivation that overlaps with most people's general aim to deal with his discomfort.

The Judgment Theory

This one is straightforward to grasp. It merely proposes that when faced with a new piece of information or idea, a person's reaction is dependent on the way he/she currently feels on the topic. What this means is that we're likely to accept something that resonates with our current belief, reject something that doesn't fit in with our thoughts, or stay indifferent to something never considered before.

Therefore, when attempting to persuade a person, it is better to determine their views on the topic to gauge whether you'd be successful and if your effort would eventually be worth it.

The Inoculation Theory

The inoculation theory supports the view that even if uninterested before in two points of view, once argued for, you are likely to pick the dominant point of view and stick with it. Here is an example:

You have never viewed a soccer game in your life, but one day you are relaxing on the beach and happen to find yourself stuck between two diehard soccer fans who support rival teams. An argument begins about whose team is better and more dominant, and they both turn to you, presenting their points like you are a seasoned fan and, after some time, ask you to judge who's better. You obviously would pick the person with the better argument to not betray your lack of knowledge on the subject. If another individual were to pose a question to you in the future, inquiring about which of those two teams is better, you'd probably find yourself arguing in favor of the choice you made then, maybe even with some of the same points were used then.

It is the power of vaccinations; the most potent initial idea always takes root.

Narrative Persuasion Theory

From experience, I think we would all accept that stories have a more enhanced effect on perception and opinions than abstract advice.

People's attitudes and views towards objects and others tend to change when they are told compelling stories of such subjects.

The theory attempts to explain the heightened effect on people if appropriately utilized. In this, the listener feels transported, which significantly affects their perception of events, making them more pronounced and vivid than they might have been if they had been expressed ordinarily and abstractly.

The Psychological Perspective

Ordinarily, persuading people would be difficult without organizing and presenting an argument properly. But if inexperience in any or both of these is coupled with an inability to understand moods and stances. Would make your task many times more likely to fail.

The ability to instantly sense and recognize a person's stance on an issue is complex, not to talk of performing the same trick on an audience. Because of this difficulty, most speakers who are attempting to introduce people to a new perspective always tend to ask questions that would enable them to gauge the audience's stance before moving on with their presentation.

After asking such questions immediately, they usually watch out for visible reactions from the audience members, maybe a smile to indicate a knowledge of the topic, sitting up to show interest, turning away, or sighing to indicate disagreement, boredom, or even a person willing to answer. These simple markers give you an idea of how your message may be received and help you map out a strategy of approach.

It is also a valuable tool as people express themselves more sincerely when they do not feel particularly in the spotlight. If you are unsure, do not refrain from asking a few surface questions to test the waters or, more aptly, to feel out the crowd.

It should also be noted that numerous people might give an adverse reaction to one-on-one persuasion and would start arguments to further their points. The moment you realize that your attempt to persuade a person has deteriorated into an idea, it is sensible for you to stride away. Very few disputes occurring outside law courts ever get settled. Engaging in one would be fruitless and time-consuming. That time is better spent elsewhere.

Chapter 9: Forms of Persuasion

Ethos

Ethos is used to demonstrate good character and credentials. The persuasion lies in the power and authority of the speaker. Classical orators used ethos, not to convince, but to fasten the already established rightness of their cause in the minds of their listeners. Ethos means "custom" or "character" in Greek. As originally used by Aristotle, it referred to a man's character or personality, especially in its balance between passion and caution. Today Ethos is used to refer to the practices or values that distinguish one person, organization, or society from others. So we often hear of the ethos of rugged individualism and self-sufficiency on the American frontier in the 19th century; and a critic might complain about, for example, the ethos of violence in the inner cities or the ethos of permissiveness in the suburbs.

Pathos

Having established character and credentials, the second type of persuasion is pathos. This is when a speaker (or crafty wife) uses her listener's emotions to further cement her case. The Greek word pathos means "suffering," "experience," or "emotion." It was borrowed into English in the 16th century, and for English speakers, the term usually refers to the emotions produced by tragedy or a depiction of tragedy. "Pathos" has quite a few kin in English. A "pathetic" sight moves us to pity. "Empathy" is the ability to feel the emotions of another.

Logos

Logos, the third type of persuasion, is the proof of the speech or point being made. Logos is persuasion by words, not hard evidence. It's a presentation that convinces the listener the conclusion given is the right one for the occasion (sort of like having the right answer all along). Logos refers to an appeal to reason based on logic. Logical conclusions come from assumptions and decisions derived from weighing a collection of solid Facts and Statistics Academic arguments (research papers) rely on logos.

An example of an argument that relies on logos is the argument that smoking is harmful based on the evidence that, "When burned, cigarettes create more than 7,000 chemicals.

At least 69 of these chemicals are known to cause cancer, and many are toxic," according to the American Lung Association. Notice that the statement above uses specific numbers. Numbers are sound and logical.

An everyday example of an appeal to logos is the argument that Lady Gaga is more popular than Justin Bieber because Gaga's fan pages collected 10 million more Facebook fans than Bieber's. As a researcher, your job is to find statistics and other facts to back up your claims. When you do this, you are appealing to your audience with logic or logos.

Deliberation

Deliberation is one of the two types of persuasion in speech advocated by Aristotle, the Greek philosopher. Also known as legislative speech, this type of persuasion is an attempt to answer questions of policy or questions of value, and to prioritize problems and proposed solutions.

Refutation

Counterpoint to deliberation is refutation. One form of refutation is the rebuttal speech. To rebut is to overcome the opposition's argument by introducing other evidence that reduces the appeal of the opposition's claim. The other form is the refutation speech. This differs from the rebuttal speech because it does seek to prove the opposition's argument is wrong, or false, but instead it focuses on the faulty reasoning or lack of support provided by the opposition speaker.

Chapter 10: Ethical Vs Dark Persuasion

Ethical Persuasion

How to persuade without manipulating? Your ability and influence to persuade are determined by how abundantly you place other people's interests first. Successful sales professionals tend not to sway. Frequently, I am being asked to explain the difference between the two. Aren't persuasion and manipulation the same thing? This may take more the form of a challenge. Ideally, this happens to be a legitimate question. Ultimately, you are trying to get an individual or group to think or do something they probably won't believe or do without your influence in both cases. Persuasion and manipulation could be referred to as cousins, with the view that one is a good cousin and the other is an evil cousin. Ideally, both tend to be based on some ideal principles of the human race, human action, and interactions.

Good persuasion and good manipulators understand these concepts and know how to use them effectively.

441 / 5000. That is why there may not be something more dangerous than a wrong person with the experience of good people. There are different principles, often the same. However, the results are very different, like day and night. The difference is the intent. In his excellent 1986 book, "The Art of Talking So That People Will Listen," Dr. Paul Swets gave a detailed explanation of both purpose and result. According to him, manipulation is intended to control, not to cooperate. It results in a situation of win/loss. Persuasion is the reverse. Unlike the manipulator, the persuader tries to boost the other party's self-esteem. The result is that individuals react better because they are treated as responsible and self-directed individuals. Also, various intentions and different outcomes are included.

The persuader is intended to serve, to damage the manipulator. And, if you don't want any harm, don't worry if that happens. The manipulator is so focused on himself and his self-interest that, like any other manipulator, an entirely self-serving organism, they only do what they feel is for their benefit and if someone has to suffer. As a result, that's how it should be. They don't know that this isn't just a good practice in life. Ideally, this is not a good business practice.

A manipulator can choose to have employees, but never a team. She may have clients but rarely get a long-lasting one and a source of referrals.

However, once established, the customer base of the manipulator continues to crumble like a stale cookie. He may have relatives and friends, but these relationships are often satisfying or happy.

Indeed, all persuaders and manipulators are conscious of nature. Also, they appear to be the cause of human motivation. However, both use their knowledge to cause a person to take the action they want to take. However, the significant contrast between the two is that while manipulators only use this information for their benefit, the persuader uses it to the advantage of the other person. How deeply you put the interests of other people first determines your power and ability to persuade.

Dark Persuasion

When people attempt to give meaning to the concept of persuasion, their answers always come in different forms. While some may set their minds on the advertisements and commercials that are everywhere in modern society, urging one to patronize a certain product or service over another makes others' minds fall back to the politicians that try to change the minds of voters to get one more vote at the polls. Both examples are correct as they are messages aimed at changing the subject's perception.

The diversion between everyday persuasion and dark persuasion is that dark persuasion does not always have a moral justification. While a normal persuader may try to persuade someone for that person's good, a dark persuader does so with motivations that aren't always good for the other person. They try to get a full grasp of the understanding of the person they wish to persuade, and they take pains to do so because they know what the biggest motivation is.

While persuasion always has moral implications, a dark persuader does not concern themselves with these implications. They are aware of them but choose to place their eyes on their objective(s) instead.

Persuasion is a psychological phenomenon in everyday life of a human being. You are either trying to persuade someone else or are being influenced. What makes the difference between dark and regular is the motivation behind it. In mass media, politics, advertising, and legal decisions, persuasion comes into play all the time. Practicing it in these fields is determined by ways of persuasion that will influence the subject of persuasion.

Chapter 11: Persuasion Vs Manipulation

The line between persuasion and manipulation is so thin that it often gets blurry. Distinguishing these two concepts can often be difficult, mainly depending on the circumstances and your perspective as an individual. Persuasion and manipulation are alike in that someone is trying to influence the decisions and behaviors in both cases. The critical distinction between the two is that manipulation is seen to be highly driven by self-interest, where one party is willing to go through any length to benefit themselves, including putting others in harm's way. Persuasion, on the other, is the more generous cousin of manipulation--there is a desire to influence self-interest, but there is often a line drawn to mark boundaries. Persuasion is the more ethical way to go about it, many will argue. However, when all's said and done, the two concepts seem to intertwine, mainly depending on the techniques used to achieve either of them.

People always have different ideas of what words mean, but to be successful in manipulation and persuasion, you need to know the different ways these terms are understood and what we mean when using them in this book. In everyday speech, influence is considered a neutral word; of course, it can persuade someone to do something that helps the persuader and not themselves, but the word itself does not imply that. On the other hand, manipulation tends to mean the ill intention of the manipulator.

The ethics of manipulation and persuasion are a topic we have explored throughout these pages, but we know that for our purposes, influence is changing someone's beliefs, while manipulation is changing someone's actions. This is easy to remember because NLP involves the neural pathways for both language (religion) and programming (step).

If you want your subject to change their behavior, you have to get them to change their thinking about their behavior. They are a thinking person just like you are, and while they have mental shortcuts that can get in the way (just like they can for you), your subject is entirely capable of talking through their judgment calls with you. In a conversation with you, they can re-evaluate their actions, and if you go through the conversation the right way, you will have the opportunity to convince them to change.

When it comes to manipulation, there is a slight difference from persuasion. The difference is that it is the right thing to ask them to change their behavior directly at some points. Now, you don't want to pull this out as your first move. This is something you build up to after a long conversation — after you accomplish steps zero and one, just as you do for persuasion. But the big difference between changing someone's ideas and changing their behaviors is here in step two: more often than not, you should directly tell them what you think they should do differently.

When NLP newcomers learn this at first, they are totally taken aback. They think, how could I possibly be told to tell them directly to change their behavior? But if you think it through a bit longer, it makes sense. What is the difference between belief and behavior? Persuasion changes belief by getting close to someone's mind and changing what is in there, and manipulation is getting closer to their mind and changing what is in there, too.

But with manipulation, there is the added hurdle of getting them to follow up on the change in thought. While it is true that all of our behavior ultimately comes from our minds, our brains are still not simple masters of our actions. Instead, our efforts are determined by multiple factors other than simply what our brain tells us to do. You eventually have to ask your subject to change their actions directly because, for new behaviors, a change in thought is not enough.

Your subject needs voices other than the one in their head, telling them what to do. They have the thought you got into their head through NLP; you are telling them directly, too. But there is still more you have to do.

Social bonds are essential to human beings. If you want to manipulate someone's behavior, unlike when you persuade them into having new thoughts, these thoughts alone are not enough. You telling them what to do is not enough, even once they have recognized you as like them. If you want to change their behavior, next, you have to change the person's social environment with the undesired behavior.

This is not a catch-all for manipulation because nothing is. After all, not in every situation will you be able to change the social environment of your subject. If they are not friends or family, but rather a co-worker, this could prove much more challenging. It only fits since manipulation is a more complicated and challenging task than persuasion.

But if this is a person whose social environment you have some control over, you have to determine what social factors lead to undesired behaviors. Is there another family member enabling their drinking or drug use? This is the most prominent example, but it is symbolic of the NLP manipulation framework in general.

All of this is to say that when you are not in control of a person's social environment, directly telling them what action they should take is a necessary and challenging part of the process. It is so hard because there is no way around it, and it is also straightforward to do the wrong way.

You have to work hard not to work too hard for them. If they can see how badly you want them to change their behavior, they will want to continue acting the way they do out of spite. Don't give them this opportunity.

Recall how with persuasion, we never addressed objections to your frame if you don't want to address the structure itself at all possible. That's because if you address the frame itself, you are acknowledging the fact that it is not the naturally occurring reality that you want your subject to see it as. However, with manipulation, the situation is different from persuasion.

With manipulation, you have to respond to objections directly because you have to tug harder than you do with persuasion. You see, persuasion is a subtler, quieter art than manipulation. This is a direct way of saying that manipulation is loud and aggressive because it is not.

But you can't be quite as gentle with manipulation. You want them to change their habits, so to get your subject to understand the gravity of the situation enough to trigger the behavior change, you must be slightly pushier than you are with persuasion. Again: don't be pushy, but you can't be as subtle as you are with persuasion.

Even when you deal with their objections, you are better off preparing for them before they come up. When you are ready for any question or complaint your subject can haul at you, it is a signal to them that you are like them, you see things from their side, and perhaps, you know better. This is Step One yet again. If you demonstrate that you are like them and can reason things out better, they will listen. You are almost ready to get into the techniques of manipulation, but before then, you need to get into the personality of the NLP manipulator.

You might think that you are born with a certain personality, and you can't do anything to change it, but this couldn't be further from the truth. The kind of personality you should adopt to get people to do what you want is one that anyone can learn.

Why is learning this personality so important? Well, it's important because you need to seem like you are positive about what you are saying.

If you seem even a teensy bit unsure in any of your speech or body language, nobody will buy what you are selling.

That's why in your body language, dress, facial expression, tone of voice, and words, you need to pull off the personality of someone who knows what they are talking about.

They have the answer to your question; they know what's what. If you can pull off that personality, you don't have to do anything else. Personality is everything — don't forget that.

Personality is so important because no matter how unlikely something seems on the surface, people will believe in it if it comes out of the mouth of the right personality. You have to believe in what you are saying to some extent if you expect to pull this off, so don't think you can playact your way through the whole thing — after all, you are not doing the personality right if you are unsure about the merits of what you are saying. But more important than anything you say is the personality you are displaying while you say it.

Not everyone has this naturally, but it is not nearly as hard to learn as you might think. The right place to start is always your breathing and your posture. You already know what the right posture to take is — stand up straight and without shaking. Now, take deep breaths like for your state control exercises. Just like before, don't breathe loudly. Breathe deeply but not in a way that anyone can tell is unusual.

The third and final thing you have to do is enter the headspace of this unshakeable personality. Everyone has experienced a moment where everything was going right for them, and that is exactly the place you need to go. Revisit that memory as though you were there again right now, and come back as the person you were in that memory.

Chapter 12: Emotional Persuasion Tactics

Emotions are a core part of our existence as human beings. Regardless of the attempts made by most of us to construct a persona that is tough and formidable in this dog-eat-dog world, we still feel things. All of us do. And many people find themselves making decisions based more on their emotional states than brutal, logical rationalization. This propensity is that emotionally manipulative people exploit through several tactics, strategies, and techniques.

The most powerful emotional manipulation techniques are covert; that is, they are designed in such a way that they change your behavior, character, and attitudes without you realizing it. They are underhanded methods that operate so profoundly that they often penetrate your consciousness, burrowing so deep that they reach your subconscious. Don't be fooled by individuals who are charming and likable around you. They could be your boss, a coworker, a friend, or even a relative, and your interactions with them could seem as normal as with any other person – but be on high alert.

Even harmless-seeming behavior can be very toxic. For instance, you may have a friend with whom you find it difficult to share negative feelings that you're having or worries that keep you awake at night. This may be because this friend always projects a conscious positivity on everyone around her and maybe even frowns when you mention something negative around her, like you're staining her vibe or dampening everyone's spirit. Your natural reaction may be to view this trait as positive or helpful. This friend is trying to make you focus on only the good stuff because, you know, life is too short to spend time complaining about bad things that may be out of your control anyway.

However, if you scrutinize this scenario intensely, you'll realize the intense manipulation that is happening underneath it all. Because of this, friend, you find it challenging to speak your mind and express the things you genuinely feel. Incredibly enough, this exterior of eternal positivity may be a coping mechanism for this person. Still, because of their quest for mental and emotional stability, the box you into your headspace so they can feel good within themselves. That's manipulation.

Emotional manipulation exists in many forms and can be employed through various techniques. Below are seven major emotional manipulation strategies.

Negative Reinforcement

Have you been in a scenario where someone did something to you that they knew you didn't like? At this point, did you feel the urge to do something to them that they wouldn't want in return? The guiding law behind this is that the manipulator understands that if they do something you wouldn't like as payback for what you have done, chances become higher that you will do something that favors them in the future.

Imagine a sibling who lets you use his car for a side hustle on the weekend. This sibling then does something that hurts you, and, angry, you go for happy hour drinks at the bar without him. This sibling then becomes cold, refusing to let go of his car keys until you apologize and do something he likes, such as promising a more significant cut of the pay you earn from using his car or doing his laundry.

The trick is straightforward. The manipulator knows that if they persist with their hurtful actions, you'll give in eventually and do what they want. This way, they not only get you to do what they like; they further increase the likelihood that you'll do similarly in the future.

Premature Disclosure

Say you work in an office, and a new associate joins the team. As a professional, you want to be careful about the kinds of conversations you have in the workplace and are very skeptical of non-work-related talks. However, this new associate has heard that you're the best on the team in a specialty that could significantly enhance her output, comes to you, and engages you in an unexpected conversation. She invites you for coffee during lunch and then opens up to you about an intimate matter. She tells you personal stories and opens up about her dreams, goals, fears, embarrassments, likes, and dislikes.

You are taken aback, shocked that someone you just met could let you in on matters so personal, but this false gesture of intimacy moves you, and you feel the burden of trust that she has placed on you become heavy on your shoulders. This is what the manipulator is counting on. You are scared about opening up, but because she has exhibited such vulnerability toward you, you decide that it wouldn't hurt to tell her a few things.

You are at first skeptical that she may not understand your perspective or accept your stories at face value, but she does, even going further to say that she has experienced similar things and feels the same way you feel.

What this manipulator has done, however, is build a false connection. She could have also done this by trying to impress you with her accolades and achievements, so you see her as a worthy and valuable colleague. Ultimately, all she wants is to exploit this make-believe "relationship" to call in special favors with you on that expertise that only you possess.

Guilt

The capacity to feel guilt symbolizes that you still have a conscience. In your drive to remain a good person, you will make mistakes and feel guilty about this. Because guilt is a negative emotion with close ties to shame and anxiety, it can be very uncomfortable, but this doesn't make it a weakness. It is a part of you. It only becomes a problem when emotional manipulators use it to control you.

As a family, society, religion, and many other forms of moral instruction have taught you to feel guilt, especially when you feel like you have harmed someone through your actions or/and inactions, manipulators seize this cow and milk it to death. When you feel guilty, you want to get back in a good place with the offended party, usually using an apology or making amends. Manipulators divert this need for penance to make you do their bidding. Because your thought process has become clouded by guilt, you are instead focused on fixing things, and you fail to see that the manipulator is making you do something that you don't want to.

Empty Words

Many emotional manipulators are skilled with the use of their tongues. They can build castles in the skies and take you across the galaxies, all through their words. These manipulators realize that most individuals have an inbuilt desire for verbal approval. People like to be told that they are loved, admired, respected, and appreciated. By using empty words to fill this need, manipulators get you to lower your guard so they can take over the reins of your life.

It's not just enough for someone to tell you that they love you. If their actions don't show this love, then there's a problem. Chances are this person is merely inflating your head, so you do what they want you to do. If you're ever confused about someone's true intentions, judge the person solely based on their actions. You'll have your answer.

Gaslighting

If you're in a relationship where you apologize all the time, feel endlessly bewildered or withdrawn, or find yourself having trouble making decisions, you may be a victim of gaslighting.

With gaslighting, the manipulator denies your perception so vehemently that you begin to doubt your ideas and feelings. By rejecting an apparent reality, they render it invalid.

Something happens, and they tell you it never did, or that it's all in your head, or that your memory is playing tricks on you, or they even go as far as to question where you got the idea. By doing this, they undermine your understanding of events and perception of reality to the point where you begin questioning your sanity.

Gaslighting should be apparent to most folk, but because expert manipulators tend to start small and increase its severity over time and also couple it with other subtle manipulation tactics, victims' perceptions are questioned so frequently and severely that they lose all trust in their perceptions. They lose the capability to function independently, relying on the manipulator's definitions of reality.

At this stage, the manipulator has already won. Having rubbished every ounce of self-esteem in the victim, the manipulator finds it easy to exercise complete domination.

Rationalization

A man hits his wife only to come around minutes sooner to issue the following apology: "I'm so sorry I hit you. You just hit so many buttons, and I lost control. I'm sorry."

The above seems perfectly sincere and heartfelt but could very much be the words of an emotional manipulator. As humans, when we love or trust people, we always want to see them in the best possible light. As a result, even when they do the wrong things, as long as they come up with an explanation that makes some level of sense and tugs at a few heartstrings, we will most likely overlook what they have done. Manipulators use this to their advantage.

Although what they have done is wrong, they find a justification that sounds logical and rational, so their bad behavior is minimized till it doesn't seem so bad anymore, and so that they can get you to stop talking about it and move on.

Creating Fear

You may observe this trait, especially with manipulative individuals close to you, such as family members or lovers. These individuals know how much you cherish the relationship you have with them and how special they are to you, so they'll use this to get you to do what they want. By sowing the idea in your mind that they will terminate their relationship with you or dilute it if you take specific actions, they manipulate you into doing things that you would not naturally do.

The fear of loss is a powerful fear that nobody wants to relive. As a result, the strategy of creating fear works in keeping you right where the emotional manipulator wants you to be. What makes it worse is that, in this scenario, the person who created the fear is the same person who can relieve you of it, putting all the power in their hands automatically.

Emotional manipulators come in many shades and guises and employ techniques vaster than the number presented above. The guiding idea here, however, is for you to develop an understanding of their techniques and strategies and understand that they could be anyone. Who knows, you may have been a victim of emotional manipulation for years without even knowing it. Now, you have all that you need to cut the puppet strings and rewrite the narrative.

Chapter 13: Self-persuasion

Self-persuasion is one of the most powerful and one of the most challenging areas of persuasion. The reason is that where the other forms of persuasion are applied from an external force, self-persuasion comes from within. So how can persuasion be used as a technique?

First, self-persuasion can be used as a method to persuade others indirectly. Self-persuasion must come from within. In other words, a person decides without being told what to think directly. Persuading someone using self-persuasion involves setting up a situation where the other person comes to the desired conclusion because of what they have learned. Given what they know, they can come to no different conclusion.

Self-persuasion is a valuable technique to employ in association with some reward. If a person behaves in a certain way and receives a benefit afterward, they will begin to see that the behavior is beneficial and conclude that it must be right.

We'll look at the techniques of self-persuasion on others more. First, let's look at one of the most beneficial ways self-persuasion can be used: As a means of personal development.

Personal Development

We all have parts of our life that we would like to improve. It's just human nature to want to get better and strive for something more. But getting the change we wish to see in our lives is difficult because we find it hard to reason our way into the proper behavior. Persuasion techniques don't work well when we try to use them on ourselves because we realize what we're doing. It's like trying to use persuasion tactics on another person overtly. If they know we're trying to persuade them; they tend to fight against what we're asking them to do.

Our minds are the same way. So how do we end up doing things we don't want to do over and over again? One way is that we accidentally create habits that aren't beneficial in our lives. Because these tend to be associated with a reward, we do them repeatedly until the pattern is formed. For instance, we eat candy because it tastes so good, but we create a habit of taking in a large number of calories that aren't good for us.

We eventually figure this out and try to make changes, but our old ways are too easy to fall back on. We've got bad habits holding us back.

According to researcher and self-improvement specialist James Clear, the reason is that your body is continually building habits. Oxford University researchers found that adult humans have over 40 percent fewer neurons compared to newborns. Clear says that this is because your brain is actively pruning away connections between neurons that don't get used, and at the same time, reinforcing the links that you use regularly. This makes your brain work more efficiently, making it much harder to change.

Because the habit is such a solid subconscious force, you can use it as a method of self-persuasion by building new habits that help you.

Habit Stacking

The term 'habit stacking' comes from S. J. Scott's 2014 book by the same name. In their work, Scott and Clear propose that you 'piggyback' a valuable habit that you want to create onto a pattern that you already have. For example, you need to do a better job of loading the dishes in the dishwasher regularly, instead of just leaving them in the sink. You have a habit of listening to your favorite podcast every day. If you change your podcast habit to hearing in the kitchen when it's time to load the dishwasher, you'll soon create a habit of loading the dishwasher while listening to your podcast. The new, desirable behavior connects with the existing practice.

This works the best with small tasks that can easily combine to treat them as one habit. The power of habit stacking is to make excellent and easy habits interlocked so that you always do one with the other. Eventually, the perfect pattern becomes just as strong as the original habit because of the pruning of neuron pathways to favor what we often do and eliminate what we don't do often.

From Many Small Habits Come Big Change

This system of self-persuasion works best with small things that can easily do along with something else. But what if we want to make a significant change? Divide and conquer is the strategy here. Please take a look at the significant change you want to make, and divide it into smaller components that all work together to reach the larger goal. Like any complex project, you can take your bigger target and separate it into several smaller tasks.

Those smaller tasks can be stacked together with existing habits you already have to make a more significant, long-lasting change.

For example, let's take a look at weight loss. The easiest way to lose weight is to eat less and exercise more. Sounds simple, but we all know how difficult those steps can be. Let's divide it down into more minor changes. Eating less can be accomplished in several steps. First, make a habit of using your reusable shopping bags at the store, and only buy what you can fit into those bags. If the food doesn't come home, you can't eat it.

When you get to the store, or anywhere for that matter, quit parking close and instead use your regular weekly shopping habit to get exercise by walking to and from your car. Make your driving and errands into an exercise habit every day by parking farther and farther from your destination. Add an app to your phone to count your steps, and you'll see how quickly this adds up. When you make your meals at home, dish them up on smaller plates and put the leftovers away before you eat. Like to eat from a drive-through? Use that habit to cut your food consumption by making a habit of throwing away half of what you order before you leave the lot. You'll either lose weight or lose the habit of going to the drive-through and wasting the food.

Do you stop for a fattening coffee every morning? Try changing your order to lighten it up, or order a smaller size. Or, change your order altogether and grab a healthy muffin for your breakfast instead of eating it at home.

Once you get to the point you hardly notice that you are doing these small things, add a little more change to the habit. Walk around the neighborhood before you sit down to watch TV, or watch your favorite show only while on the treadmill or stationary bike. Making these minor additions to existing habits will start to make a difference over time.

Making a Well-Worn Path

When attempting to use self-persuasion to make any changes in your behavior, it's best to set up a path for yourself ahead of time so that you have little chance to go astray until you've established the new actions into a habit. Chip and Dan Heath, in their book Switch, compare our behavior to the relationship between an elephant, a rider, and their path. You can direct the rider, being our conscious mind, only so well when the reason is our own. The elephant, being our emotions and subconscious mind, will take some direction, but in the end, it will go where it damn well pleases.

But the elephant can be controlled ultimately by the path it is on. If the course is well-defined and challenging to stray from, even the most substantial elephant must follow along. To change a behavior, shape the path for your elephant so that the habit will form quickly.

Recognizing Self-Persuasion Tactics

We all like to think that we are immune to the control of others and that we are free to make our own decisions. With the advent of the Internet and after social media, the positive thinkers were calling this time the new Age of Information, where all information would be available to all people, all of the time. Never would people again be without the valuable facts they needed to make the best decisions about their life. People would find peace and understanding as we all started to see much more central ground because we had a better sense of shared experience worldwide. Each person would be able to make their voice heard.

How is that working out? Not so well. Some people think that this is the most divided nation, mainly along political lines. If you were to judge public discourse only by what you see online, you would expect to see rioting in the streets. When you talk to people face-to-face, though, you see that things are not nearly so black-and-white. What's going on?

Much of what you're seeing is persuasion in overdrive because of the Internet. As you've seen in the principles and techniques we've given you for influence, communication is a crucial component to the persuasion of all kinds. The always-on nature of communication today has just increased the communication channels we all have available to us ten-fold-times-ten.

But isn't that supposed to make us all more intelligent and more well-informed? Getting all of those facts at the tap of a screen should make it, so we never get fooled. How can so many people become to so many disparate decisions on what is right and wrong? As usual, the human mind is at fault.

Why Analyze People

Analyzing people is something that various people in different capacities utilize. The most basic reason you may decide to analyze someone is to understand them. When you have an in-built technique of understanding others, you will discover that having a cognitive instead of an emotional connection is critical to establishing a genuine connection with someone else's mind. Consider that you are trying to land a deal with a significant client.

You know that the agreement is critical if you hope to keep your job and possibly even get a promotion, but you also know that it will be a difficult task to manage. If you can read someone else, you can effectively allow yourself to know what is going on in their mind honestly. Think about it—you will tell if the client is uncomfortable and respond accordingly. You will tell if the client is deceptive or withholding something—and respond accordingly.

You can tell if the client is uninterested, feeling threatened, or even just annoyed with your attempts to influence him or her, and you can then figure out how to reply. When you can understand someone else's mindset, you can regulate yourself. You can fine-tune your behavior to guarantee that you will be persuasive. You can make sure that your client feels comfortable by adjusting your behavior to find out what was causing the discomfort in the first place.

Beyond just being able to self-regulate, reading other people is critical in several different situations. If you can read someone else, you can protect yourself from any threats that may arise. If you can read someone else, you can understand their position better. You can find out how to persuade or manipulate the other person. You can get people to do things that they would otherwise avoid. Ultimately, being able to analyze other people has so many critical benefits that it is worthwhile to do so.

Developing this skill set means that you will be more in touch with the feelings of those around you, allowing you to claim that you have a higher emotional intelligence simply because you come to understand what emotions look like.

You will be able to identify your feelings through self-reflection and learn to pay attention to the movements of your body. The ability to analyze people can be invaluable in almost any setting.

When to Analyze People Analyzing people is one of those skills that can use in almost any context. You can use it at work, in personal relationships, politics, religion, and even just in day-to-day life. Because of this versatility, you may find that you are constantly analyzing people, which is okay. Remember, your unconscious mind already makes snapshot judgments about other people and their intentions, so to begin with, you were already analyzing people.

Now, you are simply making an effort to ensure that those analyses are made in your conscious mind so you can be aware of them. Now, let's look at several different compelling situations in which being able to consciously analyze someone is a critical skill to know: In parenting: When you can analyze other people, you can begin to use those skills toward your children.

Now, you may be thinking that children's minds are not sophisticated enough to get a reliable read on, but remember, children's feelings are usually entirely genuine. In essence, they have their feelings that they have, and though the reason behind those may be less than convincing to you as a parent, that does not in any way dismiss their feelings. By recognizing the child's emotions, you can begin to understand what is going on in your child's mind, and that will allow you to parent calmly and more effectively.

In relationships: When you live with someone else, it can be straightforward to step on someone else's toes without realizing it. Of course, constantly stepping on someone else's toes is likely to lead to some degree of resentment if it is never addressed. Yet, some people have difficulty discussing when they are uncomfortable or unhappy. This is where being able to analyze someone else comes in—you will tell what your partner's base emotions are when you interact, allowing you to play the role of support.

In the workplace: Especially if you interact with other people, you need to analyze other people. You will see how your coworkers view you, allowing you to change your behaviors to get the company image that you desire. Beyond just that, you may also work in a field that requires you to get good readings on someone in the first place.

Perhaps you are a doctor; to begin with, you may need to tell how someone is feeling and whether they are honest with you. Maybe you are a lawyer, and you need to analyze the integrity of your client and those that you are cross-examining. Maybe you are a salesperson who needs to tell if you are convincing in your attempt to close a deal.

There are some obvious and crucial differences between Persuasion and other types of mind control, such as brainwashing and hypnosis. While these two requirements should isolate the subject to change their minds and identity, Persuasion does not require isolation. Manipulation is used on one person. Although Persuasion can also be done on a single subject to change their minds, there is also a possibility of using it on a large scale to change the minds of a whole group or even an entire society.

For this reason, Persuasion is a more effective mind control technique and perhaps more dangerous because it can change the minds of many people at the same time instead of the mind of just one person at a time. Several people make the mistake of thinking they have an immunity to the effects of Persuasion because they think that they will always see every sales pitch that comes their way.

They believe they will always be able to use logic to grasp what is going on and then find a logical conclusion to it. Thanks to the fact that people are not always going to fall for everything they hear if they use logic, this may be true. It is also possible to avoid Persuasion because the argument does not augur well with the person's beliefs no matter the strength of the argument. However, some people know how to use persuasive messages to encourage people to patronize the latest gadgets or products in the market.

This act of Persuasion is very subtle, so the subject will not always identify it, so it will be quite hard for them always to be able to form an opinion about the information they will get. Whenever Persuasion is mentioned, one likely thinks of it in a bad light. This is because they automatically think of a conman or salesman who is always trying to get them to change their perspective and eventually push them until this change is achieved. While dark Persuasion is prominent in sales and conning practices, there are also ways that Persuasion can be used for good, like in diplomatic relations between international bodies or in public service campaigns. The difference only lies in how the process of Persuasion is brought to play.

Dark Persuasion is a branch of Dark Psychology, and it is very effective in its way. Dark Persuasion is something that is used often. What are the principles of Dark Persuasion? The first Brainwashing Brainwashing is the practice of taking over someone else's capacity to think. Naturally, we all have unique thinking patterns, and we all have the power to think critically about what is going on around us.

Brainwashing takes away this power, and it puts that power into the hands of whoever is doing the brainwashing. Cults use this technique heavily, as it allows them to recruit and retain members.

Brainwashing has many different implementations, but the principle remains the same throughout. A person is first brought into the fold of the new scenario. They are told that they matter, worthy, and have a place to be in the new milieu. They must separate them from the outside society to do this. The brainwashed person is convinced that this new way of thinking is a way to live better and happier.

A person is often the center of the brainwashing, centered as very wise or smart. This person will be the 'leader' of the cult, and the person who is being brainwashed will start to think of this person as their new family director. This is all part of the breaking down of the self. Their sense of self must be broken down.

In cults, this will often already have happened when the person joins. Cults look for people who are weakened by loneliness, suffering, or isolation. When a person has a good sense of self, they are less susceptible to brainwashing. Thus, this must be attacked and broken down to convince that this new way of living is the best. Brainwashing might also employ guilt to convince a person that they are in the best environment. Brainwashing will have people feeling guilty about their past lives,' and they will be presented with a solution for their guilt. Guilt and shame are potent emotions, and people will do whatever they think will work to get away from these emotions.

Guilt and shame are what people feel when they are sad and ashamed about themselves. These negative emotions drive people to search out a solution, and often the solution can be manipulated by others in the form of brainwashing. The brainwashers present the possibility of salvation. The possibility of salvation comes in the form of accepting the new ideas or format of the brainwashers. It comes in the form of accepting that this new person or group can save them.

Leniency is presented to the person. Rather than being told that their past transgressions are something that they will never escape from, they are told that they can escape it if they reach their new goals with the brainwashing. This feels good, and it is hard to turn away from the possibility of salvation. Another form of Persuasion is hypnosis. Hypnosis works on a few basic principles. The first is induction.

Induction is where a person is helped along to a state of suggestibility or relaxation. This is a state wherein they are put at ease and are made vulnerable to messaging.

The person who is being hypnotized is welcomed into this vulnerable state, and it is from there that they can be persuaded. After a person is put through an induction, their defenses are broken down, and they can receive suggestions. The suggestions may come in many different formats. Some people seek out hypnosis to bring themselves away from bad habits, like smoking or other addictive habits. In this format, the person would go through the initial process of induction, and then, the hypnotist will make suggestions to them about how to quit smoking and messages relating to why they shouldn't smoke anymore.

The hypnotist's suggestion in this formula will include statements like "You don't need to smoke. You don't have cravings. You don't have the social need to do it. You don't feel pressured to do it". The suggestion can be in any direction, and there are very subtle ways in which a person can be suggested towards any goals. A hypnotist might use positive messaging that might include positive feelings about the person's self or the world.

Chapter 15: Tips on How to Talk to Anyone

Breaking the Ice

First things first: time to say "hello." For many people, this is the most challenging part of meeting new people. Each social situation carries its own set of rules and pitfalls to be navigated. Each new person is a mystery--with their likes, dislikes, histories, and personalities. How do you know what to say to them in particular? How do you know that what you say will be taken well?

Let's say you are meeting a new coworker for the first time. You say hello and state your name; then you drift into silence while you search for what to say next. The silence drags on until your coworker either attempts to keep the conversation alive or gives up and moves on. Even though your silence was simply the product of shyness and anxiety, your coworker may see things differently; they may think that you are unfriendly or take your silence personally and think you don't like them. They will be wary about talking to you and unsure of your competence. You hardly say that this can hurt your work relationship and your job.
Similarly, at a social gathering, long awkward silences can make the other participant think you are dull or disinterested in them, and they will be likely to move on to someone else for better conversation. After all, no one likes to talk to a statue. Too much of this will leave you bored and ready to go when you could be having a great time making new friends and building lasting relationships. But fear not--breaking the ice is not a rugged mountain to climb.

Mastering non-verbal Communication
Imagine you are talking to a coworker in your company break room. While she is carrying on a conversation with you, she is also toying with her phone and not making eye contact. Would you imagine she is interested in your discussion or simply killing time until it's time to go back to work?

About half of your message is carried through your words any time you speak. The other half is taken through nonverbal cues: your tone of voice, facial expressions, posture, and gestures. No matter what you say, if your nonverbal cues don't match your message, they won't believe you.
Take the example above; the distracted coworker might be fully engaged in her conversation with you, but her body language says she is bored and disinterested. Likewise, even if you know that you are giving someone your complete attention, if you look at your shoes, turn your body away from them, or fidget with your keys or phone, the other person has no reason to believe you are focused on them. No one wants to talk to someone who doesn't want to be engaged.

So, can you make your body language match your message? Can you control your facial expression and gestures? Can you make the person you are talking to feel like you are interested and focused on them? The answer is yes to all of the above--you can make your body language match your verbal language easily. But, would it feel forced? Can others sense when you are trying too hard to make eye contact and smile? The answer is no--if you know how to use body language to your advantage.

Become a Genius of Small Talk
Now that you've exchanged names and greetings, what comes next? If you are talking to someone to achieve a goal, ask something from them, or learn something, you could be direct and tell them what you want. While this is often fine, some people find the natural approach off-putting. Also, if you are at a party or event and want to meet people or make contacts, you need to engage in the art of small talk.

Small talk is just what it sounds like--a conversation about unimportant matters or current events. Some topics may include the weather, current events, sports, or work. There are some people who dislike and avoid small talk, but you can use it as a tool to learn about and gain rapport with others and to let others get to know you. There is an art to it, however. It would be best if you were careful of talking for too long or dominating the conversation, or you may come off as self-absorbed and inconsiderate. Also, your topic of discussion should be appropriate for the setting and for who you are talking to. Always know what topics are open to debate and which topics to stay away from.

Get them Talking About Themselves.

Once the small talk is over, it's time to get your neighbor, coworker, or acquaintance talking about themselves. As we've seen, people like to talk about themselves, and you can learn a lot about them from not only what they say, but what they don't say.

You want to develop a natural rhythm, however, and not rapid-fire a hundred questions at them; after all, this is a conversation, not an interrogation.

Let's see this in action. At a party, you meet and start talking to someone. You engage in small talk, learn some of her interests and what she does for a living, and begin to ask her questions about her hobbies and job. After a few rounds of questioning, she starts getting bored and anxious and starts to look for a way out of the conversation. Just as you can talk too much about yourself, you can ask too many questions about another and be just as unpleasant to talk to. The key is to follow these steps to make your conversations exciting and dynamic while also learning about others.

Find Your Commonalities

In a world of over seven billion people, it's easy to get lost; you meet a stranger with whom you have nothing in common. But the world is a lot smaller than you might think. Everyone on Earth has something they love, something they hate, something they've lost, something they hope to gain. We are all much closer than you might think.

In a conversation, especially with someone you don't find much to say, it's important to find commonalities--shared interests and experiences. Commonalities help us break down barriers and learn more about each other. Say you are at work meeting a new supervisor for the first time. She went to a different school than you did, grew up in a separate area, has other hobbies and interests. In short, you are simply two different people. When you think about giving up on the conversation, she mentions that her last job was at a company you use to work for. This opens up a new area of discussion and gives you both a chance to see how you are alike, not how you are different.

Why is this important? In the above scenario, it never hurts to have a good working relationship with a supervisor. If you both see each other as "different people," likely you won't be able to communicate as effectively with each other. If you can't communicate effectively with your work higher-ups, you aren't doing your career any favors. But why would this be important in any other situation--say, with a coworker or other acquaintance? Why should you care about being able to find commonalities with anyone?

There are benefits to establishing an even playing field with anyone for a few reasons. First, it helps to put people at ease. Imagine meeting with a prospective client and finding that he tends to act obnoxiously.

He makes unreasonable demands and refuses to cooperate when you don't give in to them. Very likely, he feels you are in a position of power over him, and he feels the need to prove that he won't allow himself to be taken advantage of. Taking a few moments to find your commonalities shows him that you are here to work with him, not against him. Second, it can help to stave off arguments. In a statement, people focus on what is different about them, not what is the same. By finding your commonalities, you can show the other person that you are not two members of opposing teams with the goal of "winning" over each other, but simply two people whose ideas on some subjects differ.

Give Genuine Compliments

Suppose you are talking to a coworker who recently and completed a work project. You congratulate him by saying something along with the "Great job on the Johnson project." Your coworker mumbles a thank you and goes on about his business. This probably wasn't the response you were expecting. Sooner, while getting a drink with some coworkers, you compliment a lovely coworker with, "You are beautiful." She tenses and looks nervous, then excuses herself from the conversation. What went wrong?

We've seen how people enjoy talking about themselves, and we've learned a few ways to ask questions to allow them to do so. But what happens when a lull in the conversation stalls any attempt to keep them talking? What if your compliment is met with indifference? What if you sense nervousness in them? How do you counteract their anxiety? Everyone likes to receive a genuine compliment. But, if given the wrong way, a compliment can serve to make a person feel indifferent, uncomfortable, or even embarrassed.

Be a Magnetic Personality

Anywhere you go, there always seems to be someone, or perhaps a few people, who are surrounded. People gravitate to them, want to talk to them, want to hear what they have to say. Being on the outside and looking in, it is easy to think they are "magical" or have something you don't have.

The truth is, anyone can learn to draw people towards them. By now, you have the skills to strike up a conversation with anyone; now it's time to learn how to make people want to talk to you. Whenever you see a new person, there is something about them that makes you want to meet them. At a social gathering, you may be drawn toward someone who has an infectious laugh, an easy and confident manner of speaking, or they may seem to make people around them happy. Not everyone is born with a magnetic personality, but anyone can learn to develop one.

Introduce Humor

The first thing many people think of when they hear the word "humor" is something, like a joke or story, that was designed to be funny, to make people laugh. Certainly, it never hurts you to have a few jokes in mind when talking to people, as long as you keep them appropriate to your audience. Clean, family-friendly jokes are always appropriate, so save your edgier jokes for when you know your audience better. Here are some more tips on developing a good sense of humor. Be witty. Sarcasm has a certain humorous appeal but focuses on negativity. Wit, on the other hand, focuses on being clever and funny in any everyday situation. It can be a difficult skill to learn. Watch comedians, and pay attention to their timing and delivery. Keep in mind, however, that a large part of being witty is spontaneity. If being spontaneous is difficult for you, practice making jokes and witty observations with a friend. If you find something funny, chances are at least some other people will as well. Remember jokes and witticisms that make you laugh, and repeat them to others--when they are appropriate, of course. You wouldn't tell a sexually explicit joke at a church function, you wouldn't tell a "dumb blonde" joke to a blonde, and you shouldn't repeat racist jokes anywhere.

Conclusion

We hope you found it informative and able to provide you with all of the tools you need to achieve your goals, whatever they may be.
We have laid out the foundational principles of persuasion in this book, along with the tools and techniques you'll need to put persuasion to work for you. With a better understanding of how persuasion is being used in a variety of ways, in a variety of situations daily, we hope that you'll be able to navigate persuasion to your benefit and guard against the effects it can have on your life. You'll be prepared to examine your own motivations while cutting through the hype of others.

We live in a treacherous society where things are not always what they seem. More often than not, they are not as they appear, and this analogy applies to people as well. A person may not be as in love with another person as they seem. A boss might not be as appreciative of his employees as he may seem. A mother may not have the loving motherly instincts that we expect. Two friends may secretly wish each other the worst even though they smile on each other's faces. A politician with a reputation for doing well and helping people may be part of a secret society that has a mission that is opposite to this.

There are so many ways in which facades are maintained in everyday life, and it is a pity that this facade often hides something obscure. This dark intent is not clear or overt to the people that it victimizes. It does not state itself plainly. It does not give victims who are unaware of its existence the chance to fight back. This is why so many people are hurt and harmed by relationships with people they thought they could trust.

HOW TO ANALYZE PEOPLE

Introduction

You may always find yourself convinced to do whatever it was that the other person wants to do, or you may even find yourself doing something entirely unrelated to what you would normally do, to begin with.

You may realize that you are behaving in ways that are entirely out of character for you with no real understanding of why you have chosen to do so. This may be because you have someone well-versed in dark psychology in your life.

Maybe you want to be the one controlling other people. You want to be the one that can sway others to do what you want, whether through persuasion or manipulation (and yes, the two are different). Regardless of why you have chosen to pick up this book, you will find something within this book for you. Within these pages, you will be guided through everything dark psychology entails.

You will learn how important it can be to understand it, as well as several situations in which you may find dark psychology useful.

Being interested in dark psychology, whatever the reason, you can rest assured that you won't be disappointed with such a study. It is interesting to find within the dark psychology the possibility to study each individual's mind; since it is the only way to explore man's human mind better, to understand even the smallest detail of their body language, thus discovering everything.

You learn to persuade a person, to dupe every behavior of him to get what you want in return. This book is the best tool you can rely on, as it will be able to provide you with more detailed information on how to act or not. On the other hand, if you are leafing through these pages, you are very interested in this dark psychology form. You will use these tools of manipulation and persuasion only to defend yourself from possible cheating and defend your person, thus obtaining vital information to be used when you feel like it or the opportunity. The opportunities will be crazy.

Chapter 1: The basics of dark psychology

Dark Psychology Defined

Dark Psychology is an investigation of the human condition as it is identified with the psychological idea of individuals to go after others propelled by criminal and additionally degenerate drives that need a reason and general suspicions of instinctual drives and sociology hypothesis. All of humanity can mislead different people and living animals. While many control or sublimate this inclination, some follow up on these driving forces.

Dark Psychology tries to comprehend those contemplations, sentiments, recognitions, and abstract handling frameworks that lead to ruthless conduct that is contradictory to contemporary understandings of human behavior. Dark Psychology expects that criminal, freak, and harsh practices are purposive and have some balanced, objective arranged inspiration. Dark Psychology hypothesizes there is an area inside the human mind that empowers a few people to submit horrible acts without reason. Right now, he has been authored the Dark Singularity.

Dark Psychology places that all humanity has a repository of malicious aim towards others running from negligibly prominent and short-lived contemplations to unadulterated psychopathic degenerate practices with no firm discernment. This is known as the Dark Continuum. Moderating elements going about as accelerants or potentially attractants to moving toward the Dark Singularity, and where an individual's deplorable activities fall on the Dark Continuum, is the thing that Dark Psychology calls Dark Factor. Brief acquaintances with these ideas are outlined underneath. Dark Psychology is an idea this essayist has thought about for a long time. It has just been as of late that he has, at long last, conceptualized the definition, reasoning, and psychology of this part of the human condition.

All societies, all beliefs, and all humankind have this famous disease. We are destined to the hour of death; there is a side prowling inside every one of us that some have called insidiousness, and others have characterized as criminal, immoral, and obsessive. Dark Psychology presents a third philosophical build that sees these practices as unique about strict authoritative opinions and contemporary sociology hypotheses.

The individual isn't keen on his kindred men who have the best challenges throughout everyday life and gives the best injury to other people. It is from among such people that every single human disappointment springs.

Dark Psychology sets some individuals to submit these similar demonstrations and do so, not for influence, cash, sex, retaliation, or some other known reason. They offer these awful demonstrations without an objective. Rearranged, their closures don't legitimize their methods. Some individuals disregard and harm others for doing such. A possibility to hurt others without cause, clarification, or object is the territory this author investigates. Dark Psychology expects this dark potential is unfathomably mind-boggling and significantly increasingly hard to characterize.

Dark Psychology accepts we as a whole have the potential for predator practices, and this potential approaches our musings, emotions, and discernments. As you will peruse all through this composition, we as a whole have this potential. We all have had contemplations and emotions, one after another or another, of needing to carry on ruthlessly. We, as a whole, have had musings of needing to hurt others seriously without kindness. If you are straightforward with yourself, you should concur you have had reflections and sentiment of requiring to submit intolerable acts.

Given the reality, we view ourselves as a kind animal category; one might want to accept we figure these contemplations and emotions would be non-existent. Lamentably, we as a whole have these contemplations, and fortunately, never follow up on them.

Dark Psychology presents some individuals who have these equivalent contemplations, emotions, and discernments; however, follow up on them in either planned or rash manners. The undeniable contrast is they follow up on them while others mostly have brief musings and sentiments of doing as such.

Religion, reasoning, psychology, and different doctrines have endeavored fittingly to characterize Dark Psychology. It is genuine; most human conduct, identified with malicious activities, is purposive and objective situated. Yet, Dark Psychology accepts there is a zone where purposive manner and objective arranged inspiration appear to get shapeless. There is a continuum of Dark Psychology exploitation running from considerations to unadulterated psychopathic aberrance with no apparent soundness or reason. This continuum, Dark Continuum, assists with conceptualizing the way of thinking of Dark Psychology.

Dark Psychology tends to that piece of the human mind or all-inclusive human condition that takes into consideration and may even affect savage conduct. A few attributes of this social propensity are, as a rule, its absence of evident regular inspiration, its comprehensiveness, and its lack of consistency. Dark Psychology accepts this all-inclusive human condition as unique or expansion of advancement. Let us take a gander at some fundamental principles of improvement. Initially, consider we advanced from different creatures, and we by and by are the perfection of all creature life. Our frontal projection has permitted us to turn into the summit animal. Presently let us expect that being zenith animals doesn't make us expelled from our creature impulses and savage nature.

The more prominent the sentiment of mediocrity that has been encountered, the more remarkable is the desire to succeed and the more brutal the passionate disturbance. Expecting this is valid if you buy into development; at that point, you accept that all conduct identifies with three essential impulses. Sex, hostility, and the instinctual drive to self-continue are the three crucial human drives. We and all other living things act in a way to multiply and endure. Hostility happens for the reasons for denoting our region, securing our domain, and, at last, winning the option to reproduce. It sounds normal. However, it is never again part of the human condition in the perfect sense.

Our capacity of thought and recognition has made us both the zenith of species and the pinnacle of rehearsing severity. If you have ever viewed a nature narrative, this author is specific you wince and feel distressed for the eland torn to shreds by a pride of lions. Albeit merciless and lamentable, the reason for the viciousness fits the transformative model of self-conservation. The lions execute for nourishment, which is required for endurance. Male creatures battle until the very end, on occasion, for the ritual of a region or the will to control. Every one of these demonstrations, rough and cruel, development clarifies.

Rebellious people will consistently mistreat others, yet they will always view themselves as oppressed. At the point when creatures chase, they frequently stalk and execute the most youthful, most fragile, or females of the gathering.

Even though this reality sounds psychopathic, the explanation behind their picked prey is to lessen their likelihood of injury or demise. All creature's life acts and acts right now. All their fierce, rough, and bleeding activities identify with the hypothesis of advancement, characteristic determination, and impulse for endurance and generation. We, people, are the ones to have what Dark Psychology endeavors to investigate.

Speculations of development, regular determination, and creature senses, and their hypothetical precepts appear to break up when we take a gander at the human condition. We are the main animals on the substance of the earth that go after one another without the explanation of multiplication for the endurance of the species. People are the main animals that go after others for incomprehensible inspirations. Dark Psychology tends to that piece of the human mind or all-inclusive human condition that takes into consideration and may even induce savage conduct. Dark Psychology accepts there is something intrapsychic that impacts our activities and is against developmental. We are the main species that will kill each other for reasons other than endurance, nourishment, domain, or multiplication.

Scholars and religious journalists throughout the hundreds of years have endeavored to clarify this wonder. We will dive into a portion of these recorded understandings of detrimental human conduct. Just we people can hurt others with a total absence of bright sane inspiration. Dark Psychology accepts there is a piece of us since we are human, which energizes dark and awful practices. As you will peruse, this spot or domain inside the entirety of our creatures is widespread. There is no gathering of individuals strolling the substance of the earth now, previously, or later on who don't have this dark side. Dark Psychology accepts this feature of the human condition needs reason and coherent discernment. It is a piece of us all, and there is no known clarification.

Dark Psychology accepts this dark side is additionally unusual. Unusual in the comprehension of who follows up on these risky driving forces, and considerably increasingly erratic of the lengths some will go with their feeling of benevolence nullified: some individuals assault, murder, torment, and abuse without cause or reason. Dark Psychology addresses these activities of going about as a predator searching out human prey without plainly characterized purposes. As people, we are amazingly risky to ourselves and each other living animals. The reasons are numerous, and Dark Psychology endeavors to investigate those hazardous components.

Inspect the idea of Dark Psychology and comprehend the root and improvement of mental wonders rousing people to display savage conduct without any evident objective inspiration. This author understands his undertaking to prevail at this is beside unthinkable, yet he trusts Dark Psychology will encourage an enthusiasm for additional investigation.

There have been plenty of logicians, incredible masterminds, strict figures, and researchers who have endeavored to conceptualize aptly Dark Psychology. For this essayist, Dark Psychology epitomizes every past hypothesis and clarifications for human severity. Dark Psychology exists all around all through the human species and shows itself as savage conduct (tendencies) without bright, reasonable inspiration. Assessment of Dark Psychology and its developmental establishment is crucial. It doesn't recommend that Dark Psychology is a piece of our developmental legacy, yet we believe it is fundamental to research the transformative establishment of Dark Psychology. Dark Psychology resembles a bug-catching network's endeavoring to catch every single past hypothesis of human exploitation and convey them to others, motivating mindfulness and empowering mindfulness.

The more perusers can imagine Dark Psychology, the more ready they become to diminish their odds of exploitation by human predators. Before continuing, it is imperative to have, in any event, a negligible understanding of Dark Psychology. As you proceed through future compositions extending this build, this essayist will broadly expound on the most significant ideas. Following are fundamentals important to ultimately get a handle on Dark Psychology as follows:

· Dark Psychology is a general piece of the human condition. This build has applied impact since forever. All societies, social orders, and the individuals who live in them keep up this aspect of the human condition. The most generous individuals known have this domain of shrewdness yet never follow up on it and have lower paces of vicious musings and sentiments.

· Dark Psychology is an investigation of humans as it identifies with people groups contemplations, emotions, and recognitions identified with this inborn potential to go after others without clear perceptible reasons.

Given that all conduct is purposive, objective situated and conceptualized through usual methodology, Dark Psychology advances the thought the closer an individual attracts to the "dark opening" of unblemished underhandedness, the more outlandish he/she has a reason in inspirations. Even though this essayist expects flawless malice is never come to since it is boundless, Dark Psychology accepts some approach.

· Due to its potential for distortion as abnormal psychopathy, Dark Psychology might be disregarded in its inert structure. History is loaded with instances of this inactive propensity to uncover itself as dynamic, harmful practices. Present-day psychiatry and psychology characterize the mental case as a predator without regret for his activities. Dark Psychology sets there is a continuum of seriousness extending from contemplations and sentiments of viciousness to extreme exploitation and savagery without a sensible reason or inspiration.

· On this continuum, the seriousness of the Dark Psychology isn't regarded less or increasingly egregious by the conduct of exploitation, yet plots out a scope of cruelty. A straightforward delineation would think about Ted Bundy and Jeffrey Dahmer. Both were extreme sociopaths and shocking in their activities. The thing that matters has Dahmer dedicated his monstrous homicides for his hallucinating requirement for friendship while Ted Bundy killed and savagely dispensed agony out of sheer psychopathic fiendishness. Both would be greater on the Dark Continuum; however, one, Jeffrey Dahmer, can be better comprehended using his insane urgent should be adored.

· Dark Psychology expects all individuals have a potential for viciousness. This potential is intrinsic in all people, and different inner and outer elements increment the likelihood for this possibility to show into unstable practices. These practices are savage, and now and again, they can work without reason. Dark Psychology expects the predator-prey dynamic gets mutilated by people. Dark Psychology is exclusively a human wonder and shared by no other living animal. Brutality and disorder may exist in different living life forms. However, humankind is the main species that can do as such without reason.

· A comprehension of the fundamental causes and triggers of Dark Psychology would better empower society to perceive, analyze, and conceivably diminish the threats inborn in its impact.

Learning the ideas of Dark Psychology serves a twofold valuable capacity.

To begin with, by tolerating, we as a whole have this potential for fiendish permits those with this information to decrease its likelihood of ejecting. Besides, getting a handle on the fundamentals of Dark Psychology accommodates our unique developmental reason for attempting to endure.

This is to instruct others by expanding their mindfulness, making a change in the outlook of their world to improve things, and motivating them to teach others to attempt upon the way of figuring out how to diminish the likelihood of succumbing to those controlled by the powers investigated by Dark Psychology. If you have been a casualty of the Dark Psychology guided predator, don't feel mortified because we as a whole encounter some type of exploitation at once or another in our lives. It is a piece of the human condition, yet made a deal to avoid being surely known. A terrible reality, Dark Psychology encompasses us standing by quietly to jump. Dark Psychology incorporates all types of coldblooded and brutal practices. We need just gander at the silly cold-bloodedness of creatures. Being a devoted pet darling, creature maltreatment to this author is both awful and psychopathic. As ongoing investigations have proposed, creature misuse relates to a higher likelihood to submit savagery against humanity.

Demolition and youngsters have to play violent computer games are gently contrasted with apparent viciousness; however, they are specific instances of this all-inclusive human element this present essayist's hypothesis delineates. By far, most of humanity denies and shrouds its essence, yet at the same time, the components of Dark Psychology unobtrusively hide underneath the surface in every last one of us. It is widespread and wherever all through society. A few religions characterize it as a genuine substance they call Satan. A few organizations have confidence in the presence of evil spirits similar to the guilty parties causing harmful activities. The most splendid of numerous societies have characterized Dark Psychology as a mental condition or brought forth by hereditary attributes that went down from age to age.

This endeavors to analyze Dark Psychology's starting point and nature to see how the normal, very much mingled individual can end up in the news, having carried out a monstrosity nobody could have anticipated. Anytime during the day and for the duration of the night, since the start of written history, abominations delivered by one human on another are boundlessly happening. Albeit grim, it is astonishing how lovely individuals might take an interest in, or permit, such detestations to happen.

A considerable number of these barbarities are clear from the beginning of time. The holocaust during World War II and the ethnic purging by and by happening in neighboring nations are a couple of models. As portrayed above, Dark Psychology is fit as a fiddle and requires a genuine investigation. As you keep on investigating the precepts and establishment of Dark Psychology, a psychological system of understanding will gradually create.

Dark Singularity

The Dark Singularity is a vague idea like the meaning of singularity at the focal point of a dark gap. In the end, when this author endeavors to outline the concept of the Dark Singularity, he utilizes space science and cosmology as a similitude to depict this idea. In astronomy, the singularity is irrefutably the focal point of a dark gap that is fantastically little yet thick in mass outside the scientific ability to grasp. The hypothesis recommends that the singularity is so dense and ground-breaking, present-day laws of material science and their numerical conditions become snared.

A dark gap is the broad field of room encompassing the singularity; thus, abundant light can't get away from its grip. At the focal point of all cosmic systems just as our own, the Milky Way is a mighty dark opening with an interminably little singularity at its middle stuffed with great vitality. The Dark Singularity is made of immaculate underhandedness and unadulterated malignance. The individual who comes nearest to the Dark Singularity is the progressed and serious insane person who misleads others with negligible inspiration or reason for his activities.

The Dark Singularity is drawn closer, however, without appearance. The closer individual methodologies the Dark Singularity, the more deplorable and vindictive their conduct becomes. Simultaneously, their usual way of doing things turns out to be less deliberate. Nothing we start during our life expectancy happens heedlessly. Even though his way of thinking may seem at first solid oversimplified, it is very mind-boggling.

Given this reason, the motivation behind why individuals are considerate is that it serves that individual to be so because they receive the benefits of acknowledgment by their friends, friends, and family, and network.

Youngsters instructed to be thoughtful, mindful, and contributory have more prominent degrees of feeling acknowledged and being a piece of a gathering. For Adler, feeling some portion of or a substantial requirement for acknowledgment by others was the reason for sound utilitarian conduct. Taking his hypothesis of all manner being purposive to the far edge of the range, malicious practices fill a need too.

Individuals who carry on in threatening or non-tolerating ways were reacting to a profound feeling of inadequacy. At the point when individuals see they are not part of or not acknowledged by a social gathering, they move into negative bearings. Under this principle, Dark Psychology expects that 99.99% of all conduct is purposive. Like Freud and Jung, Adler bought into the way of thinking of Teleology.

Besides, as people progressively become debilitated, detached, and their social condition turns out to be gradually divided, the more they lash out towards others in unstable manners. A prime model and fast delineation would be the narcissistic mental case. The narcissistic, insane person is amazingly childish, discovers, gets a kick out of misleading others, and intentionally exploits others without regret. The idea of purposive conduct is vital to the comprehension of Dark Psychology.

This essayist emphatically accepts all human conduct is 99.99% purposive. The left finished 0.01% is he varies from Adler. This 0.01% is the Dark Singularity. The supposition of all manner as purposive is essential to understanding Dark Psychology, yet shifts somewhat in the severest type of vindictive human behavior (s).

The second hypothetical precept characterized vital to Dark Psychology is the idea of abstract handling. We, as a whole, have contemplations, emotions, and activities in which perceptions and full of feeling states impact conduct. Then again, an individual's behavior impacts his insights and feelings. Characterized as a framework or what is known as a group of stars, the ternion or trinity of human experience is contained as a circling arrangement of musings, feeling, and practices. Adler added abstract handling to this arrangement of human experience.

Youth encounters, birth request situating, relational peculiarities, nature of a social acknowledgment, and the elements of mediocrity versus prevalence worked in a way over make an individual's perceptual encounter and direction of connecting with his reality.

The most effortless approach to comprehend emotional handling and the perceptual structure is by envisioning a couple of shades. Your eyes speak to genuine reality, and the shadows talk to your separating instrument, mutilating the truth of the brutal daylight. Consequently, your "perceptual shades "channel misshape and modify how you decipher data and react in like manner.

Reality exists and happens each minute surrounding us. Sensitive handling channels our world to both shields and shields us from what we feel might be counter shown to our purposive objectives. If the human creates in a situation where he sees being a piece of, having a place with, and acknowledged, his emotional handling sifting system permits input that is considerably more exact. Individuals associated with what he sees as a debilitating domain, their abstract handling gets mutilated and tangled with self-centeredness and narcissism.

As to Psychology, the objective is to accept that all individuals channel their reality utilizing emotional preparation. Those individuals who are forceful, vicious, or oppressive are wearing a couple of world-renowned shades that are nearsighted and foggy. These individuals see others are out to hurt them and move to attack or control them first. Their abstract preparation mutilates their regular conventionality, kind acts, and benevolence. Demonstrations of consideration become alien encounters or used to manage their social condition guided by a usual childish way of doing things.

Social Interest is the arrangement of observations, considerations, and sentiments converted into big-hearted practices. Expressed, the more prominent an individual feels acknowledged by others, the more they think some portion of, and the higher the feeling of having a place legitimately interfaces with an individual's Social Interest. Individuals with high Social interests are innately kind, sacrificial, giving, and open. These characteristics of Social Interest further set their abstract handling to be confident and humane. High Social Interest rises to low Dark Psychology sway.

At the point when an individual feels disheartened, doesn't feel some portion of, doesn't encounter a feeling of acknowledgment, and sees his reality as segregating, he is at a higher hazard for showing useless unfriendly responses. Identified with purposive conduct, abstract handling, and Social Interest are vital to understanding Dark Psychology.

A segment of the data significant to understanding Dark Psychology is a diagram investigating youngster improvement, relational peculiarities, and different variables that work to formalize Dark Psychology. Even though it is highly unlikely to precisely characterize why and how a few people go to the dark side, there are regions for an investigation that help to clarify how the "laws of likelihood" exist in the improvement of individual character building. Different territories examined incorporate mental disease, a character issue, and liquor/chronic drug use as impetuses to freak conduct. Psychological and liquor/substance misuse doesn't clarify the savage manner. However, this essayist agrees these unsettling influences add to the comprehension of Dark Psychology.

Contemporary sociologies explore the territories of psychopathy, narcissism, and character issue. These profiles are charming and fuel a significant part of the enthusiasm for the field of legal and criminal psychology. Given this present essayist's examination, there is, by all accounts, a complex blend of these three characters scattered builds that make genuinely tyrannical individuals. When this essayist has introduced Dark Psychology thoroughly, will be elective clarifications to lewd conduct. Another component of Dark Psychology examined will incorporate attackers, pedophiles, and vicious sexual guilty parties.

When you have a grip of Dark Psychology, you will, at that point, evaluate others' activities as being conceivably hazardous. Keep in mind; Dark Psychology incorporates all lawbreakers and freak practices submitted upon others. Albeit numerous individuals are interested in the conversation of the sequential executioner and insane person, most by far of predators chasing human prey are not occupied with murder or sexual abnormality. If this author were to make a gauge, he would put the level of human predators at generally 70% of the all-out pool of individuals who are out to exploit others, however, which are not engaged with murder or sexual abnormality. 30% have been evaluated to incorporate lawbreakers, freak, and savage guilty parties where physical contact is arranged. The thing that matters is most by far from humankind has never followed up on those considerations. For them, their Dark Factor is raised, affecting them to move toward a path towards what many characterize as shocking, and this essayist describes as a direction quickening towards the Dark Singularity.

For them, it is never again about being sympathetic and kind. Their abstract preparation hues the entirety of their musings, feelings, and observations with obscurity and venom. Sooner or later in the improvement of the human predator, he/she activates his considerations and sentiments and starts down the long street of what contemporary criminologists call psychopathy. Inside time, their emotional handling channel gets separated from encountering regret. They come to see that the exploitation of others is merited by the individuals who are too sincere even to consider protecting themselves.

Given that a vast segment of human improvement encompasses social acknowledgment, the predator, some way or another, moves into the field where his Dark Factor turns into a functioning power energizing a desire for the decimation of others. When driven by the domain of psychopathy, he has entered the final turning point. Similarly, as light can't get away from a dark opening, the human predator can't get away from the way towards the Dark Singularity. Meetings led by scientific profilers and research researchers with indicted famous mental cases have demonstrated the hypothesis of quickened development towards the Dark Singularity.

Not just have maniacs disclosed an impression of encountering a feeling that their malevolent demonstrations quicken in recurrence, yet also, their experience of going about as predator takes on an addictive quality. Utilizing cosmology by and by as an illustration for Dark Psychology, the closer issue moves toward a dark opening; the quicker mass quickens and can failing to swing ceaselessly from the dark gap's high gravity. Meetings with sociopaths precisely emulate this general law of astronomy.

As society moves further into what is characterized as the Information Age loaded up with advanced innovation and the internet, Dark Psychology and its effect on humankind will be tried at more prominent rates. Given the cloak of namelessness, the internet offers all humanity; the inquiry remains if the evil viewpoints living inside us all will perceive there is a domain of free rule called the advanced universe.

Chapter 2: The Dark Triad

The dark triad is a collection of character traits present in every person. These acts refer more to individuals with a difficult to control personality; in fact, such actions can make the manipulator lose control, leading him to senseless and cruel gestures.

When one of these elements is found that completely dominates the manipulator, it is identified that such behavior leads to its destruction, even if in some cases it can be creative. Those who exhibit such a dark triad are very intelligent and crafty people; they are very attentive to everything around them. For this reason, they are easy to get what they want and do what their written predictions have imposed on them.

They won't stop at anything or anyone, as long as they don't get what they want first. They will pretend to be interested in your well-being, in your most fragile feelings, until they reach their purpose.

Be careful if you find yourself in an individual who shows one of these manipulative traits because it is not sure to walk away slowly without fighting it. Winning against them is not an easy battle; it would undoubtedly lead you to a deep wearing out of which it will not be easy to be able to get out freely.

Narcissism

In the first line, we deal with his narcissism. Narcissism is an attitude that tends to exhaust the personality in the exclusive consideration and exaltation of itself. They are presumptuous people who want to be the center of attention, forcing each individual to do what he orders. They are not interested in worrying about others' feelings; their only purpose is to make sure that the person in question does what he proposes. Otherwise, it would be the end of any story.

But there are also the smartest narcissists because they can also indulge in losing their prey, making them so pleasant and fascinating to get to know. All this is just a strategy phase because as long as they are praised, they are perfectly calm; on the contrary, they become another person when they do not receive the attention they expect. They are very selfish.

It will make them become like no one can ever imagine, raising a sort of barrier in front of them. Conversely, everything would be great; the critical thing that they are treated as they wish, and everything can go smoothly, thus moving on to the next move.

They completely mind control freaks. Everyone must follow their orders, and everything must be as they order, so that everything is under their circle. If he somehow lost control of the situation, the narcissist would do anything to get it back at the cost of destroying everything in his way.

Usually, this type of manipulation already arises from a childhood age, often caused by the abandonment syndrome, the feeling of being isolated and not considered by the affections you love. All this has repercussions on adulthood.

Machiavellianism

Such behavior falsely covers undeserving gestures, adopting subtle behaviors to get what you want through deception. Machiavellian individuals display a rare intelligence, so they rely entirely on what their minds suggest without using illicit mechanisms.

So, it's up to you to choose whether to share your time with a Machiavellian personality, since either you go against them by destroying them, or you agree with them.

This feeling is already born from the pubic age, and maybe they cannot understand their gestures and what they can lead to in the future.

Psychopathy

There is also a psychopathic mind, that is, not feeling any emotion. They cannot feel any empathic feeling towards themselves or towards someone, not understanding in the least what others think. They have no remorse, they do not feel the need to understand the gestures they made with superficiality, and all this can only be classified as mental problems. They are utterly devoid of emotion as if their brains are completely shut off from that feeling.

However, this behavior can also be due to the brain and a psychological, emotional disorder caused by childhood dramas, by an adverse event that inevitably causes you a considerable injury. All this leads the individual to completely dissociate himself from the world and his feelings, closing in on himself.

The Dark Triad in Action

Even one reason for having the dark triad within one's being is enough to be called a sick individual. Especially when the various dark forms come into effect altogether, in that case, there is no longer any sense of humanity. Their only obsession is to harm others.

There is no solution to be able to deal with this mind, although there is the best possible intention to help them, for this reason, it is easier to walk away. After all, these are elements that can also occur in our person, with the only difference that we allow them to emerge totally from our ego. We can control or stop these impulses because we are carried by a remarkable ability to control. When it happens, we can deal with our feelings. I think no one wants to be consumed by their emotional and psychological state.

Chapter 3: Dark Psychology Tactics

Dark Persuasion

Dark Persuasion is a branch of Dark Psychology, and it is very effective in its way. Dark Persuasion is something that is used often. What are the principles of Dark Persuasion? The first is Brainwashing.

Brainwashing is the practice of taking over someone else's capacity to think. Naturally, we all have unique thinking patterns, and we all have the power to think critically about what is going on around us. Brainwashing takes away this power, and it puts that power into the hands of whoever is doing the Brainwashing. Brainwashing has many different implementations, but the principle remains the same throughout. A person is first brought into the fold of the new scenario. They are told that they matter, worthy, and have a place to be in the contemporary milieu. They must be separated from outside society to do this. The brainwashed person is convinced that this new way of thinking is a way to live better and happier. A person is often the brainwashing center who is centered as very wise or intelligent. This person will be the "leader" of the cult, and the person who is being brainwashed will start to think of this person as their new family director.

To make sure that the person adapts and accepts this new milieu, their sense of self must be broken down. In cults, this will often already have happened when the person joins. Cults look for weekend people by loneliness, suffering, or isolation. When a person has a good sense of self, they are less susceptible o being brainwashed. Thus, this must be attacked and broken down to convince a person that this new way of living is the best.

Brainwashing might also employ guilt to convince a person that they are in the best environment. Brainwashing will have people feeling guilty about their "past lives," and they will be presented with a solution for their guilt. Guilt and shame are potent emotions, and people will do whatever they think will work to get away from these emotions. Guilt and shame are what people feel when they are sad and ashamed about themselves. These negative emotions drive people to search out a solution, and often the answer can be manipulated by others in the form of Brainwashing.

The possibility of salvation comes in accepting the new ideas or format of the brainwashers. It comes in assuming that this new person or group can save them. Leniency is presented to the person.

Rather than being told that their past transgressions are something that they will never be able to escape, they are told that they can run it if they reach their new goals with the Brainwashing. This feels good, and it is hard to turn away from the possibility of salvation.

Another form of Persuasion is hypnosis. Hypnosis works on a few basic principles. The first is induction. Induction is where a person is helped along to a state of suggestibility or relaxation. This is a state wherein they are put at ease, and they are made vulnerable to messaging. The person who is being hypnotized is welcomed into this vulnerable state, and it is from there when they can be persuaded. After a person is put through an induction, their defenses are broken down, and they can receive suggestions.

Some people seek out hypnosis to bring themselves away from bad habits, like smoking or other addictive habits. In this format, the person would go through the initial induction process, and then the hypnotist will make suggestions to them about how to quit smoking and messages relating to why they shouldn't smoke anymore. The hypnotist's request in this formula will include statements like, "You don't need to smoke. You don't have cravings. You don't have the social need to do it. The suggestion can be in any direction, and there are very subtle ways in which a person can be suggested towards any goals. A hypnotist might use positive messaging that might include positive feelings about the person's self or the world.

There is the military application of this process, which is pretty well-known. Initially, the soon-to-be soldiers enter boot camp with their heads still in the mode of being back at home. Their goals are not formulated yet, and they are used to the comforts and privacy of home. They must be broken down first to accept the messaging of the military. They enter boot camp, and they are put through rigorous physical training and emotional damage.

Their first experience in the boot camp is that everything is crazy and uncontrolled. They are given the message that they are powerless and that everything is against them, except their fellow soldiers. They are thrust into a world that is pure chaos and evil. They are told that nothing will save them, that nothing matters except to achieve whatever goal they must work on in that very moment. This is how they are broken down: they must learn that they are worth nothing, empty, and not valid. This is the classic formula of Brainwashing and hypnosis. The first phase works as the breaking down, or the induction, of the mind.

This is where people are put into a state of suggestibility. Then comes the possibility of salvation. In the military case, what will save them is working hard, being tough and bonding, and working cohesively with their colleagues. The fellow soldiers and the commanding officers are the families and only friends of the soldiers. They are taught that they are worthless than dirt unless they are work-in toward a common goal with their fellow soldiers.

This ultimately creates a very cohesive, well-working unit of people who believe that they can only function in this environment. They know that they can do this because they are forced to be in such a terrible environment and make it out alive. They were able to get through these awful conditions because they could rely on one another for help, and the commanding officers gave them a rest at the end of their terrible exercises. This is an excellent illustration of Dark Psychology at work; the military can be known as an institution that has these principles nailed down to a well-oiled machine of science and psychology.

From car dealerships to governmental organizations to interpersonal relationships, dark persuasion tactics are something you always have to look out for. It takes some self-knowledge and exploration, but you'll be able to unmask the dark persuader if you give it some thought.

First, you should try to learn about your responses in certain situations. When you go into a sales situation, you should recount your goals before entering and try to center yourself. Then, as you enter into the battle of the sales situation, you should try and recognize your responses to the problem as challenges come up.

The dealer might try to tell you what you want. This is a standard dark Persuasion method for people trying to sell you something. The salesperson will tell you, sometimes quite literally, that you want something that they have, even if it is something that you don't need or want. Are you able to tell them no? I don't want that?

It takes some strength of personality to pull this off; after all, persuasive people can be tough to go against the grain with. When the dealer tells you that they have a car that you have to have, and they start to pressure you, try to see how you feel in your body at that moment. Are you feeling grounded? If not, try and remember that you have two feet on the floor, and you are there in space, standing somewhere. You are not floating above the ground. You are strong and planted in your position.

Another way to maintain groundedness is to relax. It would help if you remembered that whatever you are doing is your right and your place to be doing. When you allow your body to get uncomfortable and for stress to manifest in your body, you allow yourself to become ungrounded and uncensored, leading to a lack of strength. People who are grounded, strong, and centered are not easily persuaded of things they don't believe in. Weak people are more easily persuaded. Why is this? You can think of human relationships and cognition somewhat like a gravitational pull.

A planet, or any large mass in outer space, has a particular gravitational pull, which will pull in objects with a floating group in outer space into its orbit. They will then be locked into orbit with the planet, and they will be connected, in a sense, to the earth. This is similar to human spirits. We are all floating around, and we get sucked into the gravitational pull of other planets and large masses. Their power and persuasiveness serve as the pull of gravity, and before you know it, we are stuck and connected to them.

This happens a lot with people who lose their family or support system. Left without people to help you out, you are easily susceptible to tricks of the mind and persuasive techniques. You should make sure that you have a positive support system to help you out if you feel that you are going up against someone using dark manipulation tactics.

Another critical aspect of preventing yourself from being persuaded is confidence. If you have confidence in yourself that you will face someone trying to convince you and come away wholly yourself, safe, and accomplishing your goals, you will be more likely to be able to do it than someone who is not confident. Confidences are something that goes against all the principles of dark Persuasion. Someone using unclear persuasion principles is not counting on meeting someone satisfied in their web of deceit. They are looking for the people who have no sense of self, the people who have nothing to say when you ask, "who are you?"

Intuition

Intuition is critical here. Sometimes, it may be difficult to tell who uses dark persuasion techniques, whether for their goals or another overarching goal of an organization, or whatever. Intuition is key to detecting when these techniques are being used against you. Let's say you start a new job. It is a sales job, and you are taken to a group interview where you are asked to convince the manager that you are suitable for the job.

Group interviews, well, they aren't the best sign, but you are looking for a job right now and need the money, and you decide, whatever, you will have a look. You do well in the group interview, and you are selected as one of the people who will be joining the team. You start the training process, and you notice that something is off. When you are participating in the training, you are shown videos and told how to operate. You start to see that some of the videos tend to denigrate the people who are being trained. You notice that people go along with it and agree that this job is very honorable and that they should be ashamed of their past. The management then tries and convinces you that this job is one of the only jobs out there and that this is the only job you'll be able to get, so you better not quit. Then, you are started to be told how incredible the benefits are and that you might be able to make a fortune at this job if you work hard. You should pay attention to your intuition in this situation because it should warn you about every one of these persuasion tactics.

Your intuition will recognize these as evil because we have a natural sense of self-protection as humans. Evolutionarily, we have become accustomed to protecting ourselves in the wild. Before humans developed an agricultural system and modern civilization, people had to defend themselves from the pure elements of the world, which were very threatening. People had no sense of what might be happening in nature or with animals; there was no science to tell us about the weather, no books to read about the history of the world, no way to know whether it is going to snow tomorrow or rain the next day. An earthquake could be seen as a very terrifying and mysterious event.

Through the centuries of living like animals in the wild, humans have developed an evolutionary capacity to understand their intuition. It is not precisely thinking or cognition; it is not a feeling; it is somewhere in between. It is a gut instinct that tells you when you are being played. It can also tell you when you are experiencing true love and when you should jump into something with your whole heart. But intuition has a great capacity to protect us. Your intuition will be going off when someone tries to use dark persuasion techniques against you. Learning to tune into intuition might be difficult, but you will eventually get there. Maybe you saw a slight smile in the corner of their mouth, or perhaps the story didn't add up.

Whatever it was that allowed you to get some insight into their condition, that's what intuition is. Intuition is letting yourself trust yourself to see into someone else's soul.

We all have that capacity, and in fact, we all can read peoples' minds. It is just something that people rarely recognize and even less often learn to develop and embrace.

Another essential part of defending yourself from dark persuasion tactics is to learn how to say no. Saying no, in all its different forms, is what will save you from being put into the grinder. Sometimes saying no is putting the answer off. This is called the delay tactic. By not answering at the moment, you are delaying the need to answer at all, which gives you time to think about your options and consider whether or not you are being manipulated for some purposes that are not in your best interest. This is an excellent tactic in situations that involve sales or personal relationships. By saying, "give me some time to think about it," you are allowing yourself some time away from the pressure at the moment to give some thought to the idea of if you are true to yourself.

The delay method is an excellent tactic to defend yourself from dark Persuasion because much of shady persuasion tactics rely on a person being pressured in the heat of the moment. Suppose you can get out of that moment, and you can depend on deeper thinking and a better environment that will foster relaxation and calmness. In that case, you will inevitably make a better decision regarding the task at hand.

Machiavellianism As Defense Mechanism

Another thing to consider is using Machiavellian principles to defend yourself. If whatever is being presented, you should ask yourself further away from your personal goals or closer to your personal goals. Remember, you should be focused on yourself in this mindset. This is not the mindset of helping people, although there are many situations where it is better not to adopt a Machiavellian attitude. Suppose you are in a position where you need to provide support for other people or are in a situation where you already trust the person you encounter. In that case, the Machiavellian mindset is not appropriate. However, when you are trying to defend yourself from manipulative people or people who do not have your best interests in mind, you can lean on this mindset to help put up defenses.

The Machiavellian mindset is, at its core, selfishness. Most people think of selfishness as a negative thing. However, it would help if you rethought this. Selfishness is an essential human trait. It is not something that you should employ all the time, by any means, but you should be able to use selfishness when appropriate. After all, in a situation where you are being challenged with dark Persuasion, you are against them. It is fight or be killed. So, to defend yourself, you must become selfish. Your foe in this battle does not deserve help or kindness. You are the one who deserves support and service from yourself. Could you not give them an inch? Ask yourself what is best for you At that moment, whether it lets the other person down or not. Some people are so wired towards being a helper, and a giver that standing up for themselves is very foreign and very different. You might find that this is true for you, and you will have to switch over from a mindset of a helper and pushover into someone who is self-interested and wants to help themselves.

Understand the Motive

When you can detect that you are being manipulated or persuaded, the first step is to examine the motivation for the manipulator. When you are presented with a situation where you are convinced to do something, you should first investigate the possibility of monetary gain.

If it is a business that solicits you for time or patronage, ask yourself if you need those services, and ask if your life is better off with or without those services. If it is a charitable organization, do some research into whether they do what they say and if they should be trusted.

There are also other reasons that people might be trying to sue you. There are many ways that people are subjected to scams that get you to provide information about what you do online or other activities. This may seem pretty benign at first, but you will realize that you are being taken advantage of if you look into it. Development companies for apps and other online services work these days to look for ways to collect information about you. Why is this information valuable? Because it helps them to be able to target other people in their services and manipulation.

Remember, if the situation is not equitable, you are probably being manipulated. To unmask the dark persuader, you should be able to see why entering into some agreement benefits you rather than the deal being one-sided.

Get to The Root of Things

Human psychology is such that we are pointed to ignore the deeper levels of our situations to survive. The will to survive is very implicit and profound in the consciousness of a human. We have all kinds of automatic responses and habit patterns that become standard parts of our lives. We do not question them. They become ingrained in the everyday truth with which we live. So, to develop critical thinking and problem skills, we have to learn how to get to the root of things. This will take some introspection, and you try to break down the repression and suppression of thoughts and feelings that have built up. This is not uncommon; many people have repressed ideas, reviews, and desires and never observe them or become aware. It takes bravery to look inside the soul. This is our takes, ultimately: to look inside the soul. If you can trust your instincts, you will be able to think critically and solve problems at the deepest level. If you put a band-aid on the wound, you will treat the symptom but not the cure. To understand the nuance that exists in most of our interpersonal and personal problems, we must be able to detach from emotion and look at ourselves with pure determination.

This requires us not to get distracted by petty or unreasonable desires. When faced with a problem, we must ask ourselves: are we getting down to the underlying causes? Ben is an intelligent kid and has a great head on his shoulders. However, he has developed some behavioral problems. He seems to have gotten stuck in a scenario where his only friends are the ones who cause trouble. They cause the distraction of other students, disruption in class, and vandalize parts of the school without getting caught. Ben is not a bad kid; he likes excitement and adventure, and these activities provide him with a sense of challenge and excitement. He takes on these rule-breaking activities and uses his understanding of critical thinking to get away with it.

His teachers try to tell Ben to stay away from these friends because they are a terrible influence on him. They punish him for being distracting. Ben is given detention once a week for the next three months. The teachers think that if they use behavioral modification to punish the boy for bad behavior, he will learn the rules and avoid the behaviors. However, what they are ignoring is that Ben has family troubles at home and not experiencing the sense of stability he needs. The problem is not the symptom behaviors that come out as a result. He doesn't feel grounded in his family life and cannot play the role of a successful student in school, as he would like. If he can deal with the stressors involved in his family life, he will focus more on school.

If you are easily manipulated, you will be easily convinced that Ben's problems are whatever his teacher says they are. Teachers can often be very manipulative with parents because they want nothing less than to investigate the issue. Partly because it is not their job, and partly because people tend to want to do the least amount of work possible.

People will try to get in your way; you must detach from emotion and be a neutral observer. Using critical thinking skills is very important; you must cut through the silliness to get to the essence of a problem. The nature of a problem could be unexpected. It would help if you remained open to the chance that the solution you are seeking is right under your nose or right under something else that your eyes have already crossed. How good are you at looking people dead in the eyes and disagreeing with them? This will be easier for some than others.

Persistence requires knowledge to back up your claims, and it requires confidence in your actions and confidence in yourself as a person. Industry can come from many things. Some parents like to encourage their kids to get involved in sports for this reason. Athletic training can sometimes provide modeling and techniques to become a persistent, excelling person. So, what happens if you run into Stacy in accounting and she disagrees with the deadline that is perfectly reasonable and that you have the right to set? You must get to the root of the problem first and take into account all of the already available information. This could be experienced in the past with Stacy; it could be files that you have that she has met deadlines on in the past or her emails that she had recently sent to you. Whatever data you have to gather, make sure you have compiled it and maintained an awareness of all of the information you already have.

Chapter 4: Deception Tactics

The deception can include several different things, such as masking, camouflage, diversion, hand sleight, lies, and hiding. The agent will monitor the subject's mind because the issue has faith in them. The agent believes what the agent says and could base their plans for the future and shape its universe on the agent's staff. Deception is an omission and lying form of communication to persuade the subject's world to serve the agent the best.

1) Lies: This is when the agent provides information that is different from reality. This knowledge is presented to the subject, and the issue must understand it as the truth. The subject cannot understand that false information is being fed; if the subject understands that the data is wrong, he or she will not speak to the agent, and he or she will not be fooled.

2) Concealment: This is the other form of deception that is very common. The agent will not have lied to the client directly, but he will ensure that the critical information needed is never a subject.

3) Equivocation: The agent makes conflicting, vague, and conditional statements. It can also save your face as an agent if the subject returns later, claiming they have been deceived.

4) Exaggeration: It happens when the agent overestimates a fact or stretches the facts to some degree to transform the story as it wishes. The agent may not lie to the subject directly, but they will make the current situation a more significant deal so that the issue bends to their will.

5) Avoidance: This occurs when manipulators don't give straight answers or move the discussion into a different topic utilizing diversion tactics. In a dialog, avoidance occurs by rambling or otherwise talking endlessly in a meandering fashion. So, their ultimate game is to confuse the target, which makes them question the authentic version. When a manipulator changes the topic, it can be gradual and not entirely obvious.

Main Components of Deception

While deciding what factors display during deception may be difficult, specific components are typical of fraud. It is often not apparent that these elements existed unless the agent told a blatant lie or was caught in deception. Camouflage, mask, and simulation are the three main components of fraud.

1) Camouflage is the first dimension of deception. This is when the agent tries to conceal the facts so that the target does not know that the information is missing. The agent can mask the facts so that the target can honestly find it hard to learn by chance about the deception.

2) Disguise is another component of the deception process. It occurs when the agent depicts themselves as other people to the subject. This is more than simply changing the suit someone wears in a film; the agent tries to change their entire personality to deceive their target. One is to dress in interactions with the agent, sometimes as someone else, so that they cannot be identified or recognized. The agent will do this to get back into many people who don't like them, change their personality to make people like them, or otherwise advance their goals. In some situations, the word disguise can be the agent who disguises the true nature of a proposal hoping that it hides any controversial effect or motive for such a proposal.

3) There are three essential techniques that an agent can use in simulation.

The first is mimicry, where the agent is unknowingly depicting something similar to themselves. They could be talking about someone else's idea and give credit to themselves by saying that the idea is theirs.

Fabrication is the second technique where an agent will use something in reality and change it to become different. They can tell a story and add embellishments to make the story sound better or worse than it was. While the main story may have happened, it will have things added on top of it and change the whole narrative.

Lastly, we have a distraction as a form of simulation. This is when the agent tries to make the subject concentrate on something other than the facts, usually baiting or proposing something more appealing than the reality of the matter.

For example, when the husband is having an affair and feels that the wife is starting to learn about it, he may take a diamond ring home to confuse her.

How to Use Deception

Psychological research is the sector that mainly uses deception as it is necessary to determine the actual results. The explanation behind this deception says that people are susceptible to the way they look both to others and themselves and that their self-awareness can distort or interfere with the way the subject is compared to doing research in normal circumstances, in which they do not feel examined. The deception is intended to make people feel more comfortable so that the agent can get the right results.

The agent may be interested, for example, in knowing which circumstances a student could cheat on a test. If the agent specifically investigates the student, the subjects are unlikely to confess to lying, and the agent could not make out who tells the truth and who does not. In this scenario, the agent should use a distraction to get a clear picture of how cheating fraud occurs. Alternatively, the agent could suggest that the study is about how intuitive the subject is; even in the process, you can say that you can look at someone else's answers before offering your answers. This analysis includes the conclusion.

Alternatively, the researcher may suggest that the research seeks to find out how insightful the subject is. The issue may even be advised that they have the opportunity to look for answers from someone else before providing their solutions. After the deception experiment, the agent should ask the subject what the fundamental nature of the trial is and why the deception is required. In addition, some agents will also give a brief description of the results between all participants when the study is carried out.

It is often problematic for the subject to decide that deception exists unless the agent slips up and either tells a flat or straightforward lie or contradicts something already real. It is often tough to detect if fraud occurs because no signs are present.

Deception, however, can put a great deal of pressure on the mental workings of the agent because they need to find out how to recall all the comments they have made on the subject so that the tale remains plausible and consistent. One mistake on the agent's part and the issue will tell something is wrong.

The agent is more likely to redirect information to tip off the subject, either via non-verbal or verbal signals, because of the pressure they have to keep the past straight. Researchers believe that identifying deception is a mental, dynamic, and complex process that often differs from the message being exchanged.

The Interpersonal Deceit Theory shows that deception is an iterative and complex mechanism of control that exists between the agent who manipulates information in such a way as to make it different from reality and the subject who then tries to find out whether the message is valid or not.

The agent's acts shall be linked with the actions of the issue after the message is received. The agent must disclose nonverbal and verbal details during this exchange, which will lead the subject to deceit. The subject might tell at some points that the agent has been lying to them.

Chapter 5: Skills and Tools

To discuss the phenomenon that happens inside our subconscious, it is necessary to mention the great Sigmund Freud's name, since he was the most influential psychologist and philosopher. He lived in history, especially for how he could concretely develop psychoanalysis. It is the conscious source of material that is easily accessible. The top of the iceberg is the smallest part of the iceberg, however, and if you dive deeper, you can see that most of the iceberg exists underwater. This is what Freud thought about the proportionality of the human psyche. He felt that most of the human mind was not at the surface but rather down below in the depths. Most of the unconscious was down where it wasn't easy to access, and he thought that people didn't show their true selves unless they were put in a position where this material could be uncovered.

Freud called the different parts of the psyche the Ego, the super Ego, and the id. It is the most primal part of humanity, and it is the only part of the psyche which is within us from the very moment we are born. It might seem dark and scary, but it is the most natural part of us.

It is the part that tells us what is doable and controls our reality orientation. The Ego is the part of us which "converts" the Id's drives into behavior.

The Super-Ego is the moral component of our psyche. The super Ego tells us what is appropriate and ethical in any given circumstance, and it tells us what we think is okay and what we believe is unacceptable.

The Id and the Ego are engaged when people use Dark Psychology and Dark Persuasion. When a person uses these tactics, they hire the subconscious, which partly lives in the id and partly lives in the Ego.

The subconscious mind is made up of all the memories and associations you have and all the experiences with different people. Have you ever tried food that you had a terrible reaction to or gotten food poisoned? His happens to many people, and many of them discover that they are no longer able to eat that food again for many years after this experience. This is the subconscious at work. If the food in question is carrots, then you will find that the next time you encounter carrots, you will be disgusted at the thought of eating them. You will find them repulsive and unnatural. This is because your subconscious has internalized the experience of discomfort and disgust with that particular food. In reality, you know that the food will be fine in future adventures. Still, you cannot encounter that food and engage with yourself rationally because you have integrated that awful experience into your psyche. The subconscious is instinctual and has a lot of animalistic qualities to it.

The subconscious is responsible for the sexual drives which we have. It is governed by the pleasure principle, which states that we are driven by pleasure, and that pleasure is the ultimate motivator. This is why advertising works well when it engages ideas of sexual motivation and other forms of fun. The old saying "sex sells" is ever prescient to this day. Think about the phenomenon of sexual attraction. You might understand consciously that you are married, and happily so, but you will still find yourself wanting to engage in sexual conduct with others, even though you have agreed with your partner not to do so. It is always present, lurking, and is the most feral pressure. Sexuality is often part of Dark Persuasion tactics. A leader is often handsome in physicality. This is part of charisma, and it is a very effective way to engage in someone's subconscious drives. Sexuality and other base drives are an essential part of dark Persuasion. Sex and drugs have always been a way to control and manipulate a population.

Memory

Memory is a tricky thing. One person might remember it as a situation in which they were victimized. Memory can fade and come back within a lifetime. Is it a pleasant memory or an unpleasant one? Sometimes the unpleasant memories are what stick out the most.

As the names would suggest, long-term memory is when you keep something in your mind for a very long time. Short-term memory is where thoughts or experiences are stored while your brain decides to file them in your long-term memory or let go of them. Implicit memory is something that you don't have to try for. This is riding a bike (if you've already learned to do so). You already know how to do it, and you don't have to try to do it. Ti is also the type of memory you are using when you brush your teeth or walk around.

Your muscles do not have to be directed to do these things because you already know how to do them. Autobiographical memory is your memory of how your life has progressed.

This is similar to intuition. These are very closely related concepts. Intuition and subconscious memory are when you are integrating memories of the past, but you don't know when or where they are coming from, and you don't precisely know the content of this memory. This will be something you can lean on to identify instances when you are being manipulated or persuaded, brainwashed or deceived. FI you can tap into this mysterious system of the subconscious, you will be able to defend yourself. Ways to Train the Subconscious

Allow yourself to believe the unbelievable.

To change your habits or way of thinking, you must fight back against the impulse to believe that nothing can ever change. This is one thing that often gets people stuck; it is the belief that the way they are now will be the way they are forever. Banish this thought, for it will only leave you undeveloped and will keep you away from self-realization.

Permit yourself to be successful.

Many people have in their subconscious the belief that they can never be as successful as they want. Some people have complexes from growing up poor that tell them that they will never have enough money and always act as though having enough money will never be an option for them. Some people think that they can't be creative, or they can't do a specific type of job. You have to switch this thinking, and when you find these thoughts arising from your subconscious, you can tell yourself consciously that you are capable; you can be successful.

Resist others' projections.

We are all subject to the projection of others. The point is when a person has beliefs or feelings about themselves, and they think that all other people are like them. They start to believe that everyone around them matches them in some characteristic or habit. It would help if you allowed yourself to reject their thoughts about you. Resist their attempts to put you in a box.

Give yourself some positive reinforcement.

The very essence of resisting Dark Persuasion is understanding the dark forces at work and giving yourself the opposite information. Understanding Dark Psychology means that you will have to engage in the darkness just a little bit. However, once you do this, you will have to balance out your energy with some positive thinking. If you can give yourself positive messages to balance out the gloomy darkness, you will find that you can overcome all manipulation and deception.

Be honest about your success.

Don't be humble. Of course, being humble is a virtue, but only up to a point. Being humble will eventually lead to your downfall. You need to stand with Machiavelli on this point and let yourself be able to praise yourself wholeheartedly. Individualism is one of the central tenets of Western culture, and this means embracing yourself, your needs, and your way of living. Celebrate yourself. Tell yourself that you are the one who deserves success.

Envision your future.

Be bold about your future. If you are always envisioning a lot full of pain and suffering, you will probably be working toward making that real. If you can create a future vision for yourself that is one of success and domination, you will be much closer to creating that in reality.

Point out your weaknesses so that you can work on them.

Your subconscious will play tricks on you. Sometimes, it will make you think that you are perfect and have no flaws, which is not the case. Most people have one or two areas that they can work on. If you can point these out to yourself, you will find that you can morph more closely towards self-realization.

Embrace gratitude.

Embracing gratitude is all about fostering a healthy self-image, which will help you on your path to self-realization. Some people have damaged their subconscious, and they get bitter and weakened because of past failures. You must learn to resist this urge, and you must find gratitude in the world.

This will make your defenses stronger, and it will teach you that there are things that are worthy of your pursuit of happiness.

Could you identify what you want and get it?

Stop messing around and keeping yourself from getting what you want. If your goal is a specific career path, then ask someone if you can be his or her apprentice. If you can learn on your own, do your research and start to learn how you can achieve this goal on your own. Read books, the internet, and ask other people how they have achieved what you want to achieve.

Get rid of your attachment to the "how."

The "how" is not essential. The subconscious will sometimes push you towards judgment, and you will find that if you have a voice that makes you towards a conclusion, this will start to create a space between what you want and where you are.

Remember, this is a sort of paradoxical task because the subconscious is not something we can readily access. You have to make suggestions and observations about yourself. You can't directly train the subconscious. What you are doing by employing these tactics is more akin to creating an atmosphere. You make the conditions for the garden to grow by encouraging your subconscious to be able to grow in the ways that it can.

It would help if you also tried to keep neutral thinking in play when enacting these strategies for the subconscious. This is a self-reflexive act, and to complete it, you will need to separate yourself, the researcher, and the subject. However, there is a way to defeat this self-bias, and that is through mindful self-reflexive practices. You must be able to consider yourself as another being rather than yourself. You must be able to consider yourself a character in a book, which you can analyze and read, rather than your self which you need to protect.

Chapter 6: How to Analyze People

Understanding and knowing about ourselves through self-analysis is vital to learn more about who we are individually and how outside people, environment, and circumstances impact us. Often, we may overlook or dismiss aspects of our personality and behavior that are picked up or readily noticed by someone, who may use this trait to either help or exploit us. Sometimes, we may try to understand or assess someone, so we know why they act or behave in a certain way and how we can adjust to relate and communicate with them effectively. In some cases, spouses of abusive partners may understand a specific personality disorder and whether it is an underlying reason for the abuse or toxic behavior. On the other hand, we might try to figure out how a person can be positive and ambitious despite experiencing setbacks in life to learn from them and understand their internal methods for coping and conquering their goals.

Before we can adequately evaluate someone else, it is vital to learn self-analysis. We need to become comfortable with our inner thoughts, emotions, and behavior before we can assess someone else as to how we communicate and act towards others, which impacts them. When we review a situation where there is a conflict, we may immediately look at the other person(s) before considering our role in the discussion, debate, or argument that resulted. Even if there is no fault of our own, it's essential to rule out any influential markers or perceptions of us the other people may have had, such as a gesture or tone that could be misunderstood. For this reason, and to begin on a neutral level, begin self-analysis steps.

Self-analysis is defined as an internal evaluation of your thoughts, behaviors, and resulting actions. It is a way to enhance self-care by delving into our thoughts and emotions to understand ourselves better.

1. Consider all the negative, positive, and neutral attributes you would attach to you. Suppose you find that most of your characteristics of this analysis shift towards the negative; you may be too critical or demanding on yourself, whereas if there are many positive traits you can think of in yourself. In that case, this is a sign of confidence. Neutral and a balance of everything may balance acknowledging what you are good at and finding areas for improvement. Overall, you should gauge your self-perception and determine what that is and whether it's positive or negative.

2. Consider other people's feedback, and be sure to ask a variety of people, not just those who are critical in general or anyone who would shy away from being honest and upfront. You could ask them to assess their thoughts of you constructively, looking for points of improvement along with positive traits. It's best to obtain a cross-section of different people and opinions, with little or no coaching, so the results are more honest and valuable.

3. When you receive the feedback, consider that not all terms are necessarily entirely negative or positive, depending on who uses the time to describe you. For example, independence is often seen as a positive trait. However, it is seen as less collaborative and team-oriented to some people, which may be helpful in particular work and organizational environments. Some people may consider a competitive nature healthy and natural, while others see it as unfavorable in certain situations. Some attributes are always well regarded, such as reliability, fairness, and innovation, whereas others tend to be vastly regarded as unfavorable: arrogant, ill-tempered, and indecisive. Aggression may be frowned upon in situations where patience and care are needed. In contrast, an abrasive environment may accept, even embrace, some forms of perceived aggression as a sign of strength, even where it is not.

4. Once you have collected all the feedback and have a good list of attributes to work with, build a list or table and move each of the items under their appropriate category:

Which items are considered valuable skills, characteristics, and abilities? These may include a sense of responsibility or accountability, diligence, honesty, hard-working and reliability.

Do you have hobbies and areas of expertise that help you develop? Do you play an instrument, speak more than one language, enjoy reading, sports, or an artistic pursuit?

How would I describe my relationship with family, friends, neighbors, and colleagues?

What goals do you have currently, and what milestones are you looking to achieve?

What are my areas of improvement?

There are some key benefits from self-assessment, which include the following:

Self-criticism, in a constructive way. When you assess your feelings, actions, and behaviors, your perspective moves outside as you look within. Often, we can be critical about ourselves, which can be habitual, though constructive criticism can give us a balanced view of what we can improve upon, to reduce what we're not content with

Receiving constructive feedback from others is of great benefit and allows us to see who we are from the outside without attempting to attempt this ourselves. Contrary to what many people think, others may have a more favorable view of you, offering some new ideas and advice that can benefit self-improvement.

The combination of feedback and self-perception creates a comprehensive view, or 360 degrees of perspectives, which can paint a complete picture of reflection.

There is a potential to build confidence. When we take the self-assessment approach, this can become part of a self-care pattern, where we aim to take care and improve ourselves together.

Gaining a fuller perspective of who we are, what we experience, and the world around us is a valuable way to achieve a greater understanding of reality by viewing our world through several lenses and viewpoints. Once we are aware of our perception and how it may differ from reality, we can take a more pragmatic approach to experiences in life and how we make decisions.

Techniques on Analysis: How it is Done?

Reading People, Observing Body Language, Various Methods of Communication and Cues

Reading people and analyzing their behavior is essential for understanding their cues and various reasons for acting in specific ways. Looking for strings is not tricky, and many signs can be picked up in body language, positioning, and other non-verbal expressions.

Close Proximity/Positioning:

When you first meet someone, most people will allow a reasonable amount of personal space between you and them. The average personal space allowance is about eighteen inches, or close to this distance. Suppose you ride subway trains or other means of public transportation that require close contact with other people. In that case, you notice how most will try to maintain a space of at least a few inches in between them and others for safety and security. Most people will offer a handshake, though an embrace is often reserved for people you know more intimately or work with closely. If someone you first meet tries to close or minimize the gap between you and them at an early stage in your relationship, it may be a sign they feel comfortable and want to foster that connection.

This can also be a sign that a person you've only just met to gauge how close they can get to you and how far you will let them. They will observe your reaction and whether you welcome their close contact or feel intimidated by it. When this happens, it can be a manipulator's way to learn your comfort zone and what they can and cannot get away with. If you find yourself in a situation where someone is trying to get too familiar too fast, consider it a warning sign, or at least a position to monitor, for your safety.

Hand Gestures:

People who strive for control tend to rub their hands together or their neck with their hands. This can be a clear indication in some people, though it may also signal that a manipulative person feels guilty or anxious about what they're going to do. Consider how some people get sweaty palms when they tell a lie or perform a dishonest act. They may also react this way when trying a manipulative tactic or trickery and may feel conflicted about it. Other people who are more skilled in persuasion may not exhibit these symptoms because they are well practiced and no longer feel uneasy about their actions.

Another hand gesture common among manipulators is when the fingers are spread, with the tips outstretched, forming a tent. This is usually done while sitting, with their hands developed this way on a table or over their lap. This can signal a strong urge to achieve and maintain control over people and situations.

Eye Contact:

When eye contact is maintained, this means you are being taken seriously and listened to. There may be many reasons why keen attention is being paid to you and what you say, especially when someone can know more information: they may be trying to assist you for your benefit or learn something new. If someone is manipulative, they may be listening for cues or signs of inadequacies that they can use against you. Shifting eye movements or avoidance can indicate a lack of interest or occur due to distraction.

Generally, bodily movements that impede your space or make you feel uncomfortable are often used by people who want to establish control. It is their way of invading your space physically and making you feel as though they are powerful. When a manipulator does this, they often look for cues from you: do you shrink back and try to avoid their covering nature, or do you stand firm to them and assert yourself? Someone looking for easy "prey" may be more accessible to target, but only if they are receptive to the manipulative techniques.

For example, a salesperson may be eager to close a sale. In their determination, they use clear language towards the potential customers, highlighting the benefits of their selling. In doing so, they may create an extended comfort zone, where the customer feels obliged to allow them to continue speaking to them. They may touch your arm or pat you on the back, as a friend would, gauging how receptive you are to their closeness. For some people, these actions make them feel "trapped" as if they need to commit to the sale, where others may feel compelled to buy into the "benefits" of becoming a consumer.

A salesperson is crafty but careful in their tactics; they may be able to sell to someone who doesn't want to buy the product but does so because of pressure. In this way, persuasion moves into a more potent form of manipulation.

Chapter 7: The Benefits of Dark Psychology

Remember, while dark psychology may be based upon looking at how the dark personality types prey on people, that is not all that it is suitable for—it is essential to understand these abilities and skills. In understanding comes the power to protect and prevent, after all.

Nevertheless, as you have been exposed to several malicious usages from several of these techniques, let's go over the ethics of dark psychology, as well as the benefits that may arise from it. Dark psychology does not have to be the harmful concept that it has become because of the people that wielded it—you can reclaim it.

Is Dark Psychology Evil?

For the million-dollar question: Is dark psychology evil? It does not have the capability of being good or evil in the same sense that gravity cannot be good or bad—it simply is. As a force without free will, it cannot possibly be labeled with a human construct such as good or evil without any way to control itself. However, that does not mean that it is necessarily safe, nor does it mean that it cannot be used in hurtful manners.

While dark psychology itself is not evil, evil people can use it. Just as it is not about the gun being evil, but rather the one wielding the gun that determines how bad the situation is, dark psychology is entirely at the mercy of those wielding it. If the individual who uses these techniques uses them for evil purposes, taking advantage of these techniques to steal and abuse is his failure and no one else's. He will have to address that failure for himself and no one else, which is significant.

Of course, that means that the inverse is true as well—it cannot indeed be a reasonable force either. While dark psychology may not indeed be good, it can be used in ways that are beneficial to people, and throughout the book, you were exposed to several. Is it awful to influence someone to buy a car that will truly serve their own family? Is it wrong to control someone to no longer have crippling anxiety at the idea of taking a final exam? What about hypnotizing someone to have insomnia no longer? You would be hard-pressed to find anyone who would claim that any of those were bad decisions or wrong, even though they all used techniques common to dark psychology.

Remember, as dark psychology has been studied, people have gained access into the minds of predators capable of far more than the average person. The average person is not going to be intentionally manipulating and harassing people on the regular—he is going to be minding his own business. He does not have any interest in preying on other people. So, would that average person have a use for dark psychology? Several other techniques can be used on yourself as well. You can anchor yourself to create your coping mechanisms, for example, or you can choose to self-hypnotize to help yourself build self-confidence. These are not evil.

Ultimately, whether the art is good or evil, one thing remains true—it is all about how it is used that determines how welcome the use of it is.

Reasons to Use Dark Psychology

There are several reasons that one may intentionally learn dark psychology. They may want to use these methods to help themselves—perhaps they were victims of a dark personality type in the past and want to understand why.

That insight is invaluable, and gaining the reasons why and how someone could entirely and utterly dismantle someone's personality can be therapeutic somehow. In understanding how you have become vulnerable, you can remove those vulnerabilities to figure out how best to fight them off.

Some people may learn about dark psychology out of sheer curiosity—we are fascinated by what scares us. After all, horror is a massive genre in movies for a reason! You may find that learning how the insides of an evil individual's mind works are just as fascinating as it is terrifying, and for that reason alone, you want to keep reading on how they do what they do.

Other people may read simply because they want to fight back. When you can recognize dark psychology, you can prevent it from being effective. So much of dark psychology is all about identifying vulnerabilities and exploiting them.

If you know those vulnerabilities and about the common exploits, you can side-step them. You can avoid falling for them and instead work on strengthening your skills to protect yourself.

Effectively, dark psychology is incredibly flexible, as are the techniques. The same methods that can utterly destroy someone else can also be used to better everyone involved. They can make you more likely to interact with other people simply because you will have a better understanding.

Above all, you will be able to protect yourself with ease. At the very least, you will be able to rest easy knowing that the dark personality types will be far less likely to pull a fast one over you simply because you know what to expect.

The Insight of Dark Psychology

Dark psychology is unique in the sense that it opens the window for us to see through the eyes of the narcissist, the Machiavellian, or the psychopath. In understanding how these techniques work, you can precisely see what spurs these people to act in the ways they do. You can figure out why people want to behave these ways and what they stand to gain by doing so.

While you may never want to manipulate others yourself, you may find that the insight of understanding why is critical, especially if you are in the position of healing from a relationship with one such person. When you can understand the other person's mind, you may be able to recognize it for what it truly is—disordered.

Beyond just that, though, the insight provided in understanding dark psychology allows us to see what made us so vulnerable to its grasp in the first place. You will know what each of these techniques plays off of, and in knowing what they use, you can figure out how to shield from them. Consider that NLP directly influences the unconscious mind.

When you know that the unconscious mind is one of the most commonly attacked parts of the mind when trying to control someone else, you can remind yourself always to do self-checks, understanding why you do what you are doing at any time.

You can ask yourself if the behaviors you are doing at that moment are your own or common for people who are usually manipulated. You can figure out if the thought in your mind that drives you is your own, or if it seems out of place or contradictory to an idea that you know you have had for ages.

Effectively, when you can recognize the thought processes of yourself about dark psychology, you can figure out whether you have been manipulated in the past. Knowing that is critical to realize if you are a victim or proactive enough to avoid victimization altogether.

However, what is true, despite the insight that you have gained, is that you have earned knowledge. You know what is possible in the world.

You have knowledge about the mind and some of its secrets. You know the predators that you may never have been aware of in reality. That is invaluable. Knowledge is power, and if you can wield that power bravely and proudly, you will be able to protect yourself.

Conclusion

Dark Psychology is one of those topics most people will avoid. They worry that it's unethical to use it to get what you want. However, if you are willing to use the techniques and practices we have discussed in this guide, you will find that you will be able to go further than you can imagine with any other method.

The more practice you can do, the easier it will be for you to succeed against your actual goals, and you will get everything you want in your life.

Once you can successfully employ any of the techniques mentioned above, it is essential to consider whether you are using it ethically. Our ethics generally evolve from our internal value system. Before choosing to influence another person in any way, it is usually a good idea to take a step back and ask yourself whether you would like to be in your subject's position.

DARK PSYCHOLOGY AND MANIPULATION

Introduction

The human mind is undeniably complex—it is responsible for everything we are as people. It determines who we are, what we like, and how we interact with the world. It is complex enough for us all to have very distinctive personalities. However, despite this complexity, the human mind is surprisingly predictable. We may have our differences, but our minds work with the same tendencies at the heart of it all. You can influence someone else, without them realizing what you are doing, in all sorts of different ways. From changing what you have said to change your body language to alter how you talk, you can adjust the way people respond.

This is hardly anything new—if you are a salesperson, you have probably been guided through ways that you can frame how you respond to those around you to try to get them to buy. If you work with children, you have probably been taught what you need to do to help facilitate a learning environment that will help them. If you work in law enforcement or something else that will involve you needing to exert your authority, you are taught how you can use your body language to be seen as dominant. Ultimately, you can make use of how you act, how you speak, and how you hold yourself to ensure that you can control the way other people respond. This is primarily because, while people can think and act independently, the vast majority of what we do and how we feel is directly related to how we respond unconsciously.

By taking advantage of the unconscious mind, you can control other people. You can take control of other people. You can come up with ways to influence the way other people think, and in taking control of their thoughts, you can take control of their actions. You will be introduced to how manipulation, as a form of social influence, works. You will learn about what manipulation is and the ethicality of manipulation. You will learn how to manipulate other people effectively, and you will be guided through the role that emotions play in influencing others. You will then be guided through several very different forms of emotional manipulation and how they work. You will be guided through several different methods that can be used to manipulate others. In particular, you will take a look at emotional manipulation to allow you to better influence behaviors. You will learn about methods of mind control and how you can genuinely control how people interact with others.

You will take a look at Neuro-Linguistic Programming, a technique used to influence how people around you interact by tapping into their unconscious minds. You will learn to understand the power of persuasion and how you can better influence how you will control others without them even realizing it. Finally, you will know how you can use your body language and hold yourself to help you influence everyone else.

Being able to influence and control other people can be incredibly useful. It can help you learn how to influence others better to guide them to make decisions right for them. In being able to influence other people, you can ensure that you are in control at the end of the day. You can influence someone to do what you know is best for them. If you know that someone is more likely to act in a way that would be harmful or not benefit someone else in some way, you will be able to change the practices in which they are more likely to behave. Doctors can use this to encourage people to make treatment options suitable for them. Salespeople can encourage people to purchase other items. If you have a friend that is especially prone to making bad decisions, you can influence them as well—and this book will teach you to do exactly that.

Remember, the actions of others are dependent upon how you encourage other people to behave. The way that you approach other people can directly influence how others behave. It can allow you to change how people behave, but you also need to remember that you ought to respect how people think. It would help if you appreciated the fact that people should, by and large, have that autonomy that they deserve. If you choose to manipulate other people, you must accept that you are taking that risk for yourself. It would help if you recognized that the consequences that come with it would be yours to take. Nevertheless, it could be that sometimes, the risk is worth it. Sometimes, it could be worth it to spend time manipulating others, and if you think that is the case, then that is your prerogative.

Chapter 1: What is manipulation.

It is the act of changing someone else's thoughts, feelings, or behaviors without them being aware of it. It can change how someone is acting, essentially pulling their strings and influencing them directly. It attempts to exploit the other person to change either their thoughts or behaviors through methods that are often considered indirect or deceptive. Because manipulation works primarily by keeping the other person out of the loop, it can quickly become very effective. It is essentially escaping detection to allow for manipulation to occur.

The defining factor of manipulation relies on the person being manipulated not knowing that they are being manipulated. This is often done through covert aggression, but not always. It can sometimes be done to advance the betterment of the manipulator, but not always. It can sometimes work in ways that harm the individual being manipulated, but not always.

That is not outside of the realm of possibility—you can learn how to influence and control other people, and it is not as hard as you may have initially thought.

Think about it this way—you are being asked to change your belief in something you are doing. Perhaps you were told that you could not eat meat on the job at your place of employment, and then in tandem with telling you that you cannot eat meat on the job, your manager also educated you on the reasons you should not consume meat at all. If you were to agree that the reasons for not eating meat were valid, you have internalized the message—you believe that it is right to avoid eating meat, and so you change your habits as well.

Identification

Identification is a little bit different from the other two. With this particular form of social influence, you rely on the fact that people will naturally influence people they admire. When someone admires someone else, such as a celebrity, they naturally want to align with the thoughts and beliefs of the one that they identify with. The result is that ultimately when they do relate to someone else, they are going to attempt to emulate them. After all, mimicry is one of the most sincere forms of flattery, and when you mimic a celebrity or someone else that you admire, you are being influenced.

Reasons to Manipulate

Ultimately, people use manipulation because they want to see a change in either the behaviors of someone else or want to see a difference in someone else's thoughts. They are usually driven by one of several reasons, but the result is often the same—they want to change someone else. They want someone to behave differently for some reason, or they want someone to think differently for some reason or another. Some of the most common reasons to manipulate others include:

• For advancing one's purposes: Some people find that they are entirely comfortable taking advantage of other people. They treat those around them like steps to further and further in life without struggling. These people generally do not empathize with others—they view other people as abused and controlled or as tools to allow them to get further ahead.

• For power: Some people feel like they need to get ahead, and they need to feel powerful to do so. They feel like they are only secure when they have that feeling of superiority. They will intentionally manipulate people, not because they need something else, but because they want to feel that power over others for their benefit. This is very dangerous—these kinds of people do not care about others. They have no qualms about hurting other people and will not hesitate to do it. They think that the peace of mind they get from doing so will be worth it.

• For control: Similarly to needing power, other people do so to control those around them. They feel like they can only remain stable and in control if they can exert that level of control onto those around them. It becomes widespread, then, to see people who will reach out to control other people to feel better in general. Control gives people a sense that they are not entirely helpless. It allows people to ease their anxiety about something when they feel like they can control something around them—even if that something is someone else.

- For fun: Some people want to control those around them because they feel like it will be fun. They decide that they will move forward by figuring out how to interact with others.

   They will, for example, try to get someone to do something else to see if they can do it—it becomes like a challenge for them.

- Unintentionally: Some people inadvertently end up manipulating others. They often do not attempt to use other people, but it winds up happening anyway due to self-control, self-awareness, and lacking that essential element of empathy.

- Impulsively: They do it on a whim without actually planning it out. They are not attempting to be destructive—they lack self-control over their behaviors. In response, they may also manipulate people in an attempt to preserve their image that would otherwise be challenged by the impulsive behaviors in the first place.

For some covert plan: Sometimes, the manipulation is intentional and happens to manipulate someone into doing something that will fit an agenda. For example, think of those scammer phone calls that go out when people decide to influence others who are more likely to be vulnerable to doing something for them or get them to pay for gift cards and mail them somewhere.

How Manipulation Works

Several psychological theories explain how successful manipulation works. The first and perhaps the most universally accepted theory was a renowned psychologist and author George Simon. He analyzed the concept of manipulation from the point of view of the manipulator, and he can up with a pattern of behavior that sums up every manipulation scenario. According to Simon, three main things are involved in psychological manipulation.

· First, the manipulator approaches the target by concealing his or her aggressive intentions. Here, the manipulator seeks to endear himself to his prey without revealing the fact that his ultimate plan is to manipulate him or her. The manipulator accomplishes this by modifying his behavior and presenting himself as a good-natured and friendly individual who relates well with the target.

· Secondly, the manipulator will take time to know the victim. The purpose of this is to understand the psychological vulnerabilities that the victim may have to figure out which manipulation tactic will be the most effective when he ultimately decides to deploy them.

·

Depending on the scenario and the complexity of the manipulation technique, this stage may take anywhere between a few minutes to several years. For example, when a stranger targets you, he may take only a couple of minutes to "size you up," but when your partner or colleague seeks to manipulate you, he or she may spend months or even years trying to understand how your mind works.

· If the manipulator successfully hides his intentions from you, he is in a better position to learn your weaknesses because you will instill some level of trust in him, and he will use that trust to get you to let down your guard and to reveal your vulnerabilities to him.

· Thirdly, having collected enough information to act upon, the manipulator will deploy a manipulation technique of his choosing. For this to work, the manipulator needs to marshal a sufficient level of ruthlessness; this means that the manipulation technique chosen will depend on what the manipulator can stomach. A manipulator with a conscience may try to use less harmful methods to manipulate you. One that completely lacks a conscience may use extreme methods to take advantage of you. Either way, manipulative people are willing to let harm befall their victims, and to them, the resultant outcome (which is usually in their favor) justifies the damage they cause.

Simon's manipulation theory teaches us the general approach that manipulators use to get what they want from their victims. Still, it also points out something significant: Manipulation works, not just because of the manipulator's actions but also because of the victims' reactions.

In the first step, the manipulator misrepresents himself to the victim: If the victim can see through the veil that the manipulator is wearing, the manipulation won't be successful. In the second step, the manipulator collects information about victims to learn about his or her vulnerabilities. The victim can be able to stop the manipulation at this stage by treating the manipulator's prying nature with a bit of suspicion. In the third stage, the manipulator uses coercive or underhanded techniques to get what he wants from the victim. Even in this stage, the victim may have confident choices on reacting to the manipulator's machinations.

Understanding both the victim's and the manipulator's psychology makes it possible to figure out how you can avoid falling victim to other people's manipulation. It can also help you become more conscientious so that you don't unknowingly use manipulation techniques on other people around you.

Let's look at the vulnerabilities that manipulators like to exploit in their victims.

The first and most prevalent vulnerability is the need to please others. We all have this need to some extent; we seek to please the people in our lives and total strangers. This is technically a positive quality that helps us coexist in our societies, but it's a weapon that can be used against you as manipulators.

Many of us are willing to endure certain levels of discomfort to make other people feel happy; we feel a certain sense of obligation towards one another, and that's just human nature. The closer we are to certain people, the greater the need to please them. For example, the need to satisfy your friend is higher than your need to please a stranger.

Manipulators understand this, and they use it against their victims all the time. If a manipulator wants to get something big out of you, he will first take the time to get closer to you, not just to get to know your vulnerability but also to increase the sense of obligation you feel towards him.

The second vulnerability is the need for approval and acceptance. We want people to love us, think of us as members of their groups, and choose us over other people. This feeling can be addictive, and it can give other people (incredibly manipulative ones) a lot of power over us. The vast majority of manipulation victims have close personal relationships with the manipulators; in other words, they have an emotional need to gain the acceptance or approval of the manipulator. The remaining manipulation victims can be manipulated because they want to be a part of something (a group, a social class, etc.).

The third vulnerability that manipulators like to exploit is what psychologists refer to as "emetophobia" (which is the fear of negative emotions). To some extent, we are all afraid of negative emotions; we will do lots of things to avoid feeling angry, scared, stressed, frustrated, and worried, etc. We want to lead happy and fulfilled lives, and anything that makes us feel "bad" is a threat to that sense of fulfillment.

So, in many cases, we will do what manipulators want to alleviate that "bad" feeling. Manipulators know this, and they use negative emotions against us all the time.

The fourth vulnerability is the lack of assertiveness. Assertiveness is low quality; even people you may generally consider to be assertive are likely to cave in if manipulators push hard enough. Even when you are willing to stand your ground and to say "No," manipulators can be very persistent, and in the end, they can wear you out.

The fifth vulnerability is the lack of a strong sense of identity. Having a solid understanding of identity means having clear personal boundaries and understanding one's values. Unfortunately, these qualities aren't so strong in most of us, leaving us open to manipulation. Manipulators succeed by pushing our boundaries little by little, making them blurry, and then taking control of our identities.

Finally, having an external locus of control and having low self-reliance are also critical vulnerabilities that manipulators love to exploit. It means you view yourself through other people's eyes. It means that you are extrinsically motivated. When you have low self-reliance, it means you depend on other people for sustenance and emotional stability. It means that if support systems in your life are taken away, you can easily find yourself leaning on a manipulator, which leaves you at his mercy.

Manipulation is a Part of Human History

Looking at history, we will see that some of our most loved historical figures practiced manipulation. During the United States founding, our founding fathers had to use socio-political manipulation to help set a revolution in motion. Using various economic manipulation tactics on the other colonies and colonists, joining their cause would benefit them more than the British. Secondly, many political games had to be played, all using deception and manipulation to help get the right people to lead the country.

Manipulation had to be used in its persuasive form here so that the right person could get the proper backing. This was not evil nor bad; it showed how the covert tactic of playing into a willing pawns card could allow for everyone involved to win. Imagine, too, that they had to manipulate the British for quite a while before things indeed were sent into emotion. They had to work them into trusting and believing them.

These same kinds of manipulative games have been used for good by many significant figures in history to manipulate their opposition into doing what is right.

Think of the rallies and marches during the civil rights movement. It did so much good by manipulating and playing on people's emotions and wants for a just society. This is not malicious manipulation, but evil must enact significant change in this world.

Knowing that manipulation is not always an evil wantonly committed for sin makes it much easier to understand the tactics people will use. In a significant part complimenting and persuading someone through charisma is, in a sense, manipulation. You tell them what they want to hear, whether it approves or being a shoulder to cry on for someone. Almost every friendship that is healthy has this give and take. For a large part, these are simple altruistic forms of manipulation that allow and help both sides win and accomplish a goal of theirs. Charisma and persuasion two topics I mentioned earlier. Persuasion and charisma are the simplest forms of human manipulation.

Manipulators work by making someone come across as if they are the type of person who loves and cares about you and would drop anything if need be to help you with something. This glib or charm is a manipulative tactic that one could use to gain friends. You are putting on a front that people want, and as a result of this, they then become drawn to you easier and wish to spend time with you or do stuff to you.

This manipulation on a social scale is not for harm but companionship. The issue is that the word makes manipulation sound bad and evil. But the truth is that doing simple things that social charmer does, like mirroring body language, buying someone food, or constantly asking about their interests and ignoring yours, is essential human interaction. You can get people to trust you and even help you get ahead in life, mainly if this kind of interaction occurs in the social world.

Manipulation and Success

You could argue that to a certain degree, without some influential people in society who used manipulation to get their way to the top, the world would fall apart. Maybe we would not be so successful. This manipulation is far more different from the much more sinister mind manipulation. It is simple to understand the term mental manipulation.

Simply put, mental manipulation occurs with the nefarious act of playing mind games, making you feel guilty for not buying or doing something, getting you to question your judgment.

This covert manipulative behavior can become so common that we often don't recognize it until it is too late, by which point we have befallen the consequences of said manipulation. Avoiding these consequences is a great thing to be capable of doing. That is why it is good to know what mental manipulation is due to its subtlety. This type of manipulation – mental manipulation – is perhaps the most common form of manipulation you will encounter in your day-to-day life.

Mental manipulation shows its face a lot in relationships with friends or other people you care about. As a result, the people who do this are very good at it and hide it well. Besides being such a common form of manipulation people will use, it is essential to realize that there are many varieties of mental manipulation to which you could easily find yourself as a victim.

Consider times when you are speaking with a group of friends, and one person tries to make you feel guilty due to you choosing not to buy them a costly gift for their birthday. They then might try mental manipulation to get you to fall for the trap of "oh well, I have done all these things for you; do you not think it is fair if you get me XYZ."

Behavior like this is where manipulation becomes evil and unacceptable. This is not trying to sway someone over to your side of thinking for a good reason or trying to survive in a time of crisis. Understanding the subtle moral differences in manipulation makes it easier for you to appreciate how to learn about different manipulative tactics as a whole and how you can go about defending from and using them as well as giving you the valuable ability to know how to avoid people who could potentially try and manipulate you in person, this includes the media and everything else we see. Since they all use manipulation tactics, understanding this is half the battle.

Examples of Manipulation

Body language is a potent tool needed for mastering how to manipulate people. If you can honestly understand how body language works and analyze it, you will be in control of the other person, though in a tactical manner.

Body language works as a compass by telling you essential things about how the person is feeling and what they are thinking in the present.

This information will help you understand how they think about their environment and what is going on around them and how they feel about you, and their interactions with you or anyone else with whom they may be sharing interactions. Knowing this information means that you have a tremendous upper hand interacting with the person. With it, you now know when you should approach them and how, which manipulation and persuasion strategies you should use, what wording would likely work best on them, and even the exact timing of when you should be able to tip them in your favor ultimately.

As you can tell, body language is an essential compass in helping you effectively manipulate people. For that reason, you must understand the "reading formula," or how you will assess the three types of body language that you will be reading on the person in front of you. This formula is essential and can even be crafted into an easy-to-remember sentence, just like the one you use to remember the three steps of manipulation.

As you now know, primary body language is the part of the body language you are reading to get a general understanding of what a person is thinking and feeling at the moment. This is the first thing you want to read before you approach a person or begin manipulating them, as this will give you an understanding of where they stand and what path you need to take to get to where you want to go. After gaining this general understanding, you typically do not want to find yourself focused excessively on primary body language.

When you read complex body language signals, you want to look at two primary areas: their hands and their feet. The location and actions being taken with these two parts of the body will tell you more than almost anywhere else on the entire body.

By reading the signs being given to you by the hands and feet, you can get an idea of what the person is thinking and how they feel. In general, you want to watch the movements taking place in the hands and feet during your conversation with the person you are talking to and wishing to manipulate. Use them to determine whether you are successfully driving the person into the emotion that you need them to be in for manipulation to happen or if you need to adjust your tactics to get them there.

Please pay attention to them during the entire conversation, mainly when you use a specific manipulation tactic. These complex signals will act as a form of compass to guide you through the conversation step-by-step, on their terms that you secretly orchestrate.

Let us analyze some of the possible ways to manipulate others using his body language.

Manipulation by Mirroring the Other Person

When you consciously and deliberately change your body language to fit into another person's class and even behave like the person by learning the tone of voice, posture, facial expressions, including micro-expressions. This merely is mimicry or imitation aimed at impressing someone else.

Although, this process could be risky because the other person may get to know you are just trying to make a false impression, and it could cost you the relationship or further valuable details. It is better to maintain your natural body language than to mirror another person's traits, which has the potentials of backfiring at the end, leaving you in pieces.

Exciting and Captivating their Emotions

This step is a beneficial method of manipulating people easily by exciting and captivating their minds through their emotions and finding out the issue troubling their heart and using it as bait in luring them into doing what will be an advantage to you.

Make People to Like You

You may want to ask me, what shall I do to make people like me? No matter the intrigues and tactics you want to use in manipulating people, it may not work if they don't like you naturally. Therefore, endeavor to make yourself a likable person. The character is one of the criteria that will cause people to quickly and gullibly accept whatever you say to them. Howbeit, remember that your ultimate goal is to make everything work to your advantage, nothing less than that.

Present Yourself as a Trustworthy Person

Trust is the crucial thing in every relationship. If your friend does not trust you, he will not commit salient details to you.

One of the criteria to win your friend's trust is to share a very personal issue with him or her, and that will make him open his or her heart for you too. With this gesture, you may win the confidence of your partner, as he is poised to confide in you.

Use Your Emotions to manipulate them.

The very first step to analyzing anyone is to study their body language. Body language is something that virtually every master manipulator has learned how to read, and you must know-how, too. Body language is a language that we use to communicate beyond the spoken word. Still, you must understand how to read body language from a manipulator's perspective if you want to analyze a person effectively.

Set a Baseline

When you have a baseline about people, reading body language and other nonverbal clues becomes more accurate. Please tune in to people completely to figure out their baseline or essential behavior. This will help you relate nonverbal clues more effectively. How does someone react to different circumstances and situations? What is their inherent personality? How are their communication skills? How is their speech and choice of words? What about the voice? Are they essentially confident or anxious?

Look for a Group of Clues

Read clues in clusters, which offer a more accurate analysis of what a person is thinking or feeling. Do not make quick and sporadic conclusions based on isolated nonverbal signals.

Spotting Lies and Deception

While reading people for deception, it is crucial to keep their baseline behavior and the physical setting and culture/religion into context too. Reading or analyzing people through body language is not an overnight process, but it keeps getting accurate with practice. Try deciphering what people are thinking or feeling by practicing people reading skills at the airport, on the train to work, at the doctor's clinic, or cafe. You'll learn to tune in to their actions and behavior accurately over some time.

General Body Language Signs

If you are speaking and someone is leaning in your direction, he or she is interested in what you are saying or keenly listening to you. Likewise, crossed arms and legs are a huge sign of switching off or being completely closed to what you are trying to communicate. The person does not subscribe to your views or isn't confident about what you are saying.

This information can be precious, considering a smile is the single most significant weapon people use to conceal their honest thoughts, emotions, and feelings. It is a widely established conclusion among psychological experts that a smile is tough to fake. There has to be a genuine experience of joy or happiness for creating that specific expression. When you are displeased, the terms will not settle into their place.

Signs of Manipulation

Victims develop anxiety. After being manipulated over time, victims develop an anxiety disorder, which is characterized by warring and fearing that they are not strong enough and interfere with the daily routine.

Find it hard to trust. Trust is a rule that governs all regulations and humanization of all the interactions on the earth. Victims felt betrayal firsthand, and it is hard to overcome the fear of trusting again.

They lie to project a particular image of themselves for others to comprehend.

They feel depressed. They have mood swings that include emotional highs and lows and affect sleeping, activities, judgment, and inability to think clearly.

They don't remember to take time for themselves and forget self-care is a priority. As Dodinsky said, "Be there for others but never leave yourself behind." Most likely, they are stressed, and they are running everywhere, taking care of everyone to hide their depression.

Unhealthy coping patterns. Coping skills are habits that victims develop to deal with stressful situations after being manipulated.

The practices help them feel better physically and psychologically, which allows them to perform their daily routine. They engage in strategies that they give problems later in their life.

Examples of Manipulative Behaviors

The motive behind the manipulator varies from mischievous to unconscious, and it is always important to know the environment where the manipulation is taking place. Such practices are:

- Verbal abuse – It is an act of criticizing or bullying another person, especially people in an intimate relationship. It is a negative form of communication to harm the other person's emotions. Gaslighting – Its form of psychological manipulation, where a manipulator makes the victim become doubtful and question their perception and sanity.

- Dating a person who manipulates and isolates you from your family and friends.

- Withholding info – Psychopathic people withhold information so that they don't feel vulnerable and can control the situation or relationship.

- Passive-aggressive actions – Manipulators act indirectly aggressive relatively than direct aggressive. They show resistance to demands from loved ones and constantly procrastinating and acting stubbornly.

- They deploy sex as a means of accomplishing or achieving something. It happens when manipulates almost realizes that they are manipulated.

Implicit threats: They are suggested, implied, or expressed indirectly and are not said clearly. The manipulator issues such warnings to be in control of the relationship.

No More Being A Push Over

Are you sick of being pushed around and caving in to someone's demands because you care about them? It will boost your confidence, and in the end, hopefully, the people you love the most will look up to you and respect you.

The whole idea is to keep the people in your life but make them understand that you are not one to be taken advantage of.

There are ways to stop allowing others to manipulate you without changing who you are as a person. Being firm is a critical quality to gain. Are you a parent? Do you let your children get away with anything because you love them so much that you want to give them the world? I hope your answer is no. Structure and firmness are essential to growth.

The tools you use as a parent (if you are one) can be used for any person you encounter. Since you are already on the mindset of being firm rather than mean, you can let the person know you are serious, and hopefully without making a scene.

You may not be 'friends with your co-workers. Therefore they may not have that inner concern for you that close friends, family, and romantic partners have. There is a difference between earning your place and being used to do all the work that isn't necessarily fun.

Family members who take it upon themselves to push you around are difficult to wrangle with, but fear not, it can be done. It takes finesse, and much like with children, you have to be consistent. You can't allow them to do something one time without expecting them to push even further the next. If you want your family to respect you and take you seriously, you need to let them know you mean business and that there are certain things you will not accept.

People don't always have the same beliefs, and in a romantic relationship, things can get tricky. You have to decide if what that person is doing to you, and possibly to others, is something you can overcome. If it is, then keep clear boundaries. If it's not something you can live with, then maybe they aren't the right person for you. People have differences. It can be exciting, or your personalities can clash.

In the end, the overall goal is to stop being pushed around and to show others that you are a strong individual who demands a certain level of respect. But first, you must respect yourself. Once you do, getting rid of the 'push over persona' will be reachable, and your life will be much smoother and less stressful.

How to Outsmart a Manipulator?

Psychological manipulation is always going to be a very loaded and heavy-handed issue. It can often be referred to as lying, deceiving, skewing, distorting, gaslighting, intimidating, guilting, and other such things. Sometimes, the person who is manipulating you might be a parent, sibling, boss, classmate, coworker, or romantic partner, among others. That's why manipulation is such a complex topic to handle. It can take various tactics, and multiple agents can also employ it. This is why it can be increasingly difficult for someone to identify and deal with a manipulative person.

You were exposed to the many different feelings, sensations, and experiences you might have should you ever find yourself in a manipulative relationship environment. As long as you keep your eyes peeled and make an active effort to seek these red flags out, it shouldn't be a problem. Now, it's a matter of dealing with these people and managing their advances.

First, evaluate whether the person is more of a systematic or unconscious manipulator. The more routine, profound manipulators are almost certainly beyond reach. They can have grand visions and don't care who they have to get by to pursue their goals; they may enjoy controlling others, perhaps they have had childhood traumas and issues that lead them to exploit others for fulfillment.

These people are more aware of it and aggressively pursue their manipulative traits. If possible, whatever the case may be, keep your distance from these types of people. It can be so easy to burn bridges with someone if you know that they have manipulative tendencies and that they would be so willing to advance their interests at your expense. That kind of selfishness should warrant a cutting of ties.

There will be times when the person who is manipulating you is someone you have a deep bond and connection with. Even a chance they are not consciously aware of their behavior themselves.

For instance, if your parent, partner, or friend is manipulating you, it's not going to be so easy to break that relationship off entirely. Instead, it becomes an issue of managing this individual. They might not have bad intentions, and they might take offense to the fact that you are accusing them of being manipulative. That is why you have to be extra cautious and sensitive when you broach the issue with them.

First, Be Safe

If you know that you are in danger whenever you are with this manipulative individual in your life, always make sure that there is a third party present. You can never really know what they might do to you if the two of you are alone. It would help if you had that mediator, someone who would help bridge the two of you. You can always call on a mutual friend, a shared loved one, or a trusted confidante.

The point here is that the confrontation process should never be conducted recklessly. And a lot of the time, that means having someone else in the room to be with you.

Take a Diplomatic Approach to Initiate a Dialogue

You can either choose to influence them to lessen the adverse effects, or you could confront them. The initial confrontation doesn't have to be so hot and passionate. The best approach to engaging this individual would be to be as calm and collected as can be.

You want to make sure that you are taking emotions out of the equation. Keep in mind that a manipulative person is always going to capitalize on the emotionality of a person. If you take that ammo away from them, it leaves them very little to work with. In addition to that, it's more likely that they won't react in such a hostile manner if you take a more civil approach to initiate this dialogue with them.

Using people's own words against them makes it harder to resist whatever it is you are asking them to do; if one claims to be selfless, then they would not partake in specific actions, to begin with. You have to remember that starting the conversation isn't always going to go so smoothly. It's very much likely that they will resist at first. However, it would help if you stayed persistent.

You have to emphasize the importance of this conversation. However, if they decide to engage with you in this conversation, you need to remain mindful of the following tips.

Don't Fight Back

If they are hostile with you about it, resist the urge to fight back. Negatively responding to them will only result in you playing into their games. When they get emotional, don't invalidate these feelings. Their emotions might be very authentic regardless of whether they are based on distorted truths or not. A person can still feel angry about a complete lie or fantasy. Keep that in mind.

Instead of invalidating their feelings and telling them that they're unreasonable, hear them out. With this method, you will get a chance to understand them more. The more you know them, the better it will be to manage this entire situation.

Set Clear Limits and Boundaries

Once you have heard their side of the tale, it's now time for you to air out your grievances. You don't want them to be invalidating what you're saying just because you're hysterical. It would help if you weren't beating around the bush anymore. Be courteous, but also, don't pull any punches. No matter how uncomfortable it might be to speak honestly about your feelings, you're going to have to do so. If you're interested in salvaging the relationship, then emphasize this point. However, it would help if you also noted that you would be setting clear limits and boundaries as you move forward in your relationship together. Make them understand that the integrity of your relationship is dependent on their respect for the edges that you set in it.

Chapter 2: Ways to Manipulate and Persuade People.

Manipulating People

Now you get to get into the bulk of the manipulation process! You will learn about the exact purpose of this book and how you can master it. Once you have known to analyze someone effectively, you can learn how you can manipulate them effectively! Here you will understand what manipulation tactics exist and which you should choose based on what drives your subject.

Manipulation is easy once you learn how, so take your time and focus on really mastering these steps so that you can rely on them in the future. It is also essential that you do not skip these steps before you have fully got analyzing people. Manipulation will not be nearly as effective if you have not thoroughly studied the person you are trying to manipulate, so you must take your time and master that part first. Then, mastering manipulation will become infinitely more accessible. You will likely find that it takes you minimal timing to grasp the concept and use these tactics if you have already successfully analyzed your subject!

If you feel ready, read on for the best-proven manipulation tactics out there!

Encourage Them to Say No

If you want to ask someone for something, such as for sale or something big, you often want to start by asking something that you know will say no to first. You do this by encouraging the person to say no to you through a tactic such as asking for something outrageous or unreasonable instead, then asking for what you want second.

You want to deliver it as somewhat of a two-part option, leading them to believe there is no third option. For example, you might say, "So, would you like the four-year warranty for $999, or the six-year warranty for $1099?" Here, you did not ask if they wanted to go with no warranty at all. Instead, you gave them a choice to choose between a four-year and a six-year warranty.

Since the six-year warranty is only an extra $100 and comes with two additional years of protection, this is the one you want to sell them. When you state it like this, you lead them to think about it.

Then, you can add, "Just so you know, the extra two years only cost $100 extra, and it protects against everything from damage to natural breakdown. To me, it is a necessity to protect your investment." This way, you have entirely erased the idea of "no warranty" from their mind and made it a "necessity." You have also offered them an additional two years of protection for only $100. They are more likely to go with that option since it is more favorable to the shorter warranty for nearly the exact cost.

By encouraging someone to say no to what you don't want, it makes it easier for you to get them to say yes to what you do want. Some other examples include things such as:

- "So, will that be a five-year contract or a two-year?"

- "Do you want to go on a date to the top of the Eiffel tower or the Keg tomorrow night?"

- "Would you rather stay here by yourself and wait with all of these strange people around, or come with me and keep me company while I run errands?"

By manipulating your phrasing to sound like the person only has two choices, and both are ones you have picked for them, you ultimately get to decide which of the two the person will respond to. Since you have intentionally made one outrageous or unusual, or simply one that they would most likely say no to, they are more likely to say yes to the one you want them to agree with.

Establish Similarity

People are attracted to people that they have similarities too. Creating the illusion that you have plenty in common with someone gives the idea that you are the same. Through that, you can establish trust and chemistry. This will lead to the person liking you a lot more, even if they don't already know you.

Once they feel this way toward you, they are far more likely to agree with you and want to do what you suggest. This is because they feel like you know them and that they can trust you to offer things that would ultimately be to their benefit or favor.

For example, you might say something like, "I like my TV, even though I paid $9,000 for it. Because I love relaxing after work and enjoying the game while I eat dinner, it was a no-brainer for me. I know that you like football too, and you have got to see what the game looks like on a TV with this resolution! In this example, we will assume that you have already established similarity and learned that your client is interested in football and enjoys having the best of the best.

You also get the opportunity to overcome any money resistances that they may have toward the product. As you can see, similarity gives you "pull" with the person you are manipulating.

Establishing similarity is easy. It comes from relating to what someone is saying and then sharing information that they would connect with. For example, if they say they like the color red, you would agree. Then later, you would say something like, "That is my favorite ____, especially because it comes in the color red!" You haven't directly stated that it comes in red for them. Instead, you have shared that you love red, which makes you excited. Since you already know they like red, they are more likely to feel as though they are similar to you because they would also be the type to get excited over this information.

You can do this with virtually anything. If you are on a date, for example, you can express similarity by how you feel toward your career, your goals, and your life in general. You can share similarities by listening to what memories your date shares with you and sharing similar memories that you have. Ultimately, you can create a situation where they feel like they understand you. You know them, no matter how little you may know each other.

This is more of a persuasion tactic, but it is still essential in the manipulation process. The way master manipulators do this is through a practice called "pacing." That means that they essentially mirror a person's body language and use their cues, including verbal and non-verbal cues, to generate a feeling of similarity.

Because you behave similarly to your subject, they feel like you are similar to them on a deep, psychological level. They may not recognize it consciously, but their subconscious mind will realize that you are copying them, and it will take this as a sign that you and your subject share many similarities.

You never want to be too obvious when doing this, but mirroring them to some degree is a great way to boost your morale with them and increase the pull you have when convincing them to do what you want them to do.

Inspire Fear, Then Provide Relief

One innovative and highly effective way of manipulating people is to use fear. Whether someone is emotionally driven or logically driven, they will be easily moved and controlled by fear. The trick with anxiety is to inspire fear in someone and then provide a relief solution. This is an excellent tactic for selling stuff, spreading information (such as through the media), and getting your way with virtually anything else.

This tactic works in a straightforward two-step manner: cause the other person to fear something and then give them a solution that inspires relief. To make the most of this tactic, you first want to have a general idea of what you can use to inspire fear. In other words, you will need to properly analyze the person so that you are clear on what they would be afraid of. Once you have, you want the solution you offer to be the form of relief.

Here is an example of inspiring fear and then offering relief:

News: "Today, sixteen people have died due to an attack by an unknown source. While many witnesses claim they know exactly who was responsible for the attack, authorities have not yet located the individual. In the meantime, twenty-three others are in the hospital to be treated for varying degrees of injuries, from minor scratches to extensive damage caused by the bullets spraying through the crowd.

We are exposed to forms of manipulation as the one above daily. In very fundamental reality, we are fearful because many people were shot, and the attacker is still on the loose. Technically, the relief source would be the authorities searching for the attacker. However, the news broadcaster has shifted the relief to be the news station itself as they are claiming to be the ones that will provide us with live updates and inform us when the attacker is finally caught. Therefore, instead of relying on the authorities for relief from the fear, the audience depends on that news broadcaster.

The ultimate goal is to make your product, service, offer, or solution the one that provides relief from genuine fear.

When people are afraid, they are often desperate to alleviate the anxiety and make them feel safe and comfortable once more. If you are the one who can invoke the fear (without making it look intentional) and then provide relief (without making it look staged), then you are the one who orchestrates both parts of the strategy. This means that you can quickly "sell" your solution because the person you are talking to is active "buying."

Use Guilt, Play the Victim

For people driven by emotion, manipulating feelings of guilt and playing the victim are two great ways to control people. These ways tend to be more evident if you are not careful. Still, if you plan it properly, you can use these without seeming like you are intentionally manipulating the other person. Instead, they will see that you "need" their assistance, and they will be eager to provide it.

Using guilt means that you essentially guilt someone into doing what you ask of them. For example:

- "But you owe me, remember when I helped you?"

- "You don't want to disappoint me on my birthday again, do you?"

- "I recall you told me last time you purchased her a gift; it was not what she wanted. You wouldn't want to be responsible for two bad gifts, would you?"

- "I covered your shift last week, and you can't help me cover mine now?"

- "I run all of the errands that you ask of me; why are you going to try and make me do this one, too?"

By using guilt, you can make people feel as though they are obligated to comply or agree with you. Because you can point out a genuine reason as to why they "owe" you, they feel as though they have to fulfill that obligation.

People do not like to feel indebted, and using guilt is a great way to make them feel as though they have to help you or do what you have asked. Playing the victim works synonymously with using guilt to get your way.

Playing the victim essentially means that you make people feel as though they are asking little things from you. As a result, they are more likely to comply and give in to what you want from them because they feel guilty that they were the ones "trying to manipulate you," even though technically, you are manipulating them with this tactic! It works like this:

- "I can't believe you would ask that of me!

- "I have never once treated you the way you are treating me now; what makes you think that is okay? I don't deserve this."

- "I was only doing what you asked of me; it's not my fault you didn't ask clearly!"

- "What, am I not good enough to do _____ for you?"

- "Do you think this about me? What have I done to induce you to have humility?"

When you switch into the victim card, people automatically feel as though they have been unkind to you. Then, they turn into a mode where they want to "fix" the situation. That is where you get to offer them your solution. Because they want to make you feel better, they are far more likely to say yes so that you won't be so upset anymore. Then, you get your way!

Use Logic to Appeal to Rational People

People who are logically driven are also emotionally driven, as you know. Still, they also require you to cater to their logical side if you can get anywhere with them. This is not as hard as it sounds, but it does take some practice.

Using logic to appeal to rational people mainly works through providing a lot of factual evidence and statistics that back up what you are trying to "sell" or "solve." This can work in many different ways, but ultimately you want to infuse as many facts as you can. You want to make it seem as though you know all of the critical points to decide so that they don't go and look for the facts themselves. Perhaps it is a skincare product created to help people with dry skin.

The facts in the following statement are not accurate, but they will provide you with an idea of what the "solution" should sound like:

"You mentioned you have a problem with dry skin, right? I have this great skincare solution for you. Did you know approximately 60% of the population has moderate to severe issues with dry skin? This cream was tried on a group of 100 people, and 99 of them claimed it made their skin feel smoother in as little as three days. Within a week, their dry skin symptoms had completely disappeared, and they were back to feeling comfortable and confident in their skin! It is made using a special ingredient created in our labs.

It is a patented technology designed to help cater specifically to problematic dry skin. It gets deep into the pore and infuses it with moisture, essentially hydrating it. It is like for your pores when you use this skin care product. Would you like to try some on? (Apply the lotion to their dry skin now.) It is only $39.99 for a bottle, but today we are giving away two bottles for the price of one! Here, you took the time to educate the person on how the product works fully. You incorporated many facts, statistics, and explanations as to how the product works.

Rather than solely targeting the emotional side of their problem (for example, a lowered sense of self-esteem from problematic dry skin), you appealed to the logical side of them, too. However, you were not completely focused on the logic. You did include words like "comfortable" and "confident" to appeal to the underlying emotional side, which would also need to be appealed to manipulate a logically driven person successfully.

By tailoring your solution to feature many facts, evidence, and statistics, you make it so that those with logical minds are more likely to want to purchase the product you are selling, agree to help you in some way, or otherwise engage in your solution or pitch. As a general rule of thumb, if you are uncertain about whether or not someone is logically driven, it is helpful to include a few facts in your pitch. Appeal equally to both sides and gauge their response to see how they react. If they seem to emphasize the points you have shared, share more. If they are more interested in the emotional benefits, elaborate on those. Paying attention to their reaction is a great way to continue to appeal to what they need to hear to agree with you and do whatever you have asked or take what you have offered.

Bribe Them

Bribery is a phenomenal tool. It works on getting children to complete their chores, and it works on adults when you need it. You can easily use bribery in several different situations to help get what you want. In some cases, bribery will be apparent. In others, it may not be quite so obvious.

You will want to choose how obvious you make it depending on the situation. For example, if you are trying to use guilt and bribery together to get your friend to loan you their car for the weekend, you might say something like,

"Come on, don't you remember all of the times I helped you? Don't you owe it to me? If you help me out this once, I promise to take you out to your favorite restaurant on Monday, completely on me!" Wording something like this will make it very clear that you are trying to bribe the person you are talking to.

In general, this is a better solution to use in personal relationships where you know the person, and you know what you can and cannot get away with.

If you need to hide your bribery, you can word your sentence differently. You start by putting the product in their hands and getting them to interact with it. Then, once they comment something to do with them liking the product, you say something like: "Yeah, that is a phenomenal product! Plus, we have an amazing promotion going on right now where if you purchase that product, you get a free (another product) with it! It's an incredible deal and a great way to try out a couple of new things to see what you like the most, without spending more money!" Here, you look like you are simply offering more excellent value and not trying to bribe the person into buying the product.

Chapter 3: Behavioral musts to be adopted to become a perfect manipulator

1. Similarity

The similarity is the best way to get someone to do what you want, using a foolproof method of making that person trust you. By making a similar person trust, it inevitably happens that the other person does what he wants unknowingly.

It is a method that works perfectly, especially when you want to manipulate a work situation because when emotion is in the way, it is difficult to perform.

2. Sign up for a Drama or Theatre Workshop

When manipulating a person, one has to control emotions, expressions, body gestures with the sole purpose of convincing someone that they can blindly trust the manipulator.

The fundamental thing is that to manipulate, you must know how to control your emotions. Otherwise, you risk being used unknowingly. A specific context must be adapted to each situation so that the victim does not create any doubts about your real personality.

3. Develop Charisma

The concept of charisma is hard to explain, yet it can be quickly recognized or identified when you see it. Charismatic folks have an effortless and inherently smooth tendency to get people to do exactly what they want. Do you radiate a warm and friendly vibe? Do you have a more approachable, affable, and open body language? Can you hold people into a compelling and arresting conversation even if you've only just met them?

4. Practice Reading People

Each individual has a distinct personality and a unique spiritual, psychological, and mental makeup. Everyone is not likely to respond to your manipulation techniques similarly. Every person has a different trigger point that drives them into thinking, feeling, or behaving in a certain way. Before you begin putting together an elaborate plot for manipulating someone, take some time to study their personality thoroughly.

What makes him or her tick? What is the most suitable and practical approach to getting them to do what you want them to? What are the person's most compelling fears, motives, and needs?

Here are a few tips for reading people accurately.

5. Follow an Unrealistic Request with a Reasonable One

We have used this type of manipulation at least once in our life. The manipulator exposes two requests to his victim, thus finding himself inevitably having to choose one of the two. Whatever the choice is, it is equally selected from by the manipulator himself.

The first option is tension, while the second, with slight relief, inevitably leads the prey to choose the second.

6. Induce Fear then Relief

Plenty of marketers, brand managers, advertisers, and business owners prey on consumers' fears to manipulate them into buying from them. Make the person imagine the worst situation, followed by helping them feel relieved. This sneaky little trick will help you to get them to do precisely what you want them to.

For instance, you could say something like, "When I wore your dress for the prom night, I thought I heard a horrible sound of the dress tearing. I was sure I had torn your beautiful dress. However, I realized that it was just a video one of the girls watched on her phone. Isn't that truly funny?" This reminds me, can I borrow the dress again for an upcoming weekend bash if you do not mind?

See what we did there? We took the person on a whirlwind of emotions from fear to immediate relief that the dress is still in good condition after all. They will be in a more positive and receptive frame of mind, which will increase your chances of having your way with them.

7. Induce a Feeling of Overpowering Guilt

Guilt is another excellent tool for manipulating someone into your way of thinking, feeling, and doing. This works even more effectively on people who aren't sure of themselves, do not possess a very high self-confidence (or sense of self-worth) level, or are generally indecisive by nature.

For example, if you want to manipulate a parent into allowing you to go camping with your friends, make them feel pangs of guilt that they have been highly protective of you throughout your childhood and haven't allowed you to experience life on your own. Similarly, if you want to induce guilt in a friend, list all the beautiful things you've done for them or times when you've gone out of the way to do things for them, followed by how they've let you down on various occasions.

Notice how some senior people induce guilt among their children and manipulating them into doing what they want them to by stating that the children do not spend enough time with them or do not do much for them or that they aren't going to live for too long now even though the grown-up children go out of their life.

8. Play Victim

Playing the victim card is another time-tested manipulation strategy. Often a group of people to gain political or social or some other benefit will portray themselves as a disadvantaged group to attract the support of the masses. They will manipulate popular opinion in their favor by demonstrating the unfairness they've been subjected to or the disadvantages they faced on account of belonging to a particular group, class, community, tribe, race, or religion.

People using this manipulation technique are likelier to come up with, "I do not know what I or we did. But everything seems to go against me or us for no reason." Sound like you're perplexed by why things are not working out for you or going in your favor. It will trigger a sense of sympathy and empathy in people. Make people feel that you're constantly being nice and giving to others, and no one seems to return the same sentiments.

Rather than arguing, fighting, or quarreling with people to have your way, act calm and like you've accepted the situation. For example, if a co-worker refuses to give you a ride back home from the office, tell them it is all right. "I could do with the exercise since no one is willing to help. It is wonderful."

9. Manipulation Tactics

They sniff manipulation from miles and more so if you've been using the same techniques on the same set of people over and over again. If a friend, manager, or spouse calls you out for using sneaky, manipulative strategies for having your way, never admit to it. Just open your mouth wide open, gape, and say, "I do not believe you said that." Act horrified (now you know the importance of signing up for that acting class) and hurt.

Saying something like, "I do not believe you think like this about me," will make the person feel terrible about accusing you of resorting to manipulative techniques. Under no circumstances should you ever admit to using manipulation because it will be tough to manipulate the individual into doing what you want again.

10. Flirt

We all have done this more than once. You can't simply issue orders and tell them to do what you want them to. People can't be forced to do what they want. They have to like you or, even better, adore you if you're going to cast a spell on them and drive them into thinking or behaving in a particular manner. You invoke positive emotions and give yourself the power to make a more favorable impact on the other person.

Whenever you can flirt and impress people, go ahead and do it. Throw aside your inhibitions or differences about gender, and use some suggestive expressions or touches without going overboard. A light tap on the arm or leaning while talking to someone or gently ruffling their hair can be harmless flirting and increase your likeability quotient in the eyes of the other person.

Do not be respectful, pushy, or aggressive when people are not taking too kindly to the flirting. Respect the other person's boundaries and wishes even when trying to get them to do what you want. Flirting (or using different ways to charm an individual) works well with people who have a low sense of self-worth or are lonely.

11. Hide Criticism as Altruism

You have to appear to be a nice person (even if you aren't one) if you want to get people to believe you and get them to do what you want. Harmful acts such as criticizing people's actions, screaming at them, or holding them responsible for something (whether they are or aren't) are not going to be very effective until you cleverly coat it with altruism. Present yourself as someone who always cares about reaching out to others and helping them.

Explain to them how they aren't acting in their interests, which is bothering you. After an outburst, if you regret what you just said, explain why you got so volatile that you genuinely care about their welfare and want the best for them. Ask them how you can help make it easier for them. Offer them complete support and confidently state that you will always be around for them no matter what anyone says or does.

They accept everyone to be up against them and make them accountable for it and hence get even more defensive. Instead of criticizing, if you reach out to them as a do-gooder who is more than happy to help them instead of accusing and blaming them, they will buy into what you are saying immediately.

12. Be a Pro at Overcoming Trust Issues

People who have experienced manipulation in some form on earlier occasions are wary of being manipulated and come with plenty of trust issues. They do not take too kindly to manipulation techniques. Whenever you find there are trust issues with a person, eliminate the trust barrier by sharing something increasingly confidential, secretive, or personal with him or her.

Share something related or significant to them to make it even more effective. Your story may or may not be accurate, but you must believe.

13. Sign Up for Debates and Public Speaking

While a drama class can hone your ability to control your expressions and reactions, debates will help you influence, persuade or manipulate people in a calm, balanced and unruffled manner. You will learn the fine art of gathering and coherently present your facts/arguments. A public speaking class will arm you with the ability to use your voice tone and body language for convincing people.

By becoming a powerful orator or speaker, you can hypnotically attract and inspire people to your cause like a magnet. You learn subtle yet effective strategies for making yourself more convincing while presenting ideas to people.

14. The Bribery Strategy

This is another popular manipulation technique proven to work well across multiple settings and relationships.

When you reward someone emotionally or objectively, they will feel compelled to reciprocate for that action. Just make sure they return the right way.

When you make a gesture of favor, wait for them to return the favor somehow. If they don't, tell the individual openly the vital thing that it doesn't look like blackmail. Otherwise, you would lose that person's trust. Don't let the corruption strategy get out of hand.

15. Foot in the Door Route

The foot in the door strategy is to cut the ice with the other person by making a small request that they aren't likely to refuse. Then very subtly and cleverly, go for the kill and ask for what you have in mind or want from them. What you are doing is starting a chain of positive replies.

Once someone says yes to you (for a small request), they will find it harder to follow it up with a negative reply. The trick is to ask for something small and reasonable that is very easy for the other person to fulfill, followed by what you want them to do.

16. Win at home

To charm someone to do what you ask them to do, you will need to be in a place known to you, where you certainly have a better chance of winning. The other person, in this case, will feel like they are trapped.

This is a tactic to negotiate in a place where you are familiar, ensuring you are getting what you are contracting for.

17. Let Them Talk First

When you try to sell something to someone or get them to do what you want, let them speak first. The baseline gives you a good idea about their thoughts, feelings, and behavior. You can use this to determine their positives and negatives. Keep a set of questions ready (the answers to fulfill your plan) and ask wherever possible.

18. Smother with Facts and Statistics

Overwhelm these folks by dumping a ton of research and arguments on them through "intellectual bullying." Pose yourself as knowledgeable and authoritative in a particular field, and take advantage of your expertise.

Present facts, statistics, research findings in an imposing manner. Please focus on the other person's areas of weakness and talk about subjects they have little expertise in or do not know much about. This technique can be in negotiations, professional encounters, social arguments, and just about anywhere. You gain the expert advantage and push your agenda on the person even more convincingly. It not just awards you a sense of intellectual superiority but also makes the other person feel inadequate, ultimately leading to them giving in to your demand.

Day to Day Examples of Dark Psychology

Most people assume that they understand the darker aspects of human nature. They imagine they would be able to see manipulators if they met them and know exactly what to do to keep themselves from being taken advantage of. Most people are wrong. Evil will not wear a mask that makes it easy to identify. It will blend in and gain the target's trust before turning on them and victimizing them. The victim will often realize what's going on when it is already too late for them to do anything about it.

The devil himself is known for taking the ideal form or even appearing as an angel of light. Users of dark psychology are no different. They are master shapeshifters that will take whatever form is necessary to snare their prey. Disguise and deception come naturally to them. So what does one do then? One does not have to use any of them, but they do have to learn enough to identify the threat, at least when it is present.

People around us may even use them on us in ways that are not harmful to us, not realizing what they are doing. Sometimes they may even use them for our good. Think of mothers telling their kids false facts to get them to eat their vegetables or trying to trick a drug-addicted loved one to go to a place where they'll find their loved ones waiting to ambush them with an intervention. It leaves out many more benign examples of the tricks of dark psychology and tells you of the times when there may be high stakes, and you cannot afford to be manipulated or blindsided. These can be moments where someone tries to get you to spend more money than you had intended to or act in a way that may set you down a path that could be disastrous for you.

19. They have strong opening cases

A strong opening argument can often be the deciding factor for winning and losing cases or even closing deals with potential clients. It becomes a game of controlling perspectives. The way an attorney opens before jurors, judges, and potential clients can be the crucial moment that determines how the rest of their interactions go.

This is a significant thing to remember when trying to persuade or prevent being persuaded by an expert attorney. Learning how to take in opening statements, or maybe learning how to give them, can be beneficial when trying to establish a dominant position in a persuasive exchange because that will be the northern star for the rest of the business, so remember to open strong and set a firm foundation to build the rest of your persuasion game.

20. They anticipate the most likely objections

The best attorney knows their arguments and standpoints so well that they even know the most likely stances people might take against them and prepare to react to those accordingly in advance.

They leave no stone unturned until they are confident that anyone they interact with will leave that exchange feeling like every objection was tended to and every question answered.

Chapter 4: Mistakes that make you vulnerable to manipulations.

Although anybody can be manipulated, some people are perceived to be more likely to be used than others. This may be because of our mistakes.

·   The naive–Someone that is naïve in a field lacks judgment in that field or has not gained experience. The victim finds it too difficult to believe that some people are cunning, full of deceit, and insensitive. The belief that this kind of human being does not exist makes it easier for them to fall prey to the manipulators as they feed on their naivety.

·   The dutiful ones –This is the willingness or the ability to do one's work well. This set of people overtly give manipulator the benefit of the doubt to ensure that no blame comes from their side of the bargain. Manipulators are not interested in those positive attributes. The manipulators take advantage of it, and you become their victim.

·   Low self-confidence – Here, the victims are not sure of themselves. They lack confidence in themselves and look for self-validation from someone else. Unfortunately, they may fall into the wrong hands that would cheat them in the name of friendship and later change by resorting to the withdrawal method.

·   The justifiers- This set of people try to apologize for the manipulators. They tell themselves that the manipulator has a genuine intention for whatever he does. They believe that the act the manipulator displays is justified.

·   Emotional attachment - These are people who depend on other people around them emotionally. They are vulnerable to the manipulators as by doing so; they are only being manipulated and exploited.

Manipulators are usually not in a rush. They are the ardent believers of 'the patient' eats the fattest bone. They wait till the time is ripe. When they have prepared a soft landing for themselves, then they strike.

The following tips can help you take proper care of yourself:

   Identify your needs and arrange them to suit your desire

   Handle your affairs as they are the only things that matter

   Enjoy staying alone and everything that comes with it

   Develop interest in what you like, make discoveries, and learn new things

   Identify with a group of like-minded people to share your feelings

   Find your distractions and create a means of escape that mechanism

   Consciously allow yourself to go to and fro your subconscious mind

   Experiment with different sources of joy and identify the one that suits you

   Engage in physical exercise from time to time to cool off

   Take out quality time for yourself and give yourself a treat

   Savor any beautiful moment you have and keep the memory alive

   Practice self-motivation regularly

   Keep your hope alive

You may not achieve all these once, but it would get better with time. Learn to work with yourself. Find your areas of vulnerability. Express yourself through audio records, diaries, or by speaking to yourself. Be honest to yourself, accept your flaws, open up, and tell yourself things like 'I am so tired, how can I cope with this?' Cry if you want to cry, and you would get emotional relief. Sometimes, that friendship and satisfaction we seek in others can be given to us by ourselves only. It is difficult not to resent resentment at this time, especially to people who abandoned you. See it in the light of a beggar in the street. You were in a similar situation. Do not blame those who did not help. Most importantly, avoid idealizing anyone.

Immaturity –Those who are immature cannot pass accurate judgment and tend to believe exaggerated claims.

Lack of experience –Those who are naïve lack experience and therefore do not know that there are dishonest people worldwide. They have open arms to welcome everyone, making themselves vulnerable to being manipulated.

Impressionable–The impressionable ones are easily charmed by the manipulators. They may choose to marry a man who opens the car door for them.

Trust –Honest people often believe that every other person is like them. They trust people thinking that they are honest too. They entrust themselves even to strangers. If these sets of people interview you, they are more likely to believe anything you tell them without questioning you.

Carelessness: Careless people are liable to jump into any offer without investigation or thorough questioning. They do not check things like "who was there before me," "what happened to them," "what do I gain by accepting this offer?" "what do I stand to lose?"

Loneliness –Lonely People may jump at any offer of human contact. A stranger who is a psychopath may offer companionship for a price. However, the price is usually deadly.

Impulsive –People who act on impulse are prone to making decisions at a snap. Those spontaneously in nature can see a lady on the road and decide to marry without consulting anyone.

Altruistic –Altruistic is the opposite of psychopathic. It means people who are too fair, too honest, or too empathetic. They feel too much. They can give everything they have for peace to reign.

Materialistic –They want quick money and would dare any means for making money. They are called the fast liners and easily fall prey to manipulators who know their weak points without much stress.

Greedy ones: The greedy ones can easily fall prey to a manipulator who can entice them with items that would get them salivating. The manipulator is aware of the kind of people he is dealing with, so; he knows how and when to press the right button.

Masochistic – These people neither have self-respect nor discipline. They can easily consider buying anything marketed to them because it may relieve them.

Chapter 5: Types of Emotional Manipulation

Some people are always lucky to get what they want at any time the need arises. Sometimes they do so at the expense of others; this, however, is achieved via access to the emotional bank. They can influence your thoughts or emotions to their advantage and leave you a victim and vulnerable.

Owning space

The main aim of emotional manipulation is to make you lose control of your emotions. It will involve making you stagger with emotions which, on the other hand, will make you even more vulnerable. Advantage will be taken, and they will access you and get all they wanted from you. Suppose there existed a lock to the emotions. In that case, I am sure everybody would have their feelings locked away and unlocked only to intimate relationships or where your feelings will be valued. To ensure you are off the steering with your emotions, manipulators will invite you to a place where they know it is new to you but familiar to them. This will keep you off balance; the new environment will give him or her the dominance and feeling of being in control. You are new to the place, and the manipulator will take advantage of the window between adaptability and regaining control.

Your words against you

How you talk or react speaks volumes, and emotions can be passed along—manipulators like talkative people since it is easier to access them due to the link provided. If you are the introvert type or a conservative person, it takes more effort to make you open up. Introverts would require tailored questions that will be well planned and will give you away from one by one. The manipulator makes sure the questions are aimed at the emotional state. Personal questions will open you up, and you will start speaking with feelings; this is an indicator that manipulation is taking place and working.

By asking tailored and straightforward questions that mostly are personal or involve something we like, hobbies, interests, among others, will lead to saturation with emotions. A master manipulator will take advantage of the situation and ask us questions to establish your beliefs, strengths, and weaknesses without you realizing it.

Guilt

Kind-hearted victims are easily vulnerable to emotional manipulation. Guilt will be used against you, especially if you are so sensitive you may end up giving in to their demands. Guilt will either make you give in or feel bad about yourself. For instance, you may both agree on something, and when the time comes to complete the deal, the manipulators will pretend to forget or even act as victims of your actions. By doing so, they will be finding your soft spot, and once they find it will be the target of manipulation. Guilt and sympathy will be served to you; you will fall for the play if you are not strong enough. They will influence you through that guilt since you will be under their spell, and since you now believe they are the victims, you will do all they ask to make sure your 'victims' do not suffer anymore.

Positive and negative emotions

Emotions of sadness or happiness can also be a pathway for emotional manipulation. An emotional manipulator will play with your psychology; he or she will show you that what you might be going through is nothing compared to what they have going on in their lives. By doing this, they try to exalt you and win your trust. If you fall for that and believe there are more needy people than you in the world, you will loosen up and think that you are selfish. You will no longer focus on your big problem; instead, you will focus on their 'big unfortunate events' since you will now feel pitiful. Once you trust them, you give them a key to your emotional bank, and indeed, they will use it against you.

Once you trust them, you might end up offering yourself to assist them; that, however, was their plan from the start; they will have attained their goal.

Anger

Anger is another emotion that can be used to induce emotional manipulation. Some people are natural peacemakers; they avoid confrontations and conflicts in all ways possible. Once a manipulator realizes you are this type of person, he or she will use anger, aggressive language or raise his or her voice or even drop several threats. These aggressive techniques are tailored to make tick. The secret behind this aggressive approach is to induce fear and discomfort so that you can give in hastily without taking a second to think through. Once you give in to their demands, they now get control over you and directly manipulate you in whatever direction or way that pleases them. They use this opportunity to get what they wanted from you since you will be cooperative, earning another instance of acute aggression.

Self-discipline and confidence

Being self-driven and confident is a solid barrier to the effects of emotional manipulation. With the right mindset, you become less vulnerable to emotional manipulation attacks. Insecure and sensitive people are the easiest target for emotional manipulators. They are easily spotted and accessible; they put their needs behind others and often feel the need to please. All a manipulator needs to be caring, sensitive, and urge to help out. The needy part of sensitive people exposes them. The emotional manipulator will see it as a gate pass to influencing your thoughts, perceptions, and feelings to his or her advantage. With time the emotions break open, and they are exploited easily since the manipulator was disguised as a caring and sensitive person. Surprises

Negative surprises are also another mechanism used to keep people off balance. When bombarded with the new, unexpected news that comes with a limited timeframe will lead to panic. As you panic, you get little time or none to think of a counter move. They may be good enough to trap you with suggestions as they pretend to help, yet it is a plan made to make you unstable both psychologically and emotionally.

Once you become unstable and overwhelmed by the sudden change of events, it becomes their opportunity to influence your decisions and any other emotion they are interested in. They may even consider making more moves that will bind your relationship with him or them so that they can utilize that window of opportunity created by the panic moment. You may not realize it since they appear to be assisting, whereas they use you for their benefits.

Criticism

Criticism is also a tool for emotional manipulation. The manipulator will say bad things of you, ridicule you, or even dismiss you. He or she will make sure her mission of dismantling you succeeds. Once you have had enough, you end up off balance and believe they are superior to the inferior you. You will feel so down, and their opinions will stick. The manipulator will make sure you understand that you can never be good at anything no matter what you do or invest in. This will get into you, and you will be emotionally distressed. You will feel hurt and not worthy of anyone's help. They will then pretend to have answers to your problems. He or she will give you tips and suggestions that are so genuine looking and constructive. Once these well-outlined answers transform you and get you out of it, they threw you will worship them. Once they have your attention, they can make you do what they want or influence you.

Doubt

Doubt and uncertainty are also other forms of leverage in emotional manipulation. You will receive a silent treatment until you start doubting your actions or words that you may have used the last time. The manipulators will do this deliberately to stir up the feeling of doubt; once you give in and break the silence by acting as the cause of the quiet, treatment will be an excellent chance to be taken advantage of.

This creates a window of opportunity, and they will manipulate you.

Ignorance

Pretending to be ignorant of your duties will also get things done. You may want to do something, but you want it done by someone else, let us say your spouse. She or he will note something is off and try to make it right, but you pretend to be good with it, but since they know it has to be correct, they will do it anyway.

Techniques used by women to manipulate men.

Let us also take a look at the other side because, although the heavy cases of psychological manipulation in the couple are true to the detriment of the woman, it is also true that women are those who, even unconsciously, use the most manipulative techniques to attract a man's attention.

Show their physical strengths. Highlighting beautiful breasts, making puppy eyes, wearing a pair of skinny jeans, or wearing bright lipstick are just some of the techniques women use to make men's heads spin. It's a physical matter, and the man has no defense. Even a sweet voice or whispered word in the right way can open a man's mind as quickly as you can break an egg. Crying. Any man (at least a normal man) is naturally inclined to defend a woman. If a woman is in trouble, the man rushes in, if a woman is pregnant, the man gives her place on the subway, and so on. Crying is the signal sent by a woman to make her understand that she is in trouble, that circumstances defeat her. Some women call "on command" and use this powerful weapon to manipulate the man.

Intimacy. This technique is useless to explain, and it is an extremity of the first one we have seen. She was using nicknames. It may seem nice to a guy to be called with a handle, but the woman does it only on two occasions: when she is happy and everything is fine, or when she has to convince the man to do something. The man who is used to being happy to be called by a nickname will not notice the difference between the two occasions and will perform his task.

Competition. Putting one's boyfriend in competition with others makes him do everything worthy of him. "Sophia's boyfriend vacuums the house every morning!" This technique tends to make the boyfriend jealous while his girlfriend seems to look the other way.

Cold. Ignoring, quietly making it clear that something is wrong or using the right tone to say, "It's fine!" It's an old but still effective manipulation technique.

Nagging. The man is driven by the need to lift himself from an unpleasant and annoying position, with the woman repeating the same command over and over again.

I had the last word. Whoever has the last word in a discussion is undoubtedly the dominant element of the couple. It is not easy to achieve this, but usually, if the woman has the last word, the man gets mad.

He was pretending to agree. This technique can also be used when you can't get the last word. If the discussion is prolonged, the woman ends it by pretending to agree but, of course, taking care to make the man understand that he does not agree at all. This technique uses tones of voice and gestures that disagree with the word.

She was pretending to be submissive. This is a very subtle technique that smarter women often use. It resembles that already seen of "pretending to be a victim." Pretending to be submissive makes it possible to convince the other person to act by making them believe that it resulted from their thoughts. Imagine a woman clinging to her man who fills him with cuddles, making herself small in his arms. This is an attitude of submission to which, however, can accompany the phrase "All right dear, tomorrow you can take me shopping, but only for an hour, no more.

She was pretending to be clumsy. When a woman doesn't want to do something, she can pretend she doesn't know how to do it. All she has to do is add a few flatteries and a few compliments to her partner, who can do everything... and that's it!

Chapter 6: Psychological Tactics of Manipulation

Take a minute to consider the latest state of affairs in which you desired something from every other man or woman. Otherwise, you wanted a promotion out of your boss. In an excellent global, we should ask for all of the matters we want from human beings, and they might comply. So what are you able to do to get what you need?

Here are a whole lot of sincere, moral solutions to this query. But there also are unethical answers. If you try and get what you need through deception, lies, or oblique procedures, you are manipulating.

We are not providing you with that equipment so you can go out and control others. Think about this as a caution video. Humans are looking to manipulate others every day. If you could spot the signs and symptoms of Manipulation, you may see via them and have extra management over the decisions you're making and your dating with others.

People want to feel appealing and desired. Manipulators play into those emotions using being charming. They trust that once a person starts evolved to get a bit flirty, they'll begin to be interested in the manipulator and maybe much more likely to post to the manipulator's needs.

They could say, "in case you don't help me rob this bank, I'll kick your canine." Yikes. The individual being coerced might also feel as though the effects of not doing the motion are worse than doing the action.

Silent remedy

Silence is a tremendously effective manipulation (and negotiation) device. Silence makes us anxious; if a person is silent or refuses to talk, we can also experience the urge to provide into their desires or deliver them something they need to interrupt the silence.

The reason is an exquisite example of any such manipulation tactic. People may additionally use cause or logical arguments to get what they need. They may inform someone (or themselves) something like, "in case you help me rob this bank, you will be capable of feed your circle of relatives." nothing faulty about that, right?

Regression

When two humans reason with every other like adults, it could be easy for each event to keep its ground. But while one individual reverts to performing like a toddler, matters may go haywire. People may deliver in surely because they need childish conduct to prevent.

Self-Abasement

Not all manipulation approaches involve insulting or forcing the alternative person to do something.

If you already booked an appointment, but it's no longer so clean to bypass out and now not get your nails executed.

Hardball

Hardball processes take coercion to the following level. While a person may use force to fear damage, hardball techniques genuinely motive damage or physical injury.

Satisfaction induction

For lots, pride induction is an innocent manipulation tactic. While someone invokes the pride induction tactic, they tell a person that the motion can be a laugh and that the man or woman will experience it.

Many human beings measure their fulfillment, splendor, and presence of persona trends through the evaluation of others. Manipulators realize this tendency nicely. They'll use social assessment to convince humans to take action. "Your pal at work does this for her companion." Economic praise

Manipulators may also play into someone's greed by offering them cash to devote acts they typically would not dedicate. If you had been supplied a million dollars, might you commit a criminal offense?

Who're the master Manipulators?

Allow's damage down a few stereotypes right here. Women are frequently framed as master manipulators. This isn't proper. There are not any intercourse differences in tactics of Manipulation - research suggests that males and females equally carry out those processes. How Do methods of Manipulation display Up within the big 5?

Manipulation processes show up regularly within the Prince. Folks that are more "Machiavellian" are much more likely to apply (and justify their use of) manipulation procedures. They accept as accurate that they're above ethics and get what they need, even though they get it through Manipulation. This connection is as a substitute obvious. However, there are also a few connections among Manipulation procedures and the massive five-character tendencies.

However, it does not think these techniques of Manipulation into your effects.

Extraversion

Individuals who were rating high in extraversion are much more likely to use coercion and duty invocation.

Agreeableness

Folks who score high in agreeableness are much more likely to use pride induction and motive to get what they need. These manipulation processes are maximum ethical; they convince humans that they may get something practical from taking positive movements.

Conversely, extra unpleasant individuals are much more likely to seek revenge on humans through coercion and the silent remedy.

People who rate low in conscientiousness are much more likely to select potentially crook techniques, like coercion or unlawful sorts of economic reward.

Openness

Folks who were rating excessive for openness are much more likely to apply purpose and occasionally pleasure induction or obligation invocation. Successful reasoning often calls for higher information about logic or higher intelligence.

Chapter 7: Difference Between Being "Nice" and Being "Manipulated

Aren't we always advised to be nice to others? Should we stop being nice if people are out there to manipulate our niceness?

NO. That's not right; however, there is a difference between being nice and being manipulated.

Some people CHOOSE to be friendly, while others are nice inherently. A person who chooses to be nice has control over his or her niceness. They can be nice to genuine people only and save themselves from being manipulated.

On the other hand, inherently friendly people become vulnerable in front of a manipulator. They don't have control over their social behavior, which leads to manipulation many times. Just because you don't say no to work, you get more jobs than other people in your office. The boss is always on your head with unimaginable deadlines.

It all leads back to the conditioning that you gained from your parents and school. Our teachers and parents forget to tell us about the "choice of being nice," and that skipped part creates vulnerability in our lives.

Let's consider a scenario:

One day, Victor went shopping for groceries from the supermarket. Victor was behind three people, and a little girl was behind him.

When Victor reached the counter, he allowed the little girl to buy her candies before him. The girl purchased and left but, just after that, a woman, with three children, cross Victor saying, "I am in a hurry, please."

Now, Victor has two choices. He can allow that lady to cut him, buy her items first, or stop her.

If Victor is inherently lovely, he will let the lady buy first, but that would allow others to cut him in the line too. However, if Victor chooses to be friendly, he will notice that this lady has seen him as a potential victim because of the earlier scenario with the little girl.

We all come across thousands of scenarios like this when our visible niceness makes us a potential victim for manipulators. You can choose not to allow those people to use your niceness to their advantage.

Reasons Why "Being Too Nice" is a Wrong Choice

1. People assume that you would do everything they ask in advance. This is the most significant hazard of being too nice to others. Whenever there is a problem, people burden you with that problem without even asking whether you need that problem or not. Your responsibilities are yours, and others' responsibilities are yours as well.

You say "yes" to help a person twice, and he will hand over the responsibility the third time with complete confidence that you are available at his or her service. People stop caring about your responsibilities, time, and even your emotional state. They think you are weak because you never say no to anyone, leading to manipulation and exploitation of your niceness.

2. Some wrong people get attracted to you Be too nice and get ready for "not so nice" people in your life. Even people who hide their whiny, angry, and wrong sides force all those emotions towards a nice person. In a way, your niceness allows the wrong side of others to come out and attack you.

People start demanding things from you instead of requesting. They control your moves and shift your actions as they please. This happens anywhere you go. Unlike manipulation, niceness becomes visible quickly. Your family, partner, colleagues, and even strangers give you a hard time.

3. You forget to appreciate yourself

You have an appointment with your doctor, but your boss wants you to manage a meeting for him.

Or you want to relax this weekend, but your friend has asked you to fix his bike.

Others become a priority when you are too nice. You don't know how to say no because he is your boss, or she is your friend. But guess what? Since the day you were born, you have been with yourself, but friendly people forget that and give their life to others.

Forgetting yourself in the act of niceness makes you a perfect victim of manipulation. People think of you whenever they need something and forget the moment you do that thing for them.

This leaves you hurt, but mainly your niceness doesn't allow you to learn anything from bad experiences.

4. People stop taking you seriously

When you say nothing but "yes" to everything, your point of view becomes useless to others. You are never disappointed at anything, so your children or colleagues don't ask for your opinion on anything. You never push back; hence, your projects are completed with your juniors' inputs. You lose your perspective on things or don't find the right way to express those perspectives.

There is no excellent way to say that something is wrong; hence, people with too much niceness fail to impact their surroundings, whether it is their household or workspace.

5. People think you are fake

Too much niceness makes your personality suspicious to others. People think that you are faking and your real side is not lovely. This creates a sense of distrust, which leads people away. That is why friendly people don't get promotions or find a top spot in projects. People in your life stop trusting you with important information. They think you will use them somehow while you are the one being manipulated constantly.

Manipulators around you can trigger rumors about your niceness. They can turn your friendliness into an evil thing and take advantage of that. As people feel strange about your niceness, convincing them is never tricky that you are faking it all.

6. You are unable to give tough love

People who are too lovely never thrive in a leading position. As a father, a team leader, or a boss, such people feel unable to perform.

You can't be nice to your people all the time. Sometimes, they need tough love to grow and become better, but a nice person doesn't know how to project that tough love. Pushing your staff to complete a project, or asking your kid to work harder on his skills, requires a slight roughness. It should be a perfect balance of niceness, logic, and toughness motivating people. Without this combination, you can't act as a leader.

Saying, "Please, sit down, son, it might make you angry" won't work at all. Your son would know that you expect him to get angry when you talk. Also, you can't talk in circles and try to find an excellent way to say the real thing. Sometimes, ripping off the bandage is the right way to make others realize that you exist, even if the ripping might take off a little skin with it.

Why Do Nice People Feel Angry So Often?

The thought behind being nice is that you receive happiness in return, but that joy doesn't come to you very often. If you are nice enough to let manipulators control you, it results in anger and regret.

Friendly people feel happy during an act of kindness, but they realize that they were being manipulated. The end feeling is anger towards the manipulator, as well as oneself. This only happens when the tactics of manipulators blind your niceness.

Only then can you stay happy and avoid anger.

Manipulators love when they see certain traits in a person. They carefully choose their targets who are vulnerable and too nice. Everyone has doubts, fears, wishes, gratitude, hopes, love, and other feelings, but the weak personalities are the ones that don't know about their own emotional and psychological conditions. Manipulators observe that and try to manipulate their victims. You don't have to become an unsympathetic or senseless person to avoid manipulation; understand your inner-self before a manipulator does.

Chapter 8: environmental tactics and ideas.

New environment

Usually, based on where you are, it can result in a positive and negative request. It is easier to get favors if you are out of a work environment since that place is seen as a sort of challenge to those who are better at it, on the contrary, to have a positive outcome, you need to evaluate the place well, which is in front of you. to a drink or a party with friends. Jim from Finance will be more willing to consider your requests to expedite the invoicing process if you ask him after he's had a few beers at a party compared to when he is at the office and buried in paperwork.

Make It About The Other Person

Here's the thing—you are looking to learn how to manipulate people for your gain, but you do not have to make your selling point. When a person feels that you have helped them get what they want, they will be more likely to help you get what you want too, be it knowingly or otherwise.

Quickly Dialogue

There are two reasons for this: they might not process what you are saying and do not want to look stupid by asking for clarification, or they do not want to process what you are saying because your energy is overwhelming, and they do not want to deal with it. By babbling to your customer and rattling off all the details of this and that car, the customer quickly becomes overwhelmed and settles on the next choice of offer.

To Dress in Fashion

A well-groomed gentleman who smells nice and looks great will have an easier time getting what he wants from a woman as opposed to a man who looks like he crawled out of a hole. And remember, you do not have to buy designer labels or the most expensive outfits on the planet to make a great impression—you have to make it seem like you did.

Scare Tactics

All you need to do is convince the said consumer that a very high likelihood that a particular thing will go wrong and that they need to prepare for this likelihood by buying your product or service.

The solution Is Key

There is one thing you should never underestimate. For example, when someone is nice to you but rude to someone else, obviously there is something wrong with his character. The manipulator must never underestimate this feature. He must not have double personalities; on the contrary, he must always be consistent with what he says and does. Being consistent is fundamental in this game; make everyone believe that you are the same as every individual, you will have more trust in this way from others. Once this method is adopted, you can be sure that you will have more prey available to manipulate.

Silence The Best Weapon

Silence is the best weapon for lingering someone to speak; thus, the individual will feel compelled to open a speech, allowing the manipulator to hear everything about his prey. The more information he knows about it, the easier it will be to conquer him.

Play Nice

For example, if you want a colleague to do something for you (for example, correct a report that they have messed up on), you'll want to phrase your statement in a way that absolves them of most of the guilt. For instance, instead of telling them they are a dummy and have mixed up all the numbers, ask them whether they sent the correct report and if they would like to take a second look and send another version. This gets you what you want without making the other person feel foolish, and this is exactly what you want as you need to keep getting what you want from this individual.

Carry Your Cross

You can do certain things that will make people automatically assume that you are a good and trustworthy person, even when you are not. For this reason, you will find some men walking their cute dogs (even when they are not interested in the dog) or taking their pretty nieces along to social events because these two accessories (while not store-bought accessories) give a significant boost to their appeal. A man with either of these two accessories automatically comes across to most women as a decent, nurturing, and well-grounded guy who can make a good father to a baby, be it a real one or a fur baby.

Talk To Me

To look smart, you don't need to display dialogue qualities like a guy usually does. Instead, rely on books, general culture, deep documentaries so that you can find yourself stable when you face a speech at dinner. People have a sense of trusting people better than they deem thoughtful about their emotional impact. Slowly, without having to throw all your skills headlong at once, enrich your prey little by little so that this one does not get tired of you quickly.

It doesn't matter if you haven't had a lot of experience conversing freely; remember that you can always tell other stories or make them up as long as they are credible.

On the other hand, it can only be your advantage to have a brilliant mind.

Be Trustworthy

You want to be a manipulator who stands out from the others, and above all, he is not forgotten for his skills. You want to distinguish yourself when you are close to another who, although it may be better in age for several aspects, you will be able to transmit more than any other individual.

Newbies Are Easy Targets

Newbies, be it at the workplace or any situation, are always eager to help and fit in because nobody is a fan of sticking out like a sore thumb. You will, however, have to be careful not to come across as overbearing as you want to use this newbie for as long as you can while having them think you are looking out for them.

Need For Help

Expressing a request for help in a manipulative way means that you will not only receive a courtesy favor but will ensure that you will receive complete orders.

Chapter 9: Dealing with an abusive or manipulative partner

Comprehending manipulation in a partnership

Suppose your partner appeals to your instabilities or makes you feel guilty to get his/her very own way taking over control. It can show up in different types, including passive-aggressiveness, mockery, and unjust teasing. Every case is various, and adjustment is not always easy to pinpoint.

"If you think you are being manipulated, most likely it's happening since you find yourself doing things unlike your instinct at the prodding of somebody else's dreams or requests." Be objective: Identify the indicators of a manipulative partnership.

To identify signs of manipulation in your connection, it's essential to take a look at your companion's practices with valuable eyes. " One of the toughest elements of manipulation is recognizing it. To do so, there is the need of neutrality, self-awareness, guts as well as being conscious of the patterns and practices," clarifies Ikka. Be straightforward with yourself and consider your partner's behavior without rose-colored glasses. Approach your companion with a strategy

To note out whether you can solve the problem, you have to raise your feelings to your partner. Be aware that your partner might reply to your sensations by acting angered or injured, thus attracting unsecured.

Highlight what you are feeling instead of speaking directly regarding your companion's actions. " Before approaching your companion, make a list of the ways you feel you are being controlled using 'I' declarations to ensure that you can supply concrete instances," suggests Ikka. If you stay away from any strong language, your companion will be most likely to respond favorably, and also, the conversation will be much more constructive.

"Manipulation features an unfavorable undertone. However, it's not always a resource of wickedness," says Ikka. If they're, an exit technique might be essential, she recommends.

If your companion comes to be protective and mad or is otherwise insensitive to your sensations, consider your actions carefully. What's crucial is that you identify your partner's attempt to manipulate you.

" As soon as a person recognizes that they are being adjusted, exactly how they choose to handle it will certainly differ," says Ikka. "Having the ability to determine indicators of adjustment in a partnership is the secret to either getting out of one that isn't most likely to function or managing it. It's the trickiest component."

Why people adjust

People can be manipulative because of their woundedness, discomfort, or immaturity. They tend to respond anxiously as opposed to relating easily. They lack the essential relational skills required for healthy communications.

Along those lines, some individuals have a personality problem and have pleasure in controlling others - even to harm them.

Manipulative individuals might have various reasons behind their activities. However, they usually fall under three major groups or styles.

Master. They often tend to be aggressive and also easily outraged. They're bullies.

Savior. He or she has pleased you and believes that, because they "protect" you (from whatever), you owe them a financial obligation of thankfulness for life and are anticipated to do points their means. It's for your very own excellent.

Sufferer. This person is frequently overlooked as manipulative because they're inadequate individuals.

Chapter 10: Laws of Manipulation

Can you think that your brain has been manipulated or manipulated in 1 way or the other in every waking minute of your lifetime? Not always by somebody who you understand either. Social networking, online news articles, and the more things you see and listen to in conventional media, advertising, conversations we view and listening in the office or private lives. They are some exploitation or head controller, and the majority of the moment, it is happening without you realizing it. Why, though, will be the individual head so prone to manipulation? Is it that our leader is filled with what's called "loopholes"? Let us look at the Solomon Asch experiment that was conducted in 1957. Asch completed this experimentation on conformity at a collection of psychological tests to show the level to which a person's comments could be affected by a bunch of individuals. The outcomes, Asch found, were with the ideal quantity of peer pressure, folks were eager to ignore the truth or fact which was facing them and hotel to providing a false or erroneous response to adapt to the remainder of the group.

Before That, Here Is A Fast Question.

Can you find yourself as somebody who's a nonconformist? Or just a conformist? Many men and women feel they are sometimes precisely the perfect quantity of nonconformists to stay against other people when they understand they're about something. A conformist but would like to mix with this group. While many often think they are nonconformist, the study would suggest differently, in which individuals may be more vulnerable to conformity than that they initially thought. Following is a fast test. Imagine you are now a part of a psychology experiment using many other men and women. Everybody is taking the same trial where you are shown a set of strangely contours images and requested what you can see if you consider the picture. A few participants declare that they can observe the specific concept on certain occasions, but if you look at the image, you see something completely different. Every other player in the area has an identical coordinated response. What could you do? Can you stand by what you can see? Or can you go right ahead and announce precisely the same answer the different participants provide?

That is precisely what the Asch conformity experiments aimed to detect. Conformity is an individual's inclination to go together with the unspoken behavior or principles of a social circle.

Asch set out to see together with his experiments when folks might be forced into adapting, even when they understood that everybody else in the team was incorrect. Asch's primary intention of the investigation was to show precisely how substantial conformity may be in a bunch.

After Asch completed his experimentation, some participants had been "in" about what was happening and faking to be just like the rest of the participants, and people who were unaware of precisely what was occurring. Individuals who knew exactly what was happening could act in specific ways. The goal was to see whether their behavior was likely to impact the other participants. In every experiment completed, there could be one innocent participant put with some of those "conscious" participants. There were 50 participants in the bunch, and everybody was told they'd be participating in some "vision evaluation."

From the "eyesight evaluation," people who had been conscious of precisely what was happening were told exactly what their answers were likely to function as a job that was introduced. The innocent participant had no hint they were the ones that had been blissfully oblivious. Each of the participants was provided a lineup job, and everyone needed to declare verbally that line (B or C) had been the nearest fit to the goal line that they had been awarded. Several 18 different trials were completed, and also, the conscious participants have incorrect responses for 12 from the 18 trials. Asch desired to decide whether the innocent participants could alter their answers to conform to everybody else (the conscious group) responses.

Everything was going nicely throughout the initial half of these trials, together with the conscious response, answering the appropriately given queries. But they later started providing incorrect responses, as they had been taught to from the experimenters.

The Consequences?

Interestingly enough, in the conclusion of this Asch experiment, it had been shown that 75 percent of individuals who participate in the conformity experiment went together with all the responses from the remainder of the team at least one time. When all of the trials were united, Asch found the innocent participants conformed into the group wrong response about one-third of their moment.

To ascertain that the participants can, in actuality, really gauge the suitable length of those lines they had been awarded throughout the eyesight evaluation, each participant has been requested to compose the cooperative game separately. Dependent on the outcome, the participants' Decisions were accurate, with the ideal response being selected 98 percent of their time.

Asch's experiment also appeared at just how much influence the variety of individuals present inside a group may affect conformity. If there was just another participant gift, it did not involve a player's response. If there were just two participants current (the conscious group), their replies had a minimal influence on the innocent participant's response. At the existence of 3 or more participants (conscious), there has been a substantial gap in the answers offered by the innocent participant. Asch also found that getting one aware participant supply the ideal response. In contrast, the remainder of the conscious participants who gave incorrect answers radically lowered the amount of conformity seasoned, using just 5 percent to 10 percent of their participants moving and the additional team members. Studies that were completed in the future also have affirmed Asch's findings, which suggests that social assistance was a significant component that had to exist when it regards conformity.

When the innocent participants were challenged later about why they opted to go together with the remainder of the band, though they knew that the answers were incorrect, most reacted with though they knew everybody else was wrong, they did not wish to place them at risk of being ridiculed. Some of the participants thought that the remaining part of the team had the proper responses, and they had been incorrect. The findings of Asch's experiment show the facts about conformity, which explains that it's influenced by a belief that other folks could be more intelligent or more educated, along with a desire to fit in with the remainder of the group. This "loophole," then, is really where the individual mind thus becomes vulnerable to manipulation.

Why Do We Conform?

For people who know the way the body functions, it subsequently becomes straightforward to take full advantage of their leverage. Utilizing this knowledge for their benefit, they can easily influence each of the other unsuspecting people with merely a couple of well-placed phrases or accessible commands. Manipulation quickly sets you in a place of power if you perform someone else's emotions, the most specific target.

If you can convince a person and make them feel that in doing precisely what you need them to, they'll be happy, they will be more than prepared to bend into your own rules. If you make them feel guilty enough, they will attempt to do what they can to "fix" this Circumstance. Even playing someone else's anxiety makes them an easy goal. Make them think they are at risk of losing whatever they can't manage to lose, and they will jump at any chance presented to them. If your boss should happen to dangle the possibility of facing you that you may lose your work, would not that fear-free you make anything request they request of you? Emotions make exploitation so simple.

Asch conducted further experiments and found that the reasons people become vulnerable more to adapting when:

☐ There are far more individuals present

☐ When the undertaking is more complex and we're confronted with doubt. We tend to affirm if we think others may be much better educated than we're on the topic.

☐ As soon as we see other people in a bunch with more "energy" or "influence."

Asch did find, though, that the energy of conformity will diminish when the participants could react individually or independently from other people. The additional study reveals that less agreement occurs when the individual in question has at least another individual inside the category that supports their perspective. Interesting really.

The 13 Laws of Manipulation

Manipulators may come in all sizes and shapes. As different as they might function as humans, there are particular things that manipulators possess in common with one another, and that's that they're untrue, misleading, and underhanded and can resort to using some other strategy if it means that they get what they desire after the day. They care little about your feelings or anybody else, for that matter, the people they enjoy. The one thing that matters is their schedule and precisely what they need.

Manipulators hotel to a single, two, or many tactics to attain their objectives, always at somebody else's cost.

While the strategies may vary from 1 manipulator to another, you will find legislation of exploitation. Each manipulator can utilize at one time or another:

Law #1: Reduce Your Intentions. Lying is possibly the earliest and best kind of exploitation around. Manipulators frequently resort to the strategy when they attempt to prevent twists or responsibility into the fact for their advantage. A few manipulators even hotel to lying if there isn't any true motive to do so, just booming on the joy of producing chaos or the understanding they're playing with somebody else's emotions. An expert manipulator knows how to operate this angle so discreetly that you don't actually.

Recognize the lie they spin till it is too late. There might be many explanations for why a manipulator hotel to lying. It might be to benefit from another one. To hide their actual goals so that you do not understand what they are around. Or maybe even to measure the playing area so that they could stay 1 step ahead of you. A worker who had been worried that their occupation could approach the supervisor and inquire about the chance of being laid off or terminated. To hide what is going on, the manager could tell the worker there is nothing to be concerned about if, in actuality, plans were being forced to substitute him when he's finished work on the job he had been delegated to. A colleague that has been eyeing the same advertising you're might withhold possible information so they can place themselves before you.

Law #2: Action Seeking. Just a bit of play in lifestyle keeps things interesting; however, play occurs all too often for a manipulator. Why? Since they made it on goal. Manipulators enjoy being in the middle of attention to support themselves and provide their egos the confidence boost that they think they require. A colleague at work may generate a battle between colleagues B and A by telling stories to every one of them concerning another. This ensures that while B and A are still at odds with one another, they turn into the manipulator to get "relaxation," which makes the manipulator feel significant. In a relationship, one spouse could always decide on a struggle to be sure the other's focus is on these and seeking to solve a problem that might not exist.

Law #3: Behaving Emotionally Manipulators might be exceptionally psychological people, prone to striking or perhaps hysterical outbursts if they need things done their way. Melodramatic, loud, obnoxious, over-the-top, at the slightest provocation, that a manipulator will hotel of psychological behavior, which can be the majority of the time improper in a social environment.

A few loudly arguing at the restaurant since one spouse is acting when things aren't completed their way hotels to this conduct, trusting their spouse may be ashamed enough to give in to their needs makes this a very effective manipulation method when used correctly.

Law #4: Playing Victim. Everybody feels sorry for this. They appear to have the worst luck on earth. Regardless of what issue you might be needed, they discover a means to cause you to feel guilty for talking about it by figuring out just how their difficulty will be "10 times worse" than yours. Most of us suffer from a stroke of terrible luck now and then. However, the manipulator could use that unfortunate series to reestablish their particular "victim" position and place themselves above everybody else. A buddy who plays all of the opposing sides of their own life while dismissing your issues is due to the manipulative strategy to have the attention they desire. Inform them you've had a terrible day because you had a flat tire on your way to do this afternoon, and they will explain to you how you might be lucky you have a vehicle to whine about whether they must survive the hardships of people transport. Manipulators hotel for the emotionally draining strategy to get sympathy from other people, which can be just another method of looking for attention and making sure everyone is centered on these.

Law #5: Accepting Credit Where It's Not Due. Manipulators don't have any qualms about getting one to do the majority of the legwork, then swooping in at the last minute to take credit just like they've completed the lion's share of this job. A frequent tactic that's frequently utilized in a specialist setting, particularly in-class projects or teamwork. These tricky manipulators flit around assigning tasks, apparently appearing "occupied" when they are not doing anything in Any Way. Still, if it comes time to carry credit, they have no issues about pushing you apart and accepting credit for those ideas and the job you have set in.

Law #6: Based on Me. Manipulators would like you to feel like you "want" them into your lifetime. In a social setting, you can't live with them; in a social environment, they are the "favorite" ones that everybody else appears to flock into, making you desperate to wish to be part of the group.

In a connection, they might be the spouse that always informs you, "what could you do with me" or "how could you live with me." They can favor and help you at a time if you want it most, which makes you feel nostalgic for them to come and money in on those favors at a subsequent date (using a manipulator, no prefer ever comes free of charge). Manipulators make this false belief that you want them on your own life since the longer you rely on them, the greater control they have on you, which is precisely what they desire. They prey on the vulnerable and also make themselves the "crucial friend" in your own life, basking in this distinctive status they've created. The further you lean on them for assistance, the more chances they must prey on your feelings and harness you to their benefit.

Law #7: Selective Honesty. Maybe you have felt disarmed by the way the generous person who you know may suddenly turn around and stab you in your trunk? Or felt wrong-footed if you realized you just knew half of what exactly was happening? That is because the individual who had been feeding you with advice has been a manipulator, and why you feel stabbed in the trunk or wrong-footed is they just provided you advice they needed you to understand while knowingly withholding the remainder. Selective honesty, a more highly effective manipulative strategy that may be employed to disarm an undercover "victim." A system that's now very notable within specialist settings mainly. Manipulators in the office use all of the opportunity to get ahead. Whether there aren't any people around for the same promotion on the job that the manipulator will attempt to provide themselves the top hand by withholding critical information they understand while simultaneously promising everyone else who "that is precisely what's happening." They lead one to think they are being generous with clueing you into what is occurring, but in fact, they are making sure you are two steps behind them every step along the way.

Law #8: Pretending to Make a "Buddy." Do not be tricked by the exceedingly friendly man you met on your very first day in the workplace. They might be pretending to be the buddy while collecting information about you that they can later use to your benefit. When some folks can be favorable, begin to elevate the red flag when this individual becomes a little overly friendly by asking personal or significant questions, particularly if you've just met them. This strategy is notable within a good setting, and when your stomach is telling you that something is away, it likely is. The manipulator may even exist in your circle of friends.

They pretend to be the "buddy" by subtly becoming the person in charge of the dialogue. The dialog will likely always be precisely what they dictate it ought to be, and it'll only occur when they decide it ought to occur. This "buddy" may also pressure you in making decisions by providing you hardly any time to consider doing it. Phrases like "if I am your buddy, you will get this done to me" roll off the tongue of this manipulator too readily and constantly due to their advantage.

Law #9: Non-Committal. Would you know anybody in your life that has difficulty committing to anything else? Even after you have told them how significant it is and you could utilize their service at the moment? The non-committal individual isn't a buddy of yours, and they are a manipulator. They enjoy withholding their acceptance or kindness when it means there is a chance for them to provide themselves the top hand to restrain the Circumstance due to their advantage. They are just looking out for themselves, and they'll particularly refrain from committing to anything else when it means having to assume the obligation. Becoming non-committal is a manipulation strategy frequently utilized in romantic relationships. Every time a romantic partner has been non-committal, it retains the other in their feet and keeps them coming back for longer, thereby providing the manipulator the top hand. The more time they emphasize their devotion, the bending over backward you're going to be eager to do only to receive their approval.

Law #10: Playing Dumb. Is that colleague you understand unaware of what is happening? Or are you currently feigning innocence to prevent taking on additional responsibility? Playing stupid is a manipulative strategy that often goes wrong, but should you pay careful attention, you will locate it evident within a lot of configurations. If you are currently a leader of this team project on the job, do you assign additional duty to that one team member who "was not as convinced of a thing"? Or transfer that excess obligation to the next? The worker who was subsequently "playing stupid" got off performing much less but obtaining precisely the same amount of admiration as everybody else in the category. Whenever there's a battle between a bunch of buddies, would that one buddy who "does not understand what is happening" be telling the truth? Or would there be feigning innocence, knowing how well they had been accountable for instigating the battle in the first location?

In a romantic relationship, would your spouse, who "does not understand what you are speaking about," be telling you the truth if you face them about a problem? Or would they're "playing stupid" to prevent being trapped in a lie?

Law #11: Finger in The Others. Even a manipulator will always keep their hands clear by first, never imagining duty, and second by constantly attempting to stage that the final somebody else so that they eliminate scot-free whenever there is an issue. Should you know anybody in your loved ones, friends, or perhaps one of your coworkers who constantly blames the problem about anything and anybody but themselves, then you might be dealing with a manipulator. Keep a watch for anybody who is the pattern of behavior entails constantly making someone else that the scapegoat.

Law #12: I tell you what I want you to hear. It is difficult not to feel great once you're being, and you are more prone to enjoy the individuals who are doing all of the flattering over others. When there's one individual in your life who is constantly telling you all of the situations that you wish to listen to, would not you be more prone to want to follow along spend additional time together?

It is difficult not to feel great around people such as these; however, telling you all of the situations you wish to hear isn't always the sign of a fantastic buddy. They might be buttering you up so that they could cash in on an enormous favor at a subsequent date that you are going to "delighted into assisting them with "since they have been so great for you."

Law #13: Fixing Your Choices. A timeless setting in which manipulation in controlling the other's conclusion is present is inside a romantic connection. Although you usually base or alter your choices due to your spouse, is it since there is inside you a genuine desire to make them all happy?

Or do you do it since you do not wish to risk making them mad? If you end up canceling plans much too frequently with friends as your spouse conveys their displeasure or causes you to feel bad, that is manipulation in drama.

If you refrain from wearing clothing, your spouse participates (though you like it) or prevent yourself by getting a haircut as your spouse said, "they do not like short hair," which is a subtle kind of exploitation.

Conclusion

Finally, the behavior of people is driven by needs towards their satisfaction. They offer starting points for manipulation because humans always strive for something by nature. When one condition is satisfied, the next comes and demands satisfaction. The first thing a manipulator can do is this: he can introduce what he wants to manipulate to what he intends to influence him into as the satisfaction of some need.

Manipulating people to hurt them is not a good practice, but there comes a time you need to drive people to get what you want, an example in business negotiations. Still, it should be done carefully so you don't end up negatively harming them. This technique is not what you will master overnight. It would help if you had a lot of patience to study these skills. If you are naïve, people will take advantage of you. Learning these techniques will protect you from becoming their victims. As the saying goes, "dogs don't eat dog" when you know what they know, it becomes hard for people to control and manipulate you. Just like a chess game, you must know the rules to win.

Experts have labeled classical manipulators' wolves in sheep's clothing or 'serpents in suits.' No manipulator or psychopath can excel without some elements of falsehood, selfishness, ingenuity, and mischievousness under their cloaks. You will meet these people everywhere, but one thing to bear in mind is that they are very deceptive and masked; therefore, it is difficult to identify them initially.

At the beginning of your relationship with them, they appear to be very kind, considerate, and sympathetic to find a way to get the better half of you and rip you off. Firstly, they will trust you with some confidential matters about themselves. This gesture will induce you to even divulge your secrets to them, unknowing to you that they are after your backbone to chop it off your body.

When you have confided in them based on their fake commitment to you, they will pick up your ideas and secrets and implement them even before you would have noticed it.

Military organizations, financial institutions, politicians, and the media use manipulation to achieve their professional goals despite its risks and benefits.

Although the risks outweigh the services most of the time because of the individuals or personalities involved in the act of manipulation, who may feel embarrassed, cheated, and mesmerized by the manipulator.

Therefore, as a skilled manipulator, it is advisable to maintain cautiousness and curiosity while displaying your zest in achieving your selfish motives. Emotions and logic are the twin bullets applied by manipulators in shooting down their target.

Emotional appeal is more vital than logical representation because people will listen to you, follow your instructions if your words are pleasing to their minds, and fulfill their emotional desires. On the contrary, people may be indifferent to you and even oppose your motions and opinions if your logical presentations are not symmetrical to their preconceived notions. They may label and libel you with wrong appellations that may defame your character and social status.

Nevertheless, suppose you can apply the force of persuasiveness in influencing your human targets. In that case, you will surely meet your goals successfully with no one noticing your smartness and tricks in any way.

MIND CONTROL TECHNIQUES

Introduction

Next time you are in a public space, look around you and examine the people walking around. What are they doing? Who are they with? In which direction are they going? If you can imagine that last time you went to your supermarket of choice, you can probably recall people pushing carts of food around the aisles. Maybe with their spouse and children, or with friends. Maybe alone. Each of them has one thing in common: they want to buy their groceries for the week and get on with their day.

In that sense, the motivation behind their behavior is patently visible. A father walks over to the dairy section and grabs a gallon of % two milk. He then scratches the item from the grocery list and walks towards the next thing. The grocery store is an excellent metaphor for motivation in the real world. Everyone is doing something because they have some item that needs to be crossed out from a list. At times it will be easily doable, like getting a haircut. At other times it will be complex and time-dependent, like getting a Ph.D. in astrophysics.

Whatever the case, people have motivations. Everyone has a representative grocery list they want to fulfill, whether they know what is on the list or not. There is where human psychology gets tricky. Some of us know what we want. Some of us don't know. Some of us are "open" to suggestions and recommendations. Still, others are constantly seeking direction from others. Some of us know what our moral values and core beliefs are. Others do not. One second you can be reaching for the creamy peanut butter, and the next, you are looking at the crunchy version. Or perhaps you drop peanut butter altogether and look towards the organic nut butter. Or maybe you reach for the peanut butter and mixed jelly jar.

To understand what dark psychology is, we first need to establish what psychology is as a whole. Psychology is defined as the study of the human mind, especially regarding the connection between thoughts and behaviors.

Even in the great Greek philosophers' times, scholars were fascinated by the workings of the mind and its relation to our actions and reactions.

Modern psychology was founded by a German doctor named Wilhelm Wundt. Wundt was a physiologist and philosopher, and his interest in these fields led to the development of his theories about the relationship between body and mind.

In 1879, the first psychology laboratory was founded, which is located at the University of Leipzig. He was determined to prove that the mind's inner workings could be measured and examined much like any other science experiment. He developed theories and experiments based on the following principles:

Voluntarism- **the process of organizing the mind**

Reductionism- **the ability to isolate each part of the mind**

Introspection- **the ability to perform detailed self-examination**

Using these principles and a modified experiment from his days in physiology, Wundt developed a method of testing his subjects' psyche. When he was a medical doctor, Wua ndt had tested his patients' reaction time to certain physical stimuli in a controlled environment, like a noise or a flashing light (the precursors to modern hearing or vision tests). Wundt wondered if he could similarly test the mind. The result was an experiment in which Wundt had his subjects concentrate on a metronome and then describe how the metronome made them feel. By detailing the sounds, sensations, and thoughts they had when focusing on the metronome ticking, Wundt began determining how the brain is affected by controlled stimuli. He even attempted to measure the levels of chemical activity in the brain during and after these experiments.

While Wundt's work was primitive by the standards of modern psychology, it was groundbreaking enough for him to have trained over one hundred students in the budding field, and he inspired the next generation of psychologists; Sigmund Freud, who fathered psychoanalysis; Carl Jung, who expanded upon Freud's theories and developed analytical psychology; William James, who brought modern psychology to America; and Alfred Alder, who formulated the connections between emotional needs and social skills. These men created the body of work that would blossom into the many psychology and psychotherapy branches we see today, including cognitive-behavioral therapy.

Dark psychology fascinates people worldwide, especially to a category of men who like crime. Dark Psychology studies the more evil side of an individual because he can understand people and manipulate them as he wants without them realizing it.

Persuasion, manipulation, and other forms of influence are ubiquitous. You can pick up on some apparent signs here and there, but there are also hidden secret ways that others control you, which you might never be able to comprehend fully.

Many reasons exist that can make you yearn to be a more persuasive person. Perhaps you feel as though you are already under the profound influence of others and wish to break yourself free.
Maybe you are the kind of individual that can easily fall for the charm of others, and now is the moment for you to better protect yourself against any types of influence that might happen to you.

Perhaps you are trying to sell something, maybe yourself or your brand, and you need to figure out how to get people to be more persuaded by you to help you achieve the things you want in this life. No matter where you are or what you are trying to do, you have all the tools that you will ever need to be persuasive or influential with you already.

Before getting into this book, there are a few things that you need to know to be introduced to this topic to get into the right mindset as you read through this text. First, understand that there are no two manipulators that are alike. There are no two easily persuaded people that are the same either. Though it might seem like this sometimes, significantly since you can influence a group all at once, you can't let yourself fall into a thinking pattern where you place everyone in the same category.

To be an expert, you should have an open mind about manipulation and persuasion. There are many tricks to being persuasive. You are never really ready to study the human mind and be persuasive quickly.

Don't blame yourself for not being aware of the ways that you have been manipulated in the past. Regret isn't going to do you any good in this journey, so it's best to leave those feelings of, "I wish I would have known this sooner" behind. All that you can do now is move forward, and we will help you every step of the way!

What Is Normal Psychology?

Psychology is a study of the mind and behavior that delves into people and animals' mental processes in a more complex way. The psyche is the fundamental element that gives shape to express one's motivations and act based on the information that the mind transmits. Through the psyche, a person uses thought, memory, perception, imagination, sensation, emotions, feelings, inclinations, and temperament. However, the most critical question remains: what is an individual guided by, the behavior he takes on an urgent situation, and what changes within it? The answers are broad enough because, in today's psychology, there are a large number of selections:

- *General psychology*

- *Age-related psychology,*

- *Social psychology,*

- *Psychology of religion,*

- *Pathophysiology*

- *Neuropsychology,*

- *Family psychology*

- *Sports psychology, etc.*

What Is Dark Psychology?

The most exact definition to define dark psychology is focused on mind control, as it primarily studies human behavior. The difference in dark psychology is focused on the way we act, on the thoughts, and on the actions we carry out towards others since every gesture is calculated by ourselves. When such manipulation is used, it is to be considered that one has entered a dark tunnel, tactics used only by people deemed truly evil, for the sole purpose of manipulating, infatuating and forcing someone to do what one wants for themselves and of course to the detriment for the person who suffers.

Despite this, several individuals like to receive such manipulation, agreeing to be used and manipulated for their partner. Still, others choose to fight over this injustice submitted to them.

All this is done only for a particular purpose that of completely subduing the person concerned, dominating his thoughts, gestures, and the victim's entire being.

In the study of dark psychology, we try to understand these thoughts that lead these individuals to act in this way towards others. The studies deduce that such predatory actions are entirely intentional.

You have heard many times that everyone has a dark side. All cultures and belief systems acknowledge this dark side to some extent. Our society refers to it as "evil," while some cultures and religions have gone so far as to create mythical beings to whom they attribute that evil (the devil, Satan, demons, etc.). Experts in dark psychology posit that some commit the worst kinds of evil for unknown purposes.

While most people may do evil things to gain power, money, retribution, or sexual purposes, some do wrong things because that's just who they are.

They commit acts of horror for absolutely no reason. In other words, their ends don't justify their means; they cause harm for their own sake.

The skills and methods of influencing others can be quite different. They can be used both for constructive purposes and for various frauds. The characteristics of those who manage to control people, no matter what is the "dark" in the dark psychology name.

People who successfully use dark psychology have fully understood all aspects of normal psychology. Thus, they know themselves as well as others around them. They quickly analyze others with this skill. They perceive the views, opinions, and other information from those whom they wish to influence. Such a skill can be developed independently, and you will learn all about this in subsequent chapters.

Certain stories of deception of citizens with the help of dark psychology, like those that were told at the beginning of the book, were perceived as exotic. The victims of this deception were considered unlimited simpletons.

The bulk of fraudulent "exploits" using dark psychology as a particular state of the psyche was not associated at all: the victim of dark psychological influence could not find an explanation for what happened.

As has been noted more than once, the specifics of dark psychology make the active user "process" the client in a roundabout way. He does not give direct commands to do this or encourages a person to do it as if he is acting on his initiative. The person comments ask consults, and - gets his way.

Behind his behavior is a particular strategy. One of them is speculation. The phrase stands in such a way that some phenomenon, action, or object is presented in it as actually accepted. For example, they ask you: "Will you pay in dollars or bitcoins?" The question is innocent, but you have not yet said that you intend to purchase this thing at all. The question assumes that you have already made such a decision, and it remains to solve the trifle - to pay in bitcoins or dollars, about which you begin to reflect.

I suppose that what was read caused the reader an ironic smile: a primitive ploy, visible, as they say, with the naked eye. Do not rush to conclusions. Let me remind you that the "seller" has already adjusted to you and leads you; your consciousness is no longer as critical as reading these lines. This is the basis of analyzing people first, then thinking steps ahead of them, even about their actions and reactions.

The essence of this technique is as follows: the dark psychologist makes up the text of the suggestion and then "dissolves" it is a story of neutral content. During the conversation, the "user" in some way selects the words of guidance, and they turn out to be a brilliant trap for consciousness. He (or she) will change the volume of speech, pause in characteristic places, speed up or slow down the story.

There are other tools for highlighting words and phrases to consolidate them in the subconscious. The "user" can emphasize the right places in the story with gestures, facial expressions, touching your arm, shoulder, back. He can approach you sharply, turn around, turn away, etc. If you follow them, all these manipulations are the basis of dark psychology.

Now let's think about how often this is done against our will. And how this new knowledge is about to turn your life around. But first, it is worth considering the various personality types you should get ready to come across.

Understanding the Dark Triad and What It Means

This is a fundamental concept because it will help tie together some of the other aspects discussed in Dark Psychology. The name "dark triad" may sound like something that comes from a horror movie, but it is a legitimate psychological concept that is well recognized.

The dark triad is nothing more than an identification system for the three most destructive and harmful psychological personality traits a person can have. This chapter will take some time to detail each of the traits, including narcissism, psychopathy, and Machiavellianism.

What Is Machiavellianism?

The first aspect of the Dark Triad that we will discuss is Machiavellianism. This aspect gets its name from the political philosopher known as Machiavelli. In his classical work "The Prince," the ideas, principles, and tactics used by those who seek to influence others are outlined. But how exactly does a Machiavellian person come across?

The hallmarks of this trait include:

A willingness to focus on your self-interest all the time.

An understanding of the importance of your image.

The perception of appearance.

Even the ruthless exercise of power and cruelty rather than using mercy or compassion.

To keep it simple, people who have this trait always have a strategy when approaching life. The consequences and any ramifications of any action will be thought out and then assessed in terms of how they will impact the one carrying them out.

The Machiavellian approach to the world is summed up with a simple question: "How will this action benefit me, and how will my public perception be impacted as a result?"

Machiavellian people will be masters of doing what will personally serve them well while still being able to maintain the good public image that they want. This allows the manipulator to do what they want while getting people around them to like them still.

What Is Psychopathy?

The net aspect that we can discuss is psychopathy. This will refer to a psychological condition that involves a superficial charm, impulsivity, and a lack of commonly held human emotions, such as remorse and empathy. Someone who exhibits enough of these traits can be known as a psychopath. These individuals are seen as some of the most dangerous people because they can hide their true intentions while still causing a lot of trouble.

The reality is different, and this can make it more deadly. A true psychopath is more likely to be that charming and handsome stranger who can win over their victim before they ruin those victims' lives in the process.

Interestingly, some of the top people in business score high on psychopathy personality tests. But as time goes on, it is becoming more common to see psychopathy as more of a problem to the victim and society than an issue in the psychopath's own life. Psychopaths can get to the top of anything they choose because they don't have to worry about some of the compassionate indecision that other humans will experience.

What Is Narcissism?

The third aspect of the Dark Triad that we need to explore is narcissism. You can have self-love without being considered a narcissist.

Someone who is considered a narcissist is likely to have a range of traits that are there. They will have an excessively inflated self-worth, such as seeing that their life is extra special and one of the essential lives in all of history. If this has been raised enough, they may know that they are the very most important in the whole world.

In the mind of a narcissist, they are unique, but they are superior to everyone else. They consider themselves a better person's species, higher than what ordinary people would be. And because a narcissist believes this way, their behaviors will change. The behavior you see in a narcissist will reflect the self-worth that the person has.

Some of the outward signs or manifestations of this aspect would include the inability of the person to accept any dissent or criticism of any kind. Even if they feel that someone is trying to criticize them, they will have a hard time dealing with this. This kind of person also feels the need to have others agree with them all the time, and they like to be flattered. If you are around someone who always seems to need constant praise, recognition, and approval, and if they seem to organize their lives to give them continued access to those who will fill this need, then it is likely that you are dealing with someone who is a narcissist.

These three aspects are going to come together to form the Dark Triad. When one person has all of these three traits in them, it can be a hard task to stay away and not get pulled into whatever plan they have.

Being on the lookout for these can make a big difference in how much control you have in your own personal life.

Whereas psychology is different from dark psychology as it is the study of human behavior, and our actions, interactions, and thoughts are centered with them. Some people get confused and don't know the difference between psychology and dark psychology. However, if you want to manipulate others, you need to know how to use dark psychology.

Here are a different kind of people who know the tactics of manipulating others-

a) Manipulation is an art, and you need to know the tactics to meet your needs first, even at someone else's expense. Though these kinds of people are known to be self-centered, and they are good when it comes to manipulating and intimidating others. These people are not bothered with the outcomes, but they have an agenda of self before others, no matter what.

b) Individuals who know how to use dark psychology well know perfectly well when it is emotional media time to increase the audience and sales of their products. They know and know perfectly well when their emotionality becomes tangible.

c) Some people meet clinical diagnoses, as they are true sociopaths. However, these people usually are intellectual, alluring but alongside, they are impulsive. Just because these people do not have much ability to feel remorse and lack emotionality, they build a superficial relationship and take advantage of innocent people by using dark tactics. They are not concerned about anyone's feelings and are least bothered with what others might do once the innocents know about their true face.

d) Politicians know how to use safe methods to dupe people, use them to get them to do business for the specific country, and even get votes for the government elections.

e) Some lawyers or attorneys focus solely on winning their case regardless of knowing the truth and, even after knowing the truth, using dark manipulating tactics to get the outcome of what they want to win the case. They are not bothered about justice but are only concerned about their reputation and self-esteem.

f) Individuals in companies use this form of shady tactic to take advantage of their employees, forcing them to perform better and have no qualms about whether such actions are unfair. Their efforts and wages are justified according to what they do to the company.

g) People who are involved in the sales department are usually well aware of many of these dark influencing tactics to persuade and convince other people to buy whatever they are selling. They could even disguise the customers, as they are only concerned with selling their product and earning a profit.

Now that you got to know about different types of people who may deceit you by using these dark tricks, here are the different dark psychological tactics to manipulate the people and make them do what you want them to do-

1) If you want to sell your product and wish to manipulate your customers to make them surely buy your product, you can use a decoy option. For example, if you are facing a troublesome situation to sell the more expensive of two products, by adding the third option, you can make the expensive product more captivating and appealing. You just need to make sure that the decoy option should be the same price as the more expensive option but assuring that it is less effective. It is a good strategy to increase the sale and enticing more customers towards your expensive product.

2) To win an argument, speak quickly so that the opponent has no other option left but to agree with you. If you speak faster, it will give the other person less time to process what you are saying, and they will agree with you. While you should do the opposite in case when the other person agrees with you, speaking slowly is better as it will give them the time to evaluate and analyze what you are saying.

3) You can copy the body language of people whom you want to manipulate. Imitating their body actions shall impress them and will make you closer to them, and they may start liking you. If you subtly imitate the way the other

person is talking, sitting, and walking, they would probably not notice that you are copying them, and it may get them to do as per your wants.

4) Scaring other people to make them give you what you want and need is one of the dark psychological tactics to manipulate people. Anxious people often respond positively to requests afterward as they may be occupied thinking about the danger they are surrounded with.

It would make them feel scared and would do as your saying. In addition, sometimes, even if you will not say anything, they will understand what you need and do what you would have spoken them to do for you.

5) To get people to behave ethically with you, you need to display an image of your eyes. It means you should create your image as a person who watches, notice and observe the other person by posting a picture of eyes nearby. The other people could never take you like a side option and will return all borrowed items on time.

6) Tweak such an environment for the people so that they would act less selfishly. For example, if you were bargaining in a coffee shop, needless to say, you would be less aggressive as compared to what you would be in a conference room. Usually, people tend to act less selfish when neutral items surround them, whereas if work-related objects occupy them, they incline towards more aggression and selfishness.

7) Try to keep your point complicatedly and do not make it very easy for the people to understand in a first move. To comply with people with your request, confuse them. For example- instead of keeping a price tag of your product at 4 dollars, make it 400 pennies so that people would first analyze how much dollars would 400 pennies make, and if they bargain, they will do that in pennies rather than in dollars. Or they may just think that the price given is a deal to go for.

8) If you help someone to achieve their goals or sort their problems out, the other person tends to return your favor, as they would feel obliged by what you have done for them. This way, when the time comes, you may manipulate the other person, and this is one of the tactics.

9) Try to ask a question or request a person at a time when they are mentally drained and exhausted. They would never question the request, or the chances of denial for your request are very less.

10) Always make the other person focus on their gaining, not losing. Moreover, declare the price of your product at last after telling all the features and benefits of your product. For instance, if you are selling your car for 1000 dollars, always let the other person know about its features, specifications, and benefits first. Then declare its price. The benefits will entice the customer towards the car, and then the price shall not be a constraint.

Body Language Clues: *The Basics*

Body language is a meaningful gesture to make the other person who receives it understand a lot. We are often deceived by the gestures of the body, making our mind capture gestures that in reality do not exist. , our mind sometimes processes what it would like to receive. But it's a tremendous non-verbal use for communicating with others. Most of our actions derive from gesticulating, visual and expressive movements without even realizing it. We can learn a lot from our body language signs, certainly from those of the face that transmit so many signals. The smile can give a sign of denial or approval. How to express that you are okay with words, but the facial expression ultimately proves the opposite. There are many facial expressions:

1. Disgust

2. Passion

3. Stimulation

4. Disturbance

5. Terror

The expression on our face can also make us understand if we can trust that person or not. Then there is the mouth language, which is another critical example on which to communicate as body language. A practical example is that if someone bites their lips, it means many factors, whether they are insecure or trying to provoke you. The smile remains the best among body languages because it is the first language that a person clings to in everyday life. The movements of the mouth are:

- **Folded mouth: when you are bitter, disgusted, bored, irritated.**

- **Biting your mouth: when you are anxious, stressed, afflicted.**

- **Cover your lips: when you want to hide an expression of any kind, to prevent it from being discovered.**

- **Raised or bowed lip: when you express your current mental state of how you react at that precise moment. When she is up, she is happy, but one feels disagreement or pain when bent down.**

Body gestures are also a world for expressing one's language, and they are the ones that tell the most significant interest due to the movement of the body. Here are some essential gestures:

• **A hand closed in a fist: this gesture can indicate two meanings: either you are angry or want to defend someone at any cost.**

• **The raised or lowered thumb: this gesture is used when you agree or disagree.**

• **The middle finger up: this gesture is a vulgar way to send a person to that country.**

The next goal is to look at the person's body in front of you, that is, arms and legs. Crossing either arms or legs often indicates a form of defense or sometimes discomfort towards an individual. On the contrary, when there are striking gestures in opening the arms, a sense of self-confidence, character, and physical is deposited. Here are some examples of body language involving arms and legs:

• **Arms crossed on the chest: an insecure, closed, and introverted person.**

• Hands on hips: when a person is confident, bold, and aggressive.

• Hands locked behind your back: when you are restless, anxious, angry, and nervous.

• Touching your hands and fingers: when you are impatient, whipped, anxious.

• Legs crossed or crossed: when a person feels alone, closed in on himself, and needs her space to isolate himself from everything around him.

The last phase is that of posture, very significant for body language, which can reveal a lot about a person's feelings based on our physical form. Prominent examples, if you take a seat very quickly in an expansive way, make it known that the individual wants to settle down to what surrounds him quickly. If he pretends to sit down, showing the opposite side of the body, he is an introverted person, shy, not very close to dialogue. I offer you some concrete data:

●   Free position: when the body is completely open and free from any disturbance. The person in question shows himself free to interpret with his own body every gesture and every emotion that passes freely in his head. She is free to show herself for who she is, without asking the problem that some individual judges her for her extroverted way of doing. Simply free from any prejudice.

●   Defense position: when one closes oneself between one's body with arms and legs. A significant posture indicates the state of mental health of that particular individual : anxiety, inadequate, depression.

Chapter 4: Emotional Intelligence

Emotional intelligence can realize emotions, differences, labels, manage or adapt according to the context you find yourself. These individuals can remain calm despite something negative due to a possible situation. They work to intervene positively when they are in embarrassing moments, managing to make him feel completely at ease with her. For this reason, emotional intelligence is psychological and knows how to handle any emotion with absolute firmness, managing to remain calm. Over the years, the definition of emotional intelligence was broken down into four sections: perceiving, utilizing, learning, and managing. The four abilities were all attributed to emotional intelligence with relative meanings behind them. Different models were created using these abilities, therefore, facilitating how thoughts and understanding of emotions interact. Studies show that people with more emotional intelligence tend to succeed more in various areas, including academics, careers, and talents. The ability has also been associated with providing great leadership and higher performance at work. More so, researchers agree that these people are healthy mentally as well as on their standard personality traits.

Since the introduction of emotional intelligence, different studies have been conducted with the objective of determining the actual factors driving an individual to manage emotions. Each person reacts differently when it comes to putting their feelings on the line, based on how much less severe the situation or fun. Despite this, the individual with a more enterprising emotional intelligence always prevails since he can better manage these emotions. This is commonly done because they don't care what happens to them, causing them to have a slight impact on their life, whether it's a difficult situation or not. With different groups of people, emotional intelligence has been seen to have different implications on the thoughts of these individuals. For instance, children and teens with high emotional intelligence tend to have good social interaction while those having lower abilities have the opposite. Adults with high emotional intelligence accompany an excellent self-perception socially, while those with low emotional intelligence tend to become aggressive.

Features of Emotional Intelligence

Show of Authenticity

High emotional intelligence people, especially those who are more social, tend to stick to their principles and values. When sharing about themselves to others, they usually stand by their boundaries rather than sharing everything about themselves to others. As such, authenticity does not imply that you have to share all about yourself. However, you share about yourself to people who matter and those who understand you and appreciate your thoughts and feelings.

Demonstration of Empathy

These individuals tend to demonstrate empathy to people as they readily understand other people's feelings and thoughts. They, therefore, readily connect to others and agree on what is essential. Instead of becoming judgmental and avoiding those who feel different, they comfort and make them feel important to society. Despite being empathetic, these people are cautious when it comes to decision-making, therefore avoiding agreeing to every person's motive.

Apologetic and Forgiving

Another feature of emotional intelligence people is that they quickly understand their mistakes. They usually have the courage and strength to apologize even without errors, therefore, indicating the value of a relationship. The same applies to forgive and forget, even in the most resentful situations. As such, they have emotional intelligence provides a mind that readily forgives and free from your emotions from those who hurt you.

Being Helpful

As emotional intelligence entails understanding and managing your emotions and that of others, then helping them becomes part of what the ability accompanies. As one of the most significant rewards to others, helping becomes a habit to these people, and they never tire or discriminate against others. However, they help each person in need without asking too many questions. As such, it helps those who follow similar footsteps as well as building trust among people to help others.

Always Thinking About Feelings

Emotional intelligence primarily dwells on one's feelings which often change suddenly or slowly depending on the situation or environment. When an individual has a higher emotional intelligence capability, then he or she frequently thinks about different feelings and how they may impact others. They usually ask common questions regarding their self-awareness, reflecting on everyday activities, and people who may be influenced by their emotions. As such, systematic thinking and learning about emotions provide insights used to their advantage in managing their feelings and that of others.

Benefit from Criticism

Nobody experiences fun when it comes to negative feedback, especially from people you trust and those close to you. However, these types of reputation are quite effective in life as they teach you a few lessons about a particular aspect. Besides, it enables you to learn more about how others think, mainly about you and things to change and become better in what you do. Receiving this negative feedbacks may become a challenge to others, but those with the ability to check their emotions benefit a lot. With the use of emotional intelligence, these people can learn to manage their emotions and move around calmly without focusing on the thoughts of others.

Managing Emotions

People with Low Emotional Intelligence

When low emotional intelligence people are faced with any negative emotion, they tend to become violent or rather more reactive when compared to those with high emotional intelligence. For instance, when an individual with low emotional intelligence faces negative criticism, they may initially go into denial and withdraw from a given group to avoid shame. They become lonely and prevent any form of help offered to them. In some cases, others may opt to use substances to keep their minds active and evade others and what they are feeling. Others may harm themselves by cutting, starving, purging, or engaging in dangerous behaviors. The primary drive to these activities is influenced by a lack of control of emotions which are usually hurting, such as criticism.

People with High Emotional Intelligence

High emotional intelligence people have all it takes to absorb and express reasonably how they feel about a particular sensation. For instance, when these group people are offended, they would initially pause before acting and think what their next word or rather the best harmless action to take. They would also acknowledge what the next person is feeling or have in mind before deciding on providing their contribution or conclusion of what will become. Thinking first is usually their first step to prevent escalating the problem or causing more harm to themselves and others. Another critical aspect of high emotional intelligence people is helping themselves and people affected by a given emotion. In this case, high emotional intelligence people act entirely different when compared to low emotional intelligence individuals.

Emotional Quotient (EQ) Vs. Intelligence Quotient (IQ)

Emotional Quotient, EQ, is the ability of an individual to readily learn, understand, handle, and control his or her emotions even in the most resentful situations. On the other hand, Intelligence Quotient, IQ, is the measure of one's intelligence usually expressed in a number. EQ enables an individual to focus on emotions which, in turn, acts as a management system to different emotions which may become harmful to others. More so, it involves other people's emotions, and an individual can readily manage these emotions without the need to sympathize. IQ measures the degree of intelligence calculated from standardized tests created to analyze human intelligence.

Components of Emotional Intelligence

Emotional intelligence is linked to different internal components of a person, usually within the brain, which determines how one understands and controls emotions. In most cases, people who lack control of their emotions have been associated with mental problems. While others stating that lack of emotional control is attributed to the extent of the immediate feeling at hand. However, emotional intelligence has been proven to exist among different individuals and comprises the following components.

Self-Awareness

This is the ability to recognize and learn about your emotions as well as understanding the effects accompanied by your feelings.

Becoming self-aware is determined by being able to monitor emotions, realizing emotional reactions, and identifying each emotion independently. Besides, you readily understand and figure out the interaction between your emotions and how you behave when that feeling occurs. That is, when you are an emotionally intelligent individual, you become aware of several aspects about yourself and others while keeping in mind what is wrong and right. You can readily make a choice to do wrong or wicked despite how sad, angry, or hopeless you become.

Self-awareness also builds the ability to determine the strengths and limitations for quick development of measures to avoid negative impacts to an individual and to others. As a person, you can get access to new information and personal skills; therefore, you learn from others. People with a sense of self-awareness are usually humorous, confident, and aware of the perception of others. More so, they understand what it means to be emotional despite being an everyday behavior. As among the primary components of emotional intelligence, self-awareness provides a complete guide to an individual to quickly learn what to do when facing a given emotion, which may harm both them and another person when mishandled.

Self-Regulation

Another significant component of emotional intelligence is self-regulation, which entails the regulation and management of emotions. After becoming self-aware of your feelings and the accompanying impacts on others and yourself, you are required to have a governing force that enhances how you react during these situations. However, it does not imply that an individual has to lock away his or her real emotions and hide how they feel about others, but they should express them in an organized manner. That is, regulating how you express your feelings at an appropriate time and place.

People skilled in self-regulation are mostly flexible and quickly adapt to change as well as excellent in settling disagreements among people and diffusion of tension. On top of that, they are protective, kind, caring, and do not blame themselves other than themselves, taking full responsibility for their actions. As a component of emotional intelligence, self-regulation plays a significant role in enabling an individual to quickly manage and handle all types of feelings, either positive or negative, without influencing others negatively.

Social Skills

Emotional intelligence also comprises social skills, which are the ability to interact with others correctly. Learning about your feelings and that of others and being able to control them is not enough to develop your emotional intelligence. Then, there is a need to implement these abilities into actions when interacting with others daily. When you indulge in daily communication with others and put into action this information, then you are at the forefront in managing your feelings and that of others. For example, managers in businesses have utilized the knowledge of social skills to interact with workers and clients, thus benefiting significantly in their careers.

Empathy

Empathy is the capability of comprehending other individual's feelings. It is also vital to emotional intelligence but provides more insight to an individual rather than recognizing the emotions of others. Empathy involves realizing emotions as well as reactions to these emotions, which primarily encompasses the help needed. For example, if someone is hopeless, sad, or emotionally dependent, you are likely to sense these emotions and respond accordingly as if they are yours. You tend to provide extra care and concern, allowing other people to recognize power dynamics that influence relationships. Therefore, emotional intelligence enables you to become empathetic to others and give the needed support.

Intrinsic Motivation

Unlike others, people with emotional intelligence abilities are rarely motivated by external rewards, for example, richness, fame, or acclaim. These people usually work to meet their personal needs and objectives. They seek to ensure their internal satisfaction, which, in turn, leads to rewarding their inner needs. Such individuals remain action-oriented by creating goals that are of higher standards and work to achieve. Also, they remain committed to performing their duties entirely when needed without failure. As such, the motivation allows for the achievement of essential goals in nearly everything they engage in, no matter the complexity of the situation.

More Emotional People

More emotional people tend to have low emotional intelligence and, therefore, become very reactive, especially on negative emotions. In this case, these people usually lack self-awareness, self-regulation, and other components of emotional intelligence. When someone is regarded as a more sensitive person, the chances are that they may become very reactive on occasions such as anger and become violent. When sad, they may end up becoming stressed, lonely, and eventually, being depressed. This group of people may, however, have some ability to control some of their emotions but limited knowledge about how they react to a given situation.

More emotional people may, at times, face difficulties in how they interact publicly, henceforth, cannot sustain relationships. Some of the characteristic features of more emotional people include the inability to understand other people's emotions, getting into arguments quickly, blaming others for their mistakes, and lack of empathy. Other features include difficulty sustaining friends, sudden outbursts of emotions, refusal to listen to other's views, and thinking people are usually oversensitive. More emotional people typically have no control over how they express their feelings or emotions. Therefore, they become too dependent on themselves without minding others.

Less Emotional People

Less emotional people are those individuals with the ability to control their emotions or feelings even when they are profound or negative. These individuals usually have a much higher emotional intelligence when compared to more emotional people. As highlighted above, less emotional people have the ability to suppress their emotions even in the states where these emotions seem unbearable. They may look calm and in peace even after a hurtful event. More so, they are relaxed and understanding and interact well with the general public, mainly with friends, family, and those close to them, such as coworkers.

When in an emotional state, for instance, these individuals typically respond to issues rather than react and understand the matter at hand. They are equipped with the five components of emotional intelligence as well as self-control and handle situations with their related selves. When faced with a more challenging situation, less emotional people rarely complain but work to find ways of solving the problem, which, in most cases, succeed with limited failure possibilities.

As typical human beings, however, less emotional people also undergo similar impacts of negative emotions, but due to their emotional intelligence abilities, they readily get in control of their feelings and find ways to handle these situations without causing scenes.

Emotional Intelligence History

Emotional intelligence, the ability to control emotions, originally began in 1964, where Michael Beldoch wrote the term 'Emotional Intelligence' in the paper. In 1966, another article by B. Leuner, Emotional Intelligence and Emancipation, also featured the term 'Emotional Intelligence.' Howard Gardner again mentioned the term in 1983 with an effort to describe IQ and other related types of intelligence.

In this case, Gardner stated that various kinds of human IQ at the time failed to detail cognitive ability, which, henceforth, introduced emotional intelligence in his study. Subsequently, the term began being used in multiple papers, journals, and thesis such as A Study of Emotions: Developing Emotional Intelligence, written by Wayne Payne in 1985.

The term 'Emotional Quotient, EQ' surfaced in 1987 in an article written by Keith Beasley, which introduced a similar meaning to emotional intelligence. In the late 1980s, different models emerged to prove emotional intelligence in the context of controlling human feelings. Among them include the one created by Stanley Greenspan in 1989, another by Peter Salovey, and John Mayer in 1990. As such, the term became more popular in the 1990s, with several models being developed by different scientists.

However, emotional intelligence, like most findings, has received several critics, especially on its role in the business sector and the development of leadership skills. More advanced research in emotional intelligence entails the trait and ability of emotional intelligence. Trait emotional intelligence remains considered as a generic behavior passed from parents to offspring. Ability emotional intelligence is the practice learned by an individual, henceforth, gaining the technique of controlling their own emotions.

Chapter 5: Importance of Emotional Intelligence

Emotional Intelligence is linked to various aspects of one's life, if not all. It can, therefore, be said that it can be linked to our careers, job performance, and even our success. The following are, therefore, the various ways which have depicted the importance of emotional Intelligence:

Emotional Intelligence and Job Performance

Recently, there has been a rise in emotional intelligence awareness in management-focused literature together with leadership training summits. This gives us an indication that there exists a very strong relationship between job performance and emotional Intelligence. It not only proves to exist but also has depicted an array of value in different areas. One's workplace is a representation of a social community that is very separate from their personal life. This is also a place where increased appreciation of emotional Intelligence has been on the rise, allowing people to have an understanding of themselves and even others, be conversant with hard situations, and communicating in a more effective manner. This, therefore, means that employing emotional Intelligence at your workplace might greatly improve your personal and even other individuals' social capabilities.

Emotional Intelligence entails the management of emotions which improves job performance, which in turn helps people to stay calm and think logically, thus establishing good working relationships and achievement of goals. Apart from that, there is an evident relationship between emotional Intelligence and how senior employees manage their juniors. A manager who has got a high emotional intelligence is well conversant with the stress management skills and also how to recognize and manage the stress in other people. Therefore, if we put emotional Intelligence in the stress management perspective, then the relationship between job performance and emotional Intelligence is crystal clear. This is because one's commitment to one job is highly and positively impacted by stress management.

In many instances, emotional Intelligence usually applies to all kinds of employees and not only those at the management level. The employees that are at the lower rank in the hierarchy of an organization and have a high emotional intelligence usually have got desires and abilities to establish and maintain good relationships at the workplace. Apart from that, these individuals are good in management and resolution of conflicts.

This, therefore, means that they have the capability of sustaining relationships that exists in the workplace as compared to those with either low or moderate emotional Intelligence. In the current job market, many organizations are undergoing revolution and changes in different sectors. This has made organizations have the need for employees who can easily cope up with these changes and respond to them easily. This thus clearly describes the way in which emotional Intelligence is of value.

Emotional Intelligence and Resilience

Emotional Intelligence has proved to be a valuable tool in adversity as it has the potential of enhancing not only teamwork effectiveness and leadership abilities but is also an important tool in enhancing personal resilience. The impact of emotional Intelligence on the resilience of a person is the ability of that person to cope up with situations that are stressful. It has been clearly demonstrated by research that a person who has got high emotional Intelligence usually easily overcomes stressors and their negative impacts.

Focusing on leadership, a leader is usually expected to have increased responsibilities which usually are accompanied by potential stressors. In such a case, it is important for the person to have strong emotional Intelligence in order to be resilient and battle with these stressful conditions. From research where investigations were done into the link existing between emotional Intelligence and stress, it was found out that people who showed high emotional intelligence levels were not negatively affected by stressors.

These participants did an emotional intelligence ability-based test before the threat level that was posed by the two stressors was rated. After that, they reported their emotional reactions to the stressors before being subjected to physiological stress to also assess their responses. The findings of this research showed that emotional Intelligence has a relationship with lower threats. This study, therefore, provides us with a valid prediction that stress resilience is facilitated by Emotional Intelligence.

From further research done, the relationship between high levels of emotional Intelligence, the tendency to depressive behaviors, and resilience were drawn. It was established that there was a positive correlation that exists between mindfulness, self-compassion, and resilience with the rate of burnout. In conclusion, individuals who have got high emotional intelligence levels were more resilient and could not easily fall into depression or burnout.

Emotional Intelligence has a strong link to the individual's advancement and also their performance. Apart from that, it also made a suggestion that resilience acts as a mediator between self-motivated achievement and resilience. Resilience, in this case, has got a perseverance component that acts as a motivation to motivation when facing obstacles. From the various research findings and theories, we have seen a strong relationship between emotional Intelligence and resilience. We have clearly seen how one's emotional intelligence levels affect their resilience. This, therefore, has proved emotional Intelligence to be very important.

Emotional Intelligence and Motivation

Emotional Intelligence is a key component for motivation which in turn is very vital in the achievement of success. An emotionally intelligent person will always have an understanding of what they aspire and the necessary motor skills that they would need to achieve these aspirations. There are four elements that are said to make up motivation; how we commit ourselves to the goals we set, how ready we are to utilize opportunities, self-drive to improve, and how resilient we are. Motivation is said to be a psychological process that we use to psyche ourselves into action in order to realize a desirable outcome. It doesn't matter the action we are doing; whether dedication of much time to work on a project or just to change the TV channel using a remote, without being motivated, we cannot act.

This is because motivation energizes, arouses, sustains, and directs performance and behavior. The motivation that usually comes from within, also known as intrinsic motivation, usually drives us to the achievement of our full capability. A person who is emotionally intelligent has got both skills required to motivate themselves and those needed to motivate other people too. Self-motivation is the key to the achievement of one's goals. With self-motivation, emotionally intelligent people will always be capable of impacting the motivation of employees. The ability to determine the emotions and needs or concerns of others is a great skill to possess in relation to the determination of perfect methods of motivating individuals and teams.

From a study and research did, it was found out that the emotional Intelligence of a first-year graduate was positively linked to their self-motivation to studying the respective course and choosing that course.

Another study of senior employees with very high emotional Intelligence found out that they are good in arguments, have good behavior, and great work outcomes. It, therefore, means that a happy employee is a motivated employee. The capability to be conversant with anxiety and stress is a very useful emotional intelligence tool when it comes to motivation. From the above studies and research findings, it is clear that emotional Intelligence plays a major role in one's motivation. Since motivation is a very vital tool in our actions, then emotional Intelligence is also very important.

Emotional Intelligence and Decision-Making

Emotional Intelligence plays a key role in both professional and personal development. It not only has an impact on the way in which we handle our behaviors and control our social complexities but also the approaches we take in decision-making.

Having an in-depth understanding of the emotions you feel and the reason as to why you are feeling them can heavily impact your decision-making capabilities. This, therefore, means that if we carefully look into our emotions, then we can avoid making misleading and misguided decisions.

Emotional Intelligence is a very vital tool required in the prevention of making poor decisions based on our emotions, whereby lower emotional Intelligence can make you anxious and result in you making a poor misguided decision. This does not imply that we should keep emotions aside when making decisions but discovering these emotions which might not have any relationship with the problem and ensuring that they do not influence the decision that you are going to make. Negative emotions can be a stumbling block to decision-making and problem-solving in either your workplace or even personal circumstances. Being able to recognize emotions that are becoming a stumbling block to making rational decisions and being able to effectively ignore the emotions will prevent their negative influence on your decision. This, therefore, means that decision-making at this stage will be much favored as it will not be negatively influenced in any way.

From research done through observations and administering a series of questions, it was discovered that people and organizations reaped big benefits from a practical application of Emotional Intelligence in making decisions. This study had the aim of improving emotional intelligence awareness and how emotional intelligence skills can be employed in decision making.

From the observations, it was discovered that having training sessions on emotional Intelligence is one of the most effective ways to incorporate decision-making skills and also helps you to understand the possible consequences of poor decision-making.

Having an understanding of the causes and possible consequences of emotions gives you the freedom to manage and make a decision about the feeling. For instance, if you have an argument with your spouse the go to work without resolving it, you will probably stay angry the whole day. Being angry at work, your colleague might make an offer to you, but you dismiss it without even paying attention to it. This is a kind of emotional interference that can be very dangerous to your decision-making. If you have high emotional Intelligence, then you can be able to identify this form of emotional interference and manage it, thus avoiding making decisions that are emotionally driven. This, therefore, means that emotional Intelligence is vital when making decisions.

Emotional Intelligence and Success

There are things that mean different to different people. As happiness is so is a success which everyone has a different version of defining it. But no matter no success is defined, it is clear that emotional Intelligence plays an important part in its achievement. From history, most intelligent individuals are usually not attributed to the greatest successes.

This is because IQ is not sufficient on its own to enable one to succeed in life. In regards to this, you can be the most intelligent person, but if you lack an emotional quotient, you may fail to turn down people with negative thoughts about you and even manage stress. This shows that Emotional Intelligence is sometimes even more powerful as compared to IQ in life success.

Your emotional Intelligence is the actual thing that helps you to achieve your life objectives and realize great successes. Therefore, developing emotional Intelligence would influence your achievements through contribution to your morale, cooperation, and most importantly, motivation by a great margin. In a workplace, the managers and employees who perform well as compared to others usually employ strategies that are associated with emotional Intelligence in the management of conflicts, reduction of stress, and thus achieving their goals.

In the recent past, there has been blooming evidence of a range of activities said to constitute emotional Intelligence that is now vital in determining success.

This refers to success both in the workplace and also in one's personal life. It incorporates applications that we associate within our daily lives in relationships, businesses, and even parenting. Emotional Intelligence guides one to easily manage their emotions in situations that are likely to provoke anxiety. These situations include when taking examinations at the university. It is also positively associated with success in social functioning and personal relationships.

In social relationships, success achievable with the employment of emotional intelligence skills to determine other people's emotions, then adopt their emotional states and thus regulate the way they behave. This briefly shows how important emotional Intelligence is in achieving success in the different spheres of life.

Emotional Intelligence and Communication

One's ability to have the knowledge and understanding of their emotions might aid them to be aware and understand the feelings that other people are experiencing.

Considering communication in conflict resolution in the workplace, people with great emotional intelligence levels would most probably approach the conflict in the most reasonable way possible and negotiate together with others to finally come up with a reasonable outcome. On the contrary, a person with lower levels of emotional Intelligence will not be able to solve the conflict in a reasonable calm manner thus might even end up without a solution at the end.

In the workplace, relationships are usually affected by the manner in which we can manage our emotions and also understanding the emotions of those around us. The capability to do this helps us in communicating without necessarily resorting to confrontation. If you have high emotional Intelligence, then it is beyond doubt that you are equipped with conflict management skills, and thus you will be able to put up a meaningful relationship guaranteed capacity to understand and address the needs of those they engage with.

In recent years, emotional Intelligence has been able to receive much attention that drives effective communication within individuals and even teams. On close examination of emotional Intelligence as a reason for team success, you will find that it does not only do it drives the viability of a team but also affects communication quality in a positive way.

Achievement of successful communication in relation to successful negotiation and conflict has a very close relationship with high emotional intelligence levels. In this case, individuals with lower emotional Intelligence would be so defensive in such stressful situations. This will instead escalate the conflict instead of managing it. If you have high emotional Intelligence, then this means that you have got the necessary skills to ensure effective communication without resulting in a confrontation. From this, we can easily derive the importance and great contribution that high levels of emotional Intelligence add to the achievement of effective communication.

Emotional Intelligence and Happiness

Just like any other word or feeling, happiness seems something easy but actually getting to understand it is when you will realize that it is a hard nut to crack. This is because different people have got different instances and experiences that they describe to mean happiness to them. Truly, happiness means different to different people, but undoubtedly, emotional Intelligence is a great requirement to have despite the kind of interpretation you prefer. Happiness is an emotional intelligence facilitator that contributes to each and everyone's self-actualization, which positively impacts our happiness.

From a study where the relationship between different interpersonal relations and emotional Intelligence was examined, it was discovered that individuals with high emotional Intelligence scored highly in self-monitoring, social skills, and taking an empathic perspective. Apart from that, they also scored highly in affectionate relationships, satisfaction in relationships, and cooperation with their partners.

Emotional intelligence skills are very important when it comes to reducing stress; thus, in turn, they will positively impact one's happiness and wellbeing in general. Apart from the motivational value that it possesses, happiness acts as a monitor to the wellbeing of an individual. It is also a source of a positive mood to the manner in which the person copes up and meets daily needs, pressures and challenges.

Positivity is what actually encourages the emotional energy required in the increment of an individual's motivational levels, which is responsible for getting things done. It actually helps one to be successful in what they are doing and even gets to the extent of telling them the extent of success they are actually achieving. From a study done by Furnham, it was realized that a large section of variance that is evident in the wellbeing and happiness of a person is determined by their emotional intelligence levels. This refers to their ability to stabilize their emotions, social competence, and even relationship skills. Although these emotional intelligence skills are not the only source of one's happiness, it is very vital to realize that they contribute and impact our happiness up to 50%. This, therefore, prove it to be a very vital thing which should always be put into consideration.

Happiness has, therefore, proven to be closely linked to emotional Intelligence if the research and studies detailed above are to go by. A person with high emotional Intelligence will have the necessary skills to dodge any obstructions that might act as a hindrance to happiness. On the other hand, an individual who has low levels of emotional Intelligence will not be able to cope up with these obstructions and end up always sad and stressed up. This thus proves emotional Intelligence to be vital.

Emotional Intelligence and Goals

In life, each and every person has got goals and achievements that they hope to achieve someday in life. In order to achieve these goals, there are various conditions that usually impact it either positively or negatively. Emotional Intelligence will drive you to realize self-actualization, which requires you to first get motivated. In order to have the motivation, you will need to be happy with whatever you do. This is because lack of happiness will challenge you in pursuit of the motivational levels that are required to achieve your goals.

In order to realize success and eventually achieve your dreams and goals, there is a need to employ emotional intelligence skills. If you have high emotional intelligence levels, you will definitely perform excellently in what you are doing in all aspects. The effectiveness of a person or a team in a certain process directly reflects their emotional intelligence skill level. Those with high emotional intelligence levels will perform well, while those with lower intelligence levels would perform dismally and might never achieve their goals.

Chapter 6: Mind Control

Mind control sounds like a devious plot in a movie, but you have most likely experienced it many times a day for many years and never noticed it. Mind control, or the idea of thought-reform, is a controversial theory and practice, but one that does not necessarily mean tricking and scheming. As a matter of fact, mind control can be as simple as subliminal suggestion used to steer one in the direction you want rather than the direction they were going autonomously.

There are many schools of thought in regards to mind control, but for this book, let's look at a common example of mind control to start. Color, smell, sight, sound, and taste are used on the consumer by every company selling a product to advance their customers and sales. When you enter your local grocery store, often there are fresh cut flowers at the entrance. Now, how often have you bought those flowers? Chances are, never, if maybe a time or two because you forgot a special occasion. Grocers use the presence of these flowers as a means of manipulating the subconscious of their customers. Fresh cut flowers are, well, fresh. Ripe. Pleasant. They subliminally convey their thought of freshness, and your local grocery store wants you to be thinking about all the fresh produce they have waiting for you. More often, these grocers make more on the sale of their fresh produce over name brand canned and frozen produce, and if you buy the products they have available, more of your dollars go in their pocket as opposed to mass production companies.

Product placement on television and in movies. The music you hear in a store or even an elevator. Friends that are so convincing, you can't help but agree, or you find yourself always saying yes to them.

Re-education is a very optimal but controversial tool in mind control. The ability to re-educate another person's previous thought process or beliefs is possible but can take time. At the heart of re-education sits repetition. I repeat, repetition. By repeating the same belief, idea, or thought to another person repeatedly, you impress upon them the change from their own ideas towards your own. And this repetition leads to immersion in the idea or action you want them to follow. Being immersed in an idea, the idea in question always being repeated, the idea or goal always being spoken of, leads to the individual re-examining their previous feelings about the issue. Re-examining one's feelings often leads to them coming to a new conclusion. Your conclusion. You have just exerted a form of mind control on another individual, and now they agree with you.

Priming an individual is another effective way to get what you want. Some who see this activity negatively may refer to it as indoctrination, but the goal is not to necessarily start a cult. Priming involves softening a person towards you and your ideas, easing them into the thought that you know what is best. Softening can include hours of conversation, empathizing with them, and showing them that you care or love them. You care about what happens; you understand them. Once you have a foundation of trust through understanding and priming, soft persuasion towards the new idea, belief, or action can be introduced. It is imperative that you have formed a mutual bond of respect with the person who you want to influence.

A few techniques to help you on your path to persuasion using coercion may involve thinking for others, being specific in your logic and requests, creating a real sense of urgency, and stressing the importance of your goal or idea. When presenting someone with a change in long-held ideas or requests, thinking for them takes the pressure of deciding off them. People often have enough on their mental plates as it is; you shouldn't be asking them to take on more, especially when you can do the heavy lifting for them. Explain exactly why they should see things your way, offering as many examples as possible as to the correctness of your idea, proof that what you want is not only right but is proven to be effective or accurate. Once you have specifically lined out why they should agree with you, tell them what is next and why things need to be done your way. Be friendly but as firm and confident in your pitch to them as you need be, and often discouraging questions until you are finished explaining your stance helps steer others in your direction. They often forget their questions or objections as they listen to you explain what you want, why, and what you think needs to happen next to achieve the goal. It is all about the goal.

While on the topic of your goals and what you want to achieve, it is imperative to stress the importance of what you want to achieve. If others are consistently being spoken with on how important the idea or goal is, and specifics on why it is so important, eventually they start to see your idea as more than just something you want, but an issue of utmost importance. Your thought or goal becomes something more, and it should be more to you too. It should be a movement. A goal doesn't have to be a social ideal to be a movement; you just need others to feel its importance as much as you do.

Everybody wishes to be on the right side of history, no matter how big or small the issue is. And all it takes is someone to see your want as a matter that needs to be addressed or adjusted, and where there is one person who agrees with you, there are two, and more soon to follow. Other people want it too. And it is not just important; it is imperative. And it needs to happen now. Creating a sense of urgency is another effective form of utilizing mind control techniques to your benefit. Making urgent statements or claiming that this situation is time sensitive will create an emotional response in those you wish to influence or persuade. A specific deadline needs to be in place, but the idea that this can't wait long needs to be an underlying sentiment.

The quicker you get other people on board, the more important you convince them your want is, the more urgent they believe things are, the less resistance you will run into. Repeating equals results. The more information backing your idea or goal people are given, the more likely they will let you think for them and just go with the flow. The more urgent the matter is, the fewer times people have to ask discouraging questions or second guess their shift in ideas.

Being consistent is the core aspect of implementing mind control techniques to get what you want. Consistently repeating what you want, and be consistent when rejecting old ideas or goals. Be consistent when speaking about what needs to happen, when, and why. These factors should be underlined, in bold print, repeated regularly, and the time sensitivity needs to be stressed.

Another great technique when using mind control is to ask small things of others, or asking for small changes in another's ideas, and then expanding from there. Let's use a raise from your employer as an example. If you want a decent increase in pay, don't ask for your top-dollar pay increase. Ask for a small increase in pay based on your performance and loyalty. Your boss will agree (considering you are worthy of the raise, to begin with) and think that they got off cheap, keeping you happy. After you have reached the first step in reaching your ultimate pay goal, ask for more work. Let your employer know you are more than happy taking on more responsibility. You can possibly save them money if you are doing more work than before; they may not have to hire another employee to work weekends if you are willing to come in for a few hours on a Saturday.

Now, you have a pay increase, but you have more responsibility. It only seems fair that you are paid a little more now that you are a more valuable resource for your employer to utilize. It's better they give you another slight pay increase to cover your knowledge and expertise in the workplace than bother trying to hire another employee to replace you. Do you see how simple it can be? Now, that isn't saying that you have a boss or employer this would work on, but if you are implementing the other tools you have in your fast-growing arsenal, you are now a very well-liked employee and co-worker who knows how to influence and persuade others to see things the way you do.

Your employer may dislike the idea of paying you even more than before, but sometimes it's not just your work ethic that matters; sometimes it's what you bring to the table for everyone you encounter.

The final technique of mood control we should consider is generosity. You should always strive to give more than you take from others. When you give more of your time, your effort, your attention to others, they appreciate it. They remember it. And, when the moment comes that you want something in return, it is much harder to say no, or disagree, or refuse to cooperate with another who has freely offered up so much to them. Even in circumstances or changes, others may not want to agree or get on board with; if they know that you have been offered the same courtesy by you previously, they find it hard to go against you. It falls back to persuasion, influence, and reciprocation. Most often, those that you have committed your time and attention to will return the favor.

Even if you are met with resistance by someone who you have given to, a gentle reminder of what you have done for them is often all that is needed to get them on board with what you want. Sometimes it isn't the loudest voice in the room that matters, but the most consistent and softest from the individual who has done the most to help others. That soft but firm voice can be yours; you only need to take your opportunities as they present themselves.

Who uses mind control?

Media Producers

Just as our five senses are our guides in life, they can also be our enemies and traitors. Our sense of sight and the visual processing areas of the brain are very powerful.

When we dream, we always reflect visual images in them, and usually, it is someone we remember. These images transmitted to our visual mind manipulate a powerful technique to control the mind.

Traditionally, media production was in the hands of companies and institutions. Such manipulations can use visual and subconscious mental control, taking complete control of any individual's emotions. They have been used as recently as 21st-century Presidential elections. Both experiments and personal experience will confirm this to you. Have you ever loved a song until it stuck in your head? How easy is it to get out of your mind? The power of audio manipulation is even greater when it is undetected.

Lovers

Lovers are stuck in the world they find themselves in because their way of growing up inevitably determines how they behave as soon as they reach age. If a person grew up with an alcoholic family, it is almost inevitable that they grew up the same way; it is rare who chooses the correct path. Instead, those who grew up where everything is forbidden to them, as soon as they find themselves in the outside world, can feel free or even go crazy. In short, each individual has different opinions on what could be good or bad, right or wrong. The fundamental thing in love arises when a couple tries to be together, and having two opposite characters, neither of them wants to change their way of being. When this happens, there cannot be any stable relationship. Very few couples manage to go further, even if this does not start from their being, but it becomes easier to learn by loving.

Sales people

If a salesperson asks a regular customer to write a brief endorsement of the product they buy, hopefully, they will say yes. If someone asks their significant other to take some of the business cards to pass out at work, hopefully, they will say yes. If you write any kind of blog and ask another blogger to provide a link to yours on their blog, hopefully, they will say yes. With even more yesses, it will continue to grow and thrive. This is the very simple basis of marketing. Marketing is nothing more than using mind control to get other people to buy something or to do something beneficial for someone else. And the techniques can easily be learned.

Writers

Think of writing a guest spot for someone else who has their own blog. Begin small. Send them a paragraph or two discussing the idea. Then make an outline of the idea and send that in an email. Then write the complete draft you would like them to use and send it along. When asking a customer for a testimonial, start by asking for a few lines in an email. Then ask the customer to expand those few lines into a testimonial that covers at least half a typed page. Soon the customer will be ready for an hour-long webcast extolling the virtues of the product and your great customer service skills.

Everything must have a deadline that really exists. Everyone has heard the salesperson who said to decide quickly because the deal might not be available later or another customer was coming in, and they might get it. That is a total fabrication, and everyone knows it to be true. There are no impending other customers, and the deal is not going to disappear. There is no real sense of urgency involved. But everyone does it. There are too many situations where people are given a totally fake deadline by someone who thinks it will instill a great sense of urgency for the completion of the task. It is not only totally not effective but completely unneeded. Only leave free things available for a finite amount of time. When asking customers for testimonials, be certain to mention the last possible day for it to be received to be able to be used. Some people will be unable to assist, but having people unable to participate is better than never being able to begin.

In Education

By educating impressionable children, society essentially teaches them to become "ideal" members of society. They are taught and trained in certain ways that fulfill the desires of the government and authorities, and most people don't even think twice about it.

Advertising and Propaganda

By putting advertising and propaganda everywhere, those in control are capable of eliminating people's feeling of self-worth and encourage them to *need* what is being sold, as opposed to just wanting it. This is essentially a subliminal strategy to make people feel poorly about themselves so that they will purchase whatever is being advertised to increase their feelings of self-worth.

Chapter 7: Mind Control Techniques

The technique of mind control has always existed; this becomes interesting when it becomes vital to persuade a person, especially when you happen to have to face him in the eye. This helps us keep everything under control, especially if you risk running into someone who wants to play the same manipulation game. It is not just a question of wanting to dominate. Here it is a matter of pleasure in wanting to do it, of controlling everything that happens around us, since not being able to do it would make the individual himself devoid of personal self-control.

Learn how commerce can persuade customers into buying their goods and services. Recognizing such methods will help in dealing with the power of persuasion.

Manipulators believe they are always making sensible choices, but they are not always in total control, and sometimes this gets out of hand. A very present example is when we are children; in that case, the adult influences us. We do not have the slightest control over ourselves except to indulge the parent. This is deliberate manipulation.

Many are persuaded to vote for a party because of what they promise for the future, even if they don't necessarily believe in their policies. We must be careful to understand when we are being manipulated by someone to recognize what is right or wrong in our lives. Most of the manipulation is totally done for its beneficial purposes, but in this regard, one must also know how to recognize this tool's good. From here, I propose a lot of mental tools.

Recognizing the Art of Manipulation

What then, in our everyday lives, do we need to be wary of?

Persuasive Language

Words can be so much more powerful as they inspire and encourage us, even to the point of manipulation. How many are the times you have been inspired by a good orator whose daring speech motives you into action? Words even influence when we are lost completely in a great book. The art of words can be so influential in coercing us to believe something, even when our eyes tell us differently.

Advertisers and salespeople use language to convince their goods are just what we are looking for. Using words, such as:

Affordable; Easy to use; Safe; Enjoyable; Time Saving; Guaranteed to last.

· **Politicians will use language, such as:**

"We" - to encompass you in their world.

These are all communication tactics to make us feel included, so therefore important.

· **Bullies use language along with aggressive behavior to achieve their own selfish goals.**

· **Criminal predators, such as psychopaths, sociopaths, and narcissists, are all people who learn the use of persuasive language. This is a means to get their own way and gain control over another person.**

Techniques Used in Mind Control Present-day mind control is both innovative and mental. Tests demonstrate that basically by uncovering the techniques for mind control, the impacts can be diminished or disposed of, at any rate for mind control publicizing and promulgation. Increasingly hard to counter are the physical interruptions, which the military-mechanical complex keeps on creating and enhance.

1. It has consistently been an eventual tyrant's definitive dream to "teach" normally receptive youngsters. Subsequently, it has been a focal segment to Communist and Fascist oppressive regimes from the beginning of time. Nobody has been increasingly instrumental in uncovering the motivation of present-day instruction than Charlotte Iserbyt — one can start an investigation into this region by downloading her book as a free PDF, The Deliberate

Dumbing Down of America, revealing the job of Globalist establishments in forming a future planned to deliver servile automatons reigned over by a completely taught, mindful exclusive class.

2. Promotions and Propaganda – Edward Bernays has been referred to as the creator of the consumerist culture that was planned principally to focus on individuals' mental self-portrait (or scarcity in that department) so as to transform a need into a need. This was at first imagined for items, for example, cigarettes, for instance.

Nonetheless, Bernays additionally noted in his 1928 book, Propaganda, that "purposeful publicity is the official arm of the imperceptible government." This can be seen most unmistakably in the advanced police state and the developing native nark culture, enveloped with the pseudo-enthusiastic War on Terror. The expanding union of media has empowered the whole corporate structure to converge with the government, which currently uses the idea of promulgation arrangement. Media, print, motion pictures, TV, and link news would now be able to work flawlessly to incorporate a general message which appears to have the ring of truth since it originates from such a significant number of sources at the same time. When one moves toward becoming sensitive to recognizing the fundamental "message," one will see this engraving all over. What's more, this isn't even to specify subliminal informing.

3. Simply glance back at the books and motion pictures that you thought were implausible or "sci-fi" and investigate society today. For a nitty-gritty breakdown of explicit models, Vigilant Citizen is an incredible asset that will most likely make you take a gander at "amusement" in a totally unique light.

4. Sports, Politics, Religion – Some may resent seeing religion, or even legislative issues, put together with sports as a technique for mind control. The focal topic is the equivalent all through: isolate and prevail. The systems are very straightforward: impede the common propensity of individuals to participate for their endurance, and train them to frame groups bowed on control and winning. Sports has consistently had a job as a key diversion that corrals innate propensities into a non-significant occasion, which in present-day America has arrived at silly extents where challenges will break out over a game VIP leaving their city, yet basic human issues, for example, freedom is chuckled away is immaterial.

5. Food, Water, and Air – Additives, poisons, and other nourishment harms actually modify mind science to make mildness and indifference. Fluoride in drinking water has been demonstrated to bring down IQ; Aspartame and MSG are excitotoxins which energize synapses until they kick the bucket, and simple access to the inexpensive food that contains these toxins, by and large, has made a populace that needs center and inspiration for a functioning way of life. The vast majority of the cutting-edge world is flawlessly prepped for uninvolved responsiveness — and acknowledgment — of the authoritarian tip top.

6. Medications — we can equate this to any addictive substance. However, the mission of mind controllers is to be certain you are dependent on something. One noteworthy arm of the cutting edge mind control motivation is psychiatry, which expects to characterize all individuals by their issue instead of their human potential. This was foreshadowed in books, for example, Brave New World. Today, it has been taken to considerably assist limits as medicinal oppression has grabbed hold where about everybody has a type of confusion — especially the individuals who question authority. The utilization of nerve tranquilizers in the military has prompted record quantities of suicides. To top it all off, the cutting-edge medication state currently has over 25% of U.S. youngsters on mind-desensitizing drugs.

7. Military testing — There is a long history associated with the military as the proving ground for mind control. The military personality is maybe the most pliable, as the individuals who seek the afterlife in the military by and large resound to the structures of progression, control, and the requirement for unchallenged submission to a mission. For the expanding number of military individuals scrutinizing their influence, an ongoing story featured DARPA's arrangements for trans cranial mind control head protectors that will keep them centered.

8. Electromagnetic range — An electromagnetic soup encompasses all of us, charged by present-day gadgets of comfort which have been appeared to directly affect mind work. In an implicit affirmation of what is conceivable, one scientist has been working with a "divine being head protector" to instigate dreams by adjusting the electromagnetic field of the mind. Our advanced soup has us latently washed by conceivably mind-changing waves, while a wide scope of potential outcomes, for example, phone towers, is currently accessible to the eventual personality controller for more straightforward mediation.

Mind control is more common than most people think. In many instances, it happens under what is perceived as normal circumstances like through education, religion, TV programs, advertisements, and so much more. Cults and their leadership use mind control to influence their members and control whatever they do. However, when one realizes it, they can get out and start afresh.

Chapter 8: The Secrets of Neuro Linguistic Programming

Neuro-Linguistic Programming or NLP, as it is commonly referred to, is one of the most prevalent systems of mind control in the entire universe. John Grinder and Richard Bandler invented this famous method of mind control in the 1970s. It would later gain much popularity in the new age, occult, and psychoanalytic spaces back in the 1980s. Later on, in the 1990s and 2000s, NLP started to make inroads in the political, marketing, as advertising markets. It is also very crucial to note that NLP has, to some extent, become a type of devilish and pernicious force in the entire global space, which has been studied by nearly everybody in the business spheres. Those who have mastered the techniques of this great dark psychology trait are known for owning a Rasputin-like capability of tricking persons into some incredible ways, nearly at all times.

Neuro-Linguistic Programming is used today for a variety of different things. People use it to overcome anxiety, the stress of trauma, and fears. This program is used for their benefit, but others use it for hidden desires.

We would love to say that the only place you will find NLP is in your therapist's office. However, we actually see it in everyday life. From your workplace to the ads on your social media accounts, you can actually see it everywhere. NLP does not only focus on what people say but, more importantly, focus on what people are doing. Our body language says more than our mouths ever could.

NLP has been under the debate of whether it is an actual science or if it is considered a pseudoscience.

There is a pretty broad range of techniques used within NLP, and this also makes it difficult to lock down which pieces actually work. There have been some studies performed, and oftentimes the results were inconclusive. In some, it appears as if NLP had made a true improvement in subjects with psychosis, instability, and other unwanted traits. Others worked on looking at its effectiveness to help issues like PTSD and anxiety. The results came back exceptionally varied.

Neuro-Linguistic Programming has been around for more than forty years.

It also has its place in the world of Psychology and Dark Psychology. Due to the fact that it is quite unstructured, it is difficult to show true proof of its success. There are also a plethora of different ideas and ways of executing NLP. For some, it is a very effective form of therapy that truly helps them lead better lives. For others, it may not benefit them at all. These people will need to look at more traditional therapies to work through their issues and lead happier and mentally healthier life.

NLP History

NLP is, in a way, a method of mind control. However, the majority of the credit is given to two California boys, John Grinder and Richard Bandler. They wanted to take the heart of linguistic therapy and improve it. Find the pieces that truly worked and make something better.

The three people that they studied were chosen due to the fact that they had better results with their clients than most others in their field. In fact, people found their success to be odd and uncommon. Naturally, inquisitive minds wanted to know what these people had in common and why their methods worked so well. They studied them in live sessions and via videotape.

NLP is subtle. When we think about normal hypnotherapy, we think about people falling asleep and acting out strange and silly acts. Realistically, it is used for much more meaningful purposes. For example, people use hypnotherapy to help them stop smoking or to deal with traumas of the past that may not have been coped with. NLP does things a bit differently. It is much more suggestive and not so in your face.

In the beginning, Neuro-Linguistic Programming was thought to be as helpful as products like "snake juice" from the days of the old west. Businesses were jumping on the bandwagon to learn about it so they could, in turn, use it to help them gain profits from consumers. In addition, everyone from therapists to political figures started to want the information on this type of "programming." It seriously started to blow up in terms of popularity.

Companies became interested in NLP because it can help them communicate more clearly. Businesses that use NLP have experienced better growth in their companies as a whole.

Not only can it help people become better negotiators, but it can also help them stay motivated. When you feel comfortable at work, and you feel like everyone is giving it their all, it's easy to build a solid team. Being a confident leader that pays attention to tone, body language, and verbiage will help lead to better success. Implementing the practices of NLP can promote growth for companies.

As people started to employ these tactics, they started to notice changes in their teams. Boosts in morale and productivity. Now we see NLP happening around us every day. This is not necessarily a bad thing as people that practice NLP tend to be more self-aware. In turn, they tend to make better choices that are made from rationality rather than emotions.

Pillars of NLP

There are four main points to NLP; they are referred to as the Pillars of NLP. They are Behavioral Flexibility, Rapport, Outcome Thinking, and Sensory Awareness. There is no difference in importance concerning another. It would help if you had time to evaluate each point and which is the best, to be able to understand better who to remove from your life, in this case, the fakes. The first pillar is Behavioral Flexibility. Basically, this means to go with the flow. When people can see that the tactic they are currently using isn't working and adapt their behavior, it can have great results. Being able to quickly change your perspective will allow more people to understand you.

Creating a good rapport with someone is simply getting them to trust you quickly. In addition, it is the ability to form quick relationships with people. It is easy to build rapport by using common language, being polite, and showing empathy. There are many ways to build a good rapport with a person; these are only a few.

Then we move on to Outcome Thinking. It is exactly what it states, spending the time to think about the end result of what you want. Oftentimes, people get stuck on a certain point that is commonly negative. It consumes the thought pattern and can make choosing the correct route to where you actually want to go difficult. With outcome thinking, you are always working toward an end goal. This can promote better decision-making along the way.

Lastly, we have Sensory Awareness. Being aware of the surroundings contributes to knowing what is actually going on. It can also help you easily understand how you need to behave in that situation.

The more you learn about these four pillars, the more success you will have with NLP. They are the foundation, and anyone who wants to learn NLP will spend a lot of time on each one. Knowing as many points of view as possible allows you to defend better what life puts you in front of, especially those who want to manipulate, control, or cause damage to your life. All sciences grow and change over the course of time, and we imagine that this one will also continue to evolve.

After focusing on what the yes were doing, word choice, and rapport, this therapy started to grow and focus on other aspects. In the '80s, the people using NLP were focusing on what it is that causes feelings inside of us. This helped therapists to figure out how to help someone deal with their individual problems.

More and more people started using the techniques found with NLP, but they wanted to put different names to it. To say they had come up with it all on their own.

The people in the here and now that are using NLP have a variety of different reasons for doing it. Some of it is to help themselves become better people, while for others, it is about weeding out the rats in their lives. Businesses use it in team-building and marketing techniques. The world of Neuro-Linguistic Programming is truly immense. First of all, they live freely; they can face any situation, choose, and be guided by their emotions and feelings. Understanding the behaviors and actions of people can help to clue you in on what's really going on around you. This falls into Sensory

Awareness. It is startling what you can learn from looking at someone's body position and paying attention to things like their tone of voice. People really do tell you everything you need to know with very little conversation.

Whether you are at your job or heading for a late-night party downtown honing these skills can keep you mentally and physically protected against predators. Knowing NLP techniques can also inform you when other people are using them for darker desires. Many people use these practices to become their best selves. However, others have more nefarious intent.

Obviously, when you can adapt to a situation and make well-thought-out choices, you are going to be more successful.

How Does it Work?

NLP may seem like enchantment or spellbinding. During treatment, the subject dives deep into their oblivious personality and filters through layers and layers of convictions and discernments to wind up mindful of an involvement in early youth that is in charge of a standard of conduct. NLP takes a shot at the rule that everybody has every one of the assets they have to roll out positive improvements in their very own life. NLP strategies are utilized as a device to encourage these changes.

NLP Therapy can be sans substance. That implies the specialist can be viable without thinking about the issue in incredible detail. Consequently, the specialist need not be told about the occasion or even the issue, in this manner guaranteeing protection for the customer. Other than this, we likewise have a non-exposure understanding in which the communication between the customer and the advisor is kept secret.

NLP puts stock in the flawlessness of nature in human creation. Henceforth NLP urges the customer to perceive their tangible sensitivities and use them to react to a specific issue. Indeed, NLP additionally accepts that the brain is fit for finding even fixes to illnesses and infections.

NLP procedures include non-invasive, a medication-free treatment that enables the customer to find better approaches for managing enthusiastic issues, for example, low confidence, uneasiness, absence of certainty, ruinous relationship designs (adapting to separation), and are fruitful inadequate mourning guiding.

NLP has its underlying foundations in the field of social science, created by Pavlov, Skinner, and Thorndike. It utilizes physiology and the oblivious personality to change points of view and consequently conduct.

Dark Traits of Manipulative People

Among the groups of the Dark Triad, there is a conglomeration of personality traits that are oftentimes seen in criminals. It is not a surprise to realize that most criminals have quite a bit in common. Taking notice of these dark traits is a great way of figuring out if someone has malicious intent toward you or not. There are a variety of different dark traits that we see on an everyday basis. You may know someone who is very spiteful. Anyone that does something they don't like will pay for it. Sometimes it will be petty retaliation, but it can explode into something much more dangerous, depending on who you are dealing with. Criminals tend to be spiteful, as they have malicious intent with their transgressions.

Another dark trait that you want to watch out for is egoism. Some criminals scramble their way to the top because of their giant egos and their ability to only care about themselves. Keeping an eye on a big ego can save you a lot of trouble, especially in relationships and business.

Have you ever met someone that had loose morals? You know that person that really doesn't have much regard for if what they are doing is right or wrong. Someone that even when they know what they are doing is wrong, does it anyway and then just laughs it off. This is a personality trait referred to as moral disengagement. Obviously, the ability to commit a crime and not feel terrible about it is something common among criminals, a pretty dark trait.

Earlier, we discussed Machiavellianism. That person that will go to any means to get what they want. When trying to track down criminals, these are some of the hardest to catch as they tend to also be some of the smartest out there. Even experts of NLP can have a hard time locking this trait down.

Entitlement or Psychological Entitlement is also a dark trait that we commonly see in criminals and everyday adversaries. Unfortunately, the world's sense of entitlement has gone off the rails.

Self-interest is another trait that you need to watch out for. We all have tendencies to be selfish; however, for some people, it is to an extreme. In addition, their self-interest could be used to motivate them in gaining betterment in finances or society. Those that are self-interested also tend to be extremely manipulative.

Then we have the narcissist. We spoke of the narcissist earlier, but their traits are very common among criminals. They have a need for attention and commonly an inflated sense of self. This could be in how they look, how they think, or how they act. The narcissist thinks that their ideas are the best, and therefore criminal intent goes hand-in-hand with the narcissist.

Psychopathy means that you lack the ability to empathize with people. They have an extreme lack of concern where others are involved. This dark trait can also lead to a lack of self-control and extremely impulsive behaviors. Obviously, when thinking about criminals, this trait rings true for many of the extreme horrors we have witnessed in the past.

The last dark trait that we think needs to be discussed is sadism. A sadist is a person that likes to inflict pain. In fact, they take pleasure in causing other people pain. In fact, many sadists find joy and completely tearing you down mentally.

Behavior Imitation

Behavior imitation is something that can be used for good and for bad. Oftentimes, as children, we mimic the behavior of the people around us. It helps us to learn social norms. In addition, it helps us feel like we fit in with the crowd. Many traditions have been built off of people mimicking other people's behavior.

Here again, it makes us feel as if we belong. Additionally, it can help us build relationships and understand the people around us more easily. While many people use behavior imitation for the right reasons, there are many others who don't.

Criminals who are socially awkward have a tendency to act like the people around them It is a manipulation tactic that works quite well when people don't exactly know how to behave appropriately. While some people are very good at mimicking those around them, it will be quite obvious when others are trying to do this. Cases of extreme social awkwardness will not allow the person to genuinely behave like those that are around them.

Another way that behavior imitation is prevalent with criminals is when they idolize someone or something. They will change their very persona to reflect that for which they have admiration. The new generation of Nazis mimics the ways of the old because they still believe his blasphemous thoughts to be true. This is truly scary behavior imitation.

Body Language

A person's body language is one of the biggest tells in how they are feeling and what they may be planning. Those who work on learning NLP techniques spend a ton of time studying body language.

Body language is how we speak without using words. It can suggest that you are happy, sad, open to conversation, or completely closed off from everyone. Not only is it shown through your actual body but also through your eyes. Paying attention to the eyes is also an important part of NLP. There are some truths to be found in body language that may not be what the words coming out of someone's mouth are actually stating.

It has been found that we gather more information from a person's facial expressions, eyes, and body language than we ever could from their spoken words. So, learning how to read body language can help you in just about every situation you find yourself in. Learning how shady people act can help you in avoiding unwanted issues.

When you first start learning about body language, you will be able to easily identify some emotions. The signs of this can be seen easily, but finding out when someone is anxious or uncomfortable can be a bit more difficult.

Studying non-verbal cues will take you to every area of the body. For example, slightly dilated pupils may not be from bright light but may, in fact, be due to arousal. If someone is constantly biting at their lip, it could be a sign of stalling or higher levels of anxiety in the current situation.

How a person is standing or sitting also gives us some clues as to how they are feeling. A person with their arms folded around them is less likely to want to be approached. Whereas an open stance with your hands on your hips means you are likely in control of the situation, or you may be aggressive. Learning these types of things can seriously help improve your ability to pick out a troublemaker in a crowd.

Ever been in an area and realized someone was acting kind of shifty? You know, like moving around the room frequently and during conversations they are unable to hold eye contact. Your ability to notice this is because most people have at least some basic knowledge on how to read a person's body language.

Your posture also plays a key role in what your body is saying to other people. People who slouch and tend to wrap their arms around themselves are typically closed off.

They may be feeling unwelcome or anxious. On the other hand, an open posture with your chin up and shoulders back is very welcoming. It shows that you are open to conversation, friendly, and approachable. Not only does your body language help people decide how to approach you, but theirs also helps you decide about them. The more you delve into NLP, the more pieces of body language you will pick up. It can seriously help when trying to identify those that are threatening and may have mal intent.

Language Imitation

Language imitation is another piece of NLP that should be taken into consideration. When we talk to someone, even if we speak the same language, it can be difficult for us to understand each other. Each individual has what is referred to as a common language. Common language is simply the words a person uses frequently and understands better than others. When you are in a therapy session or at work, and you are listening to someone talk, understanding what they are saying can be hard. This doesn't work well for anyone as the person listening is actually learning anything. This is a major issue and can cause massive detriment to a company or a person's mental status.

Working to hear how someone talks, the phrases they use, and the tone that they have can help you succeed in language imitation. When you can speak in common language to the person or people you are addressing, you will be much more successful. Understanding will be promoted, and what everyone gets out of what you have to say will be more beneficial. Mimicking someone's language is more difficult than mimicking their body language. Someone that is very good at picking up other people's common language can be a danger if they have intentions of doing harm.

When we speak in a common language, it promotes trust. Putting trust into someone that wants to use your language against you is obviously something you want to avoid. So, be careful when dealing with people that quickly change their voice to match those that are around them. The ones that pick up on little pieces of context and repeat them to gain sympathy, trust, or control. It may be hard to recognize at first, but the more aware you become of your surrounding, the easier this will be to spot.

Criminals tend to be good at this parrot-like behavior. They understand that to get people to like you; they absolutely need to understand you. If control is what someone is looking for, this is a good place to start and get their hooks in.

Chapter 9: Manipulation and Persuasion

What is Manipulation?

According to each individual, manipulation does not exist, or at most, it happens to people as if it can never affect us personally. But manipulation is everywhere; in any sentence or gesture towards someone else, the aim is always to manipulate, even unconsciously. Indeed if you've made it this far, obviously being used, you certainly want to regain control of your emotions. We do not want to induce you to manipulate, but to help you understand how to get out of this tunnel. I think it's time to take back your life, take control of your mind, and finally be free and happy.

How Psychology Correlate with Manipulation

Three psychological conditions that are associated with manipulation are narcissism, psychosis, and sociopathy. Before talking about how the different ways manipulators might attempt to influence others, we'll give some background on these underlying psychological conditions.

As is true of many psychological measures, NPD can be seen as existing on a spectrum; people might have it to differing degrees.

The overarching characteristics of NPD include the following:

• *A grandiose self-image that might exaggerate the sufferer's importance, talent, or achievements.*

• *Have no empathy for others.*

• *I am feeling the need to be appreciated by people.*

• *Unrealistic fantasies of power, achievement, success, or idealized love.*

• *A belief in a unique or special status that can only be understood by an elite few.*

• *An expectation of special or deferential treatment.*

• *A general attitude of arrogance.*

• *An envy of others or delusional belief that he or she is subject to the envy of others.*

• *A willingness to exploit or manipulate others.*

Obviously, this last characteristic is the most relevant to our purposes, but most of the others point towards the basic psychology of narcissism that so enables manipulation. The strong egocentric framing, the delusions of grandeur, and the lack of empathy lead to a personality perfectly willing to pursue self-interested behavior at the expense of others.

Within the broader category of narcissists, there is a spectrum of subtypes that ranges from exhibitionist narcissists to closeted ones. There are some who are unapologetically abusive and vindictive and others that are thoughtful and capable of remorse. The more fully a narcissist conforms to the above list of characteristics, the more likely they are to be considered a malignant narcissist, one capable of inflicting harm.

Antisocial Personality Disorder, or APD, is the clinical diagnosis for sociopathy. Like narcissism, sociopathy tends to be a long-lived condition, often permanent and has extensive effects. To meet the clinical definition, an APD sufferer must demonstrate a conduct disorder by the age of fifteen, which includes at least four of the following characteristics.

• *Inability to maintain consistency in work or schoolwork.*

• *Ignored social norms. May engage in illegal behavior.*

• *A casual disregard for safety concerns, either concerning the self or others.*

• *Irresponsibility, as seen on the job or in a failure to honor obligations of a financial nature.*

• *I am not able to maintain a relationship for a long time.*

• *Impulsive and lacking in ambition or planning, tending to proceed without clear goals.*

• *Easily irritated and aggressive or violent.*

• *A lack of concern with honesty. This might be demonstrated by continuous lying, conning people, reneging on debts, or using aliases.*

These first two categories are similar in both their positive and negative characteristics. Either can be intelligent, charismatic, or successful. At the same time, narcissists and sociopaths can both be controlling, irresponsible and proceed with an exaggerated sense of entitlement.

Both can be abusive, and both tend to refuse to take responsibility for this behavior. They tend to produce justifications for their worst behaviors. On a core level, both tend to lack empathy, although they may be able to fake empathetic reactions when it benefits them.

Although they do have similarities, there are important distinctions between the two categories. In the Venn diagram of disorders, all sociopaths are narcissists, but not all narcissists qualify as sociopaths. They differ in motivations. Sociopaths tend to be more cunningly manipulative because everything isn't personal for them. Narcissists are ego-driven, but for sociopaths, the ego isn't a factor. They can, in fact, be viewed as lacking a real personality. They can inhabit any persona that is convenient to a given situation. This makes sociopaths harder to identify. Their tactics shift relative to a situation. They may try to win the approval of others, but only if it acts in service of their goals. They can perform humility, seeming to show remorse, but again, this is strategic and based on an agenda. Sociopaths act with a higher level of planning and calculation. Even aggression might be premeditated.

Narcissists are more reactive. They may employ lies and attempt to intimidate but are more likely to do it without a game plan, simply reacting to a situation driven by their overactive egos. A narcissist will work towards their own success or goal of achieving some measure of perfection. They are perfectly willing to exploit others as they pursue these goals, but the manipulation is secondary and directed towards personal interests and a self-centered worldview.

Both personality types are motivated by their own interests, but only narcissists truly care what others think of them. The admiration of others is gratifying. This introduces a codependent aspect to their personalities, making them capable of being manipulated themselves.

The third category of manipulative personality type worth discussing includes psychopaths. Psychosis is distinguished by a difficulty in distinguishing fantasy and reality. Sufferers may be delusional or hallucinatory. The following list contains common traits of psychopaths.

While many of these are shared in our previous two categories, remember the important distinguishing factors defining psychosis.

• *Exaggerated sense of self-worth*

• *Fleeting or shallow emotions*

• *A lack of empathy*

• *Unwillingness to accept responsibility for actions*

• *Inability to form realistic long-term goals*

• *Impulsive behavior*

• *A lack of responsibility*

• *Inability to control behavior*

• *Superficially charming and glib*

• *Being conning and manipulative*

Psychopaths tend to mislead and manipulate others through dishonesty and a superficial charm that can come off as glib. Psychopaths may mislead in order to gain an advantage, or they might be motivated to deceive and abuse merely for their own amusement. Some simply cannot resist these negative impulses. Typically, psychopaths have developed these characteristics over the course of their entire lives. They have incorporated them into an often basically functional routine.

Sometimes the traits are even externally reinforced to an extent. As a result, they don't see these characteristics as problematic. In fact, people with high levels of psychopathy often are largely unconcerned with how they are perceived, exhibiting a willingness to demonstrate their fearlessness even if it means they will be overtly perceived as dominating. As they tend to have very little empathy, impacts such as these seem irrelevant. They do, in fact, feel that their motivations are of innately greater concern than those of others.

This contributes to delusional regard of their own motives and actions as if they served some higher purpose.

The delusional nature of psychosis also contributes to the fact that psychotics often believe their own lies. Lying is natural to highly psychotic people, but that does not mean they are always conscious that they are lying. Their detachment from reality can lead them to feel and believe what they are saying even when it is motivated by conscious deception. All of these characteristics naturally contribute to a high correlation of manipulative behavior and diagnoses of psychosis.

People with other psychological conditions or those who are in perfect mental health are perfectly capable of engaging in manipulative behavior under the right circumstances.

Persuasion vs. Manipulation

There is a fine line between persuasion and manipulation, and distinguishing them from each other is not always so easy. Manipulation is given by oneself's interest to get what one wants, not caring about anything or anyone, even at the cost of the danger itself. On the other hand, persuasion is more courteous than manipulation because there is not only one's interest; in this case, there is a shred of common sense also for the other person who wants to persuade.

People always have different ideas of what words mean, but to be successful in manipulation and persuasion, you need to know the different ways these terms are understood as well as what we mean when using them in this book. In common speech, persuasion is considered a neutral word; of course, someone can be persuaded to do something that helps the persuader and not themselves, but the word itself does not imply that. Manipulation, on the other hand, tends to mean the ill intention of the manipulator.

The ethics of manipulation and persuasion are a topic we have explored throughout these pages but know that for our purposes, persuasion is changing someone's beliefs, while manipulation is changing someone's actions. This is easy to remember because NLP involves the neural pathways for both language (belief) and programming (action).

If you want your subject to change their behavior, you have to get them to change their thinking about their behavior.

They are a thinking person just like you are, and while they have mental shortcuts that can get in the way (just like they can for you), your subject is entirely capable of talking through their judgment calls with you.

In a conversation with you, they can come to re-evaluate their actions, and if you go through the conversation the right way, you will have the opportunity to convince them to change.

When it comes to manipulation, there is a slight difference from persuasion. The difference is that at some points, it is, in fact, the right thing to ask them to change their behavior directly. Now, you don't want to pull this out as your first move. This is something you build up to after a long conversation — after you accomplish steps zero and one, just as you do for persuasion. But the big difference between changing someone's ideas and changing their behaviors is here in step two: more often than not, you should directly tell them what you think they should do differently.

When NLP newcomers learn this at first, they are totally taken aback. Persuasion changes belief by getting close to someone's mind and changing what is in there, and manipulation is getting closer to their mind and changing what is in there, too.

But with manipulation, there is the added hurdle of getting them to follow up on the change in thought. While it is absolutely true that all of our behavior ultimately comes from our minds, our brains are still not simple masters of our actions. Rather, our actions are determined by multiple factors other than simply what our brain tells us to do. The reason you eventually have to ask your subject to change their actions directly is that for new behaviors, a change in thought is just not enough.

They have the thought you got into their head through NLP; you are telling them directly, too.

Social bonds are incredibly important to human beings. If you want to manipulate someone's behavior, unlike when you persuade them into having new thoughts, these thoughts alone are not enough. You telling them what to do is not enough, even once they have recognized you as like them. If you want to change their behavior, next, you have to change the social environment of the person with the undesired behavior.

This is not a catch-all for manipulation because nothing is. After all, not in every situation will you be able to change the social environment of your subject. If they are not friends or family, but rather a co-worker, this could prove much more challenging. It only fits since manipulation is a more difficult and complicated task than persuasion.

But if this is a person whose social environment you have some control over, you have to determine what social factors are leading to undesired behaviors. Is there another family member enabling their drinking or drug use? This is the most prominent example, but all of it is emblematic of the NLP manipulation framework in general.

All of this is to say that when you are not in control of a person's social environment, directly telling them what action they should take is a necessary and challenging part of the process. It is so challenging because there is no way around it, and it is also very easy to do the wrong way. You have to work hard not to work too hard for them. If they can see how badly you want them to change their behavior, they will want to continue acting the way they do out of spite. Don't give them this opportunity.

Recall how with persuasion, we said never to address objections to your frame. In fact, if at all possible, you don't want to address the frame itself. That's because if you address the frame itself, you are acknowledging the fact that it is not the naturally occurring reality that you want your subject to see it as. However, with manipulation, the situation is different than it is for persuasion. With manipulation, you have to respond to objections directly because you have to tug harder than you do with persuasion. You see, persuasion is a subtler, quieter art than manipulation. This is a direct way of saying that manipulation is loud and aggressive because it is not.

But you can't be quite as gentle with manipulation. You want them to change their habits, so in order to get your subject to understand the gravity of the situation enough to trigger the behavior change, it is necessary that you are slightly pushier than you are with persuasion. Again: don't be pushy, but you can't be as subtle as you are with persuasion. Even when you deal with their objections, you are better off preparing for them before they come up.

When you are ready for any question or complaint your subject can haul at you, it is a signal to them that you are like them, you see things from their side, and perhaps, you know better. This is Step One yet again. If you demonstrate that you are like them and can reason things out better, they will listen.

You are almost ready to get into the techniques of manipulation, but before then, you need to get into the personality of the NLP manipulator. You might think that you are born with a certain personality, and you can't do anything to change it, but this couldn't be further from the truth. In fact, the kind of personality you should adopt to get people to do what you want is one that anyone can learn.

Why is learning this personality so important? Well, it's important because you need to seem like you are positive about what you are saying. If you seem even a teensy bit unsure in any of your speech or your body language, nobody is going to buy what you are selling. That's why in your body language, dress, facial expression, tone of voice, and words, you need to pull off the personality of someone who knows what they are talking about. They have the answer to your question; they know what's what. If you can pull off that personality, you basically don't have to do anything else. Personality is everything — don't forget that.

Personality is so important because no matter how unlikely something seems on the surface if it comes out of the mouth of the right personality, people will believe in it. You have to believe in what you are saying to some extent if you expect to pull this off, so don't think you can playact your way through the whole thing — after all, you are not doing the personality right if you are unsure about the merits of what you are saying. But more important than anything you say is the personality you are displaying while you say it.

The right place to start is always your breathing and your posture. You already know what the right posture to take is — stand up straight and without shaking. Now, take deep breaths like for your state control exercises. Just like before, don't breathe loudly. Breathe deeply but not in a way that anyone can tell is unusual. The third and final thing you have to do is enter the headspace of this unshakeable personality.

Everyone has experienced a moment where everything was going right for them, and that is exactly the place you need to go. Revisit that memory as though you were there again right now, and come back as the person you were in that memory.

The world is at your fingertips just like it was back then, especially if you carry this person inside of you. That person is necessary to succeed in manipulating people's behavior in the techniques coming up, so be sure you have your personality ready before reading.

Chapter 10: Characteristics of Manipulators

Use of Language

We have shown how powerful language can be as a prime tool of persuasion. There is more to the manipulative controller, though, than mere words. They will use tactics that mislead and unbalance their target's inner thoughts. We now understand that through language, they will:

• *Use mistruths to mislead and confuse their target's normal thinking pattern.*

• *Force their target to make a decision at speed, so they don't have time to analyze and think.*

• *Talk to their target in an overwhelming manner, making them feel small.*

• *Criticize their target's judgment, so they begin to lose their own self-esteem.*

• *Raise the tone of their voice and not be afraid to use aggressive body language.*

• *Ignore their target's needs; they are only interested in getting what they want and at any cost.*

Invasion of Personal Space

Most of us set boundaries around ourselves without realizing we are doing so. It is a kind of unspoken rule to protect our own private space, such as not sitting so close that you are touching another person, especially a stranger. A manipulative character cares nothing about overstepping such boundaries. Whether this is because they do not understand or they do not care is unclear. Initially, they are unlikely to invade their target's personal space. This shows that they do understand boundaries because once they gain the confidence of their target, they will then ignore them.

Fodder for Thought

Manipulators tend to be very egocentric, with limited social skills. Their only concern is for themselves. Everything they do in life will be in relation to how it affects them, not how their actions affect others.

Take empathy, for instance. Controlling manipulators are unlikely to ever show empathy. Empathy is a natural human emotion that aids in our survival techniques. A study by Meffert et al. indicates that those with a psychopathic disorder are able to control empathetic emotions (4c). They lack sympathy of any kind because another weakness is simply another tool for them. When they detect any weakness in their target's resolve or personality, they will exploit it. The consequences to their victim are of little importance. The target's weaknesses feed the manipulator's strength, making them bolder and often crueler in their actions.

Creating Rivalry

Another tactic of the controlling manipulator is backstabbing. They may tell you how great a person you are to your face, making themselves look good. Behind your back, they are busy spreading malicious gossip and untruths about you. This is a classic trait of a controlling manipulator as it creates a rivalry between people. Then, they can pick sides that will make them look favorable, particularly to their target. It can act as the first stage to getting close to their target. Once bonded, they can start to build up trust, making it easier to manipulate the target in the future. If you recognize a backstabber, keep them at a distance. Their agenda is selfish, so it is better not to let them into your personal life. There is no point treating them as they treat you, in revenge. It will turn out to be exhausting playing them at their own game. If they know that you are on to them, they may attempt to lure you back with praise; remember that it is false.

Domineering Personality

It is unlikely that a manipulative person will outwardly show any form of weakness. An important part of their facade is to show conviction about their views. They seek to impress, believing they are right about everything. Almost to the point that if they realize they are wrong, they will still argue that they are right. On a one-to-one level, that invariably means that your position is always wrong. As they will chip away at your beliefs, they seek to undermine your sense of self-esteem. Once they have achieved this, then there is no holding them back. They seek to domineer others, often speaking with a condescending tone to belittle their victims. Using ridicule is yet another tool against their target, merely because it will make them look better. If you ridicule them back, they will seek to turn the tables, accusing you of being oversensitive to their "joke."

Passive Aggressive Behavior

A common trait of many hard-core manipulators is passive-aggressive behavior. Because they prefer to be popular, they do not wish to be seen as doing anything wrong. Not that a manipulator would ever admit to doing anything wrong. They are experts with facial expressions that are meant to dominate and intimidate. This may include; knitting eyebrows, grinding teeth, and rolling eyes. It may also include noises such as tutting and grunting sounds. It is a very common behavior for such a character, as there is little anyone else has to say that they will agree upon. For most manipulators, it is their life's ambition to show people up by proving them wrong. This can range from the confrontational look, where they seek to stare their target down. Or, it could be in response to their disagreement on something their target said. They may smirk and shake their head, turn their back, anything to show their strong disapproval.

Moody Blues

What of the emotional stability of the manipulator? Is it that which makes them behave the way they do? Do they even know what happiness is?

Happiness is a tool used initially to help them manipulate; a happy target is more likely to comply. This, in itself, makes the manipulator happy, or at least in the sense of what they consider happiness. But their joyfulness is a perverted model of what most others consider happiness to be. Their happiness is often built on the foundations of another's misery. A misery that they have caused with their cruel manipulations. Equally though, a manipulator is prone to mood swings. One minute they are euphoric at their latest conquest. Then next, they could be completely deflated at their failure to succeed. One thing is certain for those who live with or become a target of this type of domineering character; they will be unhappy all the time.

Intimidation

One aspect of manipulation, often used as a last resort, is intimidation and bullying. Some though may use intimidation from the onset. It may in a source of authority. For example, let's take the role of a manipulative boss. You have requested a day off. They don't want to allow you your request but have no choice; it is your right. This type of person would want their pound of flesh first.

They will set goals for you to reach so it will delay or cancel your request, such as moving project deadlines forward. This way, they have their little victory over you.

Alternatively, such a manipulator may use the tactic of silent treatment. Ignoring someone to the point that it becomes obvious you have displeased them. They seek to make you feel the guilty party.

Other more direct intimidating actions may include stance. Using their height or build to tower over you, or standing uncomfortably close. Be careful as they will seek revenge for wrongdoings they perceive done to them. Nothing will go unnoticed under their watchful eye. Everyone is a potential target.

But, the weak are more likely to walk into their traps because they are the ones who are easier to dominate. The vulnerable will have little resistance and are easier to bully and coerce. Many of these traits seem more fitting to men, but women can be cruelly manipulative too.

This is a person who will never back down in an argument. Never admit they are wrong. Never apologize for anything. A manipulator will never show respect but will expect everyone else to show them respect. They love nothing more than to embarrass others. Playing the dumb one is common practice, just to force another person to explain themselves further. At every opportunity, the manipulator will jump in with some sarcastic remark, "hurry up, we're all waiting for your intellectual explanation," or "why has no one else ever heard of this?" Their sole aim is to make the other person look a fool, but without seeming to be the one who made it happen. Oh no, the victim did that to themselves because they are stupid.

Techniques of Manipulation

The approaches we can use to manipulate someone's behaviors are so numerous that they themselves could fill an entire book. Thankfully, this chapter explains the most valuable approaches with more than enough detail for you to start employing them yourself.

Take note of how each method depends on your knowledge of dark psychology and NLP — without them, you can't begin to use them reliably, and that's why this is just one part of manipulation and persuasion. Our first method has been coined as "fear and relief" — in this method, you evoke someone else's fear and then relieve them by telling them there is still something they can do.

As usual, we want to remind you of the importance of considering ethics with manipulation.

That said, using fear and relief is not an unethical thing to do in every situation, even though it is not everyone's cup of tea.

The technique of manipulation works just as you think it would — first, you talk with your subject like you always would. You start out with your state control; that way, you are ready for whatever reaction they give to this tactic. Next, you get closer to them. Despite the name, as you can see, fear is not the very first thing you start with. If you literally started with fear, they wouldn't trust you in the first place, and the relief would mean nothing to them. Perhaps the better name for this method would be the peace, fear, and relief method.

Peace is where Step 1 takes place. Match up with their unconscious brain language just like you always do for NLP. After that, you bring in the step of fear. You don't jumpscare them, but rather you give them the impression that something bad is going to happen. Whatever it is, it has to be bad enough that they will be convinced to change what they were already going to do.

There is another key part of it, too, however. Your subject needs to be relieved very soon after they were made to be scared because otherwise, they will just associate the fear with you. Your subject associating you with fear will make Step 1 much harder in the future, so it's very important that you don't let this happen. Relieve them as soon as you can, and don't let them think you scared them on purpose. This will preserve their positively valenced idea of you but still put that fear into their head to get them to change their behavior.

You cannot neglect the thinking side of manipulation. It is still very much necessary because, without it, you wouldn't be changing their minds in the first place.

We already talked about the importance of adaptability with frames with persuasion.

That is still completely true with manipulation, so keep that in mind. We just don't want to repeat all of it when you just read it, so go back over it again if you need to. But with manipulation, you need to take the structure of framing into greater consideration than you did before.

That's because if you want someone to change their action, rather than thought, it takes much more drastic measures. You need to directly ask them to change their behavior, but you also need to more directly get them to confront their ideas.

What is the structure of a frame? On a basic level, the structure is that of cause and effect. The cause is what is happening in the outside world, and the effect is how it affects the subject. Before you get your subject to change their behavior, they have a certain idea about how their actions affect them and other people.

Your job as an NLP manipulator is to show them how their current framing of the cause of the effect is wrong. When you change someone's framing, this is called Deframing. Reframing is a crucial part of the manipulation because, remember, you need to take drastic measures by getting someone to change their behaviors.

If they are thinking the same way they were before when you are done with them, they aren't going to change their behavior — just like there is no chance they are changing their behavior unless someone tells them they should directly. If no one does, they will never even stop to consider the idea that this is something they should do.

Don't forget that manipulation is a matter of both thought and action. While persuasion was all about getting into someone's mind, manipulation is still about that, but it now has an added element of action. And if you want to get someone to change their action, there is a new idea you will have to learn. It is called behavioral tone.

The behavioral tone is a lot like one's emotional intensity, but it is the intensity of one's actions. Don't get the wrong idea here because you don't want to scare anyone. But you don't have to scare anyone to come off as a strong person.

Being a strong person is what becoming a confident personality was all about. If you have this kind of personality, everyone will listen to you.

But more importantly, for the matter of manipulation, people will do what you say, as well.

If you want people to do what you tell them to do, as the saying goes, actions speak louder than words. People don't think logically in the way that everyone acts as they do. And one thing that will get them to change their ways every time is a strong personality shaking things up in their life.

These chapters are rife with information, and it can probably be overwhelming if you consume them all at once. For this reason, we absolutely recommend coming back to them.

But even though it wouldn't cover everything we have been through, we will summarize the basics of manipulation before we move on to mind reading.

Manipulation requires more overt means than persuasion because getting someone to change their behavior is no subtle matter. People's minds are easy to change without their ever knowing, but changing their actions requires changes on multiple fronts, and the mind is only one.

If people, you should try to change their social environment to stop their undesirable behavior. But if that is not possible, you need to emphasize how it is all on them to change their behavior; you need to tell them directly what you think they need to change; finally, you need to use the fear and relief method to make them see what bad things could happen if they do not change.

Now that you are clear on the landscapes and techniques of persuasion and manipulation, it is time to dive into the world of mind reading, psychic resistance, and more.

Practical examples of manipulation in the world today

Manipulation happens in every circumstance in our lives, with friends, lovers, top rank like the politicians who manipulate us, and many other relationships.

Churches

Manipulation in the church can occur in both ways. The people in the church leadership can manipulate their followers and vice versa. It is sad since most of us look at the church as the source of our peace. Most of us go for spiritual nourishment when we feel down from the church. Let us look at how pastors can manipulate their followers.

1. Lack of open and honest conversations

In some churches, you are not allowed to ask questions. If you find yourself in such a situation, you are met with excuses or dismissal for not getting the information. It is okay when there are concerns not to divulge information that will interfere with the privacy of other members. The leaders should take responsibility for their actions and always be ready to explain to the members why there are certain rules. Church information should be open to its members, and there should be transparency.

2. Leaders never admit their mistakes

We can forgive our pastors for making mistakes. After all, they are human beings, but it is difficult to forgive them when they fail to communicate. I am a human being too. When leaders refuse to admit to their mistakes and are always spinning their actions to fit those of a perfect Lamb of God, they create a difficult situation. You should watch out for some recurring defensiveness in your church's leadership. You should also watch out if the church is masking some of its mistakes.

3. They use shame as an influence mechanism

Some churches in our community use shame to influence their members. They will shame their members for giving little money, shame them for missing the service and shame them for their actions. Even with no knowledge of the world, the Bible is clear that to those who belong to Christ, there is no condemnation. Remember, none of those in the church leadership will sit on the judgment seat at the end of the world. Some act as if they have the final say on who will enter the gates of heaven. They will use the carrot and stick theory to manipulate you.

4. They are selective

First of all, you should understand that God created us all equally, and He accepts us the way we are. In some churches, they will restrict you to dress in a certain manner, they will choose people of a certain color, and they will force their members to follow some stipulated rules for them to fellowship in that church. The church should not have superficial lines but should be an all-inclusive place. The church should emulate Christ, who embraced all the rich such as Lazarus and the prostitutes, such as Mary Magdalene. Do not get me wrong; rules and regulations are important to run any organization, but rules are created to exclude a certain group of people in the wrong. Church leaders should know that they are servants.

You might find that some are not even aware of these manipulative actions, but others do it intentionally. Flipping the coin, pastors are also prone to manipulation. The church members can do it without the pastors realizing it. All the same, neither of the manipulations is acceptable. Let us look at the other side of the coin and find out how the church members can manipulate their pastors.

Compliments

Compliments are good as they encourage us and make us feel good. Now some members may use compliments to manipulate you. They will seek to influence your decisions in the church's agenda through flattery. You should watch out for such signs, as they are as bad as using criticism to bully another.

Criticisms

Impossible to avoid being criticized, especially if you have the leader's role. During conversations, some members will criticize your actions using their tone and sometimes body language. Always follow the church's rules and regulations and the teachings of the Bible. Be gentle when responding to such scenarios, and you will settle the manner amicably.

Silence

They tell us that silence is the best tool to silence manipulation, but it can also be a sign of manipulation.

You find members giving you the silent treatment to control you. The pastor should be aware of this and should not carry the burden but instead should pray for the members.

Prayers

Pastors should take caution with the people they share with their burdens. They should find trusted friends to share with their challenges, and even then, they should choose what is important to share and what is not.

Families

It can be intentionally used or unintentionally, but in the end, the other party ends up doing something they did not want to do in the first place. In our homes, parents can manipulate their children, and the children can manipulate their parents as well. Children have an early exposure at an early age that they can get what they want through tantrums, and when you give in, they get control. Away from the children. Now, what are the signs that teens are manipulating their caregivers?

1. Steamrolling

Teenagers make endless and repetitive requests that are meant to wear out the caregivers to get their way. They will use the 'can I' 'how about now' language all the time—they act like a broken record that keeps playing the same song repeatedly.

2. Lying

Teenagers love to tell little white lies or omitting some parts of the truth to get what they want. They leave out some details if given, would change your affirmation to their request. Most of them also collaborate on the small lies in case the parents communicate; they will have the same information and allow them their request.

3. Retaliation

Most teenagers do some hurtful things to retaliate for not getting their way. They will not clean their room; they will dress inappropriately; they will put on loud music; all these as an attempt to get even with you. It is difficult because you cannot yell at them to stop since they are no longer children, and most caregivers end up giving in to their demands to avoid these hurtful actions.

Caregivers can as well manipulate their children, and it is bad since the children are in their developing age, and it makes their life difficult. Briefly, let us look at the signs that a caregiver is manipulating the child.

· *They do not give the child security and affirmation*

· *They are always critical.*

· *The caregiver does not allow the child to express their negative emotions*

Politics

Politicians engage the emotional system of your brains to get political mileage. They use fear, disgust, and anger and never compassion or hope. Politicians never inspire us to work together for the common good of us all. They use anger, fear, and disgust to manipulate how we vote. They influence how we feel about other candidates and their policies.

Informing you that the turnout will be high

Politicians will tell you that the turnout will be high to motivate you to go to the polls. If they told you that the turnout would be low, most would not turn out since it depresses the efforts to go out and vote.

2. Public shaming

The politicians will never shame you publicly to safeguard their reputation and their votes, but they can use other means to make you feel bad for not voting. You would get ads and letters asking you what your relatives and friends would think of you if you did not vote. It will push you to vote.

3. Making promises or threats to follow up with you

It is natural for human beings to do things in the right way when their actions are under observation. In the 2010 US election, some people received a letter to encourage them to vote. Others received the same letter, but with the addition that they will be called to share their voting experience. It brought more voter turnout than the previous general election.

Chapter 11: Hypnosis

Hypnosis can occur with or without the person's knowledge. If a person knows they are being hypnotized, they may be more aware of what is going on, but they are still susceptive to manipulation.

Hypnosis is a technique that alters a person's state of consciousness in order to make them highly suggestible to behaviors which they would not normally exhibit. It has been used historically in everything from parlor shows to intense psychotherapy and is subject to a great deal of skepticism. In the realm of dark psychology, hypnosis could be used to cause the subject to act on another's behalf or otherwise behave in a way abhorrent to their normal state of being. Because people in a state of hypnosis are often hyper-focused on the task they've been given, they are driven to complete that task no matter the consequence.

Hypnosis is used for many different reasons, and it can be used for positive change as well as negative change. Hypnosis has several elements, and they may or may not be present in different iterations of the hypnosis process. It starts with an induction. Remember in cartoons, when they have the illustration of the swirling visual effect, and some head-wrapped mystic is holding a watch with the swirl in front of a person's face? This cartoon depiction is what is known formally as the induction process.

The induction process is when a person is actually trying to change another person's state of consciousness. In order to make the person more suggestible and influence-able, hypnosis uses an actual transformation of the state of consciousness. In order to think about this, you can think about a person who is typical and awake, a person who is paralyzed but otherwise capable, and a person who is in a coma. The person who is being hypnotized is not paralyzed, but they are closer to that than normal consciousness. Normal consciousness allows the person to have too much stability and defenses. The state that is induced in hypnosis is one where a person does not have all their defenses in play.

After the induction process has been successfully implemented, then the person can be told what to do or what to think. Since the person who is being hypnotized has their defenses uncovered and weakened, they are able to take instructions without question.

One method that works in NLP as a tool for hypnosis is anchoring. Anchoring is when a hypnotist uses something very familiar to you to bring you to that induction space where you are very suggestible.

It might be a nursery rhyme, it might be a name you were called when you were younger, or it might be a song. This works to engage your subconscious, and it tricks you into thinking you are safe and allowed to be engaged in the suggestions.

Another NLP –based method for hypnosis is the NLP Flash. The flash works by switching the reward to punishment or the punishment to a reward. So, if there is something that you like to do which you are trying to stop doing, like smoking cigarettes, the hypnotist will make you think about a cigarette, and then they will make you experience something very uncomfortable, like an electric shock or some other kind of physical or emotional pain. This is a very dark method and can have very deep implications.

Hypnotism can be a very strong way to persuade someone against their will. It may not be as secretive as the other methods of persuasion, but it can be used without your knowledge.

The next major method of Dark Persuasion is manipulation. Manipulation comes in many forms; what we will talk about here the most is manipulation in interpersonal relationships.

The first is putting down the other person. The manipulator often will have to be very sneaky about this technique. Obviously, if there is someone who puts you down, you will not like them, and you will start to avoid them. So, the manipulator often starts out as a close friend or a confidant.

They build trust in the relationship before diving in. Then, at some point, they will start to disparage the other person in what they do, how they look, or other parts of their personality. The manipulator often knows exactly how much they can push buttons, and they know how far they can go before being recognized as a manipulator. Along with their technique also comes the making the other person feel guilty.

The manipulator makes the other person feel like they have wronged them, rather than the truth, which is that they are being tricked. The manipulator will make the person feel like they have some sort of debt to the other so that they enter into a sort of pact where there is inequality.

Ultimately, what happens is that the manipulator puts the person down, which makes them feel bad about themselves, and it makes them feel like they don't deserve to stand up for themselves.

Another technique of manipulation is lying. Lying may be one of the more straightforward techniques of the manipulator. Lying is something that can start small and morph into a larger problem. The manipulator knows how to keep a person stuck in their web of illusions. Overall, they create a larger illusion of what the "truth" is. They try to create something that appears true to the manipulated person.

The lies might have to do with any number of subjects. If the manipulator wants money, they might lie about how poor they are and make themselves seem broke and desperate. If they want loyalty, they might make up lies about how important the other person is to them. If they want a job, they might lie about their experience in that field and make it sound like they are very successful. If they want sex, they might lie about a whole host of subjects.

Chapter 12: Brain washing

Now that we know where brainwashing started, let's look at the definition of the term. Brainwashing can simply be defined as a process where a person or a group of people make use of some underhand methods to talk someone into changing their will to that of the manipulator. When discussing this topic, it is important to delineate between honest persuasion and brainwashing, as there are several ways that people persuade one another these days, especially in the field of politics.

A very easy way that people persuade others to conform to their will is by stating a few things that could typically induce a yes response from the target. They then use some statement of facts as the icing on the cake. For example, consider the speech below: "Are you tired of paying exorbitant fares for your child's schooling? What about the rising prices of gas and power supply? Are you concerned about the constant riots and strikes? Well, a good point to recall that the government has mentioned the country is gradually drawing close to recession and that the prices of fuel will continue to rise as they see the greatest drop in the economy since the end of the civil war. If you want the country to change for the better, vote democrats." The truth is that you may not want to agree with the fact that these are brainwashing techniques that may come off as subtle persuasion and that they are techniques in the hands of manipulators.

Some of the common manipulation techniques that you should watch out for include:

Isolation:

When trying to brainwash a person, one of the first things usually done is the isolation of the victim from their family, friends, and loved ones. This is to ensure that the victim will not have any other person to talk to besides the manipulator. So, the victim will get all their ideas and information from the manipulator while avoiding any likelihood of a third party stepping in to ask what is going on.

Attack on the victim's self-esteem:

Since the manipulator has successfully isolated the victim, he must look for a way to break his will and self-esteem. They will then use the process to begin to rebuild the victim in whatever image they wish to.

The only way a person can be brainwashed is if the person manipulating them is superior to them. This attack on the person's self-esteem would manifest in the form of intimidation, ridicule, or mocking the victim.

Mental abuse:

The manipulator will try to brainwash their victim by putting them through a phase of mental torture. They will do this by telling lies to the victim and making them feel embarrassed by telling them the truth in front of other people. They can also bully these victims by badgering them and not leaving room for them to have any form of personal space.

Physical abuse:

Manipulators understand there are many physical techniques that can be used to brainwash the victim. These techniques include depriving the victim of sleep and making sure that they stay cold, hungry, or causing bodily harm by exhibiting violent behavior towards them. The manipulator can also make use of some much more subtle ways like increasing the noise levels, making sure that there is a light that is always flickering on and off, or raising or lowering the room's temperature.

Playing repetitive music:

According to a study, if a person plays a beat repeatedly, especially a beat that has a range of about 45 to 72 beats each minute, it is possible to introduce an extremely hypnotic state. This is because repetition is much closer to the rhythm that comes from the beat of the heart of a human being. This rhythm, however, can cause an alteration to the consciousness of the person until they reach what is known as the Alpha state, which is where the person becomes 25 times more suggestible than he would ordinarily be when they are in a Beta state.

Allowing the victim to only have contact with other brainwashed people: When the manipulator is brainwashing a person, they ensure that the victim does not encounter any other person/people besides those that are already brainwashed. This is to create room for peer pressure. This is more prevalent when a person is a new member of a group. In such a case, the person will typically adhere to and promote things that the other members are saying, which will secure them a space with their new company.

Us vs. them:

This also has to do with the possibility of being accepted by a group. The manipulator makes the victim feel like there is an "us" and a "them." So, they are offering the victim a chance to choose the group they wish to belong to. This is done to gain absolute loyalty and obedience from the victim.

Love bombing:

This technique has to do with attracting the victim to the group through physical touch and by sharing some intimate thoughts with the victim. Emotional bonding is also used in this technique through a show of excessive affection as well as constant validation.

All the above mentioned are a few ways to brainwash a person. Once a person is brainwashed, it is usually very difficult to get them back to normal. They develop more rigid neural pathways than other people, and this could be an indication of why it is always very hard for a brainwashed person to double-check their situation by rethinking it once they have been brainwashed.

Manipulation normally occurs when an individual is used for the benefit of others. It is a situation where the manipulator comes up with an imbalance of power and goes ahead to exploit his victim just to serve their main agendas. Those who are manipulative are the kind of people who will disguise their own desires and interests as yours. They will undertake all they can to make you believe that their own opinions are objective facts. They will then act as if they are cornered. Manipulators will pretend to offer assistance so that you can improve your attitude, performance and promise that they will assist you in improving your life in general. The hidden truth is that the main aim of these people is to control you, and not control you, as they want you to believe. They also want to validate their lives and make sure that you don't outgrow them.

Once you have given these characters back to your life, getting rid of them will not be easy. They will appear to flip flop on issues and act so slippery when you want to hold them accountable. They also tend to promise you help that doesn't seem to be near.

People can be easily manipulated when they opt to put up with behaviors that are passive-aggressive. According to a recent study that was published in the Journal of Social & Personal Relationships, offensive people tend to interfere with the general performance of an individual. The study also noted that ignoring those who are negative could do you more harm than good. When these people are ignored, the research states that their productivity and intelligence are increased. The participants were asked to ignore or talk with random people who had been earlier asked to either be offensive or friendly.

After interacting for about four minutes, each of the participants was offered a thought exercise that needed them to have a better concentration. The study later noted that those who ignored the negative individuals performed way much better than those who engaged the negative individuals.

The researchers then summarized that ignoring some people in a serious social interaction is one better way of conserving the mental resources of a person. The best strategy is to avoid those who are negative in their speeches and actions. But at times, that can't be enough. A negative person can also be manipulative and sneaky at times.

The truth is that being manipulated is not a good thing. The only possible worse thing than manipulation could just be admitting our dirty little secrets. Each time we realize that we have been manipulated, we feel not only stupid but also ashamed and weak. And all that doesn't stop there. If we continue to fall for the tricks that these people lay on us, they will leave us with an awful feeling about everything around us. Instead of being hurt for another time, the best thing to do could just be not to trust anybody.

Manipulation can only be successful if the target fails to recognize it or just decide to allow it. But regardless of all that, there exist certain things that you can do to recognize that you are under manipulative powers. Some of the ideas may not be desirable or possible for your situation, but that's just fine because every situation and every person is totally different.

Know all your fundamental rights

One of the single most imperative guidelines, when you are in this similar situation, is to know all your fundamental rights. But that's not all; you should also recognize when any of those rights are being violated. Remember that you are at liberty to stand up for yourself and make sure no single fundamental right is being violated. Again, you should not forget that you might forfeit these rights if you cause harm to other people. He is aware of some fundamental human rights.:

- *Each individual must treat you with absolute dignity and respect.*

- *Everyone is free to express their wishes, emotions, and feelings.*

- *The right to give no as an answer and maintain that without any guilty feelings.*

- *The right to set up one's own standards and priorities.*

- *The right to take care and safeguard yourself from being emotionally, mentally, or physically threatened.*

The mentioned basic rights show the extent to which your boundaries are supposed to reach.

The mental manipulators are particularly interested in depriving you of your rights so that they can fully control you and take advantage of you. However, you still have the moral authority and power to state that you are fully in charge of your life and not the manipulator.

Maintain a distance from these people

As noted, one of the surest ways of detecting a manipulator is to check if the individual acts with different faces when in front of various people and situations. Whereas all of us have mastered this art of social differentiation, the mental manipulators are masters when it comes to dwelling in extremes – where they show great humility to one person and rude to the other. They can also feel so aggressive at one point and totally helpless the next minute. When you see this kind of behavior in people whom you are close to, the best thing to do is to keep a healthy distance. You should also try to avoid engaging with these people until you are really forced to do that. Remember that some of the top causes of chronic psychological manipulation are deep-seated and complex; therefore, saving or changing these people cannot be your job.

Stop Self-Blaming & Personalization

Given that the manipulator's agenda is to know where your weakness is and exploit it, you may even throw the blame game on yourself for not doing your best. In such situations, it is very imperative to reassure yourself that you are not part of the problem. Remember that you are just being manipulated to feel bad about your actions and surrender your rights and power in the end. It is vital to consider the kind of relationship you have with the manipulator as well. Some questions you might ask:

- *Am I respected?*

- *Is this relationship 1-way or 2-way?*

- *Am I satisfied being in this relationship?*

The answers to these issues will offer you the most important clues about whether the problem is with the manipulator or with you.

Probe the Manipulators

Mental manipulators will always make demands or requests from you. They do this to make you go the extra mile so that you can meet their needs. At times, it can be very important to put the focus back on the manipulator each time you hear certain solicitations. Ask them some analytical questions to check if they are fully aware of their scheme's inequity. Ask them if their actions appear reasonable to them or if what they want from you is all fair.

When you step out to ask some of these questions, you are simply placing a mirror so the manipulator will be able to view the real nature of his/her ploy. If the manipulator happens to be a master of self-awareness, then he/she will definitely withdraw and back down. Real pathological manipulators, on the other hand, will dismiss the question and insist on having things done their own way. When this takes place, ensure you stand up for your fundamental rights, and the manipulators will definitely flee.

Say No in a Firm and Diplomatic Way

Saying no is a firm and diplomatic way is what can be defined as real communication. When it has been articulated in an effective manner, it will give you an opportunity to stand your ground and maintain the best working relationship. It is important to remember that one of your basic human rights is to set your own standards and priorities. It is also within your rights to say no without feeling the guilt, as well as the right to pick your own healthy and happy life.

Set the Consequences

When a mental manipulator persists in violating the boundaries that you have made and is not hearing your "no," you will be forced to deploy the consequences. The ability to be able to point out and assert the consequences is one of the most important skills that you can deploy to resist the efforts of a manipulative person. When they are articulated in an effective manner, consequences will stop the actions of the manipulative person and even compel them to stop the violations and respect instead.

Confront the Bullies in a Safe Way

One fact that is not known to many is that a mental manipulator can turn into a bully when they intimidate and harm others. It is important to note that bullies only prey on those they regard as the weakest, and you can make yourself a target when you remain compliant and passive. They will often back up when their target starts to stand up for their rights. This is a common practice in office and surroundings, as well as in schoolyards.

Think about the long-term consequences of the actions you undertake

As opposed to just doing what is easiest and fastest, do not forget about the consequences that your actions can have. Remember that psychological manipulators are the best when it comes to making their option the easiest, fastest, and also the least hurtful. They are also best at keeping the people focused on their current feelings. That explains why people do things they later regret. Instead of dealing with a consequence, later on, make sure you choose to do things that you won't be forced to rethink.

Conclusion

Dark psychology is at work in the whole world. You might not like this truth, but you can't modify it.

I hope the knowledge you've gained by reading this will lead you forward and that your journey will be peopled with the kind of intelligent and lively folks that will make it a thrilling tapestry of experience. Sometimes the destination is fun to think about, but if we miss the journey on the way there, we miss out on the best part. Look up from the path, see who's walking with you, and then ask yourself – what did they mean by that hand movement? What does that facial expression mean? How do my own mannerisms mirror theirs? You'll figure out what it all means while you're on your way. Just don't forget to enjoy the journey. It really is the very best part.

HYPNOSIS

Introduction

The dark name triad for personality traits certainly sounds scary and dramatic. However, in recent years the interest of researchers is increasing for these three characteristics, which, when displayed in combination, compose the portrait of a man who is capable of conquering everything without anything being able to stop him.

These, when they appear at a low level that does not meet the criteria for a complete diagnosis, are pieces of people's personality, such as honesty or conscientiousness. How these characteristics appear is no different from any other personality elements: there are some genetic clues, but above all, the environment and upbringing play the most decisive role.

People who exhibit these characteristics tend to follow the so-called "fast life strategy." This kind of life attitude includes reckless actions, drug use, hectic love life, and interpersonal aggression. Generally, in choosing instant gratification or late earnings but with more excellent value, people with high scores in these three features choose the first option. Of course, these uncritical decisions and frivolous lifestyles have similar effects on these people's social, physical, and mental health. But let us look at each character and their products individually.

Narcissism: Considered the most adaptive and socially acceptable of the three characteristics. Narcissists are characterized by a tendency to continually seek external confirmation, attention, excessive self-confidence, and feelings of megalomania.

Machiavellianism: Machiavellian personality is characterized by duplicity in interpersonal relationships and tendencies of manipulation of others. It refers to the so-called manipulative character. It also includes a cynical attitude to ethics, a lack of barriers, and a primary interest in personal gain. People with this trait exhibit a lack of emotions, which helps them not bond with other people, making it easier to manipulate them. Often, there is a correlation of this characteristic with high achievement in the workplace: Machiavellian personalities often meet in politics, business, and generally in areas with hierarchy and potential for development.

Psychopathy: The concept of psychopathy mainly includes low emotional life and a lack of feeling of shame. In general, its characteristics are divided into two major categories: those related to emotional distancing and those that include an antisocial lifestyle.

It is worth noting that despite the similarity of Machiavellianism and psychopathy, they are distinct characteristics, which often overlap.

These three characteristics (as well as their respective clinical disorders, in the case of narcissism and psychopathy) generally occur more frequently in men. The corresponding impact accompanies each on people's lives. Psychopathy, compared to the other two characteristics, is associated with lower life expectancy and a worse quality of life. Narcissism, on the other hand, being the most adaptive characteristic, is associated with higher life expectancy: thanks to their functional interpersonal relationships, narcissists live a "full" life and exhibit high rates on happiness measurement scales. Machiavellianism does not indicate that it is significantly correlated with a better or worse quality of life.

Then, these three characteristics may exist to a high or low degree in any human being. It is important to stress that they can live separately or coexist: the existence of one does not presuppose or negate the fact of the other.

Chapter 1: Dark Manipulation

These people are usually very affordable and cold people and have no sincere emotional connection to other people.

While narcissists have something in common with selfishness and other people, there is still one thing that separates them: they can see themselves and their relationship in a realistic way.

Machiavelists don't try to impress anyone. Instead, they make themselves look who they are and prefer to see what is around them because that way, they manipulate others more easily.

Feeling the need to manipulate, because he is influenced by his selfish behavior his own needs alone to claim the attention he believes he deserves; from the need for superiority; from his self-centered behavior to meeting his own needs alone to claim the attention he thinks he deserves; from the need for distinction; from his self-centered behavior to satisfy his own needs and only to claim the attention he believes he deserves; from the need for excellence; from his self-centered behavior to the satisfaction of his own needs and only to claim the attention he thinks he deserves; from the need for superiority; from his self-centered behavior to the delight of his own needs and only to claim the attention he believes he deserves; from the need for power; from his self-centered behavior to the satisfaction of his own needs and only to claim the attention he thinks he deserves; from the need for superiority Of all the above.

This can come from feelings of insecurity on their part, even if they often seem to have strong self-confidence. If the other attempts to exert power on them, they will fight back to regain the control they feel they are losing. They also have difficulty showing vulnerable feelings because doing so can mean they cannot control and lose the victory.

It is no coincidence that the manipulating person manifests itself progressively in most cases. It is no coincidence that he chooses a person easy and with several weaknesses. This behavior is displayed at the beginning of the relationship, could more easily lead to its termination. A manipulating person learns over time, observing the vulnerabilities of the other, how he can exploit them to his advantage.

It promises to "provide" something if the other gives in to what the first one wants, e.g., I promise you that I will love you and manifest myself more as long as you are only dealing with me or know that I will be out every night if I come back and find the house untaken care of. Handling is a behavior that pretty much we've all suffered in our relationships with others. Whether these others are very close to us, such as parents, brothers, partners, colleagues, neighbors, etc., we may have been manipulative with others. Whether we know it or not. It is essential to clarify that manipulative behavior is not consciously planned but manifests itself within a context and with a victim that coincides and subconsciously encourages this manipulation.

The person who accepts this behavior usually feels disheartened with low self-esteem. He thinks that his personality is deconstructed, he cannot distinguish his desires from the desires of the abuser; more of his insecurities come to the surface and, depending on the intensity of the relationship they have between them begins and creates a connection of dependence and a confusing system of values.

Originally

Start changing yourself, not the manipulating person. Because if you focus on changing that person, his reaction will be even more manipulative. Try not to cooperate with his handling tactics and claim your initial views.

You will have fenced your space with the boundary, holding a dynamic and clear position in which the manipulating person, once he realizes that he cannot penetrate it, will begin to weaken.

Blaming someone for their behaviors and tactics will only achieve a defensive attitude that will be returned to you with more aggression and imposingness.

But speaking how you feel with their attitude, for example, I feel overwhelmed, weak, that I have no importance to you, etc., we will oblige him to take responsibility for his criticism, which usually disarms him and blocks his strategy.

It's not as easy as it sounds because manipulative people can argue, rationalize, and stick to what they believe and want to achieve. So it takes patience and mental strength, and you, in turn, insist. If you try and none of the above work, it is an excellent thing to reassess your relationship and redefine its position in your life. It is essential to know if it is worth trying and whether it will eventually manage to balance the quality of the relationship.

You may need to deal with the fear, anxiety, or guilt that has led you to comply with the demands of the manipulative person in the past.

The Art of Versatile Management

Psychology is a multifaceted science. The manipulator has to be good at what he does, especially since he can't handle everything himself if he doesn't organize the plan down to the smallest detail. Everything must be under his control with a particular method.

You Have to Feel People's Moods

It would help if you didn't think everyone's in charge. Manipulators often find a weak spot. This can be interest, faith, habit, thinking style, emotional status, etc. Psychology, books - all of this will help us understand popular management methods.

Winning Prizes

The winning payment. This kind of administration is considered the most popular among fraudsters who try to put themselves in people's trust. They tell their interlocutors that they won prizes or prizes. Naturally, if you make an effort, that might be true. But if it hasn't contributed to you, but somehow you won the award, you should consider the accuracy of the situation.

Lack of Extra Time

What is similar manipulation psychology? The insistent action on an individual or objecting to him in his favor is determined by the right moment.

The Emergence of Sense of Duty

Caring and love. The substance is that the person speaking must demonstrate a sense of duty with facts so that whoever receives the gesture can be more inclined and consenting in whatever is asked of him.

There Can Be Many Management Methods

There are many ways to defend against manipulation. As a first rule, we must listen to our sixth sense. That reveals to you more than any visible action since it is the soul that speaks to your heart. If you feel uncomfortable about a situation, you can even say no, proclaiming your rights. Don't fall for the advances; you're just being manipulated, after all.

How to fall for tricks like this?

Any communication is essentially manipulation. All we're saying, in our opinion, has to react decisively. "How are you?" By answering his question, we expect understanding, sympathy, and approval. When we don't understand any of this, for example, "What do you think of that?" We're asking an important question.

Sincere lack of communication, manipulation, which seems only ridiculous: "Shall I tell you how I did it or praise me?" Manipulation, logic, and common sense begin when it is over. Manipulation appeals to feelings.

However, depending on how the manipulator plays our emotions, there are many ways and types of manipulation, divided into six main species.

Six types of manipulation in communication:

Love manipulation. When I was a kid, they said, "If you're someone who doesn't sour so much, I won't love you." In reality, they wanted to say, "Listen to me."

"Indeed: even though it means, "We will be nice to you if you work well."

A child accustomed to this kind of treatment begins to understand that the closest people don't fully accept it, that he loves it because he does or doesn't do anything, not for what he is.

In partnerships, this kind of talk also doesn't lead to anything good. It turned out that love is a particular product that can be replaced with services or money if necessary.

Manipulation of fear. As a child, they said, "You're not going to do homework; you're going to be a janitor." Indeed: "I don't know how to get you to do homework yet." You only have one profile with him. "Although they mean this: "There are no irreplaceable ones, prepare, dear."

Most of the time, they're playing on a person's lack of awareness. Therefore, if you have regular brains about specific mythical hazards and are asked to do so or avoid them - investigate.

Come on, and I'm going to play the game for now. The problem with the chief manipulator (regardless of whether it is a mother, father, boss, or president) is that it does not have absolute authority, it is not a power, but it wants to be. He's going to calm down for a while, and then he's going to try to confirm his viability over and over again at the expense of other people's shortcomings.

When you were a kid, they said, "There are two in chemistry again? Then you'll do the dishes. Your man says, "I had coffee with Veronika sitting here alone while starving with kids." It means, "I want to meet Sergey after work tomorrow, but you're not going to let me go; you're going to cut me off." As much as they mean: "I'm going to do the job, and then I'm going to remember this."

Frequent use causes husbands and wives to start playing an exciting game that collects foreign tricks. Whoever has gathered more, won, read it - has the right to fulfill their most sincere desires. Although completely incomprehensible, why should this clear evidence be gained in such a strange and unpleasant way?

Manipulation of pride (with the idea of "above me") As a child: "Why are you afraid to jump from the tower? Are you an excellent student?" But there's this brilliant girl, clean the room, run for a beer, and now Petrovich will come to me.

"At work, they say, "We know you're a promising employee. Karl Jung, a psychologist, philosopher, and generally sensible person, said that the first half of his life is to study, find work, get married.

How does this happen in the family: "I have a headache all day, by the way, Lyutye's wives are calling us over the weekend. It's a pity you can't write. "As at work:" Remember, I had a porter. White is like that. Fluffy. He's dead.

Can I leave early? "How is this in politics:" Our Violet Party, of course, cannot win a majority in parliament. The Oligarchs aren't behind. And they don't give us normal time ... "

Features of this manipulation - A very childish school - "Marianna, my teeth hurt, can I go home?". There are very sneaky and subtle manipulators with a feeling of pain - "victims" who constantly complain about life and collect dividends - promises of encouragement and help. These "victims" are vampires. They can discuss their state of life with you all the time, but they never do anything to change anything because they're happy victims.

How to Avoid Being A Victim of a Manipulator

Logic: In a most manipulative message, since there is no link between the first part and the second ("I will not make money if you are drinking milk with friends"), we can explain to the manipulator that there is no logic in his expression. Sometimes it helps.

Step two. Strangeness: sometimes, a manipulative expression makes quite a sense, but it has a secret connotation. Putting the arm in a strange place is an exciting experience. Then tell me.

Consider Step Three: usually, the manipulator doesn't trust himself; otherwise, why manipulate it? He's trying to maintain power over others, even though he's most concerned about his behavior and his safety.

However, it is a myth that people make us feel it or give us that feeling. Emotions are within us, and no one except us can "open" and "shut it down." Are you afraid? Answer with the irony? Are you getting weak? Answer with surprise. Are you upset? Note that this is just an invitation that you can accept and reject. The manipulator is surprised.

It's customary to make fun of everything in one family, in the other - without worrying and feeling sad, in the third - blame yourself for your troubles and sprinkle it in your head.

They will be ironic, painful, and tortured more often than others, respectively, because of guilt. When these children grow up, it can be assumed that they will encounter manipulators who will play precisely in the "pioneer."

Most of the time, either remember the past - "I can't heal after my cat jumped off the balcony five years ago" - and there's also an excuse for its shortcomings and immobility. But nothing happens here and now in the manipulator. He doesn't always have time. He's busy all the time. He might have been crazy as a human being, but we're not going to do that because he wants us to feel that it will be used for other purposes.

Many have heard of the psychology of manipulation during the color revolutions of recent years connected with the socio-psychological effect on people's behavior. Before using mass impact methods on humans as a system technology, psychologists examined manipulation methods on an individual level.

How Is A Manipulator Recognized?

Manipulators are the ones where traumatic experiences in childhood prevent them from finding unity with the world or humans. Hungarian psychologists from pecs University proved that they increased their brain activity when they saw their experimental partner play honestly. For the rest of us, in the opposite case, such a surge occurs.

Characteristics of the dark:

Machiavellianism - sneaky and ruthless; they ignore every moral principle and do not worry about harming.

Psychopathy - cruelty, sympathy and empathy, shamelessness.

Narcissism is narcissism, not compassion.

Domination, sense of superiority, ambition, perseverance. Oddly enough, the owners of these traits are sexually attracted to women. They also use their charms and acting skills to spark sympathy.

First, communication may not mean anything wrong. The interlocutor's behavior and mood are worth listening to intuition when he doesn't follow the words: he puts his arms over his chest, holds them close to his mouth, throws his legs over his legs. Sometimes, intelligent and friendly behavior is seen as a human being - it's also a time to think. Especially if the interest indicates increased:

Any truth of your life. To take care of the family, to work, to hobbies, to have future views, the facts from the past, especially having a negative structure.

For this, philosophical issues begin.

He should warn:

The flat apartment. It is most often used for selfish people who quickly value it.

Self-imposed, someone's services, and assistance.

Showing love and respect. Benefits and gifts. Thanks for this; I captivated and pulled on the net.

The use of complex words reduces attention-driven special terms, non-verbal controls.

Mosaic chat: The subject begins with someone who jumps from the beginning to the beginning, ends with someone else.

The rush in the chat and the artificial time pressure for action, so it was impossible to think about what was going on in a mess. At the same time, it is possible to dramatize the results and increase anxiety.

Tense jokes and artificial humor.

"Projection." When the speaker copies the pose, gestures, etiquette "are the same wavelength."

Cutting and the theme of the theme by the interlocutor.

Basic methods of manipulation in daily communication are based on emotions and psychological weaknesses:

False love to avoid losing a good attitude towards him; a person takes care of the "puppeteer" and accepts only the personality traits that benefit him personally.

Lies and deception, denial sands.

An attitude that is not requested in return ...

The development of guilt forces the interlocutor to fulfill his "player" desires.

Depreciation. Don't claim yourself because of someone else's ambiguity. And they beat his confidence for it.

A favorite sin not only among al Pacino protagonists but also among successful manipulators. "After all, you're so great. Can you do a few more things?" The incentive method also applies to proud people.

They are punishing goods, relationships, gifts, confessions, or "lord" what do you want? And then the implicit threats to rob him.

Demonstrator anger. The requested receipt passes suddenly after receipt. It's different from intimacy.

Suggestion. Some can easily lend themselves, but they are all open to fatigue.

Trifle. Emotions, words, opponent's desires.

The irony, cynical, embarrassing the speaker.

I explained that inappropriate behavior is not so bad as the "world revolution" or for a whole reason. Sometimes with anger and likened surprise.

The reflection and condemnation of false guilt-adhesive guilt (e.g., collectively) from a particular person. Nonsense.

How to Resist Manipulation?

It would help if you were careful to remove the manipulator and not rush to decide. If a "border violation" is identified, the following methods will help counter manipulation:

Learn about the attacker's goals.

Hide emotions, show your vulnerabilities.

Be yourself.

Don't respond to provocations; don't allow you to impose destructive emotions.

Make excuses.

Ask direct descriptive questions.

Master conscious "superficial" communication to ensure that it is not existential. I mean, don't try other people's feelings in their coordinate systems.

Calculate which reactions are expected from you. Don't show it to him.

To be able to do

Don't be afraid to say that you've changed your mind, made a mistake, or you don't want to continue chatting.

If you don't like communication, let it go.

Declare that the target of the manipulator is known to you. When exposed, "puppeteer" games lose their meaning. But they don't accept the charges, at best, to change the subject. Worst of all, they're going to start pressuring your senses to make you feel wrong.

Chapter 2: Main Types of Manipulation (Examples of Manipulation and How to Apply Them)

There are several types of manipulation because it can often depend on where the manipulator is or who they are manipulating. For example, some manipulators focus on workplace tactics, and some manipulators will use their tactics no matter where they are or who they are with.

Emotional Manipulation

However, it is more potent in people known as "master manipulators" or people who will manipulate anyone to get anything they want. It is not as strong as the manipulation tactics people use when they tell someone they are fine, even when something is wrong.

At the base of this manipulation, the aim is to change the way people feel and think, which is referred to as covert emotional manipulation. They focus on your conscious awareness to control you.

First, the manipulator will get you to trust them. This will happen slowly as they don't want you to catch on to the manipulation. Once they feel that your emotions and thoughts are in their hands, they will start to tear apart your confidence. A master manipulator knows they have to lower your self-esteem to control you the way they want. They will also work to take away your identity, which allows you to become theirs fully.

While trying to break you down emotionally and mentally, they will also try to keep you away from your family and friends. One of the biggest reasons for this is to prevent people who knew you before they came into your life from coming to you because they see them as a threat. They will try to find out why you are changing, and, typically very quickly, they point their fingers at the manipulator. When this happens, your friends and family will do what they can to see what this person is doing to you and how you are being treated. Of course, you will start to notice a change within yourself. Unfortunately, it is usually after the manipulator has had control over you. You begin to see yourself change when you begin to feel different. You might notice you have anxiety, you are depressed, having trouble sleeping, you struggle trusting people you once trusted, and you become increasingly isolated ("Covert Emotional Manipulation").

In general, it is hard to spot sure signs of manipulation. Furthermore, it is often harder to spot these behaviors from people who you love and believe love you back.

In relationships, people often turn a "blind eye" to their significant other's manipulative ways because they see them as faults. We work to understand the responsibilities of each other in relationships.

While you will want to notice the personality traits, there are a lot of other signs when it comes to manipulation in relationships. This is because manipulators often let down their guard when they are at home. They are in their comfort zone and believe they can do anything, and you won't protect yourself or try to change it because you are too weak.

They will start a fight with you over something minor.

Manipulators need to win, which is frequently displayed in their relationships, especially romantic relationships. Therefore, you may notice that if you are having a minor disagreement with your significant other, they will turn it into a fight so that you allow them to win. They want you to give up and do whatever you want to do.

They are great secret keepers.

While they don't like it when you keep any secret from them, they can keep anything they want from you. This doesn't matter to you. In other words, what they do is their business, and you need to mind your own.

However, if you treat them the same way, they will start a fight, tell you that you don't love them, or become angry. If they don't know everything about you, they are losing their control. They can also keep power away from you by not letting you know their secrets.

Their actions and words don't match.

Manipulators realize that to keep you in their control, they sometimes need to give you what you want. While this can come in the form of gifts, they will usually focus on telling you what you want to hear. However, they will not follow through with their words. For example, if you feel lonely and don't want your significant other to go out with their friends again, you will ask them to stay with you.

You will ask for time alone or to go with them. They will give you an excuse for why tonight won't work, but then make a promise to spend more time with you, or both of you will do something another night. Unfortunately, they will rarely follow through with their commitment.

They will act like the victim.

There is always a time that you are going to argue with your significant other or try to stand up for yourself. This not only happens in the beginning but throughout the relationship. While you might disagree with this perception at first, they will continue to use their emotions to persuade you to believe them.

Manipulation in the Workplace

Many people deal with workplace manipulation at some point in their careers. Sometimes it is because one of their co-workers is a manipulator, while other times, it is a simple form of manipulation. For example, a co-worker manipulates you into helping them with their task or gets you to do their job. They only do this because they don't like this specific responsibility.

Sometimes you will start to notice your supervisor is a manipulator. Unfortunately, this is highly common in the workplace as many supervisors have used manipulation to get their position, mainly if they worked themselves up the ladder. However, it would help if you never assumed your supervisor is manipulative. If they are, they will typically demonstrate signs of being a manipulator, such as bullying, blaming others, making their staff look guilty, giving their team silent treatment, and distorting facts.

One way to know if you're working with a manipulator is by the way you are treated. Manipulators need to make sure you know your place, meaning you are beneath them. Therefore, they will often make sarcastic comments that make you feel inferior. For example, you come to work one day in professional attire that is more casual than your company usually wears. Instead of a white shirt and a suit, you decide to wear a white shirt with slacks. When your co-worker notices your attire, they start to belittle your clothes, making fun of your low income and how you can't afford nicer clothes because of that.

Chapter 3: What are the psychological manipulation techniques?

Ultimately, manipulation techniques run rampant. While not recommended when keeping things ethical, it is essential to understand some of these commonly used manipulation tactics. When you can recognize them, you know how to avoid them, which is crucial when remaining manipulated and unbiased. Here are nine simple ways people will attempt to get their desired results.

Convey High Expectations

When conveying expectations, you can sway where the goalposts motivate the other person to go further. It is often known as moving the goalposts; you start with relatively low expectations and slowly work yourself up to higher ones.

You do this in increments, slowly working up to whatever it is that you truly wanted.

This works the way it does because people are not likely to agree to do something that is a hassle. For example, if you are going to ask someone for a favor and want them to fix your entire car, you may first start by asking if they could do an oil change for you because you are unsure how to do it.

Controlling Body Language

As briefly touched upon before, body language can essentially be hijacked, convincing other people to believe and do certain things based on how you move. You begin this process through mirroring.

Remember, mirroring involves you mimicking the small motions of the other person. Please do not do this too obviously, or the other person will feel that you are copying them.

You want it to be hardly noticeable. For example, you could start by taking a drink immediately after they do or adjusting your sitting position every time they do.

These minor signs are essential cues for the other person; they tell the other person that the two of you are synchronizing, and as you do this, you will be able to begin controlling the other person as well.

Projection

Projection refers to the act of being unwilling to see personal shortcomings and using any available tactics to be responsible for them. While everyone may engage in point from time to time, a manipulator uses it excessively, which adds to being psychologically abusive. Instead of accepting their wrongdoings, imperfections, and flaws, a manipulator dumps them on other people cruelly and painfully. The result is that the manipulator will not drop the behavior to seek correction or improvement, and their victims feel ashamed and take responsibility for something they did not do.

An example of projection is when an underperforming employee starts blaming their bosses or colleagues for being ineffective and slowing them down, yet they are the problem.

Generalization

Typical manipulators tend not to be intellectual minds, especially in approaching issues. Instead of carefully analyzing situations and solving problems at the roots, they generalize cases and paint their victims with blanket accusations. The aim of generalizing is to compare their victims with extreme people or occurrences to gain control through indirect insults. Generalization has an aspect of stereotyping in it.

In relationships, when a manipulator is accused of something, they rush to make general accusations that are illogical. Instead of focusing on the issue at hand, they turn the blame around and make comments about their partner being too sensitive or insensitive. For instance, if a girlfriend tells their lover that they need to go out more often, the boyfriend might respond that the women are never satisfied or are ungrateful. In such a scenario, the girl feels demeaned and insulted for being female.

Intermittent Reinforcement

Intermittent reinforcement is referred to by psychologists as one of the most effective and powerful manipulation tactics. The method works by the manipulator by first giving their subject random positive reinforcement such as adoration, declaration for affection, praise, attention, and so on. This is the first step in this type of manipulation. Due to the positive reinforcement, the victim's mind becomes used to the feel-good vibes given by the manipulator to the point of addiction.

Once the manipulator knows their victim is addicted to their reinforcement, they start withdrawing. The attention and everything else they were giving is gradually removed, and the victim starts feeling like they are missing something, or they have wronged their' friend.' When asked if anything is wrong, they deny it. Later, the reinforcements start again, and the victim thinks everything is back to normal, only for the manipulator to pull out again. According to psychologists, this act increases the bond between the two while giving more power to the manipulator. The victim's happiness becomes dependent on the manipulator's wish. At this point, the subject has unknowingly become a prisoner of the toxic person and finds it hard to quit.

Negative Reinforcement

In negative reinforcement, the manipulator expects the victim to do what they want to do what makes the victim happy (reciprocate). The trick behind this act is to force the victim to do what pleases the manipulator. If they do the opposite, the manipulator also changes tune and 'revenge.' In short, the manipulator knows that their subject will read the changes and adjust to do as they want, which is outright mind control.

A partner might not be happy with their lover hanging out with members of the opposite sex in a real-life situation. So, to force them to stop it, whenever they know their lover has been hanging out with friends of the opposite sex, they become cold or start engaging in behavior that makes their partner get hurt. However, when their partner stops hanging out with the people the manipulator is unhappy with, they restore the affection and stop hurting their lover.

Arguments

When you disagree with a toxic manipulator, they turn the conversations into unrelated arguments as a way of distracting, frustrating, confusing, and discrediting you. Usually, they will deviate from the cause of the idea, which might have been a simple disagreement. In their mind, you are the problem, and they will do their best to make you pay for it. With time, you will wonder how the conversation became an argument. For instance, you might have disagreed on the taste of some food, but soon, they will have attacked your personality, career, family, and everything they can think of. Usually, such irrelevant arguments occur if you touch on an issue that injures their psychology and paints them as the problem.

Eventually, they will attack every aspect of their victim until they get hurt and let them have their way. Once they feel like they won the argument, they slow down and 'explain' calmly how the subject was wrong for pushing them into a rage.

Indirect Insults

Insults and name-calling are direct forms of abuse and aggression. A toxic person knows this and will use mind trickery not to be blamed for insulting or calling their subject names. Therefore, they will think of the raw insult and find a way to cover it with other words so it appears less brutal. The insults might be delivered in covert ways, such as using sarcasm and a calm voice tone to confuse the subject. The subject might think they are being given advice, offered solutions, helped, or taught something while in reality, they have been insulted. However, the manipulator knows that their intentions are not genuine but aim to undermine the victim's abilities and confidence. These covert insults are also known as backhanded compliments. In as much as the insults are sugar-coated, the victims are aware that they have been undermined. This leads to pain and hurts, especially since the manipulator might be somebody close such as a lover, sibling, friend, boss, teacher, or colleague.

Nitpicking

Nitpicking is also known as shifting goal posts or finding faults where none exists. In dark psychology, nitpicking is a form of criticism that, rather than helps a person, degrades them. A manipulator will move the goalposts each time their subject talks of an achievement they are proud of. They aim to make their subjects feel worthless, underachieving and fail.

During this process, when the issue opens up about something they think is good for them, the manipulator brings up more expectations to discredit their subjects. They understand that by shifting the expectations higher than their victims have acquired, they can make them feel dissatisfied and worthless.

Gaslighting

This is a manipulative tactic that works to erode and distort a person's sense of reality. It erodes the ability of a person to trust themselves. In application, the manipulator gains the upper hand by making their victims feel like they imagine things that did not happen. They will deny that something happened and move to make the victim feel crazy. When gaslighting is used, the subject has to battle with the thought of whether to trust the manipulator or stand by what they believe happened. At this time, the manipulator moves in with reasons to convince them that the victims imagine things. Often, the victim is affected so deeply that they can question their sanity.

Destroying Self-Esteem

Self-esteem is one of the human beings' most important drivers. Depending on the nature of one's self-esteem, a person can either be strong or weak, happy or sad. High self-esteem means that someone is more aware of themselves. Therefore, the manipulator will ensure they destroy the victim's self-esteem by highlighting their weaknesses and belittling them. When the esteem is lowered, a person becomes vulnerable to manipulation since their validation becomes pegged on external sources.

Lying

Lying is probably the most-used technique of manipulation. Everyone lies from time to time. However, what will distinguish normal lying from manipulation is the intent, degree, and consequence of lying. Skilled manipulators lie all the time and have variations of lies appropriately designed for specific situations. They do not feel any remorse, and when they do, they ignore it and proceed to get to their end goals. They will say anything to have their way. In definition, a lie is a false statement that is delivered as accurate.

Guilt

Experienced manipulators can make people feel guilty for something they have not done. They take advantage of the desire and conscience to be an excellent person to exercise control over you. These people know that good-hearted persons avoid wronging others, which is the weakness they will exploit. Through their conniving techniques, they make their subjects feel guilty for not doing something that they wanted to be done, yet it was the subject's right to either agree or refuse. As such, it is a favorite tool of manipulators.

Threats

One of the worst things a manipulator can undergo is to have their false sense of entitlement, grandiose, and superiority challenged at all. Whenever a victim is perceived to have committed such a violation, they are threatened. The manipulator resorts to making unreasonable demands on the victim while promising some form of punishment for not adhering to their standards. If the victim feels the threat might affect them significantly, they have no alternative but to do as the manipulator wants.

Triangulation

Triangulation is yet another super effective weapon used to manipulate people. The manipulator involves a third party in their relationship with another person. They aim to make their subject aware that a third party can be used to replace them at any time. Once insecurity sets in, the victim is forced to obey all the manipulator's wishes for fear of losing them and getting replaced. The third-party might not be directly depicted as equal to the victim, but the manipulator ensures the victim knows that someone else exists who the toxic person is fond of. If the victim asks about the third party, they are put down as being insecure, jealous, or insensitive. If it gets to this point, the manipulator has the subject under control. On the other hand, the issue attempts to put in more effort to please the manipulator to keep them around.

Conditioning

Manipulative people use conditioning, a form of training through rewarding and punishing. When a toxic person wants to take over the life of someone, they go after the traits and activities that make the victim enjoy a fulfilling life. Better put, they try to replace what somebody once wanted with themselves. Once they have succeeded in doing away with these things, they move in to make the subject dependent on them for life fulfillment. This is the human version of Pavlov dog's training where a person is conditioned over time until they detest some of the things that once made their lives complete.

Silent Treatment

It is the act whereby a person, upon feeling like you have wronged them, cuts communication then applies physical or emotional withdrawal to express their disappointment. This is something we mainly experienced when growing up. As kids, if we were denied something or when our parents punished us, we would sulk and withdraw from them until they made it up to us. I am sure you can recall this. We were once some tiny manipulators!

Passive-Aggressive Revenge

Passive-aggressive revenge is somehow similar to cold treatment in that the manipulator partially ignores the victim as a form of punishment. The only difference is that rather than cut off communication altogether, the manipulators act stubbornly. They put up fake smiles to insinuate that they are not offended, but their actions, such as body language, tell a different story. If the oppressed person tries to approach the manipulator, the manipulator comes up with a false reason to move away.

Confusing Reality

People who find themselves in the hands of seasoned manipulators find their differing opinions transformed into irrationality. In simpler terms, when you disagree with a toxic person, they will reframe whatever you have said to appear heinous and absurd. For example, if you confront them about talking rudely to you, they come up with statements such as, "So you think you are perfect, unlike me, huh?" This technique is known as confusing or misrepresenting reality. It aims to evoke guilt, yet all a person did was express their feelings.

Mind Control

In addition to controlling the physical person, manipulators are masters at mind control. They are aware that by taking control of a person's emotions and toying with them, they have complete control of their lives. This explains why toxic people create non-existent situations from thin air to throw others off-balance. They will constantly bring up disagreements followed by rage based merely on perceptions that exist in their minds. Withdrawal is a form of mind control. A manipulator knows that they can deprive their victims of certainty and psychological safety by alternating between two personalities. The more power a person has over another, the less likely it is that the victim will realize they are being abused.

Canceling Willpower

Willpower is the determination, drive, control, discipline, or self-effort to do something. Studies show that people who score high in willpower are better at regulating their attention, emotions, and behaviors. This distinct ability to manage their life makes them great at achieving goals. To the manipulator, willpower is as threatening as good self-esteem in that it would affect their rate of success in controlling their potential victims. Therefore, just like they move to attack self-esteem, they deploy tactics to cancel a person's willpower before invading their minds.

Blackmailing

Blackmailing is another favorite technique applied in the manipulation process. This is the act of using unjustified threats to gain the upper hand or have one's demands met. It also amounts to coercion. The manipulator uses this method to force a subject to please or get something they want. For this method to succeed, the manipulator takes some time to study the victim. They learn personal traits and secrets which would cause harm to the subject is exposed. For example, a man might threaten to leak a dirty secret about a lady if they do not have sex with them. Some manipulators might go as far as threatening physical harm on the subjects or their loved ones if they fail to comply with their demands.

Shaming

Shaming is an effective tool used by manipulators to attack the self-esteem and willpower of victims. A manipulator studies the subjects that the victim is proud of and targets them. By belittling and making the victim feel like they made bad decisions and should be ashamed of them, their pride and sense of self may have been lost. Toxic people like to know people's scars and wounds since they can be a powerful arsenal to use when the time comes. Manipulators can be so ruthless that they may target injuries such as abuse in childhood to traumatize their victims.

Smear Campaigns

At times, a toxic person will not control the way a person perceives. Rather than giving up, they will attempt to control the way other people see them. Smear campaigns are designed to soil a person's reputation by a third party. The explanation of such behavior is to ensure the victim has no support network to fall back on if they decide to cut ties with the manipulator. They might resort to stalking and harassing people close to the victim to tell them bad things about the subject.

Create Behavioral Consistency

Similar to consistency and commitment in persuasion, you can manipulate people into obedience and submission by creating a behavioral character. People want to feel consistent when they are doing things, and by getting an individual to do something once, you are far more likely to get them to continue doing so in the future. If you wish to use this to manipulate people, the key is in getting the initial commitment. Once you can get that initial commitment, the likelihood of the person continuing to commit out of pressure to seem consistent will get the result you want.

Social Norms and Pressure

People frequently conform to social pressure. This was even one of the principles of persuasion listed earlier. This is commonly seen as peer pressure, in which those around an individual are all doing something, so the individual feels the need to conform as well.

Repeated Exposure

Through repeated exposure, tolerance for something goes up. Think of this as similar to how a drug addict's tolerance level for a drug goes up with every usage. This works for other concepts; as the person adapts, the tolerance goes up. Often seen in abusive relationships to manipulate someone to stay, you may see someone start with lower exposure to violence or abuse. Perhaps it is name-calling, followed by an apology.

Wording

Wording can change how you perceive something happening at the moment. It is effortless to sway someone's opinion simply by changing the way you word things. You can share specific parts of facts while choosing to leave out others or use other methods to word things to make it seem one way, even if it is another.

You frequently see this in politics, with the politicians wording things that shine them in the best possible light in hopes of getting elected or getting whatever votes they were going for.

Motivate Through Limitations

Again, retouching upon scarcity and limitations that played a crucial part in persuasion, manipulation can also involve restrictions. When things are limited somehow, shape, or form, they suddenly seem more appealing. This can be the last slice of pie in the fridge, the limited-edition drink at the local café chain or even a behavior you were explicitly and explicitly told to avoid doing.

All of those are different types of limitations, and all of them then spur you to attempt to get whatever has been limited.

There are three distinct reasons we react in this way: psychological reactance, loss aversion, and commodity theory. These are relevant when things become limited, and they motivate you in different ways.

Psychological reactance refers to feeling as though you have been limited and deciding to resist it somehow. You are reacting to being limited and instead feel as though you need to do whatever that thing was that was removed.

Tit for Tat Behavior

Tit for tat behavior refers to the tendency to return what you are given. If someone gives you a dirty look, you are much more likely to produce the glare than you are to smile back. Likewise, if someone smiles at you, you are likely to feel inclined to smile in return. This sort of return exchange back and forth is referred to as tit for tat, in which people return what they are given, or they expect an equivalent deal for them.

This refers to the power balance that exists within relationships. Some people will be far more competitive and demand equality, in which they seem to create a sort of scorecard in which they can use to justify and demand certain behaviors in return.

Blackmail

The purpose of utilizing this sort of intimidation is to rely further on the subject's emotions. In regular blackmail, the target has a danger to cope with, often involving physical damage to themselves or anyone they love.

In emotional coercion, the manipulator must evoke feelings powerful enough to motivate the victim to action. Although the target may believe they are supporting their goodwill, the trickster has managed to ensure they are having the assistance and drawing out the emotions whenever required.

Putting Down the Other Person

The manipulator has other choices to persuade their target to help achieve the ultimate objective. For most situations, where the manipulator uses verbal skills to bring a target down, they may face a substantial risk of having the subject feel as though they have been exposed to a personal assault. We will be more careful with the procedure to find a way to do so without creating or ringing alarm bells.

Creating a Hallucination

The manipulator who will lie and be an expert in the creation of illusions is more successful in achieving their ultimate target. They must try to construct a vision they like and then persuade the target that this image is a reality, whether it matters to the manipulator or not.

To achieve so, the manipulator must put up the facts required to make the argument that functions against their objective.

The manipulator must plant the theories and the proof into the subject's heads to launch the deception. If these theories are in motion, the manipulator would be willing to step aside for a few days to encourage the abuse to occur in the minds of the targets during that time. Manipulation is a type of mind control that the subject has trouble resisting.

Except for brainwashing and hypnosis mentioned in the preceding paragraphs, deception may occur daily. In some instances, it may occur without any awareness or influence of the subject.

The manipulator must operate discreetly to accomplish their end objective without making the target becoming paranoid and disrupt the operation. The manipulator won't think about who they're harming or how someone may feel because most of them won't be willing to consider their targets' needs.

Chapter 4: How to Understand If Others Are Manipulating You

If you've at any point felt like something is off in a cozy relationship or have an easygoing experience, or you think you're being forced, controlled, or even feel like you're addressing yourself more than expected—it could be manipulation.

"Manipulation is a genuinely undesirable mental strategy utilized by people who are unequipped for requesting what they need, in a rapid manner. There are various types of manipulation, running from a pushy salesperson to a sincerely oppressive accomplice—and a few practices are more straightforward to spot than others.

Here, specialists clarify several indications that could signify that one could be the subject of manipulation; you feel fear, commitment, and blame.

Manipulative conduct includes three variables:

Fear, commitment, and blame.

The unfortunate casualty induces a sentiment of blame in their objective. "The injured individual, for the most part, acts hurt.

"These tactics work since they misuse social standards." It's entirely expected to respond favors. However, in any event, when somebody does one unscrupulously, we regularly still feel constrained to respond and consent."

You notice the 'foot-in-the-entryway' and 'entryway in-the-face' techniques.

Regularly, manipulators attempt one of two tactics. — Which at that point leads into a bigger solicitation—like I need $10 for a taxi. "This is normally utilized in road tricks,"

The entryway in-the-face strategy is the inverse—it includes somebody making a major solicitation, having it dismissed, at that point making a little one.

Somebody doing contract work, for instance, may approach you for an enormous aggregate of cash in advance, and after you declined, will request a little sum, he says. This works since, following the bigger solicitation, the minor request appears to be more sensible.

People control you since they figure they won't get captured. Furthermore, if they get caught, they don't figure you'll do anything.

What makes them figure they won't get captured? If you portray cluelessness or gullibility. They see themselves understanding or knowing things that you don't.

If you have low comprehension of social elements, having issues with understanding jokes, are not quick to perceive a track until it's past the point of no return, can't recognize greatness from lewd gestures, can't tell when two people are teasing, at that point, people will control you, basically because they can. They see the shortcoming and exploit it.

What's more, for what reason do they figure you will do nothing?

There are three reasons:

1.   *Because they can additionally utilize your cluelessness to state you're causing things to go up or to attempt to divert you with side contentions;*

---

2.   Because they believe they can hurt you beyond what you can break them: indeed, this is because you're most likely excessively pleasant. They realize that on account of a showdown, you won't have the option to take it far before separating;

3.   Because in your negligence, you have not framed devotions to counter deceitfulness and anything that might occur. In contrast to your manipulators, you have a social gathering for an organization, not for the support but to up in debates.

How do you understand that? I don't believe being progressively particular or less decent is suitable arrangements since they don't address the genuine reasons for the issue. The likely, long-haul account addresses every one of the three points of focus.

You have to improve your comprehension of human instinct and human inspirations. Start by observing that a great many people are not moved by ethics, whether they think they'll be compensated when seen doing right and whether they think they'll be seen fouling up and rebuffed. That implies that if you show shortcomings and offer a low likelihood of reprisal, it doesn't make a difference where you go or who you're with; somebody will manhandle that.

You have to pick up the dynamic equalization and detachment of desires with the goal that not many things can hurt you. Never anticipate the best of people since it makes you vulnerable to manipulation when you do.

Become progressively mindful of social elements. Understand that a few people become close acquaintances for social assurance, not for adoration or for the organization.

I know numerous people right now who, for obvious reasons, have endured the extreme manipulation tactics – which incorporates love-besieging, over-the-top obsessive lies, the horrendous consequence of triangulations and slanderous attacks, and practices that challenge any human explanation or clarification.

These things fly under the flag of 'manipulation.'

So, why do a few people use manipulation as a strategy?

What in the world drives people to control instead of being bona fide?

I prefer to take you on an excursion for a more profound take a gander at 'manipulation.'

Manipulation Is About Fear and Unworthiness

What causes an individual to capitalize on utilizing manipulation to attempt to verify an ideal motivation?

The main explanation is very self-explanatory – fear!

The fear that this individual won't increase an ideal outcome created from their benefits, that life and others won't give well, that life and others are situated against this individual, that others would get what they want, and that there are restricted assets in a 'no-nonsense' world that must be verified and controlled to endure inwardly, basically, or monetarily, that what my life will be if I don't get this going and will someone get the high ground over me on the event that I don't?

Presently how about we burrow further.

The fear beneath the demonstrations of manipulation originates from an individual's absence of value.

This interprets as "I am not deserving of life working out for me" and "I am not deserving of life as others are having my eventual benefits on a basic level."

How individuals see that they identify with others and life is basically how they see themselves.

So, to improve, the genuine conviction is: I am dishonorable.

The absence of cognizance happens when there is an inability to perceive that we are liable for our world. Being oblivious is the failure to make the close relationship between one's life's occasions and inner degree of being.

This relationship implies this; it doesn't make a difference what anybody intentionally introduces to the world because the passionate aim underneath that introduction is the genuine determinant of where their awareness lies and what will last unfurl.

There is no beating the frameworks of so inside, so without.

Oblivious people don't accept that this framework exists, notwithstanding the recurrent examples, the excruciating scenes, and the disgorging disillusionments. This is the embodiment of not gaining from past encounters or what inward feelings and external life appear.

This is the state of not advancing.

Oblivious people accept that manipulation in an apparent 'hazardous world' is the best approach to getting results, regardless of how these outcomes do not bring sturdy fulfillment and winding up genuinely or honestly back at the starting point over and over.

At that point, to attempt to maintain a strategic distance from the agony of this – another manipulation should be made.

For what reason does manipulation payoff beyond the underlying 'handy solution'? Since manipulation isn't a successful or genuine activity, it is thus a guarded response as an attempt to balance fear, agony, and shame.

It is a purposeful activity that isn't adjusted in the cognizance of more significant benefits.

A definitive degree of obviousness is non-understanding. By attempting to make gains using manipulation instead of genuineness, the individual outcome is non-valid.

Anything picked up from that degree of obviousness can and will make empty triumphs, continuous agony, void, fear, and more dishonor.

Dishonor is a desperate detachment from life and others – it is the fear of being disgraceful of not being adored and acknowledged by others and life as a whole.

It is a separation from oneness.

Along these lines, it is just people who feel disgraceful at the center of their control.

Stories about how to spot manipulators are viral nowadays. A fast web search will turn up hundreds, if not a massive number of pages that depict narcissists and attempts to let you know precisely how to see the warning signs and act as the needs arise. These well-expected pieces try to tell you the best way to recognize a manipulator, name them, maintain a strategic distance from them, and keep in mind that that is acceptable. I feel a profundity frequently regarding when we attempt to paint the essence of evil spirits onto people with a broad brush without consideration for subtlety, calmly tossing out findings here and names there. We never appear to truly get down to the base of what's happening and understanding the circumstance for what it is. This book is attempting to solve this to increase a superior comprehension of the manipulator. Not the slightest bit does this book look to approve or support the activities of manipulative people, but to give a stage for understanding.

I was a manipulator for a large portion of the long stretches of my life; I'll let it known. I was a genuinely terrible one as well, so allow me to disclose to you at present that this story originates from my direct understanding of what it resembled and what I'm similar to now. I needed to turn my focal point internally and practice an extreme duty to change.

This is somewhat me assuming liability for my mix-ups, incompletely instructing them to you so you may better recognize the truth about and get manipulators, and ideally give some excellent recommendations that will show you the proper behavior in like manner to limit strife and disarray.

A manipulative individual may state they need consideration when they're disturbed and need to be disregarded, at that point, appear to be tired of your quality — possibly pestered. They may forget about totally crucial pieces of a story with the expectation that you don't get it so they can cause you to appear the adversary, and unfortunately, they may convince you that you were off base. Have you encountered this or something like it? This is manipulation.

Communication

As we develop and experience an ever-increasing extent, we tend to adapt to commonly worthy communication methods with people. I never had that decision. Manipulation, in my view, is a progression of educated practices and procedures of speaking with the outside world, which is somewhat topsy-turvy. We take in our communication style from what functions admirably with others, and if we figure out how to impart from useless people, we learn brokenness. Glancing back at my trades, I was continually confused as regards the objectives of my manipulation concerning why we were unable to appear to end up in agreement — this is regularly how manipulators put on a show of being so valid in their plans, because to them, it is their source of existence. Suppose we can more readily comprehend what manipulative people are attempting to let us know in the appearing coded language they've learned. In that case, we can likely figure out how to speak with them and diffuse circumstances.

Suppose we can get familiar with the strategies used to impart unique things about what they're letting us know. In that case, we can, in any event, to some degree unravel what they're attempting to state to us — and we can react likewise, as opposed to surrendering everything over to risk, uncovering our helpless selves to the manipulator's control.

Indeed Means Maybe

Some manipulative people, they've figured out how to request things the incorrect way. "Truly" might mean no and "yes" might mean perhaps, which is a startling idea in our current reality where consent is vital for a ton of social connections.

I've thought that it was ideal to request that people affirm their point of view a few times before arriving at decisions about where they stand. I have discovered that it's perfect for giving people a few possibilities, in a happy tone, to change their feelings and express their genuine thoughts straightforwardly.

Numerous people have figured out how to say "no" once in a while when they truly need something from excessively severe guardians, at times from oppressive guardians. Not being manipulative isn't the deficiency of manipulative people; it is their obligation. The truth of the matter is, with manipulative people, "yes" consistently signifies "perhaps" and is liable to change anytime.

The Child Within

At last, most manipulators are youngsters. They are not dependable. I think what a great many people ruin as a purposeful demonstration, a well-considered, plotted, conspired up-approach to screw them over, is simply the manipulator. This isn't to overlook it — striking duplicity is rarely right. This is to state that on the off chance that we need to comprehend and figure out how to manage manipulative people adequately, we have to address the youngster inside, not to the outward veil they present to us.

This was me. I was intense, savage, bold, and accessible. Inside, I was apprehensive and startled. If an issue occurred in an individual circumstance, I would close it down, genuinely finding a workable pace out of an open café leaving the individual who I'd felt had wronged me to pay. That wasn't right, and fortunately, I've been compensated for those occasions now. It's just plain obvious, the main explanation I could be solid was by removing immense lumps of reality to make my inner world sheltered, and numerous manipulators do likewise. I required a presentation to this present reality piece by piece, and countless stunning people helped me through this procedure.

Being effective at manipulation means that you can easily manipulate companies to give you the best in deals for services and products. By promising them your praise and benefits, for example, you can essentially get them in the palm of your hand. They become far more willing to communicate with their managers and negotiate the best possible deal for you so that you will actively buy from them. Salespeople, especially those based on commission, are always eager to close a deal. This allows you to use manipulation to get the sale complete in your favor.

You can bring it up any time you get stuck doing something you would rather not be doing.

Not only are you able to use manipulation for your benefit to get out of the reunions or things that family and friends want you to help with, but you can use it at work as well. If your boss went and signed you up for something that you don't want to do, you can use manipulation to convince them to let you get out of it, or you can convince someone else to go and do the work for you.

- Housing or money problems

- Body image worries

- Divorce, separation, or other relationship problems

- Mental health problems

- Physical health problem

- Ongoing stress

- Problems with school or work

- Having a hard time finding a job or losing your job

- Experiencing a stigma, discrimination, or prejudice

- Being abused or bullied

You Are Not Your Circumstances

It would help if you learned to differentiate yourself from your circumstances. Know your inner worth and love your imperfect self. This will pull you away from the fear of failure and allow you to grow unencumbered.

Accept Compliments

One of the hardest things about improving your self-esteem is that it is hard to accept compliments even though they are precisely what you need when you feel bad about yourself. Work on tolerating compliments whenever given to you, even if you are completely uncomfortable. One of the best ways to avoid responding negatively is to have set responses to compliments and then train yourself to say them when you receive good feedback. You can say things like, "That was nice of you to say," and "Thank you."

Everybody has infinite potential and equal worth. The stronger your self-esteem is, the harder it will be for a manipulator to grab hold of you.

Chapter 6:   Techniques to Defend Yourself from Manipulation

For starters, it is good to note that it is not possible to defend yourself from a manipulative individual. The best thing you can do in this case is to make sure that you have first identified that the individual is indeed manipulative. If they happen to showcase that they are deceptive, you should ensure that you have kept a safe distance from these individuals. If they are not misleading, you can continue being friends. It is also good to note that some people may mislead others by spreading false information.

Never issue the manipulative person a warning. If you notice early on, you should leave and continue leading your life as usual. After going to them, they will look for other individuals they can manipulate to ensure that they have heeded their demands. If a person is unwell, you should go ahead and try to find out more about their condition. Since some people do lie, you can also go ahead and seek some expert advice from a psychologist or even a psychiatrist. If the person is unwell and they do not showcase any signs of improvement, you can move on and continue living your life as usual if they are not threatening you.

If the manipulative individual is related to you, you should always direct them. Ensure that you have set some boundaries and always be firm not to dare to cross the established boundaries. Manipulative individuals will realize that they will be held accountable once they showcase undesirable behaviors.

 If they understand some of the rules that you have set, they will, in some cases, be okay with that, and they will not intrude in any way. Also, ensure that you have initiated a discussion with the manipulative individual while also learning more about their character and condition. Always ask questions that will help you learn more about how they are. Always ensure that you have issued them a referral to a renowned psychiatrist or any other medical practitioner who can deal with their condition accordingly. The manipulative individuals should also be given the support that they need.

Although some of the stories issued by the manipulative individuals will appear far-fetched, you should never judge them. Although it may appear to be made up to some extent, their account is valid. If anything goes wrong, they will always use the information that they have about you to fight back.

Remember that we never choose our family members; thus, you should decide whether you will help them or ignore them. If any other people may appear to be toxic in your life, you should also avoid them.

Manipulation and abuse in romantic and other close relationships can build up with "small" occurrences, and they can end with an attempt at total control of one person over another. This is very dangerous and damaging, and you must be on alert in the early stages of manipulative behavior to get free of this dynamic before it becomes destructive. Always seek help if you feel you need it to stay safe from a threatening and abusive individual, as some situations escalate to an unsafe level.

How to Know If You are Being Manipulated and How to Defend Yourself

Psychological manipulation usually breeds healthy social influence, and it usually occurs between many individuals. The relationships, in this case, usually give or take. In psychological manipulation, one person will always benefit from the other by taking advantage of them. One individual manipulating the other constantly does it deliberately, and they often bring about an imbalance of power since they are exploiting other people for their self-benefit.

The characteristics of manipulative individuals are;

- They know how to detect the weaknesses of other people.

- Once they identify a person's faults, they will always use these weaknesses against them.

- They will always convince the victims to give up something to serve their self-centered interests.

- Once a manipulative individual manages to take advantage of another person, they will always violate the other party until the exploited person ensures that the manipulation spree has ended.

Make Sure You Are Conversant with Your Human Rights

When dealing with a psychologically manipulative individual, make sure that you know more about your human rights. It would be easy to recognize when your rights are being violated. Every person has a right to stand up for themselves while also defending their rights. If you harm other people, you may be breaking each of these human rights.

- The right to have a different opinion from that of your colleagues.

- The right to protect yourself from being mistreated mentally, physically, or emotionally.

- The right to always create your happiness while also living a healthy life.

All these human rights are meant to represent a boundary that manipulative individuals should never cross.

Some of these psychological manipulators always want to exploit people's rights so that they may take advantage of them in every way possible. The main important thing to note is that we all have the right to declare that we have power over ourselves since most people might assume that the manipulator is the one with the management. The manipulative individual does not have any control over you whatsoever.

Keep Your Distance

One of the most effective ways to identify a person who is a manipulator is by observing how various individuals behave when they are around you and when they are around other individuals. If the individual happens to behave differently when they are around different people, this character trait symbolizes they might be manipulative. Everyone has a degree of social differentiation, and some psychological manipulators may prove to be extreme in different instances. Or they may be polite to various individuals while being extremely rude to others. They may also seem helpless, and in other cases, they will showcase some aggressiveness. Avoid engaging such people unless you are forced to depend on the circumstances. It was mentioned earlier that it is difficult to learn more about why people tend to be psychologically manipulative. As a result, ensure that you have kept your distance since such individuals cannot be saved from their current predicaments.

The people who are being exploited may feel inadequate, and they may also indulge in some self-blame since they may have failed to satisfy the manipulator in different ways. In some of these situations, it is good to note that you are not the problem, although you are being manipulated. You may surrender all your rights and power to the manipulative individuals.

- Is the relationship beneficial to one party or both parties?

- Do you feel good about the relationship?

Focus on Asking Probing Questions

Psychological manipulators will always issue demands to each of the individuals they are manipulating. Some of the "offers" that they put across will seem unreasonable to some extent, but they will expect you to meet all their needs. Whenever you feel like you are being solicited unreasonably, it is good to focus on yourself by asking the manipulator different probing questions. To look into whether each of these individuals has some self-awareness, they will recognize the inequity present in each of their schemes. Some of the right probing questions include:

- Is the relationship reasonable?

- Does what the manipulator wants to seem fair?

- Do you have a say in the relationship?

- Are you gaining anything?

- What are your expectations?

When you ask yourself some of these questions, you will be coming up with a mirror meant to show you the reality. The questions are intended to ensure that the manipulator can see the truth about their nature. In an instance whereby the manipulator has some form of self-awareness, they will withdraw the demands that they have been putting across, and they will back down. Some pathological manipulators can also be termed narcissists, and they will dismiss each of the questions being directed to them. They will always insist you are getting in their way. If you ever find yourself in such a scenario, always ensure that you have applied different ideas to ensure you have outsmarted the manipulative individuals.

The best example is people who are engaging in sales. Their main aim is to ensure that they have marketed different products successfully, and they may be manipulative so that people may purchase each of the products they are selling. In such an instance, the manipulative individual will expect you to immediately answer each of their questions. They will also take advantage in different ways while also distancing themselves from the immediate influence that they have brought forth. Always exercise some sense of leadership by telling the manipulative individual you will think about it and issue them an answer at an opportune moment.

Some of these words always prove to be powerful, and since we have used an example of sales agents, the customer, in this case, is the one who is supposed to address the salesperson and tell them that they will think about it. Always take time to think about the merits and demerits present, depending on the current situation. Also, try to look into whether it is possible to come up with an equitable arrangement, or you should say no, depending on the current scenario.

Always Learn to Say "No"

It is not easy to say "no," however, you should first learn the art of communication. When you effectively know to say "no," you will be able to stand your ground while also making sure that you can maintain a workable relationship. Also, make sure that you are conversant with your human rights, most notably the area that involves making sure that you can set your priorities without incurring any form of guilt.

Always Confront the Bullies

A psychological manipulator tends to become a bully at some point. They will always intimidate or harm their victims. The most crucial point to note is that the bullies will always prey on the individuals they may perceive as weak. The manipulative individuals will go ahead with the exploitation whenever they come across a compliant and passive individual. When you make yourself a worthy target, the manipulative individuals will not hesitate to pounce on you. It is also evident that most people who enjoy bullying are also cowards. Whenever a person begins to showcase that they know their rights, the bullies will always back down. Various studies have also been carried out, and it is evident that most of the bullies have also been victims of violence at some point in their lives. Although the bullies have also been victimized at some point in their lives, it is not an excuse to bully others. Such information is meant to ensure that you can view bullies from a different perspective.

When you confront a bully, you will be confident enough that you can protect yourself against various forms of danger. In an instance whereby a person has been psychologically, emotionally, or verbally assaulted, always make sure that you have sought a counselor's services and report the matters to the legal authorities. They will take the necessary course of action. Always make sure that you can stand up to the bullies, and you may partner with some individuals who are fed up with practices such as bullying.

Set Consequences

When an individual who thrives on manipulation insists on violating your boundaries, always make sure that you are in a position to tell them "no." Always make sure that you can assert and identify consequences. Possession of such knowledge can ensure that you can handle difficult people. When a bully understands the consequences that may come about as a result of their actions, always make sure that they can learn more about the value of respect.

How to Get Rid of Manipulative People?

Some people in this world only exist and flourish because they constantly use someone to their benefit to get ahead. Manipulators can make someone else feel as if they were supposed to pay something but often pounce on hard-working, unselfish people who are more likely to be manipulated in their job. Don't let anyone leave you feeling differently. We are indeed human. It's precise because of this that we get to dwell on the view of others in everything we do. In this millennial age, the norm has been just bragging about one's wealth on social media. Many of these brags are often the reality. In the end, this leads to a loose connection with reality. This kind of self-deception can dig deep into the human psyche, and one day a victim of this may wake up and realize that only in their dreams does their perfect world exist. Depression will follow suit shortly.

The first step towards protecting yourself against persuasion and manipulation is to confront the scenario and to take the position of disrupting any illusions. Then choose consciously to see things for what they are. This agreement, which seems too good to be true, could be.

The next significant thing when you ask questions is to hear the answers. This can sound unbelievable because you will listen to the responses. We say that we listen, but we only care about the reactions we want to hear and not the answers we receive.

You would not attend the real answers to your questions because of the pain of dealing with the scenario. Actual hearing needs a certain feeling of detachment, but not reality this time around. It would help if you got rid of your feelings. It can make situations more complicated than they have to be and make you behave irrationally. It makes it so hard for your exit strategy to allow all feelings to cool down and spring. The irrational part of you may want to let everything go to hell when you face reality. Your justified anger can encourage you to take short-term measures to calm your feelings.

Addressing the Issue

The first strategy for dealing with a devious person realizes that you're being exploited, either in a job or private life. Such people will consider you to abandon everything you do when they need help and are highly overwhelming in their requirements for use. They don't see your requirements in the least bit while they require you to do something, and they see their requirements as the most profound concern. If you realize coworkers or so-called mates are putting their own needs ahead of yours, then immediately start to take measures to sabotage their efforts.

Inquire

Manipulators will even get you to do things with hardly any questions raised for them. So when you ask them a question, it changes the power balance to your side so very marginally. Ask them how or why a quest would help all interested participants or whether they believe it is fair what they are looking for. If they choose not to be truthful, you've shifted control even further to your site, as there's no justification to do something for someone less than faithful to you.

Retain Strong

In older people, clothing manipulators are pricks. They are preying on those they feel would not speak up for themselves, and they think they will still get whatever they want. Manipulators, however, lose power completely once their target is standing up for their rights before them.

They're so used to getting their bidding accomplished for them that they also have no clue what to do if someone disregards their requirements. They will often try and influence your decision to stand firm against such a manipulator. Don't let them do it. Only you can control yourself; compromising just once can lead to a slippery slope where aggressors constantly victimize you.

Use your time to benefit

Manipulators start making demands and enforce time limits that cause central pressure on their perpetrators. But it's your time. If someone you know tries to take advantage of you or demands that you complete the task over a certain amount of time, inform them that you will "think about it." Doing so is as helpful as completely tearing them down. In reality, going to string them along turns the table on the deceiver entirely because they would be the ones looking for you to learn. Of course, you do not want to be the manipulator, but allowing the aggressor a dose of their very own medicine can't harm your purpose.

Set repercussions

These are the demands that manipulators enforce on others - mandates must be fulfilled in their eyes. They will be doing their utmost to make it feel that you owe something to them and have to do what they're doing. It's they who might owe you when you do such individuals this massive favor. Make that clear to those people. This works particularly if you do have other regulations that need your urgent attention. If they find that they will end up getting to do something in exchange for you, they would more than likely retract their demand. Although they will possibly try and find another target instead of finishing the work on their own, you have at least managed to get them off you.

Act Fast

It's lovely that you have to grips with the truth of things. But it is so much more to defend ourselves against these dark, manipulative strategies. While you try to protect yourself against the claws of these manipulators, it is often intense and exciting at first. This intensity of these feelings can slowly lead to negation. The longer you take any action, the quicker the denial will begin, and if it occurs, there is a strong likelihood that you may fall back and end up being trapped on the same web.

You can avoid this by taking action as soon as you know someone is attempting to manipulate you. This can be done in the easiest way possible, as by informing a close friend about some facts of a specific scenario, all the events that will eventually lead you to liberty can be started. It would help if you understood that the fabric is made of more rigid material than glass after choosing to behave. The illusion can work its way back to your core by using fragmented parts of your feelings to help it.

A disappointed partner with whom you broke things flatly would attempt to use the other shared links in

your lives to change your mind. While the reality is that when you find that you have always been lied to, you get emotionally scarred, so you are still left untouched by the scenario. However, the priority should be to follow the path that enables you to go to this toxic condition without further harm. You're mentally all over the place. Rage, rage, hurt, and disappointment are the tip of the iceberg. But you must logically believe. Keep your head above the water and warn yourself.

Get Assistance Quickly

When you are trapped in the manipulations of others, confusion is one of the feelings you would encounter. This enables you to obscure your rational thinking and makes you feel helpless. You could even question the truth of what you're currently facing. If you continue to have those doubts, it will lead to denial. You will likely want to say that you have the whole scenario wrong.

You misunderstood specific stuff and came to the incorrect conclusion. Such thinking would lead back to the weapons of the manipulator. Develop the desire to accept a second opinion. In a health crisis, people go to another physician to get a second view. This is to clear any doubts about your first diagnosis and confirm the best therapy course for you.

Similarly, receiving an opinion from another person can assist you in discerning reality and your next steps. I recommend you choose the scene or place for this. Select a location that provides you the upper hand. That would involve some cautious planning on your part. After you face the offender and take the measures you need to get out of the scenario, the healing method must begin rapidly. The extent and severity to which you have been harmed, manipulated, or abused do not matter.

You have to be able to go through it and wait for your wounds to be "healed" rather than sitting on your bed and living in the past. If you don't do anything, an unhealthy scab might form over the wound, making you vulnerable, if not more, than you have experienced. Speak to a consultant, participate in treatment and actively facilitate the healing process, regardless of what you choose. It will not occur overnight, but you are sure you get nearer each day and with every phase of your treatment.

Have Confidence in Your Instincts

While your brain interprets signals based on facts, logic, and experience, it operates in the opposite direction by filtering data through an emotional filter. The only thing that takes vibrations is your intestine that cannot pick up either the heart or the brain. And if you can groom up to the stage where you acknowledge your inner voice and are trained to do so, you will reduce your likelihood of becoming seduced by individuals who try to manipulate you. It isn't easy to acknowledge this voice at first.

This is because we have permitted voices of doubt, self-discrimination, and the noisy voices of the critics within and without to drown out our authentic voice in our life. This voice or instinct relies on your survival. So trust that your brain cells will still be able to process stuff in your immediate area when it starts. Some individuals call it intuition, some call it instinct, and do the same, particularly when it comes to relationships.

If you've ever been doing something and felt like you were suddenly watched, then you understand what I mean. You have no eyes at the rear of your head, nobody else in your space, but you have the slight shiver running down the back of your neck, and you're looking at the "sudden understanding. " That is what I am talking about. The first step in connecting with your instinct is to decode your mind with your voices. You can do this with meditation. Forget about chatting, she said. Concentrate on your middle. You're the voice that you understand. Next, be attentive to your ideas. Don't just throw away your head's eclectic monologue. Instead, go with the stream of thoughts.

Why do you believe in somebody somehow? What's your nagging feeling about this other individual? You become more sensitive to your intuition as you explore your ideas and know when your instincts start and respond to them. You might have to learn to stop and believe if you are the individual who, at present, wants to make stimulating choices.

This break provides you the chance to reflect and assess your options. The next part is hard, and many people couldn't follow it. You can't sail or navigate this step, unfortunately. It would help if you were open to the concept of self-confidence and of trusting others to believe in your instinct. It's your fear. Every molehill tends to transform fear into a mountain. You can hear the voice better without the roadblocks of fear in your mind. Finally, your priorities must be reassessed.

Any contact you have with individuals would be viewed as individuals who try to use you, and it will quickly become the truth if you live so often. You understand how you draw what you believe in to your lives. If you always believe in material wealth, you will only attract individuals like yourself. Look at your interactions with this new view with this guide; the old, the unknown, and the outlook. Don't enter into a partnership you expect to play. You can receive the correct feedback from your intuition. Do not think this too, that if you encounter suspects, your gut will tell you to go in the opposite direction.

Preventing Manipulation

Manipulation commonly occurs when an individual is used for the benefit of others. It is a situation where the manipulator comes up with an imbalance of power and goes ahead to exploit his victim to serve their main agendas. Those who are manipulative are the kind of people who will disguise their desires and interests as yours. They will undertake all they can to make you believe that their own opinions are objective facts.

Manipulators will pretend to offer assistance to improve your attitude, performance and promise that they will assist you in improving your life in general. The hidden truth is that the main aim of these people is to control you and not control you, as they want you to believe. They also want to validate their lives and make sure that you don't outgrow them. Once you have given these characters back to your life, getting rid of them will not be easy. They will appear to flip-flop on issues and act so slippery when you want to hold them accountable.

They also tend to promise you help that doesn't seem to be near. People can easily manipulate when they opt to put up with passive-aggressive behaviors. According to a recent study published in the Journal of Social & Personal Relationships, offensive people tend to interfere with an individual's general performance.

The study also noted that engaging with negative ones could do you more harm than good. When these people are ignored, the research states that their productivity and intelligence are increased. More than 100 participants were examined for this study. The participants were asked to ignore or talk with random people who had been asked to either be offensive or friendly.

After interacting for about four minutes, each participant was offered a thought exercise that needed them to have a better concentration. The researchers then summarized that ignoring some people in a severe social interaction is one better way of conserving a person's mental resources. The best strategy is to avoid negative emotions in their speeches and actions. But at times, that can't be enough. A negative person can also be manipulative and sneaky at times.

 The truth is that being manipulated is not a good thing. The only possible worse thing than manipulation could just be admitting our dirty little secrets. Each time we realize that we have been manipulated, we feel stupid and ashamed and weak. And all that doesn't stop there. If we continue to fall for the tricks that these people lay on us, they will leave us with an awful feeling about everything around us. Instead of being hurt for another time, the best thing to do could be not to trust anybody.

Manipulation can only be successful if the target fails to recognize it or decide to allow it. But regardless of all that, there exist certain things that you can do to realize that you are under manipulative powers. Some of the ideas may not be desirable or possible for your situation, but that's just fine because every situation and every person is different.

Know all your fundamental rights

When you are in a similar situation, one of the single most imperative guidelines is to know all your fundamental rights. But that's not all; you should also recognize when any of those rights are being violated. Remember that you are at liberty to stand up for yourself and make sure no single fundamental right is being infringed. Again, you should not forget that you might forfeit these rights if you cause harm to other people. Ensure you are conversant with some of the fundamental human rights such as:

The right to be treated with dignity and respect.

The right to give no as an answer and maintain that without any guilty feelings.

The right to set up one's standards and priorities.

The right to take care and safeguard yourself from being emotionally, mentally, or physically threatened.

The mentioned fundamental rights show the extent to which your boundaries are supposed to reach.

We live in a society where people don't represent any of these rights. The mental manipulators are particularly interested in depriving you of your rights so that they can fully control you and take advantage of you. However, you still have the moral authority and power to state that you, and not the manipulator, are entirely in charge of your life.

Maintain a distance with these people

As noted, one of the surest ways of detecting a manipulator is to check if the individual acts with different faces when in front of various people and situations. Whereas all of us have mastered this art of social differentiation, the mental manipulators are masters when it comes to dwelling in extremes – where they show great humility to one person and rudeness to another. They can also feel so aggressive at one point and helpless the next minute. When you see this kind of behavior in people you are close to, the best thing to do is keep a healthy distance. It would help if you also tried to avoid engaging with these people until you are forced to do that. Remember that some of the top causes of chronic psychological manipulation are deep-seated and complex; therefore, saving or changing these people cannot be your job.

Stop Self-Blaming & Personalization

Given that the manipulator plans to know where your weakness is and exploit it, you may even throw the blame game on yourself for not doing your best. It is imperative to reassure yourself that you are not part of the problem in such situations. Remember that you are just being manipulated to feel bad about your actions and surrender your rights and power in the end. It is vital to consider the kind of relationship you have with the manipulator.

Is this relationship 1-way or 2-way?

Am I satisfied being in this relationship?

The answers to these issues will offer you the most important clues about whether the problem is with the manipulator or you.

Probe the Manipulators

Mental manipulators will always make demands or requests from you. They do this to make you go the extra mile to meet their needs. At times, it can be essential to focus on the manipulator each time you hear specific solicitations.

Ask them some analytical questions to check if they are fully aware of their scheme's inequity. Ask them if their actions appear reasonable to them or if what they want from you is all fair.

When you step out to ask some of these questions, you are simply placing a mirror so that the manipulator can view the fundamental nature of their ploy. If the manipulator happens to be a master of self-awareness, they will withdraw and back down. On the other hand, real pathological manipulators will dismiss the question and insist on having things done their way. When this occurs, ensure you stand up for your fundamental rights, and the manipulators will flee.

Say No in a Firm and Diplomatic Way

Saying no firmly and diplomatically is what can be defined as honest communication. It will allow you to stand your ground and maintain the best working relationship when it has been articulated effectively. It is important to remember that one of your fundamental human rights is to set your standards and priorities. It is also within your rights to say no without feeling the guilt, as well as the right to pick your own healthy and happy life.

Set the Consequences

When a mental manipulator persists in violating the boundaries you have made and is not hearing your "no," you will be forced to deploy the consequences. The ability to point out and assert the results is one of the essential skills that you can deploy to resist the efforts of a manipulative person. When they are articulated effectively, consequences will stop the actions of the manipulative person and even compel them to stop the violations and respect you instead.

Confront the Bullies in a Safe Way

One fact that is unknown to many is that a mental manipulator can turn into a bully when they intimidate and harm others. It is important to note that bullies only prey on those they regard as the weakest, and you can make yourself a target when you remain compliant and passive. They will often back up when their target starts to stand up for their rights. This is a common practice in offices and surroundings and schoolyards.

Think about the long-term consequences of the actions you undertake

As opposed to just doing what is easiest and fastest, do not forget about your actions' consequences. Remember that psychological manipulators are the best for making their option the easiest, most rapid, and the least hurtful. They are also best at keeping the people focused on their current feelings. That explains why people do things they later regret. Instead of dealing with a consequence, later on, make sure you choose to do something that you won't be forced to rethink.

Conclusion

Dark psychology can be terrifying, and manipulators are everywhere, but you can learn to protect yourself against them.

From here, all that's left for you to do is take some time to begin learning what you can do to help yourself both use these tools for your good and make sure that you take the time to protect yourself and everyone around you.

Ensure that you use the information that you got to work with those you care about and protect the unsuspecting. Ultimately, the tools you have provided in this book can be used for either good or evil purposes. You can choose to hurt or help. However, you have to be willing to deal with the consequences of what you decide to do.

As you read through this book, you should have begun to feel more confident than you have been before. You should be ready to get out there and get started with your newfound information that you have gained. Don't let yourself be taken advantage of and learn that you, too, can fight back, protect yourself and ensure that you can maintain yourself and your integrity. We knowingly see dark psychological strategies in our daily lives. The manipulators secretly strike us, and we couldn't even know it. Manipulators use techniques in that matter, consciously. Some secret manipulators deliberately say and do stuff for influence and leverage to have what they want to get.

You are probably not sure how to start or where to start from in your quest to protect yourself from dark psychology.

Given that the content of this book is comprehensive, you must give yourself time to learn the protection techniques one by one. A good starting place would be an in-depth understanding of NLP. As soon as you can read people's thoughts using NLP, you will be on track to protect yourself and any person in your family from manipulation.

Learn not to limit yourself by believing in things that are limiting themselves. An example recently read was when a person thought birds all have feathers. It's something that defines the believer since that premise would exclude penguins. It is hoped that this book has opened your mind to the possibility of taking your learning processes further on the subject of NLP. You will be happy that you did, as the techniques briefly outlined in this book have vast potential.

BODY LANGUAGE

Introduction

As children, it is easier to point out the gestures of our bodies, as we are not yet able to hide them. From that age, children know how to express themselves right away. They freely express their emotional state very easily than an adult who always tends to hide his emotions.

Growing up, we learn to hide our emotions so that no one can read our emotional language. On the other hand, body language and communicative ones are a great way to identify an individual who has no intention of being discovered quickly.

It is the easiest way to empathize with others; it is a great way to understand them fully.

Observing the gestures and ways of doing things helps you understand the emotions that that person is feeling, how he moves, and how he gestures.

Listen to it, look carefully at every detail, and do not miss anything.

Think of the possibilities! Is your date interested in you? How can you make a more powerful impact at work?

Reading body language is an innate ability that we all have and, as mentioned, to some degree, use unconsciously.

It is the general lack of attention to body language that has caused many of our personal and professional relationships to suffer from misunderstandings, heartaches, harsh judgments, and unnecessary conflicts, all of which can be avoided if we know how to pay attention to the body language of those who are around us.

Although this knowledge may be simple, its effect is far-reaching. The various facial expressions, head, eye, and hand movements you had once taken for granted will all take on new meanings. You will begin to understand why some of your past personal and professional relationships had issues.

Chapter 1: Understanding the Psychology of Body Language

It is well known that body language has a significant impact on interpersonal relationships. People often don't notice it, but their body movements are examples of involuntary behavior that can convey their thoughts to others. Because different personality types have different behaviors, you should be aware of how you are moving since people can often measure it based on the behaviors you indicate.

It is essential to remember that the gestures we call body language say a lot about other people. These physical expressions of what we think can also display more about ourselves. The way we behave can tell others what emotions we experience.

The exciting thing about nonverbal communication is that it is a product of our biology, environment, and culture. Perhaps that is why body language can point others to our attitudes. We can inherit specific properties that influence how we project ourselves in others, but we tend to use different forms of nonverbal communication depending on our relationship with others. For example, your work colleagues are probably presented differently to your family members. Perhaps because the comfort zone varies, it becomes more careful in certain situations, which affects the way it reacts.

While some gestures are intentional, many-body reactions when we communicate with others seem more involuntary. There are a few numbers of physical signs that can give other clues about our emotional state or what we feel.

If we realize it or not, we observe and process the body language of others, especially when we speak. One way to interpret the signals of others more accurately is to be more self-aware. Pay attention to your gestures and movements when you talk. Try to understand the connection between your nonverbal communication and the words that express a thought.

Mainly young children often communicate their feelings nonverbally, even if they begin to develop vocabulary. A child's actions can usually tell him if he is angry or unhappy. Young children and preschoolers seem to have a natural ability to express themselves physically. Similarly, babies and young children can read our body language very well.

Interestingly, children's gestures to communicate their needs can help their brains develop and then contribute to verbal communication. From the beginning, babies pay close attention to an adult's face and focus on the eyes while talking to them. How do you know that? Genetics is the most logical reason; maybe the eyes are the soul's windows!

We interact with the words we speak and the actions we perform, and how we use our bodies about our environment and others. Unpublished communication is often the most effective because sometimes words don't express everything we want to say and say so much about us that we don't notice anything if we don't realize it.

We often do not realize what our body expresses, but body language is an effective means of communication to take into account. It points to subtler signs that point to it.

Sometimes you can say something with words, but your body language can say something completely different. For example, when you try to find friends and show someone that you are friendly but defensive and aggressive, your message seems confusing and confusing. It is essential to be aware of this to better communicate with the body what you want to convey to others. It gives your words more depth and power if you can support them with conscious body language.

If you know the message you are transmitting and are using it to project the image you want, you will get much more advantage during a job interview. You will also avoid projecting an idea that you may not want to project, such as insecurity, even if your words are safe. Your body language will express a different story and undermine what you are trying to communicate.

As you learn to protect the body language you want, you become a better communicator and interact at a deeper level with others. It is essential to know that part of body language has different meanings for people from different cultures, but there are some universal similarities. Consider what you transmit in each situation and how to control your actions. It also alerts you to the body language that others use to get more information about the interactions.

Knowledge of body language is an essential skill. With practice and self-knowledge, you can connect with others and understand more than other people's words.

You will notice a completely new reaction from people as you release the strength of body language. We all communicate nonverbally, even without having to think about it.

If you want to have a strong advantage in life, you must convey the correct signs of body language, with or without saying anything else. Here we explain how to use the power of body language.

You are responsible and trust everything you do or will say during the expected interview.

Separate the feet without completely blocking the knees. Allow your shoulders to rest, keep your hands at your sides (never in your pockets) and breathe gently. Take an open posture and enjoy a warm and welcoming facial expression as if you were willing to communicate. Depending on the situation, you can smile.

Using the power of body language while conversing

Face the other person or your audience directly and make as much eye contact as possible throughout the conversation. The permission raises your eyebrows, and brings your head close, shows that you are listening.

Do not cross your arms, do not look at the floor, and not put your hands in your pockets. These may subliminally show that you are not interested.

If you have comments, you can see them negatively but respectfully, such as: For example, raising your eyebrows, pressing your lips, and raising your palm forward, as if telling the person to pause.

Key to trust

Much of your body language can show how safe, interested, bored, annoying, or nervous you are. Keep your head in the conversation to show that you are very involved in the conversation.

You can also use some hand movements to highlight a point. When you list things, it is better to use each of your fingers while mentioning each end to help your audience keep track.

Tempo helps you create more ground if you want to communicate with a more significant amount. It also shows confidence when thinking about more things to say. Balancing arms and climbing are also good indicators of self-confidence.

Acts performed by a self-confident person say more than words. And when people say "action," they mean more than just hand movement.

The body helps send messages that are clearer than what comes out of the mouth, regardless of whether the person knows it or not.

When a person feels nervous or insecure, he shows his body language. For the same reason, he would also show his confidence if he is sure of himself.

For example, if a person has an excellent resume, they go to a job interview with a sloppy look and arrive late for the appointment, then they convey a lack of interest in that job. Paying attention to details is vital to communicate better.

Convince more efficiently by adopting the correct posture and adequate body language.

Reorient a negotiation with a closed interlocutor by spotting signs of annoyance, non-interest, etc., and correcting the shot.

- **Identify the personality of a recruiting candidate more precisely by spotting signs of   nervousness or lies.**

- **We are managing conflicts more effectively and detecting the unspoken.**

- **Identify resistance to change before it is clearly stated.**

Chapter 2: Our Bodies and The Way They Speaks

Bodily Gesture

There are types of body language. We cannot classify the different styles in the same category. Other body languages can be distinguished. So, which body language styles can be differentiated? Generally, the body language is divided into two columns. That includes; Body parts and the Intent.

So what kinds in each class can be observed?

Let us start with the body parts and the language they communicate.

- *The Head - The placement of the head and its movement, back and forth, right to the left, side to side, including the shake of hair.*

- *Face - This includes facial expressions. You should note that the front has many muscles ranging from 54 and 98, whose work moves different face areas. The movements of the face depict the state of your mind.*

- *Eyebrows - The eyebrows can express themselves through moving up and down, as well as giving a frown*

- *Eyes - The eyes can be rolled, move up down, right, and left, blink as well as the dilatation*

- *The Nose - The expression of the nose can be by the flaring of the nostrils and the formation of wrinkles at the top*

- *The Lips - There are many roles played by the lips that include snarling, smiling, kissing, opened, closed, tight, and puckering*

- *The Tongue - The tongue can roll in and out, go up and down, touch while kissing, and also the licking of lips*

- *The Jaw - The jaw opens and closes, it can be clinched, and also the lower jaw can be moved right and left*

- *Your Body Posture - This describes the way you place your body, legs, and arms connected, and also concerning other people*

- *The Body Proximity - This looks at how far your body is from other people*

- *Shoulder Movements - They move up and down, get hunched, and hang*

- *The Arm - These go up down, straight, and crossed*

Legs and the feet-these can have an expression in many different ways. They can be straight, crossed, legs placed one over the other, the feet can face the next person you are in a conversation with, face away from each other, the feet can be dangling the shoes.

The hand and the fingers-the way that your hands and fingers move is powerful in reading other people's gestures. The hands can move up and down; they can do some secret language that only the same group can understand.

How one reacts to handling and placing objects-this is not regarded as a body part, but it technically plays a role in reading body language. This may predict anger, happiness, and much more.

This includes willingly making body movements, otherwise known as gestures. These are the movements that you intended to create, for example, shaking of hands, blinking your eyes, moving, and shaking your body in a sexy way, maybe to lure someone, and much more. There are also involuntary movements-this these are movements that you have no control over. This can be sweating, laughter, crying, and much more.

Descriptive Gestures

You will find people that move their hands around a lot, while others move them just a little bit. According to research, the people that drive their hands around a lot are good speakers.

However, it is not all about moving your hands around aimlessly – you need to understand what each movement means and how you can make it work for you.

This is true because the right-hand signals will complement the words that come from your mouth.

You also explain a concept faster than before because it is like sending a message using two explanations instead of the traditional one.

Emphatic Gestures

How often do we say, "If I were you," and I mean in reality, "If I, I were in one place like yours...?" It's not easy to feel what it's like in someone else's shoes.

Someone who cannot become aware of their body language signals will never be able to register the signals of others accurately. Body language analysis requires not only a "sharp" (read: trained) gaze and a "good" (i.e., trained) ear, but probably a much higher degree of good "sense."

This word describes a good empathy without which any method of self and human knowledge will fail. (You may also know someone who has attended 30 seminars and has read 500 books on the subject and yet does not get beyond a specific limit?) Registering one's feelings and non-verbal signals means going through two essential processes:

First, one perceives a signal, e.g., one tugs nervously on the lip. Second, you register how you feel right now. This combination helps others guess what feeling may have triggered a particular signal with them. Of course, this guessing is commonly called 'interpret' because it sounds 'scientific'. However, the fact remains that scientists must also "guess" as long as they work on a theory of knowledge, that is, create. Therefore, empathy for others can be practiced by registering one's processes. We can express this again as a rule:

The more empathy a person has with their emotional world, the more they will develop for others.

And vice versa. This rule also explains why susceptible people have much understanding for others and are also very sensitive (sometimes mimosa-like) to others.

Suggestive Gestures

Studies show that the way you hold your palms will say a lot about you.

When you have your palms facing upwards, you will show positive behavior, while palms facing downwards will show negative behavior.

Palms facing up tell the person that you are welcoming and honest.

For example, if you are negotiating with a salesperson when buying something and putting his palms facing upwards while saying he cannot go any lower, he is honest, and you need to believe him.

If the palms are facing downwards, then he is more emphatic.

In the first instance, you can keep on negotiating because he might go lower, but in the following example, he won't go any lower.

It has also been known that those who talk without gesticulating are prone to talking lies than those who speak with many gestures.

If you have watched a politician talk, you must have realized that they usually use more gestures than many people.

They also like to use open arm gestures to show some honesty.

Pointing is rare in most cases with politicians because they know that it is rude.

Prompting Gestures

Verbal and nonverbal cues determine how well you can communicate with people. It is about understanding the content and the context simultaneously and communicating back in kind. Verbal cues are simple prompts in conversation that ask for your attention or need your response to something. They are very clear.

"Does anyone have the answer?"

This is a direct verbal cue prompting anyone who might have the correct answer to speak up. Everyone understands this. If you don't have the answer, you might probably look around the room to see who has so that you can be attentive and listen to their explanation. Verbal cues are straightforward and explicit. You cannot mistake them.

There is a chronological order in which ideas are conveyed.

The difference with nonverbal cues? These are indirect. They are often implied but not explicit. Indirect verbal cues can be subtle. Given their complicated nature, they are usually easy to misunderstand.

Instead of saying what they want, someone acts it out, hoping you can understand them without them having to say it out loud. Affiliation to different cultural groups, societies, and other interactions often affects indirect verbal cues. It might not be easy to read verbal cues, but you can hack it with some insight.

Here are some valuable tips:

Recognize Differences. You must first understand that people are different, and for this reason, their communication styles might not be similar to yours. Everyone responds to verbal cues differently. When you respect this, it is easier to create an environment where you can understand one another.

You are overcoming Bias. The next thing you have to overcome is your personal Bias. Everyone is biased over something in one way or the other. Most of the time, you are biased without even realizing it. This is because of the inherent traits, beliefs, and core values you live by. These affect the way you comprehend things or how you recognize challenges.

Some people who are used to direct verbal cues might find it challenging to interact with people who are used to indirect verbal cues. You might even assume them dishonest because they are not communicating in a manner you are used to. On their part, they might find you unassuming, challenging to deal with, and insensitive. Some might even feel offended, yet you both mean well.

Embrace Diversity. Effective communication is about embracing diversity. People show different emotions in different ways in other parts of the world. It is wise to learn about cultural relations, especially if you might have a diverse audience.

Practice. You can learn everything you don't know. Learning means setting aside time to practice and get used to people, styles, and so forth. Knowledge will help you become flexible and understand the differences between your preferred type of communication and other people.

Chapter 3: BODY LANGUAGE

Some believe that being a successful persuader means being pushy or manipulative. They think they will have to force their opinions and ways of thinking onto others. This is an unfortunate cultural belief because it is not correct. Using force and manipulation may garner quick results and short-term success; however, gaining long-term influence requires more natural persuasion. This continuous influence is implementing scientifically based strategies carried out with integrity. They are not done with calculated tactics, intimidating others, or deceptive maneuvers. When persuasion is used to communicate truth and good intentions, people instinctively want to be persuaded by you, trust you, and believe in you. Whatever you want them to do, they will do it and will do it happily.

Everyday life requires persuasion, and because of that, the discussion and cultural understanding of it changes day by day. Sometimes the conversation is misunderstood, as explained above.

Being capable of persuasion and not being persuaded oneself is an evolutionary necessity and is essential in everything from basic survival to cultivating wealth and success. Different cultures may require other methods of persuasion. This difference is in how persuasion processes are effective and how often they are used. To provide a short example of this, advertisers will adjust the values proposed in the message depending on the culture it is being communicated to. A brand may emphasize a community-based product that brings people together in one country and highlight individual success in another.

In the mid-'90s, two researchers developed a Persuasion Knowledge Model concept. This concept provides a structure for the analysis of the knowledge of persuasion. It also provides a method for gathering this knowledge.

The method for communicating to most people is to mix colloquial dialogue with scientific findings. This way, the general public can be educated regarding new forms of persuasion through their already established beliefs or common sense. Persuasion proficiency can become muddled when there is consistent mixing of science and folklore. The significance of ability can be inferred through communication like the title of a job position, scholarship accolades, or celebrity.

This is how we have come to the cultural understanding that used car salespeople are not to be trusted. They are reported to use overt techniques that lead to distrust in our general culture. These techniques can range from giving the car keys to the customer before buying it to alter their perception of reality to intertwining their personal life to the customer during the sales process.

The first step of commitment is to establish consistency or the concept of advancing your ideal self-image. The messages you present to this other person are then biased and based on their self-image. The next step is to encourage commitment. This is a call to action. Even a person's small act can lead to more extensive commitments later down the road. Here are some examples of how to ask for a small commitment:

• Social media following. This is a remote connection and commitment. Gain more exposure to your brand if you are a business or your image if you seek to gain personal influence.

• Watch a video. Choosing to spend their time watching something you have prepared for them is a small commitment and a non-threatening way to engage a person.

• Fill out a form. Giving information is a commitment to follow-up and discuss something further. Giving someone a phone number is a simple commitment. The more information they provide, like other means of communication or their address, the more they commit.

Context

Remember that isolated occurrences of the above actions don't necessarily indicate a lack of truthfulness. You must use your powers of intuition, along with your knowledge of that person, and keep in mind that a combination of signals is more reliable than just one signal. Research has proven that most of our communication as humans is done through body language and paints a more accurate picture than verbal speech. This means that it is of utmost importance to discern and learn this language and build our skill of interpreting and sending messages to each other.

By taking it upon ourselves to understand this unspoken language clearly, we can prevent misunderstandings and conflict while increasing our ability to keep and build friendships, ace interviews, spot dishonesty, and more. For these reasons and more, nonverbal communication skills will aid us in excelling at every pursuit we choose to follow in life.

Clusters

The most significant blunder people make while analyzing body language is to make sweeping, inaccurate conclusions based on a few isolated clues. Instead, if you want to make your predictions more comprehensive, look at a cluster of clues together. For instance, if you spot a person making excessive leg movements or sweating concludes he or she is lying when they may be nervous; you end up doing an incorrect reading. Similarly, a person may shift their weight from one side to another because the seat is uncomfortable.

It would help if you watched out for clues originating from different body parts to make the reading more comprehensive and accurate rather than looking at standalone clues. Another example is that lying may maintain consistent eye contact to mislead you into believing them. If you make a sweeping conclusion based only on eye contact, you misread the person. If you look at other clues such as sweaty palms, shifting feet, nose rubbing, feet pointed towards the exit, and others, you can collectively conclude they are lying.

Congruence

Usually, two people have a difficult encounter because they have clashing personalities. They have incompatible values. A person may say something innocent, but the other party misunderstands it. The innuendo, intention, or motivation is often lost, and no one can address the problem openly. If an individual is a victim of an offensive remark or racial slur, the best course of action is to walk away.

If you are interacting with somebody and you seem to think that his body language is becoming uncomfortable, such as looking down to the floor, rubbing his arms or the back of his head, or laughing awkwardly, take these as a cue to make him more comfortable. Aggressive body language is also a sign of disagreement.

To recover from instances like these, as soon as you pick up these types of body language, allow the other person to talk instead of you. Ask general questions that are not invasive and listen. What you can add to this discussion is by asking relevant questions for the other person to explain his personality or feelings. This will allow the other person to become more comfortable and will give you a chance to connect more intimately.

However, if a person is confused if somebody dislikes him, the best way is to ask that other person. He can clear the misunderstanding. In most cases, if a person keeps asking himself if he is at fault, he probably is. He can learn social skills and become responsible for his actions.

Chapter 4: The Meaning of Body Posture

The way you sit & stand when interacting with others can communicate a great deal about you to them without you or them being conscious about it. If you somehow find that statement a bit vague, consider this: have you ever felt "suspicious" of someone who looks nice, talks nice, & smells nice? I mean, despite the "nice" appearance, have you ever felt that deep inside, this actually may be a dubious character that's just trying to put one over you? If you have, then you may not have been aware of it, but you were able to pick up on his or her body language - particularly their body positions - on a subconscious level. You could somehow pick up on what they're about on a subconscious level through their posture. & if you can master the art of using body language to your advantage, you can easily make people trust you & be persuaded by you.

Sitting positions

A lot of people - maybe you included - aren't aware, but the way we sit can tell others much about how we're feeling at the moment or even our current mood, as well as our personality. The way we sit can project a shy or insecure vibe or launch a more confident, even aggressive one.

The Cross-Legged Position

For the most part, sitting with legs crossed projects a feeling of being carefree & open. Crossing the legs with knees spread to the side can give people the subconscious impression that physically, you're all game to take on new ideas, which can also be subconsciously perceived to mean that emotionally speaking, you're also open to some new things. Being available means, you're a person that's fun & interesting to be with, making more people be drawn to you naturally.

The Erect Sitting Position

Without thinking much about it, it's also easy to see that a person who usually sits this way is a confident, reliable, & secure one. & if you sit this way most of the time, regardless of consciously or unconsciously, people will think of you as such a person. This's because if people believe you are reliable & secure, they'll more easily trust you to do business with you. & don't get me started about how this can help you in your dating or love life.

The Reclined Sitting Position

Of all the sitting positions, this one's perhaps the one that can give you a Big Bang Theory vibe, i.e., an analytical one. Leaning back is a gesture that shows you can properly think about or observe situations without necessarily or hastily acting upon them. This also means you may be more objective than most other people to separate yourself enough from a position to think about it first before taking action. & from a relational perspective, this can give others the impression that you're a person who's very much aware of how others feel, which can also help you connect to people on a deeper level & easily earn their trust & loyalty.

Crossed Ankle Sitting Position

In most cases, sitting with ankles crossed gives others the impression that the person sitting in this position isn't only elegant & refined but is also humble & open-minded. Coupled with slightly open legs, this position conveys a feeling of being comfortable both under one's skin & in the environment.

Clutching Armrests Sitting Position

Sitting stiffly & are practically clutching at the chair's armrests shows awareness of & sensitivity to one's surroundings. & by hugging on armrests, the seated person comes across to most other people as emotionally & physically unsure because of the need to clutch on to the chair's armrests for stability most of the time.

But merely using the armrests by resting your arms on them instead of clutching to them can also give a much different impression - an opposite one. Doing so can communicate that you're a stable person – emotionally, physically, & mentally - so much so that people are predisposed to depending on you for their own emotional & intellectual stability. You'll likely become their figurative armrests.

Crossed Arm Sitting Position

Often crossed arms are often perceived as indicators of confidence, defensiveness, & strength. But it can also be taken as an indicator of being closed to new ideas or being protective of one's self, with arms crossed in front of the body being taken to mean as protection of one's body from the rest of the world. Either way, a crossed arm sitting position is a body language that says a person is neither open nor weak.

Sidesaddle Sitting Position

If you're a lady, then this one's for you specifically. The amazing sidesaddle sitting position is one where you sit with your knees to the side. This sitting position communicates a naturally sweet, caring, & delicate personality. & o it can also display a character that's a wee bit flirtatious. So choose wisely to whom you'll show this particular body position. & when you point your knees & chest to the other person, it can be subconsciously taken as being available & open to something new, i.e., a possible relationship.

Hands-on Lap Sitting Position

When your hands are on your thighs & are still, it can be construed as a sign that you're a thoughtful & shy person. Also, you can come across as a calm & collected person if you're able to keep your hands still while sitting down.

Dead Center Sitting Position

Sitting smack in the center of a couch, bench, or even table communicates to others that you're a confident person. Why? It's because people who aren't sure, i.e., insecure or even tentative, tend to worry about where to sit down - they practically fuss over where they should sit & sit in the center is very uncomfortable most of them. So by sitting in the middle, it essentially communicates to others that you're not afraid of being in the center of attention & that you can choose to sit anywhere you want to. & by subtly communicating to others that you're confident, you can also come across & friendly & bold, making it easier for you to establish rapport with others, which's a crucial skill for the business.

Legs on Chair Arm Sitting Position

This's a sitting position taken mainly by men as it also uses the spread legs position. This sitting position is also one where a person stakes his ownership of the chair & communicates an aggressive & informal attitude. While it's not unusual to see this sitting position among two friends who're whiling time away joking & laughing with each other, it's not appropriate for different, more severe situations. For example, you're a boss & your subordinate comes to you after making a big mistake at work, which's ok with you. Say your aide felt terrible about the error & he sits in front of your table with head held low & hands on his knees - a submissive body language. Let's say, after listening for a while to what your subordinate has to say, you quickly adopt a legs-on-chair arm position. By doing so, you've just subtly communicated to your assistant that you don't give a rat's ass about how he's feeling & that he's wasting your time. You're coming off as aggressively dismissing your subordinate's feelings through this position.

Now maybe the reason you're dismissing your subordinate's feelings is a perfect one: that you don't think he's done anything seriously wrong & that he shouldn't feel that bad about his mistake. Even if you verbally communicate that, remember how powerful body language can be when sharing with others - about how it's more potent than verbal communications? Therefore, even if you meant well & wanted to encourage him, your body language, i.e., the legs-on-the-chair-arm position, essentially communicates a vastly different message; one that aggressively says you're not interested in how he feels & that he's just wasting your time.

On your end, you should avoid this body language at all costs, save for informal interactions with people with who you already have deep relationships. Now, suppose you use this in a business setting. In that case, the chances are high that you'll perhaps piss off your counterparties & substantially lower your chances of being able to successfully discuss or negotiate with them & persuade them to side with you.

If the other person takes this stance during a business or even professional meeting, it's a sign that this person thinks lowly of you & believes he can get away with everything with you. That's unless you respond accordingly. How can you do so without actually coming across as angry or disruptive?

You can make a light & funny but indirect attempt to tell him that you noticed he's doing that posture & that it's not appropriate. For example, you can perhaps half-jokingly say to him that his pants have split between his legs or even putting something just in front of him at a distance that'd require him to break the position & ask him to look at that thing. If he returns to the post, continue breaking it in a subtle &, if possible, a funny way.

The Chair Straddling Sitting Position

Ages ago, it usually used to be that men used shields for protection against their enemies' weapons. These days, people whatever's available to symbolize their attempts at protecting themselves against the perceived verbal & physical attacks. & these attempts may include hiding behind an object - such as doors, fences, or even gates, & straddling a chair.

By straddling a chair, a person can also symbolically protect him or herself using a chair's backside. Moreover, such a position can make a person look dominant & aggressive, which can help fend off "attackers." & because straddling a chair requires a spread legs posture, it also allows a person to take up more space & thus, adding an extra assertion to the pose.

When you encounter a straddler, the chances are that he or she's a person with a very domineering personality who likes controlling others as soon as they become bored with their interactions. & in most cases, they're very discreet, i.e., you hardly notice them slipping into this sitting position during the exchange. So how do you handle such a person, take power back, & increase your chances of successfully persuading him or her to your way position?

As with other dominating positions, change your work so that they'll also be forced to break theirs. For example, you can stand up & go behind him or her, forcing her to turn around & break the straddling position to continue interacting with you. The chances of this working are also high because by going behind the straddler, you put him or her in a place where he or she can't cover his or her back, which's a vulnerable position that people with strong personalities don't like.

Now, what if the straddler is sitting on a swivel chair that can also very quickly turn around without having to break the straddling position?

Breaking his or her perceived dominance will require you to add another action to changing your position: moving into his or her personal space. After standing up to continue conversing with a straddler, which also puts you in a position to look down on him or her, moving into his or her personal space will also make it very uncomfortable for him or her to continue straddling the chair, which will eventually force him or her to finally abandon the straddling position & change into something more comfortable.

Standing positions

When standing up, the legs & feet are the body parts that do most of the work. & because of this, legs & feet can be an excellent source of information - whether about you or others. But how's this so?

Dr. Paul Ekman & William Friesen have conducted researches on deceptive habits & those researches have shown that people who're lying tend to give away more signals of such through lower body movements, regardless of gender. It appears that the reason for this's the consciousness of activities - or lack thereof. People, in general, are more aware of their upper body movements & gestures & aren't as conscious of lower body part ones. This's probably because the legs & feet are generally out of the lines of sight of people when interacting with others & so most people aren't able to consciously control their lower body movements compared to upper body ones. Being aware of the joint standing positions & the subconscious messages they generally send can help you effectively communicate to others & to read them with relatively high accuracy.

The Parallel Stance Standing Position

This standing position is usually taken by a subordinate & is taken by standing with both legs straight & both feet positioned closely with each other. This's a formal standing position that can subconsciously communicate a neutral attitude such as that of a child student when talking to the teacher, an army member when addressing his commanding officer, or standing in front of a panel of judges while simply waiting for their verdict during a competition.

This particular standing position is also relatively more precarious than the others because feet close together while standing is a relatively weak standing foundation compared to wider-stance ones. With this position, you can be easily pushed out of balance when caught off guard, or you can also do the same to another person.

As mentioned earlier, this's a stand taken by people who're usually neutral on a particular topic or situation, i.e., they're unsure, tentative, or hesitant.

The Spread Legs Standing Position

With this standing position, which's usually a position taken by men, subconsciously or subtly communicates a stable, stubborn, & unmoving posture. By taking this position, you can subtly communicate to other people that you'll stand your ground & you're showing your dominance. This standing position is taken with legs straight, but this time, both feet are actually positioned widely apart - typically wider than shoulder-width - & bodyweight equally distributed between both feet.

One of the main reasons this's a predominantly male standing position is average height, i.e., men are generally taller than women & thus, have higher centers of gravity. But height notwithstanding, it's also used more by men because it uses the genital area to highlight dominance through a virile look, which isn't the case with ladies. Another reason is that men usually don't wear skirts, which can make the spread legs standing position a bit challenging & uncomfortable.

And more than just convincing others to look at you with a positive view, adapting the spread legs standing position can also quickly help you feel much better about yourself when you're feeling down. Couple this standing position with your shoulders pulled back & head held high, it's a short matter of time before your motion or position will affect your emotion, i.e., you'll feel more confident & optimistic about yourself.

Foot Forward Standing Position

This position, done with one leg & foot forward, can help you send subconscious signals to other people about the direction you want to go or the person in a group you find most interesting or even attractive.

In particular, the direction or person your lead foot is pointing to is a subtle way of simply telling others where you want to go or who the most exciting person in the group for you is, respectively.

Crossed Legs Standing Position

When in a gathering, I want you to do something: observe the people around you who're standing & watch out for those who're doing so with crossed arms & legs. In particular, I'd like you to observe how far they're from other people compared to those whose legs & arms aren't crossed. You'll find that they position themselves farther from others than those whose legs & arms are open while standing. Closed portions communicate that a person has a generally closed or defensive attitude, symbolized by crossed legs that appear to deny access to the genital area. There's a good chance that crossed legs & arms while standing up merely communicate that the person feels cold & not defensive. So how'd you known? First, observe the temperature of the place. If it's hard, it's also probably done as a way to keep warm. Yet another way is to check where the hands are placed. If they're tucked between armpits, they're cold. If the legs are straight, pressed hard against each other, & stiff, chances are it's an attempt to keep warm rather than a defensive attitude.

Research has shown that when you are aware of the happenings of your own body, you can manipulate it by training yourself to have control and even mold it to have effective communication. Further research recommends that you take some breathing exercises before going into a meeting or presentation. It will help you calm and have the ability to take note of your posture and gestures while on presentation. As you have noted by now, mirroring is a good technique. Always try to be keen on what the next person is doing non-verbally and copy that. They will understand you better because this tunes your mind to communicate more truthfully at a place of relaxation.

This ensures that the body language you portray matches what you are trying to present. A mismatch may bring confusion and may not be relevant at the moment. The person you are in conversation with my mistake you for meaning something else contrary to what you intended. The secret to having control of your body language is taking your time to learn it and being aware of your non-verbal cues as you apply what you know.

The Body Language That Will Help You Take Charge of Your Space

Effective management involves individuals being able to encourage and have a positive influence. In planning for a necessary appointment, maybe with your employees, management team, or partners, you focus on what to say, memorizing critical points, and rehearsing your presentation to make you feel believable and persuasive.

Here is what you should know if you want to control your position, at work, presentation, or as a leader.

When somebody psychologically marks you as trustworthy, or skeptical, firm, or submissive, you will be seen through such a filter in any other dealings that you do or say. Your partners will look for the finest in you if they like you.

They will suspect all of your deeds if they distrust you. While you can't stop people from having quick decisions, as a defense mechanism, the human mind is programmed in this way; you can learn how to make these choices effective for you.

In much less than seven seconds, the initial perceptions are developed and strongly influenced by body language. Studies have found that nonverbal signals have more than four times the effect on the first impression you create than you speak. This is what you should know regarding making positive and lasting first impressions. Bear in mind several suggestions here:

Start by changing your attitude. People immediately pick up your mood. Have you noticed that you immediately get turned off after finding a customer service representative who has a negative attitude? You feel like leaving or request to be served by a different person. That will happen to you too if you have a bad mood, which is highly noticeable. Think of the situation and make a deliberate decision about the mindset you want to represent before you meet a client, or join the meeting room for a company meeting, or step on the scene to make an analysis.

Smile. Smiling is a good sign that leaders are under using. A smile is a message, a gesture of recognition and acceptance. "I'm friendly and accessible," it says. Having a smile on your face will change the mood of your audience. If they had another perception of you, a smile can change that and make them relax.

Make contact with your eyes. Looking at somebody's eyes conveys vitality and expresses interest and transparency. An excellent way to help you make eye contact is to practice observing the eye color of everybody you encounter to enhance your eye contact. Overcome being shy and practice this excellent body language.

Lean in gently. The body language that has you leaning forward often expresses that you are actively participating and interested in the discussion. This means staying about two ft away in most professional situations.

Shaking hands This will be the best way to develop a relationship. It's the most successful as well. Research indicates that maintaining the very same degree of partnership you can get with a simple handshake takes a minimum of three hours of intense communication. You should ensure that you have palm-to-palm touch and that your hold is firm but not bone-crushing.

Look at your position. Studies have found that the uniqueness of posture, presenting yourself in a way that exposes your openness and takes up space, generates a sense of control that creates changes in behavior in a subject independent of its specific rank or function in an organization.

In fact, in three studies, it was repeatedly found that body position was more important than the hierarchical structure in making a person think, act, and be viewed more strongly.

Building your credibility is dependent on how you align your non-verbal communication.

Trust is developed by a perfect agreement between what is being said and the accompanying expressions. If your actions do not entirely adhere to your spoken statement, people may consciously or unconsciously interpret dishonesty, confusion, or internal turmoil.

Using an electroencephalograph (EEG) device to calculate "event-related potentials"–brain waves that shape peaks and valleys to examine gesture effects prove that one of these valleys happens when movements dispute what is spoken are shown to subjects. This is the same dip in the brainwave when people listen to the language that does not make sense. And, in a somewhat reasonable way, they do not make sense if leaders say one thing and their behaviors point to something else. Each time your facial expressions do not suit your words, e.g., losing eye contact or looking all over the room when trying to express sincerity, swaying back on the heels while thinking about the company's bright future, or locking arms around the chest when announcing transparency. All this causes the verbal message to disappear.

Studies likewise find that individuals who convey through dynamic motioning will, in general, be assessed as warm, pleasant, and energetic. In contrast, the individuals who stay still or whose motions appear to be mechanical or "wooden" are viewed as legitimate, cold, and systematic.

You may have seen senior administrators commit minor avoidable errors. At the point when pioneers don't utilize motions accurately on the off chance that they let their hands hang flaccidly to the side or fasten their hands before their bodies in the exemplary "fig leaf" position, it recommends they have no passionate interest in the issues or are not persuaded about the fact of the matter they're attempting to make.

The issue is that forceful blame dispensing can recommend that the pioneer lose control of the circumstance, and the signal bears a resemblance to parental reprimanding or play area harassing.

Eager gestures: There is an intriguing condition of the hand and arm development with vitality.

Laidback gestures Arms held at midsection tallness and motions inside that level plane help you - and the group of spectators - feel focused and formed.

Innovation can be a great facilitator of factual data, but meeting in an individual is the key to positive relationships between employees and clients. Whatever industry you work in, we're always in the business of individuals. However tech-savvy you could be, face-to-face gatherings are by far the most successful way of capturing attendees ' interest, engaging them in a discussion, and fostering fruitful teamwork. It is said that if it doesn't matter that much, send an email. If it is crucial for the task but not significant, make a phone call. If it is essential for the project's success, it is advised to see someone.

Ability to study Body Language

More business administrators are learning how to send the correct sign, yet also how to understand them.

Correspondence occurs in more than two channels, verbal and nonverbal, bringing about two detailed discussions simultaneously. While an unwritten post is significant, all accounts are not the only message being sent. Without the capacity to read non-verbal communication, we miss critical components to discussions that can emphatically or adversely sway a business.

When individuals aren't installed with an activity, pioneers should have the option to perceive what's going on and react rapidly. That is why commitment and withdrawal are two of the most significant signs to screen in other individuals' non-verbal communication. Commitment practices demonstrate intrigue, receptivity, or understanding, while separation practices signal fatigue, outrage, or protectiveness.

Active participation sign incorporates head gestures or tilts, the widespread indication of "giving somebody your ear," and open-body poses. At the point when individuals are locked in, they will confront you straightforwardly, "pointing" at you with their entire body. Be that as it may, the moment they feel awkward, they may edge their chest area away – giving you "the brush off." And if they endure the whole gathering with the two arms and legs crossed, it's far-fetched you have their upfront investment.

Additionally, screen the measure of the eye to eye connection you're getting. Generally, individuals will look longer and with more recurrence at individuals or things that they like.

A large portion of us are alright with an eye to eye connection enduring around three seconds, yet when we want or concur with somebody, we consequently increment the measure of time we investigate their eyes. Separation triggers the inverse: the action of the eye to eye connection diminishes, as we will, in general, turn away from things that trouble or get us bored.

Non-verbal communication is winding up some portion of an official's close to the home brand. Extraordinary pioneers sit, stand, walk, and signal in manners that ooze certainty, capability, and status. They additionally send non-verbal signs of warmth and sympathy, mainly when supporting community situations and overseeing change. As an official mentor, I've been awed by the effect of non-verbal communication on administration results.

Extraordinary non-verbal communication abilities can assist you with spurring direct reports, security with crowds, present thoughts with included believability, and indeed venture your image of mystique. That is an incredible arrangement of aptitudes for any pioneer to create.

Chapter 6: Understanding People Through Body Language

You may be wondering why it is essential to learn other people's body language. The ability to understand other people's body language saves you a lot of time that you would have probably been researching why they did something.

Identifying People's Hidden Thoughts Through Body Language

To gain the art of understanding people's non-verbal communication is a tricky thing. You may be wondering how you can focus on learning other people's cues while you do not even know yourself fully. All of us are subconscious experts in interpreting the thoughts of other individuals around us. We developed these abilities in the woolly mammoth age since our life depended on them, and the unconscious mind would work more efficiently than the conscious mind. However, when we make this unconscious understanding aware, it does not yield a good result. Practically, we can respond with lightning speed to dodge a fist that some whiny brat throws in our way or to jump out from the form of an approaching car before we can think about it explicitly.

It's excellent; it's subconscious, and it works. But in particular, we find that most of us are much less skilled at actively knowing what everyone else in a group is thinking, doing, or determining—for example, knowing if the chief ringleaders in the group are against your growth plan or not. There are those motives to see in the language of the body. The issue is that; we simply get so much far from too little data of what others plan to do. People move, shake, continuously try to look up, down, or sideways, raise their eyebrows, roll their eyes, close their ears, and scratch their noses. What is this all about? How can you control it all in a public space and do so on time to react appropriately?

You can't do that. Too many details come to us too quickly because excess chaff has been blended with wheat. You could wonder if Janet is stroking her lip because she's worried about your idea? Alternatively, is she just rubbing an itchy chin quite often? On the other hand, you could wonder if Jack will fold his arms since he resists your best efforts to change direction for the whole cohort. Or is he just cold?

You can become insane by trying to intentionally track a room full of people's constantly shifting body cues to little use because the discussion has transitioned on by the moment you figured it all out.

In the meantime, you did not attend the discussion's helpful content as you were supposed to. Is there a route around this predicament of expecting to screen gigabytes of gushing information about some individuals' expectations, intentionally and quickly, while at the equivalence, considering the substance of the discussions?

You should know that it is possible. Instead of checking the information, for the most part, search for affirmation of your theories about expectation so that you can accelerate and limit the flood of data you have to take in.

So, the genuine inquiry is this; if you need to turn into a conscious master in analyzing other individuals' oblivious articulation of their intentions, how would you structure speculations about that articulation and affirm or dismiss them? The appropriate response is to confine your potential beliefs to not many that you've recognized before your gathering, discussion, or introduction. At that point, you can suggest the single conversation starter to your intuitive personality and utilize that oblivious ability we, as a whole, need to give a detailed, solid answer.

So, we should begin. Here are five common, helpful approaches to consider what other individuals mean:

The approaches are divided into:

-   **Open and closed**

-   **Being sincere or insincere**

-   **Being allied or opposed**

-   **Strong and subservient**

Committed and uncommitted

You can, however, add yours for specific circumstances not covered by these, and you will find that all these functions are within a large proportion of interactions between people where you need to track body language in particulars.

I'll touch every range. The aims are to spend a little time focusing on the nonverbal conversation at an upcoming meeting and choose which continuum is best suited to what you are worried about or involved in and display the crux of the problem from you and the people who care. Further, as the book addresses this, you'll let go of all the control of your subconscious mind and, as if by magic, you'll get a simple, accurate measure of what other people want.

How do you reveal the truth? Read on.

Sincerity Vs. With your oblivious personality, insincerity is the ideal approach to understanding the troubling inquiry of acknowledging a lie. Perhaps the whole picture means a steady articulation is great to grab. Dishonesty; are your eyes fixed with stupid stillness as your hands interweave anxiously? That's a crucial symbol of being insincere.

The following most significant spot to check after the face is the direction of the head. That is why you would prefer not to concentrate a lot on specific cues but instead let your conscious personality get on the general situation. So once more, ask yourself, is this individual genuine or deceitful? And after that, take in the entire individual. For those of you who are keen on the details, you'll need to know a portion of the particular 'tells' in any case. Apart from the eyes and face, search for the torso just if they turn away from you, which will mean they are telling a lie, or toward you, which means they are telling the truth. Check whether there are guarded motions against the hands and arms and indications of tumult from the hands and fingers.

Furthermore, search for opposing conduct from the legs and feet. Likewise, tune in for indications of strain in the voice. If you find that the agent is painstakingly controlled or somewhat sharp sounding than expected, the individual might be endeavoring to disguise something. The world's best master of lying has discovered that individuals who are lying delay down with an end goal to control their voice, their facial expressions, and different mannerism. In any case, even the ordinary individuals can likewise race to get past a cumbersome inclination minute. So, the primary concern to search for is a change of voice from the norm, which you should know well in a spouse or a friend.

Recognizing a liar in a public gathering is a great exercise. Specific individuals have made a vocation to identify small-scale articulations that hid real feelings. In any case, it's an uncertain science because considerably more detail is absent, and you don't have a clue why the individual is covering the feeling. Is it dread? Anger? Energy? To get that, you need to become more acquainted with the individual better, requiring some time investment.

Allied and Opposed

This category will help you note if someone is on your side or not.

How would you tell whether somebody is your ally or not? The fundamental non-verbal communication to search for to decide if individuals are united or restricted is their physical position and direction. This makes for engaging people viewing. When you're on to this part of conduct, you'll see that it is easy to get. This is particularly simple to tell when there are three individuals present, and you need to make sense of who is your ally and who is not. Search for the person who has a similar essential body direction as you. For a test, move and check whether the other individual sticks to this same pattern in the next thirty seconds.

Companions, spouses, and darlings typically reflect each other's physical direction when they're at the same place or with the public, and they do inessential understand. It's fascinating to watch couples for indications of reflection and its inverse. You can regularly recognize inconvenience in the relationship before the team knows about it.

What occurs in reflection is more significant than just understanding or associating. Since influence is enthusiastic just as a scholarly movement, it originates from deep inside the mind. When we concur with somebody, we do as such with our entire being. You can utilize this to drive understanding and make an influence. Embrace a stance, and watch others receive it. When they have, they transform it somewhat. If the others come, you're well on your approach to convince the room.

The value of your power (or scarcity in that department) will be rendered and checked by your management of nonverbal communication in the hall. The explanation is that the bodies of individuals reveal what they think, not the other way.

It's both unreasonable and clear. Our brains state themselves fundamentally, I am physically adapted with this woman, so I ought to agree with her. You should utilize this control of the physical direction of other individuals with articulacy. It must be joined with a progression of steps that incorporate different sorts of agreement building.

First, construct understanding by embracing their positions, managing their worries, and most importantly, expanding on your receptiveness to them and their receptiveness to you. What you're doing is adjusting your two discussions and utilizing them to convince others in the room. It takes extensive practice to do this with nuance and viability, yet once you ace it, you'll see that your capacity to convince others will increment immensely.

Scan the alpha. If possible, he or she would be the most significant person in the room. That's why kings and queens have had daises thrones since they started ruling others. I did a test asking the CEOs, whom I worked with, to check the revelation of power by convening a conference with the CEO in the center at a conference room table. The CEOs usually take the middle of the room to demonstrate their ability anyway, and sometimes even the head. I advised the Chief executive to sit in her chair initially, but after a while, he progressively sinks into the chair by slipping very, very, gradually forward. Yes, to the conscious yet invisible mind. The outcome was phenomenal. Those within the audience who deliberately tried to articulate their subservience to the Boss sank to escape the boss upstage. The CEOs told me they could hardly suppress their laughter on hearing that everybody at the conference table slide towards the floor.

Influential individuals also take up so much space, splaying their legs or arms or hogging more space in the room. That is why influential people get larger apartments than fewer men, and that's why tall people in their careers are significantly more likely to rise faster than short people.

Influential individuals use a host of bolder indicators of their dominance to indulge in shorter breaks, from upsetting smaller individuals to talking more. We make more or less eye contact because of their choice. They monitor the communication of the second speaker's ballet with the eye and the outside touch. That is why it requires preparation to meet the Queen, and you have to get out of the room before you enter.

All this is just voicing her superiority over the rest of us. Strong people may disappear from a discussion with this capacity, control speed, and show their power. It is arrogant, but it is successful.

Non-verbal show capacity is all about regulating your behavior, as well as others'. Once it is something that is expertly tuned to by the subconscious, you'll immediately know when you're in the company of someone who thinks she's strong because of all the signs I've mentioned, and you're all instinctively aware of.

Committed and Uncommitted

Commitment is when you close the offer, the contract ink, get the job, get the 'go forward.' It is a crucial moment, and it's essential to see it so that you wouldn't be doing the wrong thing at the pivotal moment.

What is the feel of it?

People learn from you when they are serious. They are transparent, submissive at times, always genuine, and generally well connected. It starts with their eyes; they're completely open, and you're focused. Likewise, the face is relaxed. It's going to be very close to yours more than anything. It's all about completing the sale to close the distance. That is why car sales representatives regularly shake your hand. The torso, if not engaged, is accessible and nearer to you.

There is no oppositional chatter from the arms and hands, feet, and legs. If appropriate in the situations, the person or persons may well mimic you. The act of communication is often indicated by a change of nonverbal communication, which suggests a decision has been made. Search for it yes or no. Push your subconscious mind in a higher gear at that level. It is essential to ask yourself if the person is committed.

You can say easily when you see all of the positive effects I have mentioned or the opposite. With time and above all, you are going to feel relaxed. Commitment is a logical statement, and we like to achieve it because we are social creatures.

Commitment is a kind of link that makes people feel good. When you function from your subconscious mind, you can recognize it when you see it.

When there is no such thing, people have expressed their frustration with all kinds of anger, harsh body language, and efforts to quit. A few cultural norms spread these weird moments with an abundance of understanding, positive non-verbal communication, and shallow endeavors at duty. When Westerners initially work from Asia, they frequently wind up misunderstanding the Asian act of kindness and want to conceal it as a hint of wanting to commit. This is one occurrence when your consciousness can fail you. The examinations showed that fundamental non-verbal communication is the equivalent around the globe. However, it can rapidly be secured with socially decided non-verbal communication minutes later. Without a ton of training, the distinctions can be difficult to spot.

This isn't the spot for an all-inclusive exchange of different cultures, yet there are various phenomenal references regarding the matter. It's ideal for taking societies individually, when you're going to visit another nation, instead of attempting to learn them at the same time. Precisely because our childhood profoundly adapts to the non-verbal communication we convey, and it's difficult to change when it's not natural.

Open and Closed

The first way to determine the motives of others is the most important one; their level of transparency. It is the most important since interaction will start if people are honest. Nothing good can happen if they aren't. You should be prepared to scale individuals more along the lines quickly in an almost automated way with just a little training. In reality, it takes a little time for each new individual you meet to measure the performance of conduct. The idea isn't capable of carrying out this role immediately but to size up somebody with high efficiency regarding whether this person is open to you or not within a few minutes.

Past the forehead, see the versatility of the eyebrows. How regularly and far do they move? Generally, individuals will cause the movement of their eyebrows when they're communicating with others, searching for a reaction, posing an inquiry, taking you in, etc. So, the sum and separation of movement are markers of a general degree of receptiveness. On a particular occasion, when the eyebrows are up, being open to your contribution to the event. Once more, the development might be because of an inquiry that the individual has posed to you, yet it's regarded as being open.

Presently go down to the eyes themselves. Is it true that they are limited or all the way open? You have to set up a pattern of how the individual carries on in genuinely nonpartisan circumstances. Doing this will give you a thought of whether the specific case is that of transparency or not. Individuals open their eyes more extensively when they are keen on a person or thing and close them when they are not or are effectively suspicious or careful about occasions, individuals, or activities.

Since individuals are so dynamic with their eyes, you should be mindful of precluding ecological reasons. Is a brilliant light sparkling in the individual's face? That may represent the pale eyes. It may not be because you've recently offered the individual a trade-in vehicle at a tremendous cost. Being open means having an interest, fascination, and excitement; the inverse shows the turnaround. Moreover, the general degree of lighting in the earth influences the size of the pupils, so you have to build up a standard ability to note the difference.

Flaring nostrils are the result of romance books and novels about steeds. By the by, there might be truth to the portrayals associating sexual appreciation for this piece of the face, exceptionally if pheromones are being researched on and fascination ends up being valid. It is unquestionably the situation that a wrinkled nose can show disgust, or in any event, nauseate at an awful stench. Outrageous facial motions like these are difficult to miss and effectively brought to the conscious mind. It is the subtler ones you ought to be increasingly worried about. When somebody arrives at the purpose of wrinkling his nose, they have presumably already revealed to you how they feel or are going to do as such.

The mouth is fit for a thousand minor departures from the essential entourage of a grin, scowl, shock, dread, etc. In basic terms, search for a genuine smile. That is the generally comprehended indication of endorsement from others, and consequently, individuals who grin are bound to be available to you than impartial individuals. Individuals can have a smile because of different reasons; Note that it is essential to have the wisdom to recognize a firm, troubled, or false smile from a casual, regular one that is inviting and open.

Moreover, for the torso, proximity and bearing sign degrees of transparency. On a fundamental level, the closer and more direct the other person's torso toward you, the more open that individual is, and the more distance they keep from you, the more closed they are.

What are those things hand gestures informing us concerning transparency? They are not the undeniable ones like the harmony signal or the center finger. Those are known as 'symbols.'

These motions signal purpose constantly. At the point when individuals reach toward us with loose motions, for instance, they're typically flagging transparency. Occasionally is something different, similar to one side snare to the jaw. A grasp, definitive open signal, is a blend of open hand motions and an open torso.

Receptiveness can be perused in hand itself too. What is going on with it? Is it gripped or apprehensively manipulating the other hand? Is it skittish or endeavoring to disguise itself in a pocket? Writings talk a perpetual and captivating language; they are glorious little weathervanes to the condition of the spirit inside and its purposes.

On the off chance that you do an act of watching other individuals' hands, you'll find out about the condition of their nerves, preventiveness, certainty, anger, satisfaction, distress, advantage, or fatigue, notwithstanding their transparency or deficiency in that department.

Numerous books on non-verbal communication imply direct implications of explicit motions. However, this is a trick's down. Each signal can have a significant impact. We fold our arms to pick a basic model since we're cautious, undoubted, though we're worn out, cold, or we need to shroud a growing midsection.

However, if you are searching for the response to a particular inquiry, at that point, you can give your oblivious ability something to do for you. Ask yourself, is this individual open or shut toward me? Then start searching for the information you have to make an assurance.

The ideal approach to do this is to offer the conversation starter to your intuitive personality. Solicit yourself toward the start from the discussion, open or shut? What's more, sit tight for your instinct about the issue to turn out to be precise.

When you feel the circumstance, you can begin searching deliberately for pieces of information to affirm or invalidate your underlying reading. Assume you're at a prospective employee meet-up, for instance, and you need to recognize what your odds of accomplishment are.

The primary inquiry you should consider is whether you are even in the running or not. As it were, is this an open meeting or a courtesy meeting? So, start the session by asking yourself, is this individual open or shut to me? If the appropriate response returns closed, at that point, you can be sensibly certain that another person as of now has the activity.

If the individual appears to be open, you can turn on your vitality and appeal. You might need to be watchful for an adjustment in that reading. Consider the possibility that the questioner has been open for; maybe the initial forty-five minutes of the meeting and afterward all of a sudden begins to convey a shut sign. Has the questioner decided negatively, or would she say she is just flagging that the time is up? You might need to ask some particular procedure inquiries (so anyone can hear and understand) to see. For example, "What's the following stage? In what capacity will you approach settling on a choice?" Is the inquiry to pose to your oblivious personality open or shut? On the off chance that the appropriate response is given in a shut manner, you most likely won't land the position. A bolder inquiry in that equivalent circumstance may be to ask, "how would I stack facing different candidates?"

Since grown-ups become adroit in controlling their countenances and chest areas, it merits taking a gander at the legs and feet for the fascinating counter flag. Frequently, somebody has made their face in a friendly welcome, yet the legs and feet (and the middle as well) may recount to an alternate story. The legs might be crossed away from you, flagging a shut direction, the middle might be contorted out, or the other individual may essentially expand the separation, even marginally, among you.

Decoding Body Language by Watching at the Body Movement

Understanding other people may be a hard thing to do, but once you do it, you will have conquered your way into their life, hence able to influence them in various ways. The next time you are around your friends, in a work meeting, or with kids, just look for the following and understand what they mean.

Arms and Legs Crossed Suggests Opposition to Your Ideas

Legs and arms crossed are obstructions that indicate that the other individual is not receptive to what you tell. You find that, even if they tend to engage in good conversation and smile, most of the time, the truth is revealed through body language.

Authors who were doing negotiations for their new book on reading body language study a case. They held many meetings and later showed that among all the arrangements, not one resulted in an agreement whenever one of the parties crossed their legs and feet when negotiating. Mentally, the legs and arms crossed means that an individual is mentally, emotionally, or physically stopped from what is before them. It's not deliberate, so it's so surprising.

Copying Your Body Language

Have any of you ever met somebody and found that they do the same if you cross or uncross your legs and feet? Or maybe when you're thinking, they lean their heads in the very same position as yours? In reality, that's a good indication. If we experience a bond with another person, mirroring body language comes in unintentionally. It's an indication that the discussion moves well enough and that group is receiving your message. Such information can be beneficial when bargaining, as it tells you what the other party feels about the contract.

The Story is Told by Posture

Have you ever seen someone come into a room, and you immediately knew they were in control? This influence is primarily about the body's language and often involves:

- *An upright stance.*

- *Movements with the palms facing forward.*

- *Generally open and expressive gestures.*

It's a position of authority to stand straight with your shoulders back; it seems to maximize the amount of storage you fill. On the other hand, slouching is the product of the collapse of your shape; it seems to take up less space and less energy for activities. Maintaining good posture commands respect and fosters commitment, regardless of being in a leadership position or not.

Genuine Smiles crinkle the Eyes.

The mouth can deceive whenever it applies to laugh; however, the eyes can never lie. Genuine smiles touch the ears and wrinkle the skin in front of them to build the feet of the crow.

In case you're conversing with somebody whose gaze is making you squirm, particularly when they're highly still and unblinking, something is going on, and they may be lying to you.

It's challenging to do; would I say it isn't? If someone conversing with you happens to have raised eyebrows, yet the subject of the discussion would not consistently cause shock, stress, or dread, then there is something different going on.

Misrepresented Nods Signal Nervousness About Acceptance

At the point when you're telling somebody something, and they keep nodding too much, this implies they are stressed over what you consider them or that you question their capacity to adhere to your guidelines.

A Held Jaw Sign Pressure

A gripped jaw, a fixed neck, or wrinkled temples indicate stress. The discussion may be diving into something they're on edge about, or their psyche maybe somewhere else, and they're concentrating on what's wrong with them. The key is to look for that befuddlement between what the individual says and what their strained non-verbal communication is letting you know.

Chapter 7: Body Language Myths

You have a good overview of how the different parts of the bodywork may indicate other things. Still, there are also many myths about body language that suggest unlikely or provide the wrong impression about body language. This section will cover and dispel a few of the more pervasive myths.

They Aren't Looking – They Must Be Lying!

It's pretty common to hear and read that person who doesn't make eye contact has something to hide, making most people uncomfortable. However, this is pretty easily debunked. Can you think of times when someone struggled to make eye contact? Did they seem malicious, evil, or deceptive? Most likely, they appeared nervous or shy. Eye contact is crucial because it demonstrates that you are paying attention, showing confidence and strength. This doesn't mean eye contact has any inherent moral value.

You Can Easily Spot The Liar

The truth is that people are fantastic at lying to you with their words and their body: the best way to tell whether someone is lying to you or not is to use basic reasoning. If you think about most of the lies, you tell it's clear why this is the case. Often you are lying about things you are not sure about or something that you are in some ways convinced is true. Your body wouldn't lie if you weren't sure you were lying in the first place.

On the other hand, if you know someone well and you have identified their 'tells,' which are essentially behavioral actions that they do when they lie, then you can use that as a gauge to determine if they are lying. Everyone operates on habits, and most people have tells or anchors they do when they lie, this could be as simple as sniffing their nose, tapping their fingers on the table, or rubbing their chin.

Strong And Domineering Body Language = POWER

It can be very tempting to think like this, but the reality is that you will frequently work for people that do not project power with macho stances but through subtler control of a room with self-confidence and self-belief. These people are unlikely to carry themselves with weak views or closed posture, but they may not use powerful gestures or body language all that often, even though many respect them.

Trying to attain power in a situation where it does not belong to you can wind up with you making enemies or having others feel like you are overstepping your mark. Assertive body language is helpful, but it doesn't by itself grant you power, and people will notice what it is that you are attempting to do.

93% Of Communication Is Nonverbal

The '7% of communication is what you say' statistic was mentioned earlier, and it comes from a 60-year-old study based on a few specific tests. In newer studies, researchers have not found anywhere near such an importance on what the body can tell other people. Realistically, other people are not that skilled at understanding others from body language alone.

Earlier, you should consider how you communicate with a person who does not speak your language, and while you can usually get by without speaking the same language, imagine doing so without any props or context and just solely using your body. If communication were anywhere near 93% body language, then charades wouldn't even be a game!

These statistics demonstrate how much breadth there is to the ways we communicate. The words we say are just part of a broader range of tools, and the many statistics about how this breaks down in percentages aren't as important as thinking about how you are communicating and what is significant.

Body language is diverse. To ensure that you do not portray other non-verbal communications, it is essential to learn effective body language.

The Most Significant Hints for Successful Non-Verbal Communication in Front of an Audience

Deal with Your Feeling of Anxiety

While you are standing by at the back of the stage, see the pressure in your body. Understand that some apprehensive vitality is something worth being thankful for. Though it makes your introduction exuberant and fascinating, however, a lot of pressure brings about nonverbal practices that may challenge you.

Before you go in front of an audience, stand, or sit with your weight focused and equally disseminated on the two feet or seat bones. Look ahead while focusing on your jawline level to the floor and loosen up your throat. Take a few profound "paunch" breaths. Take count gradually to six as you breathe in and out the strain in your body by making some fists and straining the muscles in your middle arms and legs. As you breathe out, permit your hands, arms, and body to relax and unwind.

Express Emotions

To draw in a crowd of people, they should be genuinely included. So, before you go in front of an audience to convey your message, focus on feelings and sentiments. How would you get a simple interface with what you will state? What is your feeling towards it? How would you need a group of spectators to feel? The more you center on the emotion behind your message, the even more persuading and unified your non-verbal communication will consequently turn into.

Get in with Confidence

Remain very relaxed, leave the podium with a great stance, head held high, and an enduring smooth stride. At the point when you land in the middle of everyone's attention, stop grinning, cause a stir, and somewhat broaden your eyes while you check out the room. A casual, open face and body tell your group of spectators that you're sure and okay with the data you're conveying.

Since a group of spectating individuals will respond to any showcase of pressure, your condition of solace will likewise unwind and console them. This may seem like the presence of mind, yet I once worked with a director who strolled in front of an audience with slumped shoulders, wrinkled temples, and squinted eyes. I viewed the group of spectator's squirm accordingly. It was a disrupting approach to start a "how about we get together and bolster this change?" discourse.

Keep in Touch

Keep in touch with the crowd all through the discussion on the off chance that you will rapidly prefer not to be there, that you aren't generally dedicated to your message, or have something to cover up.

While it is physically challenging to keep in touch with the whole crowd constantly, you can take a gander at explicit people or miniature gatherings, hold their consideration quickly, and afterward move to another group or individual in another part of the room.

Dodge the Platform

Whenever the situation allows, get out from behind the platform. A strong podium does not just conceal most of your body; it additionally goes about as a boundary between you and the group of spectators. Practice the introduction so well that you wouldn't need to peruse from a content; on the off chance you use notes, demand a video guide at the foot of the stage.

Converse with Your Hands

Speakers use hand signals to underscore what's significant and to express emotions, needs, and feelings. Those are the reasons signs are so basic and why getting them directly in introduction interfaces so intensely with a crowd of people. Suppose you don't utilize them (probably that you let your hands hang flaccidly to your sides or fasten them in the exemplary "fig leaf" position). In that case, it recommends you don't perceive the vital issues, you have no enthusiasm for the problems, or that you're not a viable communicator.

Move

Individuals people, most notably, are attracted to the shifting. You are moving side-by-side shields a crowd of people from being exhausted. It tends to be compelling to stroll toward the group of spectators before making a significant point and away when you need to flag a break or a difference in the subject. However, don't move when you are making a critical point. Instead, stop, enlarge your position, and convey that vital message.

The style of strolling passes on a ton of data about our fearlessness and our characteristics. This is one reason why non-verbal communication mentors show strolling techniques to their understudies.

Stand Straight and Face Up

The primary thing to remember is that you ought not to slump or hunch while strolling. The jaw must be up constantly. Many people look down while taking a walk. This isn't taken to be exquisite. Besides, if you slacken or hunch while strolling, you will be viewed as powerless and deprived of vitality and energy.

Terrible stance while strolling, whenever preceded for longer timeframes, can prompt back agony, hardened neck, and different genuine sicknesses.

Utilize All Muscles

It is advised to utilize all your muscle bunches in the legs while strolling. While strolling, attempt to picture pushing off with your back foot, using your hamstrings and quadriceps, and propelling yourself forward onto the impact point of the other foot. Attempt to move your foot forward, impact issue to toe. This causes the lower leg muscles to work and encourages you to keep your feet at the right edge of each progression.

Keeping a pulled back yet loosened up position of shoulders keeps up a steady and vertical segment of help while walking, alongside the straight back and jawline up pose, which makes strolling diminish the odds of damage. This stance additionally radiates certainty and quality.

While strolling, the chest area needs to become the most important factor alongside the legs. The arms need to swing appropriately to extend certainty; they must move in a littler circular segment as you walk.

The quicker you walk, the bigger the circular piece you create. The development of arms increases a superior walk.

Get the Right Speed

The pace of the walk likewise matters a great deal. While strolling, the rate must be to such an extent that you can talk appropriately to an individual while proceeding with your walk and should not seem winded simultaneously.

Walking shrewdly additionally includes not accepting too long walks as you walk. Protracting the walk extends the leg muscles pointlessly and prompts destabilization of the walk.

While having a walk, the hips must be at level, and the means must be of equivalent length—this aids in picking up the balance while strolling. In addition, the head ought not to be tilted and should be held high. Putting your heel on the ground first and not the toe is the penultimate thing to do.

Positive Body Language and Its Significance

In the corporate world, keeping up excellent non-verbal communication assumes a significant job. Great non-verbal communication is acknowledged and energized in the corporate division. Awful non-verbal communication leaves the individuals in a breakdown of the corporate arrangements, and the time organizes misfortune.

Indeed, even without wanting to show the feelings, the sentiments and feelings can be shared and imparted by the body's stance, alongside the body developments. This demonstrates the saying, "Actions speak louder than voices".

A portion of the perspectives where positive non-verbal communication demonstrates to be significant is as per the following:

Self-Assured Behavior

An individual ends up being fearless and confident by joining positive non-verbal communication. Constructive non-verbal communication empowers the individual to pass on the data and conclusion in a progressively straightforward way.

Numerous individuals enjoy the emphatic conduct of constructive non-verbal communication, and in this way, individuals with constructive non-verbal communication attract more individuals.

Non-Verbal Communication

As indicated by the investigations, it is viewed that correspondence includes 65% non-verbal and 35% verbal. It infers that the other individual sees just 35% through words, and the non-verbal communication sees the remaining 65%. The way of life, feelings, and the status of an individual are distinguished by non-verbal communication.

Thus, non-verbal correspondence is significant than verbal correspondence. Non-verbal correspondence encourages rehashing the message, restricting the words, underpinning the announcements, and replacing the sentence meaning, giving a substantial base to the terms. Significantly, non-verbal communication ought to agree with the sentiments and feelings. There ought not to be any inclination of crisscross between the non-verbal communication and verbal correspondence. This may establish other individuals under the connection that the individual is misleading.

Working Environment Success

It is exceptionally fundamental to have positive non-verbal communication in a professional workplace. It helps in upgrading the representative soul by building up working environment cooperation. Positive non-verbal communication streamlines the procedure of duty assignment and empowers to determine the contentions.

A portion of the parts of constructive non-verbal communication, for example, inclining forward, open palms, tenderly grin and direct eye-to-eye connection, helps in creating relations with different individuals, particularly in gatherings, and subsequently leads to a solid association with every one of the individuals engaged with the community.

Connections

Odd developments of the body might ruin the relations with different individuals, and the body acts in this manner, prompting confound and misconstruing the connection and individual.

The conduct with an individual relies upon the feelings and temperament of the other individual. For example, if a companion is in a positive mindset, then prodding or pulling the legs will be taken by the companion as sportive and fun. Still, similar conduct may be confused as bad-tempered conduct if the companion isn't feeling great.

Open Speaking

In an open talk, care ought to be taken regarding non-verbal communication. If non-verbal communication is either cautious or latent, it might prompt the audience to lose enthusiasm for the discourse. In this way, the effect of the lesson additionally is diminished. This is because the group of spectators and the rest 65% (non-verbal) is passed up a great opportunity by the crowd are getting solitary 35% of the correspondence (verbal correspondence). In conclusion, in open communication, positive non-verbal communication demonstrates to be extremely fundamental.

Chapter 9: Body Language & Work

How to Use Body Language to Increase Sales

By communicating with intent, can you use body language to create some form of trust with another person more quickly and reliably than leaving it all to the unconscious mind? This is a question that salespeople are very interested in, but this is true for speakers since an audience wants to trust the person on stage. The answer to this question will determine if they buy into whatever you are trying to tell them.

A great way to improve the likelihood and speed of trust building is to mirror what the other person does. This is a very well-studied phenomenon in the body language world. You can look around and see co-workers, friends, and lovers unconsciously mirroring each other and agree on things quickly, which is our body's way of telling others, "Hey, we act alike, we agree on the same things, we are working on the same page."

Effective Body Language in A Job Interview

You've polished your resume, and you've got your best business suit ready. Remember, your actions can tell the interviewer more than your words or outline. Your goal in an interview is to appear professional, reliable, open, honest, and responsible. You may feel nervous, but you also want to put the interviewer at ease and show that you can fit comfortably into their work environment.

It starts even before the interview.

The use of proper body language starts with the receptionist. Many interviewers ask the receptionist for feedback on your attitude and behavior. Assume that the person walking with you to the elevator might be your interviewer or future boss; never take anything or anyone for granted.

I know someone who joined a talent contest. On the way there, the person walking ahead of her was blocking her path. She and her friends rudely made caustic remarks about how slowly that person was walking as they passed by. Imagine her chagrin when, during the contest, the "slowpoke" turned out to be one of the judges. Even before the actual interview, be aware that you may already be under evaluation.

Be open

Avoid making barriers between you and the interviewer. Sit up straight, showing your neck, chest, and stomach area. You may not feel confident enough to do this but try it. Remember, do the actions, and your brain will follow suit.

Give a good handshake.

In this case, you want to acknowledge the interviewer's authority, so feel free to offer your hand with the palm slightly up if you think it's necessary. Allow the interviewer to take a somewhat dominant position in the handshake if they try. This will make the interviewer see you as a person who will not be challenging to work with. Take your cue from the interviewer and follow the strength of his or her grip. Mimicry will also give a good impression. Follow the interviewer's pace and stride as you're led to your seat.

I necessary, ask where you may sit. Sitting in the interviewer's space is a big no-no. Leaning slightly forward can indicate interest, but leaning too far ahead may cause you to invade the interviewer's personal space.

Allow the twenty-second size up.

Before you move on to the next tip, take a few seconds to allow the interviewer to size you up. This is entirely subconscious and natural. People typically need about 20 seconds to note everything about you from head to foot and store information they will also refer to (again subconsciously) to make their overall assessment of you. You may sit and prepare your documents to allow this to happen.

When this is not done, tension can develop as the interviewer may not concentrate and note what you say during the interview. This is a significant 20 seconds that will significantly influence the outcome of your consultation.

Make eye contact

The base of this imaginary triangle should be above the lips. Focus on this triangle to show interest. Blink occasionally in order not to stare awkwardly. Be careful not to gaze below the imaginary triangle as this could give a different meaning.

Make open palm gestures.

While speaking, use your hands to articulate your ideas. Use open palm gestures and keep your hands below your face and above your waist (make sure your hands can be seen). The open palms indicate that you are knowledgeable and willing to use what you know to help the company.

Show interest with your legs.

Keep both feet on the floor, pointing towards the interviewer. Avoid unnecessary and repetitive leg movements like shaking and jiggling, as this could signal boredom and disinterest. Women wearing skirts can appear more businesslike if they keep their knees together and avoid crossing their legs. Crossed legs can be acceptable as it signals submissiveness. It is essential not to pair crossed legs with crossed arms as this would indicate an overall opposing viewpoint or unwillingness to communicate.

Make a graceful exit.

Rise as smoothly as possible, smile, nod, and thank the interviewer. Make as smooth an exit as possible.

Powerful Body Language in Public Speaking

A person will immediately find you likable if you send them the right signals. However, sending the right signals not only makes you friendly, but it also makes the other person less defensive and more at ease. Establishing rapport makes it easier for both sides to be their true selves. The techniques are still the same, and we will go through them more briefly.

Use open signals

Smile, tilt your head, raise your eyebrows, show the palms of your hand, lean a little bit forward, and do not cross your arms or your legs.

Mirror, mirror

Mirroring says, "we are like-minded." This is the shortcut to establishing and bond with a person. If you sense that someone feels nervous around you, mirroring can help put him at ease. Of course, keep it subtle, and you shouldn't mirror the negatives.

Nod to persuade

Nodding shows agreement and interest. It is also contagious, and the other person will find himself nodding and feeling more agreeable to what you are saying.

Stroke your chin

We do this unconsciously, but you can also intentionally encourage the person to keep talking.

Ready and set

If you're the speaker, you might see the other person leaning slightly forward with one foot forward and hands grasping the sides of the seat as if ready to leave. It could mean two things - he's prepared to go because he disagrees with you, or he's prepared to take what you said to action. You'll have to check for other signals to know what it means. If you noticed negative signs before this, then you'll have to take a different approach to what you are saying.

Pace yourself

Have you ever noticed how, when you're having a conversation with someone with an accent, you find yourself gradually acquiring the accent as your conversation goes along? This is an example of pacing. It is mirroring the way a person speaks. To build rapport and enhance communication, try to keep with the other person's pace. Speaking too fast will make the other person feel tense and under pressure. Try to mirror the other person's intonation, inflection, and speaking speed. This can help you achieve excellent results when setting appointments on the phone.

Make the right approach.

You may be giving open signals that are positive, but you may be perceived as aggressive if you approach too directly. An approach from the side is less threatening. Whether consciously or unconsciously, women fear being attacked from behind, so close at an angle from the front. Men fear a frontal attack, so come at an angle from the rear or side.

Ways Body Language Impacts Leadership Results

Your body can say a considerable amount about your attitude, perspective, and even your mood. It is essential to study your body movements; one of the most obvious is the inability to stay still. This is usually a sign of nervousness, although it can be seen as passion about a subject. Crossing your arms across your chest is a defensive stance and suggests someone who will be disagreeable and stubborn; not a desirable trait when attempting to communicate with someone!

If you are unsure about the message your body language is giving out, then you should replay a conversation or speech in front of your mirror; once you are alone. You may be surprised at how your body talks; being aware of this will make it much easier to negate any adverse effects and give off the right message when communicating with people. Sharing well is essential if you wish people to see you as a great leader.

- *Be Direct*

One of the most challenging things to do when discussing an issue with anyone is completely honest. There are certainly times when being completely honest can work to your detriment. However, generally, it is agreed that the best policy when discussing an issue is, to be honest about your concerns or desires and tell the other party exactly what you wish to gain from the meeting.

It is then up to them if they wish to work with you. At the very least, you are giving them a fair warning that you are after one thing, and they may need to decide what is most important to them and their own goals.

- *Listening*

This trait is essential no matter which leadership role you undertake. It is often the most underrated and valuable skill to develop when negotiating with anyone else. Talking is necessary to communicate, and properly listening and absorbing the information is required.

Listening will do more than allow you to understand the risks and desires of the other party; it will also build trust and respect. Others will see that you take the time to listen and value that in you as a person; this will make you appear trustworthy, and people tend to respond well to trust issues.

- *Open-minded*

Becoming a super leader requires you to be open-minded regarding the opportunities available and whether these ideas come from your team or another source. It would help if you also were open-minded to other avenues of communication, whether social media or trailing a banner behind a plane.

The real trick is not in which method you use, but understanding the different venues out there and when to choose the relevant one. Open-mindedness allows anyone to contribute their ideas, regardless of their social standing or even the validity of the concept.

- *Know your Subject*

If you are talking to someone about something, be sure that you know your facts before passing on any information. If you do not know your subject, this may become apparent to anyone who does understand the subject and will ruin your credibility, which should have been well established at this point.

Understanding what you are talking about will enable you to field questions at any time, whether in a pre-arranged place or out of the blue. Being well prepared at all times will ensure you are ready for any opportunity which comes your way!

- *Read between the Lines*

It is often the case in both everyday conversations and within a more professional setting that the best information is not what is said but what is not said.

There is a great deal of information that can be tapped into if you know how to listen and understand what is not being said but is being referred to. This skill may sound complicated, but it is surprisingly easy to develop. Start by concentrating on what the other party is telling you; then compare this with their stated aim, and you will see what elements have been left out of the conversation.

You will then introduce these elements in your terms and make it very difficult for the other party to say no.

- *Flexibility*

Communicating with anyone requires you to be flexible. You must be prepared to change your approach, particularly if new information comes to light that changes the way you view a situation.

All conversations should be allowed to flow freely until a natural resolution appears. By its very nature, communication should be flexible and almost impossible to drag in a specific direction.

It is also important to note that transmission can be completed in many different forms. It is essential to be flexible about the best approach for any given situation.

- *Watch for Misunderstandings*

When discussing any issue or subject with someone, it is straightforward for the other party to 'get the wrong end of the stick.' The result will probably be evident as their responses will change. You will be able to monitor for a highly positive or negative change in their behavior and reactions; this will signal that your conversation has gone downhill rapidly.

You should then quickly correct the issue and ensure the conversation remains on track.

- *Never lay Blame*

It is effortless and understandable to look for someone to blame when things have not gone according to plan. However, blaming someone creates a bad environment for everyone on the project and is not productive in communicating or resolving an issue. The best way to move your project forward is not to dwell on the mistake but to look at what is possible to learn and improve the communication and response to an issue in the future.

Blaming someone or several others will detract from the project's aims and hinder your progress.

• *Social Media*

Not all communication is verbal or via your body language! Modern technology has brought social media to every person in the world.

It is easy to get online and create a profile on anyone or the available social media platforms.

Social Media provides you with the power and the opportunity to reach many thousands of people every day. However, you must consider the message and the image that you are portraying; too severe, and you will drive many customers away, while too relaxed will not show you in a professional light. Obtaining the right balance can be exceptionally tricky and provides an opportunity to communicate effectively with many different market segments.

• *Online advertising can be as simple as creating pop-up ads which appear when people search on specific subjects or go to certain web pages. It can also be much more involved and include building a social media account and creating a group of followers.*

Whichever route you choose to take, communicating with customers, other experts in your field or even investors is a viable but sometimes tricky option. Social media will leave you open to 'throw-away' comments by others; words which if not handled correctly, can do severe damage to your image and reputation. Again, you will need to carefully manage this form of communication to ensure your projected image is what you want it to be.

• *The process can be largely automated; you create the message and select the people you want to send it to. To work effectively, you need to divide your followers into groups, preferably by interests or age: this will ensure you send relevant information to each follower.*

An email is a powerful tool, but it is also possible to get it wrong and do severe damage to your profile and your following. It is something else that needs to strike the right balance between professional and friendly; you need to be seen as approachable, but you will never be able to answer all your followers individually; it would simply be too time-consuming.

• *Never be Afraid of Silence*

When communicating with others, whether one to one or even when giving a speech, it is essential to recognize that there will be times when short periods of silence will occur.

Silence during any form of communication allows you to collect your thoughts and keep a conversation on track. It also allows you and your audience to absorb the information and formulate an opinion; this will ensure any conversation is meaningful and valuable.

In negotiating terms, silence is often an essential ingredient and follows an offer; it is usually the person who breaks the silence first who will yield on the issue. Silence can be a handy way of communicating any message!

• *Anticipation*

One of the essential skills that must be learned to ensure effective communication with a wide range of people is to anticipate what the other party needs, wants, or is about to ask for. Understanding and anticipating this desire can be achieved by researching and educating yourself on how other people do business and react in certain situations.

Understanding this will allow you to create the exemplary scenario and assure you of achieving the correct result; most of your success will result from planning and environment, not developing your actual words.

- *The Importance of Eye Contact*

When communicating with people in person, it is essential to maintain eye contact as much as possible. Of course, too much direct eye contact may seem intimidating and a little over the top. However, get it right, and people will automatically trust you as they will believe you are open and honest. Trust is an integral part of communicating to build relationships and obtain the desired result when dealing with other parties.

One of the best tricks, in a one-to-one situation, is to focus on a spot above someone's eyes, anywhere on the forehead. This will ensure you are making eye contact without intimidating them or yourself. A group scenario will involve constantly scanning the group, pausing for a few moments on each person to ensure they feel you are creating a direct connection.

- *Practice Speeches*

Public speaking is necessary, although often terrifying, part of communicating with people. It is also a vital trait of every great leader and an essential skill to master to ensure you become a super leader.

Nerves tend to be the biggest issue when faced with a public speaking event; most people will worry about if they are liked, and their speech is appreciated. However, one of the essential criteria for giving an excellent public address is focusing on what your audience hopes to obtain by listening to your speech.

The attention should not be on you or whether you are liked; this is a foregone conclusion if your address has delivered their expectations.

It is a skill that is best mastered by practice. It would help if you practiced presenting the information via the use of a few critical prompt cards; these should be enough to keep you on track when communicating without simply reading your speech from the paper.

- *Be True to Your Values*

It is essential to know your principles and values and live by them. The reason for this is that the more you know yourself, your limits, and your values, the more comfortable you will feel in your skin.

Knowing yourself allows you to focus on delivering the right product and still stick to your chosen values. This indirect form of communication will ensure you come across as charismatic and make it much easier for others to want to follow your lead.

- *Recognize the Importance of Different Opinions*

Every member of your team and even your target audience will have a slightly different outlook on life, and this will result in a myriad of different opinions.

Recognizing the different opinions and learning to communicate with each of them will allow you to make the most of every resource you have available.

Chapter 10: Using Body Language in Flirting and Dating

Usually, a person flirts with the opposite sex using spoken words. However, flirting also involves nonverbal communication. Whatever a person says without using words can help the person get a date. If he or she can weave verbal and nonverbal communications seamlessly, this person may even begin a relationship after the first date.

In essence, if a person wants to be cautious, he has to engage with vigilant body language. On the other hand, if he wants to succeed, he has to use eager body language. Throughout meeting and attracting potential romantic partners, the focus and influence techniques of a person usually change. In completing a possible partner for the first time, each person is both cautious and vigilant. Both individuals do not know yet who they are interacting with. There is a large amount of uncertainty, and the focus of the individuals must be towards their safety. Therefore, the first strategies focus on making the other person comfortable. Once the guard is down, the relationship moves forward after establishing liking and safety.

In courting successfully with the prevention focus, the possible partner feels more adventurous and safer. In essence, he transcends from worry to wonder if he can connect with the other party. Different courtship is likely at this point. It uses slower speech and movements. It also takes a backward-leaning posture instead of leaning forward, making the other party feel crowded.

At the beginning of a courtship, both individuals must minimize dominant postures by decreasing the amount of space they occupy. As strangers, personal space boundaries are still broad, and both individuals must respect the proximity of their interactions. Gestures to avoid are aggressive variants, such as grimacing, clenching a fist, meeting the eyebrows, rolling the eyes, crossing the arms, or excessive staring. The person must also avoid highly flirtatious variants not to alienate the other. Examples of this are winking, playing with the tongue or lips, playing with sensual body parts such as the neck, shoulders, or legs, and widely opening the legs. The person must remain taut, with hands relaxed on the lap or the sides. The shoulders must be relaxed but active, and the face must be visibly happy and attentive. The latter is achieved through smiling or nodding.

The use of vigilant body language may feel a little standoffish, non-threatening, quiet, and calm because both parties are strangers.

It is best to give the possible partner personal space to support the verbal language to encourage that other party to feel comfortable. If his body language changes, his shoulders will feel relaxed. He leans in more, smiles, and makes more eye contact.

Relationships only fully succeed when the two individuals move on from the prevention focus. If partners marry, have children, or make other long-term commitments without being entirely comfortable with each other, the relationship will most likely fail. Long-term commitments put a significant strain on the couple's relationship personally. Suppose the two are not yet entirely comfortable and still act to feel secure in the relationship. In that case, the long-term commitment can worsen the situation and possibly cause the two to end the relationship.

Negative body language includes the partner moving away from the other to create space. These signals dislike what the other is asking or doing. Furthermore, adverse nonverbal movements include grimacing, turning the eyes to the side, frowning, rubbing the back of the neck, scratching nose, closing the hands, scratching eyes, facing the palms down, crossing arms, having the legs stiff and betrayed, and pointing the feet away from the other partner.

A person can figure out how the other feels by searching for various behaviors. In general, positive cues mean that the limbic system of the other is moving towards the loving, excellent, and happy direction. This other person feels optimistic about the behavior shown towards him or her.

On the other hand, the negative cues signal that the limbic system of the other partner is moving towards the disturbed, nasty and uncomfortable direction. It is best to use the information to change the approach or wait for the other person to change their mood.

Body language can play a significant role in entering and maintaining a relationship. Always remember to respond to your partner's nonverbal cues and respect his or her individuality. Focus on first building trust and comfort with each other's company before you and the other person involve yourselves in commitments.

When a man shows interest through body language, on the other hand, he's not trying to provoke a woman to make a move, but he's trying to show that he has the qualities of a good partner. This's composed chiefly of physical attributes like a good physique and attractive facial features.

How to Make a Man Like You

Ladies, the tips and tricks here may not all work in the same way for every man; remember that all men are not the same. "Men are all the same!" is a conclusion rooted deeply in blind generalization by brokenhearted women. Therefore, I strongly suggest that you take a little time to understand the type of man in your life or the kind of man you hope to attract.

However, on a general note, some things tend to catch the interest of most men, and here they are:

He was putting on his shirt. Slide into his shirt and wear it over your bare legs. Let most of the shirt buttons be left undone. Don't dress in his clothes as if you are going for some serious outing. Be as casual as you can be in his clothes. Men go crazy for these things!

He was nice to random people, especially the elderly and kids. When a man sees a woman's maternal instinct in action, like when she treats a lucky kid nicely, he is drawn to her. The same thing goes for treating older adults with kindness and respect.

The act of shaving a man's face speaks more intimately than any words you can ever tell him. You don't have to be a great barber or even get it right. Just begin and even play around with the shaving cream. Rub some on his nose and have a good laugh together. You may even fake a severe face for a while to appear as if you are giving him an excellent shave; meanwhile, you are simply giving him an uneven shave. And if you happen to be good at it, he may never visit a barber's shop ever again!

She was biting the lip. Okay, this one is very sexy to most men. When a woman bites her lip, it gives her a helpless look that activates the man's inborn desire to protect her. It also makes her look very sexy. Whether you are biting your lip or the man's lip, men will fall for this movie.

They are having deep conversations. This may not seem sexy, but men lookout for a woman who can participate in their intellectual development. While looking sexy can attract a man, if the quality of your conversation is shallow or leans only towards romance, the man may tire out quickly. A man is very attracted to a woman who can inspire him and nudge him towards achieving his life's goals through deep and meaningful conversation.

Whispers and winks. A playful woman is a man's delight! Winking at a man unexpectedly or whispering in his ear, especially in public places, are some of the naughty things that most men find very attractive in women. When you make playful faces or goof around the house once in a while, you make your man want to spend more time with you. When he recalls your active face, it brings a warm smile to his face and heart, too!

He was friends with his friends. Men are constantly torn between their better halves and their friends. If a woman makes it easier for the man by befriending the man's friends, she mends that tear, and the man adores her more. Look for common ground between you and your man's friends and explore that to become a prominent part of his life both at home and when he's out with his friends, which you happen to be also.

You are telling the story behind a scar or tattoo. This is why it catches a man's attention if a woman turns her skin into a canvass. When a man shows interest in your tattoo or looks at a scar on your skin, go into a brief story of why you choose to get your skin tattooed or how you got the spot. You are using this opportunity to tell the man about yourself. Make it an exciting story—without exaggerating, of course.

They are working out. Women tend to be drawn to men with great abs and good body muscles. The same thing applies to men. When most men see a woman working out, it turns on their interest level. Perhaps it has to do with the woman's curvatures being accentuated during workouts. Or maybe it has to do with the sense of being mindful of her body weight and physiology. Men tend to be attracted to a woman who works out whatever it is.

They see that they can affect a positive response from you. Laugh at a man's humor, and you are steadily working your way into his heart. Even when a woman patronizes a man by laughing at his dry jokes, the man is most likely to ignore the condescending attitude because her laughter boosts his manliness.

How to Make a Woman Like You

To the men, there is no one universal body language to make a woman like you because, like men, women too are wired differently. While verbalizing your feelings can make a woman like you, what you do can have a farther-reaching effect than the words you speak. Women are generally known to fall for the following male actions.

I was doing chores. First on this list is something that is not necessarily romantic but can make a woman fall head over heels for you. Home chores are usually considered to be a woman's role. When you, as a man, perform tasks like doing the dishes at home, collecting her laundry (or the family's laundry), mopping the floor, bathing the kids, and any other home chore, these little things can make a woman like you.

They are fixing things. You don't have to be an expert or a professional to fix little things around the house. Many women consider being handy as sexy for reasons men cannot fathom. She'll appreciate you more!

You are rolling your sleeves to the elbow. Talking about rolling up your sleeve to fix things, many women find the act of rolling up your shirt sleeve to the elbow sexy. This is so may not be easily understood by men, but it works. Even if you are not trying to get things around the house fixed, wait to be with her and then take your time to roll up your shirt sleeves to your elbow gradually. Be deliberate about this act, and you may end up turning her on! One more thing: this works better with buttoned-up shirts than with other types of men's clothing like sweaters.

If she's already in a relationship with you, she'll like you more. Just be confident about your style of humor, and you're good to go. Make sure not to overdo this because you can quickly tire her out. Look for appropriate times to chip in with a bit of humor.

She was listening to her. If you remember the seemingly minor details she has shared with you, she'll get a sense of being an essential part of your life. Generally, it is believed that women talk more than men, and men listen less than women do. If you can break out of this commonly held belief and listen intently to her when she speaks, it will be a massive plus for you.

You are spending quality time with kids. When a woman sees you having fun with kids or chatting and explaining things to them, it triggers an evolutionary signal that you can make a great dad; and women love great dads!

They are doing random romantic acts. Men usually think that being romantic is expensive, so they spend all the time working hard to save enough money to take the woman they like on a trip or to the most expensive restaurant in town. The problem with this is that it takes a long time before many men can afford this romantic act. Women value the little actions that show that they care. For example, bringing her a cup of coffee while she's still in bed, helping the kids with their homework so that she can concentrate on her work, helping her dry her hair without her asking, and lots of other little things can be very romantic without being expensive.

You are reacting softly to other women and animals. Women take note of how they respond to and treat other women. If you are rude to your mom or a waitress, for example, the woman in your life will take note. If you are a softy for animals, for example, a kitten, she'll also notice. She'll form an opinion about who you are based on how you treat other women and how kind you are to animals.

Be passionate about something. It doesn't matter your passion; find it and put your energy into it. A woman wants a passionate man about something – just about anything! So, put your energy into that hobby or dream and work at developing it if you're going to keep your woman interested in you.

Offer her your coat. Offering your jacket to a woman on a cold night in a condescending way will not make her like you. On the other hand, kissing her hand and bowing like a prince in shining armor while offering her your coat won't do the trick either. A woman wants to be treated nicely but in a courteous manner. Politely show her your jacket and if it is appropriate, gently brush strands of hair out of her face before she steps out into the cold.

Spotting anger

It's also necessary for us to spot anger among the people around us. Women tend to show anger differently than men. Men are vocal, and they talk directly about their offense. Mature men speak logically about what makes them upset, while less mature men tend to use transference of anger.

The facial expression of men will also quickly tell you that they're angry. Their gaze tends to be more intense, and their jaw muscles tend to become more pronounced.

On the other hand, women show anger by avoiding the topic that made them angry altogether. When asked about it, they'll say common expressions like "nothing" or "whatever." You'll know that they're mad because they'll try as much as they can to avoid giving you any sign of loving attention. This's their way of showing anger.

Knowing when she's losing interest

A man should also be aware of the signs that a woman is losing interest in him and take the necessary steps to make sure that the relationship remains intact. In most cases, women quickly tend to withdraw signs of vulnerability when losing interest. They also tend to avoid showing parts of the body that's sensitive to touch, like the wrist and the inner regions of the upper arm. They also tend to avoid exposing their necks. Dominant women who don't want to show vulnerability will want to use the space around them. When carrying a handbag, women who're not comfortable with the man they're with will cling to their bags and not let the man close to them.

A man can win back her interest by quickly making gestures that she finds meaningful. Each woman has a different definition of expressive gestures, and it's the man's responsibility to know the fitting gesture.

Chapter 11: Body language Others

Body language will betray the mind in many ways because the subconscious always acts independently and automatically during a spoken lie. This is why many amateur liars are easy to understand before they can even finish their story. No matter how convincing they sound, people will still be able to see those body language signals that contradict their words.

Face the facts

Facial expression is considered the easiest to control because we always know what our faces are doing. Therefore, it is more difficult to say in the front of a person is lying or not. However, recent research has shown that we still lack the mastery of visual expressions that our inner thoughts can reflect despite the high level of awareness of our facial movements.

Before the brain can even send a message to what it wants to say, the eyes are already sending these small complementary signals. These tributes are considered reliable indicators that the statement contradicts the true basic sentiment.

They will look down very quickly, look away, or look at you. These gestures are most commonly associated with the term "moving the eyes," which usually indicates confusion, dishonesty, and deception.

It would help if you also remembered that wary eyes do not always mean that someone is lying. They may be worried, pressured, or confused about their opinions or feelings. However, you can be sure that this person is not currently able or willing to disclose their true feelings and thoughts and tries to hide this fact from you.

Through the teeth

Unfortunately, the phone has been a valuable tool since its inception, and many people lie to us. But fortunately, you can still recognize a liar with only your ears. If you carefully and accurately observe how words are spoken while ignoring the content, you may still be able, to tell the truth from a lie.

If we hold back to express ourselves truthfully, the familiar voice becomes flatter, loses depth, and becomes more monotonous.

Another fact is that people talk less when they lie and tend to make more mistakes in their speech. Unless they are well-trained speakers (e.g., salespeople, lawyers, politicians), they are more likely to stutter or hesitate when they speak.

Somewhere above the mouth

Children often cover their entire mouths when they lie, as if they wanted to hide the source of dishonesty. This original childhood gesture is also one of the most commonly used adult gestures for lying.

When a person lies, the brain unconsciously commands to suppress untruthful words. The thumb is pressed against the cheek, while the hand is used to cover the mouth. Occasionally, some people's gestures are just a few fingers on the mouth or even a tight fist, but the message remains very similar.

On the contrary, if someone does it while you talk, they may have difficulty believing you.

Touch Pinocchio's nose

When a person does not tell the truth, he rubs himself, caresses, and scratches his nose more often than someone honest and direct. One explanation is simply that the nose is just above the mouth, and when the negative thoughts of deception enter the mind, the unconscious movement of the hand to cover the mouth is diverted to the nose.

Another ingenious reason is that lying increases tension and causes an actual physical itch in the nose. Therefore, the scratching of the nose can only be used to calm the itching sensation. However, there is a noticeable difference since the true itch in a person's nose is usually satisfied by a more obvious rubbing movement instead of a light touch or a touching nasal gesture that doubts itself.

Just like the hand on the mouth, it can be used both by the speaker to hide his illusion and by the listener who is suspicious of what he is talking about.

Don't see an illusion, don't feel doubt.

Rubbing or touching the eye area is a solid indication of doubts and fraud. This gesture is the unconscious way in which the person tries not to look directly into the eyes or face of the person who is lying to him.

When a woman is lying, she usually rubs herself gently under the eye with a small and light gesture. This is because he prefers to avoid blurring the make-up, or it could just be the kind gesture of a typical woman since she grew up in a feminine environment.

Compared to a woman, a man usually rubs his eyes with a more substantial gesture. However, when the deception is enormous, men and women share a similar motion of avoiding the listener's gaze by looking at the floor or ceiling.

Undoubtedly coming to the side of the ear, rubbing, twisting, or pulling the ear lobe is a sign of insecurity or confusion, which, when performed during the speech, signals a lack of confidence in what the speaker is saying. It also means that the listener is not convinced of the truth of what is said of you when it is performed elsewhere while you speak.

These gestures that touch the ears are the improvised, adult version that has emerged from the ears of young children who want to exclude the annoyance and reproach of their parents.

Honest feet and legs

When someone decides to lie about something during a conversation, they usually cross their arms or legs simultaneously. It indicates early self-defense against imminent challenges.

Other standard foot signals may include a constant touch of the foot and feet pointing towards the exit. These gestures indicate that the person wants to get out of the current situation and get out. Usually, when a person tries to get out of something, it leads to creating a small harmless lie, rather than telling the truth in situations where they don't want to go to work or perform a particular social function.

The honest attitude

The posture of a person who is lying is often rigid and controlled. The natural physical expression of the person is retained if he holds the truth.

There is also a high probability that they will push your whole body away from you to hide both their face and the truth.

Another language of attitude that clashes with the spoken word can be seen when someone pretends to agree with you. The fact is that this person is not convinced and refuses you and what you say.

The stressful signals

The stress signals of the autonomic nervous system are the most reliable indications or indicators of dishonesty and insincerity. Stress reactions such as sweating, pallor, and irregular breathing are difficult to hide or false. The most common and reliable indicator of lying is a dry mouth. This reaction to stress makes the liar lick more often on the lips and swallows nervously at certain times. Occasionally there are more hawks than usual.

These reactions to stress are caused by someone's increased sense of fear when lying. Such obvious stress symptoms usually occur only in dramatic circumstances.

Put it all Together

Judging by the body gestures described here, obfuscation is probably the best word of lies to define the primary influence behind everyone.

It will take time and observation to acquire the ability to accurately interpret and distinguish the many types of gestures in a given situation.

Any blowing one's nose or pulling ears does not necessarily mean that someone is lying intentionally. These so-called deceptive gestures can also be initiated by expressing doubts, insecurity, confusion, exaggeration, or concern.

The ability to determine the correct mood of a person's gestures is the actual capacity for interpretation. This can be achieved by analyzing the other signals immediately before displaying these cited gestures and interpreting them in context.

It is also essential to consider which culture someone comes from, what kind of personality, and the person's actual situation. Some cultures may not be particularly expressive, while others are dramatically demonstrative. Using a person's body language to determine if he is lying must be done carefully. You should not simply use an indicator to express your opinion. There are a number of indicators to use, and you should be aware of the many possible signals of body language that liars can give if they are fraudulent.

Always remember that a liar's body movements can mean he is cheating, but not always. It is possible to misunderstand someone and judge him wrongly as a liar. They may be very shy or inferior and may feel guilty even if they are innocent.

You must carefully consider every situation in which a person has been before the present moment. Is there some emotional carryover that makes you misinterpret?

Are there cultural factors that make this person dishonest? Be sure that your company can be typical and honest to behave as you currently are. You must also be especially careful not to have any personal prejudices or prejudices against this person that could make you want him to be guilty of lying.

Another critical factor, and probably the most important, is your ability to read a person's body language to see if he is lying.

These non-verbal signals are different and include many types of movements and gestures. These can be observed when asking questions about the truth you want to find. Each indicator should be displayed with other clues provided by the body language of the matter.

1. The subject nods or shakes his head unevenly concerning the question asked. For example, if you ask the subject a question that requires a yes or no answer and the issue answers no but moves his head up and down, it could be the physical manifestation of a lie.

2. The subject places his hand near or above his mouth. This could be a liar's body language.

3. Avoiding physical contact with other people in their environment can be a sign of fraud. This becomes even clearer when the two people are in a close relationship and usually have physical contact.

4. The person suspected of lying puts an object between himself and the person asking the questions.

You must carefully evaluate these indicators and more to express an opinion. Deciding if someone is lying is a serious matter and must be done thoughtfully and discreetly.

Conclusion

There is so much that is shared nonverbally through body language. The most critical applications of body language are to model your nonverbal expression to communicate better, observe and analyze others and use both factors to persuade and convince more effectively.

By following the guidelines outlined in this book, you will be well on your way to understanding the actual thoughts and feelings beyond what they are saying. In addition, with a bit of practice, you'll soon be on your way to making your body language work for you, which in turn will allow you to connect better with others and give a much better account of yourself. The key is sensitivity; be observant, and you will soon develop the instinct to pick up signals and respond accordingly.

Most of our body movements result from habit; mannerisms that do not mean anything at all. If you prepare yourself to read body language, you will ignore meaningless body signals. Instead, you will only choose and absorb the ones that affect your life at the proper time. Life is a game and knowing body language gives you the advantage. You can choose to win, change partner, or play an entirely different game.

GASLIGHTING

Introduction

Gaslighting occurs in personal relationships and professional relationships, and in other cases, gaslighting is used by public figures to change the perceptions of targeted members of the population. Gaslighting is a form of psychological abuse. It can make you start to doubt your ability to perceive reality correctly.

It can make you think you didn't see what you thought you saw or hear what you thought you heard; and you start to wonder if you can trust the information you are getting from your five senses. Moreover, this, in turn, will make you begin to think that there must be something wrong with you, and you will begin to doubt your sanity.

It doesn't matter whether it is happening in a personal relationship (parent to child, between romantic partners) or a professional relationship at work or even between members of the same community.

Gaslighting creates an abusive situation which can cause serious health problems if the victim continues to be in such a position for a long time. And no matter whether it occurs in a personal relationship or a working relationship, between a public figure and the members of the public or somewhere else, it is essential to be aware of the signs that you or someone you know might be a victim of gaslighting, as this awareness is the first step to getting out of the damaging situation.

The first step to take towards being free from gaslighting is to recognize exactly what gaslighting is. It is often very hard to recognize the signs of gaslighting, because they affect the mind so much that, after a long period of time, the victim doesn't trust their own thoughts.

This book discusses in detail how to distinguish gaslighting behavior from typical behavior by shedding light on the different kinds of gaslighting techniques. It also aims to provide you with information about what to do if you find yourself a victim of such a negative situation.

Gaslighting, which will be defined fully in the following chapters, is a technique used by narcissists to manipulate people. Narcissists are self- centered and arrogant people who lack empathy for others. They live in their own world and believe they are unique and special. Hence, they always seek attention and praise from others.

A narcissist will frequently use gaslighting, as a narcissist's goal is to disorient the victim to gain total control over them. A narcissist achieves this aim by gradually sowing seeds of doubt in the victim's mind, and in the end, the narcissist controls the victim to do their bidding.

In addition to promoting awareness about gaslighting, this book is written with the more precise aim of exposing the extent to which narcissists use gaslighting as a means of manipulation to control and abuse their victims both physically and mentally.

They expose the words narcissists say and the actions they take to abuse victims. It is one thing to recognize what gaslighting is, and it is another to know how narcissists use it. It is also a different thing entirely to uncover the effects of gaslighting and guard against them - or better still, avoid the effects in the first place.

Most importantly, they show you how to protect yourself and even remove yourself from the control of a gaslighting narcissist.

Chapter 1. Gaslighting

Gaslighting is the endeavor of someone else to wind your reality. Narcissists can't and don't assume liability for their conduct. Rather, they look to disgrace and accuse others of evading the awful feelings. This is once in a while referred to as projection. The problem is, gaslighting is slippery.

It plays on our most exceedingly awful feelings of dread, our most restless musings, and our most profound wishes to be comprehended, acknowledged and loved. At the point when somebody we trust, regard, or love talks with incredible conviction—especially if there's a trace of legitimacy in his words, or if he's hit on one of our "red buttons"—it tends to be difficult not to trust him. Furthermore, when we glorify the deceiver—when we need to consider him to be the love of our life, a commendable boss, or a brilliant parent—then we make it more difficult to adhere to our sense of reality.

Our deceiver should be correct; we have to win his endorsement; thus, the gaslighting goes on. Neither of you might know about what's truly occurring. The gaslighter may truly accept each word he lets you know or genuinely feel that he's just sparing you from yourself. Keep in mind: His own needs are driving him.

Your deceiver may appear to be a solid, influential man, or he may have all the earmarks of being an unreliable, fit of rage tossing young man; in any case, he feels frail and feeble. To feel ground-breaking and safe, he needs to demonstrate that he is correct, and he needs to get you to concur with him.

Then, you have admired your deceiver and are edgy for his endorsement, although you may not intentionally understand this. If there's a small part of you that thinks you're that bad with no one else - if you think you need love or your gas station attendant to be satisfied - at that point, you're gaslighting submissive. What's more, a deceiver will exploit that helplessness to make you question yourself, again and again. When someone is gaslighting you, try to convince yourself that your boundaries and perceptions are stupid and useless.

If something they say bothers you because it is abusive or untrue, they will tell you that you are overreacting or that what you are saying is stupid. They will tell you that you are overly sensitive.

Even spiritual people are not immune to this; you may be told that their behavior would not bother you if you were more enlightened.

So, in essence, gaslighting and manipulation techniques make you doubt your boundaries or make you drop your boundaries altogether by convincing you that your boundaries are stupid and invalid.

The truth is that your boundaries aren't anybody's business but yours. Nobody gets to determine what boundaries you will have. If something bothers you, nobody gets to tell you how you feel. When you impose a boundary on someone, you are not only fighting for it but, more importantly, for your right to set boundaries. Don't let anyone convince you that your boundary isn't big enough for you to take a stand. It is. Such a way of thinking is disrespectful. It's very disrespectful and dishonoring to stand on somebody else's boundary.

There is a difference between controlling somebody else by telling them how to behave and setting a boundary by telling the person not to behave a certain way to you. Reinforcing a boundary means that you will have to walk away from someone or something when they do something wrong to you. Now, realize that it's not about stopping someone from living their lives the way they want to live their lives, nor is it taking their freedom away from them. It's simply about choosing to engage with or not engage with people who behave in a certain way or who don't respect your boundaries.

Setting up an angry beast The second form of manipulation is to become an angry beast. This is where somebody tries to become angrier than you when you get angry with them, to squash your challenge or rebellion. You might even be just mildly annoyed about something and want to talk to your partner about it, but they explode at you so that you find yourself back down. You will be so shocked because you talked about something relatively small, and they just turned it into something huge. You will want to back down and not deal with that drama type. Often, you will be trying to defend your boundaries, which causes the explosion.

This beast will come to you with an emotional response out of proportion to the situation you are trying to defend. You will try to pull back, and you will not even try to defend yourself because you are not willing to face that beast. This is the goal of the deceiver. But when you are defending a proper boundary or setting a boundary, it doesn't matter what the boundary is all about, nor does it matter whether that person sees it as valid or not.

Once you have communicated a boundary and the other person says that he will not accept it, you must follow through on the consequences or be intimidated into silence and submission.

That is what the angry beast wants. Hijacking the issue The next manipulative technique is hijacking the issue.

This happens when you raise a topic that challenges someone, and he takes it off on a tangent to distract you so that you will not set that boundary or defend that boundary. For example, let's say it's late at night and your spouse hasn't come home from work.

They haven't called, and you are anxious because you have no idea where they are or if something has happened to them. They finally come home, and you confront them with how worried you were and ask them where they were and why they didn't even call you to let you know that they would be late.

Rather than answer your concern and questions, they go off on a tangent about how stressed they are at work and how you're not just getting it. They might start to get angry and accuse you of having no sympathy for them. You then find yourself on the defensive side of the conversation and even apologize to them.

Now you're no longer talking about the original topic – how late they were and why they didn't call – but talking about them and what's bothering them. In the end, they will avoid answering your question altogether. They have hijacked the conversation and turned it in a different direction. You will often find yourself sitting them down and apologizing to them and feeling like you shouldn't bother them with your little concerns.

Those who use these manipulative tactics are not doing so consciously. Their purpose is not to hijack a conversation on purpose, but they do it anyway. They don't intend to work up to being an angry beast or trample on your boundaries, but they do. They do it to control and manipulate you into always putting them first.

In 1944, a movie called Gaslight was released that changed the way people thought about manipulation and its immense power. This movie shows the story of a husband character that manipulates his wife and her life to such an extent that she begins to believe that she has become insane.

In this movie, too, just like in my life, the wife, Paula, gets completely caught up with the charms of Gregory, the man who woos and wins her. The tragedy began after the wedding due to a whirlwind relationship. Gregory begins to show his true personality so subtly that Paula begins to think that everything is alright with her husband and that she is going crazy.

The husband in the film dimmed the gas lights in the house and insisted that the wife imagined that the light was dim. His insistence and manipulation were so powerful that the poor, hapless woman begins to think that she is going crazy. And so, the name gaslighting came to be used for such devious and evil manipulative tactics to deliberately steer people away from their real lives and life experiences.

The movie itself is based on a 1938 play of the same name. Of course, the criminal husband's ultimate aim was to drive his wife to insanity so that he could put her away in a mental institution and claim her inheritance.

Gaslighting is the name used by psychologists to refer to the tactics used by people with a personality disorder to control and manipulate the lives of other people, either individuals or a group of people. These tactics are so strong and go so deep that the manipulated people tend to doubt and question everything in their own lives; their reality, perceptions, feelings, experiences, and interpretations of these experiences. Your sanity is in danger if you allow someone to control your life.

At this juncture, it is essential to differentiate gaslighting from those tactics that many people use to annoy and irritate the people around them. Gaslighting tactics have a dark quality that certain people's annoying but innocuous behavior doesn't have. You must differentiate between the two so that you don't end up judging everyone you come across wrongly.

But you must know for sure that gaslighting is a severe problem, and you must learn to discern such behavior and stay as far away from such people as possible. After all, having your reality taken from you can be quite dangerous, and if not managed sensibly, can prove disastrous for you and your loved ones.

The problematic thing about understanding gaslighting is that the behavioral signs might start very small and insignificant. For example, the manipulator could correct a small detail in a story or life experience you are narrating. Of course, their correction makes sense, and you accept it wholeheartedly. Slowly, that 'past victory' becomes the focal point and keeps rearing its ugly head in all your interactions with the concerned individual, and before you know it, you become his or her slave, completely losing touch with your reality and life.

Deliberately, you will be pushed to such an extent that making simple daily decisions might become difficult for you. Driven by the seeds of self-doubt sowed by the deceiver, you could find yourself second-guessing every decision you make. Like I already told you in the introduction chapter, even the clothes I wore became my husband's decision. At some point, the victim is likely to feel that they cannot decide whatsoever and depends on every little thing on the manipulator.

Furthermore, the aggressor will slowly convince you that his or her behavior is also your fault. The more you apologize for your behavior, the greedier the aggressor's ego becomes, and the person demands an increasing level of apology and supplicating behavior from you.

The aggressor gets so deep into his or her gaslighting attitude that you will find it exceedingly difficult to reach out and seek help from other people in the fear that they will go against your aggressor. When you are entirely and irrevocably under the aggressor's control, then the person dumps you and seeks new 'conquests.'

History of Gaslighting

While the term 'gaslighting' was introduced during the early 1940s, the concept of manipulative behavior for controlling people and altering people's imagined realities has been part of human history for a long time. The victims were 'diagnosed' with this condition. They withered away in a lunatic asylum or some other institution, alone, depressed, and completely neglected.

Can you recall the story of 'The Emperor Clothes?' What happened there? Did the intelligent salesman drive every observer on the street to believe that the emperor was clothed in the finest of garments when, in reality, he was stark naked? A little, guileless child saved the day for the rest of the people who believed that if they couldn't see the clothes on their emperor, then it was their fault.

In 1981, psychologist Edward Weinshel wrote an article entitled "Some Clinical Consequences of Introjection: Gaslighting," He explained the concept in the following way. The manipulator 'externalizes and projects' the image or thought, and the victim 'internalizes and assimilates the information into his or her psyche unquestioningly. The 'victim' takes in all the faults, mistakes, and irrationality in such relationships.

Why Does Gaslighting Happen?

Put, gaslighting is all about having control. This need for power or domination could stem from personality disorders like narcissism, antisocial issues, unresolved childhood trauma, or any other reason.

Gaslighting behavior is usually seen between people involved in power dynamics where one person invariably wields more power than the other person or people in the relationship equation. The victim of gaslighting tactics is typically on a lower rung than the manipulator and is also terrified of losing something in the relationship. The manipulative relationship's target is likely to be a codependent partner in the relationship.

For example, in a romantic relationship, the wife might feel the compulsion to put up with manipulative behavior because she WANTS to be in the relationship and desires the other things it brings. Such people are ready to change their perceptions to align with those of the manipulative partner to avoid conflicts and allow things to happen smoothly.

On the other hand, the manipulator continues to be one because they are scared of being seen as less important or significant than desired. Another critical perspective of the deceiver is that the person may not realize that they are behaving in ways that could harm or hurt the 'target.' They could be indulging in gaslighting tactics simply because they were reared like that.

For example, if a person was brought up by parents who believe in the concept of absolute certainty, then this person may not know that other perspectives can exist and that they can be right. Such people could be primed to think that anyone who has a different approach or attitude is wrong. Further, they could believe that people with these 'wrong' notions should be corrected and thus resort to gaslighting tactics, an approach found commonly in a family and among loved ones.

Some employ gaslighting to show off their dominance and power with little or no care toward the pain and agony inflicted on the target. Sometimes, the 'dominance and power' could also be a facade for manipulating insecurities and fears. Whatever it is, gaslighting is employed to dominate unfairly over other people.

Where Does Gaslighting Happen?

Gaslighting can happen and be experienced by anyone and everyone. For example, you could be a victim of such tactics from your spouse, partner, colleague, or sometimes, even a parent. Gaslighting tactics are not restricted to the personal or professional realm.

Gaslighting strategies can influence a whole group of people. There are multiple instances in which President Donald Trump and his administration can see gaslighting techniques. Most experts agree that politics is a field where spreading lies is taken and accepted as a stereotypical attitude. However, President Trump seems to have taken it a bit too far.

In the initial days of his office, President Trump - along with his administration staff - are believed to have lied so blatantly that there was a shade of arrogance and utter contempt for the American people's intelligence. It was like the concerned officials were baiting the common people, telling them to rise up and revolt against the nastiness if they can; this was a clear sign of narcissistic personality disorder.

For instance, the administration lied about the Presidential swearing-in crowd size. It was clear that President Obama's swearing-in photos were manipulated to look like the current one. It was so easy to detect this lie that for some people, it was like a war cry to the media, which was most likely to be discredited by Americans for putting such lies on their websites and publications.

At a personal level, gaslighting tactics are used by manipulative people who want to control their family members' lives. Think of a physically and emotionally abusive spouse wreaking havoc on their partner or the children in the family, and you can easily discern gaslighting behavior.

Where is Gaslighting Typically Seen?

Geographically speaking, gaslighting behavior is not exclusive to any part of the world. Wherever power dynamics are in play and where the need and desire for control over people and resources exist, gaslighting behavior can be witnessed. Multiple studies reveal that this kind of unpleasant and dangerous behavior is prevalent in personal relationships and at the workplace, and even in public life, as in the way some politicians and their coterie interact with the commoner on the street.

MHR, an HR services provider, conducted a survey in the UK which revealed some shocking numbers. Over 3000 people undertook the survey, and 58% of this group claimed that they had experienced what they believed was gaslighting behavior at their workplace. About 30% said they did not experience such behavior while 12% said they didn't know! This survey poll's disturbing results reveal how widespread gaslighting is in the UK. Some examples of gaslighting behaviors at the workplace include:

- *Taking credit for your work*

- *Mocking you, your behavior, or dres's style in front of other colleagues*

- *Setting unreasonable and unrealistic deadlines*

- *Deliberately withholding information that is crucial for the success of a project you are working on*

Most of the elements mentioned above are seemingly insignificant but add up to a lot in retrospect.

Moreover, unlike bullying, which is easily discernible, gaslighting behaviors are subtle and are meant to slowly but surely doubt your capabilities and value to the organization. Such attitudes cannot be caught until after the damage is done to the target's psyche.

Another US-based report says that 3 out of 4 people in the country are not aware of the term. This state of ignorance is despite the widespread prevalence of gaslighting behavior in the entertainment and media industries, where power-play dynamics are perhaps the strongest.

Nearly 75% of the surveyed people said they had heard of the term but did not know its meaning. The study revealed that about a third of the female population had termed their romantic partners 'crazy' or 'insane' in a severe way. About 25% of the male population had also used these two words to describe their partners.

Therefore, gaslighting behavior is not restricted to any particular geography or industry and can be witnessed in different countries, cultures, and industries.

Common Gaslighting Situations

Here are some common examples of gaslighting scenarios that could help you understand if and when various perpetrators are gaslighting you

In a home environment - Alice's father, Andrew, is a bitter and angry man who is carrying a lot of negativity right from his childhood. His power play is most evident with Alice, thanks to her dependence on him for many things. Alice's mother is the breadwinner in the family and is away most of the time at work.

Alice spent a lot more time with her father than her mother and had unwittingly built herself into a codependency situation with Andrew. She was highly sensitive to his mood swings and was always worried that some action or behavior of hers would bring on a dark mood in her father.

Whenever her father was in a dark mood, he would lash out at Alice by saying that 'You're worthless,' 'I wonder why you were born,' and quite frequently using foul language too. If Alice tried to argue back with him, he would laugh it off and say, 'Why are you so unnecessarily sensitive?'

Alice had become so accustomed to this situation at home that she did not even think it important enough to speak to her mother about it that she was too busy with her work to find time for her daughter. Alice was completely under her father's control and even accepted it naturally. She believed that her father only helped her toward self-improvement and nothing wrong with him. Another common situation is when adult children manipulate their old parents. Here are some examples you will find in several homes.

In a romantic relationship - In most people's eyes, Julie's life could be seen as being ideal. Married for over five years to her first love, who is now an adoring husband, financially secure (her husband, John, is an investment banker who rakes in the moolah). With two beautiful children, Julie might look like there is no shortage of happiness in her life. And yet, she knows what she is going through. Before her marriage, Julie was an artist with some great skills.

After she got married, John did his best to prevent his wife from advancing her skills and making a name for herself in the art world. He always found fault with her work and made her feel worthless. Every time she tried to paint something, he would say, 'A lousy artist like you will not make it in the art world, which is filled with brilliant artists. Your work will never be as good as it gets, so don't waste will not just focus on looking after your family.

Also, he would always bring up a bad experience that she had had during her early artist days. She had created a painting and wanted feedback from a famous artist who was a good friend of her husband's. The man had said that her skills were way below even an average artist and that she should not even try moving forward. Julie's husband never failed to bring up that comment and used it to make her believe that she was fit for nothing more than taking care of the family.

Julie's husband used that one bad experience and feedback to remind her of her worthlessness continually, and repeated practice and habitual behavior enslaved her to her husband completely. Although she lives comfortably, she realizes that her life is empty. She wants to break free from her husband's manipulative ways, but he uses their children to strengthen his power over her.

Jolly was a salesgirl in a large cosmetic showroom in a workplace scenario. After working for five years, she was given a promotion to work in, which gave her a higher salary and opened up career growth prospects. Jolly was pleased with the rise and started working with her new boss, Penny.

Initially, Jolly found Penny helpful and sweet. Slowly, Penny started passing on trivial tasks to Jolly, who did them uncomplainingly. However, this did not stop and increased so much that she had no time and energy to learn anything new at the job. She was just about finishing all the work assigned by her boss, who kept her at arm's length and discouraging interactions of all kinds except giving out tasks.

One day, a department meeting was called, and Jolly was part of it. Penny addressed the other people and said, 'Meet Jolly, who has been with us for nearly three months now, and she has yet to learn the ropes of the new department. I hope she catches up soon, or else we might have to send her back after demoting her.' Jolly turned red with embarrassment and shame at this open and unexpected insult from her boss. And she realized that she had unwittingly become a victim of gaslighting tactics!

Emotional Hot Spots that are targeted

Nearly anyone can target gaslighting tactics considering the subtlety involved in the process. Very few people can discern the difference between gaslighting and simple annoying behavior. Most often, people will tend to categorize gaslighting behaviors as mere annoyance and tend to ignore them. There are some kinds of easy targets for gaslighting; certain types of people become easy targets for gaslighting. Some of them are:

Empaths - Empaths are susceptible to everything that is happening around them. One can often absorb positive and negative energies from their environment. Such people can be easy targets for deceivers because it is quite easy to influence them. Sending negative vibes to empaths can enhance their sensitivity to a deceiver's needs.

Insecure people: Deceivers typically target people with significant inferiority complexes. Men and women who feel unsure about themselves are easy targets considering that they are already vulnerable.

Moreover, insecure people continuously look for positive affirmation from others, which is exactly what deceivers want in any new relationship's initial stages. Gaslighting tactics start with heaping praise, often when it is not necessary and praises the victims initially, and once they are trapped, the actual color of deceivers comes to the fore.

And yet, it is time to reiterate that some deceivers are so good at what they do that even the sanest and most sensible people can become their targets. Therefore, it makes sense to be aware of the concept of gaslighting tactics and their multiple adverse effects and to be wary of such people.

Chapter 3. How to spot a Gaslighter

If there is an attribute that deceivers appear to have in abundance, it is the charm. They are generally likable people who appear to overflow tons of charm, making it difficult to identify them on the surface. There are, however, a few manners of behavior by which they can be identified, and these include:

Withholding: Here, the deceiver retains information on what they know or what is the fact by pretending not to understand their victims. They may begin sentences with phrases like "Are you trying to confound me by?" or "Please, don't accompany this again. Haven't I told you...?" It is a tactic to perplex the victim by making him/her vibe like they are off-base or misconstrued a situation.

Countering: The victim's facts are made to be false as victims are blamed for their 'carelessness' or 'jumbling things up' although the victim's memory is excellent.

Diverting: In this case, the deceiver attempts to occupy the victim or make them question themselves by changing the subject of discussion. An example is "I'm certain your crazy sister advised you to screen my calls." Or "None of this is valid; you're making them up to hurt me."

Downplaying facts: When the victim complains about an unsavory situation or communicates a fear, the deceiver laughs at the issue or downplays its earnestness, making the victim feel like a youngster with a tantrum. You hear phrases like "You're angry because of that?"

Outright denial: The deceiver will deny guarantees that they made, totally telling the victim that they never said so and that the whole conversation happened in the victim's mind. For example, "I never advised you to keep dinner waiting for me!"

Pathologizing: Especially savage deceivers may choose to play specialist with your mental health and 'diagnose' you of instability in an offer to conceal their behavior. They can proceed to make claims that you are 'unstable,' 'not all there,' 'spacey,' or 'vengeful' in an offer to unhinge their victims. They may even advise you to book an appointment with a psychiatrist, all the while acting as if they are working for your wellbeing and subsequently making you accept that something is genuinely amiss with you.

Discrediting: A deceiver will spread falsehoods and bits of gossip about you to the people within your circle under the pretense of helping you. They would pretend to be stressed over you and utilize that chance to tell others that you are unstable or acting bizarre.

They may also turn around to reveal to you that others think you are crazy as a way to drive a wedge among you and the people you would typically go to for help. Put blames on you: A deceiver will always find a way to blame you for whatever off-base they do. Attempt to have an important conversation about how they hurt you, and they will turn the discussion upside down that you will start believing that you are the reason for their bad behavior.

Shaming: Another tool the deceiver utilizes in keeping the victim calm is by unobtrusively shaming them by making victims feel inept about the fact that they have been victimized. You will, at that point, apologize to them for speaking out about a bad behavior you called out when they have convinced you it's all in your head. A husband that has been cheating may turn the tables on you by saying: "I can't trust you would think that I would cheapen our relationship in that manner! If you trust I did this, it means you have been unfaithful to me," he may say.

Use kind words to keep you daydreaming: When you call out a deceiver, they may amaze you by using kind words that may make you assume that maybe they are not all that bad after all. But suppose they utilize kind words when faced without changing their behavior or stopping the things that hurt you. In that case, they are just manipulative because, after some time, you will start thinking that you are excessively emotional.

When a person is being manipulated, cognitive dissonance is a common occurrence. You may be asking yourself what cognitive dissonance is, and the thought behind it is pretty simple. When you feel uncomfortable because it goes against your beliefs or your usual way of thinking, it is referred to as cognitive dissonance. An excellent example of this would be if you are usually an honest person and tell a lie. This will make you feel very uncomfortable.

The contradiction of the behavior you expressed as compared to your normal behaviors is quite different, and the person that does this will experience cognitive dissonance. People try to be consistent with their thoughts, behaviors, and ideas. When these items are challenged or go against your normalcy level, many people will try to change this lack of agreement by overly explaining their behavior or action. This makes it more comfortable and allows them to move past it.

The psychologist Leon Festinger gave the first theory behind cognitive dissonance. He claimed that most people would do their best to find internal consistency. Festinger's thinking is that we all feel the need to remain consistent with our behaviors and our belief systems. When they are inconsistent, it leads to internal disharmony, which is something everyone will try and avoid if they can. People will go to great lengths to find inner balance after experiencing cognitive dissonance. Various factors will impact the amount of dissonance that a person may experience. One of those factors is how concrete they feel in certain beliefs that they hold. Another factor is how consistent they are in their beliefs over time.

Thoughts and mental actions that are very personal, such as your understanding and belief in yourself, can cause more significant dissonance inside you than other beliefs. The higher value something holds in you internally, the greater the dissonance you will experience if you go against that belief. It is normal for people to have thoughts that clash; however, this tends to come and go as most people strive to have consistent thought patterns, behaviors, and beliefs. The more dissonance a person experiences, the more pressure they will experience to find balance and relieve uncomfortable feelings.

Cognitive dissonance affects each person's thoughts, actions, and behaviors in surprising ways. We can see cognitive dissonance in every part of life.

This happens when the behaviors conflict with a person's belief system; it happens when dealing with the personal identity area. Now let's look at an example of cognitive dissonance to clarify what we are talking about. · We see cognitive dissonance frequently occur when people are making purchasing decisions.

Let's say you are very conscious of the environment, and you do your very best to make green decisions. One day you buy a new car to find out that it is not very eco-friendly. This will cause cognitive dissonance because you care about being friendly to the environment, yet you drive a car that is not very friendly to the environment.

The dissonance can be reduced by the number of ways to make the belief and the behavior go together better. You could choose to sell your new vehicle and get one that is going to get better mileage and be friendlier to the environment, or you could decide to cut down on how much you are driving the new car.

Some may choose to utilize public transportation or even ride a bike to work. Each one of these is a solution to help resolve the dissonance that is being experienced. They all help bring balance. There are various ways that people will try to find balance when experiencing dissonance. Minimizing the drawbacks of a decision or action is one-way people do this.

A great example is to think about people who smoke, and they may take the time to convince themselves that the risks are being blown out of proportion. This helps their minds to accept the bad habit of smoking and, in turn, alleviate the dissonance they experience when they smoke and think about it being bad for their health.

People will get rid of the uncomfortable feelings caused by cognitive dissonance to look at the beliefs that outweigh the dissonant action.

This is done by looking for new information to change their old thinking patterns. Even if it isn't exactly correct, this new information can allow the uncomfortable feelings to dissipate, leaving the person feeling more balanced and at ease.

People will also try to reduce the significance of the belief that conflicts with how they normally feel. An example of this is the person who works in an office building and sits in front of a computer all day. They know that sitting for long periods of time is unhealthy, but it is hard to change it since it is their job to sit in front of that computer.

Rather than change their behavior, they will try and justify the action of sitting all day. They do this by telling themselves that they eat healthily and exercise once in a while will be enough to combat the negative effects of sitting all day. This helps to lessen the dissonance they are experiencing. The last way people deal with cognitive dissonance is to change the conflict occurring inside. By changing a belief so that it coincides with other beliefs, the dissonance will be alleviated. This change of belief systems is effective when dealing with dissonance, but it is also quite difficult. If you are trying to change your core values and beliefs to deal with dissonance, it will be a challenge.

More other than not, people will find other ways to deal with the cognitive dissonance that does not require them to restructure their entire thought process and beliefs on a particular subject. Let's not forget that cognitive dissonance can be very annoying. When your beliefs and actions don't match up, it can take a toll on your ability to make decisions that will benefit you.

Whenever we notice a cognitive dissonance, we can consider it as an opportunity for growth. When dealing with a gaslighting narcissist, cognitive dissonance can give you a great clue as to what is going on. If you find yourself doing, saying, or agreeing with things that go against your values and beliefs because of what someone else is saying, it is a good sign that you are being manipulated. Our bodies do a great job of helping us understand the experiences that unfold in front of us daily. You can use cognitive dissonance to your advantage so that you maintain the beliefs and values that ring true to you rather than allow yourself to be influenced by a nefarious manipulator.

Effects of Manipulation Manipulation can come in various forms, and unfortunately, there are a variety of different negative effects that come with it. Whether you are mentally or emotionally manipulated, the effects can be devastating.

Sometimes they are short-term effects that can be moved past relatively quickly, while other times, they are long-lasting and can impact your life forever. When you know the effects of manipulation, you are better equipped to handle them, and your life will be able to improve more efficiently.

Psychological and emotional abuse occurs when people are manipulated, and unfortunately, they are not superficial wounds that will heal. It is likely if you have been abused with manipulation that you will carry the scars for the rest of your life. Seeking help is sometimes the best course of action, depending on the experience that you have had. When it comes to mental manipulation, you may find that you have problems with trust, security, respect, and intimacy, and these are only a few of the issues that you may be facing. We will take the time to look at the short- and long-term effects of mental and emotional manipulation.

The gaslighting tactic is both mental and emotional abuse. So, if you have or are dealing with a narcissist who uses gaslighting, you are very likely experiencing some of these effects. Recognizing them can be the first step toward finding improved health and happiness. The Short-Term Effects of Manipulation: · If you have been mentally or emotionally manipulated, it can be tough to understand what is unfolding. You may feel surprised or confused by events.

The feelings of "this can't be so" are widespread. You may question why the people closest to you are acting so strange, even if they aren't acting odd at all. · It is also likely that you will question yourself if you have been through or you are going through this type of abuse.

You may wonder if your memory is deceiving you, or you may feel like there is something wrong with you, in general. When everything you do is questioned, this is the result. Gaslighting will frequently cause this effect as you will always be wrong or challenged by the relationship's narcissistic party. · If you have experienced mental or emotional manipulation, another short-term effect could be anxiety and hypervigilance. People become vigilant toward themselves and other people to avoid further manipulation.

They will avoid behaviors that make things chaotic or end in outbursts. Anxiety will rule them, and any extra chaos could lead to a breakdown so, they will avoid any and everything that may cause that. · Passiveness is another effect that comes from being psychologically and emotionally manipulated.

Often, more emotional pain comes when you take action in a mentally or emotionally abusive relationship, so being passive becomes part of everyday life.

It is important to note that being passive can be hard to break, especially during times of emotional stress. In everyday life, being passive can become a big flaw. · The feeling of guilt or shame is also a common effect of mental and emotional manipulation. When you are constantly being blamed for the harmful actions taking place in your life, you start to believe that you are the cause. This lousy behavior on yourself can lead to shame or guilt. This is only going to make you feel worse, and it is an unfortunate side effect of being with a narcissist or a manipulator. · Avoiding making eye contact with others is another short-term effect of mental and emotional manipulation.

When we don't make eye contact with people, it allows us to feel smaller like we can hide inside of ourselves and that you will take up less space. This is a common thing to do when someone is hard on you all the time and makes you feel as if you are insane. We think that it helps to protect us in some way. Fortunately, this is a side effect that tends to go away rather quickly after we remove the toxic manipulator from our lives and start being around people that genuinely care for us in healthy ways. · The last short-term effect that we would like to mention is the feeling that you need to walk on eggshells around people. When you live your life with an emotional or mental manipulator around, you will never be able to tell what will upset them next.

Due to this fact, you will start to obsess about everything you are doing. The obsession takes place because you are trying to avoid causing any outbursts, and it can bleed over into other relationships that you may have. While there is nothing good to be said about being manipulated psychologically or emotionally, we can take some solace because if we can move away from these abusive relationships, the above issues will likely resolve.

There are side effects of these abuse types that will not go away quickly. There are side effects of emotional manipulation that could stick around forever. Seeking professional help to figure out a course of action to help you heal is often the best place to start. Let's look at some of the long-term effects that one may experience if they have suffered or are suffering from mental or emotional manipulation. The Long-Term Effects of Manipulation: · One of the 1st and most devastating long-term effects of mental manipulation are the feelings of isolation or complete numbness.

Many find that they feel they are no longer a participant of the world but have become observers. All those things that made them happy before now don't make any sense because they don't make them feel anything anymore. When someone no longer recognizes their emotions, it leads to a sense of hopelessness. Many fear that they will never accurately feel or experience their feelings again. This long-term effect does not have to last forever.

If you can get out of the abusive relationship, you can find healing for your damaged emotions. · Another long-term effect is constantly seeking approval. People who have been emotionally or mentally manipulated will likely be exceptionally nice to every person they come into contact with. Their goal is also to please others.

They will likely be extremely focused on their appearance, and they will constantly be striving to accomplish more and more goals. They will do their best to be perfect in every way so that others will approve of them.

While some of these things don't seem so bad, keep in mind that it will be extreme, which is not good. · People who have suffered the abuse of manipulation are often left with resentment feelings. This resentment can be seen in different ways like impatience, frustration, irritability, and blaming.

When you have been treated poorly, it can be tough to witness anything other than that negative behavior. So, releasing feelings of resentment can be pretty tricky, especially if you are going at it on your own. ·

Depression is another real threat to those who have experienced manipulation. Depression is something that may never be overcome once it has taken a hold on your life. It takes a lot of work to dig your way out of the effects of depression. When people are depressed, they start to lose faith in those they care about and care about them.

They feel purposeless in their life, sad and lonely. It becomes hard for them to believe in themselves or anyone else, which takes a lot of time to heal. · Another long-term effect that may be experienced is the excessive judgment of yourself and others.

Because a narcissistic manipulator will constantly judge you, you will evaluate yourself and others much more critically. Here will be very high standards for things like appearance and behavior. This can lead to problems within your relationships, including your relationship with yourself. As noted, long-term effects can be devastating and impact your life negatively in just about every aspect.

There is hope in returning from these adverse effects after you have removed yourself from a manipulative situation. Remember that there is nothing wrong with admitting you need help and seeking it out. You really can find a lot of healing through therapy or groups, which will help you become yourself once again, allowing you to start enjoying life truly.

Chapter 5. How Gaslighting Narcissists operate to make their Victim Think that they are Crazy

So, we mentioned that narcissists have a hand in gaslighting, but what do they do/ they are giant manipulators, and they play a significant role in changing others' reality. Here, we'll discuss how they gaslight others and why narcissists are bad news for many people.

What Is a Narcissist?

By definition, a narcissist is someone with a narcissistic personality disorder. Those who are narcissists tend to have an overly inflated sense of importance, a need for admiration and attention in their relationships, and often don't empathize with others.

Narcissists only care about themselves. They don't worry about you or the guy next to you, but instead, they're only in it for their benefit. However, they have an incredibly fragile ego that will shatter and is very vulnerable if they're hit with the smallest amount of criticism.

Narcissists are textbook manipulators, and they're not fun to deal with. This type of personality causes many issues in different life areas, and you may run into one of these types without even realizing it. Typically, though, those who have narcissistic personality disorder are unhappy in a general sense if they're not given the admiration they want. They may find all of their relationships unfulfilling, and others may not like being around these types of people.

So how does a narcissist come into your life? Well, those that suffer from this love latch onto those that will excite them up, making them feel like they're special or unique, and in turn, enhance their self-esteem as a result. They may desire an immense amount of admiration and attention and have difficulty taking criticism in the slightest. They often see all criticism as defeat.

They are incredibly envious of your accomplishments, to the point where they will want to undermine them. However, they can. This can be anything from snarky achievements regarding your success to underhanded comparing of others.

Narcissists love to use gaslighting too, but we'll get to that in a bit. For now, let's talk about how they will undermine you. If you do something great, they'll try to belittle it, saying that it's not worth it, and you need to do better.

Sometimes, if the narcissist is a parent, they'll compare you to your sibling or someone else in the family. They often will try to belittle anything you do, turning you into a mess in response.

It's not good, and narcissists in general only care about themselves. Of course, many times, only a tiny fraction of people are actual narcissists. Still, in general, there are more male narcissists than female narcissists, and you often will run into them when you're dealing with bosses, coworkers, or even people you may be friends with or date.

But, how can these people use gaslighting? Well, they do so in a very crafty manner.

Narcissism and Gaslighting

Narcissists love to use gaslighting. It's their favorite, most preferred tool of gaslighting. Why is that? Well, it's because it's the perfect way to make you think you're crazy, to undermine what you think is right wholly, and to tell you that your way of thinking is wrong basically.

Remember, gaslighting is a very sneaky way of making you feel like your reality is so distorted to the point where the person will question their sanity or even their memory. Their goal is to make it so that they're right, you're wrong, and that's all they want from this.

The goal is to make you think you're crazy, which we'll get to in a bit. There are other tools narcissists will use, but gaslighting is their bread and butter.

"Oh, I never said that."

"Oh, you remember it wrong. Clearly, you should get yourself checked out."

If you've ever heard those two things before from someone, you're dealing with a Grade A Narcissist.

Narcissists use gaslighting because it's how they love to hide the abuse they're inflicting upon you. In essence, gaslighting is lying straight to your face, with one singular goal in mind, to be the ones in control, the center of attention, and you're nothing.

Every time a narcissist gaslights you, they're wholly ruining what sense of reality you have, making you realize that it's nothing, and they're everything.

They want to break you down slowly but surely. Memory is one of the easiest ways to do this. Why is that? Well, it's because they know that if you can't remember things right, you're not going to be able to trust yourself, distorting your perception and reality that comes with this.

So yes, it does happen like that, and the goal is for you to entirely rely on the abuser to tell you what's real so that over time the abuser is the one in control of your life, the one taking the reins here in the game.

The Art of Making Others Crazy

This is something that a lot of narcissists use gaslighting for. Remember, gaslighting is refuting anyone's reality, making it so that what they think is right really isn't.

When a narcissist gaslights, they will put down and refute anything that you say. They will do this to make it sound like they're the ones who are right when in reality, it's their mind games.

It's all a game for a narcissist. They want to make it so that your reality isn't correct. While you might believe that you're right, the narcissist will tell you right away that you aren't. Over time as you continue to be refuted by the narcissist, you start to doubt your reality. You start to think that you're the bad guy when in fact, it's just your narcissist playing games.

When a narcissist gaslights, they can change the view that you have of people, in general, being good. You might think that people, in general, are good, which they are, but often, if you have a narcissist in your life, this person will not protect your feelings. Someone you may think is good turns out to be wrong, and someone that you thought was bad turns out to be good since that's how the narcissist wants you to believe.

A narcissist will use gaslighting for the sole reason of, they know exactly how to manipulate you. You start to doubt your own reality, and over time, you start to wonder if maybe you are crazy. After all, after so often, you may wonder if you're not right in the head. But remember, more often than not, narcissists were the cause of this, and they're the reason why you think this way.

Often, narcissists will start by buttering you up, making you feel loved and appreciated since that's what they want you to believe. After a while, they will begin to, over time, begin to treat you like crap. When you call them out on it, they'll start to mask their true feelings, and you'll be seeing a different side.

But the reality is, that mask that they put on is, of course, their mask, and the abusive nature that they've had till now is their true form.

They will tell you what you think is what happened isn't what happened, but that's how it is. But of course, in the world of the narcissist, they'll only make you believe what they think is right.

Gaslighting takes away everything that you think is correct, which then causes you to follow what they feel is how they're manipulating you in reality.

You're basically forced to believe that you're crazy, or if you don't think you're crazy, that the abuser is wrong, but you can't stand up for yourself. They will either manipulate you until you believe you're wrong and they are right or drive you to the point of insanity.

Deceivers and narcissists love this. Because they know that, once you discount your own beliefs enough, you'll start to think that you are crazy and slowly begin to believe them.

Making People do What the Narcissist Wants

This is done because most of the time, when you start to discount how a narcissist acts, they will immediately gaslight you, saying that it didn't happen this way.

You notice your narcissist abuser is acting gross and mean, and you see that, for example, they're flirting with other girls. They totally are, and you call them out on it, but they will immediately say that isn't the case, tell you that you're crazy, that you're making stuff up, and tell you whatever you saw was wrong.

Deep down, you know what the truth is. That the actions you saw were valid, but over time, this person will continuously tell you that you're crazy and didn't really hear or say what was said.

You start to doubt your reality, and you begin to wonder if you remembered everything right. Perhaps you didn't catch the other person flirting with girls. You start to go silent on it. When in reality, your narcissist was totally doing that, didn't come clean, and now this person is seeing girls, and every time you call them out on that, and their trust and validity, basically tells you that you're insane, and you're wrong.

You stop fighting the narcissist after a while. You notice that every time you fight them, there really is no end to it and the fact that you're constantly told that you're crazy every time you do isn't a good thing for you either. So, what do you do from here?

The answer is most people tend to give in to their abusers.

Instead of doing what they feel is right, calling out the abuser, and recognizing the toxic traits, you start to do what the abuser wants. Whenever you gaslight, you start to feel like you're wrong and that the narcissist is right. You're pretty much duped into believing that the narcissist is the right person, and you're wrong, making your reality practically nothing.

If you let this continue, you're feeding the supply of narcissism that the other person craves. You may start to perceive things wrong, and often, it gets to the point where you swore it was that way, but maybe your stuff is gone because the narcissist hides it, and then they claim that you're irresponsible and not worthy of trust. They will then tell you that you're wrong and crazy, and they'll start to make others think that you're crazy.

They will even pit others against you to isolate others. Often, they'll try to put you against others, so you drop them, and the only person in your life is the narcissist. They'll make up lies, and you can't trust anyone but the person who is gaslighting you.

When in reality, the one who is gaslighting you is the last person you should trust!

Deceivers don't realize just how harmful they are, or maybe they do. They will start to make you question even the most random of strangers. You might begin to brush off someone's actions as being harmless, but the gaslighted will call it flirting, and soon, you start to attack anyone who comes at you.

Have you ever seen this? Maybe you've experienced it. You will hear about how someone was looking at you the wrong way, you start to grow weary and angry with the other person, and over time, those relationships break down since you think they can't be trusted. When in reality, it's the narcissist who can't be trusted because they're the one putting you in this direction.

A narcissist will hurt everyone in your life literally, pit you against the friends and family you have so that you're distracted from what the narcissist is doing, which is feeding you harmful lies.

It's a messy situation and not something that most of us want to deal with.

So yes, a narcissist will use gaslighting. It's the prime tool of narcissist because they know that they can bend others to the will that they have, making it very easy to manipulate them, and that's why many narcissists will smile at you with a warm, fake smile and then stab you in the back whenever you turn around or put your family and friends against you, so the only person you can rely on, is the narcissist themselves.

Chapter 6. The Effects of Gaslighting

Psychological Health: it happens gradually, affecting the person's self-esteem. They may come to accept they merit the abuse.

1.   Gaslighting manages to Effect of Gaslighting   One of the first serious effects is that which affects a person's manipulate emotional ties. The aggressor can influence a person's social life. The individual might also isolate themselves, believing they are unstable or unlovable. Effects of Gaslighting   One of the first serious effects is that which affects a person's psychological health; it happens gradually, affecting the person's self-esteem. They may come to accept they merit the abuse.

2.   Gaslighting manages to manipulate emotional ties. The aggressor can influence a person's social life. The individual might also isolate themselves, believing they are unstable or unlovable.

3.   In fact, the effects of Gaslighting can persist even after escaping from the abusive relationship. The person may even now question their discernments and have difficulty making decisions. They find it difficult to voice their feelings for fear of being invalidated.

4.   Gaslighting may lead a person to create mental health concerns. Uncertainty and constant disturbance are two common factors that contribute to anxiety. A person's sadness and low self-esteem may lead to despondency. Post-traumatic stress and codependency are common developments.

5.   Some survivors can confide in each other and constantly keep themselves on guard while avoiding further manipulation.

The individual can blame himself for not being able to stop Gaslighting first. All this causes a refusal to show vulnerability, thus creating tensions in future relationships.

Recovering from Gaslighting

Gaslighting is a form of abuse. People can grow to distrust everything they feel, hear, and recollect. Getting validated is one of the most important things for a survivor.

The individuals who have encountered gaslighting may also wish to look for therapy. A therapist is a natural party who can reinforce one's sense of reality. In treatment, an individual can modify their self-esteem and recover command of their lives.

Various mental health problems caused by abuse, such as post-traumatic stress disorder, can be treated by a good therapist. With time and backing, a person can recoup from gaslighting.

Are You Gaslighted? Pay attention to whether you recognize yourself in at least one of these experiences or feelings.

1.   You constantly think back to yourself.

2.   You ask yourself, "Am I that sensitive? Twelve times each day.

3.   You regularly feel confounded and even insane at work.

4.   You're continually saying 'sorry' to your mom, father, sweetheart, boss.

5.   You wonder now and again if you are a "sufficient" sweetheart/wife/representative/companion/little girl.

6.   You can't get why, with so many beneficial things in your life, you aren't more joyful.

7.   You purchase garments for yourself, goods for your apartment, or other personal buys in light of your partner, considering what he might want rather than what might cause you to feel incredible.

8. *You often rationalize your partner's conduct to loved ones.*

9. *You end up denying data of loved ones, so you don't need to clarify or rationalize.*

10. *You realize that something is off base; you can't communicate what it is to anyone, not even yourself.*

11. *You begin lying to maintain a strategic distance from the put-downs, and reality turns.*

12. *You experience difficulty settling on basic decisions.*

13. *You reconsider before raising blameless subjects of discussion.*

14. *Before your partner gets back home, you go through a list in your mind to foresee anything you may have fouled up that day.*

15. *There is a sense that you used to be a different person — increasingly sure, progressively carefree, progressively relaxed.*

16. *You begin addressing your better half through his secretary so you don't need to reveal to him things you're apprehensive about may agitate him.*

17. *Feel like you can't do anything right.*

18. *Your children start attempting to shield you from your partner.*

19. *You get yourself angry with people you've generally coexisted with previously.*

20. *You feel sad and dreary.*

Gaslighting tends to work in stages.

From the start, it might be generally minor—in reality, you may not see it. At the point when your partner blames you for intentionally attempting to undermine you by appearing late to his office party, you attribute it to his nerves or expect you didn't generally mean it or maybe even start to ponder whether you were attempting to undermine him— but then you let it go. Inevitably, however, gaslighting turns into a more significant piece of your life, distracting your musings and overpowering your feelings.

Eventually, you're buried in full-scale sorrow, miserable and dismal, unfit even to recollect the person you used to be, with your perspective and your sense of self. You may not continue through every one of the three phases. But for many women, gaslighting goes from terrible to more awful.

Stage 1: Disbelief Stage 1 is portrayed by disbelief; your deceiver says something over the top—"That person who approached us for bearings was extremely simply attempting to get you into bed!"— And you can't exactly accept your ears. You think you've misjudged, or perhaps he has, or possibly he was simply kidding. The comment appears to be so unusual; you may ignore it. Or, on the other hand, maybe you attempt to address the blunder but without a ton of energy. Possibly you even get into it a long time ago, included arguments, but you're still quite sure of your perspective. Although you'd like your deceiver's endorsement, you don't yet feel frantic for it.

Stage 2: Defense Stage 2 is set apart by safeguarding yourself. You scan for proof to refute your deceiver and contend with him fanatically, frequently in your mind, frantically attempting to win his endorsement.

Stage 3: Depression gaslighting is the most challenging of all: downturn. Now, you are effectively attempting to demonstrate that your deceiver is correct because then perhaps you could do things his way and at long last win his endorsement.

Chapter 7. Signs you are Being Manipulated with Gaslighting

The signs of gaslighting can be hard to see, especially for the person manipulated by this tactic. The effects of gaslighting are highly detrimental. If you can recognize its signs as it is happening, it gives you an advantage and the possibility of getting out of this toxic situation before it destroys you and your life.

Often, people who care about you will recognize the signs before you can. They may try and talk to you about the issues they are seeing, but you may not be willing to hear them if the effects of gaslighting have already taken hold.

When someone you trust or once felt that you could trust comes to you and expresses their concern over signs of gaslighting, you should spend time reflecting on what they have to say to ensure that you are not a victim of this horrific abuse.

We will discuss a variety of different signs that you may witness if you are being gaslighted. Becoming a victim of gaslighting can impact your life negatively in every way. By looking over the following signs, it may become easier to understand what is going on, which can, in turn, give you the clarity and confidence to remove yourself from your current situation.

If you find yourself doubting your own emotions, you may be experiencing the repercussion of gaslighting. Often people will try to convince themselves that things aren't so bad. They will assume they are too sensitive and that what they see as reality is tragically skewed from fact. If you have never had an issue with doubting your feelings, it can be a perfect sign of gaslighting tactics.

Alongside doubting, your emotions will come challenging your perceptions of the events that unfold in front of you, as well as questioning your judgment.

Many people manipulated by gaslighting will be afraid to stand up for themselves and express their emotions. When they do the gaslighting narcissist, it makes them feel inadequate or inferior for doing so. If you find that you are choosing silence over communication, it is a pretty good sign that gaslighting is present in your relationship.

At one point or another, we will all feel vulnerable or insecure. These are normal feelings; however, if you are gaslighting, you will feel this way consistently. You may always feel like you need to tiptoe around your partner, family member, or friend to ensure that they don't have a negative outburst. Additionally, you will start to believe that you are the one causing problems for them instead of the reverse.

The gaslighting narcissist will do their best to sever ties between you and the people you care about. This can leave the victim feeling powerless and completely alone. The narcissist will convince their victim that the people around them don't care. They will try to convince the victim that everyone thinks that they are crazy, unstable, or flat-out insane. These kinds of comments make the victim feel trapped. It also causes them to distance themselves from the people who care, which, in turn, makes them even less controlled than before.

Another sign that you are in the grips of the abuse from a narcissistic deceiver is feeling that you are crazy or stupid. The narcissist will use different words and phrases to make you question your value. This can become extreme because the victim may start repeating these derogatory comments. The sooner you can see the sign of verbal abuse, the sooner you will be able to decide not to let it deconstruct your sense of self-worth.

The gaslighting narcissist will do their best to change your perception of yourself. Let's say that you have always thought of yourself as a strong and assertive person, yet all of a sudden, you realize that your behaviors are passive and weak. This extreme behavior change is a good sign that you are succumbing to gaslighting tactics. When you are grounded in who you are and what your belief system stands for, it will be harder for the narcissistic deceiver to get you to be disappointed in yourself. When you can recognize that the viewpoint of your worth has changed, it can give you the motivation to take back control of your own life.

Confusion is one of the selfish favorite tools. They will say one thing one day and then do something opposite the following day. The result of these types of actions is extreme confusion.

The behaviors of a narcissistic deceiver will never be consistent. They will always try to keep you on your toes to be in a constant state of anxious confusion. This gives them more control. Finding that your partner, family member, or friend is exceptionally inconsistent with their behaviors should clue you into the fact that you are likely in a toxic relationship with them.

If your friend, partner, or family member teases you or puts you down in a hurtful way, too, then minimalize the fact that your feelings are hurt. It is a surefire sign of gaslighting. By telling you that you are too sensitive or that you need to learn how to take a joke, they are brushing your hurt feelings to the side. Someone who truly cares about you, even if teasing, will take the time to acknowledge the fact that they hurt your feelings. If you are constantly being questioned about how sensitive you are, be aware you could be succumbing to the abuse of gaslighting.

Another sign that narcissistic gaslighting occurs is when you constantly feel that something awful is about to happen. This sense of impending doom starts to manifest early on in gaslighting situations. Many people don't understand why they feel threatened whenever they are around a specific person, but after further investigation and getting away from the narcissist, they know it altogether.

Gut feelings should always be listened to, so if your body tells you that something is not right between you and another person, you should remove yourself from the situation before things get terribly out of control.

There are always times in our lives that we owe other people apologies; however, when you are in a gaslighting situation, you will spend a plethora of time apologizing to people. You will feel the need to say I'm sorry regardless of if you have done anything wrong or not. You may be apologizing for simply being there. When we question who we are and our value. It leads us to apologize profusely. If you notice how much you are saying, I'm sorry is increasing, and the things you are saying sorry for are minimal, you may be in a gaslighting situation.

Second-guessing yourself or constant feelings of inadequacy when you are with your narcissistic partner, family member, or friend are excellent signs that they are gaslighting you. If no matter what you do, it is never good enough, you should be aware that you may be being manipulated.

When it comes to 2nd guessing yourself, we're not just talking about second-guessing your decisions but second-guessing things like your memories.

You may wonder if you remember things as they happened because your narcissistic abuser constantly tells you differently. If you have never had a problem recreating and discussing your memories and suddenly trying to figure out whether or not what you are saying is true, you may want to take a closer look at the person you are dealing with instead of looking at yourself.

Another sign that you are succumbing to gaslighting powers is functioning under the assumption that everyone you come into contact with is disappointed in you in one way or another.

Constant feelings that you are messing things up are daunting and unrealistic; however, it is incredible how many people don't recognize when this is happening. They start to apologize for all of the time and assume that they will make a mess of things no matter what they do, which will lead to others being disappointed in them.

When someone you are in close contact with makes you feel as if there is something wrong with you, it could also be a sign of gaslighting. We aren't talking about physical ailments; we are talking about feeling like you have fundamental issues. You may sit and contemplate your sanity and reality. Unless these were problems for you before entering into a new relationship, you should pay attention to the sign.

Gaslighting can also make it extremely difficult for you to make decisions. Where you once made solid choices for yourself, you now have a sense of distrust in your judgment. This can make decision-making extremely difficult. Instead of making their own choices, many victims will allow their narcissistic abusers to make their decisions for them. The other alternative is not making any decisions at all. This could have highly negative impacts on a person's life.

One other great sign that you may be dealing with a gaslighting situation is when someone you are close to constantly reminds you of your flaws. Sure, a bit of constructive criticism is welcomed in most people's lives; however, when your weaknesses or shortcomings are constantly being pointed out by someone that is supposed to care about you, it is a clear sign that something is wrong. It would help if you never despised who you are because of a narcissist's heinous comments. So, if you take a step back and look at the people in your life, it will be easy to figure out who genuinely cares about you and who is trying to control you based on how they speak to you.

Along the same line, where a deceiver will tear you down, they will seldom admit or recognize their flaws. If their shortcomings are pointed out, they will likely become aggressive.

The deceiver is almost always on the offensive and ready to attack. This means that they will have an inability to recognize their inadequacies, and they will quickly place the blame on you if you try and point them out. They are excellent at playing the victim. Additionally, misdirection will be used so that they can turn things around and continue to dote on your shortcomings even if they are fictitious.

Another sign that a deceiver is manipulating you is when you start to make excuses for their bad behavior. People will go to great lengths to cover up the abuse they are facing and dealing with daily. They tell themselves and everyone else that things are OK or even better than OK. The victim will come up with a variety of excuses as to why their narcissistic counterpart is acting the way they are. These excuses are not usually accepted by the people questioning the victim; however, the victim will continue to make excuses rather than admit there is an actual problem.

Recognizing these signs can be difficult when you are involved in a gaslighting situation.

When these signs are being pointed out to you by friends, relatives, or other people that care about you, please take a moment to stop and think about what they are saying. Accepting the signs of gaslighting abuse can be difficult, but it is also necessary for preserving your happiness and sense of self-worth.

It is important to note that the longer you are in a relationship with a gaslighting narcissist, the harder it will be to recognize the signs. Spending the time at the beginning of a friendship or a connection to truly get to know the person and decide whether or not continuing on with them will lead to toxicity can save you from devastating abuse. Remember that people are not always what they seem, so being mindful and present in each moment as it occurs is imperative to keeping yourself safe.

Chapter 8. Things Narcissists Say During Gaslighting.

Stuff Your Gaslighting Abuser Says

If there's one thing I've learned from interacting with people who have had to battle being with a manipulative deceiver, it's that without fail, the abusers all seem to have specific choice phrases that they all use. It's almost like they all graduated from Gaslight University or something. **Here's what your abuser will say:**

1. You're only acting this way because you're so insecure.

2. You're too sensitive!

3. Stop being paranoid.

4. it's not a big deal.

5. I was only kidding!

6. You take things too seriously.

7. You're acting crazy right now.

8. You know you are little nuts.

9. You're just making all that up.

10. Stop being so hysterical!

11. Can you be any more dramatic?

12. You're so ungrateful!

13. That's all in your head.

14. No, that never happened.

15. You're lying. No one believes you. I'm not buying your nonsense.

16. If only I had been more careful.

17. We've had this conversation before. Don't you remember?

18. Don't you think you're maybe overreacting?

19. If only you had listened to me.

20. You always jump to wrong conclusions.

21. You're the only person I've ever had all these issues with.

22. I'm discussing, not arguing.

23. I know what you're thinking.

24. What does it say about you that that's what you think?

25. The only reason I criticize you is that I'm looking out for you.

26. Don't take every single word I say so seriously.

27. You need to get better at communicating.

28. Calm down.

29. You're overthinking this. It's not that deep.

30. What if you're wrong again, just like the last time?

Think about the exact context where these sentences are said to you. Were you talking about sex? Family? Money? Habits one or both of you have? You'll notice that these phrases often pop up when the conversation is centered upon that.

It's a sad truth that, for the most part, the victim is a woman, and a gaslighting narcissist is a man. The reason for this polarization of genders in narcissism is that, often, women have learned to doubt themselves and to apologize whenever there's a problem or disagreement with their significant others. Men, however, are not socialized this way.

Now comes the tricky part. Decide what to do with the narcissistic person in your life and the best outcome. This can depend greatly on your circumstances and the person at hand.

Getaway

Typically, extreme narcissists lack normal levels of empathy, don't pull their own weight, and tend to make the people close to them miserable within the space of a few weeks or months. They are unlikely to have a great deal of insight into their damaging behaviors and are unlikely to have an epiphany compelling them to change.

It may be tempting to try and open their eyes to the cause of their problems, help or change them, but this is far more likely to misfire with defensiveness or lead to resentment (depending on how extreme they are).

Relationships you could potentially cut off include romantic partners, friends, and ex-colleagues, and family. Suppose you are not legally bound to remain in contact with someone – such as engaged in a business, joint ownership of property, administration of a will, or where a dependent is involved. In that case, you have the potential to cut away if you need to.

Less drastic steps include taking a break or managing the situation. Breaks can help gain clarity, but it depends on the relationship at hand and whether you deem it worth saving. If abuse is currently involved in the relationship, an immediate cut-off should be instigated, rather than attempting to make the best of it.

It's important to choose the people you spend time with wisely because humans tend to adopt the characteristics of those around them. Professor Nicholas Christakis of Yale University explains this in terms of the ripple effect, whereby altruism and meanness ripple through people's networks and become magnified. Whatever enters your system - including the actions of your peers, colleagues, and family - will affect your personality development and outlook. Surrounding yourself with good people will make you behave in more kind and empathic ways.

Avoid the inner circle.

If you need or want to keep a narcissist in your life, it is much safer to do so at a distance rather than as part of their inner circle - who become privy to their chaotic changes in temperament. Creating justifiable distance (but remaining warm) allows you to be a welcome part of their life without suffering so many falls from grace. They may well start to think of you quite fondly. However, get too close, and you may become an undervalued part of the furniture, without your own identity or boundaries to respect. Also, you are giving more opportunities for your words and actions to be misinterpreted as threats or competition, and you are far more likely to have your fingers burned.

While you may have identified the narcissist as a damaging individual, many people (particularly those under their control) will never be able to see the situation. This can feel incredibly unfair and unjust to those who can, particularly in the family or romantic cases, if they are directly affected by narcissistic control, abuse, or manipulation.

It is usually those people who "question" the status quo that the harmful narcissist finds most threatening and subsequently suffer most acutely at their hands, as the narcissist feels compelled to bring them down to maintain their position.

If the narcissist is a family member, particularly a parent or a partner, this can be particularly damaging, with the victim often trained to unquestioningly agree or go along with the narcissist's opinions to maintain their love and their favor. Those that follow receive their rewards, while those that question are isolated, ridiculed, and ousted, often labeled as a "black sheep," "troublesome," or "combative."

Avoid narcissistic injury

Sometimes, cutting the chord on a narcissistic relationship is not an option. You may feel you should at least try and continue a non-abusive relationship, in which case avoiding "narcissistic injury" is key to preventing conflict.

In the minds of narcissistic people - both healthy and extreme - they are competent, have unique and special talents, and are accomplished. In healthy narcissists, any credible threat or challenge to these self-beliefs can be handled carefully, objectively, and proportionately by the individual.

Threats to healthy narcissists don't include other successful or accomplished people - they may be positively competitive but not derogatory. If a healthy narcissist takes a blow to their self-esteem, negative feelings may be processed without a meltdown or flying into a rage. On the other hand, extreme narcissists tend to exist in a world of hypervigilance. Any perceived threat or challenge is likely to be aggressively countered. Failing to do so could result in painful crashes to their self-esteem (narcissistic injury), as their opinion of themselves are overinflated, delicate, and variable. This hypervigilance includes people they see as threatening, so it may be beneficial for you to lie low and purposely reduce your traits that may make them feel competitive or destructive about themselves.

Avoid exposing them

Exposing the narcissist and getting the "truth" out to see can be appealing and feel like the right thing to do. You may think this is the best solution for them, you, and anyone else involved - that they will suddenly see clearly and take responsibility for changing their behavior. Forget about being suitable for a moment and bringing the truth to light.

Pointing out that the narcissist is not as incredible as they think can result in a considerable backlash, that you then must be around and may not be able to escape. They are not ever going to agree with you, as they are tied to their elevated identity. Rather than changing their minds, they will be more likely to despise you for your opinions simply.

Admire and listen to them

Being amenable is probably the most passive technique you can take, but so long as you are not already on the narcissist's "naughty list" can effectively pull you through difficult times until you reach calmer waters or can end the relationship. Clinical psychologist Al Bernstein suggests that remaining quiet and allowing the narcissist to come up with reasons to congratulate themselves is easy, effortless, and requires nothing more than listening and looking interested.

Admiring them, their achievements and qualities as much as they do can be a fast route into their "good books." So long as you avoid getting too close, this position in their excellent books can allow you to maintain a happier status quo with the narcissist still in your life.

Accept them

Rejecting a narcissist, whether in reality or their perception, is likely to make them feel incredibly hurt or angry - as it causes a severe narcissistic injury. A jilted lover may feel a great deal of pain when the source of their affection no longer wants them. So, too, a narcissist feels deeply aggrieved when a source of narcissistic supply - or anyone else for that matter - decides that they are not "good enough."

Extreme narcissists – ever hypervigilant - may feel rejected because more ordinary people would not. Being too busy or not having a good enough reason to deny their request for your company or collaboration can quickly be taken to heart and result in an unexpectedly intense response. It's best to give them a legitimate reason beyond your control than to show that you're choosing to reject them. Being too busy to meet or see them is best if your logic is irrefutable, like having to work late to meet a specific deadline, attend an essential wedding, or are booked onto a vacation or trip elsewhere.

Avoid showing weakness

If you show a narcissist what it is, that makes you vulnerable, or what it is that you want, they may at some point use it against you when they want to manipulate you. Narcissists will frequently learn what it is that you want most from them and set about denying it so that you are in a constant state of "need." If a narcissistic mother does this, she may control her children through their neediness for her love. The same goes for a romantic partner. They'll ration your supply of what you enjoy most from them to keep you controllable and pliable.

If they know your most significant concerns or fears, they may leverage these to manipulate you. They may even use you as a distraction from their inner turmoil when they experience crashing self-esteem by needling you on your points of weakness to make themselves feel strong again.

For example, an NPD manager suffering a meltdown of anxiety after a disastrous sales pitch may proceed to milk his staff for reassurance on his performance, whilst then moving the conversation on to subjects that he knows are extremely personal and emotional for them - transferring his fears to them and feeling better himself.

By not conceding any weaknesses to a narcissist and always taking a diplomatic "I know I'll be happy either way" approach, their power will bring you down while raising themselves higher is lost. This may take on the appearance of a cat and mouse game until eventually, the narcissist must concede that you are not "easily pinned" or risk exposing yourself and being seen as a pessimistic and negative person.

Give them an "out."

You can give them the opportunity to stop playing manipulative games by offering them an "out" such as: "You're uncharacteristically pessimistic today. You're usually such an optimist! Is there anything wrong?" and in doing so, call them to return to their "higher state of glory" without continuing their attack. Subconsciously, they may even be aware that you successfully navigated their manipulation and decide to give you a wider berth in the future or that they need to keep you on the side.

If the attack is particularly vicious or nasty, avoiding emotions but maintaining a cool, calm, and empathic approach can work well to bring them back around. Whether you believe it or not, providing them with a defense that effectively excuses their behavior will be much appreciated - as it helps them to avoid a crushing sense of shame and subsequent denial loops and simply feel that they are understood and forgiven. You may even be surprised to find that this approach results in a voluntary concession and what may seem like the beginnings of a more responsible course, but this should not be anticipated or expected.

Don't expect fairness.

Extreme narcissists are likely to be far more concerned with getting what they want than ensuring that everyone is treated fairly. Reward their behavior rather than their words so that they only get what they want when you get what you want too.

Extending credit or accepting promises from an extreme narcissist is a dangerous leap of faith that may not be rewarded. Lack of follow-through is just as likely to occur because the narcissist forgets their agreements - their attention being consumed with themselves and their own concerns rather than remembering their obligations.

They want to look good.

You understand what a narcissist wants means that so long as you avoid triggering narcissistic injury, they may be able to be worked with. You may even be able to maneuver them if you start to think like them.

Extreme narcissists want to look good. If you can align what they want with what you want, you may achieve great successes together. Alternatively, you may be able to manage and alleviate them to make your life easier or until you can leave the relationship.

Understand their narcissistic supply

Narcissists need people to gain a narcissistic supply. You might compare that a healthier person needs others for mutual love and support. Still, as we proceed higher up the extreme narcissism scale, the need becomes more one-directional and desperate in nature to prevent painful relapses to a place of low self-esteem. So, what exactly do they want from you?

Highly narcissistic people often prioritize relationships and career choices based on how much praise or attention they can receive. Many selfish people hamper their development (or never develop a range of interests in the first place) by making choices for praise and success over other forms of enjoyment. If they have chosen you as a part of their life, it may be that you provide a high level of narcissistic supply.

If you have not been chosen voluntarily, you may find that your relationship quality depends on how readily you give narcissistic supply or whether you question or criticize them.

Taking responsibility for not damaging their wellbeing - while protecting your own - is as essential for them as it is for anyone else. You would not feel great about filling the liquor cabinet in the home of an alcoholic, nor should you feel great about pedaling exorbitant approval and attention onto this already dependent individual. Moderate and considerate amounts to avoid attack or denigration are enough for you to get by.

An audience

Narcissists often want an audience. They may spend a great deal of time talking about themselves. This serves their need to feel special (since they are always the discussion subject). They also let other people know how much they have accomplished in life. And the result of this is that they get lots of praise from other people.

Status

Presuming they don't feel threatened by high-status people, they may want to associate with them to feel superior to others. If you think you classify as "high status," this may be what they are using you for. In this case - check your score for narcissism.

It is not unknown for narcissists to flock together and form superficial friendships and relationships to "show off" to others and highlight how special they both are, such as in a "trophy" partner / wealthy-partner relationship. Alternatively, they may want company from someone lower than they are to compare themselves to, for a similar sense of superiority.

Some may choose a mix of friends - a bunch of successful equals to go out and "show off" with one or two best friends to feel superior to, impress, and revel in their attention.

Sex

It may be that the extreme narcissist does not engage in sexual relationships for the emotional value it has, but for sex and sex alone. They may revel in their ability to seduce, in their sexual performance, or in the sense of higher status or dominance within the sexual dynamic.

Love

Narcissistic people like to feel that someone loves them and wants to be with them. Depending on how they view themselves, this may result in higher infidelity or cheating levels. If a narcissist defines themselves as "good" or "moral," then cheating itself (or engaging in any generally scorned upon activities) could result in crushing shame and self-loathing, making it less likely to happen. On the other hand, if the narcissist is reluctant to see their partner as an equal, the likelihood of cheating increases.

Avoid flooding them with supply.

If you are concerned about providing a narcissist with supply, keeping them in line can be aligned more with what they don't want. Being all about appearances, narcissists feel more shame than guilt. They don't want to look bad.

Asking them to consider their reputation may make them think far more carefully than asking them to view other people's feelings. If they think others will poorly perceive their actions, they are far less likely to act. This can be achieved by asking them what people would think about what they did or asking probing questions to trigger them into having an alternative idea themselves.

Chapter 10. Ways to Stop a Deceiver in Their Tracks

If you've read up to this point, then chances are you're probably thinking of a long list of people that have just got to be narcissists or deceivers in your life. However, as a caution: Not everyone is a narcissist just because you have a little tiff here and there. Also, keep in mind that you might recollect past events through the narcissistic glasses, so everyone might seem to be that way.

With that said, if you've asked yourself the questions listed in this book and have observed for yourself that you are dealing with a deceiver, how do you deal with them? Let's get into that.

Putting an End to Gaslighting

Pay attention to the pattern. One of the significant reasons gaslighting is so effective is that, for the most part, the target is entirely ignorant of what's happening. The minute you move from ignorance to complete awareness, you will have successfully taken back some of your power. You will find it easier to shrug off the Narcissist when they start playing games again.

Keep in mind that the deceiver might never change, no matter what you do. Sometimes, the only way there can be any change is with a professional's help. Gaslighting is all that the manipulator knows how to do, so you cannot expect them to give that up in favor of logic or reason. There is no other better coping mechanism that they know. This is not to say that they should not be held accountable for their actions. I'm just making sure you know not to hold on to the hope that they will change. They could, but don't hope for it. Accept that they're wired the way they are, and only professional therapy can help them become better people.

Remember that gaslighting behavior is not necessarily about you. It all comes down to the fact that the deceiver needs to feel like they're in charge. They need that rush of power. At their core, the deceiver is riddled with insecurity. The only way they know how to get rid of that feeling is to make others feel less than they are or give themselves the illusion that they are better than everyone else. Keep this in mind, and you will not bother internalizing anything they say or do anymore. You will be better positioned to manage the relationship you have with them or end it altogether.

Try to create a system you can rely on. Dealing with a deceiver on your own is no walk in the park. It helps to have other people you can talk to who will validate your perception of reality and your sense of self-worth. If you've noticed that ever since you got involved with the Narcissist, you've somehow been cut off from the people that matter to you, then now is the time to reach out to them. Do not buy into the Narcissist's lies about how no one else can love you the way they do. That is not true! Commit to spending time with your friends and family. Make appointments, if you must. Treat these appointments with as much commitment as you would a business meeting. The less isolated you are, the less of a hold the deceiver can have on you.

Spend a long time thinking about whether you want to keep investing in the relationship. This is crucial, especially since dealing with the deceiver's shenanigans eats away at your peace of mind, self-worth - and even your health. Is the deceiver your manager or your boss? Then take proactive steps to find another job, making it a non-negotiable agreement with yourself that you're moving to a different, better job. If the deceiver is your lover and you'd like the relationship to continue, then keep in mind that you'll both be needing some therapy. You will have to make a non-negotiable aspect of your relationship if you decide to stay.

Start to build your self-esteem back up. It would help if you took some time to remind yourself of everything about you that is amazing, no matter what the deceiver has said to make you think otherwise. You might need to begin journaling so that when you are low or starting to buy into the insidious lies they have packed your head with, you can reopen that and remind yourself of your awesomeness.

Don't just write about the great things about you. Write about times when you felt the most alive, the most joyful. As you do this, you will naturally find yourself craving those times again and taking action to liberate yourself and your mind.

Be open to getting professional help. It's difficult being the victim of gaslighting. Your self-esteem, sense of self, and sanity will have taken a beating. You might find that you're slow to make decisions, constantly unsure of yourself, and always wondering if you're good enough. You might even be suffering from depression or anxiety.

Suppose you find that you're overwhelmed by feelings of helplessness, uncertainty, hopelessness, and apathy. In that case, chances are you need to seek the help of a professional psychotherapist right away so that you can rebuild yourself after the devastating damage caused to you by the deceiver.

Change Is Possible

There it is. The answer you've been hoping for, waiting for with bated breath: it's possible for people to change, no matter what personality disorder they have been diagnosed with. Think of these diagnoses as a shorthand way of describing certain people. You can never use one word to encapsulate a person's life. When terms like extrovert, introvert, or Narcissist get bandied about, they imply a permanence to the individual's personality. That's not always the case.

It helps to consider that these disorders are not necessarily descriptions of who people are in summary. It would be more accurate to think of these labels as the perfect descriptions for behavioral and inter-relational patterns and nothing more. The same applies to narcissistic personalities.

Born of Vulnerability

Many researchers believe that Narcissistic Personality Disorder is a result of growing up in conditions where it's not safe to be vulnerable. The Narcissist as a child, had to accept that it was a sign of imperfection to be vulnerable and that showing any vulnerability meant that they had no worth.

This theory is why there's often a connection made between insecure attachment styles and narcissism, meaning the Narcissist is driven to control all their relationships because they are afraid to be in a position where they need to depend on someone else.

The Narcissist is adept at keeping people from knowing who they are. They will refuse to acknowledge their vulnerabilities or opt to suppress them or project them onto others so that they can keep crafting the person they want to be about others. For the Narcissist to change, they must be willing to be vulnerable.

This means leaving themselves wide open to emotions that they have suppressed and denied over the years.

The trouble with narcissists is not that they are unable to change; it's that they are unwilling to because it would mean that the identity of the person they have struggled to craft will be blown to bits. In a narcissist's mind, all the relationships which they have failed at offer more reason why they should remain the way they are.

Understand that Narcissist defines themselves by how others perceive them. A narcissist can't be a narcissist if they don't have anyone to put on a show for. They need to be the center of attention, so they love to spotlight awareness from those who bother to stick around them. Over time, of course, their performance starts to get old. The Narcissist knows this and is constantly running, scared that others will realize there's nothing to them. This is one reason the Narcissist refuses to change, as they are more confident than ever that the fix is not to come clean and be vulnerable but to put on a more vivid show and pile on some more makeup to conceal all their flaws.

When the Narcissist Finds True, Secure Love

When the Narcissist happens to find someone who cares about them and is not just sticking around for the flash, they're still deathly afraid that this person will think they're not worth it. The fear they feel is a subconscious one that they are not aware of, but it is genuine. This fuels the Narcissist to do things like shift blame and guilt onto their partner or act all grandiose.

When their antics are exposed to the light of day, and everyone sees them for what they are, they get angry because they've slipped up and alienated everyone who mattered to them. Rather than change their ways, this causes them to double down on who they are. They become even more narcissistic than ever before, ironically leading to the abandonment and rejection that they're so afraid of.

Breaking the Cycle

There's nothing else to do to help the Narcissist but break that vicious cycle. As gently as you can, you need to throw a wrench in the works whenever they try to control you, create distance between you, blame you, or defend themselves. This means letting them know in no uncertain terms that you're willing to have them in your life, but not on those terms. What words, then?

You should show them that they can join you in the sort of intimacy where they can be loved for who they are, flaws and all. They only need to be willing to let that happen.

The point to take away from all of this is that narcissism is simply one way of relating to others, and you can always change the way you connect with people. It's not going to be easy for narcissists to let themselves get so vulnerable to allow intimacy, but it is possible.

The Narcissist to who wants to Change

If you happen to know someone who's a narcissist but has expressed the willingness to do better, then you can let them read the book. Here is a list of things the Narcissist will need to do to become a better person. This is addressed to the Narcissist, not the victim.

Learn to recognize and respect boundaries. When you do, you'll find that you stop losing relationships and improve them. You must understand where you end, and another begins. You need to realize that other people have their own beliefs, thoughts, and emotions, and they can be completely different from yours while remaining valid. **To help you know boundaries better:**

- *Listen twice as much as you speak.*

- *Use other people's names when you write to them and if you talk to them, too.*

- *Get curious about the people around you. Ask questions to learn what matters to them and what's new in their lives. Don't be inappropriate in your asking.*

- *Be mindful of creeping into other people's personal space and time. Always ask permission first before you do.*

- *Rather than issue orders, ask open questions. Don't ask leading questions. Don't assume you know better than others.*

- *When others make a choice that is different from yours, respect it. You won't always get what you want, and that's OK.*

Be genuine, always, in all ways. You will find it more refreshing than lying, pretending, and manipulating others. How can you be more natural?

- *Keep your word. Don't make promises if you know you can't keep them.*

- *Did you make a promise you can't follow through on? Then own it.*

- *Don't make others feel like they have been deceived through your actions.*

Observe yourself often so you can grow in mindfulness. The more you observe, the better you can see how you cause problems in your relationships and push people away. Assume that there's the usual you, and then there's your higher self who observes you from a higher point of view. **Here's how to be more mindful:**

- Ask your higher or observer self whether whatever you're about to say or do will have good or bad consequences.

● Ask your observer self if your actions and words are all about you showing off or building a great relationship with others.

● Feel like you just did or said something off? Ask your observer self how it would feel if someone said or did that to you. Then apologize and make amends quickly.

Be willing to seek professional help. All of this will serve you to make an individual become complete.

Don't fight with this alone. A good psychotherapist can help you. All you have to do is be honest to make lasting changes. It's going to be so worth it in the end because you will finally discover your authentic self, and your relationships will be better for it.

Do forgive yourself. This is the only way to get the healing you need. It's also the only way to be more comfortable with being vulnerable. An added plus is you'll finally be able to flex those empathy muscles. It might be hard to forgive yourself, and you may sometimes find yourself crippled with remorse. Just be kind to yourself in moments like this. Focus on the fact that you can do better. It is not your fault that you have not been allowed to be yourself. You have done everything possible to move forward. Now, you can rediscover yourself. Be OK with being human. You won't be perfect. You never were. You have flaws, but that's OK! Learn to be comfortable with yourself.

This is the way to allow rich, beneficial, loving relationships in your life; this is how you grow. It would help if you were OK with who you are. Be OK with being true to yourself, even if it means being vulnerable.

It's going to take you some time. Be patient. You will find yourself. You will also learn that the thing you feared the most is not accurate. The people who love you don't up and leave just because of imperfection or five. After all, we're all flawed in our way.

The Trouble with Emotional Abuse

The trouble with emotional abuse is that because it leaves no scars you can see, it often gets dismissed or is almost impossible to spot when it happens. Make no mistake: the damage from emotional abuse is genuine, and it can last a long, long time.

When you're psychologically abused, the other person is saying and doing things to make you think whatever they want. Generally, the goal is to make you confused, disillusioned, and dependent on them for your sense of self-worth and identity. It is an incredibly hurtful, despicable thing to do to another person and can lead to genuine mental health issues like depression, Post-Traumatic Stress Disorder, and anxiety.

Unmasking Emotional Abuse

There are many myths about emotional abuse, which do an excellent job of camouflaging it so that it's hard to detect. Let's rip the mask off, so you can have an easier time figuring out whether you or someone you care about is being abused.

Myth #1: Emotional Abuse is always accompanied by physical abuse.

It isn't. There can be emotional abuse with no physical abuse; this often flies under the radar.

Myth #2: Emotional Abuse is nowhere near as damaging as physical abuse. This is just pure falsehood. If it hurts, then it hurts. It is not a productive argument to say that one form of abuse hurts more than another. Abuse is not OK. If you're being abused, you deserve better, and you need all the help you can get.

Myth #3: Emotional Abuse only affects women. Abuse can happen to both women and men. There is no exception. Also, it happens in other contexts besides relationships, such as at work and with friends.

What to Do If You're Being Abused

If you're emotionally abused, then you're constantly criticized for everything you say and do. You're blamed all the time, even for things that could never be your fault. You're made to feel ashamed. Your deceiver constantly threatens to hurt you physically or do something they know you don't want them to. You feel like you have zero control over your life, as the abuser takes all your power away, sometimes even going as far as controlling your finances so that you have no choice but to stay with them and do whatever they want.

If you recognize yourself in the paragraph above, you need to do something. You need to reach out and ask for help. There is no shame in that. Asking for help is one of the bravest things you can do, especially when you're in a situation where the abuser has wholly worn you down and out.

Talk to anyone you can about what you're going through. Confide in them, and not only will you have someone on your side, but you will also be able to occupy your time by hanging out with others besides your abuser. Work on getting more and more people to talk to who will back you up.

Have a safety plan in place. While there's not necessarily physical abuse going on along with the emotional abuse, it's still important to be safe. This means you need to think up plans for how you can escape from the relationship whenever you are finally ready to up and leave the abuser.

Don't Make Excuses for the abuse.

Often, people will fall back on mental disorders to justify when they do what they do. They don't talk about it like they want to make genuine change. It's just a copout for them to keep treating you the way that they always have.

It's not uncommon for the person abusing you to try to make light of the situation or try to blame you for a reason they're acting the way they do. It can seem like your significant other doesn't know when they do what they do or are utterly incapable of realizing the implications of their actions. However, this is just more smoke and mirrors on their part.

They know what they're doing. The whole point behind being seemingly unaware is to make you feel even less sure of yourself. Next thing you know, you start wondering if you're not overly dramatic or delusional! I want you to know that your abusive partner is very aware of how they're hurting you, and they always are in control of how they act disorder or no. Want proof?

They will decide when to abuse you and how far they will push it. A perfect example is when they threaten to hit you but don't. Or when they use you in ways that you can never really tell others because there's no proof, and it can seem like you're making something out of nothing.

They only ever abuse you, not others. If they indeed had no control over their actions, wouldn't they beat everyone in their lives? But they don't, do they? That's because they can control themselves. If they suffered from a disorder, then everyone in their life would get the same treatment, not just you.

They escalate their terrible behavior. When it's a matter of having a disorder, there can be changes in the person's state of mind. Even then, though, there is a consistency in how they behave. However, you may have noticed your abuser will sometimes choose not to abuse you for a while. Other times, they will steadily ramp up the abuse as your relationship goes on. This is more proof that they really can decide to be different or better.

You need to keep in mind that regardless of whether the deceiver has an actual mental health problem, you are not the one to be held accountable for how they treat you! It's possible to be diagnosed with a disorder and still choose not to act out in controlling, manipulative ways. They will need to acknowledge their issues and be open and willing to seek the help that they need. Please, always remember that you're not the reason they act the way they do, and therefore you're not the cure they need. They must own their actions, and they alone can take the first step they need, to change themselves.

Chapter 11. A Match Made in Hell: Narcissists and Empaths

There is one specific union that is never going to end well. We are, of course, talking about the match between a narcissist and an empath. The reason is that both are at opposite ends of the empathy spectrum, and as a result, they clash constantly.

This chapter will explore why narcissists and empaths are a terrible match, but we're also going to discuss the fact that this is a match that happens more often than you would think.

First things first, we need to explore what an empath is to understand why this union is one to avoid at all costs.

What is an Empath?

There is a difference between someone empathetic and someone who has empathy. A person who has a heart can understand others' feelings and put themselves in their shoes. Each person varies according to the degree of empathy they possess. Someone can be a compassionate person, e.g., have a high amount of empath, but that still doesn't make them an empath.

An empath is someone who takes others' emotions as their own due to their extreme sensitivity. For example, an empath may be standing next to someone in the line for the bus, and that person may be feeling angry about something that has happened that morning. As a result, the empath will begin to feel angry, but they have no reason to feel angry themselves. They're picking up on the other person's vibrations and emotions and exhibiting that emotion as their own.

Empaths are not rare, and many people have this tendency in their lives. While it is considered a gift, the person who has it may not feel it so! Life can become very overwhelming for people who are so sensitive to emotions around them, and many empaths find large groups to be very draining. As a result, they will either avoid large gatherings or leave quite early. An empath also has to find ways to manage their "gift" to stop it from taking over their lives.

In addition to being sensitive to emotions, empaths are also drawn to people in need. Empaths are very pure and positive people, and they like to help others who may be going through a hard time or maybe suffering somehow but not vocalizing it. The problem occurs when an empath cannot draw a line between their own emotions and another person's emotions, and they find it extremely difficult to walk away from those in their life simply because they can feel their pain and their general emotions.

The main traits of an empath are:

- *Usually introverted but can be extroverted too,*

- *Like their own space and time alone,*

- *Can become overwhelmed in large groups,*

- *Highly sensitive,*

- *Very intuitive,*

- *They can quickly become overwhelmed when in a relationship and needs to learn how to step back a little and take their own space whenever required,*

- *Often give too much of themselves, as they usually have big hearts,*

- *Their senses are highly attuned,*

- *They often need to be around nature to feel calm.*

Aside from absorbing the emotions of others like a sponge, one of the most significant risks of having this empathic gift is the fact that empaths are a massive target for narcissists and other "energy vampires." An energy vampire is very hostile or very manipulative and finds it easy to suck the life out of an empath, who is willing to give to the point of exhaustion. The solution to protecting yourself from these people is to have a lot of time and space for yourself.

Why is there an attraction between narcissists and empaths?

Now we know what an empath is, why are empaths and narcissists a standard coupling?

There is an attraction on both sides here. Firstly, the empaths recognize the narcissist struggle, e.g., their lack of confidence and their underlying struggles. The empath can feel this, but they also have a nurturing side that makes them want to make things better. Of course, we know that nobody can make a narcissist better, but the empath intends to try.

Also, narcissists are, as we know, incredibly charming and can trick people into thinking they're a wonderful person, when underneath they may have other intentions. Because an empath always wants to see the best in people, they tend to fall for the charm. You would think that their intuition would allow them to see past this smokescreen, but the narcissist is an expert at deception and often manages to slip beneath the radar.

A narcissist is attracted to an empath because of their opposite nature. Remember, narcissists don't have empathy like non-narcissistic people. An empath is the opposite and has compassion by the bucket-load. This intrigues the narcissist, but they can also see that this may be a person who can easily be manipulated. As a result, the narcissist makes a bee-line for the empath, showing their full charm armory.

While every relationship is different, the chances are that a union between a narcissist and an empath will follow a prevalent path. The narcissist will charm the empath completely, and the empath will fall entirely underneath their spell. The narcissist will then begin their gaslighting techniques as the empath starts to show their confidence and tries to have their own life outside of the relationship.

The empath struggles to understand why the narcissist is causing them distress because they look for everyone's best. As a result, the narcissist uses tactics to empathize with their thoughts and feelings, confusing because they're already overwhelmed with emotions due to their empathic nature.

Empaths feel everything very deeply, so when the narcissist hurts the empath, they will feel it ten times amplified. This causes a rollercoaster relationship to begin, with ups and downs, crazy highs, and crashing lows. The highs and lows are addictive, and the endless gaslighting and charm offensive make them stay.

A relationship between a narcissist and an empath is very similar to a relationship between a narcissist and a regular person. However, the difference is the depth of feelings that an empath experiences.

As a result, they will have highs and lows which exhaust them, and when this occurs in conjunction with all the other emotions, they're picking up on a day-to-day basis, the effect can be highly damaging.

Is There a Future For This Relationship?

Put simply, no. There is less chance of this relationship surviving than any other narcissistic-affected relationship. The emotional highs and lows will make the relationship impossible to stay.

The empath will have a tough time leaving the narcissist, and it will probably take several attempts to go through with it. Despite that, it is hoped that the empath eventually finds the strength to walk away.

This type of relationship has no future. The narcissist will drain every last drop of positive out of the empath and leave them completely overwhelmed, emotionally confused. They will question their sanity to the point of exhaustion.

Of course, the empath will desperately want to "fix" the narcissist, and they will try time and time again to do it. In the end, however, they will realize that it's just not possible, and they will give up and move on - at least, that is the hope.

How a Narcissist Can Severely Emotionally damage an Empath

A narcissist will use the empath's emotional sensitivity against them. This is a weak point in the narcissist's eyes and something they don't understand. Feeling everything so deeply is so intoxicating to the narcissist, so exotic and different, that they want to explore it and find out more about it. They then realize that this is an "in," something they can use alongside their gaslighting tactics, and it works very successfully.

An empath is generally a very pure and good person. They try to help, and they try to see the good in others, but their emotional sensitivity is their undoing in this situation. They also try time and time again to the right the case, make the narcissist see the error of their ways, show them that they understand and want to help, but remember, the narcissist sees no error in their tracks. In the narcissist's eyes, they're not the one to blame; the empath is. By blaming the empath, they damage their self-esteem and self-worth to a very severe degree.

The constant bombardment of gaslighting makes the empath feel like they're going crazy and will work entirely against the overwhelming feeling of experiencing emotions outside of their head. As a result, the empath may suffer an emotional breakdown due to complete exhaustion.

An empath will struggle severely with a relationship touched by narcissism because they simply cannot understand themselves. Both sides are totally at odds - the narcissist doesn't understand the emotional sensitivity of the empath and the empathy they show with almost everything they do. The empath doesn't understand the narcissist's total lack of empathy and how they can be so cold and unforgiving, yet so charming and giving when they want to turn on the act. The empath may know that something isn't right, they may want to walk away, but their need to see the good in everyone keeps them where they shouldn't be.

Put simply, an empath could suffer mental health damage by staying in a relationship with a narcissist, and that will take professional help to right and overcome. They will struggle with building lasting, trusting relationships in the future. They may also turn against their emotional sensitivity and empathy and see it as a hindrance rather than a positive trait or a gift.

A narcissist has the power to destroy an empath.

Points to Take From This Chapter

We have explored in this chapter how a relationship between a narcissist and an empath can be harmful. You might not have known much about empaths before this chapter, but now the hope is that you understand much more.

Perhaps you're an empath, or you're very emotionally sensitive yourself. In that case, you need to be very wary of anyone in your life who might be exploring your sensitivity.

A narcissist will see an empath as easy pickings, a natural target, and someone easy to manipulate. To turn the tables, you need to identify the signs, and you also need to develop the strength to walk away.

The main points to take from this chapter are:

- *An empath accepts the emotions of others as his own due to his sensitivity;*

- *Empaths are usually introverted, quiet, kind people who try to see the best in everyone;*

- *Empaths can also become overwhelmed by emotions very quickly, and they feel everything very profoundly;*

- *Narcissists are attracted to empaths because they are curious about their empathy, but also because they may see them as an easy target;*

- *Empaths are drawn to narcissists because they want to help, but also because they're a target for the charm offensive, which often comes at the start of a relationship;*

- *A relationship with a narcissist may be enough to cause an empath to have an emotional breakdown or burn out reaction if the manipulation is severe enough;*

- *The empath will feel the hurt and pain of the treatment by a narcissist very deeply but will still want to do their best to help their partner;*

- *Empaths are likely to need a lot of help and support when walking away from a narcissistic partner. They may heed professional help to allow them to develop loving and trusting relationships in the future.*

Chapter 12. How to stop being manipulated by a deceiver

Gaslighting has become a hot topic today because it is a harmful manipulation tool, either an emotional, psychological manipulation thing that is happening to many people than we even realize. So before now, we have talked about what gaslighting is and how you know that you have been a victim of gaslighting, and the tactics that deceivers use.

As stated before, gaslighting is a subtle way of avoiding responsibility after that person has done something terrible. In extreme cases, it is a way to abuse or gain power over somebody in harmful practices emotionally. If you haven't read the chapter that talks about gaslighting signs or know if you are being gaslighted, then go and do that now because if you haven't done that, you won't understand what this chapter is saying. It won't make sense if you don't recognize what gaslighting is and if you don't realize it is happening to you. So we are going to talk about some ways to deal with gaslighting.

Clarify yourself

And the first thing is to clarify to yourself how you know you're being gaslighted and then write it down. Write down the specific things done or say to you that makes you know that you are being gaslighted. Write down specific examples as they come up and write down what this person is making you feel crazy, question yourself on, make you feel like you are losing it, and question your sanity. Those people use specific tasks to Gaslight you. It is leaking, and it's up to you, and if you're not aware of what the person is doing, you might not even realize that it is happening to you.

Do some ground exercise.

The next step is to start carving out some grounding exercises and take some time to shut up and stay still with yourself to start connecting with yourself again. You might take some time to do some deep breathing. Whatever those grounding and meditating exercise is doing it to start connecting with yourself again because gaslighting makes you doubt yourself. It makes you. You believe yourself.

It makes you feel like you can trust yourself again. So you need to start taking time to connect with yourself; furthermore, you need to take the time to start tuning into your inner wisdom and tune to your ability to believe and trust yourself. Because that has been taken away from you, if you haven't gaslighted for a long time at some point in your life, you need to reconnect with yourself to start to realize that you are being manipulated. You need to trust yourself and see that this person is meant to mess with you and throw you off. It would help if you got things backgrounded by taking the time to connect with yourself in your thoughts, beliefs, perceptions and really ground yourself in that stuff.

Decide whether you want to continue the relationship.

The next one is if it is someone that is currently in your life that is plating you this week, and if it is becoming a big issue, then you might need to decide whether you want to continue the relationship. So you need to determine if you need to distance yourself from this person or discontinue the relationship altogether. This is a tricky thing when you are made to feel small weak, or made to feel insignificant, stupid, crazy, insane. You need to take it seriously and decide if it is worth continuing in that relationship. Even though there are certain times that these people will be caring, loving, and excellent and allow you to have a great moment with them, but other times, they try to make you feel small, stupid, or crazy, so you need to listen to yourself and decide if it is worth it. Decide if that person is worthy of staying in your life since that is how they treat you and make you feel low and take away from you your ability to handle confidence in yourself.

Reach out to a trusted loved one or friend.

The next thing to do is to reach out to somebody like a friend or a trusted loved one and tell that person because; chances are if you have been a victim of gaslighting for an extended period. And it has ever affected your sense of self-worth and ability to trust yourself; then you need to do some healing that is not just going to go away. It would help if you dug into it because things like that will impact your core beliefs. It will start to manipulate your self-worth, so you need that intervention to heal from it and be able to move forward from the wounds, the pains, the hurt, and the damage that this might have caused you. So this is something that you need to take seriously.

Take a Stand

The last one is to take a stand and not let yourself continue to be a victim. Once you recognize that the gaslighting is happening, you want to see what the person is doing. You need to stand up to them and say something like, I know what you are doing, and I'm not going to fall for it. No matter how hard they try to convince you, and no matter which Tactics they're using, try to stand up to them and say that that's not what happened, you are lying, you are making this stuff up. Try to take a stand and take your power back instead of being a victim or allowing yourself to get manipulated or even abused in this harmful way.

If you're doing some of these things and implementing some of these strategies, then it will help you to be able to regain your sense of clarity, and then you will start to trust yourself again. You will be able to connect with yourself and even believe in yourself. You will be able to trust your senses, memories, perceptions, and version and your interpretation of reality, and you will be able to stop people who are playing mind games with you.

Having healthy boundaries is good in everyday life, especially in Gaslight. It would help if you put in those boundaries, say no way, this will not happen to me, and I am going to fall for this. I'm not going to let you treat me this way. Having healthy boundaries is Crucial.

Dealing with the Narcissist

Now that you've realized that there is a narcissist in your life, what should you do?

Take a step back and analyze the situation.

Determine how bad the situation is. Try to understand the narcissist's background and the degree of his narcissism. Note or recall what drives him to narcissistic rage. Recall how he tries to punish you. Be aware of the tactics that he uses. Do all these objectively. Being carried away by emotions, shouting, or crying will only feed the narcissist. The narcissist has already painstakingly set up a strong image or reputation, and you might not come across as credible when you tell others, so you have to do your homework.

Accept that the narcissist will not change.

They are hoping that you will be able to knock some sense into the narcissist or that you could explain, and things to enlighten him will not work. As far as the narcissist is concerned, he has done no wrong.

Seek help.

Find people – friends, counselors, religious leaders, or parents- anyone you can confide in and who can give advice and emotional support. They can also provide feedback from a neutral viewpoint.

Set boundaries.

Write down which boundaries the narcissist cannot trespass and a consequence if they do. Writing things down before talking to the narcissist will help you speak without sounding emotional.

Be realistic.

Know the narcissist's limitations and work within those limits. It will only be emotionally draining and a waste of time to expect more from the narcissist than capable. Do not expect him to learn to care because he can't.

Remember that your value as a person does not depend on the narcissist.

Please don't punish yourself for getting into a relationship with him. Instead, focus on rebuilding your self-esteem, meeting your own needs, and pursuing your interests.

Speak to them in a way that will make them aware of how they will benefit.

Instead of voicing your needs, pleading, crying, or yelling, learn to rephrase your statements by emphasizing what the narcissist will gain from them. You have to learn to appeal to their selfishness. This is a way to survive situations that you cannot escape.

Bring up your ideas to the narcissistic boss when there are witnesses. Having others around to hear your opinion will find it difficult to claim credit for it.

Find proof of or document any abuse.

Use technology- CCTV or video recordings, for example- to document instances of abuse. Find witnesses to back you up.

Do not fall for the narcissist's tactics again.

Refresh yourself on his tactics and be on your guard against falling for them again. The narcissist may try to use pity, projection, or hoovering. This time, be wiser. It may take practice, as you may have become used to being the "Echo" or codependent. Being aware will help you to resist.

Leave.

The best way to deal with the narcissist is not to. For the sake of your emotional and physical well-being, not to mention your sanity, it would be best to leave. If you go, expect various tactics from the narcissist to either make your life miserable or get you (actually his supply) back. You will also undergo a period of distress akin to mourning when you leave. To overcome this problem, you need to seek help and support from someone. Do not be hard on yourself for having allowed yourself to be deceived by the narcissist. Your experience will make you stronger, wiser, and ready for a healthy relationship in time. In the meantime, focus on your interests and rebuilding your self-esteem.

Chapter 13. Narcissistic Personality Disorder

A narcissistic personality disorder is a disease that affects approximately 1% of the population, with a higher incidence of males than females. It is characterized by excessive arrogance, lack of empathy, and a great need for admiration. The primary marker of a narcissistic personality is grandiosity. They believe they deserve special treatment; they are interested in borrowing vanity and power.

Narcissistic personality disorder should not be confused with a person with high self-esteem. The difference between a person with high self-esteem and a narcissist is humility; someone with a lot of self-esteem can be humble, a narcissist cannot. They are selfish, overconfident, and ignore others' feelings and needs. Also, the disorder hurts a person's life. In general, one may be dissatisfied with one's life and be disappointed when others do not admire it and are not given the particular attitude or care it needs. All vital areas are affected (work, personal, social ext), but one cannot realize that their behavior negatively impacts their relationships. People do not feel comfortable with a selfish person, and they will feel dissatisfied with their work, social life, etc.

Symptoms and characteristics of narcissistic personality disorder

Some Of the Symptoms and Characteristics of a Narcissistic Personality These are:

- *Concern for fantasies, successes*

- *Faith, which is of great importance, only feels understood and connected to people who believe they have high status.*

- *They need and require constant admiration.*

- *Exaggeration of your achievements and abilities.*

- *Feel for rights or privileges.*

- *To envy others and have too much conviction that others envy.*

- *Think and talk most of the time in yourself.*

- *Suggest unrealistic goals.*

- *The expectations of others to provide exceptional services.*

- *I believe that no one can question their motives and demands.*

- *Take advantage of others to get what they want without the hassle.*

- *Arrogance, arrogance.*

- *Easily rejected and injured. · Strong desire.*

- *Responding to criticism with shame, anger, and humiliation.*

Narcissistic personality disorder: causes

There is no definite cause for narcissistic personality disorder, but researchers agree that environmental and genetic factors play a role in the development of the disease.

Some of the genetic factors show that people with a narcissistic personality have less gray matter in the left insula, the part of the brain associated with empathy, emotional regulation, compassion, and cognitive functioning.

The healthy development of man shapes many of the narcissistic personality traits. Researchers believe that the onset of the disorder can occur when there is a conflict in interpersonal development. Some examples of contextual factors that may change the developmental stages of "normal" include:

· *Learn manipulative behavior from parents or friends.*

· *To be overly praised for appropriate behavior and overly criticized for inappropriate behavior.*

· *You suffer from childhood abuse.*

· *Incompatible parental care.*

· *Being very pampered by parents, friends, family*

· *To be too delightful without realistic feedback.*

· *Receive many compliments from parents or others about their appearance or abilities.*

Narcissistic personality disorder: treatment

Psychotherapy

Psychotherapy is one of the keys to approaching the treatment of narcissistic personality. It helps a person connect with other people more adaptively and better understand their own and others' emotions.

If a person has a narcissistic personality, you may not have heard of the diagnosis. Studies show that they usually do not receive treatment, and if they receive it, progress is slow because it is based on personality traits that have formed over the years. Therefore, it takes years of psychotherapy to make changes. To connect more appropriately, we need changes that make us take responsibility for our actions. **This includes:**

· *You are accepting and maintaining relationships with classmates and family.*

· *They tolerate criticism and failure.*

· *Understand and regulate feelings.*

· *Minimize the desire to achieve unrealistic goals.*

Initially, group therapy was thought to be inappropriate because group therapy requires empathy, patience, and the ability to relate to and "connect" with others. A person with narcissistic personality disorder presents with deficits. However, studies show that long-term group therapy can benefit them by providing a safe context where they can talk about their boundaries, receive and give feedback, and raise awareness of themselves and their problems.

Of cognitive-behavioral therapy, in particular, the scheme-focused treatment produces excellent results. It focuses on restoring narcissistic schemas and strategies to deal with them while confronting narcissistic cognitive styles (perfectionism).

There is no specific treatment for this disease, but sometimes these people may experience depression or anxiety, and psychotropic medications can help. People with a narcissistic personality can abuse drugs or alcohol, so treating addictive problems can help this disorder.

Criteria for Narcissistic Personality Disorder

1. The exaggerated notion of personal importance is not based on reality.

An inflated view of oneself is one of the main ways narcissists give themselves permission to dominate and control others. Narcissists believe that their priorities, interests, opinions, and beliefs have more value and are more important than anyone else's. Not all narcissists show the world their grandeur; some appear to be very humble or even shy to the outside world, but this will dominate their coexistence when they are in intimacy.

2. The concern with fantasies of success, wealth, power, beauty, and love above normal.

Narcissists often have a fantasy-filled life and are rarely satisfied with the ordinary, however satisfying or beautiful it may be. This preoccupation with fantasy prevents the narcissistic personality from leading an accurate and stable life. They feed desires for wealth, fame, power, or status obsessively.

3. The belief that you are a special and unique individual can only be committed to or understood by exceptional people.

This idea is an integral part of a survival mechanism that helps them cope with the world. They often define themselves by what they consider their unique qualities and inform us of those qualities as soon as we know them.

4. The intense need for admiration.

Love me, watch me, pay attention to me. Narcissists tend to magnify and be their reference.

5. Feeling of worthiness.

Standard rules, regulations, and behavior patterns infuriate narcissists, who think they are so unique that they do not have to obey reasonable expectations or respect appropriate limits. They may be equally plagued by hard work, illness, or injury. On the other hand, the rules they impose on others must always be respected.

6. The tendency to exploit others without feeling guilt or remorse.

Depending on the other characteristics of his personality, the narcissist may induce us to do all his work for him or, for example, take our money, allow us to pay his bills, receive gifts without ever giving, charge more for services and pay less, leave waiting for hours around the corner in the rain, without considering that this behavior is disrespectful. Your sense of worthiness makes these behaviors normal, preventing them from feeling guilty or remorseful.

7. Lack of significant empathy.

The narcissist has very little ability to put himself in someone else's shoes. Your pain, problems, and point of view dominate the universe. Perhaps nothing more reflects the narcissist's behavior than the inability to understand and identify with others' experiences. This is particularly true when the person who needs understanding is someone the narcissist is exploring: his current target (loving, working, family, or friend).

8. The tendency to be envious or to imagine oneself the envy of others.

The narcissist has difficulty adjusting to a world where other people seem to have "more" or "better" things. Narcissists often fail to recognize that they are envious and turn sentiment into contempt.

9. Arrogance.

Narcissists often have a snobby attitude toward people they think are not up to their "high" standard of intelligence, competence, accomplishment, values, morals, or lifestyle. Believing that the other is inferior helps them reinforce and inflate their conviction of superiority. Demeaning and criticizing others makes them feel good about themselves. They are often homophobic, racist, discriminatory of all kinds simply because they think they are superior to a specific group.

1.   The excessive vision of the self, rather than a solid self-confidence, reflects an extreme concern for supposed excellence.

2.   Active and competitive when looking for status, since their value is measured according to the status they have

3.   If others do not recognize that status, they think they deserve it, and they feel intolerable mistreated, get angry, become defensive, or depressed. If they are not known as superiors, their belief of inferiority and lack of importance is activated.

4.   He is hypersensitive and experiences very intense feelings in response to the criticisms of others.

5.   They need, at all costs, the recognition of people whom they consider essential.

6.   They do not tolerate discomfort or negative affection. They reject the vital circumstances requiring inevitable sacrifice and tolerance towards others, such as marriage. He thinks that he does not have to make concessions and yield to the other.

7.   If limits are placed or criticized, they become very unpleasant and defensive.

8.   They show a very demanding and insensitive appearance, show little interest in emotionally supporting the other. Their characteristic is that they are big scammers; they are very difficult to influence.

9.   When others react to their exploitation and get angry with him, the narcissist thinks that what happens to him is that they are jealous of him.

10. Carefree of the feelings of others, very self-centered. When they have a conversation with others, they can feel unique personal interests. Although they can be warm in a first interaction, they immediately show arrogance, hurtful comments towards each other, or insensitive actions.

11. They often envy others' successes and discredit the people they see as competitors. Spend a lot of time comparing yourself to others

12. The worth of others lies in others' ability to admire him. The narcissist likes people who offer him devotion.

13. He feels very comfortable giving orders because he believes he is the only one who has the truth. Compared to him, the others seem mediocre; they are only mere apprentices or aspirants to be like him.

14. In the face of an argument, they can misrepresent the conversations to make others feel guilty. To justify the lousy treatment that it gives to others, they look for more or less solvent reasons that excuse their lack of consideration towards others, placing themselves in the best possible situation.

15. Their apparent loquacity facilitates access to others, but those friendships lack the intimacy component. Finally, they are perceived as boring conversationalists.

16. Behind its facade, there is an excellent feeling of incapacity, incompetence, and lack of pleasure in any achievement. Everything they do is aimed at sustaining their fragile self-esteem.

17. The difference between self-esteem and narcissism is according to Bushman and Baumeister (1998): "High self-esteem means thinking well of oneself, while narcissism implies passionately wanting to think well of oneself." For the narcissist, self-esteem results from external success; they do not trust their worth.

18. They take great care of their image and their manners since they continuously sit in a shop window. You can demand the same from nearby people, influencing them to behave in a model way, and if you don't get it, criticize and ridicule them, thinking that it is "for your own good". But if the people around them fulfill their wishes, the narcissist can feel their shadow, so he criticizes them in the same way.

19. Since the image is everything, the situations in which it may be exposed to others or to the possible criticism of these poses a great threat.

20. For your person to look, they exaggerate their merits and minimize those of others.

21. They dismiss emotions such as sadness or anxiety because they think that feeling something like this is "weak." They do not like to talk about their problems or their negative emotions because they fear being seen as fragile. They do not want to feel vulnerable since it is a symptom of inferiority. He prefers to offer an image of imperturbability.

22. They have big unrealistic dreams of job success and looking for ideal romantic love. They possess many fantasies of power.

23. They give great importance to material possessions and, in general, in everything that implies recognition by others.

24. He presumes to lead a different type of life, and this is how he can be involved in insecure businesses, risky sports, lots of sexual conquests, repeated plastic surgery. Whenever there is the possibility of standing out from others, it will.

25. You experience lasting feelings of boredom, meaninglessness in your lives, worthlessness, emptiness, feeling impoverished from an emotional point of view, and craving more profound emotional experiences.

26. It has a sense of corruptible morals and ethics, has changing values and interests, and belittles unusual and conventional valuesand norms. You can show sexual behavior that includes promiscuity, lack of inhibition, and marital infidelities.

One way to protect yourself from future abuse is to stay in close contact with your emotions. If we don't learn from our mistakes, history could repeat itself. It can be necessary to take a long hard look at your own needs to determine if you can have these needs met within your current relationship. Self-reflection requires honesty. Honesty can be painful, but through this pain, we can complete a metamorphosis.

This tactic of manipulation can keep victims glued to an abuser's side. Self-love can be a powerful wedge, allowing the abused partner to become the comfort that they're so desperately seeking from the abuser. No matter the outcome, staying or leaving, we must learn to care for ourselves. A person who doesn't value themselves will accept demeaning and degrading behavior because they feel they deserve it.

You deserve to be happy. Your situation may feel hopeless, but I can promise you that you have it within yourself to make any decision you need to in the interest of self-preservation. Admitting to yourself that you're in an abusive relationship can feel slightly like taking a step toward the edge of a cliff that drops into oblivion, an unknown abyss. You know that you are comfortable in this misery, but this isn't happiness.

Taking these next steps takes courage.

Forgiveness

This isn't forgiveness for abuse; that will come later. This is an honest look at the relationship. It is essential to understand that you have been a victim of abuse and have lived through these situations. Something inside has been ashamed and afraid to take any ownership of this hardship. Listen, you have wounds that you will need to heal.

There are reasons that you gravitated toward an abusive partner, and that is something that will need to be addressed one day. For now, forgiveness.

You are worthy of attention, love, and kindness. Begin to manifest these things by caring for yourself. Understand that you had a hand in this dynamic and forgive yourself.

This is the first step toward trusting yourself again. There are so many ways to process the guilt that we feel in these situations, and you can choose what works for you. Reflection is enough for some, but others find it helpful to write yourself a letter.

Invest in Yourself

Abusive relationships have the potential to rob us of our confidence. Narcissistic partners want you to feel as though you are silly and irrelevant, and your goals do not matter. It is much easier to lord over another person if their spirit is broken. Loving oneself can be the most challenging thing in the world when it feels like everything is against you. Any average human being dropped in a situation such as this is miserable and sad.

Make a plan to begin gluing the shattered pieces of yourself back together. This sounds like a vast and abstract undertaking, but it doesn't have to be. Learning to love yourself again can be as familiar as coming home to an old friend. We are going to take it to step by step. Human beings are uniquely cognizant, which affords us a measure of control over our lives that the rest of the animal kingdom is missing. Situations (like abusive relationships) can force us into a fishbowl and take away this control. It can be so easy to overlook that we can be what e want to be. We can make it so easy to love ourselves by becoming our hero. Be the sort of person that you would love and admire.

Make a list of the qualities and values that you want to embody. List goals and milestones that you want to achieve. It can help if you close your eyes and picture a person you admire; this person can be a role model or someone you have entirely made up. What makes this person so admirable to you? Independence? Bravery? Fashion sense? There is nothing too silly. You are authoring the following changes that will occur in your own life. This list may have as many entries as you need. The following is an example to use as a template should you become stumped:

Who I want to Be:

- **Creative**

- **Funny**

- **Brave**

This list is a way for you to take back your self-image from your abusive partner's hands. It is your job to decide who you want to be. You decide what you value, your hair color, your goals, and how you handle conflict. You don't have to see yourself through the eyes of someone who is incentivized to keep you down.

Now that you have created your list break it down entry by entry. This is going to be a map to achieving your goals. Working on your list will give you a project to focus on when the days become dark, and it is a fast-track way to relearn self-love. Creating these lists also inches us closer and closer to self-reliance. Each goal from your list is now a new list, with steps that you can take to achieve these things. Example:

Creative:

- **Research different creative mediums.**

- **Buy the sketchbook or supplies needed to begin learning new skills.**

- **Use art to express anger or sadness.**

Experiment with other methods.

No goal or quality cannot be broken down in this way. Take the pen back from your partner and begin writing your own story again. Stimulate these healthy conversations with yourself because this communication will be necessary moving forward.

Find an Outlet

Protect yourself from an abusive partner's words, and it can be essential to find an outlet for self-expression. Journaling could be a great way to document the abuse and rise above it. There is a lot of unreleased tension in victims of abuse. Stress and anxiety have become a staple of everyday life. Any moment might bring another fight.

Vent your anger or sadness through a journal or other artistic medium. Allow your mind to rant and rave about the things that you are feeling. Having a way to relieve some of the pressure can be vital in abuse cases. It can also be helpful to find an interest to focus on and is a great way to learn a new skill.

Research

In the same way, you bought this book, begin obsessively consuming material about narcissists, codependents, or abuse. There is a particular mystery to how our brains work in these situations. Sometimes we can be unsure of our actions and motivations.

Demystifying abuse will allow you to pull back the veil shrouding the abuser. The only way that you are going to believe that your partner has something wrong is if you are faced with the facts over and over again. Learn the patterns of abuse and clinical definitions.

Absorbing articles, videos, books, and other literature on the subject will also allow you to predict your partner's next moves. The abusive partner may seem erratic and unpredictable, but there are reasons behind every behavior. Every name that you have ever been called out of malice.

Both narcissists and codependents require validation in the same way. This validation is achieved through manipulation and sometimes name-calling and random fights. A narcissist can seem loving one moment and vile the next, but this is just another part of their process.

Learn everything that you can while you are trapped in this situation. Anticipate the attack and allow the words to roll right off of your skin. When you understand the motivation, then the fights stop seeming so personal.

Exercise

Eating and living in a passive way is often related to depression and stress. Take back your wellbeing by taking care of your body. This will help improve the way that you feel physically and your self-esteem. Exercise will also help fight all the negative emotions with the brain chemicals. Exercising for just thirty minutes a day can drastically allow you to change how you see yourself. Abuse will slowly and deviously steal away your confidence and happiness.

Doctors recommend exercise to treat both anxiety and depression. Endorphins are released that encourage an overall calm that can combat negative feelings brought on by your surroundings. The movement can also induce a meditative state that allows you to forget about the troubles that await you when returning home.

Challenge Your Comfort Zone

When your life feels stale, prison-like, and depressing, it can be challenging to spring back to life. Challenging yourself to escape this comfort zone is hard, but it can also be an enriching experience. There are so many volunteer organizations that would love to have assistance. This nature's social activities may also allow you to find new friends and reestablish a support system.

Your partner will object to these ventures, especially if they are narcissistic. It can be a good idea to shrug off their watchful eye and do some activities that you are interested in. If you are concerned that they will be angry when they find you, remember that they are angry (for sport) constantly anyway. There is no winning, so you might as well take care of your own needs.

Self-soothing

Break free of the abusive trauma bond by becoming the person you turn to for your comfort. Do not allow your partner to take away the pain of a fresh fight by becoming a different person right in front of you. Learn tactics to calm yourself down, as this talent has the potential to save you from the bondage of an abusive relationship.

When you need to calm yourself:

Use cozy blankets in a quiet room.

Read a book until your body feels less stressed.

Listen to relaxing music or play a podcast to drift along on the tone of a stranger's voice.

Sometimes, it can even help you feel the anger and sadness and then go about your day.

Baths are an excellent way to calm down. Candles can also be helpful. Learn about the things that work to relax you and reach those the next time you are upset. Abusive partners will dangle comfort over your head so that you bend to their will. Behaviors like this make a narcissist feel powerful. Learn to be your hero and your light in the dark.

Praise Yourself

If you are dating a narcissist, your self-image has been ripped to shreds. The narcissist is doing this for their gain. Their view of you has nothing to do with who you are. Begin to shake off all that negative and toxic commentary and challenge yourself to replace it with words of encouragement. There are so many areas where you excel. You have so many brilliant ideas. You are so resilient.

Next time your partner is calling you names or mocking you, pretend that they are doing these things to a friend.

You would tell that person that the abuser was all wrong and worthy of love. Treat yourself with the same respect.

Stop the Comparison

Comparing yourself to others can add another toxicity layer to an already toxic sandwich. Your relationship isn't good right now, and there is no need to hold yourself up to someone who has it together at the moment. You are learning some of the most important lessons of your life, and it isn't easy.

Spending too much time on social media can damage your confidence further. Avoid the things that do not make you feel good. Your journey is entirely different from those around you. You are dealing with a situation that many people would not be strong enough to make it through.

Time for Yourself

To maintain your sanity in the chaos around you, you must spend time doing the things you love. Music, swimming, hiking, or dancing would all be great examples of activities that allow for escape and relaxation.

You must keep your relationship from defining your life.

Your partner may object to you spending time without them around because they would rather you not have the chance to calm down. Do whatever you need to do to go out on your own without your partner for your sanity. There need to be boundaries set that your partner will not cross.

Activities that allow for reflection can also be a good idea. Meditation and yoga will help to solidify your overall mental health. Learning to keep your center in the face of chaos can be a valuable skill to have in these situations.

Therapy

When in an abusive relationship, it is not always easy to turn to a therapist. A professional will be the best way to help yourself get out of it. Therapy will also allow you to reclaim your sanity and stolen self-esteem. A professional can offer you specific guidance for your situation.

Talking to a professional is the quickest and most effective way to address your mental state and your relationship condition.

The therapist will help you to see your situation objectively. This can also help to restore your self-worth.

Is There Anything to Save?

Use these same eyes to look at your partner. Make a list of qualities you require in a mate or a relationship. These are the things that are important to your happiness and wellbeing in general. Do you want independence within your relationship? Do you want a partner who doesn't lash out in anger?

Objectively, if you are making no excuses for anyone else's behavior, can your partner be the person you need them to be? Have you been looking at this relationship in rose-colored glasses? Do not allow fleeting moments of kindness to obscure mountains of bad behavior.

Codependency is a profoundly rooted behavior that can take lots of effort to change. In a relationship ravaged by codependency, both partners must be willing to take steps to change their behavior. Therapy is likely going to be necessary because personal accountability is lacking from the controlling partner's side. You know your partner better than anyone else, and it will take so much honesty to be able to move forward in a way that benefits both parties.

Empathy is the deciding factor. Has your partner ever done anything for you without expecting repayment? Do you believe that your partner is attached to you or what you can do for them?

These questions are also dependent on the level of control that your partner is exerting upon because if abuse is involved beyond manipulation, you need to leave.

If you are involved with a partner that you suspect is a narcissist, things will not change. Empathy is necessary for the relationship to evolve into something that isn't harmful toward both parties. There are extenuating circumstances (such as shared children) that force some victims to continue relationships with narcissist partners. Extensive therapy is needed to keep the abusive partner in check, and these situations involve the victim forgoing a healthy romantic relationship.

Unless children are involved (and usually even if children are involved), the most sensible course of action is to go. Narcissists panic when they have been threatened with being alone. They will not move on until they have found someone they consider better. These individuals will pretend that they will change their behavior to save the relationship; they may even believe this.

The fact of the matter is that narcissism is a slow poison. Most psychologists that this disorder is incurable and will be a detriment to anyone close to the abuser.

A narcissist will promise change. Their behavior will get better for a few weeks or maybe even a month. They may even want to save the partnership. These partners can't act in opposition to their nature for very long, and their nature is to serve themselves through the oppression of those closest to them. If you are in the blast zone, then you are always at risk.

How to Know When it's Time to Go

For those in narcissistic relationships, this research is likely a sign that the end is drawing near. You have probably made up your mind already when it comes to the dissolution of your relationship. Most readers of this book are either retroactively reading about their experience or are entering the miserable stage of limbo right before the trigger is pulled—the stage where you are left wondering if you will ever find the courage to say the words.

If you are teetering on the edge of singledom, listening to your own body can be a clue to your deeper desires.

Do you still enjoy spending time with your partner? Do you dread being in the same room with your significant other? What does your body tell you about time spent together?

It's time to leave ASAP if there is physical violence in your relationship. When you are caught in a cycle of abuse, it can be best to make up your mind and wait silently for an opportunity to run. Empowering yourself is the best thing you can do for your future. Leaving is a provocation and should be done swiftly and quietly. Have people in your life on standby, ready to assist you with your escape when you give the word.

Readers involved in codependent relationships must assure that their partner is willing and capable of change. If the offending party is comfortable with the partnership's dynamic, this is a strong indication that nothing will change. Never feel guilty for taking steps to ensure your happiness. Further attempts at manipulation sign that you are doing the right thing. You are not responsible for the feelings of others.

Those who leave partners who have controlled and belittled them throughout the relationship have this deeply ingrained view that they are unworthy of love. Victims believe that no one else would want them if they leave such a situation.

Their hobbies, interests, values, and looks have been torn apart for so long that it can be hard for them to see themselves as worthy.

The fights are always manipulated to seem like the victim is deserving of the abuse. The victim made a tiny mistake, so the abuser is justified in exploding. No matter what the victim does, it will never be enough to stop the flood. If you have found yourself asking your partner to stop criticizing your every move, you may be one of these victims. Do you believe that you have been treated like a partner should be treated? If the answer is no, then it is time to formulate a plan.

Conclusion

Gaslighting is a kind of psychological mistreatment. Somebody who is gaslighting will attempt to make a victim question their impression of the real world. The deceiver may persuade the victim to believe that their recollections aren't correct or blow up over nothing. The abuser may then present their contemplations and emotions as "the genuine truth." Deceivers/narcissists can cause a lot of injuries. On the off chance that you are involved with a deceiver/narcissist, it might have damaged you in ways that you aren't truly aware of yet. Contemplate how the deceiver/narcissism might affect your perspective on yourself and your general surroundings. Just as being able to speak your feelings helps you connect with them—and with the energy to stand up for yourself—so does express your emotions differently.

Gaslighting is the favorite tool of a narcissist, and a narcissist will seek to keep you under control by gradually eroding every bit of your sanity. Doubting your senses is in no way healthy for you, and you have to be aware of how narcissists operate to avoid the mess of dealing with them in your future relationships.

Millions and millions of people worldwide are finding their authentic voice against gaslighting and are now enlightening more people about the damaging effects of gaslighting. It is no understatement when I repeat that countless people have fallen victim to this form of abuse at one point or the other in their lives. The good news is countless survivors have fought their way through depression and other devastating effects of gaslighting and are now living healthy lives. With the proper management techniques, any victim can get over the emotional abuse and mental manipulation to go on and lead a productive and fulfilling life.

My thoughts are with you, and you can find strength because you can make it through the trying times. Use that strength to carry yourself through until you find your true self again.

The next step is to get all the help you can, find a support group, and start making plans for yourself.

Please remember that Inner Strength + Emotional Support + Plan = Independence and Freedom.

UNLIMITED MEMORY

Introduction

If you want to improve your memory? Do you want to improve your brainpower so you can learn better, recall more, and work more efficiently? Perhaps you aspire to be a superhero with a perfect memory that can recall any kind of material, including facts and numbers, people's names, and events. Or maybe you want to focus and concentrate on eliminating wasted time, stress, and mistakes at work.

I have everything you need in this book, Unlimited Memory. As you read, you will learn actionable steps to get the results you want by improving memory and boosting your memory's capacity. I'll also show you how to use memory enhancement drills to train the brain to remember better, think and learn quicker. This book lays out a strategy for improving your memory while also providing a challenge for your mind, body, and soul. We have a complete kit, including food, exercise, stress management, and memory aids.

Helen was constantly forgetful, and she didn't understand why. She couldn't remember where she put her car keys, ID, or phone numbers, and she couldn't even remember her appointments. It caused her a lot of stress. Then she asked me how she could remember things better. I recommended she try memorizing lists of information like phone numbers or grocery lists. Besides, I advised her to picture each item on the list or even in a series of numbers. Once she visualized the items on her list, she could not forget them. Then Helen applied this method to her daily routine. It changed her life. She had trained her memory to remember things in the short term. Therefore, she wouldn't have to worry about losing her keys or purse.

In this book, you will learn basic skills and more advanced strategies, including mnemonic devices, the memory palace, the military method, and much more. I will train you to develop a photographic memory that enables you to remember faces and names, numbers, dates, foreign languages, and even game cards. I will also show you how to improve your reading skills. Also, I will talk about the foods that will enhance your memory.

You'll be amazed by how you will this to improve your memory and concentration. I want to invite you to come on this journey to enhance your brainpower.

It would be best if you worked on improving your memory today so that you can be as sharp as ever. Then you'll be able to be your most successful and satisfied self.

Think about the greatest inventors and scientists of all time, like Albert Einstein and Thomas Edison. Both possess excellent memorization skills because their craft revolves around various formulas and computations.

Maybe you have already tried several ways for you to have better memorization skills, but none of them worked. There is an excellent quotation by Thomas Edison, which I applied to my mindset, and I believe that is why I achieved this particular feat in my life. "I am not a failure. I've just discovered ten thousand forms that aren't going to work." – Thomas Edison. With this mindset, you will become successful in your crafts, just like they did, and just like I did. Having a good memory is crucial to achieving your goals in life, so I will reveal the method that I used to make my memory exceptionally better.

People have often told me they would be willing to give a million bucks to attain an unlimited memory like mine. I certainly wouldn't mind a million dollars, but the price is just what you paid for this book, plus the little time you will spend reading and applying it. Once you have begun this journey, you are only a step away from maximizing the potential of your unlimited memory.

Continue reading this book to learn how you can start remembering more, stressing less, and living a more meaningful and productive life right now!

Chapter 1: What is Memory?

What exactly is memory? It's a tricky question to answer but put, memory is a process that involves storing, acquiring, and recalling information. Not all memory is the same, however. There are three types of memory—sensory, short-term, and long time. But before we get into the various forms of memory, let's take a closer look at what memory is.

We can break down the process of memory into three parts, encoding, storage, and retrieval. When information goes from sensory input to our brain, it needs to change form so that the brain can understand, process, and store it. Think of it like exchanging currency when you're traveling to a different country. The currency of your home country is useless unless you have it converted. There are three ways it can encode this information, which is visually, acoustically, and semantically. How do you remember a telephone number? If you see the number, then that means you're using visual encoding, but if you're repeating it to yourself verbally, you're using acoustic encoding. Evidence suggests that the primary encoding method for short-term memory is acoustic. It means when a person is rehearsing for something, like a play or concert, the information is held in short-term memory, and they'll forget it soon after the play or show. The primary encoding method for long-term memory is semantic, which is when you give something meaning. It means that giving meaning to information helps you retain that piece of information for far longer.

How long does memory last? According to research, most adults can store 5 to 9 items in their short-term memory. People used to think that memory worked like slots and that the maximum number of places for short-term memory was 7. But, if we connect pieces of information, we can hold a lot more information in short-term memory. Unlike short terms memory, long-term memory is thought to be pretty much limitless.

How is memory retrieved? Everyone has forgotten something, whether it's forgetting to bring your calculator to a math test or forgetting your keys in the car. The brain forgets almost every day. Forgetting is when the brain fails to retrieve information. The way your brain retrieves from short-term memory and long-term memory are very different. Short-term memory is retrieved sequentially.

When somebody is asked to remember a list of numbers and then is asked to remember the 6th number in the sequence, they will go through all numbers in the order they heard of getting to the 6th number. By contrast, long-term memory is stored by association. It means if you go upstairs and suddenly forgot why you went upstairs, going back into the room where you first thought about going upstairs can jog your memory and make you remember why you wanted to go upstairs. Keeping information organized can help when it comes to retrieving data from the brain. Organizing means keeping records of time, sorting alphabetically or by size. If somebody has given you a list of tasks to do, sorting them out in a sequence, such as a sequence of time, can make it easier to memorize. A lot of people think they know about memory. But the fact is that memory is a curious phenomenon that scientists are only just beginning to comprehend. It means various myths have been spread among the people, and you need to know how to tell apart tale from fact.

Myth number 1 Memory is like a video recorder.

Many people fall under the assumption that memory behaves like a video recorder, and the eye is the lens. It is a common misconception among people; after all, a video recorder is the closest thing relatable to memory for many people. In a US survey, more than 63 percent of participants said they strongly believe that memory works like a video camera because it accurately records everything we see and hear. It cannot be further from the truth. Memory is a very fickle thing as it can be easily distorted and manipulated. Researchers Bernstein and Loftus examined half a dozen studies that examined whether researchers could plant false memories into people. The false memories in question were to do with food preferences, such as liking asparagus despite never trying it.

In one experiment, the participants completed questionnaires that included a personality and food history test. A week later, they were brought back to the lab and told their answers were fed into a machine that generated a profile of their childhood experiences with food. One of the findings was that they either got sick after eating hard-boiled eggs or felt ill after eating dill pickles. After learning about this, the participants completed the same food history questionnaire. The participants that were falsely told they had gotten sick from dill pickles or hard-boiled egg showed significantly less preference towards those food items.

Myth number 2 People can have a photographic memory.

It's a common belief that some people have a natural talent to take photographs with their brains and can retrieve the photos with 100 percent accuracy. It is, of course, not the case. There are some amazing feats of memorization, such as memory champion Lu Chao who set the world record for reciting pi to the 67,890th digit. But unfortunately, Lu Chao does not possess a photographic memory. What has allowed Lu Chao to achieve it can put down such incredible feats using mnemonic devices and thousands upon thousands of hours practicing.

Myth number 3 People forget things over time.

Many people think memories decay over time. Studies reveal that memories do not degrade like a reel of film. Most memories are forgotten almost instantly after an event. For this reason, eyewitness testimonies are not held in high regard in the court of law.

Myth number 4 Confidence indicates an accurate memory.

Being confident that your recollection is correct does not mean it is. Some factors can increase your confidence in memory despite it not being authentic, such as repeated questioning. The unfortunate result of being asked the same question over and over and receiving the same response is that it convinces you that what you're doing is right. Everyone has different levels of confidence when it comes to memory recollection. Somebody can be very confident in their memory, despite being wrong most of the time. Likewise, someone can have shallow confidence in their memory even though they're right. Another related myth is that having an emotional experience leads to more accurate memories. Memories connected to an emotional experience often are remembered more vividly, making people confident that things went exactly how they remembered them. But in actuality, these memories are just as prone to being distorted as any other.

Myth number 5 Traumatizing memories are repressed and can be recovered years after they have occurred.

Many people believe that traumatic experiences, such as an abusive childhood, are hidden deep within the brain and can be somehow recovered with the help of a hypnotist.

Studies on child abuse victims suggest they do not forget the traumatic experience. When somebody has a memory "recovered," it is far more likely that the memory in question has been fabricated or highly distorted. A hypnotist cannot recover memories because memory does not behave like a video recorder. We do not remember every detail. Evidence has suggested that hypnotism can do more harm than good by giving people a confidence boost in their memory, whether the memory is accurate or not.

Myth number 6 Amnesiacs forget who they are.

The idea that people who suffer from amnesia lost their long-term memory is a myth dramatized by Hollywood. The fact is, amnesiacs, do not possess the ability to create new memories. To be more specific, they cannot convert short-term memories into long-term memories. It is why an amnesiac may be able to tell you about their early lives, but they have trouble when it comes to remembering what they ate for lunch.

First, we have to understand how memory works in our brain. How do we even remember anything? When you read something, for example, the word 'dog,' you see that dog and the word 'dog,' you combine the two, and from the eyes, it will reach a particular area in our brain where the picture and the word are stored. So you have the concept of a dog. The next time you see the dog, you don't have to learn it anew because there is already data in your brain for that word and picture. It is called imprinting, where what we see and how we process it becomes stored in our brain. If you try to remember what you saw, you are retrieving the information from where the data was first stored and bringing that memory to your consciousness. So even without the dog actually in front of your eyes, you can recall the dog. Days and days may pass by without seeing a dog, and you can still remember the dog. So we can say that you already have a memory of the dog.

We have to understand our brain as having three kinds of memory storage: short-term memory, long-term memory, and working memory storage. The difference between the three is when it remains in the warehouse or decay and the amount of information it can store at that time.

Short-term memories have a limited capacity. Your brain can only store so much in short-term memory. For example, if you have a list of 100 items, you will only recall a specific number, and the rest will be gibberish to you. If you notice phone numbers, they are just seven digits because the theory is that the brain can take in only $7 + 2$ items. If it tells you to remember the words "batter, cook, fish, grass and nincompoop," you can still actively recall it in a second. You can even recognize it in five seconds. If you try harder, you can even remember it longer. But if you weren't consciously memorizing it, after an hour, it disappears. It is what we call memory decay. Information that is stored in the short-term memory only has a fixed time before you forget it. If you want to remember it longer or want to remember more information, it must transfer them to long-term memory storage.

The long-term memory has a bigger storage space and has a more extended decay period. You will be able to remember voluminous information from the books you read five years ago to your childhood experiences or the articles in the Constitution. You can divide the long-term memory into two: explicit and implicit memory. Explicit or declarative memory refers to events, facts, details, names, and numbers. It answers the question, what is it?

You can recall your birth date, the name of your teacher of the fourth grade, examples of amphibians, the presidents of your country, the person you met yesterday, and the dish you like. Implicit or procedural memory refers to the use of objects or how to perform activities. It answers the question, how do you do it? You will remember how to drive a car, cook fried fish, perform a Heimlich maneuver, spike a ball, and shoot a gun. Since all of these memories are placed in long-term storage, you stay there longer. For example, you may not have been driving for a while, but after a few tries, you can go again. It takes a long while to retrieve these memories because they are stored in deeper sections of the brain. So you might have a difficult time recalling a classmate's name, but eventually, you'll get to it. The memories here are not strictly permanent. They can decay through age if not accessed frequently or because of a disease.

The transfer from short-term memory to long-term memory is essential for you to remember things. It is called consolidation. The more you repeat recognizing an object, the more neurons are fired, and the same pathway is activated repeatedly. The repletion and association with other aspects such as emotions or previous long-term memories can transfer the new information to long-term storage. If you do not consolidate information, the information is discarded and forgotten, thrown into some garbage bin, and is inaccessible in your memory.

Working memory refers to the memory you used for your current needs to perform a function. It combines short-term and long-term memory to address a current situation. When you take a test, you are using your working memory. You try to incorporate what you just read an hour ago with the ones you studied weeks ago. It is the memory storage you use for what you are doing now.

If you report a presentation, you have to access both recent and past information to deliver it perfectly. If somebody asks a question, you answer with your short-term memory, and then this is supported by what you know in your long-term memory. The working memory facilitates the retrieval of information from both these sources.

So remember the differences between these three memory storages. They all have a function. For example, you don't need to remember everything in a list, which is not essential. So there is short-term memory storage to filter what is necessary and what is not, what should be transferred to the long-term memory and what should be discarded.

You don't need to memorize the whole telephone book because that only crowds your brain storage. You only need to store information that is relevant and meaningful to you. There must be a good integration of all the storehouses. Failure to consolidate means you might read something and not retain anything.

It is a problem with schooling. Students invest a lot of their time researching, so they don't remember any of what they know. They listen to the teacher, and it seems they remember. After a while, you ask them what they learned, and they forget. You spend hours memorizing a list of Constitution articles or formulas for a test.

You do very well. But during the examination at the end of the semester, you forgot everything, so you have to review everything from the start. It's such a waste of time to go over something you have already memorized before, but you have to remember it again.

You also have to distinguish between studying for an exam and studying to remember. Is there a difference? Sometimes, students learn for an exam to pass a single exam. After that exam, they can flush all the information out until such time that they will require you to retrieve it again. But if you are studying to remember, you want to retain the information beyond the exam scope.

It is more complicated and time-consuming but more efficient. It is recommended if the information is relevant to your life or your line of work. For example, during college, we had to enroll in different courses that weren't required for the path we were in, but the school needed us to take them. If you were an engineering major, you take engineering subjects for your concentration, but you have to take Basic English or Foreign Language or Philosophy.

It may be all relevant and essential to your life, but not to such a degree more than your introductory engineering courses. So students will try to study for the exam on English or Foreign Language and Philosophy, but after the exam, they tend to forget what they have learned because they aren't going to use it frequently anyway.

But, if your concentration is an engineering and you will be an engineer, you should study to remember because this is important and will be frequently used in your line of work.

You will take courses that will rely on basic engineering principles, so you have to go back repeatedly. It will be good to understand and memorize the first time around, so you don't waste effort to relearn it.

How do we remember anything? I will explain the basic principles of memory and learning that you have to understand before proceeding to techniques. You might dwell on memory techniques, and after a while, you will forget what they were for.

If we know the basics of how memory works, we can even personalize our way of learning and memorizing. Each person will have a particular form of remembering. For example, I really cannot study with music on. I cannot concentrate if there is background music, especially a song I am familiar with.

But some people can learn better with music on. They feel the mood or rhythm; they associate the song with some details, so they remember. So everyone will have a particular way of memorizing. But there are fundamental principles of memory we share in common.

These are attention, meaning, relevance and understanding. If you examine the chart below, there is a particular sequence followed. At the very bottom, we see attention. On top of it is meaning, followed by relevance, followed by understanding, and only then can memory be found.

Therefore, most people are unaware of (or unconcerned about) that we have seven different memory types. However, suppose your work includes essential tasks that require optimal cognitive functioning as you make those vital split-second decisions. In that case, you should know about how your brain absorbs new knowledge, generates memories, and easily retain the correct information.

1. Sensory Memory

In the sensory system from which it entered, sensory memory consists of sensory information stored in an unprocessed form. This form of memory is short-lived but has a vast capacity (0.5-3 seconds). Even if it was not originally the focus of consideration, sensory memory accounts for our ability to remember something after it has been said. Therefore, sensory memory has rescued many relationships.

Sensory memory enables a person, but for only a few milliseconds, to remember an input in great detail. Sensory memory helps individuals for a brief duration after the initial stimulus has ceased to retain memories of sensory information. It allows people to instantly recall great sensory details about a complex inspiration after its appearance. An unconscious response considered to be outside of human control is sensory memory. The "raw data" that offers a snapshot of the overall sensory experience of a person is the information reflected in this type of memory. Sensory memory information has the shortest time of retention, varying from mere milliseconds to five seconds. Just long enough to transfer it to short-term memory, it is retained.

No manipulation of the incoming information occurs in sensory memory as it is rapidly transferred to working memory. During this transfer, the amount of data is significantly reduced because the working memory capacity is not significant to cope with all the input coming from our sense organs.

Sensory memory types

Each of the five primary senses (touch, sight, taste, sound, and smell) has its subtype of sensory memory. Still, only three of them have been extensively studied: legendary memory, echoic memory, and haptic memory.

- **Memory iconic**

Sensory inputs to the visual system run into iconic memory; so-called icons are referred to as the mental representations of visual stimuli. "The duration of iconic memory is about 100 ms. one of the times when we see" light trails "is an iconic memory. It is the process when bright lights move quickly at night, and you perceive them as making a trail; this is the image that is represented in iconic memory.

- **Picture**

Light trails: Because of the memories stored in sensory memory for milliseconds, you interpret a blinding flowing light as creating a straight line in classic memory.

- **Echoic memory**

Echoic memory is the sensory memory branch that the auditory system uses. Echoic memory, but only for 3-4 seconds, can hold a large amount of auditory information. This brief amount of time immediately follows the auditory stimulus presentation; this echoic sound is replayed in mind.

- **Haptic memory**

Haptic memory is the sensory memory branch used by the sense of touch. Throughout the body, sensory receptors detect feelings such as pressure, itching, and pain briefly held in haptic memory before disappearing or being transported to short-term memory. When evaluating the necessary forces for gripping and interacting with familiar objects, this type of memory seems to be used. After about two seconds, haptic memory appears to decay.

2. Short-term and working memory

For a brief period of recall, short-term memory, which includes working memory, stores data for things that have happened recently. Short-term memory is the capacity to hold a limited volume of information in an active, readily accessible state for a short period. It is different from our long-term memory, where a lot of information is stored later for us to remember. It is capable of temporary storage, unlike sensory memory.

How long this storage lasts depends on the individual's conscious effort; the time duration of short-term memory is assumed to be on the order of seconds without rehearsal or active maintenance.

- **Short-term memory capacity**

For the quick recall of information, short-term memory acts as a scratchpad. To understand this sentence, you need to keep the beginning of the sentence in your mind as you read the rest. Short-term memory is increasingly declining and has limited capacity.

George Miller, the psychologist, suggested that human short-term memory has a forward memory period of about seven plus or minus two items. More recent research has shown that this figure is approximately correct for college students remembering digit lists, but the memory period varies greatly with populations studied and content used.

The ability to remember words in order, for example, relies on a variety of features of these words: fewer words can be recognized when the terms have a longer spoken duration (this is referred to as the word-length effect) or when their speech sounds are close to each other (this is referred to as the phonological similarity effect). When the words are highly familiar or frequently occur in the language, it can recall more words. Information chunking can also contribute to an improvement in the ability of short-term memory. A hyphenated phone number, for instance, is easier to remember than a single long number because it is divided into three parts instead of appearing as ten digits.

Rehearsal is the process in which data is retained by mentally repeating it in short-term memory. The information is re-entered into the short-term memory. The information is retrieved each time, thus keeping the information for another 10 to 20 seconds, the average short-term memory storage time. In short-term memory retrieval, disruptions from rehearsal also cause disturbances. It accounts for the desire to complete as soon as possible a task held in short-term memory.

- **Working memory**

- **Sketchpad for visuospatial**

In the visuospatial sketchpad, visual and spatial information is treated. It indicates that it is possible to remember knowledge about the location and properties of objects. Semi-independent systems are the phonological loop and visuospatial sketchpad; you can maximize the amount you can recall by engaging all systems at once because of this.

- **Key executive center**

The central executive integrates and integrates its operations with the phonological loop and the visuospatial sketchpad. It also connects the working memory to long-term memory, monitors long-term memory storage, and handles storage memory retrieval. The storage process is affected by the length of time during which data is stored in working memory and the quantity of data manipulation. Data or information is kept for an extended period if interpreted semantically and presented compared to other information already retained in long-term memory.

3. Long-term memory

Encoding and consolidation of information include the process of moving data from short-term to long-term memory. It is a property of time; the longer a memory exists in the short-term memory, the more chances it will retain it in the long-term memory. An object's meaningfulness or emotional content will play a more significant role in the long-term memory of its retention in this process.

This higher retention is due to an increased synaptic reaction inside the hippocampus, which is essential for storing information. The limbic structure of the brain (including the hippocampus and amygdala) is not generally directly involved in long-term memory. Still, by playing it like a continuous tape, it chooses relevant information from short-term memory and consolidates these memories.

Long-term memory is used over long periods, ranging from a few hours to a lifetime, for storing information. We have to consolidate it into a long-term memory now if we want to recall anything tomorrow. The last semi-permanent stage of memory is long-term memory. Long-term memory has the potentially limitless capacity, unlike sensory and short-term memory, and information can stay there indefinitely. A person would refer to the data in long-term memory when doing nearly any operation, also known as reference memory. It is possible to break down long-term memory into two categories: explicit and implicit memory.

- **Implicit memory**

Implicit ("unconscious" or "procedural") memory contains processes for executing actions, in contrast to explicit (conscious) memory. Over time, these behavior evolve with practice. One instance of implicit memory is athletic abilities. You learn the basics of a sport, practice them repeatedly, and then, during a game, they flow naturally. Another example of implicit memory is rehearsing for a dance or musical performance. Recalling how to tie your shoes, drive a car, or ride a bicycle are everyday examples. Without conscious knowledge, these memories are accessed; they are naturally transformed into actions without understanding them. As such, to most people, they can also be hard to teach or describe.

In the semantic scripts mentioned above, implicit memories vary in that they are usually activities involving movement and motor control, while writings appear to emphasize social norms or habits.

- **Explicit memory**

Explicit memory, also related to declarative or conscious memory, requires memory of reality, ideas, and events requiring the knowledge to be consciously remembered. In other words, the individual must consciously think about retaining the data from memory. This type of information, hence its name, is specifically stored and retrieved. It is possible to further subdivide explicit memory into semantic memory, which concerns reality, and episodic memory, primarily involving personal or autobiographical knowledge.

- **Semantic memory**

Semantic memory contains abstract factual awareness, such as "Albany is New York's capital." It is for the kind of information we learn from books and school: faces, locations, details, and definitions. When taking an exam, you use semantic memory. A script is considered another form of semantic memory. Hands are like blueprints of what, in some cases, appears to happen. For starters, if you visit a restaurant, what typically happens? You get the menu card, you order your meal, you eat it, and you pay the bill after that. You learn these scripts through practice and encode them into semantic memory.

- **Episodic memory**

For more contextualized memories, episodic memory is employed. They are usually memories of particular moments in one's life or episodes. In addition to who, what, where, and when or what occurred, they involve sensations and emotions associated with the incident. Recalling your family's trip to the beach will be an example of episodic memory. Autobiographical memory is usually seen as either similar to or a subset of episodic memory (memory for discrete events of one's own life).

A flashbulb memory, which is a highly informative, extraordinarily vivid "snapshot" of the moment and conditions under which others heard a piece of shocking and consequential (or emotionally arousing) news, is one particular form of autobiographical memory.

Many people, for instance, know precisely where they were and what they were doing when they learned of the September 11, 2001, terrorist attacks. It is because it is a recollection of a flashbulb.

Semantic and episodic memory are closely linked; it can improve memory for facts with fact-related episodic memories and vice versa. The response to the factual question, for example, "Are all apples red?" By recalling the time you saw someone eating a green apple, you might remember.

Chapter 4: The Nature of Memory

Is human memory really unlimited?

Scientific research into this subject indicates that the memory capacity of the average human brain is of an order of magnitude greater than was previously thought. According to one study, our estimated memory capacity has increased, by a conservative estimate, by a factor of 10 to at least one petabyte. In other words, the human brain may be able to store an astonishing 1,000,000,000,000,000 bytes of information. That is enough memory capacity to store, for instance, 13.3 years of high-definition video. Google processes over 20 petabytes of data every day, while Facebook (at the last count) had some 60 billion images, which equals 1.5 petabytes of storage.

Such studies into the brain's natural storage capacity constitute a significant advance in understanding human neuroanatomy. They could be a step closer to creating a complete "wiring diagram" of the human brain. Since the brain contains several billion neural synapses, researchers now believe that their calculations point to truly outstanding human brain processing power levels. No doubt considered in terms of the typical usages we need to put our memory storage abilities. Human memory is practically unlimited to all intents and purposes.

Why, then, do people want to improve their memory?

Well, at the most "human" level, our memory is so important to us that we often say in ordinary parlance that "a person does not die so long as others remember him or her." So memory can make us immortal in the eyes of others if you will. Memory is also essential in the race by medical experts to find a cure for Alzheimer's disease, which essentially dehumanizes people by stripping them of their short- and long-term memories, leaving them a mere shell relative to the vibrant and vital person they once were. The above are just two instances in which memory is fundamental to our sense of self-identity. It is similarly the case when we remember memories of childhood, which contribute to helping us understand the family and social context that we came from as individuals. Happy childhood memories, for example, are apt to last a lifetime and become something to treasure during the adult phase of life. However, memory has also shown itself to be highly selective, with the ability to repress negative memories accumulated during one's life in the interests of "good mental hygiene."

Memories come to us with such force and vitality sometimes that it cannot eradicate them in the ordinary course of events. The memory of someone you have deeply loved, for example, remains with you throughout your life. It contributes to the emotional pain and sense of loss that we feel when we are bereaved. It cannot erase memories of this strength with any machine known to man. But most important of all, memory in middle and old age becomes a repository of all the experience and distilled wisdom that the person has accumulated up to that point. By reflecting on past experiences concerning the present circumstances of our lives, we can avoid stumbling into the same habitual errors and mistakes that we have made before.

"Vagueness in recollection" is something that can be quickly resolved and fixed in our modern culture, which is marked by relentless movement and ever-increasing amounts of strain, making us more able to cope with the tremendous demands put on us by our daily lives. Having digital agendas and to-do lists, placing sticky notes around the house, and Googling for the information you need at your fingertips sometimes does the trick. Still, there is no replacement for an optimally functioning physical memory. People with wonderful memory are slowly becoming the exception rather than the norm today since we use so many electronic aids and devices as memory crutches. Think how much better off you'd be if you could commit everyday lists and professional appointments to your short-term memory.

Think how much more fulfilled you'd be if you could commit treasured moments of your life to your long-term memory through visualization techniques, filing them away in your mental filing system for lifelong recall (instead of depending on digital images can erase from a hard drive in seconds). Imagine how popular you'll be when you can accomplish simple but sometimes onerous tasks like remembering people's names at a party, not to mention all the details about them. Such memory-related attributes coalesce well with aspects of "emotional intelligence" (EQ) and contribute to improving your health in the present and give you a much better quality of life in the long term.

Chapter 5: What factors affect memory?

The archiving process is influenced by many factors, including the emotional content of our experiences are made and the strength of a memory. Every situation you go through the experience and tend to leave your mark on our neural networks. Some impressions are healthy, while others are fragile. The most beautiful are the connections of neurological systems involved in the storage process. The best and most apparent is our brain's memory—a lot of factors that influence the storage process. When we have an electrical memory in our mind, it has turned into different parts of our brain. They continue to get new information and, at times, changed if we are going through similar experiences in the future.

Because our memories depend on the neurological network, their strength or weakness depends on how neural cells behave in the brain. If the neurons in our minds tend to die or move to the newly formed circuits, a memory linked to fade becomes confused or loses definition at all. There are several studies on human consciousness. When we remember a recollection, any researchers believe that it goes through consolidation and can change based on the degree of error involved in identifying it. Let us move to look at some general factors that affect the storage process.

- The first is the ability to retain information, which depends on the memory traces of the past in our brain.

- The next factor that affects storage is the health of a person. If you are healthy, you can keep what you have learned in a better way, a person who suffers from health problems.

- The aging factor is essential when it comes to remembering things. Young people have a more exceptional ability to remember things than older adults.

- As mentioned above, interest is one of the most important factors when it comes to storage. If you love music, you will remember the words, the melody, the names of the singers, and their songs. Not only to be able to store something related to music, but you'll be able to do so quickly as well. Also, you will be able to retain the information for a while.'

You cannot store items in a better and more effective if you are not willing to learn. Several factors may affect our availability.

We are not ready to keep things; why do we not like them, sleepy, or simply tired of consuming information. Any of these things will wear you down mentally, and you'll find yourself stopping to say no to anything that would. Therefore, you must be ready for Polish Memory.

How much information can you remember?

Some experts believe that people who have the memory of extraordinary luck may contain more information than an average person can imagine. Experts believe that there is virtually no limit to store information. Our brain is not like a memory card that plugs into a phone or a camera. It cannot run out of memory. We do not need to empty before filling with new information and practices, and you can register an unlimited number of facts and unique experiences without overwriting existing content.

The ability of the brain to store information is virtually unlimited.

Experts have tried to find the meter that can measure our mental volume. When approaching a conclusion, they are stunned because individual cognitive companies are represented by a particular person or a person with a brain more.

If we look at our daily routine, we realize that we tend to forget a lot of information in the evening. It 'the fact that man has a capacity for virtually unlimited storage.

It creates room for the question of whether we have infinite memory, so why have we forgotten a lot? Since we can remember some words of a speech than an hour from our history teacher. In addition, 'indeed, it suggests that if we make an active effort to understand and aware of everything that has been said, we will memorize every word in this speech.

There are about one billion neurons in our brains. Each of them can form a thousand connections with other nerve cells, which can amount to Katherine connections. The neurons are coupled with each other so that each one can help with many memories. Here is how you can expand the mind of our brains. This regular activity of our brain allows us to renew our memories of the past and integrate new.

The researchers believe that memories are formed in the connections that neurons are formed between them and in all neural networks.

Memory behaves differently for different people. Some people can recall the tiniest facts from ten years ago, and others can't remember what happened the week before. How we can improve memory depends on how we handle some information. For example, it is often difficult for us to remember what we have read from the Internet because our brain is convinced that we can easily find this information online. With that in mind, some experts believe that the Internet affects our ability to retain information, making it easier for us to find and source information. Moreover, from this fact, we can conclude that the more we challenge our memory, the better and sharper it becomes—it 'like a piece of iron.

Factors contributing to the storage

Our memory is just another function of our brain, and we need to be in the right mood or mental state to perform brilliantly well. We can only get better take some steps in the right direction. The health of your storage capacity depends on how you shape the memories of the available information and how you remember that information when you need it in the future. Sharp memory indicates a healthy brain and has the power to make life easier and more enjoyable. Imagine how frustrating it is when we cannot remember anything, despite many attempts. A strong memory can improve our quality of life as we grow older with time. We can cherish the successes and moments that we spent with our spouses, siblings, and children.

Exercise: Exercise and sports can make a big difference when it comes to fine-tuning our memory. Yoga is perfect for the heart. It keeps the blood oxygenated and provides a significant flow of blood to the brain. It 'also good for our lungs that purify the blood and play a role in keeping the mind healthy. If the filtered blood supply to the brain, there are opportunities to have an efficient brain function. People who have a habit of doing regular exercise have a better memory function, even when they enter old age. Regular exercise also helps to preserve the memories better. It also reduces the risk of our capture of certain health conditions such as diabetes,

Are you getting enough social memory to help you perform better? Experts believe that the state of social development we are in our lives affects memory. Very social people tend to have sharp minds.

They enjoy a healthier love life, marriage, and partnerships with friends, which positively influences their brain function. It provides a healthy boost to their memory function.

Sleep: Sleep is something that is considered the most crucial factor to affect our memory. Some suggest that after a two- to three-hour class, students should be able to have a good night's sleep so that the knowledge they've learned can be consolidated in the brain and transformed into long-term memory. Besides, this may be true. Take few moments to think about your life. Can you remember a night when you had a brilliant sleep? Now, you remember the day when you woke up and found that the performance level has been raised, no matter what you did that day, such as work, study, sport, or cooking. A short nap has the power to refresh your brain to make it work better for the next few hours. Therefore, the point is that the quality of sleep is paramount.

- **Writing habits:** this seems to be a conservative tradition, but it works well if they desire to remember things for a long time. Just write stuff in the form of bullet points or prepare a list in numerical order to place them. I propose to do on the list because we write in bullets or numbered much more comfortable to remember than the information is filled in one piece. If you make this a habit, it is more likely to remember many things for an extended period. For example, I remember these points to sharpen your memory for a long time; that is why I chose the format for their writing in locations so that you can put your mind and keep them in place (Schwartz Bard).

- **You are eating healthy food:** a good, wholesome diet influences the strength of your storage. If you have a routine to consume lots of fresh green leafy vegetables and beans, you will probably have a brilliant mind and a sharp memory. Saturated fats, such as meat and dairy products, intoxicate the brain, so avoid frequent use. Fish is perfect for you two or three times a week, but do not fry it. Remember to eat the fruit also. It 'essential to feed the memory is that green leafy vegetables have a powerful effect on the improvement of cognition and memory process.

Some more vitamins and nutrients play a role in building competent cells, the food our body, including the brain, and protect our minds. They include some antioxidants such as quercetin and vitamins.

Vitamin D is vital for memory because it regulates the flow of calcium in the brain and regulates the growth of cells. The increase in vitamin D can help improve the functions of our minds. You can buy some add-on to run its deficiency in the body.

- **Mental exercises:** we talked about the importance of physical activity such as exercise and sports to improve our memory function. In addition to this, we should start some mental activities like solving puzzles, playing scrabble, chess, and other such games that challenge our mental capacity. Here is how we can improve our storage capacity (Schwartz Bard).

- **Stress factor:** whether the conditions of the brain have the right, as some chemical substances can increase stress on memory consolidation, which is the most crucial step to remember certain things. But this is not always recommended. It should reduce the factors that negative stress to reduce the portion of forgetfulness.

As a result, these are a few of the reasons that contribute to the storage phase in our brains. In addition to this, there are certain factors that elimination can help improve our memory. The main thing is smoking. Smoking can seriously damage your storage capacity. Smokers are most likely to forget names and faces compared to non-smokers. Smokers are usually sensitive to some psychological issues such as depression, which can be one of the main risk factors for Memory (Schwartz Bard).

Chapter 6: Train Your Brain

Here's a little secret you may never have guessed: humans who can accomplish notable malleable feats like memorizing the order of a shuffled deck of cards or thousands of random numbers of photographic memories in minutes. They have regular minds like you and, yes, me. This past weekend I competed at the fifteenth annual USA Memory Championships — an Olympiad testing their power to remember "mental athletes" in the place. Lucky for me, I discovered some tricks for Nelson Dellis from a man who ruled for 2 years. Here are the strategies Nelson taught me that you could start incorporating into your day-to-day life to strengthen your memory.

Memory Technology Anyone Can Learn

Although my memory is high-quality, I am terrible with names. I am so horrified that I forget the title of a person before he even declares it - it's like I don't even want to hear it. After a conversation/training session with Nelson, however, I was in a position to notice the names of dozens of strangers in a minute or two.

My Memory Training Boot Camp

My boot camp for this tournament began two weeks before the competition. I received two bottles of solid brain DHA, a T-shirt, a coaching manual, and a list of events, including a 15-minute memoir of a 50-line unpublished poem and a 5-minute memoir of a shuffled deck. Leaves. I seriously had no notion of what was happening once.

Draw and anchor

In my coaching session with numbers, that grid of numbers used to be the most intimidating part, but he taught me how to see it, so it was hardly the least intimidating. (I must admit, I have determined to match the wide variety, on leisure time, only in the remaining minutes.) There are two stages for all the recall challenges, whether you are playing an unusual mental game. / Whether you are into a hobby or not. Trying to keep in mind the place where you parked your car:

In turn, Genius does not like to consider boring things and cannot latch on to people with more and more visuals (like names and numbers).

Locate an adjoining place to place or anchor mental pictures where you have potential in your "memory palace" in your experience room, keeping them in mind.

So, for example, to remember names and faces, he asked to take a character like Nelson's and turn it into an image with the help of connecting it with a celebrity like Nelson Mandela, on his big nose Tried. Nelson starts crawling inside his nose, thinking about Mandela. The more vivid, erotic, sexual, or unusual, the better.

For the name, how the spell is spelled is not what it sounds, though how it sounds. Break it into syllables and flip pictures.

An iconic area should have a piece of cloth, an eye, a mustache, or whatever the person stands for you.

During the competition, one of the pictures featured Neil, who I thought was a science fiction, fantasy, graphic artist, Neil Gaiman, so I drew a skull on his sunglasses, which led me to name him, helped to keep in mind. In any other photo, there was once a woman named Laurie, as I knew in the school classroom, so I imagined a tissue container under her nose. I think I got at least two of those names.

My churning boot camp manual suggests that Joe would probably be sloppy Joe for the image, and if the character Joe is a mole on the anchor's face, you can imagine a sloppy Joe lick from Joey's moles. Total.

In a nutshell: When you meet someone: hold him and say his name, make a photo from one of his identification syllables, and place that photo on the anchor/feature selected for that person. The next time you see that person, you will see that photo at that ceremony and immediately note his name. (Don't state what specific feature you've got to understand the image you chose or the image you created, and don't try to stare at this feature!)

Kevin Spacey Fencing Donuts with Sneaker On My Couch to remember too many digits and random cards, similar integral techniques are still applied; however, more profitable strategies and structures are also needed.

We all have used the Dominic system, invented using the reminiscence champion Dominic Breen, which explains the number of letters. We convert the numerals into two-letter initials for humans and related moves and objects to visualize them more. So, for example, the variation, because it is round, is A, 0, and since it is beginning, one gets a two-letter translation. Many human beings use Ozzy Osbourne as their person for that number 0; speed can behead a bat and object a bat. It is easy to consider Ozzy Osbourne beheading a bat from 0 to a set of numbers.

But for the system to work, you have to make it personal, so to memorize the deck of cards, out of every thirty-two cards, I have to create a character with motion and object. Jack of Hearts grew to fry my husband's eggs, and the thing was once an egg in a pan. King of Spades used to be Kevin Spacey lit a cigarette, and the item was ever lighter. Edward Sizzordhands was ever hedging trim, and the object was once hedged. And then you want to find a familiar place to shop for information. In my memory palace, I walked through my house, started at my front door, and placed these familiar people or numbers on my furniture.

For day-to-day use, the memorial castle helps memorize a list or sequence of things. Start a journey in a place that you are very familiar with, say, your home, start from the door of your house. So for a grocery list, the example goes, think of a container of milk flowing to your door, and when you arrive inside, perhaps two massive steaks that strike in your foyer. Continue to your living room to watch the pretzels dance on your rug.

Again, the more animation, exaggeration, and senses you can put into your memory palace or journey, the higher your memoir. And the more you strengthen your memory and keep working to sharpen your mind, the greater your chances of dealing with Alzheimer's disease. If you don't think you are a visual person, then other senses are sounds, smells, touches. In everyday life, pay more attention to how things sound and feel and feel, which will likely enhance your visual skills. Start doing additional searches and paying more attention in cases.

If you want to instruct a memory chamber, remember to lug this great identity in the game, two competition training software, and the Memnetics Forum. And maybe we'll see you next year at the Reminiscence Championship!

Nelson and various intellectual athletes, including a team consisting of highly faculty children from Hershey, PA, make it look easy, albeit one that takes severe education and practice as a remembrance. Most of my hours of training have been spent just developing the card gadget and working out the number system, which was not remarkable in the case (because I was early on time, but instead with 100 humans to remember.

I used 10 characters for each digit as I needed them; they come from a video of 123—bad idea. I am a very long Muay up in my head was caught singing a video loop). I could make about half of the cards at home in five minutes, although in the competition, amazed and distracted, I got about 1/2 the whole way. I headlined about 0.33 faces, thanks to practice with that exciting intro game I referred to above.

In the end, I came in 36th out of 46 of all the mental athletes who competed — probably no longer bad for anyone who would not make any sense, having previously come across such an aspect. Was dreaming of and who was fully educated for some hours over a week. As Joshua Foyer also tells the training-to-shampoo story, there is hope - if you teach like a world-class mental athlete.

What, at that point, is the primary strategy for building a superior memory?

When you achieve adulthood, your memory is relied upon to have made an enormous number of neural pathways that naturally help you with dealing with and audit information quickly, handle fundamental issues and execute continuous assignments within any event mental effort. Nevertheless, on the off chance that you, for the most part, stick to tattered frameworks (Taking a rehashed type of way of life with no adjustment in your day by day schedule), you aren't giving your mind the affectation it needs to keep creating and moving up to improve efficiency. You have to shake things up every so often!

Memory, as solid quality, anticipates that you should "use it or lose it." The more you work out your mind to process things regularly, the better you'll have the alternative to process and remember information quicker and input it all the more viably into creative thoughts. Regardless, not all activities are equal. Notwithstanding, to guarantee satisfactory memory improvement, you have to break your day-by-day calendar and challenge yourself to use and develop new personality pathways.

It gives you something new. Despite how intellectually mentioning the activity is, if it's something you're starting at now extraordinary at, it is not a better than average personality that works out. The development ought to be new and out of your standard scope of commonality. To fortify the psyche, you need to keep learning and developing new capacities.

It isn't straightforward. The best personality boosting practices demand your complete and close thought. It lacks that you found the activity testing at one point. It ought to at present be something that requires mental effort; for example, attempting to make sense of how to utilize AutoCAD programming for compositional plans proficiently.

So below are a few things to employ to help boost your brainpower and thus improve on your procession speed:

Expand on your Aptitude

Treat yourself after reaching a Milestone.

Prizes bolster the mind's learning procedure. The more enthralled and involved you are in the campaign, the more likely it is that you will continue to participate, and the greater the benefits you will reap. So pick exercises that, while testing, are as yet charming and fulfilling.

There are a significant number of ways contemplation can generally build your memory; intellectual competence, center, and knowledge.

Handle your Health issues in Time

Sometimes, we feel our health is taking a massive plunge to the negative, and it is not farfetched. Assuming this is the case, there might be a care or lifestyle issue to a fault. It's not merely dementia or Alzheimer's ailment that causes memory misfortune. There are numerous infections, emotional problems, and meds that can meddle with memory. Health Issues like Coronary illnesses, hormonal diseases, Diabetes, hypertension, etc., can affect your memory improvement if not handled in time and accurately and, in some cases, could lead to protracted disorderliness.

Meditation

Utilizing the most recent in X-ray mind imaging innovation, a milestone 2000 Harvard College study found that in both the short and long haul, reflection specialists regularly and helpfully expanded the neural mass (dark matter) of the cerebrum locales related with long and transient memory, centered consideration, profound idea, and in general intellectual competence while all the while calming the electrical action inside the areas associated with uneasiness, sorrow, dread, and outrage.

As opposed to the generally acknowledged logical assessment of so many decades before now, the neuroplastic nature of our minds implies that our innovative possibilities are not set in hereditary stone. There are sure things we can do to improve its presentation.

Along these lines, much the same as your leg muscles, you can helpfully assemble the quality and even the size of your mind in the most beneficial and generally common ways. At that point, what is the ideal approach to fabricate a superior memory?

The possibilities of having the option to assemble a superior memory through contemplation are enormous.

Having a super-solid and right mind opens the entryway to a fantastic exhibit of life-changing advantages. To assemble your mind to ever more elevated levels, your sensory system needs exercise.

Luckily, the neurostimulation from consideration offers your whole tactile framework an uncommonly productive atmosphere, enacting too positive changes all through your body, especially your cerebrum.

In time, your whole tangible framework revises and advances itself on progressively increasingly critical levels, setting up another structure of neural pathways, opening up access between your left and right cerebrum sides of the equator like never before.

This "full personality get to" or "complete personality synchronization," as it's known among setting up scientists, can transform yourself from various perspectives, including boosting your psychological bent, level of knowledge, memory, and understanding.

Science has marginally discovered a trace of something increasingly critical concerning thought's mesmerizing display of memory-boosting benefits.

Eat a Brain-Boosting diet

So also, as the body needs fuel, it makes the brain. You, in all probability, understand that an eating routine reliant on specific items, vegetables, whole grains, "sound" fats (for instance, olive oil, nuts, fish), and lean protein will give heaps of favorable therapeutic circumstances. However, such an eating routine can, in like manner, improve memory. For mind prosperity, in any case, it's not actually what you eat—it's likewise what you don't eat.

The going with sustaining tips will help bolster your academic ability and decrease your threat of dementia:

Get your omega-3s: Research shows that omega-3 unsaturated fats are precious for mental prosperity. Fish is a particularly rich wellspring of omega-3, freezing water "oily fish, for instance, salmon, fish, halibut, trout, mackerel, sardines, and herring.

Eat more foods grown from the ground: Produce is loaded down with malignant growth counteraction specialists, substances that shield your neural connections from hurt. Splendid results of the dirt are astoundingly adequate deadly growth counteraction specialist "superfood" sources.

Drink green tea: Green tea contains polyphenols, inconceivable malignant growth counteraction specialists protected against free radicals that can hurt neurotransmitters. Among various points of interest, balanced usage of green tea may improve memory and mental sharpness and moderate personality development.

Drink Alcohol with some limitation: Taking Alcohol with strict constraint is essential since Alcohol affects the body synapses. Regardless, with some control (around one glass a day for women; 2 for men), Alcohol may improve memory and insight. Red wine appears to be the best decision, as it is rich in resveratrol. This flavonoid lifts the circulatory system as the main priority and reduces the peril of Alzheimer's affliction.

Another eating routine-related effect on memory is the mounting research that eating berries can help with warding off memory decline.

An evaluation from the School of Investigating and the Landmass Supportive School found that updating a standard eating routine with blueberries for twelve weeks improved the processing speed of the working memory. It saw the effect of this just a few weeks into the study.

A study on female specialists over the age of 70 found that the people who had by and mainly eaten at any rate two servings of strawberries or blueberries consistently had a moderate diminishing in memory rot. (The effects of strawberries might be asking to be refuted, in any case, since the California Strawberry Commission to some degree upheld that survey and another assessment focusing on strawberries suggested that you'd need to eat around 10 pounds of strawberries every day to see any effect).

More research is required now; science is moving closer to perceiving how berries may impact our cerebrums. Blueberries are rich in flavonoids, which appear to strengthen the existing relationship as a main priority. That could explain why they're helpful for long stretch memory.

Conclusion

Memory helps us to know where we come from, thanks to the happy childhood memories that are a vital treasure in adulthood. Besides, memory can also be selective. We accumulate so many experiences throughout life that the mind has excellent mental hygiene and tends to remember more the positive than the negative.

Memory has such force that for this reason, it is so difficult to overcome a breakup of partners because it is impossible to forget someone who we have loved. Even a machine can't destroy your memory.

From the vital point of view, memory based on the wisdom of experience is very important because thanks to that mind, you can reflect on new skills, you can avoid not stumbling twice in the same stone by remembering the past through the memory.

In today's society, marked by the rush and the labor pressure, the absences are a form of forgetfulness that it can correct. For example, I have an up-to-date task schedule or some notes on pending errands into visible parts of the house. Memory also has its limits, for example, tiredness.

Therefore, it is beneficial to look for tools to remember better professional quotes, birth dates, or critical data. Also, thanks to the writing of a diary, you can even have a more vivid memory of your life, just as the photographs help you connect with your memories because a picture is worth a thousand words.

Remembering the happy moments of the past is an act of emotional intelligence that improves your health in the present to have a better quality of life.

If it is so vital to human life, how to work it? Let's take a peek at how we can improve our memory.

Understanding the Memory

We have two forms of memory; short-term memory and long-term memory (technically, there is a third, a long-term memory, which lies between the other two, but let's not complicate the matter better).

Short-term memory is an active buffer, such as computer memory lost when the machine is turned off.

Your short-term memory is minimal. In essence, you can only manage with a certain amount of items, usually around seven at most. When you insert one more thing into your short-term memory, another one comes out. You can see the short-term memory in action, for example, the instant you look for a phone number and mark it. It might seem strange since the short-term memory is limited to approximately seven items, that you can memorize a ten-digit number. But fortunately, human memory is more flexible than a computer, whereas in this, everything consists of simple bits-0 or 1 human memory can hold an image or a word as a single point. Known telephone codes, for example, are a single item and leave spaces for other information.

Long-term memory is a different matter, with an unlimited capacity. It has all the power for anything that it can remember. But storing something in memory in the long-term is not as simple as it is in the short term. Using short-term memory is an act of desire that takes place immediately. On the other hand, recording something in long-term memory takes a lot of work.

It is here that lack of training in brain use becomes a real disadvantage. Unless you understand how the brain works, the actions needed to record something in memory seems to be extravagant. However, once it is understood that the images are kept on a species map, it becomes more pronounced. To fix something in memory, it is better to see it in the form of an image, given the success of pictorial representations of information as mental maps, with the most precise possible figures. To keep it there, it is also necessary to make recapitulations that ideally should emerge immediately after the material is known.

Forgetfulness

Is it reasonable to ask yourself why you forget something once you have it in long-term memory? After all, it would be beneficial if we could remember anything we have recorded in our memory. Forgetfulness is a simple process. When something has been "forgotten," it does not necessarily mean that it has wholly abandoned memory. It is more likely that it is partially lost or that the correct paths to reach it have not been traveling. It has all happened to us that we have forgotten something, and then it comes up unexpectedly a few hours later. It is clear that it had not erased our memory; it was misplaced.

EMOTIONAL INTELLIGENCE

Introduction

It seems almost strange to think that the concept of emotional intelligence isn't well taught in a lot of modern societies. In Western culture, specifically, young children are told to "keep their chin up" and not cry over the little things. Anger is considered a negative, explosive emotion that should never be expressed. Some of these biases are even used to target specific genders. Young boys and men are often chastised and teased for crying. The act becomes an emasculating scenario.

Interestingly enough, emotions are a vital part of humanity. Having a full range of emotions and being able to feel and express them is a near biological imperative that makes humans well, human. Take an individual who has an antisocial personality disorder. One of the primary components of this disorder is not feeling remorse for their actions or compassion for the feelings of others. They are incapable of feeling that and are classified as having a disorder. Yet, people who allow themselves a full range of emotions are teased, told they are "too sensitive" or that they are weak.

It seems almost hypocritical, doesn't it? Unfortunately, the stigmas that surround the expression of emotions lead to individuals hiding their emotions, bottling them up, running from them, or flat out denying them. What is the harm in that, you ask? Well, unfortunately, bottling emotions, ignoring them, and denying them leads to a culture of emotionally stunted individuals who can't empathize, sympathize, or relate.

Alright, that's going a little too far ahead. Think of yourself as an emotional being. These emotions are directly linked to your behavior, thought patterns, and how you relate with others. By acknowledging emotions and healthily expressing them, you give yourself self-awareness, you can manage your own life better, and you can manage relationships better. Interest in emotional intelligence likely stems from a desire to improve certain aspects of your life that have been impacted by your negative relationship with your own emotions.

When an emotion isn't properly expressed or felt, it becomes like water trapped in a dam. The pressure grows and grows as every situation you encounter while bottling up that emotion adds its pressure to the dam. Finally, when the dam breaks, the emotional tidal wave that explodes can quite literally run roughshod all over your life. This is commonly seen in people with anger management or explosive anger issues.

No emotion is immune to the proverbial dam. They can get trapped behind. Unfortunately, when the tidal wave is unleashed, it is often over one single drop that broke the pressure. That drop might be small and insignificant, but the entire weight of the tidal wave comes out with it.

This means that a seemingly simple event can be the trigger and result in a much more catastrophic emotional release that has been building up for a long time. As a result, the person, or situation, that receives the brunt of the explosion might be completely undeserving of such an outburst. They just happened to be the final straw, or water drop to stay with the dam analogy. These releases can then cause problems in your relationships, familial relationships, and even in your career and professional relationships.

It isn't just relationships that can be impacted by emotional intelligence. Performance in school or in your career, your physical and mental health, and your ability to socialize all hinge appropriately on your emotional intelligence.

So, what is to be done about it? Well, learning about emotional intelligence is the first step in gaining the upper hand and improving yourself. This book is going to be your starting point for knowledge and information about yourself as well as how you can improve your emotional intelligence. Despite what society tells you, you can empower yourself to live an emotionally healthier (and healthier overall) life.

Maybe you can't think of any specific situations that you might benefit from a higher E.Q. or E.I. (emotional intelligence). Here is a list of a few scenarios that can become much less stressful if you are aware of your emotional intelligence:

- Meeting deadlines, especially tight, stressful ones

- Giving and receiving feedback

- Not having enough resources

- Dealing with difficult relationships

- Coping with change

- Handling setbacks and perceived failures

As you can see, many of these potential situations are quite broad. Therefore, emotional intelligence can be volatile in a wide range of areas in your life.

With so many areas that emotional intelligence can help with, it seems like an obvious choice to begin working on your emotional intelligence. Going to be a vital tool in your transformation.

Harvard Business School did a comprehensive research study that's results determined E.Q. is vital to success. It was deemed twice as important than I.Q. and technical skills in determining who was successful (What is emotional intelligence? 2019, para 4).

Scientifically speaking, emotions are known to come before thoughts. Emotions can change the way the brain functions. They can impair the cognitive process, the ability to act interpersonally, and even inhibit the decision-making process.

Thankfully, emotional intelligence can be improved. Much like programming a computer, your mind and emotions can be "taught" or "programmed" to react a certain way. The emotional side of your brain and the rational side of your brain are separate. Emotional intelligence is based on how these two portions of your brain communicate. By improving their communication, you grow your emotional intelligence.

Your emotional intelligence pathway starts in the spinal cord of your nervous system. Before you can have a rational thought or reaction, your senses travel from the spinal cord directly into the front of the brain. Before these senses reach your rational brain, they pass through the limbic system, where emotions are generated. Biologically, emotions are triggered before rational thought (About emotional intelligence, 2020, para 11).

The human brain is essentially like a supercomputer, constantly processing information. The neural connections that allow you to process information and react are always changing and growing. When you learn new skills, acquire new information or knowledge, those connections change and grow. This is a lifelong process and is called plasticity (About emotional intelligence, 2020, para 12).

The process isn't instantaneous, though. It takes time for those connections to form and for the brain to begin processing information more efficiently across those new connections. This is why it is possible to improve your emotional intelligence, but also why it takes a certain level of commitment to make such a personal change.

That being said, having a higher emotional intelligence can quite literally change your life. Harvard Business School, a renowned and well-respected institute, postured that E.Q. contributes to success!

This can be career success, personal relationship success, or just reaching your personal goals in life. Consider what success means to you and what commitment you are willing to make to achieve it. All in all, reading this book and giving yourself new skills to carry with you through daily life isn't a very arduous commitment.

Imagine reaching all your goals and successes. It is a very elating, validating, and empowering vision, isn't it? Of course, it is! It should be. The opportunity that is presented within this book is one that will help you bring that vision into reality. It might sound almost surreal, but the science and the methodology exists to show how beneficial E.Q. is to success. That is what Emotional Intelligence offers you, a chance, and the tools you need, to make your success.

You've already taken your first step to change. Just by purchasing and opening this book, you're on the path towards improving your emotional intelligence. Skills that you will learn about and improve are going to increase your self-awareness, improve your self-management, raise your mindfulness, help you with managing relationships, and increasing your social awareness. These major points impact everyone's day today, including you.

Now, to be clear, this is not a book on how to control your emotions or how to stop feeling certain emotions. E.Q. is all about managing emotions.

That means learning how to express them appropriately, acknowledging the full range of human emotion, and applying them to the situations you are in throughout your daily life. It is about living with them in harmony. Understanding that will give you an advantage in relating to yourself and others.

It is never too late to decide that you are ready for a change, but has there ever been a better time than now? One of the factors that emotional intelligence creates ease around is change. Don't let your emotions hold you back this time. It is time to expand your emotional toolkit, starting right here with emotional intelligence.

Chapter 1: What is Emotional Intelligence?

You are not a robot. You can feel. This is why people, events, and situations evoke different emotions in you. Sometimes the gap between your emotions and reactions seems so negligible that you react to these emotions before realizing. At other times, you are more conscious or deliberate about your reactions. But as an intelligent human, your behavioral responses shouldn't be at the beck and call of something outside your control. Indeed, you can choose your responses by widening the gap between emotion and reaction. To achieve this, you need to improve an aspect of human intelligence known as emotional intelligence.

What is Emotional Intelligence?

Emotional intelligence is your ability to recognize and manage emotions within you and others. It is being in constant touch with your inner state of being or frame of mind and the things that trigger these emotional states.

Every emotion you feel is a form of feedback. A highly emotionally intelligent person can take the information provided in the feedback to influence their behavior in positive ways. The feedback can also be used to relate better with those around them.

Conversely, people with low levels of emotional intelligence rarely pay attention to the feedback from their emotions, especially at the initial stages. When they do, it is usually late. At that point, they simply let go of the oars and allow the strong currents of what they feel sweep over them and cause havoc or hopefully lead to good.

Your emotions can temporarily freeze your ability to think rationally and make you behave in ways that you will regret later. For example, someone did something that made you so mad that you acted rashly before realizing you shouldn't have said or done what you did. When regret becomes a constant feature in your daily life, it indicates a low level of emotional intelligence. You are not living to your full capacity as an intelligent human being. Something else is in the steering wheel of your life, and you need to change that fast!

You can be rich, famous, powerful, and brilliant, but without emotional intelligence, there is a yawning gap in your attitude that needs to be filled.

Your intelligent quotient (IQ) can get you all the accolades in the world, but to be truly great and successful, you need a high level of emotional intelligence. In other words, you are an emotionally intelligent person if:

• You are fully aware and in touch with your emotions for most of your day. You are rarely taken aback by stressful people or situations.
• You can be intentional about your responses as a result of being aware of your emotions.
• You respond to and influence others intelligently.
• On the other hand, your emotional intelligence level is low if:
• You can't stand people. You are easily offended and react hastily.
• When you look back, you always blame yourself for not responding as you should. You were either too harsh or too soft. You seem to be carried away by how you feel at any moment, and your feelings instead of rational thinking heavily cloud your decisions. You feel bad and judge too quickly, or you feel good and make rash decisions.
• You are not willing to consider other people's viewpoints. You tend to be always rigid about your ways. You have a made-up mind even before you seek other people's opinions.
• People think of you as an excellent professional but a poor friend. You find it difficult to connect with people beyond the surface level. You think of other people as the tools you need to achieve your aims or as a means to an end. You do not inspire and influence people positively. Instead, you live your life mostly in reaction to others. You might have a great fortune, but you live an unhappy life.

Elements of Emotional Intelligence

Briefly, emotional intelligence comprises of five fundamental components, namely:

1. **Self-Awareness**: this refers to the ability to recognize and understand your emotions and feelings accurately, and how they affect your disposition or frame of mind. Essentially, it is the first tool you need to identify your strengths and weaknesses to know the part of your life that need work. Getting better at every other aspect of emotional intelligence depends largely on how well you can use the self-awareness tool.

2. **Self-Regulation (Self-Management):** this is the ability to hold yourself back from reacting to the first random impulse that occurs to you. It takes a lot of practice to gauge different situations rationally before responding consciously. Self-regulation or self-management is not about muzzling your emotions. Instead, it is about threading the middle path between primitive reactions and temperateness.

3. **Self-Motivation:** this is the ability to propel yourself forward regardless of challenging situations. Self-motivated people don't easily throw in the towel, get disoriented because of uncomfortable emotions, or give less than their best under pressure.

4. **Empathy (Social Awareness):** this refers to the crucial skill of identifying and understanding how other people feel. Managing how you feel while being oblivious of how others feel can damage your relationships. Being socially aware requires putting empathy into practice in all your interactions and relationships. With the right amount of empathy, you can place yourself in other people's shoes to feel and understand their perspectives. But because it is a delicate skill to master, it can easily be misunderstood and abused.

5. **Social Skills (Relationship Management):** this is the ability to build stronger relationships by recognizing and managing the emotions of other people and influencing them positively. It is an offshoot of developing sound social awareness and a natural consequence of bringing all the other components together. It is a vital skill for improving communication, effectively handling and resolving conflicts, and dealing with awkward situations.

To become a well-rounded human being, you need to work on all of these components consciously. Since they are closely linked, improving one aspect usually results in an overall improvement in all the other aspects.

What Is an Emotion

In many years, psychologists and philosophers have been having a spirited debate on emotions and various types like happiness and sadness. They have been trying to determine their nature if perceptions about various philosophical dynamics or cognitive judgments are about the satisfaction of set objectives. Various theories in neuroscience explain several suggestions on how a human being's brain can generate emotions by combining bodily perceptions and cognitive appraisals. If something thrilling in your life happens to you today, it is natural and very normal to develop an array of emotions such as happiness or sadness if it is a painful situation. There is a dualist view traditional that explains that a human being's body consists of a soul and a body. In this case, the soul is believed to be the one that experiences all mental states and emotions. However, this view can be disregarded and just termed as a motivated inference or a wishful thought since there is no substantial evidence that immortality and the soul exist.

Today, there exist two main approaches, scientific approaches, that can be employed in coming up with an explanation of what emotions are and their nature. Cognitive appraisal theory is one of the approaches, and it explains that emotions can be said to be judgments on how the situation you are in currently meets the goals you have set. According to this theory, emotions such as happiness are believed to be an expression of goals being fulfilled. On the other hand, sadness and emotions depict unfulfilled goals and disappointments in life and can refer to a form of anger towards a stumbling block to your goals. Another theory that tries to explain what emotions are is that of William James, together with others. They came up with an argument that emotions are just perceptions of various changes in your body in different situations. These body changes that depict emotions include mental reactions and physiological stages in life.

These two theories, psychological perception and cognitive appraisal can be integrated to develop a unified definition of emotions. With an understanding of these theories, it is crystal clear that the mind controls and determines all sensations and perceptions based on the different situations we are in. We can, therefore, describe emotions as one's mental state that is associated with their nervous system linked to the chemical changes that take place in the body. These chemical changes are usually linked to your feelings, thoughts, degree of displeasure or pleasure, and behavioral responses.

Emotions can also be termed as negative or positive experiences linked to certain patterns of physiological functions in the body. The bottom line is that emotions are responsible for all the cognitive, behavioral, and physiological changes that we undergo in our bodies and how we react to them.

Basic Emotional Responses

There are various types of emotions that have different natures and also varying influence in the way that we conduct ourselves when with other people and even generally how we live. These emotions, if not controlled, may tend to control us. They can even harm the choices that we make in life. Apart from that, these emotions are a determiner to what our thoughts are in different situations that we face daily. Understanding these emotional responses will also give us a strong foundation to advance, discussing how we can use them to rewire our bodies and minds to attain a better and healthier life.

Happiness

This is one of the emotions that people have used different approaches to attain; it thus tends to be vital. Happiness is referred to as a nice emotional state which depicts feelings of joy, contentment, well-being, gratification, and satisfaction. This emotional state is usually expressed through facial expressions like smiling, body language like a relaxed stance, and even a pleasing voice tone.

Sadness

This is another emotional state that is the opposite of happiness and is depicted by feelings such as grief, hopelessness, dampened mood, disinterest, and disappointment. This is a very common emotional state due to different stressful life experiences that we undergo daily. Having prolonged sadness might be hazardous to your health, specifically mental health, since it can advance over time to become fatal depression. Its severity usually varies as it depends on the cause and the extent at which you can cope up with it.

Fear

Fear is a very powerful emotional state that plays a vital role in one's survival. When faced by danger or any situation that seems threatening, you will get into a flight or fight response situation.

At this point, you will find that your muscles become tensed and with an increased heartbeat and respiration rate. This will trigger you to either fight the danger or run away from it instead. This emotion is usually depicted by widening eyes and other psychological reactions like rapid breathing and heartbeat.

Disgust

Disgust is an emotional state that happens when you are disappointed or bored due to failure to achieve something. It can also be as a result of unpleasant sight, smell, or taste. This emotion can be depicted by the tendency to move away from disgusting you, other reactions like retching or vomiting, and even facial expressions like curling your upper lip. This emotion might even make you forever hate something that once disgusted you, which can be hazardous.

Anger

Anger is one of the greatest and most powerful emotions depicted by agitation, hostility, antagonism, and frustration. Just as fear, it is also capable of triggering your flight or fight response. There are various ways in which anger is usually displayed, and they include facial expressions like frowning. Body language, like turning down someone in a harsh manner, can also be a sign of anger.

Identifying Emotions

To use your emotions the right way, you need first to identify the emotions the right way. Let us look at the best way to identify the emotions:

Understand the Trigger

The first step towards identifying the emotion is first to know what caused it. This will help you to describe the events that led to an emotional event. In this step, try to stick to facts alone.

You can write down the event that led to the emotion to have it clear in your mind.

Why Do You Think It Happened?

The following step is to identify the possible causes that led to an emotional event. This is crucial because it determines the meaning that you give to the situation that happened. The type of emotional event that led to the issue will determine how you react to the event in question.

How the Situation Made You Feel?

The following step is to determine how the emotional event made you feel both physically and emotionally. This will help you see whether the emotion resulted in a positive or negative reaction.

You need to notice both the positive as well as the negative emotional and physical reactions that you felt when it happened. Notice any physical feelings that you experience, such as tightness in the body.

What Was Your Reaction

You need to ask this question so that you understand your urges. However, for the process to be effective, you need to make sure you are completely honest. It might be painful to admit some of the urges that you felt when the event happened. When we face some situations, we, at times, get strange urges to react differently. Some of the emotions that we go through might make us regret it in the future.

You need to compare your reaction at the moment that things happened and how you usually react normally. This will tell you whether you managed to control the urge, or you failed to do so.

What Did You Do and Say?

The following step would be to understand what you said or did due to the emotions. Even though you didn't manage to respond correctly, you need to be honest with yourself about how you handled the situation. You also need to understand how the decision you made impacted on the situation. This can be a good learning experience for you.

Once you evaluate your reaction, you can then use the situation to learn how to handle another situation that might arise.

How Did the Reaction Affect You Later on?

The final step in identifying the emotions is to understand the consequences of the actions that you took. If you said some words during the event, how did they affect you? On the other hand, if you acted in a certain way, how did it affect you in the future?

So, if you find yourself being overly attached to your emotions after, you need to ask yourself what happened and take the time to observe how you react when it happens. Go through these steps so that you can recognize your emotions. Once you practice and get used to these steps, you will be able to identify your emotions the right way and then choose the best way to respond to situations.

Emotional Intelligence in Action

High emotional intelligence is not merely an abstract subject; it shows up in real-life behaviors. The following are only but a few out of the many ways it manifests. These are some of the difficult aspects of emotional intelligence. Recognize them and find ways to practice them more often in your life to get better at using them.

1.   **Forgiveness**: You can give other people the chance to hold your emotions hostage when you refuse to let go of past hurts. Resentment is anger turned inward – the only person getting hurt is you! Unfortunately, those with a low level of emotional intelligence can't seem to recognize that fact. Those who cause your emotional pain may have long moved on, but if you don't forgive, you won't heal from that emotional wound. When you forgive, you demonstrate a high level of emotional intelligence and set yourself free to move forward.

2.   **Bringing the Best out of Others**: When you commend, encourage, compliment, appreciate, and inspire people, you are meeting one of the most innate emotional needs of humans – the need to be acknowledged. Emotional intelligence enables you to focus on people's strengths instead of their weaknesses. Since we all crave acknowledgment, it is natural that people will feel drawn to you if you recognize and appreciate them. But besides wanting to be around you, the constant focus on their strengths makes them get better while minimizing their shortcomings.

3.   **Giving Helpful Feedback**: Emotional intelligence helps you present criticism in a way that allows the recipient to see that you are focused on making them better clearly. Conversely, if you lack emotional intelligence, your criticism of others would be because they do not live up to your standards.

Taking Pauses: Perhaps one of the most elusive practices of emotional intelligence is taking conscious pauses just before reacting. Taking deliberate pauses before responses is not a show of uncertainty, fear, or reluctance. Instead, it shows that you are mentally weighing your options before speaking or acting. It is an easy concept to understand theoretically, but difficult to put in practice.

However, when you get the hang of this skill, you will save yourself from making long-lasting decisions based on fleeting emotions.

Are You Emotionally Intelligent?

 Most likely, you will be able to identify areas for self-improvement along the way as you read this book. The quiz below is intended to help you gain even more clarity on what your strong areas are and where your weaknesses lie as far as emotional intelligence is concerned. If the results show that you are emotionally intelligent then you can keep doing what you have been doing. If at the end of the test you realize that you have not been behaving in a manner that is emotionally intelligent then this is not something that should make you feel bad. Rather, this should serve as motivation for you to do better and be better.

Feel free to start this test whenever you are ready. If it is not right now, you can stop reading now and come back later, or jump to the conclusion. If you are ready to take the quiz now, then proceed. The rules of the test are simple. Answer true or false to the statements below and then tally your score at the end. Remember to be truthful with your answers. You must remain objective and honest if you wish to truly get a reasonably accurate picture of your emotional intelligence.

Emotional Intelligence Quiz

You can identify what you are feeling most of the time and use extensive vocabulary to label it. You do not just say you are fine or not fine. Rather, you can clearly tell when you are feeling frustrated, disappointed, angry, overwhelmed, sad and so on. TRUE OR FALSE

You have never thought of yourself as self-absorbed, selfish or self-serving to the point where you do not care about what is going on around you. You are naturally curious to find out more about the people around you. Even if you are on the introverted side, you are happy to just observe to learn more about the people you meet in your everyday life. TRUE OR FALSE

You adapt easily to change. You are flexible in your thinking and you believe that change is as good as rest. You consider a change to be one of the more exciting things about life. TRUE OR FALSE

You are well aware of what your strengths are and can also clearly articulate your weakness. You know the people you get along with and the people who tend to grate on your nerves. TRUE OR FALSE

You are not easily fooled by people. You can easily judge a person's character even when they are trying to pass themselves off as something else. When it comes to people, very few things catch you by surprise. TRUE OR FALSE

You consider yourself to have a pretty thick skin. You do not walk around looking for things to be offended about. You can appreciate self-deprecating humor and do not mind being the butt of a joke unless it crosses respectable boundaries. TRUE OR FALSE

You learn from your mistakes without wallowing in them. You know that it is human to make mistakes from time to time. You see failure as a chance to learn and not as an indication of your self-worth. TRUE OR FALSE

You forgive those who have wronged you because you understand that it is the right thing to do for yourself. Grudges have no place in your life, and you move on easily from other people's transgressions against you. TRUE OR FALSE

Whenever you have to interact with a toxic person, you know how to handle them in a way that doesn't drain you emotionally. You try as much as possible to see things from the toxic person's perspective; however difficult this might be. You know how to protect your energy while handling toxic persons. TRUE OR FALSE

You do not pursue perfection because you understand that it is just a concept that exists in people's minds and not in reality. You do not demand perfection from yourself or your loved ones or even the people you work with. You simply want to be able to say that you did your best under the circumstances that you were in. TRUE OR FALSE

You know when you need to take a break from the stresses of everyday life, and you do so unapologetically. You have never felt obliged to be available to everyone and everything 24/7. You can switch off and unwind easily because you know it is important for your overall health as a physical, mental and emotional being. TRUE OR FALSE

You are cautious about what you allow inside your body. You know that what you eat has a significant role in how you feel and know better than to allow toxic stuff into your system. You watch what you eat without being obsessive about it. TRUE OR FALSE.

You consider sleep to be a priority. You do not stay up all night doing things that can be postponed to tomorrow. You know that sleep is an important part of your life because it allows your brain to rest and recharge. You tend to sleep at the same time every night. TRUE OR FALSE.

You speak kindly to yourself. Negative self-talk has no place in your life. You do not allow yourself to be harsh or judgmental toward yourself. You forgive yourself for your mistakes and look for ways to improve yourself instead of beating yourself up for every flaw that you might have. TRUE OR FALSE

You are confident in who you are and do not look to others for validation. You are proud of your accomplishments and know how to celebrate your wins, big and small. You do not lose your sleep over other people's opinions because you know the opinion that truly matters is what you think about yourself. You do not allow anyone to come into your life to steal away your joy. TRUE OR FALSE.

Chapter 4: Understanding Empathy

Empathy is the ability to understand the emotions of other people. The term empathy has also been used to describe the range of experience. Meanwhile, empathy is like keeping yourself in the situation of others and understand others' emotions about what they are thinking of. Psychologist Edward B. Titchener introduced this term in 1909. Many people watching other people in pain and sympathetically respond to them and give a clear vision to show that empathy is not a universal response to the suffering of another person.

You may think that it is the only type of empathy, but you may be wrong the empathy may be of three types let us have a look at this.

Types of Empathy

Affective Empathy

Affective empathy involves the ability to understand the emotions of another person and respond to them correctly. This kind of emotional understanding will show concern for another person's well-being.

Somatic Empathy

Somatic empathy involves a sort of having a physical reaction in response to what someone else is suffering or experiencing. Sometimes people may experience it physically what another person is feeling. It is like when you see someone else feeling embarrassed; then you might start a blushing or upset stomach.

Cognitive Empathy

It involves the ability to understand the mental state of another person and what they might be thinking in response to that condition. This is something that a psychologist refers to the theory of mind or thinking to understand what other people are thinking.

These are three types of empathy that a person must have to enhance their emotional intelligence. Without understanding the emotions of others, you are not able to understand the feeling and connection with other people. It is also necessary to enhance this empathy, as this is the second most important concept of emotional intelligence.

Explanation About Empathy

Human beings often load with several kinds of emotions, and they are often capable of selfish, even cruel behavior. But there have been certain theories proposed to explain empathy. According to neuroscientific theory, research has shown that the specific areas of the brain play a vital role in experiencing and responding to empathy. But mostly these are focused on cognitive empathy. Whereas according to emotional explanation, the philosopher Adam Smith prescribed that sympathy makes us able to understand things in better ways, which can involve a feeling of empathy for both real as well as an imaginary character. But according to prosocial explanation, the empathy served as an adaptive function and rules for the survival of species. It leads to the helping nature of people, which will directly help in benefiting social relationships. This is because we are natural creatures that experience emotions. Though different theories with different opinions but the context is the same as behaving and understanding the emotions. When people experience empathy, they will easily able to engage in social behavior and understand emotions in a better way.

What Benefits You Will Receive from Empathy

You can receive several benefits that you experience from empathy in which some of them are;

• Empathy allows you to build up a social connection with other people. You can understand it by thinking and feeling the situation of people. People will respond more easily in social situations.

- Empathizing with others will help you to control your emotions. The regulation and controlling of emotions are very important because it will allow you to control and manage what you are feeling and how you will express it in front of others.

- Empathy enhances the helping nature of an individual towards others. You are more likely to help others and yourself when you experience empathy.

The people who lack empathy will not be able to raise their emotional intelligence and often feel distressed and distracted, and they are not able to feel social connectivity. But have you ever wondered why people lack empathy?

There may be some reason why people lack empathy like;

- They fall to the victim as cognitive. Cognitive biases influence the way people assume the world around them. For instance, people attribute to the failure of other people while blaming their external factors. These sometimes makes you unable to understand and perceive the emotions of others

- The people also lack empathy who fall victim to trap them in their thinking by showing that they are different from other people and also do behave the same as they do.

The people who lack empathy also blame others for falling off and their circumstances. However, there are many reasons for lacking empathy. But there will be some reason for enhancing your empathy. You might also be thinking of how it will enhance your empathy? Can I do it on my own or I need some help?

Here's the thing, you are either an empathetic person or you're not. You cannot switch empathy off or on whenever you feel like it. You also cannot refer to that one time when you were empathetic in 2009 and then try to pass yourself as a person that is full of empathy. In order to be considered empathetic, you must commit to the skill in your everyday life in the same way that a person needs to tell the truth on more than one occasion before they can be considered truthful.

Lucky for you, becoming more empathetic is actually pretty easy. The biggest problem you will face on your journey toward empathy is yourself. Why? Because nine out of ten times, human beings tend to be self-absorbed. Empathy calls for you to leave some room in your life for other people and their thoughts and feelings. Here are some practical tips that you can apply in your life to get better at empathy:

Tip #1: Listen More Than You Talk

A Greek philosopher named Epictetus summarized the importance of listening more than talking like this: We have two ears and one mouth so that we can listen twice as much as we speak. Unfortunately, the world today is such that everybody is talking, and nobody seems to be listening. As long as you are talking, you will never really be able to tell what the other person is thinking or feeling. It is vital to take a pause and let other people talk because that is the main avenue through which thoughts, perspectives, and emotions can be communicated.

The best kind of listening is what is referred to as active listening. In other words, you must listen in a way that shows you are invested in the conversation. Sitting across from your conversation partner without saying a single word or while staring at them blankly will only make them feel uncomfortable and uncared for.

Active listening is pretty easy to achieve. The first thing you will need to do is put away all distractions aside. This means that you should not check your phone for Facebook updates while your friend or colleague is pouring their heart out to you. Checking your phone or doing other things while your friend is trying to have a heart-to-heart conversation with you is incredibly rude and in poor taste.

Instead, put away all distractions and focus your attention on the person speaking. Steady eye contact lets them know that they are important and that you are paying attention.

Now, you do not want to get all creepy with your eye contact to the extent where the other person begins to feel as if you are staring. A clever way to maintain appropriate eye contact is to lock eyes for five seconds and then look away. During this time, you should not be staring but rather gazing at them softly and with compassion.

However, ridiculous the story might be, never roll your eyes at a person who is opening up to you about something. Remember, they are feeling those emotions and thinking those thoughts because the experience was valid to them. Even if you believe crying over a dead goldfish is being overly dramatic, do not let these thoughts show on your face.

At the same time, you want to ensure that your active listening is peppered with just the right type of insightful questions. Ask open-ended and non-judgmental questions that help them draw out the root cause of their troubles. The idea of active listening is to stimulate the other party to arrive at a solution of their own making. All along, the other party will believe you solved their issue when in fact you just listened and gave them a platform to rant and bounce off the solutions they already had in their mind.

Let's say, for instance, your friend comes to you complaining about their partner. They have been together for two years and your friend is starting to feel as though she might not be the right partner for him based on how she has been behaving.

Friend: I don't know, it just feels as though she is taking me for granted.

You: Why do you say so?

Friend: Just the other day, I came home early and cleaned the house and did the laundry just so that she could relax and enjoy our date night. She cannot enjoy a date night as long as the unfinished household duties are at the back of her mind. And you know what she said?

You: What did she say?

Friend: Nothing. Absolutely nothing. She did not even act as if she had noticed all the hard work, I put into it.

You: Have you considered talking to her about it?

Friend: No. Not really. Do I have to?

You: It would help to get her perspective. What do you think her perspective is?

Friend: Well, she does the same household duties and I do not exactly hold a parade for her. I guess she did not see the big deal about me helping.

You: …

Friend: Oh yes, that's probably it. Why is it a big deal when I do it and not a big deal when she does it? I should probably check the social conditioning I have received on the expected gender roles in society.

You: Yes, like the fact that dads are parents too and not babysitters.

Friend: Ha-ha, exactly!

The whole point of this conversation is to show you that you can flow with your partner without imposing your beliefs and perspectives on them and still allowing them to get as much as they want off their chest. Soon enough, they will get to their a-ha moment where they solve their problem and go on their merry way. The fact of the matter is that you will get the credit for the solution and they will leave believing that you are the epitome of empathy.

Tip #2: Allow Yourself To Be Vulnerable

Being vulnerable is scary. Allowing other people to see the most sensitive parts of you can feel like making yourself a sitting duck. However, it is important that other people see you for the human being that you are. We are all flawed in our different ways, and we have our own fears and flaws. We feel things and we worry too. When someone is brave enough to be vulnerable with you, do yourself a favor and allow yourself to show that side of you that you would rather not show under any other circumstances. Self-disclosure is not intended to take away attention from the other party. Rather, it is a means of creating mutual understanding and making the other person feel that you understand what they are going through.

Let's say for instance your friend comes to you with marriage troubles. They have run into tough times with their spouse after using up the graces of the honeymoon period.

They are confused and cannot figure out what they need to do to fix things. One way of being vulnerable with them is letting them know that you also experienced the same phase when you got married. You are not trying to speak ill of your spouse or marriage, rather you are letting your friend know that it is human to go through what they are going through. After this disclosure, your friend will feel more connected to you and more trusting of what you have to say regarding their little problem.

Tip #3: Put Your Assumptions And Judgments Aside

We all have preconceived notions about things that are based on our own experiences and understanding of issues. When a friend is lamenting their misfortune, it can be tempting to rush to what we think we know in an effort to give them some comfort. Unfortunately, doing so is often a problem rather than a solution. As difficult as it may be, it is crucial that you put all your assumptions and judgments aside and focus on seeing the world as your friend sees it. Empathy is patient. It is not something that is rushed so that you can move on to the following person who needs it. Many times, empathy requires that you shut up about what you know and allow the other person to tell you what they know or think they know.

You will not always interact with people who share your world views. You might even have friends who believe in the most ridiculous things. Regardless, you must always be prepared to try and understand where they are coming from, instead of trying to change who they are.

Tip #4: Use Your Imagination

Chances are high that you will need to be empathetic toward people who are going through experiences that you have never gone through. In such instances, how are you expected to be empathetic? It's simple really. You just have to use your imagination. You do not need to have gone through labor to know that childbirth can be a very painful experience. You only need to imagine how excruciating it must be to use your body to bring forth a human being into the world.

You can fire up your imagination through reading and also by allowing your mind enough space to roam uninhibited. Your mind can take you on adventures that no airplane can, so whenever possible, let it guide you.

Of course, if you have not experienced something, do not use your imagination to lie to others. A man who uses his imagination to tell a woman in labor that he went through the same thing five years before is an outright liar. And you know what does not go well with empathy? Lies. Lies do not quite fit into the same space as empathy.

Tip #5: Tune Into The Welfare And Needs Of Others

Empathy is not something you throw at others when you wake up in the morning or when you show up at work. For there to be empathy, there has to be something that hinders the well-being of another person. You cannot empathize with another person simply because they exist. You can, however, empathize with another person about the heartbreak or hardship that they are going through.

Every human being has what they prioritize as their major needs outside of the universal basic needs. When these needs are not met, a person might consider themselves to be undergoing suffering. For example, if you have a need to be loved (and most people do), getting dumped by a significant other can induce a whole lot of suffering.

Chapter 6: Self-Awareness

In simple terms, self-awareness is knowing oneself. This may bring to mind the popular Greek Maxim, "Know thyself", which perhaps most simply insinuates self-awareness. Self-awareness is being aware of one's unique self as independent of one's environment and in relation to one's environment. Self-awareness involves understanding the unique elements that makeup oneself.

One can further describe self-awareness as being aware of what you are thinking, doing and experiencing.

It is as simple as this: if you had an opportunity to live with a replica of yourself for a day, would you recognize how you think, your usual physiological and emotional response to varying situations, the kinds of judgments you make, your abilities, your preferences?

At the core of self-awareness is self-focus. The study of self-awareness is believed to have been pioneered by Shelley Duval and Robert Wicklund in 1972 when they proposed the self-awareness theory. They proposed that focusing on oneself as opposed to one's environment would enable people to compare themselves with their own internal standards. These standards will become the benchmark with which individual thoughts, feelings, and actions are judged. The disparity in a person's character and internal standard leads to dissatisfaction in oneself. This dissatisfaction will, in turn, make that person constantly seek self-improvement or behavioral change in a bid to match his internal standards. Self-awareness is considered one of the most important tools for self-control.

There are three main points that are detailed when talking about self-awareness. The first is our emotional self-awareness. This is when people not only acknowledge their emotions, but they understand and trust their emotions. The second point is self-confidence, which is when people believe in themselves. They have the confidence that they will succeed in their goals and reach their full potential. The third point is self-assessment, which is when people know their strengths and weaknesses.

Your Self-Knowledge Will Grow

We all think we know ourselves well. However, there are a lot of characteristics that we are unaware of because we aren't mindful of our emotions. The way we feel tells people more about us than anything else. While you know you are a good person, you don't know all of the characteristics which make you a good person. You might think of the times you donated to a charity or helped a friend, but what else makes you a good person?

When you strengthen your self-knowledge, you will be able to help yourself problem-solve. We all struggle to find out why we lack motivation from time to time or why we react a certain way. By building your self-awareness, you will be able to learn about your triggers and how they affect you at a deeper level.

Your Relationships Become Stronger

When you are self-aware, you strengthen your communication skills. You are more aware of your emotions, which makes you want to discuss them. You will also understand your feelings. You will know why you feel a certain way and be able to figure out what you can do to improve the situation or your emotions. Furthermore, you become more aware of the way other people are feeling. You know when they are feeling sad, angry, or happy, and you are able to empathize with their emotions.

You Become More Mindful

When you strengthen your self-awareness, you not only become more mindful of your actions but also your surroundings. Mindfulness is remaining in the present moment. You don't let your mind wander to the point of forgetting about what you are doing.

For example, if you drive the same route to work every day, you might find there are sometimes where you wonder how you got to work so quickly. You think back to your drive and don't remember passing half of the landmarks. This is because you allowed yourself to get lost in your thoughts, which means you become mindless.

You Will Become More Motivated

Motivation is something that everyone possesses. The key is how strong our motivation is to reach our deadlines, goals, and dreams. We find ourselves struggling with motivation for various reasons. When you become self-aware, you can learn why you struggle with it. You will analyze your actions, thoughts, and see when your motivation started to deteriorate. You can then take steps to keep yourself from becoming unmotivated frequently. You will also be able to realize when you are about to lose some of your motivation. This will allow you to switch gears. For example, you will start to take care of yourself. Through your analysis, you might realize that you don't take enough breaks. Once you start scheduling a few more breaks throughout your day, you become more motivated.

Your Mistakes Will Help You Grow

Another benefit of self-awareness is that you will come to learn that your mistakes help you grow. No one likes to make mistakes, which is why most people hold on to their mistakes for a long period of time, sometimes for years or even the rest of their lives. The truth is, while the mistake to you is a big deal, it isn't that huge for the other person. Most people understand that mistakes are made, and they want you to learn from your mistakes.

With self-awareness, you will become more cognizant of your mistakes. But you will also become more aware of why you made a mistake and how you can keep yourself from repeating it. When you are able to think about why the mistake happened, you will find yourself growing from your mistakes.

You Will Learn Your Limits

We all have limits. These limits tell us when we are becoming overwhelmed and need to take a step back. Our limits tell us how much of one situation or another we can handle. Your boundaries will often tell you what your triggers are. For example, through analyzing your actions, you realize that you are quick to anger when you are stressed. Therefore, you are able to look at what factors make you feel stressed and create better limits for yourself. When you find yourself struggling to maintain your boundaries, you are able to look at your actions and find ways to help you enforce your limits.

How to Strengthen Your Self-Awareness

Don't worry if you are one of the millions of people who struggle with self-awareness. Like the other three pillars of emotional intelligence, self-awareness is a characteristic that you can develop over time.

One of the first steps to take to develop your self-awareness is acknowledging your emotions when they occur, and critically analyzing why your emotions have arisen. This is the general process when it comes to developing self-awareness. Once you start to get a grip on your emotions, you are able to notice your strengths and weaknesses. From there, you can use your strengths to takes steps toward reaching your ideal person. You can acknowledge your weaknesses and continue to build on them.

Keep a Journal

I wouldn't spend too much time on how to keep a journal. This is one of the best ways to get to become aware of your emotions, actions, and thoughts.

Get Out of Your Comfort Zone

We all create a comfort zone. This is our security that keeps us from discouraging emotions. In order to become more self-aware, you need to face these uncomfortable situations and emotions. You need to find ways to handle these emotions, so when they come up, you're not surprised, and you can think and act rationally. Plus, getting out of your comfort zone will allow you to see your true potential.

Take Another Look at Your Values

Values are the rules and guidelines we were taught as children, learned from a mentor, or established ourselves. Our values help us reach our ideal self. However, we sometimes find ourselves ignoring our values for various reasons. For example, we might find ourselves following a bad habit which goes against our values. You might also start to hang out with someone who doesn't necessarily follow your values. Because you like this person, you find yourself following their values instead.

To get a better idea of ourselves and develop our emotional intelligence, it's important to review our values from time to time. Analyze your actions and compare them to your values. Where can you improve? Is there a value you've pushed off to the side for a reason? Ask yourself if you like the change. If you do, then continue on your path. If you don't like the change, then take a look at your actions and see how you can make them match up to your values.

Predict Your Emotions

Another way to strengthen your self-awareness is to try to predict your emotions in certain situations. To do this, you want to think about situations you can find yourself in. For example, you can think about how you will react when you realize you won't make a deadline for your project. If you have found yourself in a position like this before, you can think about how you reacted. If you haven't been in the situation before, you will want to ask yourself how you believe you will act. Are you going to be angry? If so, why? Do you believe you would be excited? Don't overthink the way you will react; simply allow the probable emotions to come to your mind.

Once you have a situation and know your emotions, you can think rationally about the way you want to react. Even if you believe anger is a rational emotion for the situation, you want to think about how you will react to this anger.

Create a List of Your Roles

We all have several roles in our lives. For example, you are someone's child, you might also be someone's sibling, co-worker, parent, etc. Whatever role you have, write it down. Think of everything from being a godparent to an acquaintance to someone at your job. You even want to think about your hobbies. For example, if you like to draw or paint in your spare time, you are an artist. If you like to write, you are a writer. Write down every single one of these roles. One of the perfect places to write this list would be in your journal. Leave space so you can add to the list and there will be a time you become more aware of one of your roles. For instance, if you have neighbors, one of your roles is being a neighbor. This is often a role people overlook.

Don't just create a list of roles. You also want to describe them. Discuss your responsibilities with each role and how they make you feel.

Be honest with how each role makes you feel. After all, you don't need to share this list with anyone. It's to help you get to know yourself and your emotions better.

Get to Know Your Triggers

We all have triggers. These are the actions other people take that make us react in a certain way. For example, you become angry after learning your friend lied to you. While you still remain in contact with them, you become withdrawn and don't trust them as much. Therefore, lying is one of your triggers.

You will be able to find out your triggers once you start to recognize your reactions or thoughts to situations. When you take time to ask yourself, "Why do I feel angry?" or "Why do I feel sad?" You will be able to pinpoint the cause of your emotions, which is your trigger.

Look at the Bigger Picture

Even though we don't like to admit it, we have a very narrow view of the world. Humans naturally think that they are the most important person in the world. We often feel like our problems are bigger than they are. If we start to take a bird's eye view of our situations, we are able to look deeper within ourselves.

By looking at the bigger picture, you will be able to step in before you react. You will start to recognize your triggers, which will allow you to take a step back and think about your next steps. This will also allow you to learn a little more about your reactions to your triggers.

Pay Attention to Your Emotions with the Media

Media is all around us. It doesn't matter if we are checking out social media on our phone or turning on the television or radio. You are going to hear about any local and national news no matter how hard you try to scroll past it.

One of the best ways to learn about your emotions is through the headlines you read and hear. It's hard for us to disguise our emotions when we are told information we never knew about before.

Therefore, when you hear about an assault in your area, you are going to react in a natural way. You are not going to think about your reaction.

When you hear the news and you react, take a step back and think about your reaction. You can write about this moment in your journal to give you a chance to understand your reaction. Once you analyze your reaction, ask yourself if this is how you want to react to that news. Is there something that you want to change? Remember to be honest with yourself. Sometimes we aren't proud of our emotions. This doesn't mean they are wrong, or that we shouldn't feel them. It just means that we want to find a way to acknowledge them and learn how to control them.

Your environment has a big impact on the way that you feel. The place you spend most of your time is going to weigh on your mind subconsciously. If you surround yourself in that kind of environment constantly, it's all you're going to know and all that you can identify with. You may not be actively thinking about your surroundings, but it's there in the back of your mind.

If you find it hard to remain positive throughout the day, do a quick scan of your surroundings, and observe what the sources of negativity may be. Your cluttered workstation? The toxic colleague who is constantly complaining and talking negatively about other colleagues behind their back? Maybe that pile of paperwork you've been postponing for a while now and haven't gotten around to doing yet. Once you've identified a potential source, ask yourself what you can do to rectify the problem. Can the source be removed entirely? If it can't what else could you do to spend less time around this negative source in a week? Cultivate a positive environment for yourself, one that is going to make it easier to nurture these positive emotions and help you grow. Change your environment, and you change your emotions.

Other things influence your emotions:

Music

Music can affect both our physiology as well as our emotions. It is a ubiquitous phenomenon. We make music, and almost everyone listens to music daily. Music sets the right mood, bonds you with others, and it even creates shared experiences. Listening to the music that you and a friend associate the memory with can bring you right back to that moment as though you were reliving it all over again. So, why does music have the power to influence our emotions?

Music has the power to instantly change your mood. Try a little experiment on your own. Pick two pieces of music, one happy and upbeat, and the other more ominous and gloomier. Close your eyes and play excerpts from those two pieces and observe the way you feel as you immerse yourself in the melody. Did you notice how you automatically started bobbing your head a little to the upbeat, happy music? Maybe even smiled or did a little jig on the spot?

Whereas the more ominous music probably made you feel a little sad, and you couldn't wait to switch back to the upbeat music again because listening to that felt so much better. Why does music influence the brain in this way and more importantly, how do we use this to our advantage to feel happier?

Some research suggests that we spend approximately 40% of our waking hours listening to music. As humans, we can create, respond, and move to the beat of the music. We grow up surrounded by sound and music. It is in our environment everywhere we go and a part of who we are. Children clap their hands when they hear music even before they learn how to talk. We play music to get over a breakup. We dance and have a good time when we're singing along to our favorite tunes. Music in the movies can send chills down your spine, create excitement, even give you goosebumps when it's time with the scene perfectly. This has a lot to do with the connection between music and the brain

When you're listening to a song you find pleasurable, it activates the reward area system in your brain the same way drugs and alcohol do. The right hemisphere of the brain is given preferential treatment when it is activated as we listen to a song, we find particularly emotional. Interestingly enough, this area of the brain is still activated even if you're just imagining the tune in your mind. Music is renowned for its therapeutic properties too, proving successful in the treatment of clinical depression and seizures. If you want to deliberately regulate your emotions, it turns out music might be the way to go.

Music influences our emotions because of the expressive emotional movement it creates. Every emotion we express has an accompanying movement or expression. When we're happy, our tone of voice is higher, we sound jubilant, and we probably walk with a spring in our step. Someone who is unhappy, on the other hand, is going to sound less than enthused and probably drag their feet when they walk.

Just by listening or visualizing the way the footsteps sound, you can gauge the emotion the person might be feeling. Music affects our emotions because of the expressive movement they create. Like the way you feel like bobbing your head and dancing automatically as soon as you hear something upbeat and lively.

Conclusion

Part of being emotionally intelligent is not just knowing what to do, but actually doing it. Truly emotionally intelligent people know that it is a lot harder to actually do what you say you are going to do, or to put your knowledge into work than it seems. As a result, they place a great deal of their personal effort in learning about how they can actually enforce what they know to be true about emotional intelligence.

You need to start practicing becoming self-aware, recognizing your own emotions, and becoming deeply familiar with what emotional experiences and expressions feel like and look like for you. This way, you can develop a deeper awareness of your emotions and start creating even more space for you to increase your emotional intelligence.

When you become aware of your emotions, you also need to focus on how you can respond to your emotions in a way that harnesses them and supports you in using them toward achieving your goals. Remember, it is important that you always choose to respond to your emotions, and not react to them, as this is how you refrain from experiencing emotional hijacking. Emotional hijacking is what happens when you act on your impulses and your emotions take over to the point where you struggle to experience logic and reason around your emotional experiences. While everyone can experience emotional hijacking, it is far more common in people with a lower EQ who struggle to actually navigate their emotions in a healthy manner.

Despite how cheesy it may seem, keeping a journal truly is a powerful opportunity for you to track, monitor, learn about, and work with your emotions. A journal will support you with understanding how your emotions work and why they work that way so that you can begin to find new ways to navigate your emotions. These new methods for mnapproaching your emotions will support you with creating a much stronger method for logically, rationally, and intentionally navigating your emotions for your own personal benefit.

Remember that this is not something you develop overnight, or even over a few weeks, but instead is something that you develop and improve over your lifetime. There is always room for growth and improvement with emotional intelligence, and if you truly want to master self-discipline you are going to need to continually focus on learning and mastering emotional intelligence, too.

Emotions are predominantly sited in the unconscious implying that we have significantly less control of how emotions occur.

It is for this reason, that body language is critical in determining the true status of an individual as the unconscious impacts much of the body language. With all these developments, emotions are highly manageable.

Many people are victims of settling for an unhappy life not because they want to but rather, a sense of helplessness about their circumstances. They don't think it's possible to change moods so easily, they think it's a difficult and even worse, an impossible task. Guess what! It's not even a task at all, it's just a way of life. The way an unhappy mind works is that it thinks its circumstances are divine- that their mental suffering is punishment from the Gods for being naughty at one point in their lives. An unhappy mind always focuses on the negative. The problem is that they are looking for happiness in the wrong places.

This has nothing to do with perfection, it's more to do with caring for your health- mentally, physically and emotionally. Although a happy state doesn't mean complete eradication of unhappy feelings. Having predominant unhappy emotions causes harm to both a person and the environment. Unhappy people are always to be avoided- nobody likes to be around negative energy. Leaders ensure to be on their brightest mood- not faking but genuine happy feelings. They are able to discipline their selves by these simple daily acts in which the reward promises a serene, peaceful and happy life.

MENTAL TOUGHNESS

Introduction

Mental strength is a going worry among people, associations, and nations. It is a significant subject of extraordinary reference, and with the consistent increment in total populace and rivalry, the presence of firm rivalry which cuts over each division of the world economy and business has clarified that each individual who expects to endure must have to learn the rudiments of being a survivor.

It is interesting to know that long age standing discovery of the term "survival of the fittest" has come to prove the existence of a common factor that leads to surviving, and that is the "fittest." Now the question you should be asking yourself right now is, "am I mentally tough enough to fit into the hard situations in society?"

Therefore, mental toughness is not just a topic; it affects every individual on the planet today; on the off chance that you are intense intellectually, the odds of your endurance in the advanced also quick-creating world are sure. As the population continues to increase and with limited jobs, how do you intend to survive this information age?

This is the ideal opportunity for you to search internally and know how you can genuinely turn out to be intellectually intense. I will open up your eyes to the facts and actual reality of the nature of the world, and you will see what is happening.

Then you will have the option to figure out where you have a place by and by, how you can free yourself from where you are, and graduate or jump to your chosen business throughout everyday life.

You can take your destiny into your own hands and chose where to be and when to be and achieve greater heights. Mental toughness is associated with certain factors and characteristics that will bring out the very best when you decide to make a change.

The issues identifying with progress can be found in individuals with mental durability. Thus, influential individuals are typically intellectually intense, there is something that drives them to turn out to be exceptionally fruitful, and one of those variables is identified with being intellectually extreme.

It will make you rediscover yourself and become a champion by right and merit.

Nothing comes simple in life aside from you are brought into the world lucky and wealthy, and even as at that, you may lose the wealth that you have acquired if you don't have the mental strength or arranged to accept accountability for your life, for some have had the chance of acquiring incredible riches. They are unable to expand with it or manage it well.

Being mentally tough is for both young and adults.

So take the opportunity provided here and equip yourself for that challenge that comes your way.

Be a different person, stand out from the crowd, be a leader in your area of life and become the champion that you have always dreamed of becoming; the time is now. Follow the simple steps to become mentally tough to be a survivor and a victorious person.

Chapter 1: What Is Mental Toughness?

Mental toughness is the strength of the mind to fight against circumstantial pressures, stressors, and challenges in which you are staying. It is an exercise of the mental power to overcome the shortcomings that create problems for you without blaming others. When practiced regularly, mental power exercise helps you perform better to a large extent against the prevailing difficulties and barriers. Today's hustle and bustle activities have indeed made life more complex and stressful. If you look 100 years back, you could see that people would live their lives in a poor habitable and dietary condition. They were unhappy but not stressed because they were mentally sound and robust. Today people feel more stressed than their ancestors due to a lack of mental strength.

Key Components of Mental Toughness

The main characteristics of mental ability can be sub-divided into three components, viz., emotion, behavior, and confidence. These three components play a crucial role in helping you become a more resilient and self-driven person. Let's discuss the components one by one.

Emotion: It is a state of mind that involves a feeling in a situation or relationship with other people. Your feelings in a case affect almost all activities surrounding you. It extends from home to your workplace and even to your societal relationships. Similarly, the relationship with others consists of a relationship with your family members and even your colleagues and friends. It also includes your neighbors. Without emotion, you cannot connect with the people or the situation.

Let's take an example. You have prepared a new project for your company in which you are emotionally involved. You have been asked to give a demo of the project before colleagues and higher officials. It can bring a new opportunity to expand the company's business and profit. If the project becomes successful, the chances are that you will be promoted to a superior post. Here, emotion is your mental strength. When you demonstrate your project, few colleagues pass on negative remarks and opinions, asking some questions. You strongly argue in favor of your project logically, and at the same time, you ignore their questions and do not hear them with due respect. Being ignored by you, colleagues, and higher officials can reject the project even though it has a new possibility. Here, emotion is your mental weakness.

From the above example, it can be said when emotion is mental strength, it can create opportunity, but when it is a weakness, it might hinder your success. Here, emotional weakness has dramatically affected the professional attitude, and the chance of the new project is lost in all respect. So, it would help if you controlled your emotion before emotion controls you and proactively express your emotion to the colleagues to make the best choice.

So, to achieve a strong mental ability and resiliency to overcome the weakness and eliminate any threat to your growth, you have to exercise and perform the followings three skills:

Apply emotion proactively to your task only and not to the people or situation. Focus on thinking to solve the problems. It is a mental exercise that increases mental strength and controls emotions.

Identifying your own emotion is not enough. Identifying other people's emotions on the same issue is equally important to reach a conclusive decision. This mental exercise increases your emotional intelligence to understand and manage both the people and the situation.

When you can manage and control your own emotion, you will achieve the ability to appreciate or cool off other people's emotions. This exercise creates an emotional awareness in you, and emotional intelligence increases your level of performance.

Behavior: The skills you develop in exercising the three above-mentioned mental exercises will help in all activities and relationships in your life. You will feel more considerate and compassionate, which will help you to build a strong bonding in any relationship. Your behavioral characteristics will rebuild.

However, neither the people nor the situations allow you to keep going on. When one barrier after another comes, or all doors start closing, being a mentally strong person, you should not continue the task, which may cost you more. It will be wise to quit the situation humbly and compromise the wrong path as it might lead to failure.

Confidence: Confidence is believing in your mental strength and ability but not in an aggressive attitude. While you are exercising emotional intelligence and rebuilding behavioral characteristics successfully, you will handle any social events, work, relationships, and family empathetically.

Researchers have shown a person's brain thinks about 50,000 to 70,000 issues a day, in which you boost yourself on thousands of cases while avoiding the rest with a fear of failure. So, exercising mental strength helps your brain think the issues differently to be more productive instead of leaving the problems due to fear of failure and sporting an armor of confidence.

Importance of Mental Toughness

Every person has mental strength, but it varies on the level of toughness that a person possesses. The higher the level you own, the bigger the goals you achieve. Here, you will find the importance of mental toughness to be more productive and successful in life.

Mental Strength Promotes Your Armor of Confidence – When you ambitiously run behind a long-term goal, you may likely experience self-doubt at any point in time. Then you should ask yourself about the ifs and buts that have brought a negative wave in you and created a low level of confidence. If you are mentally sound and robust, analyze the negative thoughts, adjust your attitude towards people and situation, and start working on marching forward towards the goal. This will promote your mental strength with the armor of confidence and recharge motivation.

Mental Ability Drives the Motivation – When you stick to the goal, motivation plays a crucial role as a driving force in you to keep moving on. However, psychologists have shown that the graph of the basis of a person is not linear; instead, it is a wave-like curved line. So, it has ups and downs. When motivation is at its peak, your mental strength is high enough to handle the people and situation. When it is at the bottom, you need to re-examine cognitive Ability by digging deep into yourself to rediscover yourself. This practice will tune your motivation further.

Mental Toughness Tunes Unhealthy Criticism – Exercising mental strength helps you out to tune unhelpful advice and unworthy criticism from the people surrounding you. The cognitive Ability helps to stay firm with the truth with values and emotions regardless of the criticisms thrown at you unless you make a mistake.

Mental Power Helps to Learn from Mistakes – When people judge something wrong, decide something wrong, apply something wrong, a mistake happens. Suppressing the error creates another wrongful action.

A mentally sound person accepts mistakes humbly, analyzes the error, identifies the error cause, and repairs the damage. This way, you can get the courage to learn from the error.

Mental Strength Imparts Courage – In a long-term journey towards a goal, you may not stay all the time in a comfort zone. Regularly practicing mental strength helps you develop the courage to go beyond and extend the boundary within your tolerance limit. However, you should keep a backup in case of any setback to avoid discomfort. This can increase your courage to move forward resiliently.

Mental Power Helps to Bounce Back in Case of Setback – Mentally weak people give up in case of any setback or failure without giving any effort for the next time. On the contrary, mentally strong people think that failures are the pillars of success. People work their mental Power, analyze the causes of failure, tune the emotions, reconstruct the thoughts, and get back from the failure by performing better than before. People with high mental Power have a high level of self-worth and high tolerance level to accept failure regardless of being ridiculed by others. Regular mental power exercise gives you the emotional strength to treat failure as throwing a stone to future success.

Mental Power Controls Emotion: In the paragraph "Mental Ability Drives Motivation" above, it is already explained that motivation can be high and low. Similarly, emotion gets tall and quiet during the journey of activities in life.

Thus, success also brings high and soft as it is synchronized with emotion and motivation. If you do not have the skill to control the feelings, the temptation of the situation will hold you, and gratification from your life will be a far-fetched dream. This situation invites immeasurable risks. Exercising mental Power is the critical way to control your emotion, boost motivation, and build the path of success. Building mental power also helps you develop a solid resilience to overcome failure and bounce back with complete confidence. This is an inevitable necessity of life to face challenges in any sphere of activities.

Chapter 2: Characteristics of Mentally Tough People

We as a whole would have run over explicit focuses in our lives where our psychological sturdiness was scrutinized. It might have come in the form of a toxic friendship, a dead-end job, or a destructive relationship. Regardless of the challenge, you need to be strong, change your perspective towards life, and be proactive if you want to be successful. It sounds pretty simple. Who wouldn't want good friends, a happy relationship, and a satisfactory job? It isn't easy to be mentally tough when you feel stuck. The ability to break free of the bonds holding you back and creating your path takes courage that only mentally tough ones possess. It is interesting to see how intellectually extreme individuals put themselves beside every other person. Where others see an incomprehensible obstacle to cross, they know a test that should be survived.

In 1914, Thomas Edison's factory burned down, and several precious prototypes were destroyed, and the damage amounted to $23 million. Edison's reply to this unfortunate incident was, "Thank heavens every one of our missteps was caught fire. Presently we can begin new once more." Edison's response sums up what mental toughness is about. It is about having a positive outlook towards life, seeing opportunities, and taking the necessary action even when things start looking bleak. There are a couple of characteristics that all those who are mentally tough share, and they are as follows.

1: They Are Emotionally Intelligent

One of the building blocks of mental toughness is emotional intelligence. If you cannot understand and tolerate negative emotions and turn them into something productive, you cannot be mentally tough. Moments that put your mental toughness to test are testing your emotional quotient as well. Your IQ or intelligence quotient is fixed, whereas your EQ, or your emotional quotient (emotional intelligence), isn't, and it can be improved if you are willing to work on it. When you can analyze a situation objectively and not emotionally, you will make a better decision. If positive and negative emotions can easily sway you, you open yourself up for manipulation.

2: Confident

Your mentality can influence your ability to achieve success. Mentally tough people will firmly believe in Ford's notion. If you don't feel confident about yourself and your skills, you cannot expect someone else to feel sure about you. People often tend to mask their insecurities by merely projecting confidence instead of being confident. A confident person will always stand apart compared to all those who are indecisive, doubtful, and skittish. Their faith often inspires others as well.

3: They Are Good at Neutralizing Toxic People

It is exhausting and quite frustrating to deal with difficult people. Mentally tough people can take control of their interactions with toxic elements around them. If you want to be mentally strong, you should be able to identify negative emotions like anger and not let these feelings get the better of you. Take a moment and try to see the problematic person's point of view and try finding some common ground or a solution to the problem. Even when things are going south, a mentally tough person will prevent the toxic person from bringing them down.

4: They Can Embrace Change

Mentally tough people are pretty dynamic and are capable of embracing change. They embrace change and adapt themselves to any situation as well. They are well aware that the fear of change can stall their progress and prevent them from achieving success. A mentally tough person would look for any likely change and devise a plan of action that will help him make the most of the possible change. Keep an open mind and check for ways to capitalize on such change. You will be setting yourself up for failure if you keep doing things in the same way while ignoring any changes.

5: They Can Say No

If you want to reduce your chances of experiencing stress and depression, then learn to say "no." Saying "no" is, in fact, good for your mental health. Communicating "no" not only helps you in avowing unnecessary burden, but it will also help you in prioritizing your work and cutting off toxic people from your life. While saying no, a mentally strong person would steer clear of phrases like "I don't think" or "I am not certain." Whenever you are saying no, say it with confidence.

Learning to say no will help a person concentrate better on the tasks they have on hand instead of taking on more work than they might honor.

The mentally tough ones have good self-control, and they can say "no" not just to others but to themselves as well. Stop taking action impulsively and instead follow the rules of delayed gratification.

"No" is quite a powerful word, and it can help you in protecting your valuable time. Don't make use of phrases like "I am not sure," "I don't think I will be able to," and so on. If you won't take on any additional commitments or feel that you have got a lot of work to do, then don't take on any new obligations. Just say no. If you get stuck with something that you won't do, this will only create additional stress and pressure and eventually burn you.

6: They Know That Fear Causes Regret

If you never take a chance, you will never know what could have happened. Unless you try, you can't say. Instead of lamenting over the opportunities you didn't take, it is better to control your fears and make the leap. Don't be afraid of taking risks. However, this doesn't mean that you will take on any risk blindly. Death isn't the answer. The worst thing is regret. Regret about the things that you could have and should have done. Guilt can eat you up from within. Mentally tough people know that fear causes disappointment, which is where self-awareness steps in. Mindfulness will help you in adjusting among abiding and recalling. Harping for a long time on your mix-ups will make you on edge and aware, though overlooking them builds your odds of rehashing them everywhere.

7: They Can Embrace Failure

Failures are widespread, and everyone has their fair share of losses in their lives. Mentally tough people are capable of embracing their failures. No one can experience success without knowing what failure is. When you can acknowledge that you are on the wrong path, are aware of the mistakes you are making, and can embrace your losses, you will only achieve success.

8: They Can Let Go of All the Wrongs

Mentally tough people are aware that what you concentrate on will determine your emotional state. When you stay fixated on a problem that you are facing, you tend to create and drag on the negative emotions, which stalls your progress. When you start focusing on yourself and the circumstances you are in, you will feel a sense of personal efficacy, which helps generate positive emotions and improve your productivity. Keep your mistakes at a safe distance, learn and adapt from them, but stop dwelling on them for prolonged periods.

9: No One Can Limit Their Joy

If you derive your sense of pleasure and satisfaction from comparing yourself to others, your happiness no longer lies in your own hands. You are essentially giving up control of your happiness to someone else. Those who are mentally tough would feel good about something regardless of what others think. Please take people's opinions with a pinch of salt. Mentally strong people know that irrespective of what others think of them at any given point in time, one thing is for sure, they are never really as good or bad as others seem to believe. It would help if you stopped comparing yourself to others; physically, socially, or financially. You will always have people around you who have got more money than you have, have a better social life, or are more successful in their respective careers. Instead of focusing on what others have, you should focus on yourself.

10: They Won't Limit the Happiness of Others

A mentally tough person won't be critical of others because he or she knows that everyone has something different to offer. Jealousy, envy, and resentment can drain you out of your energy and suck the life out of you. Mentally tough people will never waste their energy worrying about what others think of them, and they certainly won't spend their energy sizing others up. Instead of allowing all sorts of negative emotions to manifest, you should concentrate on channelizing your energy towards something more positive and something beneficial. Celebrate others' successes and rejoice in their victories; it won't diminish your accomplishments. Learn to radiate positivity.

Chapter 3: Assessing Your Mental Strength

Are you mentally tough? Do you wish to be mentally tough? If so, why? There are numerous misconceptions about what mental toughness means and why everyone should master its art. Mental toughness is about having the ability to manage your emotion in the face of adversities and the ability to uphold productive behavior always despite the circumstance surrounding your environment. Like developing physical strength, building mental strength requires a lot of hard work, time, and energy input.

Additionally, just like you track your physical workout progress, it is also advisable to track your mental toughness progress and determine the areas where you have improved and where you need to put in more effort. However, assessing mental toughness may not be as simple and straightforward as setting physical workout results. This is because you can determine a person's physical strength and workout progress just by looking at them, which is not the case for mental toughness assessment. In some cases, a qualified psychologist may be required to conduct a thorough mental toughness assessment on an individual, especially among elite athletes who rely on their mental toughness to win. However, for people who are trying to develop mental toughness for their benefit, it is possible to assess progress at home by answering a few crucial questions as noted herein. The effects of mental toughness are felt by an individual and are more internal than external. Therefore, an honest self-reflection exercise is paramount to developing and maintaining mental toughness. It helps understand your strengths and determine the areas that require more input to enhance your mental strength.

The personal conversations you have when alone are core ate boosting your overall well-being. Though it is common to be harsh to yourself at times, talking to yourself about some of the issues that affect you or the challenges you may be facing like you would to a best friend is very healthy and core at developing mental toughness. However, it is essential to reason realistically because having negative thoughts can always be damaging and prevent you from being productive or achieving your goals. On the other hand, too many positive reviews can also be harmful because they do not prepare for negative eventualities. Your brain is only designed for success and not failure. So, it will be hard for you to accept and move on when a failure occurs.

How Do You Keep Your Behavior Productive?

Developing mental toughness is all about understanding when you should change your behavior and when you should change your environment as well. There are times when you can work on improving self-discipline to deal with temptation better, and there are times when the only thing you can do is change your environment so that you can bring out the best in you. Other times, productive behavior entails doing the things you would not wish to do. It may also be about performing behavioral experiments that help you prove your pessimistic predictions false. Mastering mental toughness helps a person respond to different hardships effectively and overcome obstacles with ease. This way, you can make better choices about yourself and when your decisions are not very popular.

This can be easily misdiagnosed, and it occurs more often than we think. This enables consumers to create a level of self-conception that is hard, perhaps impossible, to accomplish by other means. It allows them to work with customers. In addition, this measure is a normative measure that allows for evaluating where a change happened before and after a program. Similarly, assess mental toughness and aggregated outcomes with organizations and entire populations is feasible to gather views on a central aspect of culture. That is essential as well. There is a clear link between cultural and behavioral impact. While the study demonstrates that our mental toughness has a genetic factor, our mental toughness reflects our experiences. We have learned to be mentally challenging or emotionally delicate based on the unfolded events in our lives. Consider the present "snowflake generation" discussion. It's a warning. There is no implicit necessity for our mental hardness to evolve. Instead, self-awareness and reflection are essential to our lifelong journey. Some mentally delicate people will gladly stay as they are and profit from studying and adopting methods that the mentally difficult ones will embrace.

Chapter 4: How to Develop Habits and Set the Right Goals

Transformative habits are habits that you can employ in your everyday life that considerably aid growth. Adopting these habits and putting them to work in your life will put you on the right track to learn all there is to know about something, use it to its fullest, and have an endlessly renewable interest in that subject.

Let's look at five transformative habits to keep when learning about something.

Have a burning passion.

People who perform the best are the people who love what they do. As a result of that love for what they do, they spend time and energy on it that everyone cheering them on will never see. Being devoted to your craft means more than simply being there when others can see you.

Take the lead, stay interested in your passion, and develop a passion for being the best at what you do.

Dream big.

The dreams we have for the future are what keep us working hard and running toward the horizon. Knowing that bigger and better things wait for us on the other side of the hurdles we face is a huge motivator that will help us to smash through those hurdles. There is nothing wrong with aiming for the stars with your set goals. They will only serve to help you.

As you find your dreams set on higher and higher goals, you will find that your understanding and your skill will continue to grow to support those goals. These things are connected, and aspiring to be more does have a massive effect on your growth and development.

Being dedicated to a craft, job, task, hobby, sport, etc., means more than being present for the parts that others will see. It means being there for more than just the fun parts, the glory, the excitement, and the joy. It means being there for the mundane, boring, tedious, grinding details of it as well. Self-discipline is a huge part of success in general.

If you can control yourself to do what needs to be done, when it needs to be done, you have a better chance of reaching unimaginable success.

Be willing to be coached.

This is important, so pay close attention: no one ever learned anything by acting like they already understood it. Be willing to be taught, be ready to learn, be willing to be corrected, be willing to be corrected, and always be on the lookout for new information on the subject of your interest. There is always a way to learn something you want to know.

The most crucial point is to be willing to let someone teach you something. No one will think less of you for the questions you ask when learning your skills. If you let your pride get the better of you while you're learning your craft, however, you will lose the respect of others, as well as their support. You will also be cutting yourself off at the knees regarding further improvement or honing of skills.

Desire to be challenged.

Once you allow the challenging aspects of your craft to leave the area, you will lose interest. The best way to keep a muscle toned is to flex it. Think of your brain like the muscle it is. It needs to be worked and challenged and exercised to retain what it's learned its elasticity, and its ability to make things work!

Setting challenges and goals for yourself can give you things to work toward, and it can keep your interest fresh! Remember that if there is no one with whom you can compete, you can always compete with your former self.

While we're on the subject of habits, some habits could benefit you as someone looking to succeed. These are known as the habits of influential people. They are the habits that, if you keep them, they'll keep you on the right track and primed for success!

Let's take a look at those habits now.

Don't work yourself to death.

Striving for a sustainable lifestyle in which you can get all your work done while still affording adequate time to take care of yourself is the most important thing.

If you can achieve this, you can ensure that you will be effective in the long term. This is a sustainable, recuperative, and rechargeable approach that allows you to take the time to do the things you need to do. Work is not your entire life, and you would do well to treat it that way!

Be proactive.

Getting out ahead of things is always a great idea. Don't live your life hopping from urgent task to urgent task. Take the time to look ahead, see what will be needed shortly, and account for it. This will leave you with fewer fires to put out.

Have a clear vision for what your future should be and systematically work toward bringing it into being!

Have your ending in mind from the start.

If you know where you're going, you can more accurately decide what you should be doing right now.

Prioritize

It can be easy to get snowed under with all the things that lay before you, ready to be done. To stave off that panic, the most efficient thing to do is prioritize. Find the things that need to come first and get a jump on them. As you systematically work through the things that need to get done right now, you will find yourself rolling into the future and setting up tasks that will need to be done later.

Something could have a timestamp on it that tells you it needs to get done right now. However, it might be something that you can delegate, or it might not be necessary for you at all to complete. Be sure to factor this into your evaluation before working on it.

Keep it fair.

When you're looking at the outcome of any arrangement that you're looking to make, don't try to come out on top. Coming out on top is a concept that movie villains use, and it doesn't do anyone any actual good. Through litigation and the trouble it takes to manipulate people into these situations, it's not even worth it in the end.

Go into partnerships and arrangements with the idea that they are mutually beneficial for both of you.

If you can achieve that, you're doing great. Having an honest mindset when you go into business with someone is the best way to make sure you're both getting what you need from the company and that nothing will go awry.

Hear before being heard.

Be sure that when you're presented with a problem, you do your best to hear all there is to be said about it from as many angles as available. Once you have all the information, you can throw in your input and go from there to resolve it.

If you jump in too quickly to be heard, you could discourage someone from coming forward, you could muddy the perception of what occurred, it could stir the pot, and you might be missing out on pertinent information that could more easily help you to resolve.

Be willing to hear others before insisting that you be heard.

Synergize.

This is a trendy word that is used throughout business and strategy. If you can put your sense of self-gratification aside so that you and your colleagues can share in the success, you will find the sensation to be even more significant in measure for each individual involved.

SMART Goals

Now that we've taken a look at the types of habits that can be the most beneficial to us in our goals, let's take a look at a method for setting goals! The plans you select should meet five criteria to ensure that your focus is in the most economical and prudent place. Doing so will save you extra effort and help you increase your chances of achieving the goals you're setting over time.

Let's look at what SMART means!

- **Specific**

- **Measurable**

- **Attainable**

- **Relevant**

- **Time-based**

We'll break this down by letter so you can see precisely what your goals should look like as you're setting them in your day-to-day and your long-term planning!

You want to state what you'll do, and you want to use action words when you make those statements. For instance, if your whole goal is, "I want to be rich," there aren't a lot of specifics in there, and the only verbs in the statement are "want" and "be." Those aren't particularly active words, and this statement doesn't fall into specific categories.

Now, if you were to say something a little bit more, you could say something like, "I want to develop a new app that will generate $50k in its first year." This is very specific and features words that show action. Now, once you set this over-arching goal, you can further break down the specifics of that goal. To do this, you can ask yourself some simple questions:

· **"What do I want to achieve with this goal?"**

· **"What is my timeline for this goal?"**

· **"Do I want to work with someone to achieve this? Who?"**

· **"Are there conditions or limitations with which I should be thinking at this stage?"**

These questions give you an excellent base for understanding your goal, all the intricacies that will come with it, and it gets you into the right frame of mind to begin working on it.

Measurable

Our goals can be hard to quantify when we're in the beginning stages of them. If our ideas are too nebulous, it could be hard to tell if we've even been looking in the right places. Ensuring your goal is measurable means taking the time to identify the things you will see, hear, feel, and sense when you achieve your goal. It means taking the quantifiable elements of the plan you're setting and working with them. For this aspect, you will want to gauge measurable results. While being happy is an excellent result for achieving a goal, it's hard to quantify. Try looking for something like, "I've gone from needing to walk with a cane to being able to walk a 5k." These are quantifiable, measurable results that are tangible. Defining the physical specifications of the goal you're working on achieving is a great way to make it easier to visualize and execute.

Attainable

This part of the process can be a little bit hard to swallow. If it isn't, you owe it to yourself to be reasonable and state that it is not currently attainable. This doesn't need to mean that you can't work your way up to it eventually, but if you start to go right for it out of the gate without setting up the preliminary steps, you could be setting yourself up for heartache. Make sure that, whatever you're shooting for, you're keeping in mind the real-world obstacles that stand between you and that goal!

Relevant

Is this goal relevant to you and what you want for your life? Ensure that you're not setting goals based on what others want for your life. Your goals should be the things that you want to accomplish. Take a look at your motivations behind your goals and determine if they're relevant to you!

Timely

Give yourself a deadline! Remember Parkinson's Law! The time allotted for a task will inevitably be taken up by the needed things to complete it. Put together a flexible timeline for your goal and all the functions relevant to that goal. Make sure that you make adjustments as you learn about how long things take and find out more things about your capabilities.

Chapter 5: How to Change Your Mental State and Increase Mental Toughness for Personal Success

Now that you have a clear idea of what your hidden potentials are, please step back and allow yourself to feel good about them. This shows you in no uncertain terms that you're not worthless, not by a long shot. You have the raw ingredients. It's there; it's just beneath the surface.

I need you to recognize the list of your hidden and obvious potential. Now, look at that list and allow yourself to feel good. Allow yourself to conclude that you're not entirely worthless, that there's nothing wrong with you, and that nothing is missing with you. You have the raw ingredients for success.

Of course, turning potential into reality takes work. Still, it's a tremendous victory for you even to recognize that you have all these things going for you. There's no need for false modesty. There's no need to sabotage a positive feeling by saying: "Well, everybody has potential." Or "I'm just a face in the crowd because everybody has potential that they're not developing."

Forget that. Just focus on the fact that you have this potential, and you have the choice to develop them so you can live up to your most total capability. You have it in you. This proves point-blank that you have the ingredients for greatness; you need to connect the dots; you need to mix the ingredients.

It's not like you're going to have to get something that you currently don't possess proactively. It's already there. I need you to wrap your mind around this, and I need you to feel good about it.

Take Your Passions and Build on Them

Develop yourself by developing your passions. If you're passionate about specific activities, then pursue them by all means. The more you do something that gives you fulfillment and happiness, the more you invest in your purpose. The more you do it, the more you invest in your self-esteem. How does this work? Well, it's straightforward; the more you develop your passions, the more competent you are with them. They're no longer just potential; this is no longer just a theoretical set of traits that would be nice to develop. When you work on them and sharpen them and build them, they affect your reality because you can see their impact.

For example, if you like to sing in the shower, you might want to pursue your passion for singing. You can start the battery, take some singing lessons and then venture out to open mike night at a local club, bar, or hall. Now, everybody's lined up to sing, so you don't need to feel out of place.

However, when you get up there and face that crowd, and you bare your soul, that is a tremendous victory. You've come from somebody who is hiding this immense personal light under a bowl by singing in the shower to somebody who found the nerve to sing in front of the public. That's a victory. It doesn't matter what happens next; what matters is that you could make that journey. That is a massive transition.

You celebrate yourself when you develop your passions. However, there's nothing wrong with you. You are worth respecting, you are worth loving, and you are worth something. The more you accept yourself, the more your self-esteem grows. The secret here is to be mindful of the process. This is crucial; you're not just enjoying the journey.

Now, don't get me wrong, there's a lot of value in that. But this is purposeful; you must also pay attention to the character you're building. You know you're doing this for a reason; you're doing this because you have low self-esteem, and you want to build it up and transform it so it can project into greater and greater levels of self-confidence.

This is very hard to do unless you keep a laser focus on your transition from somebody shy and suffering from inadequacy and low self-worth to somebody who feels that they can actively change their waking reality. In other words, somebody operating from a place of tremendous self-confidence.

Self-Esteem is based on Accomplishment

Now, a lot of people might think that this is terrible news. After all, we live in a modern society where self-confidence is supposed to be a door prize. Most school curriculum emphasizes self-confidence instead of making sure kids go through the traditional curriculum to achieve academic excellence.

The old standard had it right. Self-confidence comes later; there is a precursor to self-confidence.
It's like building a massive tower. You can't make the tower on sand; it's going to sink. It's going to tip over and kill people inside the building. I mean, this is common sense. You can't just build self-confidence without foundation. And that's why you need to first focus on your passions, your interests, discover more about them and then make the transition from feeling good about your potential, challenging your potential, celebrating your potential, and celebrating yourself to self-confidence.

Like I said earlier, the world doesn't care about your feelings; all it cares about is what you do or what you achieve. By entertaining your passions, polishing them, and engaging in them, you start accomplishing things. You start getting good at your interests.

Again, taking the example of singing, it's one thing to sing in the shower and have the voice of a small puppy being tortured to death. It's great you're getting in touch with your inner passions. It's great that you've identified your need to bear your soul through singing. However, you can't leave it there. You have to polish your passion. You have to get good at it. If your voice sounds like a small puppy being tortured to death, then you need to keep working on your passion until you say good.

Do you see how this works? This is where Accomplishment comes in; this is where the real world steps in. It's easy to feel good about subjective things like, oh, you have to get in touch with your passion, and you have to bare your soul by entertaining your love. That's all well and good behind closed doors, but ultimately, you have to have external validation.

In other words, you have to get good enough at it so you can objectively say I've accomplished something. I've taken something that I was interested in and passionate about, and I have worked on it to such a degree that other people would agree that I am good at it. In other words, I have achieved. This is crucial because otherwise, all this progress would be subjective. It would just simply be self-serving and private. That's not going to move the needle as far as your self-esteem goes. Genuine self-esteem is built on Accomplishment. When you become good at something, you allow yourself to feel good at it and say to yourself: "I'm good at something. I'm accomplished at something." By doing so, you carve out your own space; this is one space that nobody can take away from you because you worked at it. Do you see how this works?

Self-esteem is based on Accomplishment. It is not a priori value that somebody drops on you because you showed up. It's not a door prize; it's built on something solid. In other words, you worked at it, and that's what makes it real. You have to keep working on your passions; you have to get good at them. I know this will be painful for many people reading this, but I need to say it. You have to allow yourself, after a certain point, to be critiqued. You have to subject yourself to an objective standard. Before this point, everything is subjective. Everything is all about your feelings. How it feels great, how you feel validated, how you think honored; that's all well and good.

However, the moment you take your passion and subject it to external review, that's when you know when you have truly accomplished it or not. If not, that's okay. This is where the trait of resilience comes in. You hit a bump on the road and suffer a setback; that's okay.

Because if you're truly passionate, you would draw from that internal energy and get the power you need to keep pushing.

Build on the Objective Foundation of Excellence

When you become excellent at something, you feel more confident. You have the solid and objective foundation for this self-assessment that you are good at something. It's not just wishful thinking; you're not just hypnotizing yourself or engaging in self-delusion. This is really because it can be traced to actual accomplishments. Compare this with showing up at a school and everybody getting an A or participating in a sport, and nobody loses because everybody gets a medal. There's nothing to work for because whether you try hard and sacrifice or slack off, the result is the same.

You're Only as Good as Your Last Victory

When was the last time you hung out with people that keep reminiscing about the good old days? They would tell you: "Oh yeah, five years ago I was making a million bucks a month," or "Ten years ago, I was traveling all over the world." While those kinds of statements may be significant in rehashing shared memories, they get old and stale sooner or later. They can get downright annoying. You see, the world focuses not only on the results you produce but also on the here and now. In other words, can you produce good results now? While the gravity and enormous value of what you did in the past do hold some sway, the more distant the Accomplishment, the less the world cares. It has a short-term memory, like it or not.

This is why you need to understand that when it comes to producing Accomplishment, you're only as good as your last victory. Don't rest on your laurels. Allow yourself to be constantly engaged, constantly refine your skill sets, challenge yourself continuously.

This leads to continuous improvement; you're always looking for the next bigger and better thing to do as far as your passions go. This gives you a tremendous competitive advantage compared to people trying to do what you're doing. They can't hold the candle to you if you are passionate about this because you constantly improve yourself. The difference is like black and white because you are invested in constant improvement.

Ride the Spiral Staircase to Greater Self-Esteem

Believe it or not, a constant improvement in your passion leads to greater and greater self-esteem. It starts with your desires. You then improve on them, so you produce better and better results. You then get some objective validation. People would tell you: "Wow! You're singing better now than before," or "You're making more money now than before," or "You're living in a bigger house now than before," or "You're more respected now. Then before."

Whatever the case may be, and whatever your passion may be, there's an increase in objective validation. This then boosts your self-esteem because you tell yourself in no uncertain terms, "I'm doing something right. I took my passions, improved on them, and I can objectively test that I've reached a higher level.

When you feel greater self-esteem, your level of passion increases; your passion "gas tank" is refilled, and you have more energy to go to the next level of improved action, objective validation, and on and on it goes. It's an upward spiral of greater and greater self-esteem. With each increase, there's also a more excellent projection, meaning there's an outward manifestation; your self-confidence is more apparent. People who are good at what they're doing become more confident. The more confident they become, the more successful they become because the world sits up and pays attention. See how the upward spiral works?

Chapter 6: The Psychology of Willpower, Motivation, and Discipline

You are getting up every day to go to the gym, setting aside time for studying every day, rehearsing daily for a show or performance, or training each day for a sports event. The truth is, you will not always feel like working out, or studying, or doing anything productive; somedays you will want to do the bare minimum. So, what will keep you going when willpower and motivation fail you?

Mentally tough people understand something that most people do not. Motivation and willpower are undoubtedly good to have, but they come in waves. They are emotions, and just like any other emotions, they come and go depending on the circumstances, your environment, and a host of other factors. In essence, your motivation is not always up to you. Sometimes someone may say something discouraging and make you feel worthless, or you may be facing circumstances that take the wind out of your sails.

What this means if you are relying on willpower and motivation alone. You will have a problem being consistent. One day you are raring to go; the next, it's all you can do to get out of bed. This is what happens when your emotions influence your productivity. Think of people who start every year with grand ideas of turning their life around. They follow through on their resolutions until somewhere in mid-January, then gradually begin to fall back to old behavior patterns.

So, they do not make it the main reason behind what they do. Instead, they invest in plans, schedules, and habits. They understand that consistency and self-discipline are the only tools that will keep you on track no matter your mood or the circumstances.

When you prioritize habits and action plans over motivation and willpower, you are no longer going on emotions alone. Self-discipline ties you to specific actions regardless of your frame of mind. When you create habits and action plans, every day, you wake up knowing what you have to do, why you have to do it, and when it needs to be done. This ultimately is more beneficial for productivity than motivation will ever be.

When you are waiting around for motivation or inspiration, you end up wasting valuable time. You end up procrastinating and putting off important decisions and tasks because you are not in the right frame of mind. Mentally tough people realize that if they establish daily habits, create schedules for themselves and stay focused on the goal, they have a better chance of success than someone who sits back waiting for a dose of motivation or inspiration.

Think of pro-athletes. They practice every day without fail. The team's star player will show up for practice just like the weaker players will. They do not tell the more talented players to sit at home and wait for game-day since they are already good. It does not matter how good you are at something or how talented you are; if you are not consistent and disciplined, things will start to go south sooner or later.

Let's consider writers for a moment. They bring words to life and create content for other people to enjoy. If, on the one hand, you have a writer who only writes when they feel motivated, and on the other, you have a writer who has a schedule where they write at least two thousand words per day, who is likely to be more productive? Undoubtedly the writer with the program will be more effective because moods or emotions do not drive him. He has a plan of action, and he follows it consistently every day.

Many people fail to achieve their goals because they do know what they want but rather because they do not have a plan of action. You want better grades, but how are you changing your study routine? You want a healthier body, but what changes have you made? Without a plan, you will simply be going on motivation and willpower. As soon as the reason starts to wane, you give up and revert to default settings.

Motivation is not a plan, and it certainly is not consistent. Why do yo-yo dieters always end up putting back on all the weight they had lost? It is simply because they focus on the result instead of investing in the process. Instead of cultivating self-discipline and perseverance, yo-yo dieters rely on motivation and willpower. Ultimately when the motivation fizzles out, they find themselves right where they started. They jump to the next fad diet, not realizing that it is not the diet that needs to change but rather their approach.

Mental toughness is about taking deliberate steps to make your dreams come true.

You do not wait for inspiration to hit or for the moment to feel right; you start and make daily habits that then become ingrained into your everyday life. Without self-discipline and consistency, the short story is that motivation and willpower will only take you so far.

Self- Awareness

There is no escaping yourself. Everywhere you go, well, there you are. This may sound pretty insane, but it is probably one of the most important realizations you will make in your life. Your attitude, your beliefs, your values, and your emotional baggage follow you around in every situation. They are the invisible coat you put on each day before you go out to face the world. These beliefs, attitudes, and values influence how you see yourself, see others, and approach challenges and opportunities.

Every relationship they get into seems to end the same way? Or someone who always hits a plateau at work no matter how many times they switch jobs. They always think the next opportunity will be their breakthrough, only to end up in the same situation they were trying to escape.

These situations, where life seems to be unfolding in similar patterns repeatedly, occur because of the baggage you carry around with you. If you behave the same way in your current relationship that you did in your last one, why would the outcome be any different? If you work in the same way you have always done, why would your boss suddenly notice you? Recognizing the role that we play in the circumstances that unfold around us is crucial in breaking cycles of dysfunction, broken dreams, and unhappiness. Find the enemy within before you look for the one on the outside.

If you are blind to your own self-limiting beliefs, you will never conquer your demons. You will always be fighting the same problems in the same way and wondering why your life is going round in circles. Self-awareness is the only way to realize how we sabotage our success.

How often do you talk yourself out of doing things that you know might be good for you? You tell yourself, I don't have the experience. There is no way I would get a better job, or I am too fat; it is too late to start exercising or never get into college. Why bother studying? What do you say to yourself? Are you your own worst critique, or are you cheering yourself on?

Self-sabotage is challenging to beat because it is intrinsically tied to who we think, our self-esteem, and our identity.

You will often hear people say things like, oh, I do not like to socialize, that's just the way I am wired, or I am just terrible at Math; there is no way I am passing that test. When you box yourself into a specific identity, you effectively stop yourself from even trying. The more you do it; the more limited your opportunities become because your mind is closed to things that do not feel comfortable or familiar to you.

To become mentally tough, you need to understand that your own beliefs are the biggest hindrance to your success. You have to stop seeking ways to reinforce your beliefs and instead embrace things that make you question the identity you have created for yourself.

For instance, if you hate socializing, make it a point to go out every weekend. Do it every weekend without fail until it becomes a habit. It may be hard at first, but the more you do it, you will start to realize that nothing is daunting about it. The point here is to challenge who you think you are by doing something you would never do. Even if you never really get to like it, you will learn how to cope with uncomfortable situations and grow in the process.

Do not get so caught up in sticking to an image you have created for yourself that you miss out on opportunities that have the power to change your life. If you think about it, most of the labels you have put on yourself are simply shields you have developed to protect yourself and to avoid feeling vulnerable.

You tell yourself you are underqualified so that you do not have to take a chance on asking for a raise, or you tell yourself you are too fat so that you do not have to challenge yourself by working out. All these little lies we tell ourselves are all about holding on to the identities we have created for ourselves. They make you feel safe because you do not have to push your boundaries or step out of your comfort zone. You can sit back and say, that's not my thing, no point in trying.

The more self-aware you become, the easier it will be to bust the self-limiting beliefs and stop self-sabotaging. Before you make a decision, ask yourself, why am I choosing this instead of the other? Am I afraid to challenge myself? By questioning your motives, emotions, and triggers, you will start to unravel all the little ways in which you derail your progress.

Chapter 7: Disciplined Like A NAVY SEAL

The unbeatable mind is solid and rigid. It is resilient and relentless. It is determined, and it has the willpower and the drive to succeed. We all want an unbeatable mind and often get frustrated when we fall short of what we wanted to accomplish because we could not stay focused and determined. Focus and determination are both products of having mental strength.

Traits of the Unbeatable Mind

1) Mental Competency
2) Emotional Intelligence
3) **Resilence**
4) **Willpower**
5) A Winner's Mind
6) The Ability to Focus
7) They Surround Themselves with Other People Who Are Mentally Tough
8) They Avoid Trying Too Hard to Go Against the Grain
9) Expect Delayed Gratification
10) Consistency, Consistency, Consistency

Trait 1: Mental Competency

The first trait that you must possess to develop and sustain a certain level of mental toughness is mental competency. Having a sound and sharp mind is the first thing you need to gain mental toughness. Mental competency is the ability to make sound judgment decisions. Thus, it is essential to pay attention to and take care of your mental health before developing your mental competence. Disorders such as bipolar disorder can cloud your judgment and make it very difficult for you to develop mental toughness.

Don't assume that your mental health and mental competency do not change when certain things in your life change. If you experience a death or a severe emotional loss or are going through post-partum depression, or you just entered menopause, take the time to get your mental health checked out.

Trait 2: Emotional Intelligence

Emotional intelligence can be characterized as a type of emotional competency, similar to mental competency for emotions.

Having a low level of emotional intelligence can make it very hard to succeed in areas of life that involve other people. For instance, a person who lacks emotional intelligence may find it hard to achieve in relationships because he cannot identify and understand the emotions of potential dates and mates. This may lead to a significant amount of communication issues, a lack of enjoyment in the relationship, and the inability to form relationships altogether.

Moreover, having a low level of self-awareness can cause you to identify your own emotions improperly. You may fail to realize how you truly feel about a person, job, or issue because you could not touch your feelings. This can lead to less satisfaction in these areas of your life. A person who has mastered emotional intelligence skills is more likely to do things that lead to a higher level of satisfaction for him or her because he or she knows himself better.

However, people who excel in the area of emotional intelligence may find it very easy to deal with people and gravitate toward people. These people tend to gravitate toward other people because people tend to reach them well. Two key factors have a significant impact on how people react to them, and these are 1) empathy and 2) an increased ability to communicate with others.

People who can empathize with others are more likely to make other people comfortable around them and feel relaxed. Furthermore, people tend to think that the empathetic person cares more about their day or how they are doing than people who have not developed the skill to emphasize with others. This can lead to deeper connections. Thus, a person who has emotional intelligence and can empathize with others is more likely to have more positive, strong relationships with people than a person who does not know how to empathize with others. And these vital connections are a support system upon which a person can build more mental toughness.

A person with emotional intelligence has better communication skills. Understanding the emotions of others can keep you from saying things that are off-putting or offensive, both that can quickly end a conversation and convince the other person not to communicate as much with you in the future.

Communication skills are derived from the ability to understand emotions and speech; it includes reading and understanding the use of body language, personalities, and more. Much of communication is about listening. To be a good listener, you should learn to listen actively. Do not just stand there passively as a conversation is taking place; that a strong interest in the words that are being said. Hand gestures are also suitable for you to notice. Take in the whole scene and make a judgment with that in mind.

Trait 3: Resilience

Resilience is the cornerstone trait of mental toughness. Many people consider resilience to be the definition of mental toughness. Resilience is the ability to persevere and persist even through the challenges that life brings you. It is the ability to dust yourself off after a setback and get back up and try again and again until you succeed. Resilience helps people overcome the challenges and obstacles that they find when they start trying to achieve a specific goal.

One of the factors that play a role in resilience is self-confidence. You must have the confidence to succeed. Confidence is the belief that you can accomplish the goal you have set out to accomplish, that you are good enough, and deserve to achieve your goal. To achieve a lofty goal, you have to believe that you can.

Therefore, confidence is also the ability to limit and control your negative beliefs in yourself so that they do not outweigh the positive ones telling you that you can succeed. Many people have formed a significant amount of negative thoughts about whether they can be something they want to be or do something they want to do throughout life. People may have been led to believe that they are limited by where they are from, how much money they have, their skin color, looks, and more. These beliefs tend to reside in the back of people's minds and stop them from believing that they can achieve specific goals in life and that they need to 'stay in their place' and dream the type of dreams that were made for someone like them.

Peers, teachers, classmates, and more may have discouraged a person from trying to achieve specific goals instead of encouraging them to go after them. Therefore, resilience is the ability to get past these negative affirmations that have been placed in our minds, sometimes over the years, and to reprogram ourselves to see our chances of achieving these goals in a more positive manner.

Trait 4: Willpower
Willpower is the determination needed to do things such as lose 50 pounds, stop smoking, stick to an exercise routine, and many other things in life. Willpower is the ability to not give in to your harmful desires. It is the ability to resist the temptation to make changes in your life that will improve your life from its current state. In a survey conducted by the American Psychological Association, it was found that the number 1 barrier that most people cited to making positive changes in their lives was the lack of willpower. Therefore, according to the American Psychological

Association, the most limiting factor that people face is not the lack of money, lack of education, or the lack of time; it is the lack of the ability to resist harmful temptation.

To quit smoking, you need to withstand the urge to do so; but, the majority of people who try to stop smoking fail because their desire to quit is not as strong as their desire to smoke one more cigarette. Even though smokers who want to leave may be aware of all of the adverse effects that smoking can have has on them, such as a wide variety of health problems, high cost, stained teeth, walls, and more, people still lack the sheer determination to quit the habit. However, a person who has mental toughness can channel this determination and use it to quit smoking effectively. And willpower is the key to success in most of the goals you have in life.

Trait 5: A Winner's Mind

Mentally tough people have the right mindset to achieve the task they set out to achieve. They believe that they can do it and have a positive attitude and the likelihood to succeed. Having a winner's mind is about having the drive to push forward and not allowing yourself to take no for an answer. People with a winner's mentality do have the willpower necessary to achieve the goals and dreams; in fact, this is something that many people with a winner's mind never even bother to call into question, unlike the rest of us.

Certain aspects are present within the winner's mind. A winner's mentality is grateful for what he or she has. Being thankful for the things you have allows you to have a positive attitude despite the things you lack. A winner is glad for the everyday things that he or she was blessed with that will allow him or her to achieve his or her goals in life.

A winner's mind thinks positive thoughts. Many people allow their minds to be clogged with negative thoughts. This is detrimental to their spirit, mindset, and likelihood of achieving the goals they set out to accomplish. Winners concentrate on positively seeing things. Winners try to surround themselves with a positive vibe and group of people altogether so that their mindset is connected to positivity.

In addition, a winner's mind is always ready and open to learn more and enhance the skills that the person possesses. Winners are constantly learning and developing and evolving to stay on top of their game.

Winners are constantly setting new goals. Once you reach one goal in life, a winner would not be satisfied to sit back and be content that he or she had achieved that particular goal. Winner's tend to set new goals immediately after completing one goal; fulfilling one the first goal offers encouragement and confidence that the next goal that is formed can be achieved as well. Winners also tend to set these goals in progression, or series, one right after the other, knocking them off like a to-do list. This helps to keep you motivated and striving to achieve more and more.

Trait 6: The Ability to Focus

We've all seen people who do not have a solid ability to focus and are easily distracted. There is a good chance that you are one of these people if you have not taken the time to develop your mental toughness. Mental strength improves your concentration. A significant number of exercises designed to help you improve your mental strength are focused on engagement. Many high-performance athletes have tunnel vision when in their athletic performance mode to have a total and complete concentration that allows them to excel. This focus is necessary to make split-second decisions on dealing with other players to come out on top. Many people who have never participated in these types of activities do not understand the kind of focused zone these athletes get into and may have never honed their skills to get to total focus on the play at hand.

Trait 7: They Surround Themselves with Other People Who Are Mentally Tough

People with mental toughness tend to surround themselves with other mentally challenging people. You often find that athletes and entertainers of a certain level tend to associate with each other, and you may have assumed that it is because they are celebrities or because they are highly paid. You may not realize that their work ethic may be part of why they gravitate towards each other. Their careers are so demanding that other people may not understand this and may disagree with doing the same amount of work they are willing to put in. These high-level performers keep each other on their toes and encourage each other.

And these people all possess a high degree of mental toughness which tends to feed off each other. They can encourage each other to stay strong and work hard. They illustrate what mental toughness is in a given situation; they support each other and more.

You rarely see a person who seems to be strong mentally and emotionally closely associated with significantly weaker someone in these two categories. This is because, although the stronger one may rub off on and have an effect on the weaker ones, the weaker one affects the stronger one as well. The stronger one is being pulled down, and the weaker one is being pulled up toward a joint average strength. This is often uncomfortable for both people. It can be frustrating for the stronger person who may wonder why the weaker one fails to show as much willpower, determination, and drive. It can be belittling for the more vulnerable person who may experience insults and a condescending attitude from the other. Thus, it is beneficial for both people to associate more closely with someone on their level of mental strength. This means that if you desire to develop your mental strength, you need to identify and surround yourself with people who possess mental power. And you may have to eliminate or reduce association with some people who may keep you from reaching higher levels of mental strength.

Trait 8: They Avoid Trying Too Hard to Go Against the Grain

No, it would help if you did not always try to go with the flow and fit in. And the people who are known for having very high levels of emotional intelligence stand out; however, there is nothing wrong with trying to fit in a little.

Constantly trying to buck the system can get tiring and become frustrating. In addition, this can place more stress and mental strain on a person. This takes up space in a person's minds and takes a good deal of his or her time that could have been spent on something else. Furthermore, trying to be different can take a toll on you emotionally.

Trait 9: Expect Delayed Gratification

People with mental strength do not need to reap immediate benefits for their work and actions. They are okay with the services coming in time for their work and the time they put in. Seeking instant gratification can keep you from achieving what you could have achieved if you understood that the payout for the work that you put in does not always come immediately. Sometimes, it may take years to see the fruits of your labor. It is still essential to keep going to see the benefits of your work. Honing your mental strength will allow you to see that rewards are not the only good thing you receive from your hard labor. There is the pride of a job well done and accomplishing your goals. You can also enjoy helping others in some way. And the rewards for your hard labor will come in time.

Trait 10: Consistent, Consistent, Consistent

People with mental toughness are consistent. Consistency goes along with expecting delayed gratification and patience; however, it does differ slightly. When watching an NFL game, you often hear the quarterback being judged on his consistency. One great play or game is not enough; to be the starting quarterback whom the team builds their offense around and has kids wearing his jersey, he must be consistent through the game's plays, game after game.

Chapter 8: How to Develop State of Mental Strength

This is the part of the book where we tie everything together and connect the dots back to mental toughness. Everything we've talked about so far is one small part of the mental toughness mindset, so learning how to implement all of it will give you the complete picture. Each strategy will also include a simple action step for you to do so that you're not just reading about how to improve your mental toughness—you're doing it.

Mental toughness gives you the ability to tune your responses and react in ways that help you move forward. It also makes you more aware of all the opportunities you may have missed in the past due to the blinders you put on when life gets hard. In truth, it's about becoming your lifestyle.

Putting Everything Together

This will be a bit of a recap of everything we've covered so far so that you know exactly what your next steps should be. Do yourself a favor and get a journal or even a notebook so that you can track your progress. Whenever you rely on mental toughness to get you through something, could you take note of it? Even when you feel like you failed to be mentally tough, write that down, too, and ask yourself why you weren't able to apply toughness to the situation. This isn't for anyone's eyes but your own, so be honest and open. You won't become mentally tough overnight. If it were that easy, you wouldn't have to read a book about it. It's going to take time and practice, and a journal is a way for you to visually see the steps you've taken and the progress you've made.   So, let's take a look at the attitudes and actions you need to have and bring to build up your mental toughness.

Get Out of Your Comfort Zone

You'll never learn mental toughness if you never have to rely on it, and you won't have to in your comfort zone. If you skip this step, you might as well skip everything else because it won't do you any good. Cut the cord, burn those bridges, leap, and leave your comfort zones far behind. Nothing life-changing will ever happen in there because life never changes.

That's another thing you need to remember and take to heart—change is good. It's better than good—it's essential. You'll never find out your true potential if you stay the same from when you're born until you die.

The moment you break away from your comfort zone is when you'll discover yourself. Nothing in your life will change if you don't change first, and the only way to do so is to get away from your old life and habits.

That's right—, every single day for at least a week. Whenever you're in a situation that kicks up your fight-or-flight reflex, choose fight. It's going to be nerve-wracking at first, but that's the point. Once you start to get comfortable with fear and the feeling of apprehension that goes along with it, you'll realize that it's not so bad after all. There's no better way to learn how to master your fear than to run toward it.

Develop Habits Without Waiting for Motivation

Hopefully, you realize by now that motivation is a sham. If you haven't, I challenge you to stay motivated for an entire day while doing something you don't find fun. Time waits for no one, so don't waste it trying to find the motivation that just isn't going to come. To use your time and brainpower wisely, you need habits.

That's one of the biggest secrets of mental toughness—learning how to automate specific processes so that you can focus on situations that require more attention and quick thinking.

When your brain is bogged down, trying to make decisions about the little things, you have less power to devote to more pressing matters. In essence, that's why habits are essential.

There's a lot of advice you'll find out there about the best ways to build habits, but it's genuinely a simple process. Do something repeatedly, then reward yourself for doing it. Presto, you've just created a pattern!

It can be a little tougher if you're trying to replace a bad habit with a more positive one, but it follows the same principle. Tell your brain to do something, convince it that it's worth the effort, and your brain will want to do it all the time.

Furthermore, it can either be a significant change to your routine or small addition to your day. It just has to mean something to you. Don't forget to implement the cue-action-reward cycle. Pick a cue, decide on an action, then have a reward ready when you complete that action.

If you're keeping a journal, track your progress. If you forget or miss a day, but a lovely big red X next to the date, not as a punishment but as a visual reminder. When you get to the end of the month, congratulate yourself and keep ongoing. Lifestyles are built one habit at a time, so take that first step.

Embrace Good Stress and Manage Bad Stress

This is the aspect of mental toughness that can be the most confusing. We either can't tell the difference between good stress and bad stress or don't use good stress effectively, or we let bad stress cause us to freeze in our tracks. Don't make the mistake of thinking that all our stress will disappear when we become mentally tough. The difference is that it won't have mastery over you anymore. When you can channel good stress into your work and use it to propel you forward, you succeed. When you can recognize where bad stress originates from and work to overcome it instead of letting it overwhelm you, you win.

Action Step: Chances are, you encounter a stressful situation every day. First, recognize whether it's good stress or inadequate stress. Then, if it's good stress, find a way to use it to help you. If it's bad stress, realize that you don't control the situation, only your actions. Although you may have stopped everything and let the pressure get you down or make you panic in the past, you're now going to wave hi to it and continue walking. You'll acknowledge that it's there, but you won't give it any more thought.

Additional Strategies

The strategies don't end there. Mental toughness can be built from many habits and actions, and you should do your research once you finish this book to see if there are any in particular that resonates with you. However, before we conclude, I'll leave you with a few final strategies to be mentally tough and live up to your highest potential.

There's one common thread you'll notice in every one of these strategies: they all incorporate what you've been taught so far. Some rely on habits, others focus on getting out of your comfort zone, but all aim to help you succeed in life, no matter what success means to you.

Limit Distractions

Why is it that every time we want to get work done, the forces of the universe come together to provide every possible distraction? Coworkers, TV shows, Facebook, that new restaurant around the corner you've been dying to try—all of them seem to want to pull you away from your work. These are the things that feel comfortable (although with coworkers, that's not always the case) and provide us with immediate gratification, which we don't get from work.

It's usually at this point that we seek out that ever-elusive motivation to guide us to the right decision. However, instead of waiting for something that never comes, get into the habit of tuning out or limiting distractions automatically so that you don't have to decide between productivity and time-wasters consciously.

An excellent way to do this is by building a routine (that later becomes a habit) to get you into "work mode." Soon, it won't be seeking distractions because it knows what to do next. There's no need to decide between work and distractions anymore. Work is what you usually do after this routine, so you'll do it. That's the power of habit.

Action Step: Develop a "work time" routine that's as simple or complex as you want, although simple is probably better. Before you sit down to work, do something that you can easily do every single time you're about to start working. You can make a cup of tea, set certain supplies out on your desk, put on a playlist, or do something more refreshing. Then, get right to work. It's like a Pavlovian response—ring the bell, and the dog drools. Only, in this case, the bell is your routine, you're the dog, and you're working instead of drooling.

Chapter 9: Improving Your Emotional Intelligence Using Mental Toughness

Train your brain is necessary to stay calm under pressure. In case of any disaster, it helps you look beyond what happened. It gives you prudence to observe the elements of tragedy with a new lens, examine your thoughts, get the shortcomings, recompose the actionable parts in a new frame and get the work done seamlessly. However, life does not always follow an easy-going road, and everyone has to face failure. So, do not worry about your loss or do not feel sad due to negligence. Your mental strength is your true friend who always stays with you like your shadow. It stays with you in success and as well as failure. So, it is always with and all you need to strengthen it more.

Practice Meditation

It has been proved repeatedly that meditation can improve the level of mental toughness you have. Even soldiers who are about to go on a mission or are being trained for combat are advised to practice meditation and for a good reason. They do not become too emotional in their career, or in other words, their mental toughness is improved.

In the world of mental toughness, there are usually three types of people. The first one is the marshmallow. As the name suggests, these people are very soft, both inside out, and so any tiny amount of pressure on them can cause havoc. They have a soft inner core but a hard shell. They are more challenging than marshmallows, but at times, even they can buckle up after a prolonged period of stress. The last group of people in the rocks can handle everything put in front of them. When a person learns to adopt a lifestyle that includes a regular time set aside for meditation, then he/she eventually starts developing a growth mindset. In this mindset, people do not see their failures or obstacles as negative things but rather learn from their mistakes and life events. You will learn to harness the power of meditation and then use that energy to stay positive throughout your day. Your idea of mental toughness will be elevated to a whole new level with this new routine of meditation. On average, a person has over 70,000 thoughts in a day. What meditation does is that it helps you seek that quiet place inside your head that is present but is hidden under the pressure of all those thoughts weighing you down. But people often confuse meditation with mindfulness. Mindfulness is a different thing, and you can say that it is a type of meditation.

But with the help of meditation, you will be able to analyze so many thoughts that got buried in your subconscious, and you will be able to do so without being judgmental at all.

The first way meditation promotes mental toughness is that it helps you enter a calm state. When you are relaxed, you have the time and concentration required to judge which thoughts are worthy of your attention, and thus, you can invest your time in them. You will also learn a rational way to respond to anxiety in your daily life. Moreover, with meditation, you can distinguish between noise and static. Your recalling power will increase, and you will also learn how you can control your mind not to get affected by any distractions. In short, meditation can improve your capacity to handle stress and thus enhance your level of mental toughness.

Don't Beat Yourself Up For Things You Cannot Control

There will always be things in your life beyond your control, which is the ultimate truth. When people cannot get over the fact that they can't control everything, they become control freaks.

Thus, if you want to train your brain to have mental toughness, then you need to stop picking fights on every small matter that comes your way. Frankly, you need to understand that everything is not worth it to waste your energy fighting over it. There will always be some troubling times you have to face in your life. But don't fret or don't give in to depression just because you cannot control the situation. The simple fact is that the problem cannot be handled.

Yes, you can influence people, but you can never, or rather you should never force your will upon others. For example, you can do everything you can to make the party good, but you cannot do anything to make the people have fun. It is their own decision and choice. Sometimes, the feeling of being a control freak intensifies, even more when you tend to jump to catastrophic outcomes which might not even happen. So, judge your thoughts and think about whether you are indulging in such a practice or not. Usually, it won't be as bad as you believe it to be.

As already mentioned, you can practice meditation, or you can also do something you love. Practice anything that is stress-relieving to you.

You can even go out and have a good time with your friends if that is what you want. For example, if you are thinking 'Important members of the board are going to be present at the meeting' then you need to tell yourself 'I can handle it.

Give a Name to Your Emotions

Dealing with your emotions is essential in all aspects of your life and not only when it comes to mental toughness. When you name your emotions, the process is called labeling, and it is also the first step for everyone towards effectively dealing with their emotions. You have to pinpoint what you are feeling, and sometimes you might label your emotions as something that it is not.

There are so many reasons why labeling your emotions is a difficult task. For starters, right from your childhood, you have been taught that it is necessary to suppress your strong emotions. Moreover, sometimes there are unspoken organizational and societal rules that stop you from expressing your actual feelings. Or sometimes, a child is never actually taught how they should speak up and say what they are feeling. These things cumulatively act as a barrier to correct labeling of emotions.

The most common emotions visible in a workplace setting are stress and anger, or at least that is what they are labeled as. But in most cases, these two labels mask way deeper emotions than they seem to be. The tendency to avert from showing or talking about one's emotions is a growing concern in today's world, significantly when mental health issues increase each day. When you avoid speaking about your emotions, you automatically create a distance between you and your emotions. This affects your ability to identify how you feel at a particular moment.

As already mentioned above, sometimes adults label their emotions, but they do it in the wrong way. For example, if someone feels sad, instead of saying 'I'm feeling low,' they might say, 'My eyes got watery, nothing more. You must spend some time every day with yourself, and you must acknowledge that you are feeling what you are feeling. It would help if you also thought about how these emotions affect or affect your decision-making abilities. Whether it is about something that happened in your workplace or your personal life, if you have some feeling on your mind, it is more likely to get spilled all over your life and create havoc.

I am not saying this just because I want you to be precise. No, that is not what I mean. I mean that when you use the correct vocabulary, you will also gain the power to describe your emotions correctly.

An accurate diagnosis of your feelings is essential if you want to respond correctly to them. Also, don't stick to basic descriptions like angry or sad, as sometimes your emotions are way more intense than that. Being angry might also mean that you are grumpy or annoyed. It would help if you labeled your feelings the way they are.

Maintain a Balance in Your Emotions with the Help of Logic

Whether it is a family dilemma or a financial crisis where you need to make crucial decisions, being mentally strong is very important. But for that, you need to implement logic to balance your emotions. So, if you see that your feelings are running high, take a stand immediately and increase your level of rational thinking. If you are confused about how you can achieve this in your life, then here is a tip that works for most people—whenever you are making a choice, consider the pros and cons and write them down somewhere.

When you finish your list of pros and cons and reread it, you will realize many things and may even be able to separate your emotions from your decisions.

Decisions are something you cannot spend your day without. Even if you are not doing anything and simply chilling at home, there will be several decisions cropping up in your mind, for example, 'what should I eat for lunch?' Do you see it? Your daily life is filled with so many small and big decisions that sometimes we even tend to look past them. If you plan to quantify your decisions in a day, then don't try to walk on that path because it is nearly impossible. Your decisions are not always huge. They can even be hidden in mundane things like whether you want to get a coffee or make yourself some tea.

It is often said that their emotions influence 80% of the choices made by humans. So, do you favor logic or feeling when you are making some decisions in your life? Unsavory situations in life can arise at any moment, and they are all due to momentary lapses in your judgment. Yes, you might feel constant friction in your mind when you are trying to create a balance between emotions and logic, and your emotional self might even try to break free and dominate, but you have to deal with it all if you want to achieve mental toughness.

Chapter 10: Risk Management Toughness

Every opportunity comes with an equal chance of failure or success. This means that you must be willing to take a risk to seize opportunities and take chances. People who have risk management toughness are not afraid of failure; they are more fearful of the options they will miss by not taking any risk.

To cultivate risk management toughness, you need to be comfortable with uncertainty and challenging yourself. For instance, if you believe that you are better at one thing over another, you always go for opportunities that align with what you think you are good at. While this approach may be safe, you never really learn anything new by always doing the things you have always done.

People with risk management toughness are the ones who are not afraid to disrupt themselves and do something different. They challenge their beliefs and do not hesitate to go against established norms or accepted practices if that is what it takes to reach their goals. This kind of mental toughness gives people the mental strength and willingness to take risks and reinvent the wheel led to the startup revolution.

Founders of mega-companies like Uber, Airbnb, and similar startups took extraordinary risks to get where they are today. In the natural sense, the biggest taxi company in the world should have taxis, yet uber does not own any taxis. The founders of Uber found a way to disrupt the system and go against typical and expected. It is only by taking a risk that other people would have labeled crazy or impossible that such startups can change the definition of what is expected and what is not.

This same concept of disruption and taking a risk by venturing into the unknown has made Airbnb such a huge success. These companies did not just go along with the accepted business practice, but rather, they found a way to revolutionize their respective industries and create a new normal. The thing about risks is that the size of the risk is almost always equal to the potential payoff. Therefore, it takes extraordinary mental toughness to take on such huge risks when you cannot be sure of the outcome.

While you may not be looking to found the next mega startup, it is essential to borrow lessons from these startup founders who took significant risks to achieve extraordinary success.

The truth is, no one gets to such heights by playing it safe. You must be willing to take chances even when they feel unsafe or threaten your sense of security. This requires mental strength and a willingness to embrace uncertainty.

For most people, fear is the main driving force behind their actions. When you become risk-averse, you will always be limited to what you know and what feels safe. This is why risk management toughness is crucial for people who want to achieve extraordinary outcomes in their lives.

Risks do not always have to be huge to pay off. Sometimes simply doing something you would not normally do can get you past a hurdle you have been dealing with for a long time. To see different results, you must be willing to do something different. That is a simple fact of life. Avoid getting into thinking traps where you have closed yourself into a safe box that defines what you can and cannot do. Test your limits, your beliefs, and your abilities by trying something new and opening up your mind to new perspectives.

Ultimately the most significant hindrance that people have to achieve their goals is to stay within a specific comfort zone. This desire to avoid uncertainty at all costs makes people risk-averse and resistant to change. Think of people who are stuck in dead-end careers because they are too afraid to rock the boat. They know that they can do better, but they remain stuck in limbo because they do not want to risk failure. This is a classic example of how adopting a risk-averse mindset can cripple you and prevent you from making progress in your life.

Overcoming the Fear of Failure

When you think of all the reasons why you hesitate to seize an opportunity or take a chance at something, you are likely to find that some fear fuels your hesitation. Fear comes in many forms. Sometimes you may find other excuses to explain why you are not doing what you need to be doing, yet all these excuses cover up fear.

You may say you do not have enough qualifications, or you are not ready for the challenge, or that you do not have enough capital to start, and so on. When you get into a habit of being driven by your fears, any challenge that comes your way and threatens your security is quickly classified as a threat. Once you identify it as a threat, then you do anything in your power to avoid it or get away from it. This is why some people will never step up at work when there is an opportunity or take a chance by doing something they have never done.

Ultimately when your fear of failure is much bigger than your passion or commitment to your goals, you will never muster up enough courage to go after what you want.

They even have the business plan all drawn up and have identified the product they want to offer. However, at the thought of leaving a cushy job that offers job security and a source of regular income, they balk at the risk involved in starting a business from scratch. Ultimately their brilliant ideas remain just that. They spend their time dreaming about the future they wish they had but could never have the courage to pursue.

When you fear the driving force behind your choices, do not be surprised if you end up living an average existence doing average things. A lot of people confuse being risk-averse with being careful. People with risk management toughness can weigh their opportunities against what they stand to gain or lose by taking a risk.

A measured risk means that you have done due diligence, come up with a plan of action, and then made a decision fully aware of what you are taking on. Just like you, people who take risks have concerns about safety and security. However, they are also passionate enough about their dreams to take calculated risks if it means they have a shot at achieving their goals.

If you find yourself constantly choosing the safest option, you may be denying yourself the chance to seize potentially life-changing opportunities. As much as you want to seek security and comfort, you should understand that there is a price you pay for safety. More often than not, this price passes upon opportunities that would have allowed you to realize your dreams.

The fear of failure is such a powerful de-motivator because when we fail, we have to confront our shortcomings. Nobody wants to die or feel like they do not have what it takes to succeed. Many of our emotions and confidence are invested in who we think we are. So when you are forced to confront your flaws, then you end up feeling like, in some way, you have lost your identity. This is why most people will shy away from doing something new because they are more comfortable doing what they already know.

Failure is only a deterrent for going after your goals when you let them become more potent than your passion. People who have risk management toughness find a way to manage their fear of failure to not stop them from chasing their dreams. They feel the fear but do not let it overcome their determination to succeed and pursue their goals.

Like every other emotion, your fear of failure is tied to an underlying trigger. These could be anything from childhood events that made you feel insecure or unsafe, or past experiences that ended up in failure, or just an inability to stretch your boundaries. Whatever it is that is the root of your fear; unless you confront it, you cannot develop risk management toughness. Most of our fears stem from unresolved underlying issues that have preconditioned us to think in a particular way. For example, you may be carrying around a belief that you do not have leadership skills because you did not do well in leadership roles at school. The problem with these kinds of assumptions and generalizations of your abilities is that they are all based on who you were in the past.

The fact is that we all grow and evolve with time and experience. So if you remain adamant in judging your abilities based on past mistakes, you are essentially stripping any lessons you learned from your past failures. Stop attaching labels to yourself and learn to view yourself objectively. Do not think of yourself as "the guy who botched the presentation last month." Just think of yourself as the guy who has an opportunity to do something great. Ditch the labels and the self-limiting beliefs and gradually taking risks will not be so daunting.

To overcome your fear of failure, learn to dissociate reality from the assumptions that you have made based on the past. Even if you have made mistakes in the past, it does not mean that you cannot learn and do better given a chance to try again. Mentally strong people do not seek comfort in an identity based on the past.

They are comfortable trying new things and challenging their beliefs because they understand that it is the only way to grow.

When a child is learning to walk, they must first get up. They will fall many times before they finally get their balance right, yet the falling does not stop them from trying until they finally master the ability to walk. If a minor child has enough courage to get back up when they trip, what stops you from trying something new? This same analogy applies to the unique things you will try in your life. In most cases, you will fail the first few times you try, but what you will learn in the process will be worth the effort.

Whenever you choose to pass on an opportunity because it feels too much of a risk, consider what you will miss out on. If your dream is to start a business, but you are too afraid to move, think of the freedom and independence you are missing out on. Consider all the opportunities you are missing out on by not taking the leap and following your dream. When you focus on what you stand to gain by taking the risk, then the fear will still be there, but it will pale compared to what is at stake.

Think of all the things you procrastinate about due to the fear of failure. Consider the many ways in which your self-sabotage by giving in to fear. You remain stuck in unhappy situations that you are fully capable of changing because the thought that you are risking failure by trying leaves you unable to take the necessary steps.

In the larger scheme of things, the choice that you have to make is between going after your goals by taking a risk or giving up on your dreams to avoid the risk of failure. This is essentially a choice between unhappiness and uncertainty. You can never be thrilled unless you pursue your goals, and yet the fate of the unknown prevents you from taking a chance. So, ultimately you have to choose whether you want to be unhappy in your comfort zone or chasing fulfillment by embracing uncertainty.

If you are always thinking of the worst-case scenario, every challenge or opportunity will inevitably seem like it is bound to fail. Train yourself to have hope and positive expectations.

Negative thoughts can keep you from seeing things objectively and cloud your judgment. Always weigh the possibility of failure against the chance of success. Negative thoughts lead to procrastination because they push you to keep putting off the things you are afraid of taking on.

Procrastination then affects your productivity, and you become prone to indecision and inaction. You find that when big moments come, you choke, and you cannot decide whether to move forward or stay where you are.

When faced with great opportunities, you will balk at the chance to do something different because there is a risk involved. The net result is that you will find your life is going round in circles and not making any progress towards your goals.

In the same way that negative thoughts lead to inaction and procrastination, positive reviews increase productivity and push you to become proactive. Hen faces opportunities or challenges; you jump at the chance because your expectation of success is much higher than your expectation of failure.

Positive people know that there is a possibility of failure, but they understand that failure is just a normal part of the journey to achieving your goals. This mindset causes positive-minded people to have higher risk management toughness and a greater affinity for taking chances. When you are mentally strong, the possibility of failure does not deter you because you understand that failure is part of the process and not the result.

Until you learn to stop the negative self-dialogue, you will always keep sabotaging your progress by feeding your fear. The more afraid you become to venture out of your comfort zone, the fewer opportunities you will be able to identify and seize. Your mind will remain closed off to new ideas and perspectives because anything that challenges your beliefs and identity feels risky and uncomfortable. A mindset refers to the established attitudes and thoughts you have created over time. People with a fixed mindset believe that their skills, talents, and abilities are predetermined and fixed, so they always priorities innate ability over learning. People with fixed mindsets think that to do something; you need to have the natural talent for it or have some pre-existing qualifications.

On the other hand, people who have a growth mindset embrace learning through experiences and challenges. They do not look at challenges in terms of how well equipped they are to face them, but rather what they can learn by trying something new. To cultivate a growth mindset, you need to open up your mind to learning and changing the way you think.

These two mindsets explain why it is not always the people at the top of their class who are successful. No matter how high your IQ is, if you do not take a chance on opportunities, challenge yourself and take risks, your brilliance will stagnate. On the other hand, people who believe they can increase their skills and abilities by testing and pushing themselves are more likely to get ahead because they take risks that the average person would not.

Building a growth mindset where you embrace change and taking risks will help you make new habits and look at life from a different perspective. A growth mindset helps you see failure not as a definition of who you are but as a regular part of learning and growing. To get past the limitations of a fixed mindset, prioritize education and hard work over talent or innate abilities.

Many talented people do nothing with their talent because they do not work hard enough. Stop worrying about your IQ or what talents or skills you may be lacking and focus on learning by pushing yourself to try new things. Learn to take risks by taking on challenges and doing something that you would not normally do.

Neuroscience has proven that our brains are plastic. You can always learn anything that you do not know, and any bad habits that you have created can be replaced with good ones. There are no limits to what your brain can learn and unlearn, but you have to be open to new experiences and change for this to happen. Do not create limitations on your abilities or your skills.

People with risk management toughness are not afraid to have flaws because they know that they are not permanent. Instead of avoiding challenges, think of them as a way to discover new 6things about yourself, expand your horizons, and reach your goals.

It is not caused by the size of the challenge or any other external circumstance. Fear comes from your insecurities, self-limiting beliefs, and the negative self-dialogue you constantly engage in. This means that to overcome the fear of failure, you need to change how you think about yourself, your abilities, and your beliefs.

Before you try and change the situation, first change yourself by questioning your assumptions. Only then will you be able to overcome your insecurities and embrace the uncertainty that comes with taking risks.

The Perfection Fallacy

One of the biggest reasons people procrastinate and hesitate to take risks in pursuing perfection. Perfection is when something comes with all the desired qualities and guarantees in such a way that it is 100% of what you want. Ultimately there is no such thing as perfect in reality because perfection in itself is an idea, and so it changes from day to day. What you thought was ideal yesterday might seem flawed today, and so, in essence, the pursuit of perfection is a never-ending mission in futility.

I am sure that you have at some point bought something that you thought was perfect. You thought this is just perfect when you saw it; it is everything that I wanted. Once you get home with your new purchase, the perceived perfection may last a couple of days or even weeks. However, sooner or later, you start to notice minor flaws here and there, get tired of it, and then eventually discard it. This often happens because perfection is an idea; what looks perfect today will fall short in some way or other tomorrow,

While going for perfection when shopping for goods or services may be a good, albeit somewhat misguided, idea, the pursuit of perfection can become a dangerous obsession if you make it a way of life. The perfection fallacy occurs when you start waiting for things to be just "perfect" for you to take action. You are waiting for the perfect job opportunity, waiting for the perfect soulmate, waiting for the ideal market conditions to start a business, the perfect time to start losing weight, and so on.

Of course, since these perfect situations do not exist, what you end up doing by chasing perfection is nothing worthwhile. People who are always waiting for all their ducks to line up perfectly in a neat row before they can make a move never really get around to doing anything with their lives. They remain stuck in the same situations year in year out because they do not want to take a risk and do something that will not be perfect.

It is commonly said that perfection is the enemy of good. This is because perfection keeps you from acting even when there is a clear opportunity ahead of you. You become so afraid of taking chances because you do not want anything to go wrong.

So you end up just choking at crucial moments and missing out on opportunities to do something great or try something new that could bring you closer to your goals.

Concert pianists, professional athletes, and even theatre performers always keep rehearsing and practicing their craft. So by practicing constantly, they get even better at what they do. With each repetition, they get better at what they are good at, improving their flaws. Perfectionists miss out on the opportunity to get better and work on their deficiencies because they do not try. They want to start at perfect for perfectionists instead of starting at good and working their way up to perfect.

You cannot start from the top; you have to do it bottom-up. The lesson in this simple truth is that you need to start with what you have to get anywhere. You start where you are and gradually build up on the abilities you have, your skills, and your knowledge until you have what you need to achieve your goals and dreams.

You may never end up being perfect. However, when you take a chance and start something, in the end, you will be better than you were when you started. Instead of waiting for things to fall neatly into place, start with what you have and start where you are. As you go along on your journey, you will keep increasing what you have, learning new things, and getting better with each challenge and failure. Some of the most successful people will tell you that the moments in their lives that are most memorable are the ones where they challenged themselves, overcame difficulties, and discovered things about themselves that they never knew.

People who cultivate risk management toughness understand that you must be willing to take the first step to get anywhere in life. This means that sometimes you have to be ready to start with good enough to get to what you want. Unless you take a chance on what is in front of you and work to make it into what you have envisioned, you will always be waiting for an ideal that will never come.

You do not need to have millions of dollars to start a business or just the perfect product or service to become an entrepreneur. When companies go to market with a minimum viable product, it is not because they are too lazy to finish the product. They want to make improvements to the product based on user feedback and the reaction they get from the consumer.

Imagine if you spent millions of dollars on a product only for you to launch something that consumers did not want. You would end up having to pay even more to fix the flaws and change the product again.

As we have already said, perfection is not set; it is an idea that shifts from day to day.

The success of using a minimum viable product for businesses is that it allows companies to start with what they have. Once they have started with a primary outcome, they can improve it as they learn more and more about what their consumers need. They rely on user feedback as a source of valuable information to fine-tune the product and improve on it until it meets the consumer's needs as best as possible.

You may not be going into business, but having a minimum viable product to start with works in any dimension. It simply means that you start with something good and then fine-tune it and make it better as you go along. The key here is that you create. You do not obsess over the small details; you do not wait for the wind to blow just the right way or any other excuses you use to delay action. Start with your minimum viable product, whatever it is, and then learn as you go along.

If you want to lose weight, do not wait until you have money to join an expensive weight loss program. Both of these are free, but they will get you started on your journey. When you get too caught up in doing things just a particular way, you may end up wasting valuable time, yet you had everything you needed to get started all along.

If you want to start a business, you do not need to have millions in capital. Plenty of successful companies started in people's basements as they worked to build up their money. If you are determined to see your goal through, then you will not let the minor inconveniences and details stand in your way. Most of the time, we use perfection as an excuse to delay action because we are afraid to take risks or push ourselves out of the safety of our comfort zone.

Your dreams will gather dust in a drawer somewhere as you wait for just the perfect moment to act or get moving. Build your risk management toughness by embracing uncertainty and getting over procrastination. Train yourself to take the first step. Most people find that once they take the first step, then the rest are not so hard to take.

Break down your goals into smaller steps that will help you to focus on the process instead of the result. Stop wondering whether the outcome will be a success or not, and commit to what you need to do today. When you build discipline and invest in the process, the results will take care of themselves. So, all their energy and focus are usually on the preparation process.

All this means is that worrying about perfection does not add any value to your outcome. Your efforts and energy should be on the actions you can take to ensure the result you want. The product may not be perfect, but it will always be better than staying stuck in the same situation because you are busy waiting for things to be just right before you make a move.

Risk takers are not bold because they know the outcome of waiting for them down the pike. Instead, they get their confidence from knowing that they will get where they need to go if they keep doing the right thing consistently sooner or later. Trust in the process and guide you to the result you want. At the end of it all, whether you succeed or fail, you will still be a better person than you were when you started.

Conclusion

The truth you cannot deny and avoid is that everyone needs mental toughness as long as we are all humans. When the theory of survival of the fittest was propounded, other ideas later emerged, which postulates that some living things will have to struggle for their survival. Those living things that were better adapted to changes in their environment will survive the changes in their environment. Therefore, you should know by now that there will always be changes in our life and environment; the question is, "how well will you be able to adapt to such changes?"

Secondly, ask yourself, "have you developed those features that will enable you to carry out your adaptation"?

Then it is evident that one of the distinctive features you will need to develop is your level of mental toughness. Whether you like it or not, you need to set yourself mentally. It will start somewhere; you may be scared right now about how to begin; let me tell you something, your waiting days are over, the simple truth now is that you have to get things started; taking actions is what you need. By the time you start with a single step that you decide to take now, you will sooner or later look back and see the distance you would have covered.

Don't wait any longer, take that bold step in the right direction, follow the basic principles and teachings as explained in this book, step by step and one at a time, always refer back to the contents and read to gain mastery of the various approaches and directives given to advance further.

Be mentally tough, and you will be victorious forever!

Let's hope it was informative and able to provide you with all of the tools you need to achieve your goals, whatever it is that they may be. How amazing it must have been for you to realize that your mind is the primary determinant of where you are in life. It determines how quickly you move or how much you hesitate.

For these reasons, you need to ensure that your mind is continually tough to withstand the challenges that come about and to keep yourself moving ahead. It helps when you work on yourself, using your abilities as a benchmark for future improvements, but you could also get inspiration from the works of great men and women that have achieved success in their lifetimes.

See what they did when the odds were against them. See what happened when they listened to other people rather than their voices. Use their lives as lessons for your own life. You do not have to teach yourself to learn; other people make excellent illustrations.

Thank you, and good luck!

MENTAL MODELS

Introduction

Mental models are deeply ingrained assumptions or generalizations that influence how we understand the world and how we take action. Some other words we use for mental models are perspectives, beliefs, assumptions, and mind set, to name a few. Mental models are often the greatest barriers to implementing new ideas in organizations, but they are also the area of organizational learning where organizations can make the most significant impact.

Unfortunately, assumptions, the word most often used to refer to mental models, have a negative connotation to most of us. Well, you can fill in the blank. Assumptions, nonetheless, are the only way we can make sense of our complex world. It is not possible to have complete information about every situation we encounter, so by their very nature, our assumptions or mental models are incomplete and therefore flawed. For the most part, however, our mental models serve us well.

There are those occasions, on the other hand, where our mental models lead us astray. A great example of how imperfect mental models can be comes from the ancient parable of the blind men and the elephant, where several blind men are feeling different parts of an elephant and describing it. The descriptions by themselves are inaccurate, but when combined into one, give a clearer albeit still flawed description of what an elephant really looks like. Mental models are like puzzle pieces that we need to fit together into a larger whole. As different mental models are recognized, another piece falls in to place, and we see a clearer picture, but in this work, we do not have the top of the puzzle box to guide us. We must grope along like the blind men.

Mental models affect what we see in situations and create reinforcing patterns of behavior.

Chapter 1: What are Mental Models?

Mental models are cognitive frameworks that contain multiple representations or versions of how the world works. They are often used to help us deal with difficult problems, make important decisions, and comprehend complex information. To illustrate how mental models help us organize information, Schön (1983) told the following story about George's man. George works on a dairy farm. He is responsible for supervising two machines that process milk. One of the machines must be shut down every night so that it can be cleaned. The problem is that no one else knows how to shut down the machine, and if it isn't done properly, it might break.

Mental Models As Camera Lenses

Mental models function as a type of camera lens that can be focused or unfocused, zoomed in or out to see larger or smaller details. They help simplify our perception and understanding by categorizing information and forming patterns (often across different categories).

Mental Models As Related to Strategy

Mental models help us identify strategic issues and plan future options. They are used to form hypotheses and predictions or make connections between different elements of our knowledge of a situation.

Mental Models as Diagnosis Tools

Mental models can serve as useful diagnostic tools when combined with the scientific method. The problem with using mental models in this way is that they may be inaccurate. We often assume that the things we already know about a situation alone are enough to understand it. Still, there's always more we don't know yet, and using mental models is like trying to see through a camera lens that's too blurry--we're going to get only a partial view.

Mental Models as Adaptive Tools

A mental model is a form of tacit knowledge (i.e., it is subconscious, difficult to articulate, and difficult to transfer). Mental models are often used as adaptive tools. This means that they help us make sense of our environment by helping us understand how different elements in our reality interrelate to support or oppose certain actions.

This type of thinking helps us predict consequences and make good decisions (i.e., they're tools that help us adapt to the environments we find ourselves adjusting to).

How we form mental models?

Mental models can be formed in several ways. They can be self-generated, such as the mental model that reveals complex systems by considering them as feedback loops. They can also be generated from other mental models, such as when we think of complex organizations and their relationships from a system's perspective. When used in this way, mental models usually involve seeing patterns within information and creating categories or classifications to simplify understanding.

Benefits of mental models

Mental models help us make sense of and predict complex situations. They also provide a simple, often visual way of depicting different relationships and the elements that go into those relationships.

1.   <u>Mental models help us do and think about things in a more orderly, organized way.</u>

2.   Mental models can help us to predict possible future actions and consequences.

3.   Mental models help us organize complex events into identifiable aspects or categories to see relationships more easily.

4.   Mental models are used to formulate hypotheses and predictions about complex systems-based issues (e.g., organizational behavior from a system's perspective).

5.   Finally, mental models help us adjust to a given situation by making sense of what is happening to us, the necessary course of action, how it will affect other parts of our lives (see Adaptive mental model).

Chapter 2: The Origin of Mental Models

Mental Models That Block Creativity

"I cannot do it." "I do not have the capacity." "I will not try because it will not work."

These are typical phrases that we repeat in difficult situations that require going beyond the ordinary. But maybe it's time you re-thought the use of each phrase and line you speak. The human unconscious sometimes imposes barriers on our actions. These are the so-called limiting thoughts, which make us fear new and different experiences. That kind of reasoning only leads to the commonplace and prevents something creative from being externalized. Do you know those traditional phrases, the clichés like "every politician is a thief" or "blonde is dumb"?

The point here is to leave such expressions aside and allow yourself to go further, to understand the meaning behind each story, and not just repeat what most propagates as truth.

Discover your Mental Models

You may know the origin of your mental models, but have you stopped to wonder why they affect you in a certain way? Trying to find out what these patterns are and understand what they mean is appropriate for your thoughts and emotions.

Want to understand how? Check out the following tips, which I have collated and listed below:

Self

The first question you should ask yourself is: do I know myself?

Looking at yourself and seeking answers is the first step in understanding how you relate to people and the world. Aggression, for example, is a fairly common feeling among those who try only to stifle the struggles they daily struggle within to find out what they expect from life.

Respect

After all, the natural way is that of respect for contrary opinions. But this is also an exercise you must bring about. Each individual has his/her mental model, created from their personal, cultural, and other experiences - and there is nothing wrong with it. The important thing is not to make it the only option.

By performing these activities, you will be much closer to discovering and controlling your thought patterns. Now, I am guessing that the following question will be the logically next query on your mind:

The Influence of Mental Models on Corporate Results

The success story of Southwest Airlines, a Texan airline, shows what we have just said. The company, which has giant competitors such as Delta and United, is the only one to profit for 43 consecutive years. Since its foundation, it has an open mental model that allows identifying market trends.

While the other companies are investing in state-of-the-art aircraft, with class A, B, C, and D cabins and multi-stop flights, Southwest has more modest aircraft models without stipulating socioeconomic divisions for passengers and non-stop travel. This type of business grew out of the perception that a specific consumer had purchasing power but not enough to pay for all the luxuries of an air trip.

Looking at the service differently made it possible to enter a segment that had not been explored until then. Hence, you might ask, "Oh, but have not competitors tried to repeat the business model?" They tried, but they did not have the same success as we mentioned before. This happened because the public did not buy the idea and preferred to continue flying with the company that, from the beginning, was dedicated to it.

How Does The Mental Model Of Leaders Impact On Company Performance?

Believe it or not, mental models of leaders do impact company performance a lot. Any and every decision made by a company's leaders is in some way based on their mental models. That is, the impact is direct and appears in each of the choices made.

Brief Conclusion

Mental models are present throughout our lives, and they start existing even before we were born. As much as you might try to ignore them, they will appear in your decisions. They are so natural that we often do not even notice them. The important thing is to know how to use them in our favor in a way that impacts our actions positively. To get there, do not forget these three words: self-knowledge, empathy, and respect.

Understanding the mental models that are part of your life is fundamental to understanding human behavior as well. Mental models can determine a person's success or failure. When I ask anyone I talk to on the topic or even otherwise as to what this means, some people look at me apprehensively and are waiting for a tip. Still, the question is mine, and I always try to extract the answer according to the general knowledge of the group. When you understand the concept and seek to associate it in practice, the journey becomes less painful.

Understanding the basis of human behavior and the keys to personal fulfillment depends on understanding the meaning and importance of mental models in your life. Whether you know it or not, mental models define your ability to act and react to the simplest things and the hardest things in life; that is, they define your behavior. First, it is necessary to know the sources of mental models and the way they are formed. According to Daniel Goleman, author of the bestselling book called Emotional Intelligence, the sources of mental models are the way humans organize and give meaning to their experiences. According to Goleman, human behavior is conditioned by mental models, and these, in turn, are defined based on four assumptions:

Biology: labeling the human being's ability to perform based on its physiological limitations. Does someone is tall or short, black or white, hairy or bald, fat or thin, beautiful or less favored in terms of beauty should be a factor of inclusion or exclusion in the job market? For many companies, this is how it works, unfortunately. Have you ever read a job advertisement in the newspaper with the following words: Do you need a Chubby Secretary, short, and everything which more or less means something about appearance and less about skills or intelligence?

Language: is the medium in which the consciousness of the human being is structured. When you hear a Northeasterner, a Santa Catarina, a gaucho from the pampas, a Paulista from the interior, or a carioca with a conversation with that typical accent of his region, what comes to your mind? Do not say you've never labeled someone because of your accent? Enjoy!

Culture: within any group - families, industries, organizations, and nations - collective mental models develop from shared experiences. Thus culture can be considered a collective mental model. If you are the child of Jew, Italian, Greek, German, or Japanese, it does not matter, and there is a set of values or assumptions typical of each culture. Somehow, this affects relationships, hence the difficulties of admitting the union of people from different roots in some cultures. Personal experience: concerns race, gender, nationality, ethnic origin, social and economic condition, family influences, level of education, how our parents treated us, siblings, teachers, and childhood partners. The way we begin to work and achieve self-sufficiency is also the fruit of our personal experience, which is key to our success.

Because of all this, some phrases become common in your daily life, and when you least expect it, inadvertently slip, without the least concern for the reflection of your words. What counts for one country or culture is not necessarily valid for another. Have you ever uttered any of these phrases?

All men are equal! It means that your father and that person you both admire are also. You cannot trust women! Even your mother, your wife, and your sisters?

All politicians are equal! Including that his relative, who had been very hard-fought and found a job for his entire family that was in trouble?

The little with God is enough! Believe me, if this is true, the most you will achieve is definitely that 'little,' and at the same time, you will continue to envy the rich for the rest of your life.

This is not going to work, and it has always been like this here! This is one of the most well-known mental models in organizations that are doomed to fail.

I'm poor, but I'm happy! Do you know some poor, in the literal sense of the word, happy?

The important thing is to win! More important than winning is contributing and not being overwhelmed by defeat. If the world were made only of victors, learning would not exist.

Chapter 3: Principle of reason

A principle of reason guides us as we make decisions and take action because it helps us ensure that our behavior is goal-oriented and complements our values. Principles of reason are also known as moral theories.

The Pareto principle

The Pareto principle states that "the majority of the effects comes from the minority of causes."

The idea that we should maximize our private utility (or at least minimize the damage done to us) has led to many ethical debates, such as that between Utilitarians and deontologists.

The ethicist John Broome is probably best known for his ethical theory, which uses a principle of reason to determine right and wrong. He stated that people should always maximize their receiving (or keeping) of benefits and avoid harming others (or not gaining the benefit of others' harm).

The principle of reason has also been used to support the theory that an act is right if it follows a rational procedure. The idea behind this theory is that it would be counter-productive to base ethical decisions on sentiments, as this could lead to irrational decisions.

The Pareto Principle can be used to decide how to distribute costs and benefits when planning resource allocation.

The philosopher John Rawls used the principle of reason to find a universally acceptable set of rules for social order. Rawls states that rational individuals would agree on the following principles:

In smaller social groups, the application of these ethics may differ, depending on circumstances. For example, some cultures allow an individual to kill their child if it is a danger to society, or when a judge sentences someone to death during a wartime regime; however, this does not contradict the principles stated above since they are generalizable and the reasons for which they are applicable are generally justified for maintaining social stability or situational necessity.

The principle has been used to support a new form of rational egoism, a version of ethical egoism that suggests that one should always act to maximize their self-interest.

The principle also has implications for the debate about freedom of speech and censorship. If the principle of reason is applied to this area, there are limited circumstances in which it may be right to restrict someone's freedom of speech for the greater good. For example, certain forms of hate speech are only allowed if they are relevant and contribute something meaningful to the debate. There is no intent to cause harm or provoke violence towards others based on their race, religion, or sexual orientation. This would allow the debate to be put forward without causing harm to social cohesion.

Social Contract Theory argues that individuals can only fully and freely decide in conditions where they have agreed on principles with others. This freedom requires the existence of law, equal treatment for everyone, some form of the impartial legal system, and a public voice capable of influencing the use of power. The authority which gives one such power is usually called an "overarching Law." Without these conditions, one cannot fully fulfill their rights as a rational, autonomous individual and therefore cannot make free choices unless coerced by another person or entity.

John Rawls has used the principle to find a universally acceptable set of rules for social order.

Confirmation bias

("also called confirmatory bias") A cognitive bias occurs when the human mind selectively focuses on information that confirms one's preexisting beliefs or hypotheses. It is a logical fallacy in that it does not take into account contradictory information; for example, believing in

The principle was first used by Aldous Huxley in his novel "Brave New World," saying: "I say dully: "See what you like… See everything through my eyes."

The principle of reason has also been used to support the theory that an act is right if it follows a rational procedure. The idea behind this theory is that it would be counter-productive to base ethical decisions on sentiments, as this could lead to irrational decisions.

The philosopher John Rawls used the principle of reason to find a universally acceptable set of rules for social order. Rawls states that rational individuals would agree on the following principles:

In smaller social groups, the application of these ethics may differ depending on circumstances. For example, some cultures allow an individual to kill their child if it is a danger to society, or when a judge sentences someone to death during a wartime regime; however, this does not contradict the principles stated above since they are generalizable and the reasons for which they are applicable are generally justified for maintaining social stability or situational necessity.

The principle has been used to support a new form of rational egoism, a version of ethical egoism that suggests that one should always act to maximize their self-interest.

The principle also has implications for the debate about freedom of speech and censorship. If the principle of reason is applied to this area, there are limited circumstances in which it may be right to restrict someone's freedom of speech for the greater good. For example, certain forms of hate speech are only allowed if they are relevant and contribute something meaningful to the debate. There is no intent to cause harm or provoke violence towards others based on their race, religion, or sexual orientation. This would allow the debate to be put forward without causing harm to social cohesion.

John Rawls has used the principle to find a universally acceptable set of rules for social order.

The 10/10/10 rule

The 10/10/10 rule ("also called the 1/1/1 rule") is a simple thought experiment that aims to demonstrate the importance of social cohesion. It proposes that it must be necessary, important, and true if something is to be said. Typically, the speaker will use this principle to debate some contentious issue to encourage people to speak more constructively.

William Connolly first put forward the idea in his book "The Fragility of Things: Self-Organizing Processes, Neoliberal Fantasies, and Democratic Activism." The 10/10/10 rule is reversed to 1/1/1 in the normal form of the postulate of Mathematical Democracy (also called the 1/1 rule).

Using this rule in the real world is a matter of debate: some organizations adhere to the principle, while others adopt alternative decision-making methods.

In technology circles, it is common for software engineers to be encouraged to think in terms of the 10/10/10 rule as a means of preventing bad code from making it out into the world.

The rule is used in debate training to ensure that debates are restricted to those things that are necessary, important, and true.

The rule has been used in educational settings to prevent unhelpful debates in the classroom.

Circle of Competence

Julian Luce proposed the Rule of Competence in his 1957 essay, "The Ethics of Democratic Planning."

Luce argued that the Rule of Competence should not only be used by planners to ensure that they had a broad knowledge of what was going on in their political domain (particularly local affairs) but also by citizens to ensure that they did not criticize actions or projects within the domain of others.

The rule can be summarized as: "Within the limits of our competence, we should stick to our affairs and speak out only when we know enough about them."

For example, citizens who are not experts in financial matters should hold back from calling for public spending cuts, and so on.

The Circle of Competence allows each party to remain within their sphere of influence.

The Rule is often misrepresented as "Do not criticize" but should be seen as encouraging active engagement with problem-solving within one's area of expertise rather than engagement with others across political lines.

Maslow's Hierarchy of Needs

It is important to state that the Circle of Competence and Maslow's Hierarchy of Needs are not mutually exclusive and related.

Maslow's Hierarchy of Needs is about how a person's needs are met, whereas the Circle of Competence is about how each member contributes to meeting those needs.

The main reason for this connection can be found in Maslow's statement that "We are motivated by the nature of our psychological survival needs" (1943: 453).

Although these needs for a constant food supply and safety may not be directly affected by political participation, participation indirectly affects this need.

Parkinson's law

Parkinson's law is an adage in management and human resources. It states that meetings inevitably become longer as the number of attendees increases. One interpretation is that when a group becomes larger, members attempt to include more people by taking up more time.

However, there are also many other principles from Parkinson's law that can be applied to healthy interactions: work expands to fill the time available for its completion, you should not put off difficult tasks until tomorrow because they will take twice as long tomorrow, etc.

Eisenhower box

The Eisenhower box is a management method designed by U.S. President Dwight D. Eisenhower to effectively manage workable processes and outcomes within an organization to achieve successful goals and objectives. The box is a diagram of three concentric circles. The outer circle represents the organization, the second circle represents the group of people within the organization, and the inner circle represents interacting with each other.

The Eisenhower box addresses problems that have two primary causes:

It is recognized that problems can never be completely removed from an organization (in part because people are human and we all have flaws). The Eisenhower Box helps organizations deal with these problems to effectively manage, organize, and execute work within their organizations.

The Eisenhower Box helps solve these problems by addressing them in a hierarchy like:

Eisenhower's Decision Matrix also applied the Pareto Principle, which states that 20% of our efforts account for 80% of our outcome. This means that we should focus on the most effective part of our activities and remove the less effective ones. It also implies that we should not spend time on frivolous tasks or in unimportant meetings because they will ultimately be ineffective.

These methods encourage healthy interactions between people and help define what actions will be most effective for reaching a goal. In contrast to harmful interactions, it is more about what you do to achieve your goals, not just how you interact with others.

The misinformation effect

The misinformation effect is how the amount of incorrect information we receive in a given period can influence how people behave over time.Suppose there is a mechanism by which people can be misguided by misinformation regarding information that they are exposed to or about an issue. People tend to seek out and follow incorrect information if this is sufficient to achieve their goals, whereas they tend not to do this if their goals are met without being misled. This tendency can be measured and studied, but there is the possibility that people only respond in this way when they fail to achieve their objectives by taking into account all the available options.

Ambiguity effect

The ambiguity effect tends to prefer an uncertain option that has a chance of a positive outcome over a more certain option with an outcome that is negative. The term ambiguity effect is used in prospect theory to describe the idea that people feel better about their outcome if they receive one lottery ticket with a chance of winning than if they receive two tickets with a smaller chance of winning. The term ambiguity effect also means that people prefer the two-ticket option, regardless of whether or not it wins, if they do not know how likely they are to win with one ticket versus two tickets.

Chapter 4: Writing and Inquisitive? The Best Mental Models to Help You

The Socratic Questioning Technique

This will be a mental model that has been devised to inspire some critical thinking along the way. This technique will employ a set of questions that will enable someone to learn about their fallacies, their unfounded assumptions, and limiting beliefs. And by this discovery, the person will be able to think more critically. You will continue to work with this one until you can come up with the right answer that makes the most sense of the situation.

The Why Iteration

The next mental model that we will take a look at is known as the Why iteration. This one is going to be where you ask the why question five times at a minimum. The point of this one is that you want to get to the root of the initial response rather than stopping at some superficial point along the way. The assumption with the Why Iteration is that the first response is rarely the final one, and relying on this first response will not give you the true picture of things you need. Here we see that the more questions we ask, the closer we can get to the root of the matter.

You can consider each Why to address a specific layer in the structure. And you also have to consider the problem as a type of root that has five layers down. The first why you ask is going to be able to address the respective portion of the root in the first layer, but four other portions and four other layers you need to spend some time on before fully understanding the problem.

One thing to keep in mind with this one is that the five is not empirical but more encouragement. Some structures could have fewer numbers, and others are going to have more. Don't use this as an excuse, asking why two times and give up. Work at adding in as many different layers to the problem as you can, and see what a difference it can make.

The NLP Meta Model

The NLP Meta Model is going to be similar to the Socratic model that we talked about before. It will help us make some deep inquiries into information that word labels may not avail. What a person says is often just a small percentage of the entire information that that person holds, basically just the tip of the iceberg. It is not always the intent of the other person to filter out the information. Still, they may do it to shorten up the conversation if needed or just to give you their perception of the most important information. In the process of perceiving information from a sensory organ, the brain:

1. Deletes a bit of the sensory information to make it easier to do the processing.

2. Distorts part of the sensory information based on what experiences you have had in the past.

3. Generalizes the sensory information, especially if the information was repetitive.

These will be done to effectively utilize the limited space in the memory, fit the existing mental models, and prioritize the functional benefits. Thus, to help us get a clear picture, we need to ask some specific questions that we can recycle or reconstruct the deleted portion of the message, straighten out the part that is distorted, and unwrap some of the generalizations so that e can get more information out of this person. A good example of what this is going to look like when we work with the NLP model includes:

1. Distortion: I am sure that he is feeling jealous. I am sure that his congratulation message is not genuine.

2. Deletion: No one likes seeing me successful. When people tell me they do, it's always a fake compliment.

3.   Generalization: All women are gold-diggers.

From the statements above, you can see that there is so much information that we are missing out on, which is being withheld from this. Using the NLP meta-model, you will ask a specific set of questions to that other person to figure out the root of that statement. T

his is also a good option to use in therapies because it gives you the ability to understand the problems of others better or help them understand their problems more deeply.

The Response Bias

Response bias occurs when an interviewee will respond that is not based on the facts but is more based on some of the other factors nearby. It could include some factors like the desire to please, fear, a desire to look politically or socially correct, a desire to conform, and even a desire to avoid telling the other person the truth.

Because of this bias, researchers, journalists, and more need to learn how to not overly rely on a given response without putting it to strict empirical test and proof. You want to make sure that you are getting the right answers from others, rather than getting this bias that will distort the kind of image you can get from the other person. If you can learn how to take away some of the bias and get the other person to feel more comfortable and open around you, you may find that they will give you better answers without the bias, and this can do some wonders in the process.

Chapter 5: The Role of Mental Models

After looking into some of the best mental models you can find, it is imperative to delve into the role of these mental models. Certainly, this is something that might have crossed your mind as you wonder how the models will help you. So, why mental models? What makes these models relevant in your life? Of course, you now know that mental models allow you to understand how this world works. The varying models provide you with clear-cut information on comprehending how different thought processes can boost your thinking capacity.

However, it is still worth questioning why and how these models can positively impact how you think and perceive the world around you. Looking at the array of mental models, it can be argued that mental models can assist you in solving your problems faster. Challenges are part of our daily lives. This is what people have to go through to achieve their goals, in the short or long run. To ensure that people achieve their goals, decisions have to be made. Accordingly, mental models come in handy to make the decision-making process easier.

Concerning what has been said, mental models can guide the design of the approach you will be taking to handle a particular situation. It will help you and your team settle for an optimal strategy to solve a problem in business. If there are problems you are facing, mental models can guide you on the best approach.

When Jeff Bezos was in a dilemma about whether to start Amazon, he looked for a framework to guide him to make the right decision. As such, he came up with the regret minimization framework. Using this framework, he pictured how he would feel in the future depending on his decision. In this case, Jeff had a good feeling about starting Amazon, and he was sure he would not regret the decision to quit his job and start the company. Therefore, his model provided him with the motivation to make a sound decision easily and effectively.

From Bezos's example, there are three things that we can notice here. First, the regret minimization framework he used gave him confidence in the design he was using. He dared to make a big leap to start Amazon. You should bear in mind that he was a senior vice-president at the company that he left. So, he was not quitting because he was not earning well. For that reason, quitting his job was not easy. Without confidence, this is something that he would have just brushed off.

Secondly, the framework that Bezos used provided him with clarity. After coming up with his model, it was now clear that he would regret not implementing what he had in mind. The framework gave him a reason to understand that this was the right direction to take.

Third, Bezos's framework was rooted in the idea of focusing on the long-term consequences of a particular decision. He envisaged himself 80 years after starting Amazon, and he was sure that he would regret it if he didn't work on his vision. His mental model gave him a reason to believe in the continuity of his strategy.

Therefore, the advantages of using mental models in your life can be summed up as follows. It helps you gain:

- Confidence in your approach

- Clarity in direction

- Continuity of strategy

Confidence in Your Approach

You can never be sure about anything that you want to do. However, this doesn't mean that there is nothing that you can do to make your decision-making process simpler. Using mental models gives you confidence that the approach you are using has been proven and tested by other successful people in society. Once your mind acknowledges that your framework is based on solid research, you will have the energy to pursue what you have been thinking of. This is because you are more convinced that it will work. You have solid proof, and nothing can stop you.

Besides, if you are working with a team, the mental models you use allow them to believe the approach you plan to use. In a way, when they comprehend how your approach works, they will grasp your understanding of the solution and embrace it.

Leverage Luck and Intent

Since we agree that the world is full of uncertainties, there is room for luck in what we do. Basing our argument on the probabilistic thinking mental model, numerous variables will contribute to succeeding in anything you do. Believe it or not, luck is one of them.

The funny thing is that most individuals would want to attribute their success to certain facts. They will give plenty of excuses to justify that the decision they made was accurate. The reality of the matter is that luck influences how we succeed. When using mental models to improve your thinking abilities, you are more comfortable opening up to the world of possibilities. That's not all, and you will also acknowledge the variables that contribute to your success. Simply put, you will embrace the uncertainty that this world puts you through. Accordingly, mental models will be the right tools to steer you in the right direction.

Mental models provide you with the evidence you need to rely on your approach. They are a language that you can read and understand. Language helps you to communicate with other people. It gives you the ability to interact with others and to know what they feel. In the same manner, mental models are a language that you can master. The good news is that you will not be the first person to use them. Thousands of people are using these models to solve their problems with ease.

Differentiate Between Solutions

Undeniably, the more models you grasp, the more informed you will be. For you, it will be easy to distinguish between solutions that can be reached by using these models. The point here is that models give you the advantage of perceiving this world from different perspectives. Hence, you will not be limited to one solution. You can decide to utilize distinct frameworks to solve the diverse problems you might be facing.

Accept that Ideas Match Needs

Another good thing about mental models is that it provides you with the right platform to confirm that your approach is ideal. In this case, when using any mental model, you will embrace the notion of a higher level of thinking. For instance, before making any decision, you will want to compare your decisions to what renowned scholars would do if they were in your situation. Eventually, this puts you in a situation where you decide based on what you have validated to be realistic.

Avoid Politics

The confidence that you have in your approach will prevent you from second-guessing. You know what is right and what is wrong. Therefore, you will want to choose the best path with a proven track record. Certainly, this is important, more so when working in groups.

Some individuals might want to engage in trial and error to solve their problems. Making wild guesses on what you should do can easily bring any successful business to the ground. A mental model would save the day as it would provide the best interpretation to decide what you ought to do.

Clarity in Direction

In addition to giving you confidence in your approach, mental models will also provide you with a clear direction on how you should think and act. Throughout your decision-making process, you will want to have a clear strategy for doing things. The people around you should notice that you have a different approach to solving your problems.

Engage in the Whole Experience

There are numerous situations that you will be faced with concerning decision-making. The problem that you deal with today might not be the same problem that you handle tomorrow. Regardless, if you have mental models to turn to, you will always emerge victoriously.

Use Your Approach to Your Advantage

Looking at Maslow's hierarchy of needs model, there is no doubt that people love to feel good about their achievements. Meeting self-esteem and self-actualization needs will give you a reason to be happy about yourself. Mental models will steer you to make the right decisions that impact your life positively. The compounding effect that you will gain from your achievements will boost your self-esteem. People will respect you. They will look up to you for assistance whenever they feel stuck. Thus, your sense of direction in life will give you an added advantage as you will accomplish some of your personal needs, as argued by Maslow's model.

Transform Yourself

There is an overall transformation that will be taking place in your world. People around you will be the first to notice that you have changed. As you take your time to learn more about mental models, you will advance your knowledge. You will garner deeper insight into how the world works. Accordingly, it will not be a daunting task for you to make sound decisions.

It is also worth noting that your metamorphosis will be evident through the life goals you will achieve. Indeed, making the right decisions and succeeding in your ambitions go hand in hand. For that reason, you will be glad that things seem to work your way. This is the power of mental models. It delivers you results in remarkable ways.

Continuity of Strategy

Continued use of mental models will provide you with a sense of advancement in how you do things. Besides finding it easy to make decisions and solve problems faster, your new way of thinking will help you better control your life. Most of the decisions that you will be making require you to look into the future. Frequently, you will want to consider the long-term consequences of your actions instead of just paying attention to short-term gains.

Mental Models Will Help You Change Gradually

At the beginning of this manual, we pointed out that transforming your decision-making process is a lifelong journey. It is not something that you can do overnight. There are numerous mental models that you need to comprehend to become a good decision-maker. The learning process will also not be complete if you fail to put into practice what you learn. Therefore, you must practice the new thinking frameworks that you will be learning from this manual.

Practice makes perfect. You don't have to be an expert in applying mental models to how you think and approach your problems. However, with constant practice, you can polish your critical thinking skills.

Simply put, mental models provide you with the frameworks that you need to make informed decisions in your life. Their role is to bestow you with confidence that your approach toward making certain decisions works. Often, we are skeptical, not knowing the best moves that we should take. This is a common experience, more so when faced with big life decisions. However, with the help of these models, you can understand life from varying perspectives.

To gain the best from these models, you should equip yourself with knowledge by learning how to apply distinct models in the problems that you face. The more you know, the better. We live in a complex world, and for you to grasp a solid understanding of how things work, you must have several mental models in your thinking toolbox.

Chapter 6: Cognitive Bias

In our world of instant gratification, we are constantly told what to think and feel. The media is relentless in its drive to get us talking about certain subjects and sell the latest fad without any thought for what may be the other side of the story. As a result, as individuals living in society, these biases shape our thoughts and prevent us from thinking critically.

The beliefs that we hold can cause problems if they lead to negative consequences such as bullying or discrimination towards others with different beliefs. To understand the bias, we must first explore the cognitive mechanisms in play.

Cognitive biasing used to be defined as the idea that 'the mind has it is own built-in biases and rules of thumb which are more likely to produce errors than logical deductions.'(Barkley & Jensen) Taken at face value, this is a fairly simple concept, but it can become rather complicated when examined in more detail.

How Does Cognitive Bias Work?

Cognitive biases are common but difficult to recognize that people typically have when making a decision. These patterns can be helpful and prevent someone from making rash decisions, but they're also likely to lead to errors in judgment.

The goal is not necessarily to avoid the mistakes created by cognitive biases but rather to identify them before acting on our judgment. Here's how cognitive bias works:

For example, doing independent research that confirms what you already believe is an example of confirmation bias. The result is not just self-satisfaction but overconfidence in your conclusions with the potential for harm because you don't consider alternative possibilities.

Another example is our tendency to perceive things in terms of black and white. Here's an example: "You're stupid because you think there are two kinds of people, right-wingers and left-wingers." This describes the major cognitive bias known as the "Us versus Them" effect. Those who identify are also susceptible to cognitive bias. Stereotypes are an example of this, where those who believe in stereotypes about groups of people often perpetuate them even when it's against their own group's interests.

Cognitive biases tend to be particularly insidious because they can cause us to make choices that seem logical at the time but lead us into unforeseen trouble. For example, when we recognize that some in our group are unprincipled, we may change the rules to exclude those people. This may seem logical at first, but it's not always the best choice.

Cognitive biases can also be unintentional and unknowingly influenced by your surroundings. For example, when threatened with aggression, you might become more aggressive because it is a defense mechanism. In this case, your aggression is not an intentional behavior but rather a reaction deep within you.

These biases are very common in today's society and have a major effect on our lives.

Causes of Cognitive Bias

There are several causes of cognitive bias that have been defined by professors Mark Novick and Steven Quartz. The three main ideas are "why we do it" or the "why" theory, "how we do it," or the "how" theory, and "what happens to us when we do it."

These three theories combine to form the many causes of cognitive bias.

The first reason people put in their biases is that they were abused or neglected in some way. This may have caused them to become afraid and assume everyone else is worse off than them. Therefore, they feel the need to fight to protect themselves. However, this is not an acceptable or good way to do such things. The second reason is that they were probed negatively by others when they were growing up. They learn that good people and bad people tend to stick with one side of the story without looking at other possibilities. Finally, some people may have been told as a child that "They are the only ones who know what is best." As an adult, this becomes true for them also.

This causes their overconfidence in their decision-making skills and inability to see alternatives or think objectively about problems and solutions.

Here are other causes:

Cognitive Biases and Education

A person's education plays a huge role in everything they experience. This has made many people believe that cognitive bias is only academic. However, cognitive bias can happen at any point in one's life. Instead, any situation you encounter could cause you to apply bias in your head and avoid thinking for yourself. Therefore, the best education is the one you give yourself! The more experiences you have with different situations, the less likely you will make mistakes when making decisions. However, there are some common characteristics of a person who tends to be biased (the "why" theory).

"Us versus Them" effect

This is a common trend in the world. People tend to stick with one group or side, often without knowing enough about them to make an informed decision. For example, rich people are usually looked down upon by poorer people who decide not to associate themselves with them without looking at whether this is true or not. This often leads to one-sided and biased opinions that may be incorrect. In the worst cases, when bias and lack of knowledge are combined, it can lead to prejudice (prejudging) and discrimination (choosing sides).

Labeling Theory

Many people tend to accept a person's actions based on the label placed on the person. This is often a bias because labels are set by others and not always accurate. This is really true when someone wants to raise their status or when they want to avoid people who have gained more power than them. For example, if someone has been labeled as "stupid" by others, they may decide not to do well in school because it will further lock them down in their social class. Those who don't fit into one of these labels may feel like an outcast and may cope with this by being different from everyone else. If a person's intelligence is not acknowledged and they keep doing well in school, it can make them feel fake.

Cognitive biases are very common and often lead to bad decision-making. The first step to avoiding biased decision-making is to become aware of them and know when they affect you. This way, you can learn to avoid them or see them as something that is no longer affecting you (e.g., cognitive therapy).

Cognitive bias should not be confused with logical reasoning. Cognitive bias is an emotional process, while logical reasoning does not involve emotions (like fear, love, etc.).

Several studies are showing the positive effect cognitive biases have on decision-making.

An Overabundance of Information

Bias is not all about information, and when it comes to cognitive bias, the key word is information. People oversupply themselves with information. This can lead to poor and uninformed judgments, if you know what I mean! That's why people believe they will do better on a test if they study for three hours instead of two because their information has increased by a full two hours.

Other examples of this overabundance of information are the belief that we have more knowledge than we do or that our data processing ability is enough to make us highly intelligent.

When we believe we know more than what we do and oversupply ourselves with information, we are more likely to make poor decisions.

We don't know what we don't know, and because of this, we are more likely to fall prey to cognitive bias.

People tend to believe whatever they are told as opposed to independent research. In other words, our beliefs about something are not based on facts but rather on our own opinions and opinions of others. This is an example of confirmation bias or the "I believe so because I said so" effect. These beliefs can be very dangerous because they can cause us to overreact or act inappropriately based on our criteria without considering alternative possibilities that are more beneficial for us and those around us.

This bias makes us certain that we have enough information to decide when it may turn out otherwise in reality.

Another example of confirmation bias is when you believe something based on your own experience but does not acknowledge the experiences of others even if they confirm something else entirely.

This is another huge bias that affects more than 75% of the population.

This bias causes us to think we are in control when in fact, we are not. This can lead to inadequate planning and a lack of effort altogether because we do not see it as necessary or in our control, to begin with. We tend to make less effort when the effort isn't what we would like to be or a lot more effort towards our interest.

Connecting the Dots

We are bad at connecting the dots. We don't connect the dots and tend to believe that they do not exist. Or when they do appear in front of us, we simply ignore them and continue with the same old what we were doing before. This makes decisions boring and hard to find solutions for because we focus on our answers instead of thinking objectively about a problem and reaching a better solution for everyone.

This bias also tends to be overconfident in our knowledge about science topics such as gravity or evolution, even though it has been proven many times that we still don't fully understand everything.

This is one of the most common biases that young adults have. This can be due to a lack of experience, fear, and impulsiveness.

This bias causes us to generalize from one particular experience and apply it to all situations in life. It's based on the idea that this will always happen and doesn't consider anything else, and we are more likely to make the same mistake repeatedly. This mainly affects our view of people.

This bias causes us to form judgments about someone else based on an isolated event or situation without taking their performance over time into consideration. For instance, if you can't make a presentation in front of everyone and they happen to see this, it can easily lead to your belief that "I suck at making presentations" instead of "I simply had a bad performance that one time."

This bias also makes us think only about ourselves and ignore what others think or may be going through.

The more common term for this is "The sunk cost fallacy." We keep investing money into something we know is not good for us because we have already invested so much

Time Is of the Essence

"Time is of the essence" is a term that is used in many different situations. This quote refers to "Time is of the essence" when predicting things happening in the future. For example, if you're late for an appointment, then you know that "Time is of the essence." This can have a huge effect on your life and how you spend a lot of time on things that are not beneficial. It also affects our ability to stay focused and what we do during our spare time.

If something isn't happening, it's most likely because we are saying or doing something wrong. We often overlook the fact that there may be something wrong with the circumstances or our environment. Instead, we only look at ourselves.

We tend to think that if we worked hard enough, then anything is possible. This is not true and can lead us to work on things that are not beneficial for us. We also think that we are in control regardless of the circumstances when we aren't.

This bias is an example of being optimistic even though it's proven repeatedly that this belief can cause us to do things without thinking about them first or without giving them enough thought before taking action.

This makes us believe that we can solve a problem using the same methods that didn't work the first time. We think that we can get successful results if we just try harder or think smarter. However, we will often fail and end up causing more problems than we had in the first place!

We tend to only stick to one way of thinking, limiting our ability to develop a diverse group of solutions and ideas.

Cognitive Bias vs. Logical Fallacy

A logical fallacy is a pattern of reasoning that is weak and can be refuted. For example, an argument with this pattern of reasoning "There are no books, therefore there are no people in the house" or "This medication is not working because I still feel pain." However, a cognitive bias is not a pattern of reasoning that can be refuted, making it very difficult to recognize.

Cognitive biases affect our perception based on past experiences.

Research has shown that you must acknowledge your own biases to overcome them. A cognitive bias refers to situations when we allow emotion or memory to interfere with our thinking process and lead us down the wrong path. It is important to be aware of these biases so that we can avoid them. Awareness is the first step, and it will make it easier for you to recognize when these fallacies are happening in your own life. The next step is to counter-balance the bias in your thinking by using a logical argument or approach that will allow you to think more objectively about the situation.

Cognitive biases like fear, social pressures, greed, and even love are factors that can affect how we act and what we do in any given situation. This makes recognizing cognitive bias even more important because our actions are often based on what we feel instead of what someone may try to force us into believing. Overcoming cognitive bias takes time and hard work.

1. Characterize the Real Problem

This is a big deal. Guarantee that you are taking care of the exact problem. What's more, guarantee that you explain the main driver of the problem and are not merely treating the side effects. There are various strategies to decide underlying drivers - cause mapping, fishbone graphs, and so forth. For me, the least demanding is to utilize the Five Whys. Ask an inquiry and to each answer, pose For what valid reason? Once more. Doing this multiple times ought to get you to the underlying driver of the problem, which might be altogether different from what appeared to be the problem initially.

2. Characterize the Real Problem

I need to rehash this since it is so significant. Decide the actual problem and comprehend it. Toyota is reasonably celebrated for its problem-tackling savvy in consummating its creation strategies. As per Toyota, the way to their technique is to invest more energy in characterizing the problem and moderately less time making sense of the arrangement.

3. Get the Facts

Burrow deep and get the certainties to genuinely comprehend the idea of the problem and the potential solutions. Examine to give the realities a chance to do the talking rather than gut nature. As Wharton Professor Peter Cappelli says:

4. Use Hypothesis

As occurs on the CSI network shows, make the best conjecture regarding the answer for the problem toward the start - characterize the initial hypothesis. At that point test, this initial hypothesis digging deep to decide if the assumption is correct or off-base. At that point, change the theory as the realities direct. This utilization of approach has been the premise of the logical strategy for the last few hundred years. There are two points of interest to problem understanding utilizing a prediction. To begin with, the initial hypothesis gives you a system, a method for clarification, to see every one of the realities and information you are gathering. Second, by considering it a hypothesis that still should be demonstrated, you abstain from getting to be secured on an answer and are progressively open to altering your perspective as the actualities manage.

5. Keep the arrangement basic

Your group must actualize any answer to a problem. Accordingly, keep the arrangement as basic as could be expected under the circumstances. Have the option to disclose the solution for the question unmistakably and precisely in 30 seconds or less. Keep the activity things to take care of the problem to three or less. Think 80/100. Go for the arrangement that tackles 80% of the problem. However, that is 100% implementable by the group instead of the 100% arrangement that is probably not going to be appropriately actualized.

6. Don't re-design the wheel

Not at all, like in school, copyright infringement can be significant. If someone has an astute thought or approach to take care of your problem, by all methods, lawfully use it. "Not concocted here" disorder is sheer self-importance.

7. Increase energy in problem illuminating

In circumstances where you have multiple problems to unravel (for instance, a business turnaround, new market improvement, or a securing), cull the low hanging, yet significant, natural product first; take care of the simple problems. This gives force, demonstrates advancement, and gives your group certainty. At that point, center around proceeding to hit singles, not grand slams. The best approach to progress is to take care of several little problems.

8. Think about the time

Take a gander at the time component in problems and problem comprehending. In any arrangement, figure the first way to guarantee that you do first what should be done first. Additionally, ensure that the agreement can be executed in a reasonable timeframe. With most problems, solutions that take longer than a couple of months will probably fall flat. The energy will cease to exist; top administration will proceed onward to another "basic issue." To best take care of a problem, actualize your answer before the day, before the week, before the month is out.

Think Big, Think Differently and Become More

Achievement is a perspective. Our tangible results, goals achieved, authentications earned, or abilities developed are the aftereffect of our contemplations. What's more, if musings lead to activities, activities lead to propensities. Our tendencies are what decide our possible character and fate - would this rationale not recommend that to achieve great things, we should initially develop the capacity to plan for an exciting future? But then, preparing to stun the world isn't sufficient. We additionally need to think suddenly, boast, trust more, act huge, act now, and act reliably to wind up incredible and achieve our goals and dreams throughout everyday life.

It is critical to recollect that reasoning massive isn't equivalent to thinking beyond practical boundaries; indeed, I would contend that they are unique. Everybody has enormous dreams - and these fantasies are close to just expectations and wishes. It requires an alternative perspective, mental order, re-programming, and thinking uniquely in contrast to most ordinary people we are continually encompassed by. Planning for an impressive future involves activity, changing our viewpoint, defeating the voices of dread and uncertainty, having confidence in ourselves and our fantasies, developing the capacity not to stress what others state or think, and setting up goals and an arrangement that will result in enormous activities that mirror our massive reasoning.

Maybe one of the best instances of changing our perspective, re-programming our psyches, and planning for an exciting future and diversity is exhibited in one's capacity to escape the typical representative mentality. This bleak outlook isn't just inconvenient to one's potential; however, it is so generally acknowledged that it has turned out to be social. It is made apparent in activities and attitudes, for example, doing only enough work to keep your business, just doing work that falls under your duties, thinking about your calendar and needs instead of the organization's or clients, getting excited about salary increases and advancements, feeling that working for 40+ years for a pitiful retirement is some way or another attractive, and trusting that resumes, and GPA's and occupation titles are what decide your capacities and potential.

Planning for an impressive future and thinking unexpectedly, concerning escaping the usual representative attitude, would involve accomplishing more than asked or required, defining grand goals and striving to achieve them, turning into a maker and never exchanging time for cash, not trusting that evaluations or state-administered test scores or establishments went to manage your profession potential and understanding that this worker outlook extends into each part of life and is, therefore, the main reason concerning why individuals so frequently neglect to achieve their goals, dreams and become effective throughout everyday life. Those people who proceed in this unfortunate mentality develop a reliance upon a manager or organization for their professional success, day by day survival, and individual and social endorsement; and along these lines, they neglect to develop the necessary qualities for accomplishment in anything - which are: planning for an impressive future, developing self-assurance, wanting achievement, trusting in themselves and their fantasies, risking and defeating fears, gaining from disappointments, and being eager to appear as something else and do whatever is required to acquire achievement.

This representative mentality is nevertheless one model and circumstance concerning how we can think contrastingly and plan for an exciting future; similar standards apply to any condition, situation, challenge, objective, or dream. Remember, notwithstanding, that because these standards are pertinent to any defining or purpose we have - despite everything, we have to apply the rules! Therefore, preparing to stun the world is a worthless undertaking except if pursued by activity. To move toward becoming and achieve more involves an adjustment in mentality and an adjustment in propensities.

Choose now to prepare to stun the world dependably. Set up grand goals and specific designs to accomplish and understand your fantasies. Develop the capacity to think unexpectedly. Never succumb to the dominant culture of contentedness and the simplicity of average quality. Train your brain never to stress what others believe or state, and figure out how to wipe out the voices of dread and uncertainty. Submit now to doing whatever necessary - as hard and long as it might be, and notwithstanding the disappointments that unavoidably result - to achieve your goals and dreams. What's more, dependably recollect that to make great things, you should dependably plan for an exciting future, boast, and act huge!

Thinking Differently

Is it safe to say that we are pursuing the correct arrangements? Over and over again, especially on great occasions, we seek awful arrangements bargains outside our sweet spot or agreements that might be unfruitful for our organization. We waste bunches of time and assets following methods we don't generally need or have low probabilities of winning. We would be in an ideal situation, putting the time in prospecting for the correct arrangements, at that point seeking after them.

Would vital records, they say, be the correct ones? We will, in general, respect our necessary documents; we treat them uncommonly, we give various types of help, we do anything we can to hold and develop that business. We've had them as vital records for quite a long time; we can't envision not having them for some more years. However, regularly, they are not our best records; they might be our least gainful records. We may have arranged a unique evaluating, and we give more help soon as their productivity goes down. Maybe it's an excellent opportunity to rethink the amount we put resources into them, and we may even now need to keep them as a decent record. However, we might need to begin putting more into developing more current documents that are progressively gainful. Is it true that we are on autopilot in executing our business procedure? This might be an issue with experienced and fruitful sales reps. Once in a while, we jump on autopilot. We begin getting to be oblivious amid the business procedure. We start missing things, and we make presumptions dependent on experience, not the present circumstance. We start making mistakes and losing.

Do we have the right channel? Sales associates like doing bargains. We will, in general, center our time at the base of the pipe doing the last proposition, the final "pitch," shutting and arranging. These can expend our time, yet when they leave, we take a gander at our pipelines, and there's nothing there. Is it safe to say that we are separating ourselves and making unmistakable esteem? We will, in general, present a similar stale offer without genuinely understanding whether it implies anything to the client. At that point, we haven't figured out what they esteem. At that point, we show our incentive regarding what's important to them. We depend on the "old offers," yet the contenders have outpaced us.

Is it safe to say that we are concentrating on our selling procedure, not the client's purchasing procedure? We make the best esteem focus on how the client needs to purchase and encouraging their purchasing procedure.

Every day, our minds are filled with information from everything that is happening around us. As a result, we are left with the challenge of clearing our minds to pave the way for effective thinking. Allowing too much to flow in and out of our minds prevents us from thinking right. The use of mental models can be useful in helping us to think clearly. Most people use these models every day, but they might not realize that they are doing it. When thinking of how you can best relate with your friends and relatives, you are using a mental model. When pondering on how to budget for your monthly expenses, you're also using it.

Any framework used to help you in grasping something easily is perceived as a mental model. Practically, these models can be identified as the apps present in your mind. With the help of each app you have stored in your mind, you can make the right decisions. Also, the more apps you have, the easier it will be to solve the problems in your life. Why? This is because you have a wide array of tools that suit different kinds of problems you might be going through.

How to Think Clearly

Clear thinking is not as easy as you might think. It is a challenge that most people have to go through more when dealing with other stressful issues. Your ability to think can also be affected when you're feeling tired and overwhelmed.

Check Your Attitude

Your ability to think clearly will largely depend on your desires. Often, you will find it easy to sit down and think of the strategies you can adopt to achieve your goals. Of course, this is dependent on if you have goals. When you don't want to achieve something, it is also easy to think of all the things you can do to accomplish this. Therefore, to think clearly, it is imperative to be honest about your goals and ambitions. Is this something that you want in your life? Ideally, developing the right attitude will be helpful toward bringing clarity to the goals you wish to attain.

Use Your Passion

There is a good reason why successful people will always advise you to follow your passion. The reality is that you have never heard them tell you to follow your emotions. Your passion for a particular goal will help you to overcome any challenges associated with it.

Passion drains away all the negative thoughts that could deter you from thinking clearly about the task ahead. Conversely, emotions will do just the opposite. Allowing your emotions to get the best of you will make you feel overwhelmed about what you should do. Usually, you will find yourself focusing more on the obstacles that you must go through. Therefore, to think clearly, it is advisable to use passion to keep your emotions in check.

Use Negative Thinking

It might sound controversial that you should use negative thinking to help you. It is possible. Remember, we are talking about finding the right frameworks to help you understand something better. So it is worthwhile to consider how negative thinking can help clear your mind.

Believe it or not, there is a positive power in negative thinking. When striving to achieve goals, most people will embrace the idea of thinking positively. Certainly, thinking positively works in many ways. It gives your mind a chance to focus your energy on what you can do to ensure you accomplish set goals. Interestingly, negative thinking can help you understand the main reasons why you might not accomplish a particular goal. Therefore, looking at this from a positive perspective, you can take advantage of your negative thinking to bring about positivity.

Use Cool Logic

Achieving a clear focus you need on what you want to achieve might be easy in the short run. Most people find it easy to concentrate for a few weeks or months before losing track of their doing. Therefore, to ensure that you maintain a clear focus on what you desire, you should use cool logic. How does this work? Cool logic relates to the idea of concentrating on the issue at hand. You should not allow anything else to distract you. For example, if you are working on a project, your mind should concentrate on the project and nothing else. Normally, it is easy to get distracted and allow your ego to control how you think. In this case, you will be withdrawn to think about how you are better than others in doing a particular task. Ultimately, this will harm the outcome of the project.

Challenge Your Preferences

Several presumptive beliefs could affect the clarity of your thoughts. The ideas you have developed in your mind about a particular issue can deter you from thinking about anything else. Many people will want to settle for the most expensive wines simply because they believe in the notion that the price of the bottle determines how the wine tastes.

However, this might not be true if you engage in a blind taste test. You might come across something that you will like. The point here is that you should challenge your preferences by trying something that you have never done before. You will be surprised that you could make informed decisions to the least of your expectations.

Think About Thinking

The aspect of being aware of your thought processes is termed metacognition. For you to think clearly, you should be aware of how you are thinking. Therefore, you shouldn't allow your thoughts to flow freely without being aware of them. Instead, you must plan and assess how you are thinking. The advantage gained through metacognition is that you will enrich your learning experience. For instance, your self-awareness will drive you to think clearly about how to accomplish a particular task.

Ideal Mental Models for Clear Thinking

First Principles Thinking

Some problems appear too complex for us to solve. Without a doubt, this is a dilemma that most people go through in their lives. Well, you shouldn't be stuck when faced with such circumstances because you can apply mental models. An ideal mental model to use here would be the first principles of thinking. This model is highly recommended when dealing with challenging situations. The best part is that this framework will push you to think for yourself.

The first principles of thinking have been there for several years, but it recently became popular in 2002 after Elon Musk stressed the importance of using them. This framework focuses on the idea that one should think like a scientist. The reason for taking this direction is because scientists don't use assumptions. Their conclusions are often made after facts have been proven.

The first step of deconstructing requires asking yourself intelligent questions regarding your situation or problem at hand. Additionally, you must have a deep understanding of frameworks from distinct disciplines. You must get more information about varying forms of mental models. Your knowledge is required to guarantee that you can look at your problem from varying perspectives. Your next move will be to bring together the pieces you had broken down in the first step. Again, for you to effectively reconstruct, you have to practice how to do it. You could have an idea of how to do something.

However, a standalone idea cannot help you to make good decisions. You need to combine several ideas to make valid conclusions. Practicing this more often will strengthen your mental muscles. Eventually, you will improve your thinking skills and end up making sound decisions.

Thought Experiment

The thought experiment mental model can help you think clearly by solving difficult problems. The thought experiment encourages speculation. What's more, it forces people to alter their paradigms. Instead of reasoning like other people, the thought experiment model pushes you out of your comfort zone. As a result, it forces you to ask yourself rhetorical questions that are complex. This style of thinking unveils the things that you don't know and some of which you know.

The advantage of using the thought experiment is that it encourages innovative ideas by pushing you beyond your thinking boundaries. Therefore, you will not be limited to the things that you already know. One major challenge with this mental model is that it appears impractical. Nevertheless, scholars believe that it can be used theoretically.

BATNA

BATNA is the acronym for Best Alternative To a Negotiated Agreement. This mental model can help you during negotiations. Normally, there are instances when negotiations reach a deadlock. This is a situation whereby parties cannot agree on a particular issue. In such cases, there should be an ideal alternative since the parties negotiating cannot agree.

It is worth noting that BATNA should be taken into consideration even before engaging in negotiations. Before entering into negotiations with any individual, you should be aware of your BATNA. The benefit that you gain here is that:

- It gives you the best alternative in case you fail to agree.

- It gives you an upper hand during negotiation since you will have negotiation power.

- It helps you dictate your reservation point. This is the lowest price that you can accept in the deal.

Compounding Knowledge

Compounding knowledge is a mental model rooted in the economic concept of compounding interest. It can be understood as the growth that emerges from your previous growth. The framework is not only applicable in your investments, but it can also be applied to your business, relationships, and knowledge.

People are always on the verge of consuming information. What they fail to realize is that most of them consume expiring information. This is something that Warren Buffett strives to steer away from. Instead of focusing on consuming information that is not important, Buffett focuses on equipping himself with the knowledge to help him manage his companies successfully. The idea here is to learn something new that would positively change what you do.

Gaining and gathering information from time to time will undeniably lead to compounding benefits. Learning something today and combining it with something else that you learn on the following day will make you a better person. Filling your mind with expiring information that is of less importance is easy, but the reality is that it will not help you in days or months to come.

Occam's Razor

Occam's Razor is a mental model that is attributed to William of Ockham. He did not introduce the term, but his style of reasoning inspired people to come up with the heuristic. The simplest way of comprehending this concept is that the simplest solution to a particular problem is correct.

One important fact about mental models is that they complement each other. This means that you have to apply other models in your decision-making for one mental model to be effective. In addition, you should embrace the idea of gaining more knowledge about a particular matter. Don't just limit yourself to one or two models.

Chapter 9: Mental Models For Critical Thinking

Understanding issues

The world requires us to use what are called mental models. Mental models help us understand new information and compare it to what we already know. They act as a framework for thinking about things about different contexts, problems, and issues. Mental models can be quite useful in keeping information organized and making connections between the two. As an example, let's say that you're new to a city that you are visiting for the first time. You use mental models to organize all of the different things that you see as you walk around. If you were told that there were five types of cars in this area and had never seen any of these before, what would your mental model look like? You might picture a car having four wheels, one windshield and one door, two seats facing backward (the driver's seat and the back seat), and being able to transport people by road or by public transit. You might also picture a group of cars as a line, and of course, this is just one example of how your mental models can work.

Critical thinking aims to identify how we use mental models and the effects on our cognition. By doing so, we can recognize how we learn and how we organize information. We can become more knowledgeable about the discussion and debate that occurs in the classroom. We will be able to explain better why certain things are true or false. We will be able to explain how ideas are born and develop into knowledge over time. We will also discuss how our mental models grow from infancy to adulthood by learning through experience, observing others, being taught by other adults (i.e., parents), and becoming exposed to an abundance of information by whatever means available in our society.

Mental models are constantly changing and evolving as we learn, age and change. "The world changes quickly, but our minds standstill." The world changes so rapidly because it only takes one or two individuals to create a new mental model. A small group of people creates most mental models at any given time, and they can last from years to decades. "The last person who added something significant to the model was probably not alive when the preceding person added something significant to it.

Extending Your Set of Mental Models

To extend a mental model, we must take one or two ideas from it and update our existing knowledge by applying them to new situations. We can learn the basics of fixing an engine by watching people do it with their hands. But if we want to repair a car with intricate parts that are hard to track down in a book, we should at least have an idea of how something works enough that it can be explained in just a sentence or two.

When you encounter new information, you incline to make your existing mental models fit the new situation. If you make structures that are too complex for your mental models to accommodate, they will become outdated and useless when new information comes along. This is an example of the Duhem–Quine thesis, which states that you must also disprove all of the auxiliary assumptions that it is based upon to disprove a theory. Your collection of mental models will be the key factor in how you assimilate new information.

Mental models are the foundation for knowledge and education. All of our thoughts and actions have been formed by mental models one way or another, and they shape how we interact with others, and they shape how we expect others to act. Learning involves connecting parts in your mind so that you can organize them better. College classes allow you to learn more about mental models by placing them in a new context. This will help you recognize when and how they were used in the past and how they are used. Critical thinking skills are formed through the practice of reading, writing, speaking, and listening.

Mental models allow us to organize information into categories and structure the world into a comprehensible system. To build mental models, you have to identify your knowledge and what you lack in knowledge. We must categorize things we encounter in our surroundings because they might impact how we view certain issues. The ability to categorize is, therefore, an essential part of critical thinking. For example, when we encounter new information, one of the first things they do is identify whether or not it fits with our understanding of the world around us.

Mental model theory on informal arguments

A mental model as a representation of an object or concept that we use to understand a position. It's important because it helps us become more effective communicators and decision-makers. The theory suggests that we can develop our mental models. The way we form a model depends on our personal experiences, beliefs, values, and environmental interactions. There are many different mental models, such as causal models, logical models, and diagrammatic models. A categorization or "the process of grouping objects together according to shared attributes" is termed unification. Categorizations can facilitate the process of forming a mental model.

Forming a mental model is essential for communication because it allows us to view a situation from another person's perspective. When we don't understand something, we use our own experience to construct a mental model of what the other person is trying to communicate. For example, suppose you want others to understand your business idea, but they don't have the necessary expertise. In that case, they will barely understand anything you say because their understanding will be based on their own experience. However, if you can create a mental model that portrays the problem you are trying to solve, they will understand what you need from them.

Mental models can also be used as a tool for understanding other people or situations. To do so, we have only to consider what is happening around us, which helps us make assumptions about people. Knowing the kinds of questions that people ask when they are trying to understand each other can help us anticipate how they might react at certain times. We can then go about our business knowing that we will be able to answer their questions.

Mental models are not meant to replace all the dynamic interactions that take place between people; they are only a tool in the toolbox of human interaction. The whole point of mental models is to help us understand people, certain situations, and a way of approaching them.

So, where do mental models come from? We can take some from the way that people think, as well as examples or analogies. Analogies are useful for understanding the cause and effect of things. But most analogies rely on abstract thinking and identifying key variables within a situation that might change over time or might relate to each other in different ways.

Analytical Skills

Analytical skills are very useful to you in critical thinking because they help you test your knowledge. They help you show how different perspectives can lead to different conclusions. These skills are used in science, mathematics, economics, and the arts; as such, it is essential for students who plan on pursuing these fields that they learn how to utilize analytical skills. Analytical skills are also an important tool for lawyers, doctors, and people in business because they help them interpret data and see the problem from all perspectives.

A good way to practice analytical skills is to work through puzzles that force you to think things through in a different manner and a different order. These puzzles help you analyze facts, determine relationships between them, and conclude the information at hand. Other ways that you can practice analytical skills include talking with someone who has a different perspective about the same thing so that you can try and work out how they came up with their ideas.

Mental Models Can be Used in Everyday Life

Many people ignore the importance of mental models for everyday life because it's not considered a useful skill. But as an adult, these same people might encounter situations that require them to make decisions or communicate with others based on what they know and their mental models about certain issues or topics. For example, suppose you want to understand the person taking your order at a fast-food restaurant. In that case, you need to pay attention to their body language, tone of voice, and facial expressions because they will impact how they respond. If you don't pay attention to these things, you might be unintentionally rude or aggressive. In turn, they will not take too kindly to your interactions with them, and they might even be unwilling or unable to do what you ask of them.

Benefits Of Developing Analytical Skills

Analytical skills are useful in every domain because learning how to put things in different ways can help you think of different solutions. You will be able to understand the different aspects of a situation, and you will be able to look at it from several perspectives. In turn, you will be able to look at problems in new ways and develop the best possible solutions.

Critical thinking is not objective; it is subjective, and subjective is often classified as sensitive or subjective. We all know emotionally sensitive individuals, and they tend to over-react when it comes to situations. Critical thinking is used to understand the world as it is, a world that is changing every day. Society has evolved, and we have had to adapt to survive.

The problem with critical thinking and analytical skills is that most people do not realize how important they are in our lives until we are presented with a situation in which we need them. For example, you might be at a party, and someone starts talking about a movie you have seen before.

Communication Skills

Communicating effectively is important in critical thinking because it is one of the primary ways to transfer and understand our knowledge. Critical thinking has a lot to do with communication skills, and as such, it is necessary for everyone who wishes to master their knowledge and skills.

We have some different ways in which we communicate information with others. We can verbalize it, broaden it, or keep it simple while also keeping things sensitive or keeping them at a level that those listening will understand what you are talking about and think about what you are trying to say. After this, you will find that the listeners will be able to make sense of what you are trying to say, and they may even be able to ask additional questions if they need clarification.

Other communication skills are essential for critical thinking. They include finding the right words and tone and using metaphors and examples, among others. Using these techniques helps us communicate our thoughts clearly without having to use a lot of effort on our part. A phrase says, "the best way to communicate is to shut up," so when you communicate with someone else, you need to pay attention not just to what they say but also to how they say it and how well they listen.

Creativity

Creativity is an essential part of critical thinking and its success. Activities that exercise creativity include writing, art, dance, music, math, science, and problem-solving.

This is also an important factor in our everyday lives because if we are creative, we can find new ways of doing things. People who have a lack of creativity tend to become bored with the same tasks over and over again. Hence, they find other activities that involve less creativity, like watching television or playing video games.

The main idea is to put together ideas to solve problems or come up with new ideas for old ones. Creativity is also about breaking down problems into smaller parts to look at them from more than one perspective or point of view.

There are many different ways to be creative; some of these include observing, reading, writing, drawing and using our imagination. It is important to develop the creative side of our minds because it will help us solve problems and develop different concepts. Thinking creatively is a key part of critical thinking. If you cannot come up with new ideas or break apart what you know into small pieces, you will be stuck in the same situation forever.

Open-mindedness

Open-mindedness, or being receptive to new ideas, is an important part of critical thinking. It is essential for people who want to learn, and it allows them to view the world in a different light. For example, an open-minded person will see different perspectives or points of view on a particular issue. This is why open-mindedness is important because it allows us to understand the complexity of life and how everything is connected. Interpersonal communication refers to our ability to communicate with other people through language, nonverbal cues and gestures. Interpersonal communication involves various aspects and things that we can control, like posture and facial expressions, and uncontrollable things like noise levels or time constraints. This makes it important in critical thinking because if we communicate our ideas or concepts to someone else but do not put them in the right way, that person will not understand what we are trying to say. Two skills that help us to improve our interpersonal communication are listening and reading others. Reading others means understanding the verbal and nonverbal cues they give off so that you can know how they are feeling about a particular topic or idea. When you listen, you need to pay attention to hear what they are saying. This will make your conversation meaningful because you will understand what they mean by certain things even though you might not agree with their point of view or use of words and phrases.

Chapter 10: Mental Models For Personal Happiness

You may have heard the expression, "What you see is the thing that you get." It infers that our perspective on the world hinders our capacity to encounter it. Few would contend with the way that an individual who has never experienced love in their lives has a lot of trouble finding, keeping up, or supporting a top-of-the-line relationship. Likewise, on the off chance that you've experienced childhood in abject poverty, it takes a lot of personal change before you can live with bounty effectively.

For what reason is it so hard to act without uncertainty and tension? Your mind is running some broken mental models. Over our lifetimes, we as a whole receive restricting convictions that are obtained through media, childhood or unrepresentative experiences. These mental models keep us grounded rather than free and sure.

Here are eight instances of mental models you have to embrace to flourish in this life.

1. Acknowledge the world for what it's worth

For one thing, you should create an articulate acknowledgment of the world you live in.

There are plenty of awkward certainties in life that we attempt to avoid. Awkward actualities, cruel substances. The world may appear to be unreasonable, yet it's not. The world simply is. There is no inalienable goodness or disagreeableness about it. It is only a gathering of things in being.

So quit placing your head in the sand–slowly inhale and perceive the truth about it. Go up against yourself with the real world. Try not to gloss over it, yet additionally, don't get maneuvered into misrepresented considerations of fate.

As you acknowledge how things may be, you can make moves to improve them adequately.

2. Assume liability for your life

You are the essential partner in your life and, at last, the one in particular that will consistently mind. You are likewise the one with the most immediate impact on your life. That implies you are answerable for where you end up.

You may have been managed an awful hand. However, there is no reshuffling of the deck. You can play the cards you have. It's dependent upon you to progress nicely.

If you don't care for something in your life, change your disposition towards it or change the circumstance. Create dynamic adapting procedures. Try not to accuse other individuals, God or the universe. You have an unrestrained choice; you are in control. Take the valuable view to look towards yourself for progress.

3. No self-centeredness

Self-centeredness is an overwhelming feeling. It's so useless to feel frustrated about yourself. Regardless of how reasonable, it is poisonous.

Nothing is picked up by taking part in this decaying perspective. Are you down and out? Are you plain monstrous? You are 30 and as yet living in your mother's cellar? Your life may genuinely suck. However, you can't live in self-indulgence since then. Things will never show signs of change!

4. Reclassify disappointment in a learning knowledge

Disappointment has a major shame in western culture. When you come up short, you are a failure. An excessive number of individuals accept that you ought to have the option to win immediately in one way or another. That won't occur. So why not give yourself consent to suck and bomb throughout everyday life.

Gain from your slip-ups. You are not a failure since you have fizzled! The genuine washouts are those that don't attempt or who surrender too rapidly. The person who falls flat and gets back up is eventually the champ.

Make an effort not to consider a to be objective as the meaning of your prosperity. Rather, see gaining ground as progress. It won't be a straight line to flawlessness, yet attempting to push ahead through disappointment and learning is an achievement!

5. Dread is your guide

As you travel through life, you will at times end, incapacitated by dread. Feel the dread and make a move in any case. Except if you are going to win a Darwin grant, you were most likely destined for success.

Dread gives you where you need to go. However, you need to take a jump. Give dread a chance to show something you have to do. Push through. Give dread a chance to be your foreboding manual for flourishing.

6. Consider your passing

Alright, so perhaps that isn't such extraordinary news. However, it's valid. Utilize this as an update that your time is limited. One day you will be no more. It may be tomorrow; it may be in 80 years. The majority of your little triviality, fears and jealousies should fail to measure up to the enormous obscure nothingness that anticipates you. So why not take advantage of this brilliant existence of yours?

Set aside the effort to go up against yourself with this impending fate, and cheer that you are as yet alive!

Time to appreciate life much more by risking and gaining ground toward even the most straightforward of objectives.

7. Try not to take life excessively genuine

What is the significance of life? What is tremendous importance? On the off chance that you go down that hare gap, you will wind up with this answer: The importance of life is to live.

It's not extremely grave. However, it's exceptionally noteworthy. Culture and childhood may contend with something else. However, the significance of self-assertive occasions, parameters and individuals is generally misrepresented. There is no critical, more significant standard to achieve, no higher reason aside from the one you give yourself through living.

So relax. There isn't a checkpoint you need to go to accomplish a satisfying life. It's simply not excessively genuine! It is to be delighted in at whatever point conceivable. You pick how you need to live, so why not relax regardless of what individuals attempt to let you know.

8. Live in the now

To wrap things up, to genuinely flourish, you should live in the now. Figure out how to relinquish your psyche. Quit pursuing lost minutes and foreseeing potential fates.

For the most part, your forecasts are off, and your recollections are remixes of unalterable occasions. Rather, figure out how to encounter what is directly before you, no denying yet grasping the now. Regardless of whether it's through sports, nature, or contemplation, grasp the present.

Adjusting these mental models won't be a simple assignment, and it won't occur without any forethought. However, on the off chance that you help yourself remember them and make little strides towards your objectives, you will see after some time that your programming will be changed, and it will amazingly affect your life.

Change Your Thinking Change Your Life

They state an inspirational mentality decides how far we go throughout everyday life and everything else between. In any case, does this apply when you're in a situation where you feel undervalued, segregated, and misjudged?

Our frame of mind influences our connections, bliss, way of life, and achievement. Building up an inspirational demeanor makes a huge difference, notwithstanding our conditions. Factually a large portion of the individuals conceived are hopeful commonly, and the other half are cynical. This means there's a half possibility that you see life through a negative focal point.

Indeed, even the hopeful person will think that it's hard now and again to have an inspirational frame of mind due to life encounters, impact, and social molding. So whichever you are, Today is another day for fresh starts. Disregard everything your mentality has made of your life, and begin once again. Adjust it. Sand the rough spots, and start building up an inspirational outlook that changes you into the individual you need to be. Here are a few different ways, how, and where to begin.

Chapter 11: Using Mental Models for Decision Making

#1: Asking the Right Questions

Questions with 5W's: who, what, when, where, and why; can be used to help identify information before you begin working on a mental model. As you answer these questions, you'll require critical insight into the situation that you are dealing with. By asking factual questions like these and giving a direct answer, it provides you with factual information that is not biased or skewed. Once you have all the who, what, when, where, and why questions figured out, you can move on to the next step.

#2: Considering Potential Problems

One reason people experience poor outcomes from decision-making is that they work through the problem forward instead of backward. Moving forwards means tackling problems as they arise. The problem is that it leaves the person or corporation making the decisions unprepared. Rather than having an idea of what might go wrong and how to fix it potentially, they must spend time researching what is going wrong and how to approach it before coming up with a plan. This costs valuable time that people do not always have.

For example, imagine that somebody wanted to start a florist business. Even though there is the option of growing their flowers, that might not always produce predictable results, especially if they grow outdoors where they cannot completely control the environment. In addition to considering how they will grow and source the flowers, they'll also need a plan for keeping the flowers preserved until they are ordered. With a well-thought-out plan, it is much more likely that the company will experience success. If the florist shop does not take the time to plan out these different steps, they are less likely to know what to do when they need to source more flowers to fulfill orders or a problem with the coolers they store the flowers in.

#3: Consider the 10-10-10 Principle

Like the regret minimization framework used by Jeff Bezos, the 10-10-10 Principle helps you look at a situation critically before making decisions. You consider the decision and how it will make you feel 10 minutes from now, ten months from now, and ten years from now.

This is a great strategy for evaluating the short-term and long-term benefits of a goal, both in the near and distant future. As you consider the 10-10-10 Principle for each of your possible decisions, you'll find the best course of action that benefits you in the short-term and long term.

#4: Know What Has the Most Influence

When you are making a decision, some factors have greater weight than others. It is important to know what matters most. Otherwise, you'll spend so much time focusing on unimportant details that it will be hard to see how they fit into the equation and their effect on the outcome. If you can, try to break down the parts of your decision into what matters the most. Choose 3-4 areas that are most concerning to you and consider how your decision will affect each.

For example, imagine that someone is considering moving to another state. Their parents live in their current location. If they are close to their parents, the proximity might be more significant to the decision than for someone estranged from their family.

#5: Ask for Outside Perspectives

Even once you begin to remove bias from your thinking and develop mental models in many fields, it is important to remember that every person is an asset with their perspective. When you are unsure of a decision or your possible options, don't be afraid to ask a friend, coworker, or family member for advice. The only thing that an outside perspective will do is give you a chance to look at your decision differently. Sometimes, the is exactly what is needed to make a clear-headed choice.

#6: Study Similar Scenarios

Many successful people spend their free time researching various ideas, strategies, and scenarios, how people responded, and the overall outcome. By studying similar scenarios, learning more and looking at things from a new perspective becomes possible. Additionally, by broadening your research into an area, you increase your expertise. This will help with problem-solving in the future and as you lay a foundation on which you can build more mental models.

#7: Consider Several Options

As you broaden your mental models, you'll find a greater range of possibilities at your disposal when decision-making. Doing away with bias and assumptions in your thinking also opens your mind and broadens your perspectives, giving you more options. It is okay to brainstorm ideas and jot down several things. Once you feel satisfied, go through the list and pick out 3-4 that are the most likely to have a good outcome.

Considering which of your options is most viable, consider the risk, reward, and probability. Once you have chosen at least 3-4 choices, visualize each of them and possible outcomes. Most scenarios have more than one possible outcome, with some outcomes being more likely than others. You can use decision trees to help with this.

Conclusion

A model is an abstraction or simplification of a system. Models can assume many different forms—from a model volcano in a high school science fair to a sophisticated astrophysical model simulated using a supercomputer. Models are simplified representations of a part of reality that we want to learn more about. George Box stated:, "Essentially, all models are wrong, but some are useful." They are wrong because they are simplifications, and they can be useful because we can learn from them.

A mental model is a model that is constructed and simulated within a conscious mind. To be "conscious" is to be aware of the world around you and yourself in relation to the world. Let's take a moment to think about how this process works operationally.

Thinking About Systems

The human mind is very good at simulating mental models of our immediate physical reality. Things get harder when we start thinking about abstract systems. A market is a good example of an abstract system. In a market system, price acts as a signal of aggregate demand for a commodity. You can't "see" a market like you can "see" a tree in front of you. A market does not exist in a particular physical location. A market is an abstract concept that exists in the collective minds of all who participate in it. Even though markets do not exist physically, they have an enormous impact on our lives nonetheless.

When the global economic crisis hit, people started saving money instead of spending it. Retailers, in turn, dropped prices to boost consumer spending. But when consumers saw prices dropping rapidly, they delayed purchases in the hope of achieving additional savings—leading to a price deflation loop.

When the global economic crisis hit in late 2008, retailers began to struggle financially because consumer purchases declined rapidly. People were worried about the economy and started saving money instead of spending it. This started happening just before the holiday shopping season—a make-or break period for many retailers. So, in an effort to boost demand, retailers began dropping prices. This process led to price deflation, because consumers saw prices dropping rapidly and began delaying purchases as a result.

The outcome of simulating their mental models of the market informed their decision making: "I should wait to buy this because the price keeps dropping." This mental model paints a pretty picture for consumers over the short term: low prices in a down economy. As the deflationary dynamics play out over the long term, however, the picture becomes bleak. As prices spin downward, profits decline, and businesses are forced to lay off workers or close up shop entirely. As unemployment increases, consumers' perception of the stability of the economy decreases, and they spend even less (see "Economic Stability Loop").

Economists and policy makers use sophisticated computer models to help them understand markets. Consumers, on the other hand, use simple mental models when making purchasing decisions. The more sophisticated models inform policy makers of the long-term consequences of consumers' reduction in spending, so they react by trying to jump-start spending with stimulus programs. In the U. S., we've seen a few of these programs during 2009: the "Cash for Clunkers" rebate program, the first-time home buyer tax credit, and the social security payroll tax cut. As the deflationary dynamics play out over the long term, the picture becomes bleak. As prices spin downward, profits decline and businesses are forced to lay off workers or close up shop entirely. As unemployment increases, consumers' perception of the stability of the economy decreases and they spend even less.

Complex Systems

Often, it is hard for us to define the optimal boundaries for a mental model. We tend to have a narrow focus and act on short-term dynamics within our mental models. For example, in the model above, our understanding changes when we expand the boundaries to include profits and layoffs. However, we are generally not very good at mentally simulating complex systems with interdependencies, lots of variables, and delays. This is where software steps in. Using systems thinking software, we can transform our mental models into operational models that we can simulate more reliably using a computer. Doing so not only helps us create new knowledge and understanding, but also helps us construct better mental models in the future.

EMOTIONAL AGILITY 2.0

Chapter 1: Emotional Intelligence at Home

Remember, emotional intelligence will have an impact in all areas of your life. Learning how to deal with your emotions and those of others will help you live a purposeful life. You will always see the best out of every situation. When relating with other people, we always strive to present ourselves in a manner that guarantees we are accepted. Truly, whether at work or your personal life, we all yearn to feel welcomed and accepted. At times, the fear of rejection pushes us to engage in activities that we might not like. For instance, one could turn to drugs after a failed marriage. Also, it is common to see people getting depressed over their failed careers.

Undeniably, relationships are there to be mended. People are not born with friends. Folks should interact and find ideal ways of mingling. Having said this, it is imperative that you understand how to relate with people both at work and in your private life. The way you present yourself in front of other people will have an impact on the relationship you share with them. The following are recommended strategies which will help you in developing positive relations either at work or in your personal life.

People who are not emotionally intelligent tend to make for terrible partners in a relationship. Granted, emotional intelligence is not the be-all and end-all of a relationship, but it is a pretty big deal. You really do not want to be intimately involved with a person who is not emotionally intelligent because they will always fall short of your expectations, at least where emotions are concerned.

Dating a person with a low EQ can be really frustrating. It can stop you from enjoying all the comforts and benefits that come with a relationship. A partner with a low EQ can also do a lot of damage to your self-esteem. Unfortunately, many people do not know how to tell whether their partner or any other loved one has a low EQ. You may have heard your friend complain that her boyfriend is never attuned to her feelings or that he always yells when they get into an argument. While you may have known that this is wrong, you probably did not understand the relationship between such behavior and low emotional intelligence.

Signs You Are Dealing With A Partner Who Ranks Low On The Emotional Intelligence Scale:

He is not able to read your feelings

Imagine dating someone who is never able to tell how you are feeling. Sounds frustrating, right? While we are not mind readers, we are at least supposed to somewhat be able to read the emotions of our significant others. Being able to understand verbal and nonverbal cues shared by your partner is a sign of emotional intelligence.

If you have to spell out each and every emotion that you are feeling to your partner, you are dating someone who needs a whole lot of practice on EQ. Of course, your partner cannot be expected to sense your every emotion and anticipate your every need. That is a lot to ask from one person. However, they should at least be in tune with your reality. If you are crying in the darkness of your bedroom, it does not require a rocket scientist's assessment to tell that you are sad.

He has no network of friends and acquaintances

Emotionally intelligent people make friends easily because they know how to relate to people, how to make people feel listened to and understood, and how to maintain healthy relationships. If your partner just moved into town, it's okay for them to not have friends. However, if he has been living in the same neighborhood for five years and he still does not anybody that likes him enough to stick around as a friend, then you might just have caught yourself a fish that is lacking in EQ.

He behaves inappropriately

The inability to read a room is a major giveaway that someone is not emotionally intelligent. The fact that a person can stand in a room full of people and keep telling jokes that make everyone uncomfortable shows that they are incapable of reading nonverbal cues and cannot pick up on the emotions or mood of the people in the room. It can be quite embarrassing to be on the other side of such a relationship.

He is often the loudest person in the room

Now, there's nothing wrong with being extroverted. In fact, it is a good thing that extroverts exist because they fill the awkward silences that introverts leave in their wake. However, if the person you are dating is loud in a manner that is obnoxious, then you likely have a person that is emotionally immature on your hands.

Dealing with Partners Who Has Low Emotional Intelligence

Watch your tone

Some people score poorly in EQ not because they want to but because they do not know better. Your role as an emotionally intelligent partner or spouse is to bring your partner to the other side. The side where people speak respectfully and with empathy. The side where people are good listeners who do not interrupt others while they are talking. Being condescending about your superior emotional intelligence will only make your partner resentful of you.

Be realistic about your expectations

You've been suspecting that your partner has low EQ all along, and this book has cemented this suspicion by providing you with solid evidence of what EQ is and what it is not. Now what? Should you share this book with your partner and demand that they read it from cover to cover and report back to you in a week, complete with a higher EQ?

Your partner might not even be up for it. They might fight you when you suggest that they should try doing this or that. Remember that low EQ people tend to hate change. Converting your partner will not be a walk in the park. However, if your partner truly loves you and is committed to your relationship, then you can help them get started on the baby steps that they need to take for the relationship to become even more fulfilling than it is.

Remember its okay to fight

Every relationship has its fights. There can never be a relationship without fights unless the parties are afraid to share their true opinions. Fights strengthen relationships. They give a platform for partners to share the feelings that they have kept hidden deep within. Whether you are fighting about EQ-related matters or any other thing, do not feel any guilt or shame over it. Even the most emotionally intelligent people fight with their loved ones. They just know better than to yell or name-call or hit. As long as you are fighting without tearing each other down, you are on the right track.

Let the other person choose to change

You can indeed influence another person into changing by modeling the kind of behavior that is appropriate. However, you can never force a person that does not want to change to change. Change is such a personal decision that must be made by an individual when they are ready for it. If your spouse behaves in a particular manner that you find to be emotionally immature, they have to get to a place where they see it from your perspective, and then decide to change. This might take a whole lot of time and may even seem impossible at first. Sitting around, waiting for them to be ready might take up all your patience. Only you will be in a position to decide whether they are worth the wait or not.

Sometimes you'll have to walk away

At some point, you have to pull the plug on a relationship that is not working. Relationships are not recyclable plastics that you can keep and use for another purpose when you are done using them for what they were originally intended. A relationship is supposed to be positive addition in your life. If your partner is exhibiting signs of low or nonexistent emotional intelligence, including being emotionally abusive, it is well within your right to walk away. You should not only walk but run as fast as your high EQ heels can carry you. Somewhere out, there is someone who is self-aware and motivated that is bound to appreciate a respectful relationship with an emotionally mature adult such as yourself.

Strategies to Improve and Rescue Relationships in Both Your Work and Personal Life

Acknowledge and Celebrate Differences

Nonetheless, you must steer away from such ideologies. You might be different but get it clear that the world would have been a boring place if we were the same. As such, accept differences and learn to celebrate them.

Listen Effectively

There is power in listening to what other people have to say. Psychologists argue that listening is a silent type of flattery. By actively listening, you give people the impression that they are valued. You are giving them time to express themselves without interfering. With regards to creating meaningful relationships, listening stands as a fundamental thing that you ought to do.

You must realize that you shouldn't just listen, but you should actively listen to what folks have to say. There is a difference here. Actively listening implies that you listen while also showing concern. Remember, it is important to express your understanding of what the other party is feeling or desiring. After knowing what they want, you can move on to respond.

Give People Time

It is impossible to create meaningful connections with people without giving them your time. Giving people time is a special gift. Usually, we often claim that we don't have time. Therefore, by offering to spend time with friends, family, and colleagues, it means a lot. There is a lot that you will be sacrificing when you spend your precious time with individuals you care about. In the end, you find yourself developing strong bonds with those you interact with.

Unfortunately, the advent of technology has made it impossible to create beneficial relationships. Today, most people will plan for a gathering where they get to spend most of their time on their phones. This means that their presence is not felt. Technological devices have robbed people of the value that they would have generated when others create time for them. Consequently, part of ensuring that you give people the time they need, you also need to make yourself present; mentally and physically.

Improve Your Communication Skills

Communication is yet another key factor that will confirm that you create purposeful relations with people. A huge challenge experienced by most people in communication is that they make assumptions. Often, some folks tend to think that others have understood them. Making assumptions leads to misunderstandings, and this negatively affects how people relate. At work, failing to communicate effectively could lead to backstabbing and blaming each other.

Good communication at work will have a positive impact on the overall morale of workers. In this case, when a leader conveys information clearly, junior workers will find it easy to follow instructions. Synergy will also be felt if at all people are working in groups.

Poor communication will also affect love affairs. Without understanding what your partner needs, there is a likelihood that things will fall apart. Successful relationships dwell on communication. Partners who always listen to each other will find ways of solving their issues amicably.

Manage Mobile Technology

The importance of managing how you use your devices is worth repeating over and over again. Most relationships have suffered because people don't know how to use their devices. In social gatherings, it is not surprising to find people glued to their mobile phones. Undeniably, this is not the best way of interacting with people. Sure, the use of mobile technology has transformed the way we communicate. However, the bitter truth is that it is negatively affecting our relationships. Consequently, something must be done. Change begins with you; learn how to use your mobile handset wisely.

Feedback

Communication will not be complete without providing feedback to those you are relating with. To create beneficial relationships, you must provide others with constructive feedback. Don't just respond without stopping for a moment to think. You want to evaluate whether what you were about to say is pertinent. About to say is important. Other people will value positive feedback from your end. This is an essential ingredient in building a strong connection with those around you.

There is always something to gain in the relationships we enter into. Having a positive outlook on any engagement you enter into will have a lasting impact. The best part is that you will live a happier life surrounded by people you love.

Chapter 2: Emotional Intelligence at Work

In today's highly commercialized society, there is increased complexity and competition. The workforce is the forefront of this movement and developing a substantial amount of emotional intelligence can help one navigate these complexities. Whether you are an employer or an employee, possessing a high EQ can place you on a pedestal and allow you to fine-tune your skills to meet the ever growing world standards.

Getting a job ultimately means you will be integrated into a sphere where others would have varying interests and ideologies compared to yours. Therefore, the question of balancing conflicting interests arises. Your needs will differ and standards of how things ought to be done will be subject to a lot of discrepancies.

The importance of emotional intelligence as it relates to our individuality. We will discuss how EQ plays out in the workplace and why the lack of it can lead to complications and clashes. There exists a hierarchy of positions in any workplace, the vicissitudes of fate combined with the sheer force of hard work and consistency decides whatever position one hopes to occupy.

The epicurean ideology maintains that one must always remain in a job that provides happiness and a sense of fulfillment. While this is true, there is also the stark reality that we cannot all find jobs that would massage our egos and stimulate sensations of pleasure at all times. It is not alien that we should seek happiness along with the oftentimes bleak journey of life. But above all, our existence rests snugly on the basis of usefulness before happiness.

Some jobs can suck. To be frank, most jobs SUCK. A recent Forbes article reported that over half of Americans do not like where they work. It could stem from having an over-demanding boss or getting a paycheck that doesn't correspond to the amount of work you put in. While there are jobs that are mentally and physically exhausting to the point of being toxic– a major reference to 'The Devil Wears Prada', there is also the element of 'self' in some situations.

To survive, and not merely survive, but to flourish in a work environment, you have to be willing to constantly evaluate yourself. That job that seems awful and horrid beyond description may have a positive side which you unconsciously ignore because you are stuck in a vicious cycle of negativity. The most common complaint arises from the issue of stress and increased workload.

Stress takes a toll on our emotions, and emotions, in turn, can make us prone to transferring our aggression onto others, and consequently, strain our relationships with friends and family. It all plays out like a domino effect, with the first card taking root in your mind, in your emotions and how you handle them. According to the CDC's National Institute on health and safety, 29 to 40 percent of Americans are "extremely stressed" at work.

Stress is common in many jobs and it is difficult, albeit not impossible, to find a low-stress job. Considering the adverse effects of stress such as depression, anxiety, hypertension, diabetes and increased risk of heart disease, it is important for one to identify stressors and how to deal with them. Establishing boundaries, organizing your workspace, developing multitasking skills and speaking to your supervisor, can help to reduce stress levels.

Feelings of dissatisfaction and stagnancy can also arise in the workplace. There is a pressing need to do more and be more, and our jobs may not always be sufficient to satiate our need for a sense of fulfillment. Quitting your job is a crucial decision to take, and one needs the right amount of emotional intelligence to weigh the benefits and risks involved in such a venture.

Holding a managerial or executive position also requires one to be highly skilled in employing EQ in all aspects of work. The decision-making process does not necessarily have to be the sole responsibility of the leader or CEO, as employees or the board of directors may provide valid suggestions.

This does not dispel the fact that most decisions are to be made by the leader in certain circumstances. There will be situations where you make the wrong decision and that results in devastating consequences for the institution. Your ability to bounce back and create stability amidst the crisis is also a subset of emotional intelligence.

How do you know you are doing enough? What standards do you compare your level of growth to? Are you constantly comparing your output to that of your colleagues, or are you completely absorbed in your work with a singularity of purpose? EQ affects our level of productivity in no small way. To raise the bar and increase our standards, there should be a definition of what those standards are and a clear vision of the goal you wish to achieve. EQ is essential in helping you ditch the totem pole syndrome and increase your output in a healthy way.

The benefits of team performance in a work environment can never be overemphasized. Working in synergy allows for the exchange of ideas and division of labor, which ultimately leads to increased output with reduced stress to the individuals involved. As much as there are benefits to group work, there are also disadvantages. Not everyone is receptive to the idea of working in groups, as they tend to do better when working alone.

However, this may not always be possible as some jobs require you to work in groups. When this occurs, emotional intelligence is crucial to establishing good communication between team members. EQ would also enable you to balance the needs of your workers with yours. EQ is also necessary for developing good work ethics and principles around the workplace. There is security in establishing a concrete set of values and principles that will not be violated in the workplace. It is also essential in helping one think out of the box to provide solutions to problems that the institution may face. Strategies to boost and employ EQ.

It is important to develop EQ as it permeates every aspect of the work process, and the lack of it can result in dire consequences. Picture yourself walking down a bush path with many pits dug all over the road. Your eyes would be essential in helping you avoid those pitfalls and dangers. But imagine walking on that same road with blindfolds on, with only your intuition to guide you. You would be prone to falling into one of those pits, and you would walk without sureness and direction because of the fear and uncertainty that would envelop you at that moment.

Working with a high IQ represents your intuition in this analogy. But combining your IQ and your EQ (which serves as your eyes), would result in even more desirous results than you could think of. Working without EQ can increase stress levels enormously and stress leads to decreased productivity – except your gears tend to work better under pressure, but it isn't advisable to work that way constantly.

A lack of EQ would lead to a skewed decision-making process and an incorrect approach to leadership duties. A boss with a lack of empathy would invariably produce employees who work without their heart in it. Without taking the emotions of your employees into consideration, the quality of output produced would be affected.

The remedy to this situation is to create an environment where enthusiasm is harnessed and kept at its peak. An eager approach to work produces greater results than a dull, monotonous and robotic process devoid of life.

Possessing empathy also means that you show sensitivity to the plight of your subordinates or colleagues. This involves making them feel heard, understood and human. Many world leaders have a high EQ and this has helped them surmount the impossible, as they have developed an understanding of human nature. In other words, high EQ is an asset in today's corporate world.

A high EQ helps in periods of conflict. A clash of ideas is inevitable in any work setting. Individuals all have various world views and you are only bound by what the institution hopes to achieve. Staying calm and being the mediator in times of conflict proves that you have good managerial skills, and may increase your prospects of getting a promotion.

In work, you are also expected to retain your cool and professionalism even with mounting pressure. A low EQ is a liability in this case, as you would be inclined to react to pressure negatively. Feelings should be kept in check in situations like this which may seem difficult to achieve if one does not possess EQ.

Interpersonal tension in teamwork could also be a trigger for one to react in unsavory ways. If one is averse to the idea of teamwork, he/she may tend to take either of these two extremes. The first is to isolate oneself from the process and refuse to make contributions. The second is to obstinately maintain that his/her idea is superior to that of the other team members and that he/she should be the only one employed in the process. This stems from a low EQ and little to no understanding of how to work in synergy.

Having a low EQ disrupts communicative processes. Communication is key to ensuring the smooth functioning of any organization. Lack of communication skills, especially listening skills, can lead to misunderstandings and misconceptions about the idea that is to be communicated. To work collaboratively, understanding the next person is essential. Reacting to mistakes by yelling or displaying passive-aggressive behavior can be destructive to your work life and may even get you fired.

A low EQ makes one resistant and vehemently opposed to change. A key feature of high emotional intelligence is an ability to remain open-minded and to welcome change.

The organization will often undergo massive change and upheaval that would directly or indirectly affect the employees. One's response to change should be welcoming. An objective approach should be taken to situations that seem foreign.

Criticisms are also a part of learning in any work environment. A high EQ would help one understand that criticisms are meant to help him/her improve and not to stir up a malicious situation. As a leader or supervisor, a high EQ helps one give constructive criticism without being overly judgmental or having a propensity to dish out scathing remarks. A lack of emotional intelligence makes one averse to admitting a wrong and apologizing. This is detrimental to the progress of any organization, as it triggers feelings of resentment and suppressed anger.

Another disadvantage of having a low emotional intelligence is that it makes one apportion blame to other members of the team, even when one is in the wrong. It is the consequence of refusing to acknowledge a wrong.

In summary, having people with a high EQ in any organization is an asset, and sadly, the reverse is the case when surrounded by individuals with low EQ whether in the workplace or at home. A high EQ predisposes one to better interpersonal relationships, and an ability to react positively to unfavorable situations. In any corporate institution, understanding the personality and emotions of your fellow team players is a necessary skill to ensure productivity and efficiency.

Strategies to employ in order to improve emotional intelligence at work. On the bright side, it is never too late to develop a high EQ. Callous behaviors, exploitation of others, blatant disregard for the feelings of others, manipulation and arrogance, aren't the right characteristics of a leader. These may even indicate he/she is suffering from a repressed case of antisocial personality disorder (sociopathy), which can be extremely toxic to employees and subordinates.

Emotional intelligence, serves as our gateway to understanding how the 'software' of people around us operates. Getting a job propels you to establish a relationship with others. Therefore, it is imperative that we inculcate habits and principles to ensure that the relationship achieves the common goal for which it was created.

Chapter 3: Benefits of EI

We have been so focused on how emotional intelligence can affect the workplace, the family, socialization, and friendships, but we haven't really stopped and thought: What are its generalized benefits? How does emotional intelligence factor to life, as a whole?

It enables you to live a holistic life.

Long time ago, when you were a kid in primary school, you might think one thing is important – grades. Your parents had trained you to see them as the secrets to your success. So you strived hard and burned the midnight oil. You barely went out of your room because your parents expected you to earn those high grades. There was playtime, but limited. There were friends, but you were all so driven that there was really not much of a connection.

Unfortunately, you later realized that grades would not ensure your success. In fact, you would not get a job with the best resume if you had a bad attitude. People who have no experience in dealing with people would not be able to get jobs in sales, teaching, and counseling, among many others. They might be awkward around people. Introversion is different. Some introverts will still be attuned to other people's emotions because of their tendency to be quiet, attentive, and observant.

A holistic life will be achieved when you combine emotional intelligence and intellect. You think logically, but you also know how to communicate with people. You know how to engage them and to work with them in peace. Success is not just about numbers. How many people have you touched? How many people can assure you of their honesty and friendship with you?

It allows you to take care of your mental and physical well-being.

Working hard and continuous academic learning is admirable. But too much of that can also make the brain drained and the body tired. Studying and working, however, are important parts of life. You still have to go through them. When equipped with emotional intelligence, you may be able to make life a little easier. With a high level of emotional intelligence, you know how to control your emotions. Emotions sometimes also add to the stresses in our lives. We need to acknowledge and wield them properly. Giving in to them will make us susceptible to bouts of anger, to feelings of depression, and even to diseases, such as hypertension and heart diseases.

High EI also helps you manage your time more wisely. Because of this, you know which tasks to prioritize, and which tasks can wait a little bit. You don't need to scramble to get everything done all at once. Moreover, you are aware that multitasking will just mess up things. Multitasking endangers productivity because there is no focus.

It makes you more resilient.

What is resilience? Resilience is being able to bounce back from traumatic and stressful experiences. Someone who can manage his emotions will be more likely able to display resilience. One factor of emotional intelligence is being able to manage emotions. So stress and trauma may still affect you if you have emotional intelligence but you know how to bounce back.

Being able to bounce back is important. Imagine a stretchy object going as far as it can go. If it is elastic, it can go back to its original position without it breaking. That is what resilience is all about. You can find yourself in your previous state, before the stresses and the trauma, but with the learnings from those negative experiences. Not only have you recovered, but also wiser and stronger. On the other hand, low emotional intelligence may place you in danger of breaking. The emotional breakdown may have been caused by the lack of agency to analyze what has just happened and to manage extreme emotions.

It boosts your chances to become successful in life.

Being successful requires not just brains, but also an understanding of people. Even the most reclusive and talented workers may need to have such an understanding. For example, no matter how introverted a writer is, he or she must know what the target audience wants to read about. That is the interest that needs to be captured. Books that feature characters that are wooden and stereotypical show a lack of knowledge of how the human mind really works.

In jobs that require more interactions with other people, you need to use your EI. You have to understand the people you work for and work with to be able to be a success in your job.

It helps you deal with stress.

This point is related to resilience. It is all about being able to handle stress. An emotionally intelligent person has strategies that will help him survive huge amounts of stress. He is able to control the way his mind works. He can make himself focus on the bottom-line, the road to recovery, and assessing his emotions. While he may also feel the pressure, he is ready to move forward and to work hard if needed.

Emotionally intelligent people know how to organize their time, control their emotions, and analyze the situation. They are not completely free from stress, but they know how to deal with it.

It connects you to people.

Asperger's syndrome makes it difficult for someone to achieve high emotional intelligence. People with this condition may be very intelligent, but may struggle with interpreting human emotions. However, doing so is not completely impossible. They still can learn to analyze their feelings. The methodical approach may appeal to them. Now if you are a person with high intelligence, it may be your job to attempt to connect with someone with Asperger's. They need extra time and understanding. High emotional intelligence enables a person to connect with others more effectively. It is what makes the motivations of even strangers clearer, because you will be able to read gestures and not just listen to words. Knowing the typical fears and desires of people will help you in building close relationships with them.

It allows you to enjoy stories, or at least, experience them more vividly.

Stories can be more vivid in different ways when you have emotional intelligence.

One, your stories become more vivid. You can readily show emotions when you are telling people a story. They, in turn, are able to connect with you through the colorfulness of your stories.

Two, other people develop more clarity. You can better understand their point of view. The person's background and innermost desires can better explain his actions.

Three, because of your understanding of human emotion, even stories that are read (books) or viewed (movies) become a lot more expressive to you.

Chapter 4: Practical Ways to Use Emotional Intelligence

You are not reading this book because you believe that emotional intelligence plays no role in human life, and these skills serve no purpose in making your life better. You are reading because you recognize on some level that EI can be useful to you somehow. Perhaps you have EI skills, and your goal is to make them better. Perhaps you recognize that you have problems connecting with people and your goal is to try and find a way to fix that. EI can change your life, and here we focus on seven practical ways that EI can set you on the right course.

1. Self-Management And Relationship Management

Many men and women experience failed relationship after failed relationship, and they don't know why. A lot of times, this is a problem with communication, which is itself an important aspect of emotional intelligence and one that will be addressed shortly. But sometimes these problems that many people have with interaction are due to an inability to regulate our emotions and our behavior. We have seen how self-awareness alone is not enough as it can lead us to act in anger, frustration, or jealousy. One important way that EI can be used to improve our lives is by regulating our thoughts (managing our emotions better) and behaviors.

Doing this does require that we be conscious of our thoughts and understand how our behaviors are related. But as we have seen repeatedly, good EI skills means that the emotions of others are just as important as our own. Indeed, an entire book can be written on how people in the present focus a lot on self-awareness and how this can lead to behaving narcissistically, but this is a story for another time. What you need to do (or what you should do) is to learn how to manage your emotion-behavior connection. If you are more conscious of how your emotions and behaviors are linked, and you learn to care more about the emotions of others, you will see the dramatic way in which your relationships are changed.

2. Putting Emotional Intelligence To Good Use In The Workplace

The workplace is a stressful environment for most people. If you experience a lot of tension while you are at work or have feelings of anxiety around going to work, then you are not alone.

Join the millions (or billions) of people around the world who are in the same boat as you are. But going to work does not have to be a drag. Most people who dislike work usually do not because of the work itself, but because of the people. Bad relationships with others can sour all of our experiences.

Fortunately, emotional intelligence is all about improving our relationships with other people. Perhaps the difficult task here is learning how to be the bigger person. Sure, it may be natural to dislike someone who dislikes us or to feel anger towards someone who has displayed anger towards us, but all this mirroring of emotional states does is create a downward spiral that leads to damaged relationships. We can improve our relationships in the workplace by self-regulating our negative feelings towards other people and having empathy for people who dislike us or may have been unkind to us in the past. It may not be easy, but whoever said practicing EI was going to be, lied to you.

3. Using Emotional Intelligence As A Guide In Decision Making

If you are using emotional intelligence correctly (and are truly motivated to infuse your life with EI), then EI skills should eventually start to impact all areas of your life. This means that EI not only helps you improve things about yourself that need improving, like having empathy or learning to regulate your emotions, but EI also should start to impact your behavior in various important ways. One of the more important of those ways is the realm of decision making.

As human beings, the actions we take are closely linked to our emotional state, even if we are not always conscious of this. We do not always recognize that we decide to take this action or that, often thinking that certain courses of action are natural are inevitable. As you get stronger in your EI skills, you will come to recognize that emotional awareness and empathy can guide our decision making in powerful ways. And they do this to help us form better interactions with others. By allowing our EI to take on this role, we have made an important first step in improving our life.

4. Using Emotional Intelligence To Improve Your Communication

Like it or not, communication is an essential part of being human, whether you are talking about verbal communication or non-verbal communication.

Humans are social creatures, which means that communication is not only important for us to convey information to one another, but it is also important as a way that we as humans bond with one another. Although people do communicate without awareness or sensitivity to the feelings of others, doing this usually leaves one party feeling like communication was not beneficial.

By learning to use our EI skills in communication, we improve our lives as well as the lives that those we interact with. What this means practically is being aware of the emotional state of others, feeling compassion for others, having empathy for them, and using our emotional awareness as a guide for our behavior with the other person. Therefore, when you communicate, you should not only be conscious of what communication is doing for you but what it may potentially do for the other person. This is an opportunity to show that you care, to engage in an exchange where both parties care about the other person, or to have empathy even if it is not obvious to the other person (though it often is).

5. Using Emotional Intelligence to Have Better Relationships with People

By following the communication steps that we just mentioned, you are well on your way to having better relationships with people. The idea, as we stated before, is that your interactions should be just as much about the other person as they are about you. This is not only a way of showing the other person that you care, but it also establishes an unspoken connection between the two of you as it allows emotional awareness to wiggle its way into the interaction. Therefore, all the way that you behave with emotional awareness allow you to have better relationships with other people, which will certainly set you on the course of life change.

6. Emotional Intelligence as An Important Tool for Connections In Healthcare

It may be difficult for some to immediately see the connection between EI skills and healthcare, but the industry is filled with patients who feel that their healthcare providers are insensitive to their needs or their feelings. Indeed, it is believed that many adverse healthcare outcomes can be attributed to providers who misdiagnose a patient or who do not obtain an appropriate history, and this may in part be due to the inability for providers to form effective connections with their patients.

Something as simple as expressing sympathy for a patient who is going through a trial may be enough to change the outcome for that person.

This is true not only of doctors but of nurses. All in the industry can benefit from putting some effort into emotional intelligence. This will improve provider interactions with patients, which not only will improve outcomes for the patient but will provide great benefit to the provider.

7. Building Resilience with Emotional Intelligence

By practicing emotional intelligence skills and being sure to use them in all our interactions, we can drastically impact the lives of others who may be experiencing hard times. But we ourselves may have our own hard times and may need to find a way to use EI for our own benefit.

Emotional intelligence can help us to build resilience. EI can do this by combining self-awareness with self-regulation. By being conscious of our negative thoughts and how they impact our behaviors and interactions, we can then begin to regulate these thoughts. This is an essential part of being resilient. Practice this skill by adapting your negative thoughts into positive ones to improve your interactions with others, improve your ability to withstand the trials in your path, and improve your life.

Criticism is used as a tool.

People with high EI do not negatively react to criticism. They may be hurt, but a large part of them will analyze the truth in the feedback. If you still find yourself lashing out at the person who gave you feedback then there may still be some improvement needed in your level of emotional intelligence.

Scenario:

Your boss says you need to revise your report. While everything is grammatically correct, there are some points that may be misconstrued for something completely different. This may cause you to think that you have done a horrible job and will need to redo it all over again. He gives you the feedback in private. Because you have high EI, you realize you received criticism in a discreet manner. The errors were filtered while still in your company before the report is presented to client. You stick to the positive aspect.

They provide constructive criticism.

Conversely, with high EI, you will also provide constructive criticism. You tell people how they can improve instead of just telling them that their work is ugly and unacceptable. There is no malice in the way that you deliver your feedback.

Scenario:

You are the boss. You have to give feedback from time to time to ensure that work is done well in the company. You have to set standards. When you do give the feedback, you provide privacy for the employee. Instead of just pointing out the errors, you also provide advice as to what can be done to improve the work.

Buoying others with praise is natural to you.

You may have read some articles in social media about how your rude and brutally honest friend is your best friend. This may be true. People do need some dose of truth. However, if you find yourself insulting other people all the time under the pretense of being close, then something is wrong. It should be natural for you to find something to praise about another person else.
Should be no desire to be better than the other person or to discredit the achievements of others. Be truly happy for successful people.

Scenario:

You know that your co-worker always feel insecure about her portfolio. You recognize her talent and suggest that some of her artworks be incorporated into one of the company's upcoming ads. You make sure that everyone knows that it is your co-worker's art. A person with lower EI would have taken the artwork and claimed it for himself, knowing that the original artist would be too unsure of herself to counteract the claim.

You practice thinking before acting.

Some prefer being natural, as they say. They believe that people should always say and do the first thing that they are inclined to say and do. It does have a childhood quality to it. Nevertheless, being childlike is the opposite of emotional intelligence. It may be cute and refreshing, but it can also be irresponsible. You need to practice thinking before doing or saying anything. This way, you do not end up regretting something that cannot be undone.

Scenario:

At work, you see an employee acting extra shifty. There were some thefts that have been going around. So it is somewhat logical to suspect this person of having done the thefts. Instead of reporting this suspect, you may either do some discreet investigation or ask the person what is wrong. With your high EI, you might be able to spot some signs that point to a person, or at least, handle the matter gracefully.

You control and analyze your thoughts.

Sometimes people have thoughts that become uncontrollable. They change their moods and take over their lives. A repressed memory may pop up during a happy moment and completely change the mood of the moment. With a high EI, you will be able to analyze those thoughts. You can remember without having to lose control of your emotions.

Scenario:

You are a successful businessperson. Your company has been awarded for best innovation just the year before. Despite this, you know that everything is not quite there.

You had to detach yourself from family members who wanted you to do something safer, like being a doctor.

You sometimes still remember your childhood, how you were constantly bombarded with verbal abuse. Your parents used to insult and call you names whenever you made a mistake. They feel like they are good parents because they have never beaten you physically. These memories are, of course, hurtful. Your high EI will help you prevent them from taking over your life. You will, instead, use the negative emotions to drive you further towards success instead.

A sense of responsibility is active.

With high EI, you know that you have to take responsibility for your actions. Tasks that are assigned to you will always get done because you want the best for the company or the family. You understand what should be accomplished to keep the peace and the order.

Scenario:

It is late when you got home from school. Your mom is on the couch, sleeping. She looks very tired and sick. You go to the kitchen and see that there are so many dirty dishes in the sink. Instead of heading towards your room to rest, you wash the dishes. You know your mother does everything on her own, without complaining. If she forgets to do something, then she must be really sick and she needs your help.

Feelings are processed and not just expressed.

If you have to express every little emotion that you feel, misunderstandings may ensue. There are more tactical and discreet ways of expressing feelings. Before you even express your feelings, however, you have to pause a bit. What am I really feeling? Why do I feel this way? Would it hurt if I react a certain way?

Scenario:

As the company's HR manager, you meet many applicants. One of the applicants makes your boil for no reason. You do not know him and are not familiar with his name. His credentials are really good, though. Instead of just rejecting him because of your illogical feelings, you step back and analyze why you are feeling that way. You realize that the applicant slightly looks like a person you have had a huge fight with in college. He is not the same person, but the facial features are similar. You remind yourself that this is not that person you have had issues with.

This applicant may be truly useful to your company because of the skills that he possesses. You accept him.

You forgive and forget.

This is a tough one. It may take a really high EI to get to this point. You should be able to forgive people who have done you wrong. This means being able to empathize with the other person's feelings and thoughts. Instead of treating the other person as an enemy, you can think of him as a lesson learned. To forget is a little harder. What you can do is stay away from people who make you feel bad and tempted to do something drastically unacceptable.

Scenario:

One of your employees is very talented, but tactless. One time, she was dealing with clients and she said something that offended the client. It was an innocent remark like "Oh, sir. I did not know that you were related to the Martins". She did not know that the client did not want to be associated with the Martins, who were notorious for their money laundering practices. The client went off in a huff.

After the incident, the employee worked even harder than before. However, she was relegated to desk duty only. She was never allowed to put on any social events ever again. However, she started requesting being part of networking activities again. She said that she was very sorry about what happened and that she was conducting more research on each of the clients. You, with your high EQ, were very hesitant but you gave her one more chance. You also made it clear to her that she would be demoted if she ended up losing another client for the company.

Empathy is a strong quality.

Being able to understand the other person is a hallmark of high EI. You cannot respond and manage if you are not really sure as to what is going on in the first place. Empathy connects you with other people at a deeper level.

Scenario:

Mrs. Diaz has been your company's secretary for more than ten years. She was very efficient. Recently, however, you found out that she had been going through IVF treatments. At 40, she was trying to get pregnant, and she finally did. Because of her delicate situation, she incurred several tardy days.

This had never happened before. Because she has served the company well for years, you gave her some leeway and hired an assistant for her. You appreciate how Mrs. Diaz continues to serve your company even if the salary grade is fair but not exactly stellar.

You are authentic.

When you think too much before you act, you may be accused of being a pretender. This is not really what is going on. When you have high EI, you just want to analyze the situation and the person that you are dealing with before you do anything. You are still authentic. You are able to see your true self because you have studied yourself well enough.

Scenario:

They say authenticity is about getting what you are seeing. You are like that. You are the boss of the company but you are genuinely to get down and dirty when it comes to clearing up the office.

A hurricane struck your town. The office was badly damaged, but standing. After the winds had died down, you needed the help of all your employees to clean and clear up. Instead of sitting at your desk and overseeing the work, you decided you were also needed. You took up a mop and some rags and helped out. You were leading by example.

You keep a positive attitude.

Negativity is all around us. That cannot be helped. The best way to tackle it is to have a positive attitude. Even a desire to have a positive attitude and lifestyle is a strong move towards the right direction.

Scenario:

Phillip has a very stressful life. He has to travel to work as early as 6:00 am because it takes about two hours to do so. Living in the city is too expensive. When he gets to work, he has the responsibility over a team of 30 call center agents. Ten of them are new because the company has recently expanded. Phillip, who has a high EI, is aware that if he starts grumbling, he may never be able to stop. Some of the other higher ranked employees in his company rant every day. He notices that they started getting more wrinkles. Anna even has had to be hospitalized because of hypertension. He does not give in to this. During the ride to work, he meditates.

He listens to an audio with nature sounds and breathes into it. Despite the two-hour travel, he reaches with positivity that is absorbed by even his young trainees.

You are approachable.

People with high EI know that some people may be awkward in certain situations. They may be intimidated with people who are in a high position or are too quiet and reserved. People are afraid of dealing with something that they are uncertain about. Having an approachable demeanor makes it easier for others to come to you. The advantage is two-folds: you can network and connect better, while people do not have a hard time approaching you.

Scenario:

Mrs. Mills is the multi-branch manager of Easy Shopping. She has to be stern when she is on the job. However, she also keeps an approachable demeanor. Customers know that she is friendly. They do not hesitate to air their concerns. These concerns may be able to improve the company. Moreover, because she does not keep a stiff upper lip, people also approach her in a nice way. They do not shout out complaints. Even workers know that they can confide in Mrs. Mills. However, this does not mean to say that her standards are low and that she can be tempted to be unprofessional. She makes it clear that while she is friendly and warm, her expectations from her workers are still high.

You are attuned to the nuances of emotional variations.

This means that your emotional dictionary is rich. You don't just describe people as sad. You may describe them as distraught, depressed, or devastated. This means you know that Person A is distraught because she lost her wallet a few hours ago. Meanwhile, Person B is depressed and has been so for a long while. Her lethargy is palpable. Person C is devastated because his family died in a car crash. Their feelings should not be simplified to sad, because their levels of emotions vary greatly.

Scenario:

As a psychiatrist, you are able to list the characteristics of each patient vividly. You know which ones are ecstatic for no reason. It is not just about being happy because the sun is shining. There is something seriously wrong about a person jumping around with glee while the rest of his family could not understand so. You also know if a person is murderous instead of just annoyed.

For patients suffering from depression, suicidal tendencies may also be assessed. Is the patient merely sad or alarmingly suicidal? This gives you the reason to break oaths of confidentiality to save a life. This is still a very tricky situation for doctors, who have pledged to keep the sanctity of their patients' confidences.

You are not easily offended.

When you can better understand people, you are not easily offended. Instead, you analyze the situation. Did the person really mean to be sarcastic? Is it his demeanor to anyone he encounters? With your ability to walk in other people's shoes, you understand the motivations of the other person. You may get slightly annoyed, but you are willing to understand.

Scenario:

Mr. Edward is an old man in his eighties. He always talks about how respect is a very vital part of good character. His son, Leo is off to visit him one day. Mr. Edward will finally meet his grandson, Louis.

Louis has been brought up overseas. He has just gotten back to the country at the age of twenty. Mr. Edward is eager to meet him. Then, they meet. The young man's language and gestures are far too vulgar for Mr. Edward. He likes to use his phone even when talking to his elders. He even vapes in the same room. His words are full of colloquial expressions.

Mr. Edward is a little shocked. However, he reminds himself that his grandson is young and has lived away from the rest of the family for almost two decades. He is a jolly enough young man, who likes to entertain his grandpa with his adventures. Mr. Edward knows, however, that when his wife meets Louis, it will be different. Mrs. Edward will be ecstatic, but she will also be deeply disappointed. She may take Louis' behavior as a sign of disrespect towards her.

You are a good judge of character.

People who have high EI are good judges of character. They know whom they can trust and they can gauge people even before speaking with them. It is not merely a matter of instinct, but a matter of having a rich knowledge of human motivations and behavior.

Scenario:

Miss Daisy is an HR manager. She deals with many applicants every day. Their company has several branches, and it is through her that various types of people get deployed to those branches. Her first assessment of behavior is through the resume and cover letter. Are they impressive and most importantly, accurate? The second step is meeting the applicants and matching them to their resumes. Are they telling the truth? The third step is to listen carefully to the way they speak. Are they loud and fast or quiet and meek? Then, the fourth step involves watching their gestures and mannerisms. Are they simply nervous or are they hiding something? Miss Daisy believes she has always been a good judge of character. This was shy she got the job. However, her continuous work with the company provides her with more opportunity to improve her "people radar."

When bosses and employees have high EI, even bad situations get better. They do not get inflated and stretched to their limits. People truly enjoy working for a good boss. A boss with high EI is not perfect. He is not a robot, either, but he understands the human condition. If he can feel dejected, he knows that other people in the company can feel dejected, too. Employees with high EI understand when they are being corrected. They have a strong sense of responsibility of improving the company. They are not just there to sign in and out and get their salaries at the end of the month.

Finding out if a person has a high EI is more intensive. IQ can at least be verified using standardized tests. There are no standardized tests for checking EI. EI can be observed, instead. It can be felt. If things are going smoothly inside an office, a school, or a home, then chances are a person with high EI is in command in varying capacities. Someone is making sure that things are fair.

Think of your emotional intelligence as a muscle. To strengthen that muscle and build it up to where you want it to be, you need to exercise it consistently, just as you would with physical exercise.

Reflecting on Your Feelings

The first exercise that you can begin working to develop and improve your emotional intelligence is to begin by observing your feelings and reflecting on them. It is cool to fall out of reach with ourselves in this hectic world that we live in. From the moment we wake up each morning, our lives seem to be constantly on the go. Trying to manage one thing after another, taking care of ourselves often falls by the wayside, and we lose that connection to our innermost feelings. Instead of learning to focus on our emotions when they arise, we choose to do the easier, more convenient thing. We either brush it aside, ignore them, or deny them completely. Maybe even distract us from those feelings by doing something else. The more you deny your feelings, though, the harder it becomes to manage them later on. Bottling up your emotions and hoping they will just go away on its own has never proven to be an effective strategy. If it were, there wouldn't be quite so many people walking around lashing out emotionally or reacting impulsively. From now on, whenever you experience an emotion (no matter what it may be), observe it, acknowledge it, and reflect on how it is making you feel.

Make a Note of Your Triggers

This is something new because you've probably never done this before. Take your exercises towards building emotional intelligence one step further by writing down the triggers that cause you to become emotional each time you observe your feelings. What caused you to get worked up? What caused you to feel stressed? What's responsible for creating this feeling of happiness you now feel?

Whenever you make a note of every emotion you experience, write down, and make a list of the things that triggered it. Examine that list a couple of times a week. Do you notice any patterns? What is a recurring theme that you can spot? Understanding how to detect the triggers that cause extreme emotional reactions is key to learning how to manage your emotions.

After all, you can't manage something that you don't know. You need to know what you're associating with before you can start making moves to remedy it.

Keep Track Of The Emotional Triggers!

Once you have found out the reasons behind the occurrence of every emotion, write down those reasons on your list. For instance, if there is a certain person or a certain event that invokes the emotion of anger in you, then you must write down this reason under the heading of anger.

Making Use Of Those Emotions

We must never underestimate how emotions affect our thoughts. Whenever we think about a certain thing, our emotions control our reactions to that thing.

Emotions don't just tend to occur on a sudden basis. They occur due to reasons that have been supporting them for a certain period. For instance, you are getting late in the morning while driving to work. You see a car with a busted tire standing during the road. You start angrily shouting at the driver of that car to move his car away from the road. This anger didn't just occur as a sudden reaction to the flat tire of that car, but it occurred because you woke up late that morning due to which you were already late for your work.

At the end comes the task of managing your emotions. For some people, this task is known to be the biggest challenge in their life. Managing your emotions is not just a one-day task, but it requires a continuous struggle. However, once you master this task, managing your emotions might become the easiest thing on this planet.

Take a Timeout When You Need It

An emotionally intelligent person does not let their feelings overwhelm them. They always remain cool, calm, and collected. They always respond appropriately. More importantly, they know when to take time out and return to the situation with a better solution. It is easy to let your feelings overwhelm you if you're not careful. As much as you want to resolve the conflict there and then, sometimes, you need to take a time-out or a five-minute breather just to clear your head whenever your emotions are starting to get the best of you. That is the intelligent thing to do.

Start Practicing Responding

Where before this, you may have been more prone to reacting impulsively each time you had an extreme emotional reaction, now you need to adopt a new exercise. You need to learn how to respond first instead of reacting. You now need to respond to your first default mode, and you do that with self-awareness and self-regulation. By giving attention to your emotions, especially those that trigger an extreme reaction in the past, you can then learn how to regulate yourself. You can make a conscious effort to choose the next move you will make instead of letting your emotions drive you. You will do the intelligent thing by leading with your head, not your heart. This is why it is important to emulate the steps above, especially learning how to identify your triggers. If you know, something will trigger an extreme emotional response, take measures to that put a stop to that through self-regulation.

No Room for Superiority

An emotionally intelligent person is that way because of one thing – they are humble. It simply won't do without thinking that you may be better than everyone, or that someone is not on par with you, which makes you more superior. You will never achieve a leadership position if you inflict an air of superiority because no one will ever respect a leader who makes it difficult to be likable. When you choose not to be humble, you make it very difficult to achieve self-awareness because you will be blinded to your faults. It's no problem for you to point out the flaws in others immediately, but you won't be able to note the things that you are doing wrong. See everyone as an equal, not a subordinate. No matter what family they come from, everyone deserves to be treated respectfully. Display emotional intelligence by always choosing to be humble, approachable, likable, and pleasant.

Avoid Overthinking

One of the reasons that we sometimes become more emotional than we should is because we tend to overthink a lot of things. A simple matter which could be resolved easily could potentially get blown out of proportion because someone was reacting to it in a highly emotional way. To start exercising better emotional intelligence on your part, what you could do is to stop overthinking situations and just see things for what they are. You do that by looking at the facts in front of you. If something is not a fact, then don't think about it.

Observe the situation in front of you and see things as they are. Don't embellish, don't assume, and don't add on facts of your own. This is how things get more complicated than they should, and emotions get fired up when there was no need to be.

Writing Down Your Feelings

Bring paper and a pen. Note down the emotions that you feel regularly. Point out your physical reactions to each type of emotion under the heading of that emotion. For instance, you have written down the emotion of HURT, which you feel now and then. Whether you cry or feel a sense of loss, just write it down on your list. Once you have completed the first emotion and its symptoms, move on towards the next emotion.

Pour your heart out, open the floodgates of emotion, and just let it flow until you're done. When you've finished, read what you've just written down. Assess your thoughts, observe how you're feeling and reflect upon why and what triggered such emotion within you. Once you've finished and felt better, you can always tear up or shred the paper. Do you notice how you sometimes feel better after talking about your feelings with someone? It works the same way, except that by writing it down, you ensure that you always have an outlet for your emotions, even when no one is available.

Chapter 7: Busting the Myths About Emotional Intelligence

As is the case with a lot of things, there exist several misconceptions regarding emotional intelligence. Throughout this book, you've probably been able to identify the misconceptions you have had about emotional intelligence yourself, and the accompanying truth of the matter. This chapter is dedicated to busting the many myths that many people have when it comes to EQ. Some of the myths are laughable, while others are downright ridiculous. Seeing that EQ deals with emotion, it is probably not too unexpected that there would be numerous feelings expressed. Dive in to find out what is true about emotional intelligence and what isn't.

Myth: Emotional intelligence is a woman's area

Truth: Emotional intelligence is a skill that applies to both men and women.

For the longest time, the stereotype of women being more emotional than men has been perpetuated by various channels. It, therefore, follows that when most people hear of emotional intelligence, they only think of women. This could not be further from the truth. First of all, the claim that women are the more emotional of the human species is not a claim supported by biology. When scientists set out to study this phenomenon, they found out that the populations observed were more likely to behave according to the expectations placed on them by their cultures rather than as dictated by nature. In other words, women might behave more emotionally since that is what society or culture dictates from them, while men might repress their emotions for the same reason.

Seeing that we are capable of emotion, regardless of gender, there is a need to understand and manage those emotions. Even if there were a parallel universe where males were virtually incapable of having emotions, they would still be required to deal with women who have emotions. Emotional intelligence is a scale that these parallel universe males would require when interacting with the parallel universe women.

Myth: Emotional intelligence is the sole determinant of success in life.

Truth: Many factors determine whether you will be successful in life and EQ happens to be one of them.

Emotional intelligence opens a lot of doors for you in life. When you can read and relate well with people, you do not have as many obstacles than someone who has low EQ. However, EQ is not the all-inclusive package for success. Success requires a combination of smarts, hard work, opportunity or chance, and sometimes even sheer luck. Being low in the EQ does not automatically qualify you for failure. There are some professions where people become highly successful just by relying on their IQ.

An engineer, for instance, might be required to have a very high IQ so that they can easily grasp concepts. The same engineer might be very low on the EQ front and still become highly successful because their work calls for smarts over emotional intelligence. Sure, the engineer might struggle with personal relationships and will probably never hold a management position, but they will still be successful in their own right.

Myth: Emotional intelligence is about being nice.

Truth: Emotional intelligence is more than just being nice.

Over the years, nice has grown to be synonymous with being a pushover or a doormat. Whenever people hear that someone is nice, they start to imagine all manner of ways they can walk all over that person. Here's the thing: If you think of nice as the capacity to tolerate people's personalities and their quirks, then yes, emotional intelligence is about being nice. However, if your definition of nice is the person that says yes to every request and does not have a voice of their own, then you are way off from what emotional intelligence is. Emotional intelligence does not make you a yes-man.

Emotional intelligence equips you with all the skills that you need to be able to say no as many times as you need and to do so unapologetically.

Myth: You're either born with emotional intelligence or not.

Truth: You can learn to become more emotionally intelligent.

Emotional intelligence is not the same as height whereby you are either born tall or short and are, after that, doomed to never reaching the higher shelves or always being the brunt of height jokes. Sure, some people have a higher ability to grasp emotional intelligence. This might depend on how they are born, how they are raised, the experiences they have been through, and numerous other factors that they interact with as they become adults. However, most people are capable of being emotionally intelligent.

Even psychopaths who are incapable of feeling emotions like the rest of us know how to mimic emotional intelligence. If you are a fully functional human being with a wide range of emotions, then you are fully capable of being emotionally intelligent.

Myth: Everyone that knows how to charm people is emotionally intelligent.

Truth: Sometimes, there is more than emotional intelligence behind the charm.

Some of the most charming people you know are also the most dangerous human beings you'll ever cross paths with. Just because a person knows when and how to smile in your face does not mean that they are high in EQ. They might just be manipulative. Psychopaths, for instance, know how to blend in and play Mr. Sociable Guy's role to perfection. While an emotionally intelligent person will make you feel relaxed and comfortable without invading your personal space, a psychopath trying to win your trust may be more forceful, persistent, and full-on in a manner that might be uncomfortable. A trick you can use to determine whether you are dealing with high EQ or psychopathy is by trusting your gut feeling, watching whether someone's actions match their words, and noticing how you feel after every interaction. If you leave conversations feeling drained and unsure, you might be dealing with an energy vampire in the form of a psychopath rather than an emotionally intelligent person.

Myth: Introverts are not usually emotionally intelligent.

Truth: Introverts can be as emotionally intelligent as anyone else.

Introverts are known (or at least stereotyped) to be these shy and socially awkward people who have little to zero chance of being good at normal social interactions. While there may be some truth to it, this is not exactly the textbook definition of an introvert. An introvert is simply someone who prefers to look into themselves rather than turning to their external world for stimulation. An introvert is content in their own company and will often prefer to be silent rather than to talk. An introvert's worst nightmare is the extrovert, especially the kind of extrovert who does not have any emotional intelligence. Just because a person prefers to be silent does not mean that they are low in emotional intelligence.

The fact that introverts are inward-looking means that they probably already have the self-awareness bit of EQ figured out. However, because introverts tend to be so absorbed in their worlds (in the most unselfish way possible), it means that they have to work a little harder at drawing themselves out into their external environment.

Seeing that introversion is a personality type, and personalities are not known scientifically to be dynamic, introverts will often face the uphill task of opening up their world to other people. For instance, you cannot be empathetic to the suffering of others unless you are aware of this suffering. To become aware of this suffering, you must at least speak with this person to tell you that yes, indeed, they are having a bad day. This can be almost too much to ask from an introvert.

The good news is that emotional intelligence can be learned since it is a skill like any other. An introvert can pick up the cues that they need to incorporate to be emotionally intelligent, just like all other personality types. There are introverts out there who are highly emotionally intelligent. They know how to carry themselves when they are in a group of people. They understand that certain circumstances call for them to leave the security of their shells. Once they are back home, they quietly retreat to the safety of their shell until different circumstances require them to come out.

Myth: Emotional intelligence is only important for people in leadership roles or particular professions.

Truth: Emotional intelligence makes your life easier regardless of who you are.

When you are in a leadership position, your lack of emotional intelligence will be more apparent and detrimental compared to a lack of emotional intelligence in the people that you lead or any other person. It has been said that with great power comes great responsibility, and this could not be truer when it comes to emotional intelligence. When you serve as a leader or boss, your every move is in the spotlight. People will pay attention to how you speak to your juniors, how you show care and consideration for others, how you manage stressful situations, and even how you manage yourself. Your teams will also look to you to model the kind of behavior that they should emulate and to be their mentor in matters of business and relationships. Imagine being in such a position while lacking emotional intelligence. More likely than not, you are going to be highly overwhelmed.

Chapter 8: Obstacles to the Improvement of EQ

There are some things you need to be cautious of because of the adverse effect they can have on the development of your EQ.

Once you are able to successfully navigate through these obstacles, you will be ahead of the curve when it comes to being emotionally intelligent. Below are the challenges you need to surmount to rate high in emotional intelligence:

Not Realizing You Need to Change

Change is constant in life. However, it depends on the kind of change you are talking about. Change is constant because you will either get better or worse. Stagnancy does not really exist when it comes to human development; deterioration is what is constant when you are not getting better. In other words, positive changes are not constant, they demand to be deliberate and committed. It is, however, not possible to improve the quality of your life when you don't even realize or agree that you need to improve.

It is only after you have come to realize that you need to take purposeful steps to change your life that you can make the necessary changes. Hence, until you agree that you need to improve your EQ, you can never take any step to develop it. As much as it is good to have people around you that love you unconditionally, you need to be sincere with yourself to improve the areas of your life and to improve your EQ.

Not Being Ready To Change

It is one thing to realize and agree that you need to change; it is, however, a different thing entirely to be ready to pay the sacrifices attached to the positive change you crave. There are no free gifts in life. Every gift you receive was paid for by another person. No one can improve your life for you more than your own willingness to do that. Developing your EQ demands deliberate efforts that require your commitment. Hence, don't just sit there and hope that a miracle will occur somewhere that will make you suddenly begin to improve. You must be ready to work your socks off. Thus, once you have agreed with yourself that you need to improve your level of emotional intelligence, you need to also start doing everything necessary to improve in the way you handle your emotions and those of the people that come your way.

Accepting Defeat

Some people have a deterministic view about life where they feel whatever comes their way is their lot. This view makes such people accept anything that comes their way and they rarely make any attempt to take deliberate steps or concise efforts to improve the quality of their lives. Such people will see their inability to manage their emotions effectively as just their 'personality'. This is their grand excuse for acting impulsively and having difficulties with maintaining excellent relationship with others.

I am not denying that your personality has a role to play in the way you behave, but there is a lot you can do to improve the way you act. Hence, you cannot afford to throw in the towel yet because there is still room for improvement. You can either chose to do nothing about your EQ or challenge yourself to make the necessary commitment to improving your emotional intelligence.

The Wrong Company

I am not talking about a firm, I am talking about the kind of people you have around you. You cannot grow beyond the kind of influence you have around you. When you surround yourself with negative people who don't care about the way they go about life, you will find it difficult to grow in the way you manage your emotions. Be around people who genuinely care about you as such people will accept you in spite of your deficiencies and help you grow.

They will not let you be contented with your flaws; they will work in tandem with you to help you grow and fulfill your potential. When you have such people in your life, don't let pride or offense set in and make you lose them. Value such people and see to it that the relationship continues to blossom. The quality of your life depends on such people.

Not Giving Room for Growth

This is particularly important if you function in one leadership role or the other. When I said "leadership role", I am not outrightly referring to being the C.E.O. of a company. As a father or mother, you are also a leader because you need to lead your children correctly. As a leader, you must be willing to give room for growth. In other words, as much as you want people to be productive and effective, you have to also allow them to make mistakes and learn from them.

Knowing when to be stern and when to pat people on the back is key to emotional intelligence. When you allow people to grow and become better, you will have a larger heart which is unconsciously developing your EQ. Therefore, you will not only harm the people you are leading when you don't allow them to grow, but you will also hamper your own growth as an individual.

Letting Every Opinion Matter

It is important to listen to the opinion of others but every opinion must not count to you. There will always be ridiculous people who have chosen to make you feel miserable. There is no one, no matter how good they are, that is disliked by absolutely no one. Hence, you will only be denying yourself the necessary room to develop your EQ when you take everyone who criticizes you seriously.

You must be able to know the difference between people who criticize you because they want you to become better as a person and people who are all out to bring you down. People who criticize you to bring you down will hammer on every fault and try to disrupt your rhythm. You must be determined to be focused and ignore such people. Trying to please such people is pointless because there is nothing you can do that will ever be good enough for them.

Being a Destructive Critic

You don't want people to talk you down just to distract you, you should also not do the same to others. When you are concerned about bringing others down, you will not be able to grow also. You will be too busy designing new techniques to attack others to come up with ideas to improve your own life. Not doing to others what you also don't want them to do to you is a simple but important life principle.

Get busy with improving your own life and developing your own EQ rather than saddling yourself with the task of bringing others down. Never forget that people only criticize those who have decided to go out there and do something important in life. No one criticizes people who don't do anything meaningful with their lives because such people don't count. It is hypocritical to want others to be kind to you while you are always ready to attack them when they make mistakes.

Chapter 9: How to Improve Yourself

Increase Your Self-Esteem

Re-affirm your positive traits. Just as we often think negative things about ourselves, we must learn to affirm positive traits as well. For example, maybe you're constantly telling yourself, "You're a lazy person." You've been telling yourself that for so long that you are believing it and you've internalized that voice. To see yourself positively and improve your self-esteem, try telling yourself the opposite.

- Avoid comparisons. One of the toughest parts of developing your self-esteem is realizing that you cannot compare yourself to others. Too often, we compare ourselves with people around us like family, co-workers, friends, or people we don't even know thanks to the exposure to social media. Whether it's about looks, money, personal possessions or whatever it may be, the trap of comparing is that you never feel good enough.

- Identify your unique gifts. Everyone has something that they excel at. We all have our strengths and our weaknesses. Instead of focusing on your weaknesses, focus on what your strengths are and what skills you possess that make you feel confident. Whether it's your skills at work, your creative outlets, your skill on the guitar or how well you cook, it's important that you are not ashamed of what you do well and channel that energy, so you feel confident about yourself. Don't focus on your failures - focus on your successes! Be proud of your accomplishments.

- Focus on self-care. Whether you are exercising, treating yourself to a spa day or getting a good night's sleep, it's important that you take care of yourself physically to take care of your mental health. Exercise is proven to release serotonin, a neurotransmitter of the brain that creates feelings of happiness and contentment. Whether it's an hour at the gym or just going for an evening walk before dinner, take some time to exercise so you are physically taking care of yourself. Do something relaxing for yourself after a long week. Treat yourself to a cheat day if you've been sticking to your diet regularly. Whatever it is, you should focus on yourself and making your emotional and mental health a priority.

- Help others. Studies show that helping someone else or volunteering can help you feel better about yourself. It takes you out of your mindset and urges you to think about someone else. The best way to increase your feelings of self-worth is volunteering face to face such as at a homeless shelter or a soup kitchen. But if you can also donate money or provide services online, then you can also increase your self-worth. You can feel like you are part of a cause and that you are helping people. You have a purpose. This gives value to you and your time, and you feel part of a greater community. This increases your self-worth and self-esteem and how you feel about yourself.

Remind yourself that you are not your circumstances. Tell yourself over and over that even if you are going through a tough time right now, you may not be soon. Circumstances occur in our life that is sometimes out of our control. As the saying goes, "this, too, shall pass." With hard work, compassion, and patience, whatever tough time you are going through will soon ease itself. Your problems will be solved, and you will feel stronger for having gone through it. This is important to recognize your self-esteem and not let the circumstances around you beat you down.

How to Use Self-talk

The habit of positive or negative self-talk often begins early in our childhood and the people who are around us. The good news is that even if you have a negative self-talk habit, it's never too late to change your outlook. Here are some steps to help you!

- Identify how you treat yourself. It may sound silly but try and view how you talk about yourself and how many times you say negative things to yourself in the span of a day. Whether you need to write a journal or simply take some time to meditate, it can be astonishing sometimes to realize how often we speak to ourselves negatively. Use a thought-stopping method to stop yourself from saying something negative in your head.

-     Replace the negative statements in your self-talk with positive ones. When you are becoming aware of how you treat yourself and the world around you, you can begin to replace the negative statements with different neutral or positive words.

This will help you feel more positive or at least more neutral about the experiences you are going through.

Change your definitive statements into questions. Definitive emotional statements are the ones we make every day and may not even realize it. For example, when we say things like, "This is impossible!" or "I am never going to finish this," we are ingraining in ourselves a negative slant to these statements. It only increases our stress and stops you from searching for solutions to solve these problems.

How to Use Visualizations and Affirmations

Affirmations are statements with a positive tone that work to define your goal and desire and improve the way you view yourself. The technique of using affirmations is to repeat them over and over, so they are embedded into your subconscious and you finally start to believe what you are saying. By believing them, you will follow through on them and accomplish whatever goal you have set for yourself. Whether it's about your habits, your personal or professional behavior or your personality, creating an affirmation can help your mindset so you can conquer a goal. Think of it like this. Working out at the gym is for your physical body, and using affirmations is for your mind!

You want to focus on the stage of your life you are in and what you are going through. You want to replace your "I can't" with "I can." You want to remind your unconscious mind about the positives in your life and feel appreciative about the situation you are in (even if it's a tough one!). Instead of saying things like "I am never going to lose this baby weight," or "I will never understand organic chemistry," create positive affirmations to replace the negative thoughts. Instead, replace those sayings with "I am so thankful for a healthy baby and a smooth pregnancy and labor," and "I am so happy I got into one of the top universities in my state."

Here are some simple steps to create the positive affirmation you may need to get you through the day!

1.   Use the words I am in a present tense to emphasize to yourself that you Will be doing something and you will implement this behavior and thought immediately into your life. Not future tense - but today!

2.   Be positive. Always use an affirmation to say what you want. Don't focus on things you don't want, but what you hope to gain.

3.   Be brief and be specific. You want to be focused on what your goal is and exactly what step you need to achieve it.

4.   Include an action word so your brain knows that there is some activity involved that you need to do to make this goal happen.

5.   Make sure your affirmations are for yourself, not other people. This is something you will work towards for yourself and your betterment, not for anyone else. This ensures that you will feel more motivated about conquering the goal.

Repeat your affirmations to yourself every day, preferably out loud and with energy and enthusiasm! Whether it's taking a minute after you have gotten ready in the morning or saying it before bed at the end of a long day, you want to take some time to remind yourself about these statements. If you have a friend or family member that you are close with, you can have them be the ones to remind you about this affirmation throughout your journey to achieving this goal.

Visualization is a technique where you clearly work to visualize the future reality you want to be living in. The clearer and the more detailed your vision is, the more impact it will have on your subconscious mind. It is a powerful tool that can motivate you for future success in your life. For example, athletes are always told to imagine their future success, that they've won the World Series, or that they have won the Super Bowl in the upcoming season. It's not about confidence per say, but about visualizing your goal coming true, and using that feeling to motivate you to make it happen.

Chapter 10: Guidelines on Managing and Expressing Your Emotions

Emotions are powerful biological forces that we cannot manipulate consciously. Once emotions get involved, things become complicated. Here are some important tips to adhere to to manage and express your emotions appropriately.

Master The Art of Timing

When you are pressed emotionally, being considerate is the last thing on your mind. You are simply dying to let the other person know what you're feeling. Emotions have a way of pushing all our wrong buttons, causing us to become impulsive in our decisions, and before we know it, it is over just as quickly as it began. Then we are stuck with the consequences. But, to communicate your emotions meaningfully, you have to ensure that the timing is right.

For instance, if your boss has done something that has triggered you, the last thing you should do is to storm into his office when he's in the middle of a meeting with other high-rank officials. You want to make sure that the environment in which you're communicating your emotions is an enabling one. This increases your odds of achieving the outcome you had planned.

Have A Healthy Outlet

In as much as you have to practice restraint where your emotions are concerned, it is also important to have an outlet lest you become an irritable person. When you bottle up emotions inside, you risk having it burst out one day, and woe unto the person on the receiving end. Obviously, this would defeat the purpose of practicing restraint considering that you have overreacted. One of the best outlets for your emotions is engaging in a physically-taxing activity like exercising and training.

Spend time in nature

Our environment has a big effect on our emotional states. If we live or work in chaotic places, our emotions are more or less going to take on that tone. Taking time to be surrounded by nature has a calming effect on your emotions. You could take walks in nature parks, hike, or hunt in the forest. This could help raise your spirits and release all the bad emotions.

Keep The Big Picture in Mind

If you fail to get a handle on your emotions, you run the risk of throwing the baby out with the bathwater. Sometimes, you may get stuck in an unpleasant situation and feel like letting your emotions explode. Try to be wise enough to keep the bigger picture in mind. First ask yourself, what's your agenda? And how are your actions helping that agenda? For instance, say your teenage daughter is driving you up the wall. If you become hostile with her, she may end up cutting off ties with you, thus killing off any chance of you getting to guide her through life.

Learn To Distract Yourself

An emotionally intelligent person is aware of his emotional makeup; i.e., how their body responds to various stimuli. At the onset of an unpleasant emotion, rather than entertain it, learn to distract yourself. For instance, if you were working on a serious academic project and a very attractive person of the opposite sex stumbled by, you might get aroused and experience passionate feelings. Well, sexual emotion is not bad in and of itself, but considering that you're doing an important academic project, you might want to banish that sexual emotion.

You can achieve that by distracting yourself – engaging your mind in other activities. You may not have the ability to decide which emotion to experience, but when you pay less attention to a particular emotion, it tends to subside. However, if you lend your attention to a particular emotion, you tend to fuel it and end up increasing its potency.

Never React Immediately

Whenever you experience a massive emotional trigger, be careful not to give an immediate response. This will give you time to assess the real situation and come up with the perfect plan. When you give an immediate emotional response, chances are the outcome will be less than desirable. For instance, if the actions or words of a person have triggered your anger, don't erupt in an outburst. This will get your aggressor worried about your next move. Meanwhile, you can be devising your comeback plan, or choose not to do anything at all. When you're consumed by an overpowering urge to give an emotionally-charged response, both your heartbeat and breathing rate will go up. Learning to control your breath can help in regaining your calm.

Conclusion

I hope you enjoyed reading it and were learned the finer nuances of emotional intelligence, self-awareness, regulation of emotions and social relationships. I also hope it gave you plenty of actionable ideas, practical pointers and wisdom nuggets about increasing your emotional quotient or emotional intelligence.

The best part is that unlike intelligence quotient, emotional quotient can be developed over a period of time through regular practice, effort, training, and implementation. Enhancing our emotional intelligence is a constantly evolving and dynamic process that helps us grow our psychological and social abilities with time.

Emotions are never easy to understand. That is because for most of our lives, we have let them manage us. We haven't taken the time to understand them because we are too distracted by events that are happening around us. We are busy at work. We have bills to pay. We are worried about our family. But the important thing to realize is that if we do not set aside the time to manage our emotions, then we are always going to be stuck in an endless loop of negative emotions. We will never get the opportunity to break free and truly work towards things that add purpose to our lives and make us happier. And before we know it, we have already wasted most of our lives playing catch-up to our emotions. Our emotions are powerful, and they are also necessary. Without them, we might not be able to navigate the complexities of life. But the key takeaway here is that we have to use emotions to help us go through life. We should be able to understand how they influence our lives. You are not meant to merely survive life. You are meant to live it. And the first step towards living your life is to manage one of its most vital components:

Your emotions

The next step is to go out there and apply all the proven tips mentioned in this book. You cannot expect to become more emotionally intelligent by reading about it. Implement the techniques mentioned in the book in your daily life to notice the difference. You'll slowly transform from an emotionally average or incompetent person who probably struggles with his/her and other's emotions to an emotionally developed and socially adept person, who will enjoy more fulfilling interpersonal relationships.

HELPFUL STUDY SKILLS FOR MEMORY IMPROVEMENT

UNLIMITED MEMORY

For our bodies to stay healthy, we must exercise. So why do people not apply the same information to their brains? For our memory to improve, we have to train the brain, but this isn't something that must be time-consuming and strenuous, like a workout at the gym. Memory champions and psychologists agree that the key to a better memory is visualization, and the crazier it is, the better.

Mnemonics are memory techniques that make complicated information easier to remember. The ones that show the best are often rare, and the unusual aspects of life are always more unforgettable than the mundane.

To master this technique, you visualize a location that you are very familiar with, such as your home, and put the information you need to learn in this location. To improve your recall, you can allow your imagination to run wild. This technique is also referred to as a memory palace, which we will discuss a bit more later on.

Use Your Imagination

To boost your memory retention, it helps if you can thoroughly immerse yourself in your imagination.

Not everybody is born with a fantastic memory, but everybody can use their imagination to train their brains to remember more information. Boris Konrad and Martin Dresler discovered that mnemonic brain training is something everybody can use to improve their memory, not just those notable memory champions. The only thing you need is visualization and imagination.

So, if creativity has such a significant effect on memory, imagine what will happen if you made improving your imagination an everyday habit? Please try this simple activity. It takes three minutes and is a great way to practice visualization and let the imagination run wild.

Pick an object you have around you – we'll go with your cell phone.

Now, shut your eyes and take about ten seconds or so to describe how your phone looks.

Open your eyes and then look at your phone to see any other details you could have described.

Close your eyes again and describe everything that you can remember about your phone.

Once done, open your eyes again and pick a different object – we'll say it's your laptop.

Now, you are going to engage your imagination. You want to picture your cell phone interacting with your laptop in some way. Allow this to become crazy. Perhaps, your phone could have eyes and arms, and it starts to type out a book on your laptop.

Shut your eyes one last time and describe a little short story in great detail so that you bring this to life in your mind. Remember, you want it to be bizarre and funny.

It is a fantastic way to develop your visualization skills while still allowing you to exercise your imagination. When you see objects in your mind and describe how they interact, you create memorable associations that you won't forget.

Create Pictures

Now that you know and understand the importance of imagination when it comes to remembering things, let's look at the first step in recognizing what you want. We are going to create mental snapshots of events. It is a great way to remember events in your life as well.

When you engage your full attention on what is presently happening, it will encourage more substantial, more explicit memories of essential things. A person's ability to remember detailed events usually is not automatically strong. With the use of mental snapshots, you can have better success in creating long-lasting memories. If you despise your episodic memory, don't worry. Instead, you're going to be able to snap a mental picture or two to improve your odds of remembering things.

Creating photo albums, recording a video of an event, or writing it down in your journal are great ways to preserve memories. But you can't always carry around these physical memory aids.

A clear mental image that you can instantly recall is a precious commodity. There are two main types of memory, episodic and semantic. Episodic memory is the memory of events and is one type of declarative memory. Semantic memory is the recollection of general knowledge and concepts.

Your episodic memory is made up of memories of emotions, times, and places associated with a particular event that has happened to you. When you think about your high school graduation or what you ate for breakfast, you are using your episodic memory.

It's important to remember when creating a mental snapshot ensures you are entirely focused on what is happening. You could be there and soaking in most of what is going on, but you aren't connected deeply enough with the special moments without realizing it. To create a mental snapshot, you have to be able to zoom in on the little things. We'll use a wedding as an example of a time you'd like to remember for the rest of your life.

1.   Watch the scene with intent. Make sure you keep your head still. Gaze at what is going on with concentration and focus. Tell yourself that it is essential that you can remember the details of what is going on. Carefully observe all of the colors of the scene. Look at the position and arrangement of the wedding party. The dresses that the bridesmaids are wearing. The way the room is lit, how the flowers. Drink at the moment.

2.   Slowly blink your eyes. With your eyes focused intently on what you see before you, you will want to click your brain's camera "shutter" by blinking once at half-speed. You will want to close and open your eyes at half the speed they usually move. You can even imagine hearing a "click" like you would when taking a picture.

Now, you will want to take a moment to review the picture you just took in your mind's eye. Close your eyes for a second and conjure up the picture in your memory. Take a mental look at the image you just captured. If you find that your photo is a bit fuzzy, open up your eyes, take a more complex look at what you were trying to remember, and then take another snapshot.

It can be used when trying to remember just about anything. It could even be helpful when it comes to placing a grocery list as well.

Intense focus is what is essential to come up with permanent and transparent mental snapshots. Focus requires mental effort. The more you practice this technique, the clearer and more detailed your images are going to become.

It would be beneficial to take hundreds of photographs like you would with a camera if you did not attempt to take hundreds of photographs. Instead, you should use your max concentration in just a few moments that represent the entire event. For some things, one mental snapshot could be enough.

Your most lucid memories are likely connected with powerful emotions. Events that you linked to peak moments of loss, fear, accomplishment, and joy are recalled more easily and vividly.

The Rule to Remember Anything

When it comes to memorizing things, there are three steps that you can take that will help you to remember anything and everything:

You will make sure that you engage as many senses as possible; this means sound, smell, touch, sight, and sometimes taste.

You will emphasize the mental image you have created with your senses. It means that you will exaggerate it so that you couldn't possibly forget it.

You will make it exciting.

It means that you will picture your image doing something. Let's look at each of these steps a bit more.

Use Your Senses

While the mental snapshot technique helps remember things, many other mental image techniques can help remember things. There isn't one best technique; the important thing is that you make it as memorable as possible. It entails using as many senses as possible.

Of your five senses, the mind may like thinking in pictures, but the sense of smell is the strongest when evoking memories. A simple scent can unleash a rush of emotions. The smell of perfume, wet grass, or the aroma of coffee can cause you to experience various emotions.

Use smell

When you create a mental image, make sure that you try to use your sense of smell. The smell is most closely connected with your hippocampus, a brain structure responsible for your memory. The smell is also associated with the limbic system, which the emotional area of your brain. All the other senses have to move along a path to reach the areas of the brain that control our emotions and memories.

Use sight

All of your mental pictures are going to use sight because you can visualize them. As far as presence bringing up memories, an image of a landscape, bedroom, or object can bring up a moment in your life that you enjoyed. There can also be moments where we feel as if we have experienced a moment before, known as déjà vu.

Use taste

This sense may be a bit hard to use in a memory technique, but you can figure out how to add in Taste, fantastic. When we eat something, the brain will use the sensations of flavor with the information you have stored in your memory. It will look for data concerning certain things that you can relate to with the Taste, previous situations, or other types of foods with similar stimuli.

Use hearing

Next, you will want to add sound to your mental images. Everybody has, at some point, created a mental soundtrack from songs they have listened to. Our life doesn't come with a spontaneous soundtrack, but a familiar piece of music will trigger many memories.

Use touch

Lastly, you want to try to use touch in your mental image as well. Of the five senses, touch is the weakest one. Most of the time, one of your other senses will trigger a memory before you have to use the sense of touch. That said. You can still use touch in your mental picture to be sure that something will trigger your memory.

Create Emphasis

Now that you know that you need to use all of your senses to create a vivid memory, let's look at creating a mental image with emphasis that you won't be able to forget.

When it stands out, you are more likely to remember it. That means you need to make sure that your mental images stand out in some way. Here are things to remember when it comes to creating memorable images:

Substitute one item with a different item.

Has the image come alive?

Exaggerate the amount of something, which means picture a million of whatever you need to remember.

Exaggerate a proportion of the item. It could mean that the item is vast in your mind, or only a part of it is large, kind of like a caricature.

Maybe you want to remember that the capital of Peru is Lima. Lima sounds like a lemur, so you could picture a giant lemur swinging around on a tree.

Create Action

The last is, you need to bring your mental image to life. Think about when you try to remember a phone number. You might find that you move your fingers to help you remember the number. The movement enables you to remember something, so when you make your mental image move, you will remember it more easily.

Think back to the mental image of the lemur swinging on the trees. The picture had movement; it was alive.

Chapter 1: How to Improve Your Memory?

If you want to increase your memory, there are several things you can do right now, from eating blueberries to using a mixed bag of reminder tricks. If you're confident in yourself, you'll have the ability to increase your memory right away!

Trying Memory Tricks

Say things you need to remember out loud. If you experience trouble remembering whether you took your medicine each morning, say, "I just took my medicine!" right after taking it to strengthen this thought in your brain. Saying this out loud will help you remember that you did take your medicine. It also lives up to expectations if you're meeting another individual and would prefer not to overlook his name. Repeat the name actually after you learn it: "Hello there, Sarah, it's nice to meet you." It also tries to remember a place or a meeting time. Repeat out loud to the individual who invited you: "The Grand Tavern at 7? That sounds great."

1.   Improve your breathing when you need to remember something. When it's an ideal chance to study or remember something new, switch your breathing slower and deeper. More profound and slower breathing indeed changes how your brain lives up to expectations by making the brain's electrical heartbeats change to Theta waves, which regularly happen in your brain in hypnogogic rest.

2.   Keep in mind a man's name. Use a famous trick out of FDR's playbook for remembering a man's name. At the point when a man accustoms themselves with you, picture them with their name composed on their brow. It will tell the picture of that individual with their name.

3.   Squeeze an anxiety ball. Crushing and anxiety ball or making a clenched hand with your hand can help you remember a bit of data later. Before recognizing the data, squeeze the anxiety ball in your dominant hand. For an ordinary individual, this would be your right hand. When you have to recall the data, press the anxiety ball in your inverse hand for no less than 45 seconds. This simple action may be sufficient to help you remember.

4.   Chew gum. This fundamental revelation can strengthen the brain and increase your obsession, particularly if you have to remember data for 30 minutes or more. According to the British Psychological Society (BPS), visual and sound-related memory increases when a man chews gum by keeping the individual involved. However, when you have to recollect something for under 30 minutes, it is suggested not to chew on anything.

5.   Move your eyes from side to side. Christman's research exposes that moving your eyes from side to side for only 30 seconds once every day will adjust the two sections of your brain and make your memory work all the more quickly. Attempt this life hack when you wake up in the morning.

Smell rosemary. Prof Mark Moss at Northumbria University reveals that noticing rosemary can improve your memories. Bring a sprig of rosemary or smell rosemary oil once every day. The Ancient Greeks even put a sprig of rosemary behind their ears on exam days to help them increase their memories.

Using Mindful Approaches

Quit believing that you have an "awful memory." We all have them - those hateful recollections that make us want to creep under the bed to avoid the past. Terrible recollections can turn into all-devouring if you don't address the issue head-on. Facing the memories and portraying them out loud is a compelling tactic to defuse the tension they bring. It may need some investment; however, if you've resolved to prevent the memories from filling up your brain, you'll find the courage to talk about them. Delete those considerations and promise yourself to increase your memory's capacity. Commend even little accomplishments to keep yourself inspired.

1. Exercise your brain. Regularly "working out," the brain maintains its capacity increasing and goals to advance new nerve associations that can help improve memory. You will possess the brain healthy and increase its physiological functioning by raising new mental abilities - incredibly complex ones, such as learning a new language or learning to play a new musical instrument - and challenging your brain with puzzles and recreations.

Try some ordinary, fun puzzle practices, such as crosswords, Sudoku, and different diversions that are sufficiently simple for anybody. Get out of your normal range of familiarity and pick something new and testing, which makes you flex your brain strengths. Attempt to play chess or a quick-paced table game. A vast part of your brain is initiated when it takes in another aptitude. Adapting new data is also helpful, yet since skills require both the admission and yield of data, they practice a more significant bit of your brain.

Give yourself a chance to enclose a memory. Memories are incredibly elusive in the short term, and diversions can make you rapidly overlook something as basic as a telephone number. The way to refrain from losing recollections before you can even frame them is to have the ability to focus on the thing to be associated with for a while without contemplating on different things, so when you're trying to remember something, maintain a strategic distance from diversions and complicated assignments for a couple of minutes.

Improving Your Lifestyle

Using Mnemonic Devices

Use associations to remember actualities. A mnemonic is something that can use to recall things much less demanding. As is regularly the case, it could be an expression, a short melody, or something that is well recognized that we use to recollect something else that would somehow be difficult to remember. To use associations successfully, you can make a picture in your psyche to help you remember a word or an image. For example, if you experience serious difficulties remembering JFK was the President involved in the Bay of Pigs attack, picture the President swimming in a sea included by cheerful, oinking pigs. It is entirely senseless; however, this solid picture in your brain will perpetually help you connect the President with this event.

1. Use associations to remember numbers. Suppose you continue overlooking your understudy ID each time you have to use it. Separate the number into littler lumps and make pictures connected with those pieces. Suppose the number is 12-7575-23. Figure out how to make these numbers meaningful. Suppose "12" happens to be your home number, "75" happens to be your grandma's age, and the number "23" is Michael Jordan's shirt number. It is what you can imagine recalling the number:

2. Use piecing. Chunking breaks a comprehensive rundown of numbers or different sorts of data into smaller, more reasonable pieces. They were failing to recall a 10-digit telephone number down into three arrangements of numbers: 555-867-5309.

3. Use poems and similar-sounding word usage. Poems, similar-sounding word usage, and even jokes are a supreme approach to recall more everyday statistical data points. Using a mixture of regular and senseless rhymes can help you review fundamental data. For example, if you're attempting to make sense of if April has 30 or 31 days, say the old rhyme out loud: "Thirty days has September, April, June, and November." Then you'll recollect that April

does, in reality, have 30 days. Here are some different rhymes to use as memory tools: In 1492, Columbus sailed the sea blue. A child can take in the letter set by singing it to Twinkle, Twinkle, and Little Star, making the notes poem.

4.   Try using acronyms. Acronyms are another valuable method for remembering various items, such as the five Great Lakes and conjunction terms. You can apply a prominent acronym or make one for yourself. For instance, if you're setting off to the store and know you need Butter, Lettuce, Bread, and Uncage, make a word out of every term: BULB - Butter, Uncage, Lettuce, and Bread. Here are some prominent acronyms to utilize:

HOMES. The Great Lakes: Huron, Ontario, Michigan, Erie, and Superior are remembered.

ROY G. BIV. This man's name can aid you to recall the shades of the rainbow: Red, Orange, Yellow, Green, Blue, Indigo, and Violet.

FOIL. It will aid you in remembering how to increase two binomial terms: First, Outer, Inner, Last.

FANBOYS. This acronym can assist you in remembering exact organizing conjunctions: For, And, Nor, But, Or, Yet, So.

5.   Use puzzles. Puzzles are like acronyms, except rather than simply recollecting the abbreviation, you can recall another sentence made out of the first letters of an arrangement of words that you need to retain in a sure request.

For instance, you can say, "My very enthusiastic mother – Jane - sent us noodles." to remember the order of the planets: Mercury, Venus, Earth, Mars, Jupiter, Saturn, Uranus, and Neptune. You can also make up the acrostics of your claim. Here are a couple of more prominent puzzles: Each Good Boy Does Good. It is used for retaining the lines on the treble music staff: EGBDF. Never Eat Sour Watermelons. It is used for remembering the purposes of a compass in the clockwise request: North, East, South, and West. Another great sample is Never Eat Shredded Wheat which also rhymes. Ruler Philip Can Only Find His Green Slippers. Use this to remember the request of the classification framework: Kingdom, Phylum, Class, Order, Family, Genus, and Species. Please Excuse My Dear Aunt Sally. Utilize this to recall the request of operations in science: Parenthesis, Exponents, Multiplication, Division, Addition, and Subtraction.

Use the method of Loci. This method has been used since the times of Ancient Greece. This process obliges you to partner things as far as an area to help you remember the entire data plan. To use this technique, envision putting the things you need to recall along with a course you're very acquainted with or in specific areas in a well-known room or building. To start, imagine your walk to the store; then, picture the things you need to do or recall along that way.

Chapter 2: Helpful Study Skills for Memory Improvement

When the mind is working too hard to retain all kinds of information, it struggles to keep up with what's going on. The following study skills are perfect for practical use whether you are still in school and studying for an exam. These strategies can always come in handy, so pay close attention.

1.   Avoid Interference. In learning and memorizing, Interference is widespread. This kind of overlap gets in the way of your complete understanding and can confuse you. This kind of Interference does not just apply to the subject matter. It can also be an issue with names, places, dates—basically any information you are being forced to digest.

If this happens to you often, even with the simple remembering of names, the following strategies can be helpful to:

- Know the information a lot better. If you are still struggling with recalling the information, then you haven't learned it enough. Make sure to overlearn it so that you know it through and through. It is just when you are no longer committing mistakes that you can ultimately declare that you have learned something thoroughly. Overleaning stretches your memory and reduces the likelihood of encountering Interference.

- Make the information more meaningful. Maybe you're finding it hard to make the information stick because none of it makes sense to you. Any piece of information is cluttered in your brain until you bring more meaning into it. It is where the use of patterns, rhymes, and association comes in handy. These are learning codes that are very useful in avoiding interferences.

- Segregate information into different rooms or locations. Association is always a prominent feature of memorization. If you are struggling with a lot of Interference, you may want to deal with the confusion by trying to categorize the information into different rooms or locations.

If you tend to confuse people or personalities, maybe you can set your meetings in various areas to perfect segregation in your head.

- Minimize intervening activities. Are you trying to do too much? Are you incorporating too much unnecessary activities with your targeted learning? As much as possible, reduce activities in-between study time that will only bring more confusion to your mind. Sleep and meditation is the best intervening activity for revision and learning because it helps to energize the mind and body so that it is clear to take up more information.

2.   Give ample space and time for learning. People tend to cram things into one place to achieve more. You want to do more, so you will allot maximum time on something to conquer it fully. Unfortunately, this results in exhaustion, so that in the latter part of the session, your brain can no longer receive new information.

Instead of having a long revision or work-stretch, schedule intermittent periods so that you have breaks where your brain can rest from accumulating information.

- Understand the mind's limitations. Cramming too much information into your head is never a good thing. After a while, you will lose concentration, and your mind will be unable to process any new information. As a result, all subsequent efforts to cram will be useless. In other words, the brain can focus up to a point— so you have to know your limit.

- Breaks help to strengthen the brain. Whenever you give yourself a break, the mind supports you. Your mind consolidates the information it has learned during these break periods so that rest will work to your advantage.

- Understand the role of your mood. The mood is a very fickle thing, especially where revision and learning are concerned. Some days you are entirely active; some days, you are hardly able to lift a pen. By assigning more study sessions, you gain access to different moods and take advantage of the good days.

    Because what's the use of a 3-hour session when you have a crappy mood? You might as well move on and hope that the following sessions are more productive ones.

3. Break up the material efficiently. There is usefulness in knowing how to tackle a material. You must know if you have to take it as a whole or take it in small parts. Here are the different learning methods that you can apply:

- Whole method with an exclamation of small parts. It involves capturing the material as a whole to get a better picture. You go through it once, and then you go through it again, this time by devouring it in small sections.

- Whole-part-whole method. It requires that you go through the material once, ultimately, and then you tackle it in smaller sections before devouring it once again, as a whole.

- Progressive learning method. This learning thoroughly takes the material in small parts. The whole material is broken into sections and then taken in incremental value. You continue moving from one part to another until you devour it entirely.

4. Speak it out loud; Recitation is a perfect learning trick. By speaking something loudly and repeatedly, your mind can pay better attention to the information. You can try to talk to them loudly as you read and then talk them loudly from the top of your head. If you need study aids to help in retaining information into your memory bank, the use of flashcards is good. If you need to work with a study buddy who will help you with your revisions, do so. A buddy can drill you with the information to make sure that you remember things efficiently.

    Speaking out loud is good for concentration, feedback, and active learning. I start a habit of working this way, and you will find it easier to process various information.

5. Formulate a working study system. A plan is always something you can rely on because it demands processing details in a particular fashion or manner.

Step 1: Survey. It is a quick browse to get a feel of the content and give a short assessment. You go through the entire thing without actually consuming any substance.

Step 2: Question. You ask yourself several questions to quickly test your inherent knowledge about the material. Before going into detail, so as not to waste effort, you can ask questions that will focus on your subsequent actions.

Step 3: Read; this is where you read everything in detail. Most of the time, people skip steps 1 and 2 because this gets the job done; but understand that the previous steps are essential because it increases your comprehension.

Step 4: Recite; Following the advice to "speak loudly," you should take what you have learned from your reading and recite it out loud. Doing this helps to boost your ability to memorize.

Step 5: Review; are you still making mistakes? Do you already know the material through and through?

Again, there are many different systems that you can apply, and you can even form one to better suit your needs. The SQ3R is just an example, but please feel free to use it if you find it appropriate to your requirement.

Chapter 3: Steps for Memory Formation

Memories are composed of multiple pieces of information. We do not just store everything we encounter for long periods. When we create a memory, whether short- or long-term, we go through a three-step process. During each of these processes, various parts of the brain are working together to properly filter, organize, and make sense of everything you are experiencing.

1. Encoding

Encoding takes place through sensory input. What is perceived through our senses gets interpreted and passed along to the thalamus? This information is then compressed into one event, experience, or bits of data, which then gets transferred to the hippocampus. From here, the data is evaluated and, if deemed necessary enough, is passed along for storage.

The encoding process requires various chemicals and electric pulses for the proper transfer of information. Neural pathways are superhighways that this information flows on. Each time we are exposed to new information, the brain rewires itself to create pathways or synapses to travel the brain. These synapses are essential in connecting the neurons or brain cells. Broken pathways or weakened neurons interfere with transferring information from one area of the brain to another.

Encoding can be done visually, acoustically, elaborately, or semantically. Visual encoding is received from our visual senses; it also includes the mental images we create. Most visual information is only stored briefly in our visual memory. After this brief pause, it moves to long-term memory.

Acoustic encoding is done through our auditory system or what we hear. Phonological looping is vital for this type of information to be moved to memory storage. We must subconsciously vocally rehearse what we hear in our minds for it to be remembered.

Elaborative encoding is a process of using previously experienced information and relating it to new experiences. Elaborate encoding is a crucial factor in locking away information in our long-term memory. If we do not use elaborative encoding, we will quickly forget the information in our long-term memory.

Semantic encoding links our sensory input to specific details. Mnemonics and chunking information occur through this process. An example of mnemonics used in semantic coding would be identifying broccoli as a green vegetable or creating abbreviations to remember names or words. Mnemonics are tricks we use to help appropriately encode more complex information. Chunking is another method used in the semantic encoding. With chunking, we group things as a whole instead of having to organize each part. We remember phone numbers by chunking together separate numbers to create the total number. It is also how we encode words: we group individual letters to form an extended-term.

There is also a process of memory consolidation that can occur. Unlike encoding, which requires our attention and conscious effort, a merger happens at a biological level (Step 1: Memory encoding, n.d.). The most notable time when this consolidation occurs is while we sleep. When memories are consolidated, the connection between the neurons is strengthened. It requires structural and chemical changes in our brains to take place.

As time passes, the memories we access more often will form stronger synapse connections. The reverse will also occur if the memories are infrequently accessed.

2. Storage

Memory storage begins once the information from our sensory processes has been filtered. After information enters the brain, it is deposited into our working memory. In just a few short seconds, the data is then forgotten or considered important enough to move along to our long-term memory.

Our brains store thousands of bits of information that we accumulate through our lives. We don't remember every event from our past or the present moment. Only the events we deem significant will be captured and stored away for future recall. Events that we also want or need to refer to continuously will also be stored away in our brains' library of important information. It includes learned skills and processes to perform daily functions. We filter hundreds and thousands of thoughts and knowledge throughout the day, which the brain sorts and stores in less than a second.

Memories are scattered throughout different areas of the brain in a hierarchy. Information that we are interested in is stored in an easily accessible place. Information that we do not need to retain for long or is associated with things that we would not readily need available is stored at the bottom or in the back of the mind. Here, it takes up little space and energy and, over time, is forgotten.

Critical areas of the brain that aid in memory storage include:

• The prefrontal cortex is where short-term memories are stored, and It consists of both the left and right side of the brain, with each area tracking specific information.

• The basal ganglia are where our implicit memories are stored.

• The amygdala stores emotional responses and formulates episodic memories.

• The striatum stores skills.

• The hippocampus and temporal lobes store memory formation for recall. It is also where our short-term memories are stored.

• Three key steps occur when memories are stored:

1. Sensory memories are first created when we process information from our environment. This information relates to our senses—sight, sound, smell, taste, touch—and is only stored briefly. Only a fraction of the information retrieved from our environment becomes a process; we cannot fully take in everything we gather through our current settings. Information that creates the most stimulation in the brain will be passed along to our memory banks.

2. Short-term memories are created after the sensory memories have been processed.

Long-term memory is where information that has been received before is organized. The data is consolidated, processed, and stored in various parts of the brain for later retrieval.

3. Retrieval

Memory retrieval is the process in which we access information in our short- and long-term memory.

Reading and Remembering

Whatever you do when you survey the area, you will learn to read and remember what you read whenever you need it. Being able to remember without checking details is an excellent benefit for all students. Universities can place very high demands on reading a single course. So, when you have most of the information you need, make your textbooks more efficient and your exams and routine tasks more efficient. Think about what you can prepare.

Think about the difference between writing and presenting in a newspaper or textbook. The newspaper was edited and designed so that it is easy to read. Most newspaper articles are organized according to the "pyramid" approach.

Memory Training Techniques

Memory training techniques take full advantage of the natural characteristics of memory. You can order information in various ways using the methods described here. Based on what you read, you can use them individually or in combination.

Information Organization

Minimize losses and increase efficiency. It is essential to organize the information you receive. Splitting or arranging information into simple patterns is an easy first step in data collection. Put, if the brain is somehow actively involved in processing the data, it is more likely to remember it correctly. Motivate your mind to work more efficiently; the data must be focused on using visions and other sensations and converted into more memorable forms.

Improved Concentration

Focusing is an essential practice when using storage technology. Compare the memory of a TV show that you saw when you did something simultaneously with the memory of a program that was entirely focused. The first case is more accurate and less detailed than the second case.

Imagine being asked to learn to concentrate more later. Listen to the radio and answer your friends' questions. This process of checking information after first learning is also essential for improving memory.

Use the Senses

Seeing and listening are sensations that are commonly used in learning. Develops, seeing, and hearing to make it sharper. Artists are more used to seeing things in more detail and from different perspectives, so they can "see" 30% more than the average. Make a conscious effort to notice the small parts to improve your senses. For example, spend a day observing the color, nose, and ear types of your neighbors. Listen carefully to their voices - do they have the accents and phrases that they like?

Location Use

Think about how you can mentally go back in time when trying to lose something and remember where you came from. It is what your brain does naturally and is the key to the essential skills of memory training. The "travel" technique uses routes that pass through a known number of locations.

Image Creation

The basis of all memory training is to create mental images from the learned information. The most memorable thing is that it is rare. Decorate your photos according to the principles of image creation to make them unique and unforgettable. The more you pay attention to the details, the brighter the picture becomes.

Use of the Association

Your brain loves building a repertoire of related information and making connections between data. When the brain receives new information, it looks for similar long-term memory to "understand" what it is. It happens quickly and is not a conscious process. Creating associations improves your memory. By actively creating personalized links for the brain to connect, you can do some work in your memory and restore it later.

Information Storage

Organizations are the key to properly managing information in many areas of life. The library is a good example. Without a sorting and coding system for organizing books, the library would not work at all. Most offices have efficient filing systems, and all the information you need later is stored in folders in the filing cabinet. The storage technology also takes this into account when receiving new information. For example, create a framework for patterns, locations, etc., and save the data in future storage. It enables the memory to process and store information so that it can recall as efficiently as possible.

Chapter 4: The Memorization Process

How should one memorize? It doesn't matter if the subject matter is large or small; you have to find a way to learn it to make good use of it in the future. People "memorize" for different reasons. Perhaps you want to improve your skill because you want to perform better in school or at work—or maybe you want to be efficient in handling information.

The whole business of memorization is a three-step process. It will discuss different techniques, tips, and tricks in the subsequent pages, but it all comes down to a routine of organization, record keeping, and practice.

Step 1. Organize the Information

Some people are good at memorizing, but some are not. Usually, those who have a problem find themselves entirely intimidated by the amount of information they have to remember. You look at the "elementary periodic table" and wonder if it's possible to retain everything inside the boxes—without even attempting to learn the first row. Learning can be very tough, especially if there's too much to remember.

It drew the Periodic Table of Elements to make things easier. The elements are organized in such a way so that they are arranged in ascending order and blocked into groups. It makes it easy for anyone to handle the information, so even if you are not a mad scientist with direct access to these different elements, you will be able to use it.

As with the Periodic Table of Elements, you must begin by arranging all of the data so that it would not be overwhelming. You need to place it to have quick access to all the details when you need it.

Step 2. Write everything down

Initially, you have to organize things in your head—and then you have to write words down. Whichever way you arranged the information in your head, you ought to put them down on paper to visually organize it.

You can organize them according to categories, topics or merely put them in order. It would be best if you thought of a way that will make remembering them least complicated.

There are a few benefits to writing things down:

It gives you room to plan. When you write something down, you are creating some blueprint, and it directs the course of your learning. It does not matter if you are merely jotting down a list, drawing a detailed flow chart, or plotting the details in outline form; it will provide some direction.

It makes it easier to remember. Visuals are always good for memorizing. It is why flashcards work because the image helps in embedding a lasting memory in the brain.

You can refer to it for future use. With the list on hand, you can always see it when you need to. You can use it for quick recall, should you feel that the information has gotten a little cloudy.

Step 3. Take on the Challenge

As with any learning, you have to know that practice makes perfect. Therefore, you have to take what you have learned here and start a habit of actually using it. The challenge is for you to use the process to store a vast collection of information efficiently.

You can aspire to be better at memorizing things, or you can do something about it. But first, you have to determine what kind of learner you are:

1.   **Auditory Learner.** Are you someone who responds well to sounds? Do you tend to learn lyrics to songs quicker than others? Are you the type of pickup music jingles immediately after hearing it? If this describes your learning style, you are an auditory learner.

---

2.   **Tactile Learner.** Are you a kinesthetic learner, and do you have to touch, feel or experience things for them to be significant to your learning progress? Do you like to talk with your hands, are you artistically inclined, and do you love to move about? If this describes you, you're a visual learner.

3.   **Visual Learner.** Are you someone who responds well to images? Do you have some photographic memory? Do you tend to recall images quite easily? If this describes you, you're a visual learner.

4.   **Reader.** Are you fond of reading? Do you like need to read things repeatedly for you to understand and remember the text? Can you quickly make sense of words, good enough to store them? If this describes you, you are a reader.

You must identify your learning preference because there are so many ways that you can memorize things. A method that works for one will not necessarily work for you. But if you match it with your learning ability, you will be most successful in this endeavor.

Step 4. Recall

How will you know that the formula is suitable if you do not get to this point? The success of every memorization process you take will depend on the results you produce. At the end of the test, this will be determined after a presentation, and so forth.

You have to trust the process and your efforts to get you to where you have to go. Nevertheless, always keep the following things in mind:

Stay positive. Negativism has the power to cloud your mind, and this will only make matters worse. You have done the necessary work, so trust that your preparation is enough to see you through this. Do things with a smile and let your positive energy rule through you.

Be prepared. You have to be prepared for anything. If things go according to plan, then that's good, but if it doesn't, then relax. You must be calm and relaxed, so be prepared.

This process is simple, but it is relatively straightforward. You start with organizing your thoughts so that you can carry out a plan for completion. It all seems scientific, but you have to trust that some level of organization is needed for you to conquer the struggle of memorizing bulk information.

Chapter 5: Health Lifestyle to Improve Memory

Believe it or not, many of the things we do in life work against the functioning of a healthy memory! You can improve your memory and learn more quickly by making a variety of lifestyle changes. The following suggestions and tactics will assist you in determining if you can enhance your memory by altering your lifestyle.

Get Adequate Sleep

Poor quality of sleep or not enough sleep is one of the most significant ways people negatively affect their memory. When you are exhausted, your entire body fails to function at its best. Your memory is typically one of the first things to suffer because it is less important than other functions, such as your metabolism and your ability to stay mentally alert enough to perform daily functions.

Using sleep as an opportunity to increase your memory means that you have to focus on both quantity and quality. First, you need to ensure that you are getting enough hours each night. The average time people should sleep on a nightly basis is 7-9 hours, with eight typically being the optimal point. Sleeping long enough means that your body gets to go through your natural sleep-wake cycles effectively and that you wake up naturally during one of the wake cycles. It also means that your body had plenty of time to rest, restore itself, and reenergize.

Ensure that you aren't cutting corners by having late bedtimes or waking up too early. The best way to get enough hours each night is to get yourself on a sleeping schedule. Any night, go to bed at the same hour and wake up at the same time every morning. Although it can be tempting to sleep in on weekends, resist the temptation. It can completely disrupt your regular sleeping schedule, making it difficult to sleep the next night and necessitating a significant amount of effort to return to your normal sleep schedule.

Having a proper sleep schedule doesn't only help ensure that you are getting enough hours, but it also enables you to increase the quality of sleep you have each night. A schedule means that your body naturally knows when to wind down and when to wake up. You will begin to feel sleepy without exerting any effort about the time you will generally go to bed, and your body knows what to expect.

It can help you fall asleep, and it also enables you to stay asleep. If you're always having trouble getting enough sleep, consider establishing a bedtime schedule. Warm baths, warm non-caffeinated, or decaffeinated drinks can help soothe your tummy and encourage you to rest.

Chamomile tea is a great choice when you are choosing a warm drink. Lower the lights, turn off screens and other technology, too. If you want, you can keep relaxing music on down to help your mind relax. Reading or doing other relaxing activities in the last while before bed is a great way to get yourself ready for bed, too. Having a proper bedtime routine helps you relax your mind and prepare your mind and body for sleep. It can be easier on your body than simply finishing your favorite show and jumping into bed with a sense that it is still active and busy.

Make Time for Happiness and Joy

People who are neutral or unhappy all of the time struggles to use their memory effectively. Their minds are typically preoccupied with whatever keeps them sick, making it difficult for them to concentrate or retain new information. Making time for happiness and joy daily can help relieve stress in your mind and keep you in a good mood.

Making time for happiness and joy will look different for everyone, but typically it involves making time for family and friends, hobbies, and other things that bring joy to your life. Give yourself time to laugh and be merry. Play funny videos that you can laugh at, watch a comedy on TV, or even read a joke book.

Getting yourself laughing and having fun is a great way to keep yourself in a positive mood. When you can intentionally stay in a positive attitude, overall, it becomes a lot easier to learn and remember things because you aren't preoccupied with unhappy thoughts or feelings in your mind. Instead, you are more likely to be fresh and attentive and ready to learn and remember anything new that comes your way!

Eat a Healthy Brain-Boosting Diet

Your diet, believe it or not, has a significant impact on your capacity to maintain a good and active memory. People who do not eat a healthy diet struggle with memory for a variety of reasons. Eating an unhealthy diet makes your body ill, thus causing a lot of physical and mental stress. As well, certain foods can slow down brain activity and stop your memory from working as well. There are many great brain-boosting foods you can eat that will help contribute to you having good health overall, mainly including the health within your brain. Consider the following when you are eating to improve your memory:

EAT MORE:

- Omega-3's (e.g., in fish, or through supplements)

- Fruits and vegetables

- Green tea

- Red Wine or Grape Juice (in small amounts)

AVOID:

- Empty Calories

- Saturated Fat

- Excessive Alcohol

- Refined Sugar

Excessive Sugar in General

Exercise Your Brain Regularly

If you don't work out your brain and every other muscle in your body, it won't function as well when you need it to. Exercising your brain and memory is a great way to ensure that you are getting the most out of them. You can boost your memory by exercising your brain in a variety of ways.

However, there are other ways you can do this, as well. Here are ten ideas to help you exercise your brain so that you can improve concentration, increase memory recall, make learning more accessible, and have a healthier brain function overall:

- *Do math in your head instead of with a calculator (e.g., the sum of your bank account less your most recent purchase)*

- *Make a list and try to remember everything on it and see how good the memory is. (e.g., a grocery list or shopping list)*

- *Learn an instrument*

- *Take a cooking class*

- *Learn a new language*

- *Check your taste buds by labeling the ingredients in a meal without being prompted.*

- *Practice hand-eye coordination with painting, drawing, puzzles, knitting, etc.*

- *Take up a new sport*

- *Draw a map of somewhere you frequently visit entirely by memory*

- *Use words to create a picture*

Using your brain activity means that you are calling it into action regularly. When it is regularly used, your brain is given the ability to learn new things, pick up on ways to complete specific tasks faster, and ultimately become more efficient overall. A healthy functioning brain is built by having a solid brain-building exercise schedule. There are many ways to integrate brain-building exercises into your everyday life, so keep an eye out for chances and seize them as they present themselves.

Avoid Exercise Stress Levels

Much like exhaustion, heightened stress levels can cause our body to work differently. Our entire system becomes more focused on warding off stress and dealing with the side effects than it does on virtually anything else. It means that if you are highly stressed, your body and mind are going to be preoccupied, and you will struggle to use your memory as effectively as you could if you kept your stress levels lowered.

It can reduce stress by intentionally incorporating happiness and joy into your life. However, it would be best to take additional measures to look after yourself and keep yourself feeling mentally well. If necessary, talk to a counselor or a trusted friend to relieve yourself of mental stress. You can also do relaxing things such as meditating, taking a warm bath with Epsom salts, doing a mindless activity, or otherwise reducing the stress in your life. Working to get your stress levels under control regularly is a surefire way to keep yourself as stress-free as possible and still improving your memory.

Maintain Your Overall Health

Your overall health is essential when it comes to having a well-functioning memory. Being in ill health puts your body under a great deal of stress in many ways, which, as you know, can inhibit your memory and learning capacities. Additionally, there are many illnesses that people can acquire with age that affect memory.

Alzheimer's and dementia, for example, are two naturally occurring illnesses that can significantly inhibit memory function. As well, traumas to the head, head colds, and other brain-related diseases and injuries can affect your memory function and prevent you from memorizing things as well. Ensure that you look after your health overall by going to the doctor when needed and discussing any concerns you may have.

If you feel that you have been trying to improve your memory and it does not seem to be working well for you, seeking the advice of a medically trained professional may help you assess to see if any health-related issues could be slowing you down or hampering your ability to have an improved memory.

Try Aromatherapy

Aromatherapy is an excellent way to improve your memory and desire to understand new things. There are many essential oils that, when used correctly, have a memory-enhancing effect. Check the contraindications of each oil before using it, and educate yourself about how to use it correctly by using aromatherapy options. It is crucial that they are diluted in the appropriate ratio and that you only use them in specific amounts to avoid accidental injury or overdose. The following essential oils are known to enhance memory:

- *Lavender oil*

- *Rosemary oil*

- *Peppermint oil*

- *Ginger oil*

- *Bergamot oil*

- *Lemon Balm*

Ylang Ylang oil Typically, you want to dilute these in the appropriate ratio and then rub them on your temples and the insides of your wrists for maximum impact. However, you must remember to be careful and refrain from using oils that may be harsh, or that could have health-related risks.

Chapter 6: Harnessing Your Concentration

The first step to becoming superhuman is to achieve adequate concentration control. What I mean by this is the ability to work on something and give it your 100%. Today's high-speed, always-on culture makes it challenging to attain this level of focus. I would wager that most professionals today suffer from at least some sort of distraction in the workplace. It is far too easy to open a browser and check Facebook, Twitter, and YouTube accounts that do not necessarily relate to work. Some of us are hopelessly addicted to browsing these sites or playing video games in between work assignments. Don't even get me started on phones. Unless I expect a call, I leave it on silent if I am trying to get in the zone. As a rule of thumb, I leave my phone in another room until I have done my work.

I've found that those who work from home or do freelance work are especially prone to this effect. Is the assignment due in 10 days? I'll put on a movie and get started on it later. This attitude can be fatal to the longevity of any self-employed work. It is true whether you are a novelist, technical writer, copywriter, programmer, heck, anything that needs to be done in front of the computer. If you are starting, then you are in luck. If you already have a concentration mindset—you are amazing. You are on your first step to becoming superhuman already. Others need to develop the attitude, as well as the skills associated with concentration. Much of what I will write is aimed towards those who work from home and are more prone to distractions, but it can apply the ideas here in the office.

Delaying Gratification

At the heart of the concentration, mindset understands the power of delayed gratification. If you abnegate yourself from the reward now and do the work, the tips will double in time. Before I developed the concentration mindset, I could sit in front of my computer all day and get nothing done. I don't mind just six or eight hours either.

I found myself stuck in a perpetual cycle of going from one source of entertainment to the other. I would start my day, hop on my desk chair and check my social media accounts. Then I would play whatever the latest game I was addicted to was.

Maybe get some food and watch it in front of the TV or put it on YouTube.

Then I would go on sites like Reddit, 4chan, and 9gag. I'd make the rounds going through my favorite news aggregator site just to read articles for the hell of it.

Take a break, and maybe throw on another video game and do my "daily" virtual tasks. Also, porn—so much porn. And what was the result of such depravity? At the end of the day would feel like a useless piece of crap that headed nowhere and fast. One day I said that enough was enough, and I slowly started building my concentration mindset.

I equate my experience with doing nothing all day to being "doped on dopamine." I was addicted to video games, actually, but I was also mindlessly reading articles, checking social media, and watching videos.

What do these things have in common? They all stem from the same addiction, and that is the neurotransmitter dopamine. Dopamine, sometimes called the "happiness chemical," along with serotonin, takes a hitch whenever we do some pleasurable activity.

Every time you scroll your feed looking at memes, reading news, or checking your phone for that elusive notification from your crush, you are effectively micro-dosing on dopamine hits. And some people do this throughout the day. I noticed this early on my journey to develop my concentration mindset when I saw myself crawling back to these distractions.

Even when I started taking up freelance writing jobs online, I would inevitably return to my video games, Reddit, and YouTube. I would "reward" myself every several hundred words and play a quick match of Fortnite or read an article. One half turned to another, and then a few more, and before I knew it, an hour had gone by. Imagine the time sink this presented when my breaks planned for 10 minutes turned into hours.

I thought hard about this issue, and I concluded that I stick by even today: frequent micro-dosing with dopamine messes with your mind. The more you get a taste for it, the more you will crave it, and it starts a vicious cycle. The best way to get out of that cycle is not to initiate it. I ended up eliminating social media and other distractions during working days. Alternatively, if I did allow them, only at the end of the day when it finished work for that day. Who would have known that the words of my mother would bring clarity to me as an adult? "Do your homework first, play your video games later."

Sharpen the Blade

Mastering how to delay gratification takes some time and is only a piece of the puzzle. Next comes the much-dreaded "multi-tasking" phenomena that are the bane of knowledge workers right next to procrastination. No matter how you look at it, working on one thing at a time is more productive than constantly switching from different tasks. Constant task switching combined with dopamine hits in between is a deadly combination that I struggled with for the longest time. When I would change from playing a video game to going on YouTube, I was doing so on autopilot. I didn't know where the next dopamine hit would come from, and I just knew it was coming. Sometimes I would play video games while watching YouTube without any lapse in in-game performance. But just because it works for entertainment, it doesn't mean it works for productivity.

Think of your concentration as a dull blade and your work as some material your knife needs to cut through. For the most efficient cut, you want the sharpest edge. Like, single-molecule-blade sharp. It sounds counterintuitive, but the more things you work on, the higher the average time for completion is. It is a little lesson I took from my time studying lean project management and lean manufacturing techniques. Under the Kanban system, there is a central philosophy to "limit the work in progress." In an assembly line setting, the work in progress comprises all the different stages and processes that material goes through. If you imagine a car plant with a single person responsible for each step, the work in progress gets stretched out. Sure, everything is getting done at the same time, but at what cost? Assembling a car would take forever to make! Instead, if some of those stages gained a few additional workers, and it put on the other stages pause, the work at a time gets done faster.

It can apply the same principle to your work. In between reading and writing emails (or anticipating emails), doing research, checking work chat channels, and doing actual work, the work in progress is all over the place. What's more, task switching suffers from "cold starts," a term I borrowed from the cloud computing world. A server takes a little while to initialize so that it can begin serving web pages. The traditional computing model is to have a server run 24/7 so that users get immediate responses.

Still, a modern approach in cloud computing called "serverless" shuts the server down and only starts it when there is a request. Since the server doesn't run 24/7, you save on the electric bill. But since servers take a while to start up, your first response to the user will take a little longer. Each time you switch, your mind takes some time to reacclimatize to whatever it was you were working on.

Computer programming is notorious for this. It may take a programmer up to 20 minutes to get back into the "zone" after being interrupted just once. I will admit that some tasks do have a lower cold start time, but for me, the cold start for writing is exceptionally high.

Accelerated learning is an advanced learning and teaching method being used today. It is a system for enhancing and speeding both the learning and design processes. It has been based on the most recent research and has continued to prove over and over again its ability to improve the effectiveness of learning while saving money and time.

It is effective because it is based on how we naturally learn.

Accelerated learning helps you tap into new learning potential that conventional learning methods have prevented us from using. It does so by using the whole person using color, images, music, creativity, physical activity, and other ways to get people deeply involved in their learning.

The following is what people need to ensure they have an optimal learning environment:

A Positive Environment: Students learn their best when they are in a positive social, emotional, and physical environment. It needs to be both stimulating and relaxing. It needs to have a sense of enjoyment, interest, safety, and wholeness. These are essential to optimize human learning.

Total Involvement: Students can learn better when they can be active and involved and responsible for their learning. Learning isn't about watching; and it's about participation. Knowledge isn't something someone absorbs but something that a learner creates. It means that accelerated learning is activity-based instead of being presentations-based or materials-based.

Collaboration Among Learners: Students can learn the best when they are in an environment where they can collaborate. Good learning is social. Accelerated learning emphasizes collaboration with the learners in a community.

Variety Appeals to Any Learning Style: Students can learn their best when considering how they can use their senses and exercises their regular learning style. Instead of thinking that a program is one size fits all, accelerated learning looks at it as an array of learner-centered teaching options.

Contextual Learning: People can learn best in context. Skill and facts discovered in isolation can't be absorbed very well and are quick to evaporate. You understand your best from doing the work in a process that continually has you immersing, getting feedback, reflecting, evaluating, and absorbing again.

The main aim of accelerated learning is to get results. Accelerated learning is working great for several organizations.

The following are the main guiding principles of accelerated learning:

The Whole Body and Mind are Involved in Learning: Learning is not just learning with your head, meaning verbal, left-brained, rational, and conscious, but it involves the complete mind and body with all the receptors, senses, and emotions.

Learning is Not Consumption but Creation: A learner doesn't absorb their knowledge, but they create that knowledge. Learning happens when the learner integrates skill and expertise into their existing structure. Learning is creating new patterns of chemical and electrical interactions, new neural networks, and new meanings within their total body and brain system.

Collaboration Helps with Learning: All great learning will have a social base. People learn better when they keep interacting with others that are learning in other ways. Being competitive slows learning. Interactivity will speed things up. Having a great learning community has a better outcome for education than a collection of individuals.

Learning Can Take Place on Different Levels at One Time: Learning isn't about taking in one item at a time, but, instead, taking in several things at once. Good learning will engage people on several different levels, like physical and mental, preconscious and conscious. It will use all the senses, receptors, and paths to the person's complete body and brain system. The brain doesn't process things sequentially; but instead, it processes things parallel.

Learning Happens When You do the Work: People will learn the best in context. Things that get learned in isolation can't be remembered as easily and tend to evaporate quickly. We know how to walk by walking, how to write by writing, how to sing by singing, and how to live by living.

The real world is a better teacher than anything hypothetical or abstract, given it's provided time for complete immersion, feedback, reflection, and immersion again.

Happiness Improves Learning: Feeling can determine the quantity and quality of learning. Negativity will slow the learning process down. When a person is happy and in a comfortable learning environment, their understanding will excel. Learning that is dreary, painful, and stressful can't compare to engaging, relaxed, and joyful learning.

The Brain Absorbs Images and Information Automatically and Instantly: The nervous system is an image processor more than a word processor. Concrete images are easier to retain and grasp than verbal explanations. Translating verbal explanations into images will make the verbal descriptions easier to remember and learn.

Using accelerated learning techniques, you could learn a skill that would usually take months, possibly years of study. Most of us want to learn new skills, but we write it off as not having enough time, or the gifts are too difficult even to try. One of the main aspects of getting new skills is being in the right mindset.

Here are some learning tactics that can be applied when learning any technology, language, or skill:

- **Break Hard Ambitions into Small Goals**

When trying to learn a new skill, people will confuse ambition with goals. Learning how to speak French is an ambition or something one wants to do. Understanding the most commonly used words is an achievable goal.

The key to improving your learning is breaking down your ambitions into small, achievable goals. It doesn't matter if it is related to health, language, or business.

From fitness to programming, break the larger goals into small steps, and you will see that they are not all that difficult to achieve.

Use 80:20 to Help Focus on Important Information

If you haven't heard of the so-called "Pareto principle," it is a rule that states 80 percent of the results are from 20 percent of work. It is used primarily on business but could be applied to almost anything.

When dealing with the English language, 20 percent of our words make up about 80 percent of the written language. With music, 20 percent of all chord progressions make up about 80 percent of all songs. Accelerated learning makes you focus on the critical 20 percent and keeps you from wasting time on the unimportant 80 percent.

If you can learn to apply the Pareto principle to all of your learning, you will learn even faster.

- **Block out Distractions and Focus on One Task**

It is less productive to multitask than to focus on just one task. When you have broken down the main goal into achievable steps, you will need to focus on just one goal at a time. Block out your distractions, whether it is checking your emails or watching videos. Learn to spend your energy working on one task for maximum productivity.

Gary Keller stated that "You can do two things at once, but you can't focus effectively on two things at once."

- **Practice Skill to Improve Memory**

It is easier to learn or study when you can practice it. If you are learning to play pool, learning how to calculate an angle and striking the balls are simple, but if you don't put a cue in your hand, it will be rather hard to master.

To help you keep the information you have learned, you must practice. Once you have learned the basics, put them to use by making practical tests for your friends. If you want to soak up knowledge, teach what you have learned to someone else. Being accountable for another person's learning will make you pay attention and learn the material.

- **Learn to Ask Questions**

Intelligence will grow with curiosity. By asking questions about what you are studying, you will be focused on finding the answers. You will zero in on the correct information when you sift through it to find the answers to the questions you have.

- **Describe the Subject Aloud**

Try to center yourself and focus on what you are learning. Start describing the information aloud that you have researched. Talking aloud, especially at a slower speed, will make you think about and make you conscious of what you have learned. It will expose any gaps in what you know.

- **Get Friends to Help You Test Your Knowledge**

If you are a competitive person, setting some challenges for yourself is an excellent way to improve your focus and accelerate your learning. Work with friends to test your abilities and get new skills together.

You can create competitions for vocabulary, foreign languages, or who can lift the most weight. Healthy competitions are a great way to learn a new skill quickly.

. **When You Have Learned a Skill, Reactivation is Required**

We usually compare skills to riding a bike, thinking that it is impossible to forget once they have been learned. It is not valid for all skills. Skills that are based on knowledge instead of muscle memory, like languages, are easy to forget.

Reactivating this lost skill is relatively simple. It doesn't matter if it is relearning Italian or picking up that guitar in the corner. Accelerating this process of relearning a skill takes exercises to remember the fundamentals to come naturally.

The process can be as simple as watching a foreign film without subtitles.

- **Don't Work So Hard**

Ask anyone who works a nine-to-five job when they feel most productive, and almost all of them will say it is during the morning hours. Some people might work for days without any decline in productivity, but the majority of us work the best in a three to four-hour window.

This three to a four-hour window of productivity can be applied to learning, too. The time we take on learning a skill and the knowledge that comes with it is not a linear curve but more like a logarithmic one.

To maximize your learning, it is more important to work at it less. Focus on relaxing, take a break, let the information you have acquired get stuck instead of trying to cram constantly to maximize the information input.

The best way to improve retention is to reduce stress. If you can't reduce stress quickly, don't worry, most of us can't. Meditation is an effective and great way to reduce anxiety and stress.

- **Involve All the Senses**

We are multi-intelligence, multi-sensual beings. Reading gives us words through our eyes but has limits as to be an effective way to learn. Using pictures to learn is a great way. Record information on tape and listen to these. Stimulate other senses by using fabrics, chairs, or getting a massage. Eat something you usually wouldn't while you are studying. Taste could become a part of the information and could help you recall it later. Using the memory of smells is the best memory system. Rub your favorite essential oil on your wrist as you begin to study. When you want to recall this information, get out that oil and take a sniff. Stimulating your senses will help the information to come flooding back into your memory.

- **Positive Mental Attitude**

Create a positive mental attitude toward the learning process. This principle will flood your system with endorphins that make you feel good and make the training more accessible and pleasurable.

Get into your peak state using NLP, neuro-linguistic programming, to make anchors to peak emotional states. When you start to study, stretch, sit straight, smile, and approach the material with positive expectations.

- **Measure and Track Your Progress**

Peter Drucker once said, "What gets measured gets managed." An effective tactic for learning is measuring and tracking your progress.

Make charts to see your success in a particular field like your personal fitness, foreign language, or vocabulary. You always need to keep track of your growth or progress. Without these, you won't be able to tell if you are improving.

Visualize yourself practicing the skills you are learning as an expert. Use the information as an expert. It is locked inside your brain and is easily accessible to you.

Many people aspire to have photographic memories. They describe it as remembering details in detail after taking a simple, effortless mental image. Unfortunately, photographic memory is a myth. All perfect memory takes conscious effort.

Memory is a creative, not photographic, process. If you use these techniques in your daily life, you will access your innate memory capacity. It is a talent, not a unique ability, to have perfect memory.

Have you ever seen anything similar happen to you? You're taking an exam, and you know exactly which page contains the material, but you have no idea what's on that page. Or you're reading something, and you reach the end of a page and wonder, "What have I just read?"

Since you never brought the data to light, this is the case.

Consider this: When you read a book or a film, what happens? Isn't it like you're watching a movie in your head? You recall all of the characters' titles, locations, and incidents so you can imagine them—you use your creativity and innate imaginative abilities to make images when reading.

However, as people begin to read textbook content, they attempt to create a mental photograph or video of the page while ignoring their artistic ability. People with a photographic memory or others who learn easily add ingenuity to everything they know. They may have learned how to do this or may use the principles unconsciously.

Many people try to remember information by sound, repeating it repeatedly, hoping it will somehow stick. But the sound is minimal because it doesn't attach easily to other memories. A sound is also sequential; to remember information by sound, you have to start and work your way through it. However, when you see information as an image in your mind, you can jump in and out of it, which improves your understanding.

Any book that you enjoy activates your imagination and brings the information to life. You naturally get engaged in the book, and you battle to put it down because you don't want to turn the "movie" off.

Your mind is similar to an internal movie screen from which you can generate data. It is how we think and learn effectively.

Your brain creates miracles every day by converting lifeless information into pictures and ideas. When you become aware of this, every word becomes a picture drawn with letters because words are symbols of three-dimensional images. "Isn't it incredible how we take them for granted?" Arthur Gordon asked. Those tiny black streaks on the ledger. "There are twenty-six distinct forms known as letters, set in infinite variations, known as words, lifeless before someone's eye lands on them."

If your brain weren't able to make images out of symbols, learning and reading would be worthless and incredibly dull. Your brain likes pictures and is good at remembering them. As neuroscientist John Medina said, "Hear a piece of information, and three days later, you'll remember 10 percent of it. Add a picture, and you'll remember 65 percent."

Reading comprehension is also a creative process. When we create mental pictures, we excel in this field. We sound befuddled or stupid if we don't. What if I try to tell you how a car engine works, but you don't know what an engine looks like? If I don't have one to show you or a drawing to represent it, it will be challenging for you to understand, let alone remember.

The more we turn information into images or mind movies, the more we will remember and comprehend. We can make all our learning more creative and memorable if we use our unlimited imagination. It is a power that it can compare to magic.

Some people say, "I can't take pictures in my mind."

The truth is, most of us can do it with a bit of practice. About 1 percent of people may have aphantasia, which is the inability to make pictures in your mind. Most of us don't have this condition; we haven't yet trained ourselves to master and use this skill well. So start practicing and give yourself some time to learn this valuable skill.

You can learn to enhance your memory imagination system by making your mind movies exciting and "sticky." The way to do this is with the SEE principle.

The SEE Principle

S—Senses: There are only five ways to get anything into your brain, and those are through your senses: sight, sound, smell, touch, and taste. Your feelings help you mentally recreate your world. If you learn to engage your senses, you will use more of your brain and improve your memory.

Think of a horse. See it in your mind. Touch it, smell it, and hear it. You didn't see the letters H-O-R-S-E in your mind; you saw a multisensory picture of what the word represents. Mind movies become genuine and unforgettable thanks to the senses.

E—Exaggeration: Throughout this book, we will use images to represent concepts we'd like to remember. But not just any images—exaggerated, sometimes silly, and occasionally nonsensical mind pictures. Which is easier to remember: a strawberry that is average size or one the size of a house? An elephant in a green bikini, or an elephant in a pink bikini? Make your mental images larger or smaller than life. The more you exaggerate the image you're using to help you remember a concept, the easier it will be to recall later.

Exaggerate with humor; tickle your mind. There is no scientific evidence that learning must be severe. Make your images illogical. Have fun; create some exaggerated pictures to improve your memory.

E—Energize: Give your mental pictures action. What would you choose; watch a movie or a slide show with your holiday pictures? Whatever horse, a horse standing still or a horse running and moving, evokes more emotion in your imagination?

Make your mental images as vivid and colorful as you can, not dull, flat, or black and white. Use action; it brings life to even the dullest information. To help you remember things, weave, fall, stick or wrap them together in illogical ways. Make things talk, sing, and dance. Think about the creations of the great genius Walt Disney: His characters and settings vibrate with life and fun—it's why they became so beloved, and more importantly, so memorable.

The process of imagination is a fun and creative process. The more enjoyment you can put into it, the better.

When you read or hear something you want to remember, you can't just yourself remember it. You must focus on all the SEE principles and use your imagination to guarantee you'll remember that information. Even if you don't use all the methods in this book, the SEE concepts will help you focus more.

Emile Coué pointed out that "When the imagination and the will conflict, the imagination always wins." If you allow yourself to remember something without using your imagination, you will have zero retention and recall. The trick to accessing your limitless memory capacity is to use your creativity.

"This is not how I thought naturally," some people claim.

It is not my usual way of thinking; it is how I have learned to act, and it works.

The more you practice using your creativity, the more you will learn, comprehend, and develop.

Turning Abstract Information into Images

How do I turn abstract information into images?

We remember many nouns and adjectives with ease because they have concrete meanings, and we can form a mental picture of them without much effort.

It can also make most abstract words into mental pictures. Just use a meaningful thought or phrase to represent a "meaningless" word. Break up the abstract term into its sounds or find a word or expression that sounds the same as or close to it.

Consider how difficult it would be to recall the name Washington.

You can transform all complex information into something meaningful and memorable by turning it into images. In the beginning, investing your attention in this task will take a bit of effort, but then it will become a habit.

To practice, look at words, break them up, and create pictures to give them more meaning. Let's start with a few foreign words. Imagine each word by creating a SEE movie in your mind.

Here are some Spanish words:

- *Tiger is Tigre. It sounds like "tea gray." To perfect the pronunciation, imagine a tiger drinking tea that has turned gray.*

- *Sun is sol. Imagine that the sun is burning the sole of your foot.*

Some Italian words:

- *Chicken is pollo. Imagine instead of a ball, and you're playing polo with a pig.*

- *Cat is Gatto. Consider saying to a neighbor, "You've got to hold my cat."*

Some of the French words:

- *Book is livre. It sounds like a "lever," so imagine pulling a lever to open a book.*

- *Chair is a chaise. It sounds like "shezz." Imagine you're playing chess while sitting in a chair.*

Some Zulu words:

- *Dog is inja (EEN-jaa). Think of an injured dog.*

- *Snake is inyoka (ee-NYO-kaa). Imagine a snake slithering in your car.*

Some Japanese words:

- *Chest is mune (moo-NEH). Imagine money growing out of your chest.*

- *Door is toa (doh-AH). Imagine you are kicking the door with your big toe.*

Test yourself:

- *What is the Spanish word for tiger?*

- *What is the Italian word for cat?*

- *What is the Zulu word for dog?*

- *What is the Japanese word for chest?*

- *What is the French word for book?*

- *What is the Italian word for chicken?*

- *What is the Zulu word for a snake?*

Just by connecting these words with silly mind movies, you have learned 12 foreign words. You can use the SEE principle to remember hundreds of unfamiliar words by clicking just two concepts at a time. If you visualize each idea for a few seconds, it will stick in your mind and be easier to remember in the future.

It can also use this form to remember countries and capitals.

You need to bring the information to life.

- *Canberra, Australia: Imagine a kangaroo (which represents Australia) eating a can of berries.*

- *Athens, Greece: Imagine eight hens swimming in grease.*

- *Brussels, Belgium: Imagine Brussels sprouts falling out of a bell in a gym.*

Imagine a silly picture—SEE it—and you will remember all the capitals with ease.

The most important trick of maintaining a strong memory is to use the imagination to bring knowledge to life. Take responsibility for your memory.

Chapter 9: What is Photographic Memory?

In its technicality, the phrase "photographic memory" is referred to by the scientific communities as "eidetic memory." The word 'eidetic' stems from the Greek word that means "seen." One that possesses photographic memory skills can recall information in superb detail visually. Those with photographic memory are capable of taking and absorbing memory snapshots and remembering them without error. While it can utilize both phrases above interchangeably, they each have their differences. The ability to recall numbers and text is referred to as eidetic memory, while the ability to display and recover memories is referred to as photographic memory.

It seems like a superpower, right? It most certainly does, which is why many scientists and ordinary people like you and me may have a hard time believing in its actual relevance. So how can one inherit this skill? According to science, there are a few key factors that play into creating a photographic mind. They include personal experiences that life may have demanded from them, the development of the brain mixed in with a unique blend of genetic material. While the grand scheme of photographic memory seems to be one that specific individuals have all their lives, it can hone some terms of this capability by learning and practicing it.

Our brains go through many core developmental changes during the time of adolescence, which is when people have reported more times than not having the capabilities of a photographic memory. While most of us do have this sort of memory capability naturally, those with this kind can recall precise information about specific experiences or everyday life as a whole. Many of us have more of an eidetic type of memory, more so than photographic. Our memories are more like a puzzle rather than a photograph itself. To correctly recall past events, we have to piece together all the aspects of that particular memory. As humans, we are great at remembering the main idea of what occurred but leave out other details, like the colors plastered on the walls or what furniture was in the room during the occurrence.

Memory is a process, a very complex one that many scientists have yet to 100 percent or firmly grasp. They know that when we live through experiences, our hippocampus and frontal cortex areas of our brains decide what parts of the situation are worth and not worth retaining. Any challenge we face is broken down into tiny bits and preserved in various parts of our brains, then reassembled when we need them. It is why we are unable to remember every single minute detail of memories.

Chapter 9: Speed Reading

Speed-reading is not charm, nor is it a noteworthy exorbitant mystery. Proficient speed-reading classes teach a modest bunch of easy systems that assist a person to focus his or her consideration better. The eye is pulled into the movement. Speed reading procedures put that movement on the page.

You are beginning position is fundamental. It would be best if you sat up straight, place the book on the table with your left hand, and pace with your right hand.

You should, as have now been conventional peruses before you endeavor to speed read. Speed-reading will not empower you if you have issues in understanding and vocabulary. It may hurt you to attempt to race through stuff that you cannot appreciate. It would be best if you had the basics down authoritatively first.

Until you start speed-reading, take a look at the data and get a sense of what you'll be covering and what tricks you can use.

Tricks for speed-reading

For a moment, stray in fantasyland about what you would do with 15 extra days consistently. Would you start another venture? At last, take that fantasy excursion? Go through more vitality with your loved ones?

There is uplifting news: each unique little something is possible if you make sense of scrutinizing faster. We always read, from books and magazines to locales and messages to the back of the oat box. Gigantic quantities of information are pushed into us for hours consistently. Sparing just a single hour, a day on reading would give you an extra 365 hours always or somewhat more than 15 days.

Think it is incomprehensible? Reconsider. Many people read a typical of 150 to 200 words for every moment. Nevertheless, it is possible to examine 800 to 1,000 words for every moment—and some apex entertainers do. John F. Kennedy was a speed-peruse, and it is said that he could complete six daily papers every morning over breakfast. I will even show you how to go about doing it correctly.

Nevertheless, at first, find your base rate. Discover a book, check where you start, and time yourself while reading it for 60 seconds. Stamp the end; by then, limit the number of lines you read.

Finally, increase the number of lines you examined by the number of words per line (around 10, for the most part, books). This last number is your reading speed.

Is that number lower than you might want? Hack your reading speed with these traps.

1. Get your eyes checked.

Many people who encounter difficulty reading do not have a learning challenge but instead discover difficulty preparing the data. If you experience difficulty reading, enable yourself to out and get your eyes checked. It could work wonders. Furthermore, if you have reading glasses, utilize them!

2. Turn the temperature down.

Have you anytime seen that expert meetings are held in new rooms? They are kept that way for a reason: to keep you attentive. Cuddling up in bed with a book is incredible. Whatever the case might be, if you're getting up to speed read, you'll need to concentrate. Turn the temperature down to an easily extraordinary level.

3. Utilize positive remains.

If you have spent your whole life persuaded that you are a moderate peruse, speed-reading can be a nervousness-instigating task. Calm your nerves by making a situation stacked with positive remains. You require your surroundings to inspire you. Fill them with rousing quotes, photographs of those you acknowledge, and keepsakes that remind you of the person you have to turn into.

4. Go outside.

Temperature is not by any means the only ecological variable that influences how you learn. Lighting assumes a noteworthy part as well. Reading in lessen light strains your eyes. Instead, locate a quiet place with loads of aberrant daylight, regardless of whether that is an amusement focus seat under a tree or by your most prominent window. Incomprehensible? Many lights handle regular mirror lights. Skirt the fluorescent ones.

5. Tune in to the correct music.

Some people cannot read while tuning in to music. If that is you, feel permitted to ignore this tip. In any case, if you can focus, tuning in to specific sounds may loosen up you and help get you into an apex learning state. Nature sounds are flawless, yet expand music by essayists like Vivaldi or Bach functions admirably as well. Try songs that are 60 BPM (thumps every moment) — that are a standard resting heart rate.

6. Sit up straight.

While your brain will only account for about 2% to 3% of your body weight, it consumes about 20% of your body's oxygen. When you are slumped over, you make it harder for air to accomplish the base of your lungs, where the majority of the oxygen is absorbed into the circulatory system and then fed to the brain a short time later. The brain needs as exact an amount of oxygen as possible to function correctly. So if you have to examine faster, sit up.

7. Hold your book upright.

Since you are sitting up, do not lay your book level on the table! It can make you slump over once more—or more horrendous, and you will be examined at a point with the words a long way from you. Since reading is a visual strategy for learning, you have to see a significant piece of the page as you can. Endeavor to go up against the page clearly, rather than at an edge. For a prominent number of people, that infers holding the book upright.

8. Drink more water.

Your brain is included around 75 percent water. It cannot work successfully if you are got dried out. Are you feeling drowsy amid reading? Keep a tall glass of water in your work zone and taste it much of the time. Endeavor this when you are covetous, as well, since your body regularly befuddles longing and thirst.

9. Utilize a visual pacer.

Kids, who are the best learners on the planet, frequently perused by running their fingers under each line. Various educators loathe this, so we lose the capacity as grown-ups. In any case, it is truly a particular procedure to enhance reading pace and focus (which helps to understand).

Our eyes are pulled into the movement since in Stone Age person-days, missing moving greenery could infer that we were lunch. With a visual pacer, like a finger, pencil, or PC mouse, you may read around 25 to 50 percent faster.

10. Utilize your whole brain.

It is inadequate to utilize a visual pacer. For best results, endeavor it with your left hand. Why? It is to attract your right brain. Your left brain focuses on the method of reasoning and words, while your right brain is settling to creative energy and inventiveness. For a prominent number of people, reading is a left-brain handle. In any case, since we read such an extraordinary measure of slower than we did think, the show of reading can keep our right brain from incitement and make our mind wander. Utilizing your left hand as a visual pacer interfaces with your proper brain. It saves you center and propels your reading background.

Conclusion

A perfect way to help you learn more is to read out loud while you're reading. Reading the words aloud rather than just reading them to yourself means you are creating a more precise memory of the details, which will ensure you can remember the facts more readily later. Not only that but reading out loud means you're not going to lose your concentration and instantly remember that you haven't read at all but start at the text! Reading the details and then putting them into words will help you concentrate on the letter and reading out loud will slow down the tempo a little because you should be allowed to focus on what you're reading.

Our lifestyle decisions influence the mental fitness in our brains and our capacity to recall and recover information, and whether we use memory-boosting strategies in our daily lives. Although the workouts mentioned above will sound like a lot to do every day, once you get into the habit of doing them, you'll find that they can all be completed in less than five to ten minutes per day. Some of these methods seem to be very elaborate and challenging at first, but if people begin with the basics and work their way up, it becomes straightforward, and you will see meaningful results in a short period. It could improve people's memory capacity in as little as two weeks.

Natural memory enhancers are undoubtedly an excellent method to improve memory work for different reasons. One, they don't expect you to burn up all available resources. Two, they are simple lifestyle changes you can fuse into regular living exercises. Ultimately, they fill in on a par with other memory enhancers.

Lastly, reading out loud may help you better understand the points posed in the text. Even if you're reading to yourself in silence, even when a sentence or paragraph after a few readings don't make any sense, you'll always read it aloud to try to understand it better. Reading the whole time loud will help you absorb information more quickly and make sense of it for future reference.

When you're learning or practicing, memory enhancement can be a great way to improve your study.

It's essential to ensure that you remember the knowledge you gain during your course or class for years to come because you don't want to forget it all the minute you finish your final evaluation or walk the level out for the last time.